EU Public Procurement Law

ELGAR EUROPEAN LAW

Series editor: John Usher, *Professor of European Law and Head, School of Law, University of Exeter, UK*

European integration is the driving force behind constant evolution and change in the laws of the member states and the institutions of the European Union. This important series will offer short, state-of-the-art overviews of many specific areas of EU law, from competition law and from environmental law to labour law. Whilst most books will take a thematic, vertical approach, others will offer a more horizontal approach and consider the overarching themes of the EU law.

Distilled from rigorous substantive analysis, and written by some of the best names in the field, as well as the new generation of scholars, these books are designed both to guide the reader through the changing legislation itself, and to provide a firm theoretical foundation for advanced study. They will be an invaluable source of reference for scholars and postgraduate students in the fields of EU law and European integration, as well as lawyers from the respective individual fields and policymakers within the EU.

Titles in the series include:

EU Consumer Law and Policy
Stephen Weatherill

EU Private International Law
Harmonization of Laws
Peter Stone

EU Public Procurement Law
Christopher H. Bovis

EU Public Procurement Law

Professor Christopher H. Bovis *JD, MPhil, LLM, FRSA*
H.K. Bevan Chair in Law, Law School, University of Hull

ELGAR EUROPEAN LAW

Edward Elgar
Cheltenham, UK • Northampton, MA, USA

Published by
Edward Elgar Publishing Limited
Glensanda House
Montpellier Parade
Cheltenham
Glos GL50 1UA
UK

Edward Elgar Publishing, Inc.
William Pratt House
9 Dewey Court
Northampton
Massachusetts 01060
USA

A catalogue record for this book
is available from the British Library

Library of Congress Cataloguing in Publication Data

Bovis Christopher.
  EU public procurement law / by Christopher Bovis.
    p. cm.—(Elgar European law)
  Includes bibliographical references and index.
  1. Government purchasing—Law and legislation—European Union countries.
  2. Public contracts—European Union countries. I. Title.
  KJE5632.B683 2007
  346.2402′3—dc22
                                2006028685

ISBN 978 1 84542 204 2 (cased)

Typeset by Cambrian Typesetters, Camberley, Surrey
Printed and bound in Great Britain by MPG Books Ltd, Bodmin, Cornwall

For Terry

Contents

Foreword

Public and utilities procurement in the European Union (EU) represents a staggering 13.5% of the EU Gross Domestic Product (GDP), which in turn translates to a trillion Euro on an annual basis.

There are two main reasons for the regulation of public procurement in the European Union. The first reason reveals the importance of public and utilities procurement for the proper function of the common market and the attainment of the objectives envisaged by European Union law. The second reason reflects the need to bring respectively public sector and utilities procurement markets in parallel operation to that of private markets. Jurisprudence, policy making and academia have recognised the distinctive character of *public markets*.

Intellectually, public procurement regulation draws support from neo-classical economic theories. The assumption has been that enhanced competition in public markets would result in optimal allocation of resources within European industries, rationalisation of production and supply, promotion of mergers and acquisitions, elimination of sub-optimal firms and creation of globally competitive industries.

Purportedly, one of the most important surrogate effects of public procurement regulation is to yield substantial purchasing savings for the public sector. The price of goods, services and works destined for the public sector will converge as a result of the liberalisation of and competitiveness in the relevant public markets.

The regulation of public procurement reveals two diametrically opposite dynamics. On the one hand, the influence of neo-classical economic theories has given a community-wide orientation to the regulation process and has taken the relevant regime through the paces of liberalisation within the European Union and with reference to the World Trade Organisation (WTO). Anti-trust has played a seemingly important role in determining the necessary competitive conditions for the interface between public and private markets. However, we have seen the emergence of a *sui generis* market place where the mere existence and functioning of anti-trust is not sufficient, on its own, to achieve the envisaged objectives. Public markets require a positive regulatory approach in order to enhance market access. Whereas anti-trust and the neo-classical approach to economic integration depend heavily on price competition, public procurement regulation requires a system which primarily safeguards market access. Such a regulatory system could be described as public competition law. There is strong evidence that the emergence of competitive conditions within public markets would render public procurement regulation inapplicable. This development denotes the referral of public markets to anti-trust as the ultimate regulatory regime.

On the other hand, public procurement has been traditionally viewed as the main driver of national industrial policies. Preferential purchasing patterns, strategic development of national champions and interestingly, an increasing influence of ordo-liberal theories have placed public procurement as an instrument of policy not only at national level, but also at European level.

Public procurement regulation is an essential requirement for the proper functioning of the common market and the envisaged fundamental freedoms. It is also a valuable source of international trade law in its attempts to integrate public sector markets. The new generation of legal instruments intend to simplify and modernise the regime and bring in synergies with the *acquis communautaire*, as well as with the WTO regime.

The purpose of this book is to provide for a comprehensive analysis of the legal regime of EU public procurement and its interrelation with European and national policies. The Introduction provides a conceptual framework of public procurement within European Union law. It further examines the thrust and parameters of public procurement regulation and it concludes by exploring the notion of public markets.

In Chapter 2, the development of a public procurement framework is depicted in chronological order. The chapter provides a detailed analysis and critique of the first generation of public procurement acquis, right up to the completion of the first transitional period of the European Communities in 1969. It then proceeds to examine the second generation of public procurement acquis and the evolution of the GATT (General Agreement on Tariffs and Trade) Agreement on Government Procurement and the enactment of the Remedies Directives. After the completion of the internal market project in 1992, the third generation of public procurement acquis and the WTO Government Procurement Agreement took the public procurement regulation a step deeper into the integration process of the public markets. The chapter elaborates on the consolidated Directives and the first Public Services Directive, which were enacted after the completion of the internal market in 1992. Finally, the fourth generation of public procurement acquis with the enactment of the new Public Sector and Utilities Directives is investigated. Future developments such as the procurement of public private partnerships and the revision of the Remedies Directives are finally examined.

Chapter 3 reflects on the principles of public procurement regulation and in particular the public nature of the contracting authorities, the principle of transparency and its effects, the *de minimis* principle and the dimensionality of public procurement in the European Union, the principle of fairness, the principle of non-discrimination and the principle of objectivity.

Chapter 4 examines public sector procurement and the new Public Sector Directive. It analyses the principles of the Public Sector Directive, its substantive applicability, its monetary applicability and concludes by exposing the new concepts in public sector procurement.

In Chapter 5, the advertisement and publicity requirements in public sector procurement are explained. In particular, the requirements of publication of notices, deadlines for receipt of requests to participate and for receipt of tenders, the inclusion of technical standards and specifications, the contractual performance stipulated under the Public Sector Directive and finally the obligation to provide information and feedback to candidates and tenderers are fully explored.

Chapter 6 provides a detailed analysis of the qualitative selection in public sector procurement. It examines disqualification grounds and reasons for automatic exclusion. It analyses the economic and financial standing of economic operators, as well as requirements relating to their technical and professional ability. It investigates the function of official lists of approved economic operators, as well as exclusion and rejection of economic operators mentioned in those lists. Finally, it provides an insight into consortia and group procurement.

In Chapter 7, the term of public contracts under public sector procurement is investigated thoroughly. An analysis is provided of the types and categories of public contracts under the Public Sector Directive and also a comprehensive review of the jurisprudence of the European Court of Justice on the notion of public contracts and their constituent ingredients is presented. The chapter provides valuable insights into the interface of public contracts and state aid, services of general interest, needs in the general interest, as well as the notion of public service concessions.

Chapter 8 demonstrates the nature and characteristics of contracting authorities under public sector procurement. It further analyses case law on contracting authorities and in particular the seemingly important test developed by the European Court of Justice to determine contracting authorities and bodies governed by public law. The chapter analyses the functional dimension of contracting authorities and the notion of bodies governed by public law, the dependency test for bodies governed by public law, as well as the requirement for management supervision of bodies governed by public law. It proceeds with a detailed analysis of the test of commerciality and needs in the general interest for bodies governed by public law and investigates the dual capacity of contracting authorities and their effects on the applicability of public procurement regulation. It examines the connection between contracting authorities and private undertakings, and the possibility of private companies, or semi-public undertakings captured by the definition of contracting authorities, for the purposes of public procurement regulation. Finally, the chapter provides a detailed analysis of the relation between transfer of undertakings and contracting authorities.

In Chapter 9 the award procedures in public sector procurement are fully explained. The chapter provides a detailed investigation of the procedures available and the choice of participants, and in particular open procedures, restricted procedures, competitive dialogue, design contests, framework agreements, dynamic purchasing systems, electronic auctions, public housing schemes, public works concessions and finally negotiated procedures. Finally, the chapter provides a detailed analysis of case-law from the European Court of Justice on the grounds for use of the negotiated procedure with and without prior publication of a contract notice, as well as the weighting criteria for the utilisation of restricted procedures.

Chapter 10 examines the award criteria in public sector procurement by providing an overview of the most economically advantageous tender and lowest price award criteria. It further exposes the Court's stance on the meaning of the most economically advantageous tender and in particular the use of social and environmental considerations as award criteria and the grounds for rejecting a tender based on its abnormally low offer.

In Chapter 11 utilities procurement is fully explored and the concepts of the new Utilities Directive analysed. The remit of the Utilities Directive, the types and categories of utilities contracts, the types of economic operators and the types and categories of contracting entities are explained with reference to the new regime. Furthermore, the principles of awarding contracts in utilities sectors and the substantive applicability of the Utilities Directive lead to a discussion of the activities covered by or excluded from the Utilities Directive, the monetary applicability of the Utilities Directive, and monitoring and information requirements.

Chapter 12 deals with publicity and advertisement in utilities procurement and examines notices requirements on the part of contracting entities, time limits for the receipt of requests to participate and for the receipt of tenders, requirements relating to invitations to submit a tender or to negotiate, requirements for the determination of technical specifications or variants and finally, requirements concerning contractual performance.

In Chapter 13, the qualification and qualitative selection requirements in utilities procurement are analysed. In particular, the chapter deals with qualification systems and their function and operation, the mutual recognition of qualifications and the applicable criteria for qualitative selection in utilities procurement.

In Chapter 14, the award procedures and award criteria in utilities procurement are exposed in thorough detail. The chapter provides a comprehensive exposition of award procedures in utilities and in particular of the use of open, restricted and negotiated procedures, framework agreements, dynamic purchasing systems, electronic auctions and design contests. Finally, an examination of the award criteria for utilities procurement is provided by reference to the most economically advantageous tender and the lowest price criteria and the reasons and grounds for rejection of abnormally low tenders.

Chapter 15 reflects on compliance with public procurement rules at national level. It provides a comprehensive analysis of the Remedies Directives and their principles. In particular it exposes the principle of effectiveness, the principle of non-discrimination and the principle of procedural autonomy before proceeding to an analysis of the remit of the Remedies Directives and the requirements for the set aside and annulment requirements of decisions and the award of damages under the Remedies Directives. Finally, the chapter provides an insight into national legal structures and public procurement litigation.

In Chapter 16, the enforcement regime of public procurement at both European and national levels is analysed. In particular, enforcement of public procurement rules at European level covers proceedings before the European Court of Justice, interim measures as well as an analysis of the consequences of a judgment by the Court. Enforcement of public procurement rules at national level reveals a valuable picture for pre-judicial stages in review procedures, interim measures, set aside and annulment conditions, actions for damages, dissuasive penalty payments, and complaints to the European Commission, the conciliation procedure for utilities and finally, compliance with and enforcement of the rules under the WTO Government Procurement Agreement. The chapter includes a valuable codification of the jurisprudence of the European Court of Justice on the review proceedings requirements specified by the Remedies Directives.

Finally, Chapter 17 provides an epilogue and includes a summary of public procurement as a policy instrument. The chapter examines procurement regulation in the light of economic policy, anti-trust, state aid and industrial policy at European Union and national levels.

Series editor's preface

Public procurement in the EU is a matter not only of huge economic importance, but it is also an area in which there has been a massive growth of EU legislation and case-law: when Professor Bovis wrote a book on the subject ten years ago, it had five chapters; the current book has 17 chapters.

Legislation in this area was a priority in the context of the completion of the internal market by the end of 1992. However, while the EU may have the objective of an economic policy conducted in accordance with the principle of an open market economy with free competition, Professor Bovis points out that public and utilities procurement remains an area where the fundamental objective of market access requires a positive regulatory approach, given that it involves public markets.

We have therefore seen a growth in the range and detail of the relevant EU legislation, and the author initially gives an overview of how we have got to the fourth generation of legislation in this area, and of the principles of public procurement regulation. He then enters into detailed analysis of specific aspects of Public Sector Procurement and of Utilities Procurement, leading on to a consideration of the specific rules on Remedies and the more general issues of enforcement in this area of EU Law.

This book will be of interest not only to those working in the area of public and utilities procurement in the EU, but also to readers concerned with the EU's internal market, with the legislative competence of the EU, and with regulatory governance in the EU. I am most grateful to Professor Bovis for having made this material accessible to a wide range of readers.

John A. Usher
Exeter, February 2007

Acknowledgements

For the inception and completion of this book I owe a great debt to Dr Christine L. Cnossen for her intellectual generosity and the enormous amount of encouragement she has given me. Also it is with deep appreciation that I record my gratitude to Peter Cnossen and Diane Herechuk for their unconditional support.

My sincere thanks go to the publishers for their professionalism.

I am eternally grateful to Yetta Lamar, Executive Vice President and CFO of *LE Group Inc*, for her devotion, affection and esteem over the past years.

Finally, I owe an enormous amount of appreciation to Terrence G. Bramall, a person I regard as a mentor, for allowing me to share his wisdom, to taste his entrepreneurial flare and to experience his principles and disciplines. I respectfully dedicate this book to him.

Professor Christopher H. Bovis *JD, MPhil, LLM, FRSA*
Spring 2007

Table of cases

1. Introduction

PUBLIC PROCUREMENT WITHIN EUROPEAN UNION LAW

The creation and proper functioning of the common market rest in the heart of European Union law. The Treaties establishing the European Union have envisaged a system of legal, economic and political integration which is to be achieved through the progressive convergence of the economic policies of member states.[1]

The concept of the common market embraces the legal and economic dynamics of the European integration process, with clear political ambitions for its accomplishment, and presents the characteristics of a genuine integrated market. Such a market is a place where unobstructed mobility of factors of production[2] is guaranteed and where a regime of effective and undistorted competition regulates its operation. These characteristics reflect the four fundamental freedoms of a customs union (free movement of goods, persons, capital and services)[3] and, to the extent that the customs union tends to become an economic and monetary one,[4] on the adoption of a common economic policy and the introduction of a single currency. The adherence by member states to the above-mentioned fundamental principles of European economic integration will result in the removal of any restrictions or obstacles to inter-state trade. The level of success of economic integration in Europe will determine the level of success of political integration among member states, which is the ultimate objective stipulated in the Treaties.

---

[1]   See Articles 2 and 3 of the Treaty of Rome (EC).
[2]   See Articles 48 and 67 EC respectively.
[3]   The European Court of Justice has recognised a fifth freedom, the free movement of payments, which is closely related to the freedom of movement of capital, see cases 286/82 & 26/83, *Luisi & Carbone v. Ministero del Tesoro*, [1984] ECR 377, 308/86 *Ministère Public v. Lambert*, [1988] ECR 478. The Treaty of Rome provides also for the accomplishment of this freedom in Articles 67(2) and 106. The free movement of payments, a complementary principle of the free mobility of capital as a production factor, plays an extremely important role in the process of integration of public markets, and in particular in financing public projects either through indirect or direct investment.
[4]   See Article 102a EC.

Two strategic plans have facilitated the economic integration of the member states. These plans were enacted by European institutions and have been subsequently transposed into national laws and policies by member states. The first plan included a series of actions and measures aiming at the abolition of all tariff and non-tariff barriers to intra-community trade. The second plan has focused on the establishment of an effective, workable and undistorted regime of competition within the common market, in order to prevent potential abuse of market dominance and market segmentation, factors which could have serious economic implications in its functioning. The first plan, the abolition of all tariff and non-tariff barriers to intra-community trade, reveals a static effect which aimed at eliminating all administrative and legal obstacles to free trade and had as its focal point member states and their national administrations. The second plan, the establishment of an effective, workable and undistorted regime of competition within the common market, has been implemented at industry level and has an on-going and dynamic effect.

All tariff barriers appear to have been abolished by the end of the first transitional period,[5] so customs duties, quotas and other forms of quantitative restrictions could no longer hinder the free flow of trade amongst member states. Non-tariff barriers, however, have proved more difficult to eliminate, as they involve long-established market practices and patterns that could not change overnight. Non-tariff protection represents a disguised form of discrimination and can occur through a wide spectrum of administrative or legislative frameworks relating to public monopolies, fiscal factors such as indirect taxation, state aid practices and subsidies, technical standards and last but not least public procurement. Non-tariff barriers are by no means confined to the European integration process. The existence of non-tariff barriers is a common phenomenon in world markets and their elimination is the main objective of regulatory instruments of international trade. It has been maintained that non-tariff barriers could seriously distort the operation of the common market and its fundamental freedoms and derail the process of European integration.

The European Commission's White Paper for the Completion of the Internal Market[6] identified existing non-tariff protection and provided the framework for specific legislative measures[7] in order to address the issue at

---

[5]   The first transitional period covers the time period from the establishment of the European Communities until 31/12/1969. See Article 8(7) EC.

[6]   See European Commission, *White Paper for the Completion of the Internal Market*, (COM) 85 310 final, 1985.

[7]   The completion of the internal market required the adoption at Community level and the implementation at national level of some 300 Directives on the subjects

national level. The enactment of a set of Directives was deemed necessary for the completion of the internal market by the end of 1992, and the timetable was set out in the Single European Act, which in fact amended the Treaty of Rome by introducing *inter alia* the concept of the internal market. The internal market, in quantifiable terms, could be considered as something less than the common market but, perhaps, the first and most important part of the latter, as it '. . . would provide the economic context for the regeneration of the European industry in both goods and services and it would give a permanent boost to the prosperity of the people of Europe and indeed the world as a whole'.[8]

The internal market, as an economic concept, could be described as an area without internal frontiers, where the free circulation of goods and the unhindered provision of services, in conjunction with the unobstructed mobility of factors of production, are assured. The concept of the internal market is a reinforcement of the principle of the customs union as the foundation stone of the common market. The internal market embraces, obviously, less than the common market to the extent that the economic and monetary integration elements are missing. The Single European Act (SEA), as a legal instrument amending the Treaty of Rome, reveals strong public law characteristics, since the regulatory features of its provisions promote the importance of certain areas that had been previously overlooked. As a result, there has been both centralised and decentralised regulatory control by European institutions and member states over environmental policy, industrial policy, regional policy and the regulation of public procurement. The above areas represented the priority objectives in the process of completing the internal market. Public procurement was specifically identified as a significant non-tariff barrier and a detailed plan was devised to address the issue. The European Commission based its action on two notable studies.[9] Those studies provided empirical proof of the distorted market conditions in the public sector and highlighted the benefits of the regulation of public procurement.

The regulation of public procurement in the European Union has been significantly influenced by the internal market project. The White Paper for

---

specified in the Commission's White Paper. See also the *Third Report of the Commission to the European Parliament on the Implementation of the White Paper*, (COM) 88 134 final.

[8] See Lord Cockfield's quotation in the Cecchini Report, *1992: The European Challenge, The Benefits of a Single Market*, Wildwood House, 1988.

[9] See Commission of the European Communities, *The Cost of Non-Europe, Basic Findings, Vol. 5, Part. A: The Cost of Non-Europe in Public Sector Procurement*, Official Publications of the European Communities, Luxembourg, 1988. Also the Cecchini Report, *1992*, op cit.

the Completion of the Internal Market[10] and the Single European Act represent the conceptual foundations for the regulation of public markets in the member states. The identification of public procurement as a significant non-tariff barrier has offered ample evidence on the economic importance of its regulation.[11] Savings and price convergence appeared as the main arguments for liberalising the trade patterns of the demand (public and utilities sectors) and supply (industry) sides of the public procurement equation.[12] The regulation of public procurement exposes an economic and a legal approach to the integration of public markets in the European Union. On the one hand, the economic approach to the regulation of public procurement aims at creating an integral public market across the European Union. Through the principles of transparency, non-discrimination and objectivity in the award of public contracts, it is envisaged that the public procurement regulatory system will bring about competitiveness in the relevant product and geographical markets, increase import penetration of products and services destined for the public sector, enhance the tradability of public contracts across the common market, result in significant price convergence and finally be the catalyst for the needed rationalisation and industrial restructuring of the European industrial base.[13]

The legal approach to the regulation of public procurement, on the other hand, reflects a medium which facilitates the functions of the common market. In parallel with the economic arguments, legal arguments have emerged supporting the regulation of public procurement as a necessary ingredient of the fundamental principles of the Treaties, such as the free movement of goods and services, the right of establishment and the prohibition of discrimination on nationality grounds.[14] The legal significance of the regulation of public procurement in the common market has been well documented through the Court's jurisprudence. The liberalisation of public procurement indicates the wish of European institutions to eliminate preferential and discriminatory purchasing patterns by the public sector and create seamless intra-community trade patterns between the public and private sectors. Procurement by member

---

[10]   See European Commission, *White Paper for the Completion of the Internal Market*, op cit.

[11]   See Commission of the European Communities, *The Cost of Non-Europe*, op cit. Also the Cecchini Report, *1992* op cit.

[12]   The European Commission has claimed that the regulation of public procurement could bring substantial savings of ECU 20 bn or 0.5% of GDP to the (European) public sector. See European Communities, *The Cost of Non-Europe*, op cit.

[13]   See Commission of the European Communities, *Statistical Performance for Keeping Watch over Public Procurement*, 1992. Also the *Cost of Non-Europe*, op cit.

[14]   See Bovis, 'Recent case law relating to public procurement: A beacon for the integration of public markets', *Common Market Law Review*, 39 (2002).

states and their contracting authorities is often susceptible to a rationale and a policy that tend to favour indigenous undertakings and *national champions*[15] at the expense of more efficient competitors (domestic or Community-wide). As the relevant markets (product and geographical) have been sheltered from competition, distorted patterns emerge in the trade of goods, works and services destined for the public sector. These trade patterns represent a serious impediment in the functioning of the common market and inhibit the fulfilment of the principles enshrined in the Treaties.[16]

Legislation, policy guidelines and jurisprudence have all played their role in determining the need for integrated public markets in the European Union, where sufficient levels of competition influence the most optimal patterns of resource allocation for supplying the public sector as well as the public utilities with goods, works and services. Public procurement has now been identified as a key feature in the vision of the European Union in becoming the most competitive economy in the world by 2010.[17]

THE THRUST OF PUBLIC PROCUREMENT REGULATION

Whereas the regulatory weaponry for private markets is dominated by anti-trust law and policy, public markets are fora where the structural and behavioural remedial tools of competition law emerge as rather inappropriate instruments of a regulatory framework. The applicability of competition law to public markets is limited, mainly due to the fact that anti-trust often clashes with the monopolistic structures which exist in public markets. State participation in market activities is regularly assisted through exclusive exploitation of a product or a service within a geographical market. The market activities of a public entity are protected from competition by virtue of laws on trading and production or by virtue of delegated monopolies. Another reason for the

---

15   The term implies a firm with more than a third of its turnover made in its own country which has enjoyed formal or informal government protection. The term has been defined by Abravanel and Ernst, 'Alliance and acquisition strategies for European national champions', *The McKinsey Quarterly* (2) (1992), 45–62.

16   See Nicolaides (ed), *Industrial Policy in the European Community: A Necessary Response to Economic Integration*, Martinus Nijhoff, 1993.

17   See Communication from the European Commission to the Council, the European Parliament, the Economic and Social Committee, and the Committee of the Regions, 'Working together to maintain momentum', 2001 Review of the Internal Market Strategy, Brussels, 11 April 2001, COM (2001) 198 final. Also European Commission, Commission Communication, Public Procurement in the European Union, Brussels, 11 March 1998, COM (98) 143.

limited applicability of anti-trust law and policy in public markets is the fact that conceptual differences appear between the two categories of markets – private and public – in the eyes of anti-trust, which could be attributed to their different nature. In private markets, anti-trust law and policy seek to punish cartels and abusive dominance of undertakings. The focus of the remedial instruments is the supply side, which is conceived as the commanding part in the supply/demand equation due to the fact that it instigates and controls demand for a product. In private markets, the demand side of the equation (consumers in general) is susceptible to exploitation and the market equilibria are prone to distortion as a result of the collusive behaviour of undertakings or an abusive monopoly position. On the other hand, the structure of public markets reveals a different picture. In the supply/demand equation, the dominant part appears to be the demand side (the state and its organs as purchasers), which stimulates demand through purchasing, whereas the supply side (the industry) fights for access to the relevant markets. Although this is normally the case, one should not exclude the possibility of market oligopolisation and the potential manipulation of the demand side.[18] These advanced market structures may occur more often in the future, as a result of the well-established trends in industrial concentration.

Another argument which has relevance to the different regulatory approach to public and private markets reflects the methods of possible market segmentation and abuse. It is maintained that the segmentation of private markets appears different than the partitioning of public ones. In private markets, market segmentation occurs as a result of cartels and collusive behaviour, which would lead to abuse of dominance, with a view to driving competitors out of the relevant market, increasing market shares and ultimately increasing profits. Private markets can be segmented both geographically and by reference to product or service, whereas public ones can only be geographically segmented. This assumption leads to the argument that the partition of public markets would probably be the result of concerted practices attributed to the demand side. As such concerted practices focus on the origin of a product or a service or the nationality of a contractor, the only way to effectively partition the relevant market would be by reference to its geographical remit. In contrast, as far as private markets are concerned, the segmentation of the relevant market (either product or geographical) can only be attributed to the supply side. The argument goes further to reveal the fact that the balance of power between the supply and the demand sides is reversed in public markets. In the latter, it is the demand side that has the dominant role in the equation by

---

[18] See Konstadacopoulos, 'The linked oligopoly concept in the Single European Market', *Public Procurement Law Review*, 4 (1995), 213.

dictating terms and conditions in purchases, initiation of transactions, as well as in influencing production trends.[19]

In public markets, concerted practices of the demand side (for example, excluding foreign competition, application of buy-national policies, and application of national standards policies) represent geographical market segmentation, as they result in the division of the European public markets into different national public markets. It could also be maintained that public markets are subject to protection – rather than restriction – from competition, to the extent that the latter are quasi-monopolistic and monopsonistic in their structure. Indeed, the state and its organs, as contractors, possess a monopoly position in the sense that no one competes against them in their market activities.[20] Even in cases of privatisation, the monopoly position is shifted from the public to private hands. The situation is different in cases of an open privatised regime pursuing an operation in the public interest. In that case, it would be more appropriate to refer to oligopolistic competition in the relevant market. Also in privatised regimes, interchangeability of supply is very limited, to the extent that monopoly position characteristics survive the transfer of ownership from public to private hands. The state and its organs also possess a monopsony position, as firms engaged in transactions with them have no alternatives to pursue business. Access barriers to geographical public markets are erected by states as a result of exercising their discretion to conclude contracts with national undertakings. This type of activity constitutes the partition of public markets in the European Union, whereas undertakings operating in private markets must enter into a restrictive agreement between themselves in order to split up the relevant markets. Due to their different integral nature, private and public markets require different control. The control in both cases has a strong public law character, but while anti-trust regulates private markets, it appears rather inappropriate for public ones. Anti-trust law and policy is a set of rules of a negative nature; undertakings must *restrain* their activities to an acceptable range pre-determined in due course by the competent authorities. On the other hand, public markets require a set of rules that have a positive character. It should be recalled that the integration of public markets is based on the abolition of barriers and obstacles to national markets; it then follows that the type of competition envisaged for their regulation is mainly *market access competition*. Above all, this indicates that price competition is expected to emerge in European public markets only after their integration.

---

[19] See Bovis, 'The regulation of public procurement as an element in the evolution of European economic law', *European Law Journal* (Spring 1998).

[20] See Swann, *The Retreat of the State*, Harvester-Wheatsheaf, 1988, chapters 1–2.

It appears, however, that in both private and public markets, two elements have relevance when attempting their regulation. The first element is the *price differentiation* of similar products; the second element is *access* to the relevant markets. As the European integration is an economic process which aims at dismantling barriers to trade and approximating national economies, the need to create acceptable levels of competition in both public and private markets becomes more demanding. In fact, a regime of genuine competition in public markets would benefit the public interest as it would lower the price of goods and services for the public, as well as achieving substantial savings for the public purse.

The evolution of public procurement regulation in the European Union points towards a strategy for eliminating discriminatory public procurement amongst member states that have posed significant obstacles to the fundamental principles of free movement of goods, the right of establishment and the freedom to provide services. That strategy has been based on two principal assumptions: the first assumption acknowledged the fact that in order to eliminate preferential and discriminatory purchasing practices in European public markets, a great deal of *transparency* and *openness* was needed; the second assumption rested on the premise that the only way to regulate public procurement in the member states in an effective manner was through the process of *harmonisation* of existing laws and administrative practices which had been in operation, and not through a *uniform* regulatory pattern which would replace all existing laws and administrative practices throughout the Community. The latter assumption indirectly recognised the need for a decentralised system of regulation for public procurement in the Community, well ahead of the pronouncement of the principle of *subsidiarity* which was introduced in the European law jargon some years later by virtue of the Maastricht Treaty on European Union.

Since harmonisation was adopted as the most appropriate method of regulation of public procurement in the common market, and the decentralised character of the regime was reinforced through legislation, the onus then was shifted to the national administrations of the member states, which had to implement the Community principles in domestic law and give a certain degree of clarity and legitimate expectation to interested parties. Occasionally, the European Commission is criticised for not reserving for itself or other Community institutions central powers, other than those already available and at its disposal as the guardian of the Treaty, in relation to the enforcement of and compliance with public procurement rules. Critics often refer to the applicability of competition law and policy of the European Union and the regime which legally implements it through specific Regulations. However, although in principle competition law of the European Union may apply to the awarding of public contracts,[21] the *effectiveness* and *efficiency* of a regulatory regime in the public markets through basic anti-trust remedies remains a challenge for the law and for policy makers. Application of a rigid regime in a uniform way across the common market would not take into account national particularities in public procurement and a highest common denominator would probably eliminate any elements of *flexibility* in the system. Public procurement, as the *nexus* of transactions in the supply chain of the public sector, does not differ in principle from the management of purchasing practices in the private sector, which remains unregulated.

The legal instruments chosen by European institutions to achieve the objective of flexibility are Directives. Public markets and their regulation are dominated by different legal regimes and legal approaches that diverge to a considerable extent from each other. Directives, as flexible legal instruments leaving a great deal of discretion in the hands of member states with respect to the forms and methods of their implementation, can harmonise public markets, taking into account existing divergences in domestic legal systems. The appropriateness of Directives to achieve the desired degree of competition in public markets and establish a regime where optimal resource allocation benefits the public interest is unquestionable. The nature and character of Directives, as *'framework'* legal instruments, aim at harmonising existing legal systems, bringing them into conformity with envisaged Community objectives. Directives attempt to approximate different national laws and achieve a similar legal regime throughout the common market, based on the lowest common denominator amongst the systems of the member states. Divergences will inevitably remain, as the European Union lacks the powers to abolish existing domestic legal regimes and impose *ab initio* a different one.[22] Nevertheless, it

---

[21] See case *Cooperative Vereniging 'Suiker Unie' UA v. Commission*, [1975] ECR 1663, in which the European Court of Justice recognised the adverse effects of concerted practices in tendering procedures on competition in the common market. This case appears to have opened the way for the application of competition law to public procurement in the Community. The applicability of Competition Law provisions of the Treaty (Articles 81, 82 EC) in controlling collusive tendering and anti-competitive behaviour of suppliers was also the subject of Commission Decision 92/204, OJ 1992 L 92/1. It could be argued that competition law and policy apply equally to private as well as public markets, but the explicit provisions of the Directives on consortia participation in tendering procedures might limit the scope of Articles 81 EC and 82 EC on public procurement.

[22] For the constitutional aspects of the application of a Regulation in domestic legal orders, see the reservations of the French Government after the adoption of the SEA and in particular Article 100A EC, which constitutes the legal basis of all Public Procurement Directives after 1986 in Kapteyn and Verloren van Themaat, *Introduction to the Law of the European Communities*, 2nd edn, Kluwer-Deventer, 1989, pp. 470–79.

should be pointed out that Regulations aim at unification of the regimes
governing the member states' legal orders and have been extensively used in
the anti-trust field. It could be further argued that Regulations reveal all the
characteristics of instruments of public law, in particular to the extent that they
are directly applicable and produce vertical and horizontal direct effectiveness.
Apart from the creation of a uniform system common to the internal legal
orders of the member states, other notable advantages of having recourse to
Regulations instead of Directives would have been the fact that individuals
could directly rely on their provisions not only against the state but also
against other individuals before domestic courts.

Directives, on the other hand, appear to have strong characteristics as
instruments of public law, inasmuch as they constitute the legal framework
within which the state must enact rules that regulate the relevant sector.
Directives, unlike Regulations, lay down duties and obligations addressed
only to member states. Regulations, in addition, introduce rights of individuals to be respected by member states and also other individuals. Directives
resemble circulars at domestic administrative level, to the extent that the latter
provide the framework for action by central government towards the competent decentralised authority. The difference is that Directives are binding legal
instruments and may be relied upon before national courts by individuals
under certain circumstances restrictively interpreted by the European Court of
Justice (the case of direct effect), whereas administrative circulars produce no
binding effects. Directives, as Community legal instruments, were thought to
be the most appropriate method to regulate public markets in the European
Union. As mentioned above, fundamental differences in existing national legal
systems dictated the continuation of domestic public market regimes, but the
main concern was their enforcement at national level. In fact, it was the range
of procedural and substantive sensibilities and peculiarities found in the judicial infrastructure of the member states, especially the system through which
judicial review of public procurement is channelled, that prevented legal unification at Community level by means of Regulations.

Treaty provisions on non-discrimination, on the prohibition of barriers to
intra-community trade, on the freedom to provide services and on the right of
establishment, on public undertakings and undertakings to which member
states grant special or exclusive rights and on state monopolies providing
services of general economic interest, although capable of embracing the legal
relations arising from public procurement in the common market and regulating intra-community trade of public contracts according to the principles stipulated in the Treaties, seemed insufficient on their own to eliminate the
protection afforded to domestic undertakings by preferential public procurement. The diversity of legal systems within the member states of the European
Union and the differences in existing domestic public procurement rules

would have rendered the regulation of public markets ineffective, if recourse was sought solely to primary Community legislation. The negative character of the primary Community provisions which apply to public procurement, to the extent that they provide a legal framework which prohibits any obstructions, distortions and hindrances to intra-community trade and the relevant fundamental principles, could be seen as the main reason for the need by European institutions to intervene and introduce a set of rules which, although based upon the primary Community rules above, have a positive character in the sense that they allow a margin of discretion in their implementation. Owing to the decentralised nature of any regulatory form of public procurement in the common market, the normative character of the primary Community rules was diluted in favour of a process of harmonisation of existing laws and practices in the member states.

THE NOTION OF PUBLIC MARKETS

The main reason for regulating public sector and utilities procurement is to bring their respective markets parallel to the operation of private markets. European policy makers have recognised the distinctive character of *public markets* and focused on establishing conditions similar to those that control the operation of private markets. The public markets reflect an economic equation where the demand side is represented by the public sector at large and the utilities, whereas the supply side covers industry.

The state and its organs enter the market place in pursuit of the public interest.[23] However, the activities of the state and its organs do not display the commercial characteristics of private entrepreneurship, as the aim of the public sector is not the maximisation of profits but the observance of public interest.[24] This fundamental difference emerges as the basis for the creation of *public markets* where public interest substitutes for profit maximisation.[25]

---

[23]   See Valadou, 'La notion de pouvoir adjudicateur en matière de marchés de travaux', *Semaine Juridique* (1991), ed. E, no. 3; Bovis, 'La notion et les attributions d'organisme de droit public comme pouvoirs adjudicateurs dans le régime des marchés publics', *Contrats Publics* (September 2003).

[24]   Flamme and Flamme, 'Enfin l' Europe des Marchés Publics', *Actualité Juridique – Droit Administratif* (1989).

[25]   On the issue of public interest and its relation to profit, see cases C-223/99, *Agora Srl v. Ente Autonomo Fiera Internazionale di Milano* and C-260/99 *Excelsior Snc di Pedrotti Runa & C v. Ente Autonomo Fiera Internazionale di Milano*, [2001] ECR 3605; C-360/96, *Gemeente Arnhem Gemeente Rheden v. BFI Holding BV*, [1998] ECR 6821; C-44/96, *Mannesmann Anlangenbau Austria AG et al. v. Strohal Rotationsdurck GesmbH*, [1998] ECR 73. The existence of profitability deprives the

However, further variances distinguish private from public markets. These focus on structural elements of the market place, competitiveness, demand conditions, supply conditions, the production process, and finally pricing and risk. They also provide an indication of the different methods and approaches employed in their regulation.[26]

Private markets are generally structured as a result of competitive pressures originating in the interaction between buyers and supplier and their configuration can vary from monopoly or oligopoly conditions to models representing perfect competition. Demand arises from heterogeneous buyers with a variety of specific needs, is based on expectations and is multiple for each product. Supply, on the other hand, is offered through various product ranges, where products are standardised using known technology, but constantly improved through research and development processes. The production process is based on mass-production patterns and the product range represents a large choice including substitutes, whereas the critical production factor is cost level. The development cycle appears to be short to medium term and finally, the technology of products destined for private markets is evolutionary. Purchases are made when an acceptable balance between price and quality is achieved. Purchase orders are in bulk and at limited intervals. Pricing policy in private markets is determined by competitive forces and the purchasing decision is focused on the price–quality relation, where the risk factor is highly relevant.

On the other hand, public markets tend to be structured and to function in a different way. The market structure often reveals monopsony characteristics.[27] In terms of its origins, demand in public markets is institutionalised and operates mainly under budgetary constraints rather than being subject to the price mechanism. It is also based on fulfilment of tasks (pursuit of public interest) and it is single for many products. Supply also has limited origins, in terms of the establishment of close ties between the public sector and the industries supplying it, and there is often a limited product range. Products are rarely innovative and technologically advanced and pricing is determined through tendering and negotiations. The purchasing decision is primarily based upon the life-time cycle, reliability, price and political considerations. Purchasing patterns follow tendering and negotiations and often purchases are dictated by policy rather than price/quality considerations.

The intellectual support of public procurement regulation in the European Union draws inferences from economic theories. Although the regulation of

---

relevant market of public interest functions, since it cultivates competition and as a result the substitutability of supply denotes that the market is a private market.

[26]   See Bovis, *The Liberalisation of Public Procurement in the European Union and its Effects on the Common Market*, Ashgate, 1998, chapter 1.

[27]   Monopsony is the reverse of monopoly power. The state and its organs often appear as the sole outlet for an industry's output.

public procurement aims primarily at the purchasing patterns on the demand side, it is envisaged that the integration of public markets through enhanced competition could bring about beneficial effects for the supply side. These effects focus on the optimal allocation of resources within European industries, the rationalisation of production and supply, the promotion of mergers and acquisitions and the creation of globally competitive industries. Public procurement has cyclical dynamics. It purports to change both behavioural and structural perceptions and applies its effects to both the demand and supply sides.

The integration of public markets in the European Union is achieved solely by reference to the regulation of the purchasing behaviour of the demand side (the contracting authorities). The behaviour of the supply side is not the subject of public procurement legislation, although its regulation would arguably be of equal importance to the integration of public markets in the European Union. The supply side in the public procurement equation is subject to the competition law and policy of the European Union, although there is no integral mechanism in the public procurement legislation which is capable of introducing anti-trust rules to the supply side. *Stricto sensu*, anti-competitive behaviour of undertakings or collusive tendering do not appear as reasons for disqualification from the selection and award procedures of public contracts.

European institutions have assumed that encouraging the public and utilities sectors in the European Union to adopt purchasing behaviour which is homogeneous and based on the principles of openness, transparency and non-discrimination will achieve efficiency gains and public sector savings and stimulate industrial restructuring on the supply side.

The European Commission has claimed that the regulation of public procurement throughout the European Union and the resulting elimination of non-tariff barriers arising from discriminatory and preferential purchasing patterns of member sates could bring about substantial savings estimated around 0.5% of the gross domestic product of the European Union. Combating discrimination on grounds of nationality in the award of public procurement contracts and eliminating domestic preferential purchasing schemes could result in efficiency gains at European and national levels through the emergence of three major effects which would primarily influence the supply side. These include a *trade effect*, a *competition effect* and a *restructuring effect*.

The trade effect represents the actual and potential savings that the public sector would be able to achieve through lower cost purchasing. The trade effect is a result of the principle of transparency in public markets (compulsory advertisement of public contracts above certain thresholds). However, the principle of transparency and the associated trade effect in public markets do not in themselves guarantee the establishment of competitive conditions in the relevant markets, as market access – a structural element in the process of integration of public markets in Europe – could subsequently be hindered by the discriminatory behaviour of contracting authorities in the selection and award stages of public procurement. The trade effect has a static dimension, since it emerges as a consequence of enhanced market access in the relevant sector or industry.

The competition effect relates to the changes in industrial performance resulting from changes in the price behaviour of national firms which had previously been protected from competition by means of preferential and discriminatory procurement practices. The competition effect derives also from the principle of transparency and appears to possess rather static characteristics. Transparency in public procurement breaks down information and awareness barriers in public markets, and as mentioned above, it brings about a trade effect in the relevant sectors or industries by means of price competitiveness. The competition effect comes as a natural consequence of price competitiveness and inserts an element of long-term competitiveness in the relevant industries in aspects other than price (for example, research and development, innovation, customer care). The competition effect will materialise in the form of *price convergence* of goods, works and services destined for the public sector. Price convergence could take place both nationally and Community-wide, inasmuch as competition in the relevant markets would equalise the prices of similar products.

Finally, the restructuring effect reveals the restructuring dimension and the re-organisational dynamics on the supply side, as a result of increased competition in the relevant markets. The restructuring effect is a dynamic one and refers to the long-term industrial and sectoral adjustment within industries that supply the public sector. The restructuring effect will encapsulate the reaction of the relevant sector or industry to the competitive regime imposed upon the demand and supply sides, as a result of openness and transparency and the consequential trade and competition effects. The response of the relevant sector or industry and the restructuring effect itself will depend on the efficiency with which the industry merges, diversifies, converts or aborts the relevant competitive markets and will also reflect contemporary national industrial policies.[28]

From the mid-1980s, the regulation of public procurement in the European Union became a priority. The inefficiency of the relevant primary and secondary Community provisions to combat discriminatory practices and preferential public purchases by contracting authorities throughout the common

---

[28]   See European Commission, *The Opening-up of Public Procurement to Foreign Direct Investment* in the European Community, CC 93/79, 1995.

market was disclosed, as statistical results revealed significantly low cross-border import penetration in public contracts. Furthermore, a disturbing picture emerged as to the extent of differentiation of market access in public procurement opportunities in the member states of the European Union. Market access reflects the effectiveness of import penetration strategies (marketing, predatory pricing, venture alliances) by an undertaking and very much depends upon the regime of competition reigning in the relevant market place.

If scale economies were important in defining the most desirable purchasing pattern for the public sector and if competition were to increase amongst industries which supply the latter, an efficient European industrial structure would support fewer firms operating at full capacity.[29] Strategic mergers and cross-border investments would reshape the industries and reorganise the operation of firms. Within this reorganisation process, structural adjustment would constantly change in order to adapt to the new market environment introduced by the legal regime on public procurement. In the process of developing new industrial strategies, two factors appear essential: the need for integration of industrial activities[30] and the need to meet local demands.

In the past many of the advantages offered to national champions and locally operating firms in public procurement markets had discouraged the tradability of public contracts[31] amongst European industries.[32] Persistently low import penetration in protected public procurement sectors dictated a corporate strategy to the relevant industries. Before the opening up of public procurement in Europe, the typical strategic choice was low on integration and high on responsiveness, including the replication of all major corporate functions (production, research and development, marketing) in each member state. The on-going realisation of the common market and the regulation of public procurement in the European Union have been forcing undertakings to revise their strategies and to build up *network organisations* which combine local responsiveness with a high degree of centralisation and co-ordination of major supporting activities. The new strategy has the characteristics of a multi-focal strategy.

---

[29] See Dunning, 'Explaining changing patterns of international production: In defence of the eclectic theory', *Oxford Bulletin of Economics and Statistics*, **41**(4) (1979), 269–95.

[30] See Dunning, *The Globalisation of Business: The Challenge of the 1990s*, Routledge, London and New York, 1993.

[31] The term tradability of public contracts denotes the effectiveness of the supply side in engaging in transactions with public authorities in member states other than the state of residence or nationality.

[32] See McLachlan, 'Discriminatory public procurement, economic integration and the role of bureaucracy', *Journal of Common Market Studies*, **23**(4) (1985), 357–72.

The adoption of multi-focal strategies or global integration strategies involves a major shift in location patterns of key functions within firms.[33] The old decentralised multinational organisations which duplicated major functions in each country in which they operated need to transform into an integrated system of which the key elements show a different degree of regional concentration.[34] As a consequence of the new organisational structure, different types of international transactions are expected to occur.[35] Specialisation and concentration of activities in certain regions will lead to more trade between certain member states. In addition, as a result of the corporate network system, trade will increasingly develop into intra-firm trade and intra-industry trade with greater exchange of intermediary products.[36] The organisational rationalisation following the development of network organisations may result in a problem of ownership and location of corporate headquarters. Some member states may fear losing strategic control in the restructuring process[37] and may therefore resist the rationalisation process that the industry has been undergoing, by imposing various restrictions in terms of ownership or control structures of locally operating firms.

---

[33]   Porter, *The Competitive Advantage of Nations*, Macmillan, London, 1990.

[34]   Prahalad and Doz, *The Multinational Mission: Balancing Local Demands and Global Vision*, The Free Press, 1987.

[35]   Dunning, 'Multinational enterprises in the 1970's', in Hopt, *European Merger Contract*, de Fruyter, Berlin, 1982.

[36]   Vandermerwe, 'A framework for constructing Euro-networks', *European Management Journal*, 11(1) (1989), 55–61.

[37]   Tirole, *The Theory of Industrial Organization*, The MIT Press, Cambridge, MA, 1988.

2. The development of a public procurement framework

THE FIRST GENERATION OF PUBLIC PROCUREMENT ACQUIS

Public Supplies

As early as 1962, European institutions realised how important public procurement was to the functioning of the common market. The Council of Ministers adopted two *General Programmes*[1] for the elimination of restrictions on inter-state trade with a view to providing guidance to member states on the implementation of Articles 52, 53 EC (right of establishment) and 59, 60 EC (freedom to provide services). Member states had in operation rules and practices for the award of public contracts which discriminated against foreign undertakings on nationality grounds. The result of such restrictions was a significant fragmentation of the common market, in relation to public procurement.

The General Programmes aimed at the abolition of restrictions which '. . . exclude, limit or impose conditions upon the capacity to submit offers or to participate as main contractors or subcontractors in contract awards by the state or legal persons governed by public law'. The General Programmes envisaged a gradual removal of quotas established between member states for public contracts and the co-ordination of national procedures for their award to persons or undertakings of other member states through agencies established in other member states or directly to those persons or undertakings. The two General Programmes took account of the special features of public works contracts.

In 1966 the European Commission introduced Directive 66/683,[2] which required the elimination of measures prohibiting the use of imported products or prescribing that of domestic products in public procurement. The Directive was adopted in the light of the abolition of all quotas and measures having an

---

[1]   See J.O. 1962 36/32.
[2]   See J.O. 1966 P. 3748.

effect equivalent to quantitative restrictions upon trade amongst member states, as a result of the first transitional period of the European Communities.[3] However, public supplies contracts were exempted pending the adoption of a specific Directive, which was adopted in 1970. The Commission in that year enacted Directive 70/32[4] on the basis of Article 33(7) EC, hence introducing the prohibition of measures having an effect equivalent to quantitative restrictions on public procurement.

Directive 70/32 applied to all products of whatever description which were admitted to free circulation within the Community by virtue of Articles 9 and 10 EC. These were products originating in a member state, as well as third country products admitted to free circulation within the Community through a member state. The Directive indicated two types of barriers that states, territorial authorities and other public corporate bodies could impose upon procurement of public supplies;[5] (i) those preventing or inhibiting the supply of imported products and (ii) those favouring the supply of domestic products or granting preferential treatment, except treatment relating to state aids or preferential taxation.[6] The Directive in Article 3(3) listed a number of forms of discrimination against foreign goods. Among those were technical specifications, which though applicable to both domestic and imported products, had restrictive effects on trade.

The rationale behind Directive 70/32 was similar to the aims of Directive 66/683. However, Directive 70/32 was the very first legal instrument to regulate public supplies contracts in the European Communities and came into force after the expiry of the first transitional period at the end of 1969. The expiry of the transitional period, *inter alia*, resulted in rendering Article 30 EC (free movement of goods) directly effective, thus questioning the logic of introducing secondary legislation with its main thrust the free movement of goods, when at the same time primary Treaty provisions guaranteeing the principle of free movement of goods had become directly effective.

Directive 70/32 attempted to integrate markets relating to the supply of goods destined for the public sector from within and from outside the European Community. It made clear to member states that public supplies markets could not be confined within the geographical territory of the

---

[3] The first transitional period covered the period from the establishment of the European Communities until 31 December 1969. See Article 8(7) EC.

[4] See J.O. 1970 L 13/1.

[5] See Articles 3(1) and 3(2), of EC Directive 70/32, as well as the preamble to the Directive.

[6] State aids must be assessed under the framework of Article 92 EC, whereas direct and indirect forms of taxation are ultimately at the discretion of member states by virtue of Article 90 EC.

European Community, or the national borders of member states. It defined the market for public supplies as a broader field of sourcing goods destined for the public sector.[7]

In 1977, the Council of Ministers adopted Directive 77/62[8] for the co-ordination of procedures for the award of public supply contracts, based on Articles 30 and 100 EC. This Directive, which came into force in 1978, was designed to ensure more effective supervision of compliance than the previous Directive 70/32 on public supplies and also adherence to the negative obligations of Article 30 EC. The Directive imposed a number of positive obligations on purchasing bodies and contracting authorities,[9] which in turn introduced a great deal of discretion in the hands of member states. The positive obligations imposed on member states by virtue of Directive 77/62 raised a number of questions as to the direct effectiveness of its provisions. The fact that a Directive imposes positive obligations may affect the direct effectiveness of its provisions. The European Court of Justice was initially reluctant[10] to accept that the margin of discretion deriving from a positive obligation was capable of rendering the provision in question directly effective. Interestingly, in two cases[11] it ruled that even positive obligations contained in a Directive may have a direct effect.

The primary aim of Directive 77/62 was to enhance the efficiency and transparency of public markets by ensuring that conditions of competition were not distorted and that contracts were allocated to suppliers and contractors under the most favourable conditions for the public sector. Directive 77/62 introduced three fundamental principles: (a) Community-wide advertising of

---

[7]   This was the first attempt to link public procurement to the Commercial Policy of the European Communities and resulted in cultivating the ground for the introduction of common commercial policy considerations in public procurement. Ten years later in 1980, the European Commission was concluding on behalf of the member states the Agreement on Government Procurement during the GATT Tokyo Round, thus expanding the territorial application of the EC internal regime to members/signatories to the Agreement. See Bovis, 'The extra-territorial effect of EC Public Procurement Directives – The situation under the GATT Uruguay Round', *Legal Issues of European Integration*, vol. II (1993), 83–93. Also, Bovis, 'Public Procurement under the framework of the EC Common Commercial Policy', *Public Procurement Law Review*, 4 (1993), 211–20.

[8]   See OJ 1977 L 13/1.

[9]   See Article 1(b) of Directive 77/62 and the contracting authorities specified in Annex I.

[10]   See case 57/65 *Alfons Luttucke GmbH v. Hauptzollampt Saarlouis*, [1966] ECR 205.

[11]   See case C-28/67, *Firma Molkerei-Zentrale Westfalen/Lippe GmbH v. Haupzollampt Paderborn*, [1968] ECR 143; case C-13/68, *SpA Salgoil v. Italian Ministry of Foreign Trade*, [1968] ECR 453.

contracts; (b) prohibition of technical specifications capable of discriminating against potential bidders; and (c) application of objective criteria of participation in tendering and award procedures. However, the scope of Directive 77/62 was limited. It explicitly excluded from its coverage public supplies contracts by public utilities (authorities in the transport, energy, water and telecommunications sectors). The main legal reason for that exclusion was that public utilities had different legal status (public corporations or public undertakings) and operated under different regimes in member states (some covered by public law, others governed by private law, while some were in the process of privatisation, although essential control remained in the hands of the state). Directive 77/62 contained a *de minimis* rule; it was applicable only to public supply contracts with a value of more than 200 000 EUA.[12] Its legal basis (Articles 30 and 100 EC) rendered it inapplicable to products originating in and supplied by third countries outside the European Communities.[13]

In 1980 Directive 77/62 was amended by Directive 80/767[14] in order to take account of the 1979 GATT Agreement on Government Procurement (AGP).[15] The AGP committed the European Community and its member states to providing suppliers from third countries with access to central government purchasing and to some defence procurement. Directive 80/767 instituted an element of *multilaterality* in access to international public markets based on the principle of *reciprocity*.[16] That AGP became part of European Community law as it was approved by Council Decision 80/271.[17]

Public Works

Initially, Directive 71/304[18] covered the award of works and construction

---

[12]   See Article 5(1)(a) EC Directive 77/62. EUA refers to the European Unit of Account, the predecessor of the ECU. The threshold of the Directive was exclusive of VAT.

[13]   The Directive was also inapplicable to public supplies contracts awarded (i) pursuant to an international agreement between a member state and one or more non-member countries; (ii) pursuant to an international agreement relating to the stationing of troops between undertakings in a member state or a non-member country and (iii) pursuant to a particular procedure of an international agreement.

[14]   See OJ 1980 L 215/1.

[15]   See OJ 1980 L 71/1.

[16]   See Birkinshaw and Bovis, *The EC Public Supplies Directive*; *Public Procurement: Legislation and Commentary*, Butterworths European Law Service, 1992.

[17]   See OJ 1980 L 215/1.

[18]   See OJ 1971 L 185/1.

contracts after the transitional period. The Directive required member states to abolish restrictions on the participation of non-nationals in public procurement works contracts. However, it came into force after the completion of the transitional period, when Articles 59 and 60 EC concerning the freedom to provide services became directly effective, thus leaving few aspects to be implemented by member states. It now serves mainly to list professional trade activities which constitute public works.

In 1971, Directive 71/305[19] was adopted in order to enhance the implementation of the aims envisaged in Articles 52 EC (right of establishment) and 59 EC (freedom to provide services) in the field of public works procurement. Directive 71/305 was the primary legal vehicle for the opening up of public works contracts to intra-community competition by seeking the co-ordination of national procedures in the award of public works contracts. The Directive was based on the prohibition of discriminatory technical specifications, adequate and prompt advertising of contracts, the establishment of objective selection and award criteria and a procedure of joint supervision by both member states' authorities and the EC Commission to ensure the observation of these principles.[20]

The Directive's major objective was the establishment and enhancement of a transparency regime in the public works sector, where conditions of undistorted competition would ensure that contracts are allocated to contractors under the most favourable terms for contracting authorities. However, Directive 71/305 had a limited thrust. It did not introduce new tendering procedures nor were existing national procedures and practices replaced by a set of Community rules. Member states remained free to maintain or adopt substantive and procedural rules on condition that they comply with all the relevant provisions of Community law and in particular, the prohibitions following from the principles stipulated in the Treaty regarding the right of establishment and the freedom to provide services.[21]

The concept of public works contracts under the first Public Works Directive was very extensive[22] and covers those contracts concluded in writing between a contractor and a contracting authority for pecuniary interest concerning either the execution or both the execution and design of works related to building or civil engineering activities listed in class 50 of the NACE classification,[23] or the execution by whatever means of a work corresponding

---

19   See OJ 1971 L 185/5.
20   See the Preamble to Directive 71/305.
21   See cases 27, 28, 29/86, *CEI and Bellini*, [1987] ECR 3347.
22   Article 1(a) of Directive 71/305 as amended by Directive 89/440.
23   See General Industrial Classification of Economic Activities within the European Communities; see Annex II Directive 71/305.

to the requirements specified by the contracting authority. The above formula was wide enough to embrace modern forms of works contracts such as project developing contracts, management contracts and concession contracts.[24] With reference to the latter type of contracts, a public works concession is defined by the Works Directive[25] as a written contract between a contractor and a contracting authority concerning either the execution or both the execution and design of a work and for which remunerative considerations consist, at least partly, in the right of the *concessionaire* to exploit exclusively the finished construction works for a period of time. The initial Works Directive 71/305 did not apply to concession contracts, except where the concessionaire was a public authority covered by the Directive. In such situations, only the works subcontracted to third parties would be fully subject to its provisions. In any other case, the only provisions of the Directive applicable to works concessions were that the *concessionaire* should not discriminate on grounds of nationality when it itself awarded contracts to third parties.[26]

The European Commission's Communication to the Council on Public Supply contracts[27] revealed an unsatisfactory situation[28] with respect to the implementation of the Supplies and Works Directives in the legal orders of member states.[29] Subsequently, the European Commission's White Paper on the Completion of the Internal Market[30] reiterated that there was a serious and urgent need for improvement and clarification of the relevant Public Procurement Directives.

---

[24]   Concession contracts were public works projects under which the consideration for the works consists of a franchise (concession) to operate the completed works or in a franchise plus payment. For more details see the Guide to the Community rules on opening government procurement, OJ 1987, L 358/1 at 28.

[25]   See Article 1(d) of Directive 93/37.

[26]   See Article 3(3) Directive 71/305.

[27]   See COM (84) 717 final.

[28]   The list of factors responsible for the lack of success included *inter alia*: failure to advertise contracts in the Official Journal, as a result of intentional or unintentional splitting up of contracts; ignorance of the relevant rules on the part of contracting authorities or deliberate omission of these rules; excessive use of the exceptions permitting non-competitive tendering (negotiated procedures) instead of open or restricted procedures; discriminatory requirements posed by contracting authorities by means of compliance with national technical standards, to the exclusion of European standards or equivalent standards of other countries; unlawful disqualification of suppliers or contractors or discriminatory use of the award criteria.

[29]   It was anticipated that EC Directive 83/189, OJ 1983 L 165/1 was enacted in order to assist suppliers to fulfil the requirements of norms and standards referred to in EC Directive 77/62 and to eliminate discrimination arising through their use.

[30]   See COM (85) 310 final.

THE SECOND GENERATION OF PUBLIC PROCUREMENT ACQUIS

Public Supplies

In accordance with the Commission's action programme, the Council of Ministers in 1988 adopted Directive 88/295[31] amending all previous public supplies Directives. The main improvements were:

- with open tendering procedures as the norm, negotiated procedures were allowed in exceptional circumstances;[32]
- the definition of the types of supplies contracts was widened[33] and the method of calculation of the thresholds was clarified;[34]
- the exempted sectors were more strictly defined;[35]
- purchasing authorities had to publish in advance information on their annual procurement programmes and their timetable, as well as a notice giving details of the outcome of each award decision.[36]
- the rules on technical standards were brought in line with the new policy on standards, which is based on the mutual recognition of national requirements, where the objectives of national legislation are essentially equivalent, and on the process of legislative harmonisation of technical standards through non-governmental standardisation organisations (CEPT, CEN, CENELEC).[37]

Public Works

As a result of the Commission's action programme emanating from its White Paper for the Completion of the Internal Market, the Public Works Directives were amended by virtue of Directive 89/440. For the purposes of the Directive, the definition of contractors comprised any legal or natural person involved in construction activities and contracting authorities might impose a requirement as to the form and legal status of the contractor that won the

---

[31] See OJ 1988 L 127/1.
[32] See Article 7(2) of Directive 88/295.
[33] See Article 1(a) of Directive 88/295.
[34] See Article 6(1)(c) of Directive 88/295.
[35] See Article 3(2)(a)(b)(c) of Directive 88/295.
[36] See Article 9 of Directive 88/295.
[37] See Article 7 of Directive 88/295. See also the White Paper on Completing the Internal Market, paras 61–79; also Council Resolution of 7 May 1985, OJ 1985 C 136, on a new approach in the field of technical harmonisation and standards.

award.[38] The above requirement covered for the first time the case of *consortia participation* in public procurement contracts. To facilitate market access and provide as many opportunities as possible for interested tenderers, the Directive specifically prohibited contracting authorities from disqualifying groups or consortia of tenderers without corporate structure. This meant that contracting authorities must apply all the relevant selection and qualification procedures equally in evaluating an offer made by a consortium and award the contract to the consortium if the offer meets the award criteria. However, after the award of the contract and for reasons dictated by legal certainty and legitimate expectation, as well as for reasons associated with the supervision of the contract and its management, contracting authorities may require the incorporation of the consortium into a more concrete entity. As far as contracting authorities are concerned, the Directive provided a definition which was very wide and covered bodies governed by public law which is defined as being any body 'established for the specific purpose of meeting needs in the general interest and not having an industrial or commercial character, which has legal personality and is financed for the most part by the state or is subject to management supervision by the latter'.[39] There was a list of such bodies in Annex I of Directive 71/305, which is not exhaustive like that in the Supplies Directive, and member states were under an obligation to notify the Commission of any changes in that list.

Works contracts in the utilities and defence sectors and those contracts awarded in pursuance of certain international agreements were explicitly excluded by virtue of Articles 4 and 5 of the Directive. These provisions were identical to the corresponding provisions of the Supplies Directives.[40] This revealed the fact that those public contracts under the framework of the Works Directive covered mainly construction projects in the education, health, sports and leisure facilities sectors, in as much as state, regional or local authorities undertake such projects. Where entities involved in such activities (for example, a hospital or a university) enjoyed considerable independence from the state or local government, as to the undertaking of works contracts, Directive 71/305 was inapplicable, since such entities were not included in Annex I as bodies governed by public law for the purposes of the Directive in question. This seems to have limited the scope of the Directive only to cases where the state or local government had direct control over the above-mentioned entities.

---

[38]   See Article 21 of Directive 71/305 as amended. The same requirement is also found in the Supplies Directive (Article 18 of Directive 77/62).

[39]   This definition resembles the Court's ruling on state-controlled enterprises in case C-152/84, *Marshall v. Southampton and South West Hampshire Area Health Authority*, [1986] ECR 723.

[40]   See Article 3 of Directive 77/62 as amended by Directive 88/295.

Given the fact that works contracts in the utilities sectors were also excluded from the framework of the Directive, it applied to a rather modest portion of the construction sector. In order to moderate this undesirable result, the amending Directive 89/440[41] placed an obligation upon member states to ensure compliance with its provisions when they subsidise directly by more than 50% a works contract awarded by an entity involved in activities relating to certain civil engineering works and to the building of hospitals, sports recreation and leisure facilities, school and university buildings and buildings used for administrative purposes. These conditions seemed not to impose a heavy duty on member states, as only direct subsidies trigger the applicability of the Directive. Indirect ways of subsidising the entities in question, such as tax exemptions, guaranteed loans, or provision of land free of charge, render it inapplicable. It should be noted that under both the original Supplies and Works Directives, preference schemes in the award of contracts were allowed. Such schemes required the application of award criteria based on considerations other than the lowest price or the most economically advantageous tender, which are common in both regimes.[42] However, preferences could only be compatible with Community Law inasmuch they did not run contrary to the principle of free movement of goods (Article 30 EC et seq.) and to competition law considerations in respect of state aid.[43] Preference schemes have been abolished since the completion of the internal market at the end of 1992.

Another important feature of Directive 89/440 was the introduction of the regulation of concession contracts into the *acquis communautaire*. In fact, the Directive incorporated the Voluntary Code of Practice, which was adopted by the Representatives of Member States meeting within the Council in 1971.[44] The Code was a non-binding instrument and contained rules on the advertising of contracts and the principle that contracting authorities awarding the principal contract to a concessionaire were to require him to subcontract to third parties at least 30% of the total work provided for by the principal contract. Because of the lax character and non-binding nature of the provisions of the Voluntary Code, its requirements could not easily be incorporated into a binding instrument such as Directive 89/440, thus a more relaxed regime occurred. As a result, the co-ordination rules of the Directive applied to concession contracts only in respect of their advertising. The Directive's rules

---

[41] See Article 2 Directive 71/305 as amended by Directive 89/440.

[42] See Articles 29(4) and 29(a) of Directive 71/305; also Article 26 of Directive 77/62.

[43] See the Commission's Communication on the *Regional and Social Aspects of Public Procurement*, where it gives an overview of the preference schemes still existing in member states, COM (89) 400 final.

[44] See OJ 1971 C 82/13.

on tendering procedures, suitability criteria, selection and qualification, technical specifications and award procedures and criteria were inapplicable. Interestingly, Article 3(3) of Directive 71/305 on the prohibition of discrimination on grounds of nationality by a *concessionaire* awarding subcontracts disappeared from the text of the amending Directive 89/440. The reason might be that by the end of the transitional period Articles 7, 48, 52, 59 and 119 EC were directly effective and in addition, their horizontal direct effect had been pronounced by the European Court of Justice.[45]

Utilities

Initially, supplies and works contracts in the transport, water, energy and telecommunications sectors were excluded from the relevant supplies and works Directives.[46] The exclusion of the above-mentioned sectors from the framework of supplies Directives (77/62 and 88/295) had been officially attributed to the fact that the authorities entrusted with the operation of public utilities had been subject to different legal regimes in the member states, varying from completely state-controlled enterprises to privately controlled ones. With respect to the works Directives, the above justification also appears valid, although Directives 71/305 and 89/440 had very limited application in relation to construction and works projects for the entities operating in the excluded sectors.

As far as supplies contracts were concerned, a more convincing reason for the exclusion of those sectors is that the projects covered therein could not fall within the thresholds of Directives 77/62 and 88/295. Energy, telecommunications, transport and, to a lesser extent, the water industry, are technical sectors requiring state-of-the-art technology (especially telecommunications and energy). The value of the relevant contracts is very high, in comparison with (simple) supplies contracts, so the only way these sectors could have been brought within the Supplies Directive 77/62 would have been either to increase the thresholds (that is, 200 000 ECU) of the supplies contracts to such a level as to catch a substantial number of contracts in the excluded sectors or, on the other hand, to lower the envisaged thresholds of contracts in telecommunications, energy, transport and water industry sectors[47] to the level of the (simple) supplies contracts (that is 200 000 ECU). Either alternative would

---

[45] See case C-36/74, *Walrave and Koch v. Association Union Cycliste International et al.*, (1974) ECR 1423; case C-43/75, *Drefenne v. SABENA*, (1976) ECR 473.

[46] See Article 2 of Directive 77/62 as amended; Article 3 of Directive 89/440.

[47] See Article 12 of Directive 90/531; 400,000 ECU for water, energy and transport supplies and 600,000 ECU for telecommunications supplies.

have resulted in an undesirable situation. If the first alternative had been chosen, the bulk of supplies contracts would have escaped from the framework of the Supplies Directives. On the other hand, reducing the thresholds of the excluded sectors to 200 000 ECU would have eliminated the *de minimis* rule for those sectors. The principle of the *de minimis* rule is an essential condition for the dimensionality of public procurement in the European Communities, where quantitative criteria (that is, thresholds) for the regulation of a sector are chosen. The *de minimis* rule contributes significantly to lessening the administrative burdens on contracting authorities, which otherwise would make the award of public contracts a slow and costly exercise.

With respect to works contracts, the exclusion of the telecommunications, transport, energy and water industry sectors from Directives 71/305 and 89/440 could be better justified by reference to the different legal positions of the entities in question in the member states. If a privately controlled entity operating in the above sectors were to be involved in a construction project, Works Directives would be inapplicable, as the former was not included among the contracting authorities specified in Annex I (bodies governed by public law). To cover both privately and publicly controlled entities operating in the relevant utilities sectors, the Works Directives should have expanded the definition of contracting authorities; but this would have resulted in an internal disturbance in the operation of the original Supplies and Works Directives, which had envisaged as their objective the regulation of the award of construction projects and that of supplies contracts, exclusively by the state or local government or bodies governed by public law. Thus, in order to regulate the transport, telecommunications, and energy and water sectors, the only viable and reasonable solution appeared to be the introduction of a separate legal instrument, applying the same principles as those found in the Supplies and Works Directives.

A more sceptical explanation for the late regulation of utilities procurement could be the fact that due to their purchasing volume and relative magnitude, public utilities procurement constituted an important domestic industrial policy instrument. Member states appeared reluctant to subject the procurement of their utilities to the rigorous transparent and competitive regime of public works and supplies purchasing, as they have relied upon preferential utilities procurement with a view to sustaining certain strategic national industries.[48]

The European Commission was requested by the Council to follow the

---

[48] See European Commission, *Statistical Performance Indicators for Keeping Watch over Public Procurement*, 1992.

progress of the CEPT proceedings[49] on harmonisation in the field of telecommunications and to submit to the latter a timetable for measures ensuring effective competition in the field of supply contracts awarded for telecommunications services. The Commission, in its Recommendations on Telecommunications,[50] also expressed its desire to ensure that the objective of an open market, in particular for suppliers within the European Community, was being achieved without undesirable consequences for trade patterns with non-member countries. In its 1984 Communication to the Council on public supply contracts[51] and its White Paper on the Completion of the Internal Market,[52] the Commission reiterated the need to liberalise the so far excluded sectors, particularly the telecommunications sectors.

The European Parliament's Committee on Economic and Monetary Affairs and Industrial Policy presented a report to the European Parliament[53] stressing the need to extend the scope of the supplies and works Directives to cover the excluded sectors in utilities. In its Resolution[54] the Parliament approved all the Commission's and Council's actions, and called them to submit a proposal for a Directive to cover procurement activities and regulate the purchasing behaviour of excluded sectors. The Council, in Recommendation 84/550,[55] shared the Commission's wish to open up access to public telecommunications contracts, providing that governments of member states should offer opportunities for Community undertakings to tender on a non-discriminatory basis for the supply of specified telecommunications equipment and should also report to the Commission on implementing measures and practical effects. In 1988 the Commission issued Directive 88/301[56] on competition in the telecommunications terminal equipment markets.

In 1990 the Council adopted Directive 90/531[57] on the procurement procedures of entities operating in the water, energy, transport and telecommunications sectors. The regime reflected similar characteristics to the Supplies and Works Directives with some important differences as to the flexibility given to

---

[49] CEPT is the European Conference of Postal and Telecommunications Administrations, established in Montreux in 1959 and aiming at closer relations between member administrations to improve their administrative and technical services, OJ 1977 C 11/3.

[50] See COM (80) 422 final.

[51] See COM (84) 717 final.

[52] See COM (85) 310 final.

[53] See the von Wogau report, DOC. A2-38/85.

[54] See OJ 1985 C 175/241.

[55] See OJ 1984 L 289/51.

[56] See OJ 1988 L 131/73.

[57] See OJ 1990 L 297.

the contracting authorities over the choice of methods to be used to make the award process competitive.[58]

The legislative background of the Utilities Directive and the arduous process of the regulation of public utilities procurement are justified by the high complexity of the regime. The fact that public utilities often have unclear legal status or that their legal nature varies within the member states' legal systems has obviously made it difficult to introduce a single legal instrument to regulate their purchasing, although such a prolonged delay should be attributed to other factors. It may be recalled that public utilities absorb the vast majority of high technology equipment designated for public services and public interest projects. Protectionism in strategic industrial sectors has been pursued through preferential purchasing with a view either to sustaining the relevant industries or to assisting the development of infant industries in member states. The regulation of utilities procurement had to overcome not only the significant legislative barriers attributed to their nature but also the abandoning of member states' individual industrial policies through strategic procurement. In addition to those constraints, the fear of an uncontrolled flow of direct investment which would target vulnerable European-based high technology industries and the subsequent possible increase in take-overs and acquisitions, mainly from Japanese and American investors, time and again, discouraged the attempts of European institutions to integrate the utilities procurement within the common market.

The first Utilities Directive represented the most radical approach to public sector integration in Europe and its enactment coincided with the envisaged international liberalisation of public procurement during the Uruguay GATT negotiations. One might question such a strategy by European institutions, particularly bearing in mind the vulnerability of Europe's high-tech industry in comparison with those of the USA and Japan. However, the GATT regime introduced a new era in the accessibility of international public markets, to the extent that highly protectionist countries like the USA and Japan must, under the new regime, abolish their buy-national laws and policies and open their public markets to international competition, on a reciprocal basis.

The ambit of the first Utilities Directive and the scope of its application appeared more complicated than those of the Supplies and Works Directives, although the internal legal structure of all three Directives is very similar. Articles 1 and 2 of the first Utilities Directive constituted the broad framework

---

[58]   The Directive provided different implementing periods for Spain, Greece and Portugal. Spain had to implement its provisions by 1 January 1996 and Greece and Portugal by 1 January 1998 respectively. The delay in the uniform implementation of the Utilities Directive could be attributed to the preparations needed for the integration of the public utilities sectors in the respective countries.

of the Directive's application, providing various definitions and the remit of some preliminary exemptions. The first Utilities Directive devoted a substantial amount of provisions to attempting to exempt from application certain contracts or activities that have been deemed ineligible for community-wide regulation.

Apart from the normal exemptions on the grounds of defence and security and confidentiality, the major exemptions in the applicability of the first Utilities Directive were provided for under Articles 1 and 2. Radio and television broadcasting were not classified as telecommunication activities and were specifically excluded from the ambit of the Directive by virtue of Article 2. Also, bus transport services to the public were excluded on condition that their providers operated under a regime of competitive conditions, which meant that other potential contractors or suppliers of similar services were allowed to enter the relevant geographical and product markets and compete against the existing utilities provider (Article 2(4)). A similar rule applied to telecommunication services which operate within a competitive market.[59]

Under the same special exemptions provided for by Article (2) of the Directive were the cases of private entities supplying gas, heat, drinking water and electricity. Although the wording and spirit of the Directive covered private entities operating under exclusive and special rights in the utilities sectors, nevertheless under certain conditions, those entities could be exempted from the rules of the Directive. In the case of production of drinking water and production and distribution of electricity, if a private entity was able to demonstrate and prove that it did so for its own purposes, which were not related to the provision of drinking water or electricity to the public, that entity escaped the provisions of the Directive. Similarly, if a private entity was able to show that it supplied to the public network drinking water or electricity which was destined for its own consumption, and that the total so supplied to the network was not more than 30% of the total produced by that network in any one year over a three-year period, that entity was also exempt.[60]

In the case of gas and heat supplies, if the production by a private entity was related to an activity other than supply to a network for public consumption, then the first utilities Directive did not apply to that entity. Along the same lines, if the supply of gas and heat by a private entity to a public network related to economic exploitation only and did not exceed 20% of the firm's turnover in any one year, taking an average of the preceding three years and the current year, then that entity was also exempt.[61] Those exemptions

---

[59]   See Article 2(4) and Article 8 of the Utilities Directive amended by Directive 93/38.

[60]   See Article 2(5)(a) of the Utilities Directive amended by Directive 93/38.

[61]   See Article 2(5)(b) of the Utilities Directive amended by Directive 93/38.

predominantly covered entities that have research and development as their main objective in the relevant utilities sector, or that did not play a major role in supplying public networks with water or energy.[62]

There were also exemptions for entities exploring for gas, oil, coal and other solid fuels under Article 3. Entities operating in those sectors were not regarded as having an exclusive right provided that certain conditions were fulfilled. Those conditions were cumulative and stipulated that, when an exploitation right was granted to the entity in question, the latter was exempt from the Utilities Directives provided that other bodies were able to compete for the same exclusive rights under free competition; that the financial and technical criteria to be used in awarding exclusive rights were clearly spelt out before the award was made; that objective criteria as to the way in which exploitation was to be carried out were specified; that these criteria were published before requests for tenders were made and applied in a non-discriminatory way; that all operating obligations, royalty and capital and revenue participation agreements were published in advance; and finally, that contracting authorities were not required to provide information on their intentions about procurement except at the request of national authorities.[63] Furthermore, member states had to ensure that those exempted bodies and entities applied at least the principles of non-discrimination and competition. They were obliged to provide a report to the Commission on request about such contracts. However, that information requirement was less stringent than the mandatory reporting rules in the Supply and Works Directives. It should be mentioned that the first Utilities Directive did not apply to concession contracts granted to entities operating in utilities sectors, awarded prior to the coming into force of the Directive. All exemption provisions within the first Utilities Directive were subject to assessment in the light of the four-year overall review of the process.[64]

Other exemptions covered entities in the relevant sectors which could demonstrate that their service and network associated contracts were not related to the specific supplies and works functions specified in the Directive, or if they were related, they took place in a non-member state and they were not using a European public network or a physical area.[65] The member states were under an obligation to inform the European Commission, on request, of

---

[62]   See O'Loan, 'Implementation of Directive 90/531 and Directive 92/50 in the United Kingdom', *Public Procurement Law Review* (1993), 29. Also, A. Cox, *Public Procurement in the European Community: The Single Market Rules and the Enforcement Regime after 1992*, Erlsgate Press, 1993.

[63]   See Article 3(1) of the Utilities Directive amended by Directive 93/38.

[64]   See Article 3(2) to (4) of the Utilities Directive amended by Directive 93/38.

[65]   See Article 6(1) of the Utilities Directive amended by Directive 93/38.

the cases when those exemptions had been allowed. There were also provisions which allowed for resale and hire contracts to third parties to be exempt when the awarding body did not possess an exclusive or special right to hire or sell the subject of the contract, and there was competition already in the market from other suppliers or producers to provide the commodity or service to third parties.[66] Similar relaxed reporting and monitoring requirements to those relating to the gas, oil, coal and other solid fuels sectors were found in Article 8 which applied to telecommunication exemptions.[67]

Interestingly, shortly after the enactment of the first Utilities Directive, a national case[68] concerned with the definition of the relevant provision of the Directive relating to the application of procurement rules to entities operating in the telecommunication sector set an interesting precedent. Article 8(1) of the Utilities Directive provided for an exemption from the regime and for the inapplicability of the Directive when contracting authorities in the telecommunications sector operated under substantially the same competitive conditions within the same geographical market. The national court asked the European Court of Justice for an interpretation of Article 8(1) of the Utilities Directive and in particular the competence of member states to determine a sufficiently genuine competitive regime, and the criteria for such evaluation, in a geographical area between telecommunications operators in order to exclude them from the application of the Directive. In the preliminary ruling, the European Court of Justice exposed the so far controversial interpretation of Article 8(1) and the exemption schemes within the first Utilities Directive, as well as determining member states' obligation to award damages to individuals who suffered from wrongful implementation of public procurement Directives. The Court followed the Conclusions of the Advocate-General and held that a member state could not decide, when implementing the Directive, which telecommunication services were excluded from the scope of the Directive, as that power was reserved to the telecommunications entities themselves. Answering the second question, the Court maintained that in order for the criterion in Article 8(1) to be satisfied, other contracting entities had, in all the circumstances of the case, to be able to compete as a matter of fact as well as of law.

Another set of significant exemptions was provided for water authorities under Article 9 of the first Utilities Directive. Under that provision water authorities specified in Annex 1 were specifically exempt from the rules when they purchased water. They were however covered by the Directive when they

---

[66] See Article 7(2) of the Utilities Directive amended by Directive 93/38.
[67] See Article 8(2) of the Utilities Directive amended by Directive 93/38.
[68] See case C-392/93, *The Queen and HM Treasury, ex parte British Telecommunications PLC*, OJ 1993 C 287/6.

purchased other supply and construction products.[69] Similarly, there were specific exemptions for the electricity, gas and heat, oil and gas and coal and other solid fuels entities outlined in Annexes II, III, IV and V of the Directive, but only when they awarded contracts for the supply of energy or for fuels for the production of energy. For all other relevant contracts those entities were covered by the rules of the first Utilities Directive. Those exemptions were provided because of the need to allow contracting authorities to procure from local sources of supply which might not always be the cheapest, but which were deemed to place importance on regional development policies or environmental grounds, and because those purchases were central to the operations of those entities and did not form part of normal supply and works procurement process.

Finally, specific exemptions under the first Utilities Directive were provided for those carriers of passengers and providers of transport services by air and by sea. In the preamble to the Directive it was stated that, under a series of measures adopted in 1987 with a view to introducing more competition between firms providing public air services, it had been decided to exempt such carriers from the scope of the legislation. Similarly, because shipping had been subject to severe competitive pressures, it was decided to exempt certain types of contracts from the Directive.[70]

The first Utilities Directive intended to open up procurement practices in the four previously excluded sectors, mainly to EC-wide or intra-community competition. With respect to goods (and services) originating in third countries, things were more complicated. A product outside the European Community, in order to be subject to a public contract regulated by one of the European public procurement Directives, must have been lawfully put in free circulation in at least one member state.[71] Except where there had been an international agreement which granted comparable and effective access for Community undertakings to public markets in a third country (the reciprocity principle), Article 29 of the first Utilities Directive made it possible for European contracting entities in the utilities sector to reject offers from suppliers based outside the European Community and required preference for European products, where Community offers are equivalent to offers from third countries, provided the price difference between the EC product and that originating in a third country did not exceed 3%. With reference to an international agreement granting access to public markets, the first Utilities Directive opened the door for the application

---

69   See Article 9(1)(a) of the Utilities Directive amended by Directive 93/38.

70   Sea-ferry operators would be excluded in the future, but their position was kept under review. Inland water-ferry services and river-ferry services operated by public authorities were to be brought within the rules.

71   For the concept of origin of goods and their lawful free circulation in the common market, see Regulation 802/68, OJ English Special Edition 1968(1), p. 165.

of the GATT Agreement on Government Procurement to the utilities sector of
the European Communities.

The GATT Agreement on Government Procurement

The first Public Procurement Directives were inapplicable to products originating in and supplied by third countries. In practical terms the meaning of this
limitation was that a product outside the Community, in order to be subject to
a public contract regulated by one of the Directives, had to be lawfully put in
free circulation in at least one member state.[72] The Council, conscious of the
above limitation, adopted a Resolution[73] concerning access to Community
public supply contracts for products originating in non-member states. At the
same time, negotiations in the international framework were being carried out
under the GATT Tokyo Round (1973–79). Finally, on 12 April 1979, the
GATT Agreement on Government Procurement (AGP) was concluded and
became part of the Community's legal order by virtue of Article 228(2) EC and
Council Decision 80/271.[74]

The primary aims of the AGP were similar to those of the Supplies
Directive 77/62, and particularly in relation to transparency of laws and procedures on government procurement and elimination of protection for domestic
suppliers and of discrimination between domestic and foreigner suppliers.[75]
However, the AGP provisions went further than those of Directive 77/62 by
introducing more favourable conditions for tenders from outside the
Community; the AGP was envisaged as the vehicle for establishing an international framework of rights and obligations with respect to government
procurement, with a view to achieving liberalisation and expansion of world
trade. As a consequence, third countries/signatories to the AGP were under an
obligation to provide the same opportunities for access to Community tenderers in their respective public markets, as those provided by EC member states
to undertakings from those countries. Due to the above modifications specified in the AGP, Directive 77/62 was amended. The result of this amendment
was that the AGP rules were incorporated in the public supplies regime,[76]
which was the only public procurement regime which produced extra-territorial effects in its application.

---

[72]   For the concept of origin of goods and their lawful free circulation in the
common market see Regulation 802/68, OJ English Special Edition 1968(1), p. 165.
[73]   See OJ 1977 C 11/1.
[74]   See OJ 1980 L 215/1.
[75]   See Weiss, 'Public Procurement in the EC – Public Supply Contracts',
European Law Review (1988).
[76]   See Directives 80/767 and 88/295, *supra*.

The AGP (Tokyo Round) rules which were incorporated in Directive 88/295 provided that foreign undertakings, which were based in third countries but had subsidiaries within the common market, had the same access to public supplies contracts as European undertakings and could invoke and enforce Community law both at Community and at national levels. Obviously, it was required that undertakings from outside the Community have an economic presence within the common market. For such purposes, subsidiaries of foreign undertakings had to establish as corporate entities in one of the member states and be subject to the tax laws of the member state within which they operated. It should also be noted that under all the public procurement Directives, contracting authorities had the right to impose an obligation on one or more undertakings to which they wished to award a public contract, that a specific legal form or personality conducive to the legal regime of the contracting authorities be taken by those undertakings.

Suppliers which were signatories to the GATT, but not established in the Community, were subject to the GATT Agreement on Government Procurement, although they could invoke and enforce Community law. They could not enforce GATT rules, unless the competent forum (EC member state or third state-GATT signatory) provided the appropriate remedies. The AGP laid down a rather inoffensive dispute settlement and enforcement procedure, where consultation and conciliation between the aggrieved contractor and the contracting authority played the dominant role. With respect to the enforcement of the AGP rules, the Committee on Government Procurement (composed of representatives from each of the parties), as the body responsible for consultation on matters relating to the operation of the AGP and the furtherance of its objectives, had the right to authorise any measure adopted by a party aimed at suspending the reciprocity principle, between that party and a party that refused access to public markets for undertakings of the former. State retreat represented a very interesting compliance method for disputes in international trade. However, such actions often resulted in unsatisfactory consequences, amounting to trade wars between the European Communities and third countries. Undertakings which were non-signatories to GATT faced trade restrictions by member states according to Article 115 EC, which governed the European Community's Common External Policy.

Despite its promising aims and purposes,[77] the AGP-EC regime on public supplies contracts had rather limited application as (i) it embraced only its signatories, (ii) it covered only the supply of products and services that were incidental to the supply contract and not services contracts *per se* and (iii) it

---

[77] See the FIDE Congress on The Application in the Member States of the EC Directives on Public Procurement, Madrid, 1990.

applied only to centrally controlled authorities, thus leaving local or regional authorities outside its scope.

The AGP-EC regime left large areas of procurement activity unregulated by the GATT or by EC secondary legislation. Works and utilities contracts and supply of services were excluded. In its 1977 Resolution[78] the council noted that the opening up of the public procurement market in respect of non-Community countries could only be accomplished through reciprocity in treatment and mutual balance of advantages. The reciprocity doctrine or the 'mirror principle' required that non-member states provide in their domestic markets similar opportunities to those provided by European member states to undertakings coming from those countries. This meant that the element of reciprocity should have occurred between all European member states and the third countries in question. Such a scenario was rather unlikely, so the Commission in its statement in 1977 concerning Article 115 EC[79] was prepared to permit a limited and controlled use of its principles by individual member states which had established economic and commercial relations with non-member countries in public procurement. During the Tokyo Round negotiations, the Council also noted that Community undertakings were participating in contracts awarded in third countries. That finding revealed that reciprocity was a bilateral phenomenon in economic activities between a member state and a third country. At first sight, that appeared to contradict the centralised policy that European institutions sought to apply in the regulation of public procurement. In this regard, the Commission stated that, in order to prevent deflection of trade between a member state and a third country, it would authorise the former, under Article 115 EC, to exclude from public contracts certain products, originating in third countries, which were in free circulation in another member state, where similar arrangements (reciprocity effects) had been made for products imported directly. In other words, it was thought that the use of Article 115 EC might eliminate the 'free rider' phenomenon and 'protect' the benefits gained through a bilateral trade flow between a member state and a third country. From an economic point of view, this tactic may have prevented deflection and diversification of trade. However, it could well be argued that it created what is sometimes more serious: non-tariff barriers to intra-Community trade. It is often difficult, in the framework of an economic union such as the EC, to strike a balance between a common external policy and individual commercial policies pursued by one or more member states.

One could ask why the AGP did not extend its scope to cover works

---

[78] See OJ 1977 C 11/1.
[79] See OJ 1977 C 11/2.

contracts. It should be recalled that supplies and works contracts were the only regimes covered by public procurement Community legislation during the GATT Tokyo Round (1979). A possible answer might be that the coverage of supply of products was the maximum that could be agreed, at least during the first stage in the cumbersome and laborious negotiations between the European Communities and GATT signatories. Like the EC Treaties, the GATT did not explicitly prohibit discrimination by government purchasing agencies in favour of national products. Under the EC regime, discrimination for economic reasons is justified. National authorities may justify their discriminatory purchasing practices by invoking concern for employment and social equity, under the broader goal of promoting greater economic efficiency and industrial adjustment. Under the GATT regime, Article III 8(a) excluded government procurement from the principle of national treatment regarding its regulation. Thus, free movement of goods was considered, with respect to public procurement, to be the first step under the framework of the Multilateral Agreements between the EC and GATT signatories with a view to liberalising trade and preventing non-tariff barriers arising from national procurement policies.

Another possible justification of the limitation of the AGP rules to the supplies of goods only could have been that works and construction contracts involve further aspects that should have been taken into account in an attempt to liberalise their regime. They involve social and regional policy aspects, short- and long-term employment considerations, and peripheral development of the EC regions. Liberalising the public works regime between the Community and third countries would not only have brought into play free trade area considerations (free movement of goods), but would have also gone further, trespassing onto the field of economic union, where labour, capital, payments and services need also to circulate freely.

The first Utilities Directive 90/531 interfaced with the GATT AGP regime in a limited way. Except where there was an international agreement which granted comparable access for Community undertakings to the public markets of a third country, Article 29 of the Utilities Directive 90/531 allowed EC contracting entities in the utilities sector to reject offers from outside the Community. It also authorised a preference system where Community offers are equivalent to offers from third countries, subject to the price differential not exceeding 3%. The commitment of the European Communities towards international liberalisation of utilities procurement was demonstrated by its offer to the GATT AGP signatories during the Uruguay Round to eliminate all discrimination regarding contracts in urban transport, ports, airports and heavy electrical and telecommunications equipment.[80]

---

[80]   See Council Regulation 1461/93, OJ 1993 L 146, on access to public contracts

Expansion of the AGP framework to embrace supplies and works contracts in the utilities sector and services contracts was pursued during the GATT Uruguay Round.[81] The new regime introduced substantial changes in the application of the AGP with respect to types of contracts and coverage of contracting authorities, as well as remedies available to aggrieved undertakings. Works and services contracts were covered under the amended regime and the list of contracting authorities embraced not only central government departments and their agencies but also regional and local authorities and some utilities in the form of public authorities or public undertakings. Certain exemptions between the signatories did apply, but, based on bilateral agreements, the amended regime promised a significant extra-territorial expansion of European procurement legislation.[82]

With reference to EFTA countries, the European Commission reached an agreement on 22 October 1991 with the seven states (European Economic Area) to participate in the Single Market from 1 January 1993. That agreement changed the previous framework under the preferential agreement regime which was in operation until 1991,[83] to a free trade area, as the EFTA states were required to implement Community law, and incorporate the public procurement Directives in their national legal orders. The regime applied to Hungary and Poland, by virtue of their Association Agreements.[84]

The Remedies Directives

European Community law remains silent as to the availability of remedies available to individuals at national level in cases of infringement of primary or secondary legislation. To address the issue of the protection of individuals under Community law when their rights have been violated, one should first seek clarification of a crucial factor: the direct effectiveness of Community law and in particular whether an infringement of a directly effective primary or secondary Community provision may be used by individuals before national courts as sufficient ground for an action for damages against the state. As many provisions of Community legislation concerning public procurement (Directives) are deemed to produce a direct effect, the question of whether an

---

for tenderers from the United States; Council Decision 93/323, OJ 1993 L 125, on the conclusion of an agreement between the EC and USA on government procurement.

[81]　　Article XXIV 1 AGP, signed on 15 April 1994 by all the previous signatories except Hong Kong and Singapore.

[82]　　The applicability of the new GPA to its signatories was subject to its ratification before 1 January 1996.

[83]　　See Weiss, 'The law of public procurement in EFTA and the EC: The legal framework and its implementation', *Yearbook of European Law*, 1987.

[84]　　See OJ 1993 L 347/36 and OJ 1993 L 348/36.

infringement of them can be considered as a sufficient ground for an action for damages at national level is combined with the duty of national courts to afford a mechanism for effective protection (remedies) of the rights conferred on individuals by directly effective Community law. In an attempt to complement the substantive procurement rules enacted by virtue of the Supplies, Works and Services Directives and to provide a system of effective protection of individuals in cases of infringements of their provisions, European institutions enacted the Compliance Directive on the harmonisation of laws, regulations and administrative provisions relating to the application of review procedures in the award of public works and public supply contracts (Directive 89/665 EC).[85] To encompass the utilities procurement rules, Directive 92/13[86] extends the remedies and review procedures covered by Directive 89/665 to the water, energy, transport and telecommunication sectors. Both instruments are still applicable, pending their review sometime between 2007 and 2008.

The scope and thrust of the Remedies Directives focus on the obligation of member states to ensure effective and rapid review of decisions taken by contracting authorities which infringe public procurement provisions. Undertakings seeking relief from damages in the context of a procedure for the award of a contract should not be treated differently under national rules implementing European public procurement laws and under other national rules. This means that the measures to be taken concerning review procedures should be similar to national review proceedings, without any discriminatory character. Any person having or having had an interest in obtaining a particular public supply or public works contract and who has been or risks being harmed by an alleged infringement of public procurement provision shall be entitled to seek review before national courts. This particular obligation is followed by a stand-still provision concerning the prior notification by the person seeking review to the contracting authority of the alleged infringement and of his intention to seek review. However, with respect to admissibility aspects, there is no qualitative or quantitative definition of the interest of a person in obtaining a public contract. As to the element of potential harm by an infringement of public procurement provisions, it should be cumulative with the first element, that of interest. The prior notification should intend to exhaust any possibility of amicable settlement before the parties have recourse to national courts. A novelty in the Remedies Directive of the Utilities sectors[87] is the introduction of the *attestation procedure*. Member states are required to give the contracting entities the possibility of having their purchasing procedures and

---

85   See OJ 1989 L 395.
86   See OJ 1992 L 76/7.
87   See Directive 92/13, OJ 1992 L 76/7.

practices *attested* by persons authorised by law to exercise this function. Under the attestation mechanism, possible irregularities in the award of a public contract may be identified in advance and provide an opportunity for the contracting authorities to correct them. The latter may include the attestation statement in the notice inviting tenders published in the Official Journal. The system appears flexible and cost-efficient and may prevent wasteful litigation. The attestation procedure under Directive 92/13 could be an essential requirement in the development of European standards of attestation.[88]

THE THIRD GENERATION OF PUBLIC PROCUREMENT ACQUIS

Public Services

The completion of the single market project in 1992 epitomised a significant milestone in the European integration process, in that all freedoms and principles stipulated in the Treaties were properly functioning and contributing towards the objectives of the European Communities. Whilst the liberalisation of trade, as envisaged in international agreements such as the GATT or in supranational organisations such as the European Union, embraces primarily the free movement of goods, provisions regulating the provision of services are often described as inadequate. Modern economies have witnessed a shift in trade patterns from product manufacturing industries to markets where the provision of services is the predominant sector of the industry. The lack of regulation of services at a global level has given rise to economic controversies. Trade wars have been taking place and the international legal community currently attempts to adopt measures towards regulation of trade in services within the context of the GATT Uruguay Round of multilateral trade negotiations.

In line with the above considerations, European institutions enacted Directive 92/50[89] on the award procedures relating to public services contracts attempts to pave the way for liberalisation of services in public markets. The Directive followed the same principles as the rest of the Community's legislation on public procurement, namely compulsory Community-wide advertising of public contracts, prohibition of technical specifications capable of discriminating against potential bidders and uniform application of objective criteria

---

[88]   See Article 7 of EC Directive 92/13.
[89]   See OJ 92/50, OJ 1992 L 209.

of participation in tendering and award procedures. The Services Directive introduced a special type of award procedure, namely *design contests*, with reference to planning projects. According to Article 1(g), *design contests* were those national procedures which enable the contracting authority to acquire in the fields of area planning, town planning, architecture and civil engineering, a plan or design selected by a jury, after being put out to competition with or without the award of prizes. The award of *design contests*, according to the Services Directive had to follow specific rules. The admission of participants to the contest could not be limited either by reference to the territory or part of a member state, or on the grounds that under the law of the member state in which the contest is organised, participants would have been required to be either natural or legal persons. Furthermore, where design contests were restricted to a limited number of participants, the contracting authorities had to lay down clear and non-discriminatory selection criteria which ensure sufficient and genuine competition among the participants. The jury had to be composed exclusively of natural persons who were independent of the contracting authority.

Under the Services Directive, public services contracts were contracts which have as their object the provision of services classified in the Common Product Classification (CPC) nomenclature of the United Nations, as a nomenclature for classification of services at Community level does not exist. The United Nations Common Product Classification covers almost every conceivable service an undertaking may provide, although the services description is rather plain.

The Services Directive was the first legal instrument which attempted to open the increasingly important public services sector to intra-community competition. It should be mentioned that the Directives on public supplies, public works and utilities contained provisions where the provision of services was regarded as ancillary to the main contract under their regime, provided the value of the services were less than the value of the supplies or works. Such services were covered by the relevant Directive.

Specific services contracts were excluded from the scope of the Services Directive. Apart from those contracts which were covered by the relevant provisions of the Works, Supplies and Utilities Directives, and therefore not considered as services, the other contracts excluded from the Services Directive were:

(i)   contracts for the acquisition or rental, by whatever financial means, of land, existing buildings, or other immovable property or concerning rights thereon. (However, financial service contracts concluded at the same time as, before or after the contract of acquisition or rental, in whatever form, will be subject to the Directive);

(ii)   contracts for the acquisition, development, production or joint produc-
         tion of programme material by broadcasters and contracts for broad-
         casting time;[90]
(iii)   contracts for voice telephony, telex, radiotelephony, paging and satel-
         lite services;[91]
(iv)   contracts for arbitration and conciliation services;
(v)   contracts for financial services in connection with the issue, sale,
         purchase or transfer of securities or other financial instruments, and
         central bank services;[92]
(vi)   employment contracts;
(vii)   research and development service contracts other than those where the
         benefits accrue exclusively to the contracting authority for its use in the
         conduct of its own affairs, on condition that the service provided is
         mostly remunerated by the contracting authority.

Research and development services contracts were excluded from the remit of
the Services Directive. The exclusion of such contracts could be justified by
reference to the assumption that research and development projects should not
be financed by public funds.[93] However, where research and development
contracts were covered by the public procurement rules, a provision in the

---

[90]   This includes the purchase of, on the one hand, services producing audiovisual works such as films, videos and sound recording, including advertising, and, on
the other hand, broadcasting time (transmission by air, satellite or cable). In principle,
these services are covered but are given derogations in so far as they are connected to
broadcasting activities. See Armin-Trepte, *Public Procurement in the EC*, CCH
Europe, 1993, p. 101.
[91]   These have been excluded because they are not part of the Community liberalisation package for the telecommunications services market.
[92]   This refers to contracts which constitute transactions concerning shares, for
example. In the public sector, it will also include within the derogation contracts
awarded to financial intermediaries to arrange such transactions because these are
specifically excluded from the scope of investment services (Category 6 of Annex IA).
However, this exclusion does not appear in the Utilities Directive so that contracts for
the services of intermediaries who make the arrangements for such transactions would
be subject to the provisions of the Utilities Directive; see de Graaf 'The political agreement on a common position concerning the utilities services Directive', *Public
Procurement Law Review* (1992), 473. The choice of such intermediaries is often difficult in practice since it is quite often made on the basis of the perceived quality of the
intermediary or on references from existing clients and past experience. This choice
will be made no easier by the application of the procurement rules which do not necessarily best fit such services; see Armin-Trepte, *Public Procurement in the EC*, op. cit.
p. 101.
[93]   See de Graaf 'The political agreement on a common position concerning the
utilities services Directive', and Armin-Trepte, *Public Procurement in the EC*, op. cit.

Utilities Directive allowed a contracting entity to award a contract without a prior call for competition where it is purely for the purpose of research, experiment, study or development and not for the purpose of ensuring profit or of recovering research and development costs and in so far as the award of such contracts does not prejudice the competitive award of subsequent contracts which have these particular purposes.[94]

Interestingly, service concessions, although included in the draft Services Directive,[95] have been excluded from the provisions of the final text of Directive 92/50. The exclusion of service concessions fell short of the aspirations to regulate concession contracts for the public sector under the Works Directive and broke the consistency in the two legal instruments. The reasons for the exclusion of service concessions from the regulatory regime of public procurement could be attributed to the different legal requirements in member states to delegate powers to concessionaires. The delegation of services by public authorities to private undertakings in some member states runs contrary to their constitutional provisions.

The Services Directive adopted a two-tier approach in classifying services procured by contracting authorities. That classification was based on a 'priority' and a 'non-priority' list of services, according to the relative value of such services in intra-community trade. *Priority services* included: maintenance and repair services; land transport services (except for rail transport services), including armoured car services and courier services, except transport of mail; air transport services of passengers and freight, except transport of mail; transport of mail by land and by air; telecommunications services (except voice telephony, telex, radiotelephony, paging and satellite services); financial services including (a) insurance services, (b) banking and investment services (except contracts for financial services in connection with the issue, sale, purchase or transfer of securities or other financial instruments, and central bank services); computer and related services; research and development services; accounting, auditing and book-keeping services; market research and public opinion polling services; management consultant services (except arbitration and conciliation services) and related services; architectural services; engineering services and integrated engineering services; urban planning and landscape architectural services; related scientific and technical consulting services; technical testing and analysis services; advertising services; building-cleaning services on a fee or contract basis; publishing and printing services on a fee or contract basis; sewage and refuse disposal services; sanitation and similar services. *Non-Priority services* included: hotel and restaurant services; rail

---

94 See Article 20(2)(b) of amending Utilities Directive 93/38.
95 See COM (90) 372 final, SYN 293 and COM (91) 322 final, SYN 293.

transport services; water transport services; support and auxiliary transport services; legal services; personnel placement and supply services; investigation and security services; education and vocational education services; health and social services; recreational, cultural and sporting services.

The division was not permanent and the European Commission has the situation under constant review, assessing the performance of 'non-priority' services sectors. The two-tier approach, in practical terms, meant that the award of priority services contracts was subject to the rigorous regime of the public procurement Directives (advertisement, selection of tenderers, award procedures, award criteria), whereas the award of non-priority services contracts had to follow the basic rules of non-discrimination and publicity for the results of the award.

Article 6 of the Services Directive provided for the inapplicability of the Directive to service contracts which were awarded to an entity which is itself a contracting authority within the meaning of the Directive on the basis of an exclusive right which was granted to the contracting authority by a law, regulation or administrative provision of the member state in question.[96] Article 13 of the Utilities Directive provided for the exclusion of certain contracts between contracting authorities and affiliated undertakings.[97] Those were service contracts which were awarded to a service-provider which was affiliated to the contracting entity and service contracts which were awarded to a service-provider which was affiliated to a contracting entity participating in a joint venture formed for the purpose of carrying out an activity covered by the Directive.[98] The exclusion from the provisions of the Directive was subject, however, to two conditions: the service-provider had to be an undertaking affiliated to the contracting authority and, at least 80% of its average turnover arising within the European Community for the preceding three years had to derive from the provision of the same or similar services to

---

[96] This practice resembles the market testing process often employed in the United Kingdom between a contracting authority and an in-house team; see Harden, 'Defining the range of application of the public sector procurement Directives in the United Kingdom', *Public Procurement Law Review*, 1 (1992), 362.

[97] An affiliated undertaking, for the purposes of Article 1(3) of the Utilities Directive, is an undertaking the annual accounts of which are consolidated with those of the contracting entity in accordance with the requirements of the seventh Company Law Directive (Council Directive 83/349 (OJ 1983 L 193/1)).

[98] See the explanatory memorandum accompanying the text amending the Utilities Directive (COM (91) 347-SYN 36 1) which states that this provision relates, in particular, to three types of service provision within groups. These categories, which may or may not be distinct, are: the provision of common services such as accounting, recruitment and management; the provision of specialised services embodying the know-how of the group; the provision of a specialised service to a joint venture.

undertakings with which it was affiliated. The Commission was empowered to monitor the application of this article and to request notification of the names of the undertakings concerned and the nature and value of the service contracts involved.

The Consolidated Public Procurement Directives

In order to consolidate all previous legislation on public procurement and provide for a more homogeneous regulatory framework *vis-à-vis* the Public Services Directive, a consolidated regime was introduced in 1993, comprising of three Directives on supplies, works and utilities. Minor amendments were subsequently introduced to the consolidated Directives,[99] mainly covering procedural issues and issues of conformity with international obligations.

Of significance is the remit of the consolidated public works Directive 93/37[100] which embraced all relevant Community legislation relating to public works with some important amendments and clarifications of existing provisions of Directive 89/440. The Consolidated Works Directive adopted a special, mitigated regime for the award of concession contracts.[101] The provisions of the Directive only applied to concession contracts with a value of at least 5 million ECU. No rules were given as to the way in which the contract value must be calculated. For the award of concession contracts, contracting authorities must apply rules on advertising similar to the advertising rules concerning open and restricted procedures for the award of every works contract. Also, the provisions on technical standards and on criteria for qualitative selection of candidates and tenderers applied to the award of concession contracts. The Directive did not prescribe the use of specific award procedures for concession contracts. The Directive presupposed that concession contracts should be awarded in two rounds, such as in the case of restricted procedures or negotiated procedures for ordinary works contracts. However, there was no provision which prevented contracting authorities from applying a one-round open procedure. The Directive contained no rules on the minimum number of candidates which have to be invited to negotiate or to submit a tender. It seemed that a contracting authority might limit itself to selecting only one

---

[99]   See the Public Supplies Directive 93/36/EC, OJ L 199, as amended by Directive 97/52/EC OJ L 328 and Directive 2001/78/EC, OJ L 285; The Public Works Directive 93/37/EC, OJ L 199, amended by Directive 97/52/EC OJ L 328 and Directive 2001/78/EC, OJ L 285; The Utilities Directives 93/38/EC, OJ L 199, amended by Directive 98/4/EC OJ L 101; The Public Services Directive 92/50/EEC, OJ L 209, amended by Directive 97/52/EC OJ L 328 and Directive 2001/78/EC, OJ L 285.

[100]   See Directive 93/37, OJ 1993 L 199.

[101]   See Article 3 of Directive 93/37.

single candidate, provided the intention to award a concession contract has been adequately published. Contracting authorities were under strict obligations to publish a notice to the Official Journal indicating their intention to proceed with the award of a concession works contract.[102]

Works contracts which were subsidised directly by more than 50% by the states could fall within the scope of the Directive.[103] Works which were not subsidised directly, or for less than 50%, fell outside this anti-circumvention provision. Not all subsidised works fell within the scope of the Directive: only civil engineering works, such as the construction of roads, bridges and railways, as well as building work for hospitals, facilities intended for sports, recreation and leisure and university buildings and buildings used for administrative purposes are referred to as subsidised works contracts.[104] That list was exhaustive. The Consolidated Works Directive did not apply to works contracts which are declared secret or the execution of which must be accompanied by special security measures[105] in accordance with the laws, regulations or administrative provisions in force in the member state concerned; nor did the Directive apply to works contracts when the protection of the basic interests of the member states' security so requires. Finally, the Directive did not apply to public works contracts awarded in pursuance of certain international agreements;[106] nor did the Directive apply to public works contracts awarded pursuant to the particular procedure of an international organisation.[107] Several international organisations, such as NATO, have their own rules on the award of public works contracts.

The WTO Government Procurement Agreement

The public procurement legal regime of the European Union has been extended in order to cover signatories to the GATT Agreement on Government Procurement.[108] Foreign firms (from third countries) can participate in tendering procedures for the award of public contracts from public entities in the common market and vice-versa, European firms can participate in tendering procedures in foreign public markets. The GATT Agreement on Government

---

[102]   See Bovis, *EC Public Procurement Law*, Longman, European Law Series, 1997, pp. 67–8.

[103]   See Article 2(1) of Directive 93/37.

[104]   See Article 2(2) of Directive 93/37.

[105]   See Article 4(b) of Directive 93/37.

[106]   See Article 5(a) of Directive 93/37.

[107]   See Article 5(c) of Directive 93/37.

[108]   See Council Regulation 1461/93 (OJ 1993 L 146) and EC Council Decision 93/324 (OJ 1993 L 125).

Procurement embraces the following countries: the USA, Canada, Japan, EFTA countries, Singapore, Hong Kong and Israel and promises considerable improvement in reciprocal market access.

The Government Procurement Agreement (GPA) is based on a number of general principles which depict the principles of the old AGP regime. The most important of these is the principle of *national treatment*. Under this principle, the parties to the GPA must give the same treatment afforded to national providers and products to providers and products from other signatory states. Reinforcing the principle of national treatment, the *most favoured nation* (MFN) principle guarantees treatment no less favourable than that afforded to other parties. In addition to the above principles, the principle of *non-discrimination* prohibits discrimination against local firms on grounds of the degree of their foreign affiliation or ownership, or on the grounds of origin of the goods or services where these have been produced in one of the states which are party to the Agreement.

The GPA stipulates a set of procedures for contracting authorities in the signatory parties which must be followed when awarding contracts within its scope. These procedures aim to ensure transparency and openness as well as objectivity and legitimacy in the award of public contracts and to facilitate cross-border trade between the signatories. The influence of the European Community on the GPA regime is apparent, an indication of the maturity and validity of the regulatory process of the European public markets integration. The procedures are, however, less strict than those applicable for the award of public sector contracts under the Community regime, and depict the integral flexibility envisaged by the regulatory regime for utilities procurement.

The GPA intends to regulate access specifically to the government procurement markets. General market access between the signatories is in principle dealt with under other agreements, notably the GATT (on the import of goods) and the GATS (on access to services markets). The detailed scope and coverage of the GPA with regard to the entities covered, the type of procurement and monetary thresholds is set out in Appendix I of the Agreement. The Agreement applies in principle to all bodies which are deemed to be 'contracting authorities' for the purposes of the European public sector Directives. With reference to utilities, the GPA applies to entities which carry out one or more of certain listed 'utility' activities, where these entities are either 'public authorities' or 'public undertakings', in the sense of the Utilities Directive. However, the GPA does not cover entities operating in the utilities sector on the basis of *special and exclusive rights*. The utility activities which are covered include (i) activities connected with the provision of water through fixed networks; (ii) activities concerned with the provision of electricity through fixed networks; (iii) the provision of terminal facilities to carriers by sea or inland waterways; and (iv) the operation of public services in the field of transport by automated

systems, tramway, trolley bus, or bus or cable. The provision of public transport services by rail is included in principle, but there is exclusion for entities
listed in Annex VI of the European Utilities Directive, designed to exclude
non-urban transport services. However, the trust of the applicability of the
GPA in relation to utilities activities appears short in comparison with that
under the European regime. Activities connected with the distribution of gas
or heat, the exploration or extraction of fuel are notable exceptions from the
GPA's ambit.

The thresholds for the applicability of the GPA regime to public contracts
of signatories are as follows: for supplies and services it is SDR 130 000 for
central government; 200 000 for local government; and 400 000 for all
contracts in the utilities sectors (including those awarded by central and local
government). For works contracts, the threshold is SDR 5 m, for all entities.

Although in principle the GPA regime represents a significant improvement
in relation to the old AGP regime in terms of coverage and thrust, certain
important derogations from its applicability would result in diluting the principal aims and objectives envisaged by the signatories. As far as central or
federal government works and supply contracts are concerned, the Agreement
is expected to facilitate market access and enhance cross-border trade patterns
in public contracts. However, for contracts relating to services and for certain
contracts in the utilities sector, as well as for contracts awarded by local,
municipal or regional authorities, the effect of the Agreement appears rather
modest. A number of signatories have been unable, or unwilling, to offer all of
their entities or contracts for coverage in the above categories. Political and
legal particularities in the systems of the signatories have prevented similar
coverage between the parties. In addition, by applying the principle of *reciprocity* in negotiating the GPA, the result would probably have been very similar to the old AGP regime in covering central or federal public contracts. The
solution to this fundamental, apparent, deadlock was to be found in a rather
peculiar method. Each signatory should effectively negotiate with each other
signatory, to come to a satisfactory agreement on coverage based on reciprocity on a bilateral basis. This approach constitutes a significant departure from
the premises of the *principle of most favoured nation* (MFN) and has resulted
in some considerable divergence in the applicability of the GPA by virtue of
derogations and limitations imposed by signatories on access to their public
markets. Thus, for example, coverage in the utilities sector does not apply to
Canada, since that country did not commit itself to opening its own markets to
the European Community. When the Agreement was first concluded in
December 1993 there was also no coverage for utilities with respect to the
United States, but there have since been modifications to the EC–US coverage
as a result of a subsequent EC–US bilateral agreements. Also outside the
coverage of the Agreement in the utilities sector is, in relation to Japan, urban

transport and electricity; in relation to South Korea, urban transport and airports; and in relation to Israel, urban transport. There are also significant derogations for certain categories of services and for specified types of equipment.

The scope and coverage of the GPA, as well as the structure of its applicability, present a unique instrument of international law which is based on a series of bilateral agreements rather than a multilateral arrangement. This represents a significant compromise of the most favoured nation principle, which is a fundamental premise of the majority of international trade agreements. Members of the World Trade Organisation joining the GPA, at their discretion, need to reach separate agreements on the scope of coverage with all existing parties to the Agreement. The GPA has, thus, acquired a *plurilaterality* status, a fact that weakens its thrust and complicates its applicability.

THE FOURTH GENERATION OF PUBLIC PROCUREMENT ACQUIS

The New Public Sector and Utilities Directives

After a considerable amount of debate and consultation,[109] in 2004 the European Union adopted a new set of rules which govern the award of public contracts in the supplies, works and services sectors, as well as in the public utilities.[110] The new Directives reflect the 1996 European Commission's Green Paper on Public Procurement[111] and the subsequent 1998 Commission's Communication.[112] The Directives have been seen as an integral part of the

---

[109]   See the proposal from the European Commission, OJ C 29 E, 30.1.2001, p. 11 and OJ C 203 E, 27.8.2002, p. 210; the opinion of the Economic and Social Committee, OJ C 193, 10.7.2001, p. 7; the opinion of the Committee of the Regions, OJ C 144, 16.5.2001, p. 23; the opinion of the European Parliament of 17 January 2002 (OJ C 271 E, 7.11.2002, p. 176), Council Common Position of 20 March 2003 (OJ C 147 E, 24.6.2003, p. 1) and Position of the European Parliament of 2 July 2003. See also the Legislative Resolution of the European Parliament of 29 January 2004 and Decision of the Council of 2 February 2004.

[110]   See Directive 2004/18, OJ L 134, 30.4.2004 on the coordination of procedures for the award of public works contracts, public supply contracts and public service contracts and Directive 2004/17, OJ L 134, 30.4.2004 coordinating the procurement procedures of entities operating in the water, energy, transport and postal services sectors.

[111]   See the Green Paper on Public Procurement in the European Union: Exploring the Way Forward, European Commission 1996.

[112]   See European Commission, Communication on Public Procurement in the European Union, COM (98) 143.

Commission's 2000 Work Programme, which pledges to modernise the relevant legislation for the completion of the internal market and at the same time implement the Lisbon European Council's call for economic reform within the internal market. The new Public Procurement Directives became operational in member states after 31 January 2006, a deadline by which member states were expected to transpose the Directives into national law.[113]

The new Directives are based upon the principles of *simplification* and *modernisation* and the new regime maps a clear-cut *dichotomy* between the public sector and the utilities. Their separate regulation reveals the diametrically opposed nature of the contracting authorities/entities in these sectors and reflects on the process of transformation that utilities have been undergoing over the past decade. Their change in ownership from public to private has stimulated commercialism and competitiveness and provided for the justification of a more relaxed regime and the acceptance that utilities, in some form or another, represent *sui generis* contracting authorities which do not need rigorous and detailed regulation of their procurement.

The dichotomy in regulation which the new public procurement regime has established to separate public sector procurement from utilities procurement gives an insight into current market conditions and political priorities across the European Union, as well as an indication that the main emphasis should be placed on attempts to open up the public sector.

The merger of the rules governing supplies, works and services procurement into a single legal instrument represents a successful attempt on the part of the European Union to codify supranational administrative provisions which have the aim of harmonising domestic legal regimes, public or private, which coordinate the award of public contracts. The codification, apart from the obvious benefits of legal certainty and legitimate expectation, has two important implications: legal efficiency and compliance discipline. As far as legal efficiency is concerned, the new codified Directive will speed up and streamline its implementation process by member states, especially the new arrivals from the 2004 Accession Treaty, and provide a one-stop shop reference point in national legal orders, augmented by the Court's vesting of direct effectiveness upon the Directive's predecessors on numerous occasions. On the other hand, codification will enhance compliance, as it will remove any remaining uncertainties

---

[113]   See Article 80 of Directive 2004/18, regarding implementation, where member states are obliged to bring into force the laws, regulations and administrative provisions necessary to comply with the public sector Directive no later than 31 January 2006 and by that deadline to inform the European Commission of the measures they intend to introduce in order to incorporate the Directive's provisions into national laws. The application of the new rules on the postal sector has been postponed until 1 January 2009.

over the applicability of the previously fragmented regime and afford contracting authorities a disciplined method of dispersing their procurement functions. The main influence of the codified public sector procurement Directive can be traced in important recent case-law developments[114] from the European Court of Justice, in particular case-law on the definition of contracting authorities, the use of award procedures and award criteria, and the possibility for contracting authorities to use environmental and social considerations as criteria for the award of public contracts.[115]

As far as utilities procurement is concerned, the two main reasons for the introduction of a distinctive legal regime which aims at coordinating procedures for the award of contracts in the utilities sectors revolve around the relations of the state with such entities. First, there are the numerous ways in which national authorities can influence the purchasing behaviour of these entities, such as participation in their capital and representation on their administrative, managerial or supervisory bodies. Secondly, the closed nature of the markets in which utilities operate, as a result of special or exclusive rights granted by the member states, necessitates the operation of a procurement regulatory regime which ensures on the one hand compliance with the fundamental principles of the EU Treaties and on the other hand compatibility with anti-trust and sector-specific regulation in the utilities sectors.

Public Procurement and Public Private Partnerships

At European level, as part of the Initiative for Growth, the Council has approved a series of measures designed to increase investment in the infrastructure of the trans-European transport networks and also in the areas of research, innovation and development,[116] as well as the delivery of services of

---

[114]   For a comprehensive analysis of public procurement case law, see Bovis, 'Recent case law relating to public procurement: A beacon for the integration of public markets', **39** (2002), *CMLRev.*

[115]   See Communication from the European Commission to the Council, the European Parliament, the Economic and Social Committee, and the Committee of the Regions, 'Working together to maintain momentum', 2001 Review of the Internal Market Strategy, Brussels, 11 April 2001, COM (2001) 198 final. Also, European Commission, Commission Communication, Public Procurement in the European Union, Brussels, 11 March 1998, COM (98) 143. See Commission Interpretative Communication on the Community law applicable to public procurement and the possibilities for integrating social considerations into public procurement, COM (2001) 566, 15 October 2001. Also, Commission Interpretative Communication on the Community law applicable to public procurement and the possibilities for integrating environmental considerations into public procurement, COM (2001) 274, 4 July 2001.

[116]   Conclusions of the Presidency, Brussels European Council, 12 December 2003.

general interest.[117] European Community law does not lay down any special rules covering the award or the contractual interface of public–private partnerships. Nevertheless, such arrangements must be examined in the light of the rules and principles resulting from the European Treaties, particularly as regards the principles of freedom of establishment and freedom to provide services (Articles 43 and 49 of the EC Treaty).[118] These encompass in particular the principles of transparency, equality of treatment, proportionality and mutual recognition[119] and the public procurement Directives.[120] The Commission has already taken initiatives under public procurement law to deal with the award of public–private partnerships (PPP). In 2000 it published an Interpretive Communication on Concessions and Community public procurement law,[121] in which it defined, on the basis of the rules and principles derived from the Treaty and applicable secondary legislation, the outlines of the concept of concession in Community law and the obligations incumbent on the public authorities when selecting the economic operators to whom the concessions are granted.

The Green Paper on Public-Private Partnerships distinguishes two major formats of public-private partnerships: the contractual format, also described as the concession model, and the institutional format which is often described as the 'joint-venture model'. Public authorities in the member states often have recourse to public-private partnership arrangements to facilitate mainly infrastructure projects. Budget constraints confronting national governments and

---

[117]   See COM (2003) 270 final.

[118]   The rules on the internal market, including the rules and principles governing public contracts and concessions, apply to any economic activity, that is any activity which consists in providing services, goods or carrying out works in a market, even if these services, goods or works are intended to provide a 'public service', as defined by a member state.

[119]   See Interpretive Communication of the Commission on concessions in Community law, OJ C 121, 29 April 2000.

[120]   In addition to the public procurement regime, in certain sectors and particularly the transport sector, the organisation of a PPP could be subject to specific sectoral legislation. See Regulation 2408/92 of the Council on access by Community air carriers to intra-Community air routes, Council Regulation 3577/92 applying the principle of freedom to provide services for maritime transport within member states, Council Regulation 1191/69 on action by member states concerning the obligations inherent in the concept of a public service in transport by rail, road and inland waterway, as amended by Regulation 1893/91, and the amended proposal for a Regulation of the European Parliament and of the Council on action by member states concerning public service requirements and the award of public service contracts in passenger transport by rail, road and inland waterway (COM (2002) 107 final).

[121]   See the Interpretative Communication on concessions under Community law, OJ C 121, 29 April 2000.

the widespread assumption that private sector know-how will benefit the delivery of public services appear as the main policy drivers[122] for selecting a public-private partnership route. Also, the accounting treatment of public-private partnership contracts benefits national governments as the assets involved in a public–private partnership should be classified as non-government assets, and therefore recorded off balance sheet for public accountancy purposes,[123] subject to two conditions: (i) that the private partner bears the construction risk, and (ii) that the private partner bears at least one of either availability or demand risk. However, it is necessary to assess whether a public-private partnership option offers real value-added compared with the conclusion of traditional public contracts.[124]

The contractual public-private partnership

The contractual model of a public-private partnership reflects a relation between public and private sectors based solely on contractual links. It involves different interfaces where tasks and responsibilities can be assigned to the private partner, including the design, funding, execution, renovation or exploitation of a work or service. In this category, concession contracts and arrangements such as the private finance initiative (PFI) or arrangements with a similar contractual nexus create a link between public and private sectors.

There are few provisions of secondary legislation which coordinate the procedures for the award of contracts designated as concession contracts in Community law. In the case of works concessions, there are only certain advertising obligations, intended to ensure prior competition by interested operators, and an obligation regarding the minimum time-limit for the receipt of applications.[125] The contracting authorities are free to decide how to select the private partner, although in so doing they must nonetheless guarantee full compliance with the principles and rules resulting from the Treaty. The rules governing the award of services concessions apply only by reference to the principles resulting from Articles 43 and 49 of the Treaty, in particular the

---

[122]   See Communication from the Commission of 23 April 2003, 'Developing the trans-European transport network: innovative funding solutions – interoperability of electronic toll collection systems', COM (2003) 132, and the Report of the high-level group on the trans-European transport network of 27 June 2003.

[123]   See Eurostat (Statistical Office of the European Communities), press release STAT/04/18 of 11 February 2004.

[124]   See Communication from the Commission to the Council and to the Parliament, 'Public finances in EMU 2003', published in the European Economy No. 3/2003 (COM (2003) 283 final).

[125]   See Article 3(1) of Directive 93/37/EEC, and Articles 56 to 59 of Directive 2004/18/EC.

principles of transparency, equality of treatment, proportionality and mutual recognition.[126]

The Community law applicable to the award of concessions is derived primarily from general obligations which involve no co-ordination of the legislation of member states. In addition, and although the member states are free to do so, very few have opted to adopt national laws laying down general and detailed rules governing the award of works or services concessions.[127] Thus, the rules applicable to the selection of a concessionaire by a contracting body are, for the most part, drawn up on a case-by-case basis. This situation may present problems for Community operators. The lack of co-ordination of national legislation could in fact be an obstacle to the genuine opening-up of such projects in the Community, particularly when they are organised at transnational level. The legal uncertainty linked to the absence of clear and co-ordinated rules might in addition lead to an increase in the costs of awarding such projects. Moreover, it could be argued that the objectives of the internal market might not be achieved in certain situations, owing to a lack of effective competition in the market.

On the other hand, the rules applicable to the award of public-private part-nerships in the format of a public works contracts or public services contracts[128] are contained in the public sector Directives,[129] where a contract-ing authority must normally have recourse to the open or restricted procedure to choose its private partner. By way of exception, and under certain condi-tions, recourse to the negotiated procedure is sometimes possible. In this context, the Commission has pointed out that the derogation under Article 7(2) of Directive 93/37/EEC which provides for recourse to negotiated procedure

---

[126]   Although the Commission had proposed that services concessions be included in Directive 92/50/EEC, in the course of the legislative process the Council decided to exclude them from the scope of that Directive. In the *Telaustria* case, the Court stated that '[the] obligation of transparency which is imposed on the contracting authority consists in ensuring, for the benefit of any potential tenderer, a degree of advertising sufficient to enable the services market to be opened up to competition and the impar-tiality of procurement procedures to be reviewed'. See case C-324/98. See also case C-358/00, *Deutsche Bibliothek*, ECR I-4685. These principles are also applicable to other state acts entrusting an economic service to a third party, as for example the contracts excluded from the scope of the Directives owing to the fact that they have a value below the threshold values laid down in the secondary legislation (Order of the Court of 3 December 2001, case C-59/00, *Vestergaard*, ECR I-9505), or so-called non-prior-ity services.

[127]   Spain (law of 23 May 2003 on works concessions), Italy (Merloni law of 1994, as amended) and France (Sapin law of 1993) have adopted such legislation.

[128]   For example those listed in Annex IA of Directive 92/50/EEC and Annex XVIA of Directive 93/38/EEC.

[129]   See Directives 93/37, 92/50 and 2004/18/EC.

in the case of a contract when 'the nature of the works or the risks attaching thereto do not permit prior overall pricing', is of limited scope. This derogation is solely to cover the exceptional situations in which there is uncertainty *a priori* regarding the nature or scope of the work to be carried out, but is not to cover situations in which the uncertainties result from other causes, such as the difficulty of prior pricing owing to the complexity of the legal and financial package put in place.[130]

Since the adoption of Directive 2004/18/EC, a new procedure known as 'competitive dialogue' may apply when awarding particularly complex contracts.[131] The competitive dialogue procedure is launched in cases where the contracting body is objectively unable to define the technical means that would best satisfy its needs and objectives or in cases where it is objectively unable to define the legal and/or financial form of a project. This new procedure will allow the contracting bodies to open a dialogue with the candidates for the purpose of identifying solutions capable of meeting these needs. At the end of this dialogue, the candidates will be invited to submit their final tender on the basis of the solution or solutions identified in the course of the dialogue. These tenders must contain all the elements required and necessary for the performance of the project. The contracting authorities must assess the tenders on the basis of the pre-stated award criteria. The tenderer who has submitted the most economically advantageous tender may be asked to clarify aspects of it or confirm commitments featuring therein, provided this will not have the effect of altering fundamental elements in the tender or invitation to tender, of falsifying competition or of leading to discrimination.

The competitive dialogue procedure should provide the necessary flexibility in the discussions with the candidates on all aspects of the contract during the set-up phase, while ensuring that these discussions are conducted in compliance with the principles of transparency and equality of treatment, and do not endanger the rights which the Treaty confers on economic operators. It is underpinned by the belief that structured selection methods should be protected in all circumstances, as these contribute to the objectivity and integrity of the procedure leading to the selection of an operator. This in turn guarantees the sound use of public funds and reduces the risk of practices that lack transparency and strengthens the legal certainty necessary for such projects. In addition, the new Directives make clear the benefit to contracting

---

[130] For example, it may apply when the works are to be carried out in a geologically unstable or archaeological terrain and for this reason the extent of the necessary work is not known when launching the tender procedure. A similar derogation is provided for in Article 11(2) of Directive 92/50, and in Article 30(1)(b) of Directive 2004/18/EC.

[131] See Article 29 of Directive 2004/18/EC.

authorities of formulating the technical specifications in terms of either performance or functional requirements. New provisions will thus give the contracting bodies more scope to take account of innovative solutions during the
award phase, irrespective of the procedure adopted.[132]

The institutional public-private partnership

The joint venture model of public-private partnerships involves the establishment of an entity held jointly by the public partner and the private partner.[133]
The joint entity thus has the task of ensuring the delivery of a work or service
for the benefit of the public. Direct interface between the public partner and
the private partner in a forum with a legal personality allows the public partner, through its presence in the body of shareholders and in the decision-
making bodies of the joint entity, to retain a relatively high degree of control
over the development of the projects, which it can adapt over time in the light
of circumstances. It also allows the public partner to develop its own experience of running the service in question, while having recourse to the support
of a private partner. An institutional public-private partnership can be put in
place, either by creating an entity held jointly by the public sector and the
private sector, or by the private sector taking control of an existing public
undertaking.

The law on public contracts and concessions does not of itself apply to the
transaction creating a mixed-capital entity. However, when such a transaction
is accompanied by the award of tasks through an act which can be designated
as a public contract, or even a concession, it is important that there be compliance with the rules and principles arising from this law (the general principles
of the Treaty or, in certain cases, the provisions of the Directives).[134] The
selection of a private partner called on to undertake such tasks while functioning as part of a mixed entity can therefore not be based exclusively on the
quality of its capital contribution or its experience, but should also take
account of the characteristics of its offer – the most economically advantageous – in terms of the specific services to be provided. Thus, in the absence
of clear and objective criteria allowing the contracting authority to select the
most economically advantageous offer, the capital transaction could constitute
a breach of the law on public contracts and concessions.

---

[132]   See Article 23 of Directive 2004/18/EC and Article 34 of Directive
2004/17/EC.

[133]   The member states use different terminology and schemes in this context (for
example, the Kooperationsmodell, PPPs, Joint Ventures).

[134]   It is worth noting that the principles governing the law on public contracts and
concessions apply also when a task is awarded in the form of a unilateral act (for example, a legislative or regulatory act).

In this context, the transaction involving the creation of such an entity does not generally present a problem in terms of the applicable Community law when it constitutes a means of executing the task entrusted under a contract to a private partner. However, the conditions governing the creation of the entity must be clearly laid down when issuing the call for competition for the tasks which one wishes to entrust to the private partner. Also, these conditions must not discriminate against or constitute an unjustified barrier to the freedom to provide services or to freedom of establishment, or be disproportionate to the desired objective.

However, in certain member states, national legislation allows the mixed entities, in which participation by the public sector involves the contracting body, to participate in a procedure for the award of a public contract or concession even when these entities are only in the course of being incorporated. In this scenario, the entity will be definitively incorporated only after the contract has actually been awarded to it. In other member states, a practice has developed which tends to confuse the phase of incorporating the entity and the phase of allocating the tasks. Thus the purpose of the procedure launched by the contracting authority is to create a mixed entity to which certain tasks are entrusted.

Such a solution does not appear satisfactory in terms of the provisions applicable to public contracts and concessions.[135] In the first case, there is a risk that effective competition will be distorted by the privileged position of the company being incorporated, and consequently of the private partner participating in this company. In the second case, the specific procedure for selecting the private partner also poses many problems. The contracting authorities encounter certain difficulties in defining the subject-matter of the contract or concession in a sufficiently clear and precise manner in this context, as they are obliged to do. The Commission has frequently noted that the tasks entrusted to the partnership structure are not clearly defined and that, in certain cases, they even fall outside any contractual framework.

This in turn raises problems not only with regard to the principles of transparency and equality of treatment, but even risks prejudicing the general interest objectives which the public authority wishes to attain. It is also evident that the lifetime of the created entity does not generally coincide with the duration of the contract or concession awarded, and this appears to encourage the extension of the task entrusted to this entity without true competition at the

---

[135] When planning and arranging such transactions, the test involving the use of the standard forms – which include the elements indispensable for well-informed competition – also demonstrate how difficult it can be to find an adequate form of advertising to award tasks falling within the scope of the law on public contracts or concessions.

time of this renewal. In addition, it should be pointed out that the joint creation
of such entities must respect the principle of non-discrimination in respect of
nationality in general and the free circulation of capital in particular.[136] Thus,
for example, the public authorities cannot normally make their position as
shareholder in such an entity contingent on excessive privileges which do not
derive from a normal application of company law.[137]

On the other hand, the creation of an institutional public-private partnership
may also lead to a change in the body of shareholders of a public entity. In this
context, it should first be emphasised that the changeover of a company from
the public sector to the private sector is an economic and political decision
which, as such, falls within the sole competence of the member states.[138]
Community law on public contracts as such is not intended to apply to transactions involving simple capital injections by an investor in an enterprise,
whether the latter be in the public or the private sector. Such transactions fall
under the scope of the provisions of the Treaty on the free movement of capital,[139] implying in particular that the national measures regulating them must
not constitute barriers to investment from other member states.[140]
Nevertheless, the provisions on freedom of establishment within the meaning
of Article 43 of the Treaty must be applied when a public authority decides, by
means of a capital transaction, to cede to a third party a holding conferring a
definite influence in a public entity providing economic services normally
falling within the responsibility of the state.[141]

When public authorities grant an economic operator a definite influence in
a business under a transaction involving a capital transfer, and when this transaction has the effect of entrusting to this operator tasks falling within the scope

---

[136]   Participation in a new undertaking with a view to establishing lasting
economic links is covered by the provisions of Article 56 relating to the free movement
of capital. See Annex I of Directive 88/361/EEC, adopted in the context of the former
Article 67, which lists the types of operations which must be considered as movements
of capital.
[137]   See judgment of the ECJ of 4 June 2002, case C-367/98, *Commission v.
Portugal*, ECR I-4731; case C-483/99, *Commission v. France*, ECR I-4781; and judgments of 13 May 2003, case C-463/00, *Commission v. Spain*, ECR I-4581; case C-
98/01, *Commission v. United Kingdom*, Rec. I-4641. On the possible justifications in
this framework, see judgment of the Court of 4 June 2002, case C-503/99, *Commission
v. Belgium*, ECR I-4809.
[138]   This follows from the principle of neutrality of the Treaty in relation to ownership rules, recognised by Article 295 of the Treaty.
[139]   See Article 56 f. of the EC Treaty.
[140]   See Communication of the Commission on certain legal aspects concerning
intra-EU investment, OJ C 220 19 July 1997, p. 15.
[141]   See the judgment of the Court of 13 April 2000, in case C-251/98, *Baars*, ECR
I-2787.

of the law on public contracts which had been previously exercised, directly or indirectly, by the public authorities, the provisions on freedom of establishment require compliance with the principles of transparency and equality of treatment, in order to ensure that every potential operator has equal access to performing those activities which had hitherto been reserved.

The phenomenon of public-private partnerships represents a genuine attempt to introduce the concept of contractualised governance in the delivery of public services. Although the public sector has always depended upon traditional corporatism to disperse public services, there is mounting evidence that the role and the involvement of the state in the above process is under constant review. The private finance initiative can be described as an institutionalised mechanism to engage the private sector in the delivery of public services, not only through the financing but mainly through the operation of assets. The private sector assumes a direct responsibility in serving the public interest, as part of its contractual obligations *vis-à-vis* the public sector. The motive and the intention behind such approach focus on the benefits which would follow as a result of the private sector's involvement in the delivery of public services. Efficiency gains, qualitative improvement, innovation, value-for-money and flexibility appear as the most important ones, whereas a better allocation of public capital resources overall sums up the advantages of privately financed projects.

Neither the private finance initiative nor the phenomenon of public–private partnerships alters the character of the contractual relationship between the private and public sectors, for such character is predominately determined by other factors attributed to the legal order in question. The contractual relationship between the private and public sectors is determined not merely by the fact that one party to the agreement is a public authority, but mainly by reference to the appropriate forum for access to justice, or the relevant remedial availability.[142] Under both traditional corporatism and contractualised governance, the contractual nexus between the private and public sectors maintains the same characteristics, which are influenced by the disposition of the relevant legal and judicial system. What the PFI does change is the thrust of that contractual relationship. The integral nature of corporatism evolves around the notion of public ownership of assets destined to serve public interest. The PFI brings an end to the notion of public ownership and instead introduces the concept of service delivery in the relevant contractual relationship between private and public sectors. The private sector is no longer a supplier to the public sector but rather a partner through a concession. It seems that

---

[142]   See the FIDE Congress on The Application in the Member States of the Directives on Public Procurement, Madrid, 1990.

there is a quasi-agency relationship between the private and public sectors, in the sense that the former provides the relevant infrastructure and in fact delivers public services on behalf of the latter. Where corporatism was always delivered under considerable budgetary constraints, a fact that reflects not only the relative balance of powers between the demand and supply sides and the risk allocation factor in their contractual arrangements but mainly the adversarial environment and the compromised quality of the deliverables, contractualised governance appears to prioritise the value-for-money principle, which has primarily qualitative attributes.

Both corporatism and contractualised governance should be delivered through a system that guarantees accountability, openness and competitiveness. Such a system for the delivery of public services is encapsulated in the European public procurement regime, which is expected to be the most appropriate delivery process for public-private partnerships. Contractual award arrangements are entirely covered by the public procurement Directives which provide for a disciplined, transparent and relatively swift system for the award of public procurement contracts.[143] What remains is the development of comprehensive guidelines for the deployment of private finances in the delivery of public services[144] and the enactment of relevant legislation[145] that

---

[143]   One the most notorious features of the existing PFI process is the abysmally lengthy negotiation stage and the prolonged pre-contractual arrangements. This represents a considerable (recoverable) cost which would be reflected in the final deal. See *Financial Times*, 24/07/98, where it was reported that lengthy negotiations due to the lack of clear guidelines and standard contractual forms presented a serious deterrent factor in concluding PFI contracts. The average PFI gestation period is 18 months compared with eight months in traditional public procurement contracts.

[144]   A serious set-back for the Private Finance Initiative in the United Kingdom was the report of the Accounting Standards Board *(The Tweedie Report – September 1998)* which criticised HM Treasury's practice of not including PFI deals in the Public Sector Borrowing Requirement (PSBR) balance sheet. The report condemned such practices and urged the government, for the sake of legal certainty and good public sector management and accounting, to issue new guidelines for future PFI projects and treat them in the same way as traditional public procurement spending.

[145]   Prior to 1997, there was considerable uncertainty as to the legal position of the parties in a privately financed project. The relevant legislation did not provide *in concreto* for the rights and obligations of the private sector and threatened *ultra vires* agreements concluded between certain public authorities (local authorities and health trusts) and the private sector. It was unclear whether these authorities had explicit or implied powers to enter into such contracts, a situation which left privately financed transactions in limbo. As a consequence, the National Health Service (Private Finance) Act 1997 and the Local Government Act (Contracts) 1997 were enacted in order to clear all legal obstacles. Both acts have introduced a 'clearance system' where the relevant authorities must certify a prospective PFI deal with the government, checking not only its *vires* but the whole commercial viability and procedural delivery mechanism of a privately financed contract.

empowers public authorities to contractualise their governance. The public-private partnership regime needs to benefit from a simplification and standardisation process, so a kind of routine similar to that governing the award of traditional public procurement contracts can assist the demand and supply sides in delivering more privately financed deals. However, the relative volume of public-private partnerships projects is not the critical factor in determining its success. It is rather the value-for-money element that is expected to crop up through the involvement of private entrepreneurship in the delivery of public services.

Revision of the Remedies Directives

The Remedies Directives 89/665 (review procedures for public supply and public works and public services contracts) and 92/13 (review procedures for public contracts in the water, energy, transport and telecommunications sectors) were enacted in order to ensure effective implementation of the public procurement Directives at national level and to guarantee access to justice for aggrieved contractors and interested parties against illegal or wrongful award decisions by contracting authorities.

It has emerged that the progress of implementation of the public procurement acquis is not uniform. The fact that only a small percentage of calls to tender are published (16.2% for the European Union in 2002) and that the figure varies appreciably amongst member states gives little cause to celebrate. Public procurement is the weakest link in the common market. Initial consultations launched by the Commission with the member states, economic operators and their representatives have revealed that the operation of national review procedures does not always make it possible to correct implementation failures. It has also become apparent that the effectiveness of national review mechanisms in public procurement differs considerably, a fact that may discourage economic operators from tendering for public contracts.

The process of revising the Remedies Directives will not be launched until the public procurement legislative package is in force. The Commission is of the view that any amendments should merely adapt and improve upon certain provisions of the Remedies Directives, without altering the philosophy and principles which underpin their structures. For example, the principle of the member states' *procedural autonomy* will not be questioned. Thus, member states will be able to retain the power to select a court, a tribunal or an independent authority as the competent forum to deal with public procurement law. However, the unsatisfactory situation brought about mainly by the very heterogeneous operation of member states' national review procedures, and recent developments in case-law, require clarification of the existing legislative framework in order to establish greater precision and to ensure that any sanctions are effective and proportionate and have a deterrent effect on infringements of Community law on public procurement.

3. The principles of public procurement regulation

THE PRINCIPLE OF PUBLIC AUTHORITIES AS CONTRACTING PARTIES

The internal structure of the public procurement law intends to embrace all the phases of the purchasing behaviour of the demand side of the public sector as well as the utilities in an attempt to introduce the envisaged regulatory system. Of paramount importance to the internal structure of the Public Procurement Directives is the comprehensive and clear definition of the term *contracting authorities*, a factor which determines the applicability of the relevant rules. The term contracting authorities for the purposes of public purchasing regulation should not pose considerable conceptual difficulties; it should cover authorities which disperse public funds in pursuit of or on behalf of public interest. EC public procurement law characterises as contracting authorities the state and its organs, interpreted in functional terms. The term *state* covers central, regional, municipal and local government departments. The above contracting authorities are primarily responsible for the core procurement requirements of supplies, works and services in a society. The Public Procurement Directives include detailed lists of all central and regional government departments that fall under their remit. However, the state in its function as a procurer of goods, works and services does not contain a range of purchasing operations which are attributed to its *organs*. By the term organs, procurement law has envisaged all entities which somehow deliver public interest functions and has described them as *bodies governed by public law*. The latter category is subject to a set of cumulative criteria in order to be classified as contracting authorities for the purposes of the Directives. *Bodies governed by public law* must be established for the specific purpose of meeting needs in the general public interest. Although they must have legal personality, their operations should not have industrial or commercial character. These entities must be financed, for the most part, by either the central government, or regional or local authorities, as well as being under their management and supervision control.

Contracting authorities for the purposes of public procurement law also include entities which are considered part of the state and its organs *in functional terms*. The European Court of Justice has interpreted[1] the term *state* in functional terms and has considered undertakings which depend on the relevant public authorities for the appointment of their members, are subject to their supervision and have as their main task the financing and award of contracts in pursuit of public interest as contracting authorities, even though not part of the state administration in *formal terms*.[2]

The enactment of the Utilities Directive brought an end to the exclusion of procurement of entities operating in the water, energy, transport and telecommunications sectors of the member states. A wide range of these entities are covered by the term *bodies governed by public law*, which is used by the Utilities Directives for the contracting entities operating in the relevant sectors. Interestingly, another category of contracting authorities under the Utilities Directives includes *public undertakings*. The term indicates any undertaking over which the state may exercise direct or indirect dominant influence by means of ownership, or by means of financial participation, or by means of laws and regulations which govern the public undertaking's operation. Dominant influence can be exercised in the form of a majority holding of the undertaking's subscribed capital, in the form of a majority controlling of the undertaking's issued shares, or, finally in the form of the right to appoint the majority of the undertaking's management board. Public undertakings cover utilities operators which have been granted exclusive rights to exploit a service. Irrespective of their ownership, they are subject to the Utilities Directive inasmuch as the *exclusivity* of their operation precludes other entities from entering the relevant market under substantially the same competitive conditions. Privatised utilities could be, in principle, excluded from the procurement rules when a genuinely competitive regime[3] within the relevant oligopsonistic market structure rules out purchasing patterns based on non-economic considerations.

Under the Tokyo Round GATT Agreement on Government Procurement (AGP), the term 'public authorities' was confined to central governments and their agencies only.[4] The new World Trade Organisation Government Procurement Agreement applies in principle to all bodies which are deemed

---

[1]   See case C-31/87, *Gebroeders Beentjes BV v. State of Netherlands*, [1988] ECR 4635.

[2]   See case C-249/81, *Commission v. Ireland*, [1982] ECR 4005.

[3]   The determination of a genuinely competitive regime is left to the utilities operators themselves. See case C-392/93, *The Queen and HM Treasury, ex parte British Telecommunications PLC*, OJ 1993. This is perhaps a first step towards self-regulation, which could lead to the disengagement of the relevant contracting authorities from the public procurement regime.

[4]   See Council Decision 87/565, OJ 1987 L 345.

'contracting authorities' for the purposes of the Public Supplies and Public Works Directives. As far as utilities are concerned, the WTO Government Procurement Agreement (GPA) applies to entities which carry out one or more of certain listed 'utility' activities,[5] where these entities are either 'public authorities' or 'public undertakings', in the sense of the Utilities Directive. However, the GPA does not cover entities operating in the utilities sector on the basis of *special and exclusive rights*.

THE PRINCIPLE OF TRANSPARENCY

One of the most important principles of the Public Procurement Directives is the principle of transparency. The principle of transparency serves two main objectives: the first is to introduce a system of openness into public purchasing in the member states, so a greater degree of accountability should be established and potential direct discrimination on grounds of nationality should be eliminated. The second objective aims at ensuring that transparency in public procurement represents a substantial basis for a system of best practice for both parts of the equation, but is of particular relevance to the supply side, to the extent that the latter has a more *proactive* role in determining the needs of the demand side. Transparency in public procurement is achieved through community-wide publicity and advertisement of public procurement contracts over certain thresholds by means of publication of three types of notices in the Official Journal of the European Communities:

(i) Periodic Indicative Notices (PIN). Every contracting authority must notify its intentions for public procurement contracts within the forthcoming financial year. By doing so, it provides an estimate of its intended purchasing and gives the supply side the necessary time for planning and response to future contract opportunities. The publication of Periodic Indicative Notices, if properly observed, also serves as a useful indicator in determining the relevant market size for the supply side, as well as the relevant procurement requirements for a type of contracting authorities on an annual basis. The fact that through PIN notices contracting authorities produce only an estimated figure for

---

5   The listed utility activities which are covered under the new GPA include (i) activities connected with the provision of water through fixed networks; (ii) activities concerned with the provision of electricity through fixed networks; (iii) the provision of terminal facilities to carriers by sea or inland waterway; and (iv) the operation of public services in the field of transport by automated systems, tramway, trolley bus or cable bus.

forthcoming contracts they intend to award does not absolve them of their responsibility to strictly adhere to the published figure.

(ii)   Invitations to tender. All contracts above the relevant thresholds should be tendered and the notice containing the invitation to tender must include the award procedures and the award criteria for the contract in question. The invitation to tender is the most important publicity and advertisement requirement for the creation of transparent and open public markets in the European Community. The publication of the invitation to tender refers only to a particular contract or a range of similar contracts of a repetitive nature and provides the supply side with the opportunity to respond and make an offer in order to meet the needs and requirements of the demand side. The invitation to tender is part of the contractual nexus in the public procurement process between the relevant contracting authority and the tenderers/candidates competing for the award of the contract in question. It is through the invitation to tender that the supply side has a clear view of the award procedures and the award criteria contracting authorities intend to utilise, thus being able to respond accordingly. The invitation to tender represents the first step towards the award of public contracts and failure by contracting authorities to adhere to the minimum requirements specified in the Directives could invalidate the whole process.

(iii)   Contract Award Notices (CAN). This is a form of notification after the award of the contract of the successful tenderer and the price of its offer, as well as the reasons for its selection by the contracting authority. In principle, Contract Award Notices publicise the reasoning of contracting authorities during the selection and award stages of the process, but quite often price information of the successful tenderers and other candidates is withheld for reasons of commercial confidentiality. The publication of CAN notices can be used as an effective indicator in monitoring the purchasing patterns of contracting authorities, as well as in providing a picture relevant to the tradability of public contracts.

All types of notices are published by the Publications Office of the European Communities. Within twelve days (or five days in the case of the accelerated form of restricted or negotiated procedures), the Publications Office publishes the notices in the Supplement to the Official Journal and via the TED (Tenders Electronic Daily) database. Two notices are published: in full in their original language only and in summary form in the other Community languages. The Publications Office takes responsibility for the necessary translations and summaries. The cost of publishing notices in the Supplement to the Official Journal is borne by the Community.

The Effects of the Principle of Transparency

Transparency, as a principle in public purchasing has an obvious trade effect, that of price competitiveness. If more interested suppliers are aware of a contracting authority's determination to procure, an element of competition automatically occurs; this type of competitive pattern will probably be reflected in the prices received by the contracting authority when it evaluates the offers. The fact that more suppliers are aware of a forthcoming public contract and the fact that interested suppliers are aware that their rivals are informed about it, indicates two distinct parameters which are relevant to savings and value for money. The first parameter focuses on value for money for the demand side of the equation of public purchasing and reveals the possibility for contracting authorities to compare prices (and quality). The second parameter has an effect on the supply side of the equation (the suppliers), which amongst other things can no longer rely on the lack of price comparisons when serving the public sector. Openness in public procurement, by definition, results in price competition and the benefits for contracting authorities appear achievable.

However, transparency and openness in public purchasing pose a question over long-term savings and value-for-money considerations. Price competition, as a result of the awareness of forthcoming public contracts, represents a rather static effect in the value-for-money process. The fact that more and more interested suppliers are aware and do submit tenders, in the long run, appears rather as a burden. If transparency and the resulting price competitiveness are based on a *win–win* process, the potential benefits for contracting authorities could easily be counterbalanced by the administrative costs of tender evaluation and replies to unsuccessful tenders. Furthermore, the risk management factor is much higher in a win–win purchasing scenario. Price competitiveness also poses some threats for contracting authorities, to the extent that quality of deliverables as well as the delivery process itself could be jeopardised, if contracting authorities deal with different and unknown contractors. It could thus be argued here that price competitiveness, potentially beneficial as a trade effect for the demand side of the public purchasing equation, has a static character. It seems that it does not take into account medium- or long-term purchasing patterns, nor the counter-effects of competition. Two elements deserve further analysis here.

The first raises questions over the aggregate loss of the economy through transparent competitive purchasing patterns. For example, if a large number of interested suppliers submit their offers to a particular contracting authority, two types of costs should be examined. First, is the cost which is attributed to the response and tendering stage of the procurement process. Human and capital resources are directed by the suppliers towards the preparation of documents and the submission of the offers. If one of these suppliers wins the contract, the remaining suppliers will have suffered an unrecoverable loss. If that aggregate loss exceeds the benefit/saving accomplished by the contracting authority in following transparent and competitive purchasing patterns, value for money has not been achieved. Secondly, along the same lines, the evaluation and selection process during tendering represents a considerable administrative cost for the contracting authorities. If the principle of transparency complements the principle of equal treatment, the contracting authorities should give the same attention to all interested suppliers that have submitted a response. Downsizing the list through evaluation and assessment based on stipulated criteria is by no means an inexpensive exercise. Human and capital resources have to be directed by contracting authorities towards meeting that cost. If the latter exceeds the potential savings achieved through the competitive tendering route, then value for money is not accomplished.

The second element that deserves attention relates to the definition of price competitiveness in public purchasing as well as its interrelation with anti-trust law and policy. A question which arises in price competitive tendering patterns is *what would be the lowest offer contracting authorities can accept*? If the maximisation of savings is the only achievable objective in the public procurement process, the transparent/competitive pattern cannot guarantee and evaluate safeguards in relation to under-priced offers. If the supply side responds to the continuing competitive purchasing pattern by lowering prices, contracting authorities could face a dilemma: where to stop. It should be mentioned here that the European rules provide for the automatic disqualification of an 'abnormally low offer'. The term has not been interpreted in detail by the judiciary at European and domestic levels and serves rather as a 'lower bottom limit'.[6] Also, when an offer appears low, contracting authorities may request clarification from the tenderer in question. Contracting authorities face a dilemma in evaluating and assessing low offers other than abnormally low ones. It is difficult for them to identify dumping or predatory pricing disguised behind a low offer for a public contract. In addition, even if there is an indication of anti-competitive price fixing, the European public procurement rules do not provide for any disqualification procedure. The suspension of the award procedures (or even the suspension of the conclusion of the contract itself) would be unlikely without a thorough and exhaustive investigation by the competent anti-trust authorities.

---

[6] See case C-76/81, *SA Transporoute et Travaux v. Minister of Public Works*, [1982] ECR 457; case C-104/75, *SA SHV Belgium v. La Maison Idéale et Société Nationale du Logement*, before the Belgian Conseil d'Etat, judgment of 24 June 1986 of the Belgian *Conseil d'Etat*.

Table 3.1 Transparency Rates by Member State (%)

	1995	1996	1997	1998	1999	2000	2001	2002	2003	2004	2005
Austria	4.5	7.5	7.5	8.3	7.0	13.5	14.6	15.5	14.8	14.2	15.2
Belg	6.9	7.6	10.9	13.8	15.6	15.6	18.6	15.8	14.9	16.1	15.7
Den	16.4	13.4	13.4	13.5	14.3	20.9	15.8	14.5	14.6	15.2	15.8
Germ	5.1	5.6	6.3	6.5	5.2	5.6	5.7	7.5	6.8	7.2	7.4
Greece	34.1	37.7	42.9	45.1	39.9	31.9	35.3	45.7	43.2	44.8	43.9
Spain	8.5	11.0	11.5	11.5	16.8	25.4	23.4	23.6	24.2	24.9	23.5
France	5.5	6.8	8.4	11.0	11.7	14.6	16.8	17.7	16.4	16.2	16.5
Ireland	11.4	16.3	19.3	16.1	16.8	21.4	19.3	18.0	21.3	20.5	20.9
Italy	9.8	9.9	11.3	10.7	13.2	17.5	15.3	20.3	17.1	17.8	18.7
Lux	5.2	7.0	9.2	14.3	12.9	12.3	10.7	13.3	12.6	13.4	12.9
Nethlds	4.8	5.1	5.5	5.2	5.9	10.8	12.5	8.9	9.8	8.1	8.9
Portgal	15.5	17.7	15.1	15.5	14.6	15.0	17.7	19.4	20.2	19.8	20.9
Finland	8.0	9.2	8.2	9.2	9.8	13.2	15.1	13.9	14.2	15.7	15.1
Sweden	10.5	10.6	11.5	11.6	12.5	17.9	23.4	19.3	20.1	20.6	21.3
UK	15.0	15.6	17.9	16.9	15.1	21.5	21.5	21.1	22.1	21.7	21.8
EU 15	**8.4**	**9.2**	**10.7**	**11.1**	**11.2**	**14.9**	**15.4**	**16.2**	**18.2**	**18.4**	**18.6**

Source: Directorate General, Internal Market, National Statistic Offices, EUROSTAT.

THE DE MINIMIS PRINCIPLE

The Public Procurement Directives are applicable only if certain value thresholds are met. The application of the Directives is subject to monetary considerations in relation to the value of the relevant contracts. There is a clear-cut distinction in the coverage of the public procurement rules upon contracts representing transactions between the public sector and the industry of a certain economic substance and volume. Contracts below the required thresholds are not subject to the rigorous regime envisaged by the Directives. However, contracting authorities are under an explicit obligation to avoid discrimination on nationality grounds and to apply all the provisions related to the fundamental principles of the Treaties of Rome and Maastricht. The thresholds laid down are as follows.

One might question the reasoning behind the division of public procurement regulation into dimensional and sub-dimensional categories as a result of the relevant thresholds. Interestingly enough, it was thought that contracts above the thresholds laid down by the Directives could embrace the majority of the public procurement requirements in the member states, thus eliminating the danger of discriminatory public purchasing for those contracts left outside the ambit of the Directives. However, careful monitoring of procurement systems in the member states has revealed that sub-dimensional procurement appears to be at least three times the size of dimensional public purchasing,[7] a fact that renders the application of the Directives only partly responsible for the integration of public markets in the European Community.

The Dimensionality of Public Procurement

The dimensional nature of public procurement by virtue of the monetary applicability of the relevant rules introduces a *de minimis* criterion, whereby certain thresholds are utilised for the applicability of the Directives in relation to the value of the contracts. The dimensional public procurement should, in principle, encompass the majority of procurement requirements of member states and their contracting authorities. However, the legislation on public procurement has had little effect on the principle of transparency, as empirical investigation into the patterns of contracting authorities of member states concerning their publication record in relation to contracts reveals a rather gloomy picture. In comparison with the total volume of public procurement in the member states, the volume of public purchasing which is advertised and

---

[7]   See European Commission, *The Use of Negotiated Procedures as a Non-Tariff Barrier in Public Procurement*, Brussels, CC 9364, 1995.

tendered according to the requirements of the relevant Directives appears disproportionate and beyond expectation, bearing in mind the importance that has been placed upon the principle of transparency for the opening-up of public markets in the European Union. The percentages of public contracts advertised in the Official Journal by member states reveal the relatively low impact of public procurement legislation on the principle and objectives of transparency in European public markets. Clarification of the above impact of the law upon the transparency patterns which contracting authorities have established should be sought by exploring three scenarios.

The first scenario is based on the distinction between dimensional and sub-dimensional public procurement in the member states. The European Directives allow the division of public contracts into lots without any justification by contracting authorities. This in most cases may result in intentional contravention of the Directives, as sub-dimensional (below certain thresholds) public contracts escape applicability. As sub-dimensional public procurement escapes from the mandatory publication requirement, contracting authorities tend to divide contracts into separate lots. It should be mentioned that the Directives stipulate the prohibition of intentional division of contracts into lots with a view to avoiding the relevant thresholds, but the provision presents practical difficulties in its observance and enforcement. Until the time of writing, there has been no case or complaint before national courts or before the European Court of Justice relating to the intentional division of contracts into lots with lower thresholds in order to avoid the application of the Directives. The relevant thresholds which are subject to the mandatory publication requirement clearly result in a segmentation of public markets in quantitative terms by creating a *dimensional forum* which is subject to the rigorous legal regime. A *de minimis* rule applies to contracts below the thresholds, which exempts them from the provisions of the Directives. Sub-dimensional public procurement is only subject to the principle of non-discrimination at European level, whereas at domestic level, national tendering rules regulate the award of these contracts.

The second scenario is based on the excessive utilisation of award procedures without prior publication. Indeed, the Directives allow, under certain circumstances, the award of contracts through direct negotiations with a contractor. Although the European Court of Justice has condemned the above practice in a number of cases before it, the actual utilisation of negotiated procedures without prior publication is widespread.

Finally, the third scenario implies the blunt violation of Community law by member states by avoiding the publication of tender notices in the Official Journal of the European Communities.

Bearing in mind the relative absence of complaints and subsequent litigation concerning non-advertisement of public contracts before national courts or the European Court of Justice, the third scenario reflects to a large extent the underlying reason for the lack of transparency in public procurement. In fact, intentional division of contracts into lots with a view to avoiding the Directives and excessive and unjustified recourse to award procedures without prior publication amounts to a blunt violation of member states' obligations arising from the relevant Directives and also from primary Treaty provisions.

THE PRINCIPLE OF FAIRNESS

Selection and Qualification

After the advertising and publicity requirements the next phase in the public procurement process is the selection and qualification of the tenderers. At this stage, contracting authorities vet all the responses received and determine the suitability of the candidates according to objectively defined criteria which aim at eliminating arbitrariness and discrimination. The selection criteria are determined through two major categories of qualification requirements: (i) legal and (ii) technical/economic. Contracting authorities must strictly follow the homogeneously specified selection criteria for enterprises participating in the award procedures for public procurement contracts in an attempt to avoid potential discrimination on grounds of nationality and exclude technical specifications which may favour national undertakings.

The relevant provisions of the procurement Directives relating to the criteria concerning a tenderer's good standing and qualification are directly effective.[8] These criteria comprise grounds for exclusion from participation in the award of public contracts, such as bankruptcy, professional misconduct, failure to fulfil social security obligations and obligations relating to taxes. They also refer to the technical ability and knowledge of the contractor, proof of which may be furnished by educational or professional qualifications, previous experience in performing public contracts and statements on the contractor's expertise. In construction projects, the references which the contractor may be required to produce must be specified in the notice or invitation to tender. They include: the contractor's educational and professional qualifications or those of the firm's managerial staff, and, in particular, those of the person or persons responsible for carrying out the works; a list of the works carried out over the past five years, accompanied by certificates of satisfactory completion for the most important works. These certificates shall indicate the

---

[8] See case C-76/81, *SA Transporoute et Travaux v. Minister of Public Works*, [1982] ECR 457.

value, date and site of the works and shall specify whether they were carried out according to the rules of the trade and properly completed. Where necessary, the competent authority shall submit these certificates directly to the authority awarding the contracts, together with: a statement of the tools, plant and technical equipment available to the contractor for carrying out the work; a statement of the firm's average annual manpower and number of managerial staff for the last three years; a statement of the technicians or technical divisions which the contractor can call upon to carry out the work, and whether or not they belong to the firm.

On the other hand, in supplies contracts, the references which may be requested must be mentioned in the invitation to tender and are as follows:

- a list of the principal deliveries effected in the past three years, with the sums, dates and recipients involved, whether public or private, in the form of certificates issued or countersigned by the competent authority;
- a description of the undertaking's technical facilities, its measures for ensuring quality and its study and research facilities;
- an indication of the technicians or technical bodies involved, whether or not they belong directly to the undertaking, especially those responsible for quality control;
- samples, descriptions or photographs of the products to be supplied, the authenticity of which must be certified if the contracting authority so requests;
- certificates drawn up by official quality-control institutes or agencies of recognised competence attesting to the conformity to certain specifications or standards of goods clearly identified by references to specifications or standards;
- where the goods to be supplied are complex or, exceptionally, are required for a special purpose, a check should be carried out by the contracting authorities (or on their behalf by a competent official body of the country in which the supplier is established, subject to that body's agreement) on the production capacities of the supplier and, if necessary, on his study and research facilities and quality control measures. The provisions covering the contractors' eligibility and technical capacity constitute an exhaustive list.

In principle, there are automatic grounds for exclusion, when a contractor, supplier or service provider (i) is bankrupt or is being wound up; (ii) is the subject of proceedings for a declaration of bankruptcy or for an order for compulsory winding up; (iii) has been convicted of an offence concerning his professional conduct; (iv) has been guilty of grave professional misconduct; (v) has not fulfilled obligations relating to social security contributions; and (vi) has not fulfilled obligations relating to the payment of taxes.

However, for the purposes of assessing the financial and economic standing of contractors, an exception to the exhaustive list covering contractors' eligibility and technical capacity is provided for, where, in particular, contracting entities may request references other than those expressly mentioned therein. Evidence of financial and economic standing may be provided by means of references, including (i) appropriate statements from bankers; (ii) the presentation of the firm's balance sheets or extracts from balance sheets where these are published under company law provisions; and (iii) a statement of the firm's annual turnover and the turnover on construction works for the three previous financial years. The non-exhaustive character of the list of references in relation to the contractors' economic and financial standing was recognised by the European Court of Justice,[9] where the value of the works which may be carried out at one time may constitute proof of the contractors' economic and financial standing. The contracting authorities are allowed to fix such a limit, as the provisions of the public procurement Directives do not aim to delimit the powers of member states, but to determine the references or evidence which may be furnished in order to establish the contractors' financial and economic standing. In another case referred to the European Court by a Dutch court,[10] the Court maintained that the examination of a contractor's suitability based on its good standing and qualifications and its financial and economic standing may take place simultaneously with the award procedures of a contract.[11] However, the two procedures (the suitability evaluation and bid evaluation) are totally distinct processes which shall not be confused.[12]

Legal Requirements for the Qualification of Contractors

The definition of a contractor wishing to submit a tender for the award of a public contract comprises any legal or natural person involved in supplies, construction or services activities. It also includes private consortia, as well as joint ventures or groupings. Contracting authorities may impose a requirement as to the form and legal status of the contractor that wins the award. This requirement focuses only on the post-selection stage after the award of the contract and indicates the need for legal certainty. The specific legal form and

---

[9] See cases C-27/86, 28/86, 29/86; C-27/86, *Constructions et Entreprises Industrielles SA (CEI) v. Association Intercommunale pour les Autoroutes des Ardennes*; case 28/86, *Ing. A. Bellini & Co. SpA v. Regie de Betiments*; case 29/86, *Ing. A. Bellini & Co. SpA v. Belgian State*, [1987] ECR 3347.

[10] See case C-31/87, *Gebroeders Beentjes BV v. State of Netherlands*, [1988] ECR 4635.

[11] See *Bellini* case C-28/86, [1987] ECR 3347, op. cit.

[12] See case C-71/92, *Commission v. Spain*, judgment of 30 June 1993.

status requirement for contracting entities facilitates monitoring of the performance of the contract and allows better access to justice in case of a dispute between the contracting entity and the undertaking in question. The successful contractor should also fulfil certain qualitative requirements concerning his eligibility and technical capacity[13] and his financial and economic standing.

Lists of Recognised Contractors

Being listed on a register of recognised contractors such as exists in various member states may be used by contractors as an alternative means of proving their suitability, also before contracting authorities of other member states. Information deduced from registration on an official list may not be questioned by contracting authorities. Nonetheless, the actual level of financial and economic standing and technical knowledge or ability required of contractors is determined by the contracting authorities. Consequently, contracting authorities are required to accept that a contractor's financial and economic standing and technical knowledge and ability are sufficient for works corresponding to his classification only in so far as that classification is based on equivalent criteria with respect to the capacities required.

THE PRINCIPLE OF NON-DISCRIMINATION

Tendering Procedures

Participation in tendering procedures is channelled through open, negotiated or restricted procedures.

Open procedures are those where every interested supplier, contractor or service provider may submit an offer.

Negotiated procedures are procedures for the award of public contracts whereby contracting authorities consult contractors of their choice and negotiate the terms of the contract with one or more of them. In most cases they follow restricted procedures and they are heavily utilised under framework agreements in the utilities sectors. There are two different kinds of negotiated procedures: (i) negotiated procedures with prior notification and (ii) negotiated procedures without prior notification.

Negotiated procedures with prior notification provide for selection of candidates in two rounds. In the first round, all interested contractors may

---

13   See Articles 20–23 of Directive 77/62; Articles 23 et seq. of Directive 71/305; Articles 29 et seq. of Directive 90/531; Articles 29 et seq. of Directive 92/50.

submit their tenders and the contracting authority selects which of the candidates will be invited to negotiate. In the second round, negotiations with various candidates take place and the successful tender is selected. In principle, the minimum number of candidates to be selected is three, provided that there are a sufficient number of suitable candidates.

Negotiated procedures without prior notification are the least restrictive of the various award procedures laid down in the Directive and may be conducted in one single round. Contracting authorities are allowed to choose whichever contractor they want, begin negotiations directly with this contractor and award the contract to him. The Directive provides only a few rules with which this procedure must comply. A prior notice in the Official Journal is not required.

Restricted procedures are those procedures for the award of public contracts whereby only those contractors invited by the contracting authority may submit tenders. The selection of the winning tender usually takes place in two rounds. In the first round, all interested contractors may signal their interest and the contracting authority selects which candidates will be invited to tender. In principle, the minimum number of candidates to be selected is five. In the second round, bids are submitted and the successful tender is selected.

An accelerated form of restricted or negotiated procedure may be used when, for reasons of urgency, the periods normally required under the normal procedures cannot be met. In such cases, contracting authorities are required to indicate in the tender notice published in the Official Journal the grounds for using the accelerated form of the procedure. The use of an accelerated procedure must be limited to the types and quantities of products or services which it can be shown are urgently required. Other products or services must be supplied or provided under open or restricted procedures.

The Directives stipulate that, where possible, open procedures should constitute the norm. Open procedures increase competition without doubt and can achieve better prices for the contracting authorities when purchasing goods in large volumes. Price reduction based on economies of scale can bring about substantial cost savings for the public sector. Open procedures are mostly utilised when the procurement process is relatively straightforward and are combined with the lowest price award criterion. On the other hand, competition in tendering procedures is limited by using the restricted and negotiated procedures. By definition, the number of candidates that are allowed to tender is limited (five and three respectively in restricted and negotiated procedures), therefore the Directives have attached a number of conditions that the contracting authorities should meet when they intend to award their contracts through restricted or negotiated procedures. Restricted and negotiated procedures are utilised in relation to the most economically advantageous offer award criterion and suited to more complex procurement schemes. Although contracting authorities can freely opt for open or restricted procedures, the latter should be justified by reference to the nature of the products or services to be procured and the balance between contract value and administrative costs associated with tender evaluation. A more rigorous set of conditions applies to the use of negotiated procedures. When negotiated procedures with prior notification are used, they must be justified on grounds of irregular or unacceptable tenders received as a result of a previous call. Negotiated procedures without prior notification are restrictively permitted in the absence of tenders, when the procurement involves manufactured products or construction works purely for research and development; when for technical or artistic reasons or reasons connected with the protection of exclusive rights a particular supplier or contractor is selected; in cases of extreme urgency brought about by unforeseeable events not attributable to the contracting authorities; when additional deliveries and supplies or works would cause disproportionate technical operational and maintenance difficulties.

All negotiations with candidates or tenderers on fundamental aspects of contracts, in particular on prices, are prohibited in open and restricted procedures; discussions with candidates or tenderers may be held, but only for the purpose of clarifying or supplementing the content of their tenders or the requirements of the contracting authorities and provided this does not involve discriminatory practices. The need for such a prohibition is clear, since the possibility to negotiate may allow the contracting authority to introduce subjective appraisal criteria. A Declaration on the above subject has been made by the European Council and the Commission of the European Communities.[14] Also the European Court of Justice has condemned post-tender negotiations as in case 243/89, *Commission v. Denmark.*[15]

The selection process must be completely distinguished from the award process. Quite often, contracting authorities appear to fuse the two basic processes of the award of public procurement contracts. This runs contrary to legal precedent of the European Court of Justice and in particular case 31/87 *Gebroeders Beentjes v. Netherlands.*[16] The Court stated expressly that suitability evaluation and bid evaluation are distinct processes which shall not be confused. The same line was adopted by the Court in case C-71/92, *Commission v. Spain.*[17]

The competitive dialogue is a new award procedure introduced by the new public procurement Directives alongside open, restricted and negotiated procedures. Arguably, the rationale of the competitive dialogue is to address

---

[14] See OJ [1994] L 111/114.
[15] See the Court's judgment of 22 June 1993.
[16] See [1988] ECR 4635.
[17] See the Court's judgment of 30 June 1993.

the shortcomings of traditional award procedures and in particular, (i) the inability of open or restricted procedures to facilitate the award of complex public contracts, including concessions and public–private partnerships, (ii) the exceptional nature of negotiated procedures without prior advertisement[18] and (iii) the restrictive interpretation[19] of the grounds for using negotiated procedures with prior advertisement.

The competitive dialogue must be used exceptionally in cases of particularly complex contracts, where the use of open or restricted procedures will not allow the award of the contract, and the use of negotiated procedures cannot be justified. A public contract is considered to be particularly complex where the contracting authorities are not able to define in an objective manner the technical specifications which are required to pursue the project, or where they are not able to specify the legal or financial make-up of a project.

The procedure is very complex, as it has three main phases and many options within these phases. First, the advertisement phase obliges contracting authorities to publish a contract notice or a descriptive document outlining their needs and basic specifications of the project. After that phase and before launching a competitive dialogue for the award of a contract, contracting authorities may, using a technical dialogue, seek or accept advice which may be used in the preparation of the specifications, provided that such advice does

---

[18]   Negotiated procedures without prior advertisement are exceptionally allowed . . . when for technical or artistic reasons or reasons connected with the protection of exclusive rights the services could only be procured by a particular provider . . . and . . . in cases of extreme urgency brought about by events unforeseeable by the contracting authority. In cases C-199/85, *Commission v. Italy*, [1987] ECR 1039 and C-3/88, *Commission v. Italy*, [1989] ECR 4035, the Court rejected the existence of exclusive rights and regarded the abuse of this provision as contrary to the right of establishment and freedom to provide services which are based on the principle of equal treatment and prohibit not only overt discrimination on grounds of nationality, but also all covert forms of discrimination, which, by the application of other criteria of differentiation, lead to the same result. Interestingly, in case 199/85, *Commission v. Italy*, op. cit., the Court elucidated that exclusive rights might include contractual arrangements such as know-how and intellectual property rights. For reasons of urgency brought about by unforeseen events affecting contracting authorities, the Court established two tests: (i) the need for a justification test based on the proportionality principle, and (ii) the existence of a causal link between the alleged urgency and the unforeseen events (see C-199/85, *Commission v. Italy*, op. cit.; C-3/88, *Commission v. Italy*, op. cit., C-24/91, *Commission v. Spain*, [1994] CMLR 621; C-107/92, *Commission v. Italy*, judgment of 2 August 1993; C-57/94, *Commission v. Italy*, judgment of 18 May 1995; C-296/92, *Commission v. Italy*, judgment of 12 January 1994).

[19]   The grounds for using this procedure are confined to: (i) the nature of the works or services or risks attached thereto do not permit overall pricing and (ii) the nature of the services is such that specifications cannot be established with sufficient precision.

not have the effect of precluding competition. Secondly, a selection phase reduces the candidates to be invited to the competitive dialogue. The minimum number of candidates should be three but it could be lower if there is sufficient evidence of competitiveness in the process or the limited number of initial respondents to the contract notice precludes the invitation of at least three candidates. Thirdly, the competitive dialogue is opened by the commencement of the award phase. Contracting authorities must open a dialogue with the candidates selected, the aim of which is to identify the means best suited to satisfying their needs. They may discuss all aspects of the contract with the chosen candidates, ensuring equality of treatment among all tenderers. In particular, they must not provide information in a discriminatory manner which may give some tenderers an advantage over others. Contracting authorities may not reveal to the other participants solutions proposed or other confidential information communicated by a candidate participating in the dialogue without prior agreement from that candidate.

THE PRINCIPLE OF OBJECTIVITY

The Award Criteria

In principle, there are two criteria laid down in the Public Procurement Directives for awarding public contracts:

* the lowest price;
* the most economically advantageous offer.

The lowest price criterion reflects a numerical comparison of tendered contract prices. The tenderer who submits the cheapest offer must be awarded the contract. Subject to qualitative criteria and financial and economic standing, contracting authorities do not rely on any factor other than the price quoted to complete the contract. The reasons for utilising the lowest price criterion are: simplicity, speed, less qualitative consideration during the evaluation of tenders.

The assessment of what is the most economically advantageous tender offer is to be based on a series of factors and determinants chosen by the contracting entity for the particular contract in question. These factors include: price, delivery or completion date, running costs, cost-effectiveness, profitability, technical merit, product or work quality, aesthetic and functional characteristics, after-sales service and technical assistance, commitments with regard to spare parts and components and maintenance costs, security of supplies. The above list is not exhaustive and the factors listed therein serve as a guideline for contracting authorities in the weighted evaluation process of the contract award. The order of appearance of these factors in the invitation to tender or in the contract documents is of paramount importance for the whole process of evaluation of the tenders and award of the contract. The most economically advantageous factors must be in hierarchical or descending sequence so tenderers and interested parties can clearly ascertain the relative weight of factors other than price for the evaluation process. However, factors which have no strict relevance to the particular contract in question or factors which are irrelevant in economic terms are classified as subjective. It is clearly stated in the *European Commission's Guide to the Community Rules on Open Government Procurement*[20] that '. . . only objective criteria which are strictly relevant to the particular project may be used . . .'. The European Court of Justice has established[21] that the award criteria concern only the qualities of the service the provider can offer and that contracting authorities may use the most economically advantageous offer as award criterion by choosing the factors which they want to apply in evaluating tenders, provided these factors are mentioned in hierarchical order in the invitation to tender or the contract documents.[22]

The most economically advantageous offer as an award criterion has provided the European Court of Justice with the opportunity to balance the economic considerations of public procurement with policy choices. Although on numerous occasions the Court has maintained the importance of the economic approach[23] in the regulation of public sector contracts, it has also recognised the relative discretion of contracting authorities to utilise non-economic considerations, such as employment and social policy considerations[24] and the protection of the environment[25] as award criteria.

---

[20]   See [1987] OJ C 385/1 at 36.
[21]   See case C-31/87, *Gebroeders Beentjes v. The Netherlands*, [1988] ECR 4635.
[22]   See case C-324/93, *R. v. The Secretary of State for the Home Department, ex parte Evans Medical Ltd and Macfarlan Smith Ltd.*
[23]   See cases C-380/98, (Cambridge University) at paragraph 17, C-44/96, (Strohal), paragraph 33; C-360/96, (BFI) paragraphs 42 and 43; C-237/99, (OPAC), paragraphs 41 and 42.
[24]   See case 31/87, *Gebroeders Beentjes B.V v. The Netherlands*, [1989] ECR 4365; case C-237/99, *Commission v. France*, [2001] ECR 934. Also see case C360/89, *Commission v. Italy*, [1992] ECR 3401.
[25]   See case C-513/99, *Concordia Bus Filandia v. Helsingin Kaupunki et HKL-Bussiliikenne*, [2000] ECR I-7213.

4. Public sector procurement

OVERVIEW

The 1996 European Commission Green Paper on Public Procurement[1] and the follow-up policy developments adopted by the European institutions[2] highlighted the need for a modern and effective regime to regulate public procurement in the European Union.[3] The previous legal framework of public procurement assigned the supplies, works and services, as well as utilities procurement, to different legal instruments.[4] The regime was the product of four decades of legal development to open up the public sector markets to competition and introduce similar allocative and production efficiencies to those found in private markets that are genuinely competitive.

The main influences on the codification of the public procurement regime into two mainstream legal frameworks to cover the public sector and the utilities respectively can be traced to the jurisprudence of the European Court of Justice,[5] in particular case-law on the definition of contracting authorities, the

---

[1]   See the Green Paper on Public Procurement in the European Union: Exploring the Way Forward, European Commission, 1996.

[2]   See European Commission, Communication on Public Procurement in the European Union, COM (98) 143.

[3]   See the proposal from the European Commission OJ C 29 E, 30.1.2001, p. 11 and OJ C 203 E, 27.8.2002, p. 210; the opinion of the Economic and Social Committee OJ C 193, 10.7.2001, p. 7; the opinion of the Committee of the Regions OJ C 144, 16.5.2001, p. 23; the opinion of the European Parliament of 17 January 2002 (OJ C 271 E, 7.11.2002, p. 176), Council Common Position of 20 March 2003 (OJ C 147 E, 24.6.2003, p. 1) and Position of the European Parliament of 2 July 2003. See also the Legislative Resolution of the European Parliament of 29 January 2004 and Decision of the Council of 2 February 2004.

[4]   The previous public procurement regime includes the Public Supplies Directive 93/36/EC, OJ L 199, as amended by Directive 97/52/EC, OJ L 328 and Directive 2001/78/EC, OJ L 285; The Public Works Directive 93/37/EC, OJ L 199, amended by Directive 97/52/EC OJ L 328 and Directive 2001/78/EC, OJ L 285; The Utilities Directives 93/38/EC, OJ L 199, amended by Directive 98/4/EC, OJ L 101; The Public Services Directive 92/50/EEC, OJ L 209, amended by Directive 97/52/EC, OJ L 328 and Directive 2001/78/EC, OJ L 285.

[5]   For a comprehensive analysis of the public procurement case law, see Bovis, 'Recent case law relating to public procurement: A beacon for the integration of public markets', **39** (2002), *CMLRev.*

use of award procedures and award criteria, and the potential for contracting authorities to use environmental and social considerations as criteria for the award of public contracts.[6]

The new public procurement Directives have also been seen as an integral part of the Commission's 2000 Work Programme, which pledges to modernise the relevant legislation for the completion of the internal market and at the same time implement the Lisbon European Council's call for economic reform within the internal market

The primary intention behind the codification of the supplies, works and services Directives into a single legal instrument concerns the simplification of the public procurement rules and the subsequent enhancement of legal certainty. Furthermore, the codification is expected to facilitate legal efficiency and compliance inasmuch as it streamlines the implementation process by national governments and provides a one-stop shop reference point in national legal orders. The fusion of the rules governing supplies, works and services procurement into a single legal instrument represents a successful attempt on the part of the European Union to codify supranational administrative provisions which have the aim of harmonising domestic legal regimes.

THE PUBLIC SECTOR DIRECTIVE

The Public Sector Directive[7] is applicable to the award of public contracts between economic operators and contracting authorities. The term economic operator includes undertakings that are described as contractors, suppliers and service providers and has been introduced in the new Public Sector Directive for simplification purposes.[8] On the other hand the concept of contracting authority embraces a variety of organisations that fall within the remit of the

---

[6]   See Communication from the European Commission to the Council, the European Parliament, the Economic and Social Committee, and the Committee of the Regions, 'Working together to maintain momentum', 2001 Review of the Internal Market Strategy, Brussels, 11 April 2001, COM (2001) 198 final. Also, European Commission, Commission Communication, Public Procurement in the European Union, Brussels, 11 March 1998, COM (98) 143. See Commission Interpretative Communication on the Community law applicable to public procurement and the possibilities for integrating social considerations into public procurement, COM (2001) 566, 15 October 2001. Also, Commission Interpretative Communication on the Community law applicable to public procurement and the possibilities for integrating environmental considerations into public procurement, COM (2001) 274, 4 July 2001.

[7]   See Directive 2004/18, OJ 2004 L134/114.

[8]   See Article 8 second indent of the Public Sector Directive.

state, central or local government[9] and also bodies which are governed by public law.[10]

The terms 'contractor', 'supplier' and 'service provider' mean any natural or legal person or public entity or group of such persons and/or bodies which offers on the market, respectively, the execution of works and/or a work, products or services.[11] The term 'economic operator' covers equally the concepts of contractor, supplier and service provider. It is used merely in the interests of simplification. An economic operator who has submitted a tender must be designated as a 'tenderer'. One who has sought an invitation to take part in a restricted or negotiated procedure or a competitive dialogue must be designated as a 'candidate'.

The Principles of the Public Sector Directive

Articles 2 and 3 cover the principles of awarding contracts. In particular, contracting authorities must treat economic operators equally and in a non-discriminatory manner and act in a transparent way.

Article 3 includes a non-discrimination clause for the cases of granting special or exclusive rights. Where a contracting authority grants special or exclusive rights to carry out a public service activity to an entity other than such a contracting authority, the act by which that right is granted must provide that, in respect of the supply contracts which it awards to third parties as part of its activities, the entity concerned must comply with the principle of non-discrimination on the basis of nationality.

Article 6 also provides for the obligation to observe confidentiality in accordance with the national law to which the contracting authority is subject. Contracting authorities must not disclose information forwarded to them by economic operators which they have designated as confidential; such information includes, in particular, technical or trade secrets and the confidential aspects of tenders. This obligation is without prejudice to the provisions of the Directive relevant to the advertising of awarded contracts

---

[9] The definition of contracting authorities has been uniformly maintained across the evolution stages of public procurement regulation. Article 9 of the Public Sector Directive repeats verbatim the definition of contracting authorities previously found in the preceding Public Procurement Directives and in particular the Public Supplies Directive 93/36/EC, OJ L 199, as amended by Directive 97/52/EC, OJ L 328 and Directive 2001/78/EC, OJ L 285; the Public Works Directive 93/37/EC, OJ L 199, amended by Directive 97/52/EC OJ L 328 and Directive 2001/78/EC, OJ L 285; and the Public Services Directive 92/50/EEC, OJ L 209, amended by Directive 97/52/EC, OJ L 328 and Directive 2001/78/EC, OJ L 285.

[10] See Article 9, second indent of the Public Sector Directive.

[11] See Article 1(8) of the Public Sector Directive.

and to the information for candidates and tenderers set out in Articles 35(4) and 41.

The Substantive Applicability of the Public Sector Directive

Excluded contracts

The Directive does not apply to public contracts in the water, energy, transport and postal services sectors[12] which are awarded under Directive 2004/17.[13] However, the Directive applies to public contracts in the utilities sectors in so far as the member state concerned takes advantage of the option referred to in the second subparagraph of Article 71 of the Utilities Directive, which stipulates deferral of the Directive's application for up to 35 months from the deadline of its implementation by member states (31 January 2006).

Neither does the Directive apply to public contracts for the principal purpose of permitting the contracting authorities to provide or exploit public telecommunications networks or to provide the public with one or more telecommunications services.[14] For the purposes of the non-applicability of the Directive in the field of telecommunications, 'public telecommunications' network means the public telecommunications infrastructure which enables signals to be conveyed between defined network termination points by wire, by microwave, by optical means or by other electromagnetic means;[15] a 'network termination point' means all physical connections and their technical access specifications which form part of the public telecommunications network and are necessary for access to, and efficient communication through, that public network;[16] 'public telecommunications services' means telecommunications services the provision of which the member states have specifically assigned, in particular, to one or more telecommunications entities;[17] 'telecommunications services' means services the provision of which consists wholly or partly in the transmission and routing of signals on the public telecommunications network by means of telecommunications processes, with the exception of broadcasting and television.[18]

The Directive does not apply to public contracts when they are declared to be secret contracts and contracts requiring special security measures, when their performance must be accompanied by special security measures in accor-

---

12   See Article 12 of the Public Sector Directive.
13   See the Utilities Directive 2004/17, OJ 2004 L 134/1.
14   See Article 13 of the Public Sector Directive.
15   See Article 1(15)(a) of the Public Sector Directive.
16   See Article 1(15)(b) of the Public Sector Directive.
17   See Article 1(15)(c) of the Public Sector Directive.
18   See Article 1(15)(d) of the Public Sector Directive.

dance with the laws, regulations or administrative provisions in force in the member state concerned, or when the protection of the essential interests of that member state so requires.[19]

The Directive also does not apply to public contracts awarded pursuant to international rules[20] which are governed by different procedural rules and awarded through the following means:

(a) pursuant to an international agreement concluded in conformity with the Treaty between a member state and one or more third countries and covering supplies or works intended for the joint implementation or exploitation of a work by the signatory states or services intended for the joint implementation or exploitation of a project by the signatory states; all agreements must be communicated to the Commission, which may consult the Advisory Committee for Public Contracts referred to in Article 77;

(b) pursuant to a concluded international agreement relating to the stationing of troops and concerning the undertakings of a member state or a third country;

(c) pursuant to the particular procedure of an international organisation.

Specific exclusions

The Public Sector Directive does not apply to public service contracts for: (a) the acquisition or rental, by whatever financial means, of land, existing buildings or other immovable property or concerning rights thereon; nevertheless, financial service contracts concluded at the same time as, before or after the contract of acquisition or rental, in whatever form, must be subject to this Directive; (b) the acquisition, development, production or co-production of programme material intended for broadcasting by broadcasters and contracts for broadcasting time; (c) arbitration and conciliation services; (d) financial services in connection with the issue, sale, purchase or transfer of securities or other financial instruments, in particular transactions by the contracting authorities to raise money or capital, and central bank services; (e) employment contracts; (f) research and development services other than those where the benefits accrue exclusively to the contracting authority for its use in the conduct of its own affairs, on condition that the service provided is wholly remunerated by the contracting authority.[21]

The Directive does not apply to service concessions[22] or service contracts

---

[19] See Article 14 of the Public Sector Directive.
[20] See Article 15 of the Public Sector Directive.
[21] See Article 16 of the Public Sector Directive.
[22] See Article 17 of the Public Sector Directive.

awarded on the basis of an exclusive right awarded by a contracting authority to another contracting authority or to an association of contracting authorities on the basis of an exclusive right which they enjoy pursuant to a published law, regulation or administrative provision which is compatible with the Treaty.[23]

Reserved contracts

Member states may reserve the right to participate in public contract award procedures to sheltered workshops or provide for such contracts to be performed in the context of sheltered employment programmes where most of the employees concerned are handicapped persons who, by reason of the nature or the seriousness of their disabilities, cannot carry on occupations under normal conditions.[24]

The Monetary Applicability of the Public Sector Directive

Threshold for public contracts

The Directive applies to public contracts which have a value exclusive of value-added tax (VAT) estimated to be equal to or greater than the following thresholds:[25]

(a)   Euro 162 000 for public supply and service contracts other than those covered by point (b), third indent, awarded by contracting authorities which are listed as central government authorities in Annex IV; in the case of public supply contracts awarded by contracting authorities operating in the field of defence, this must apply only to contracts involving products covered by Annex V;

(b)   Euro 249 000
   • for public supply and service contracts awarded by contracting authorities other than those listed in Annex IV,
   • for public supply contracts awarded by contracting authorities which are listed in Annex IV and operate in the field of defence, where these contracts involve products not covered by Annex V,
   • for public service contracts awarded by any contracting authority in respect of the services listed in Category 8 of Annex IIA, Category 5 telecommunications services, the positions of which in the CPV[26]

---

[23]   See Article 18 of the Public Sector Directive.
[24]   See Article 19 of the Public Sector Directive.
[25]   See Article 7 of the Public Sector Directive.
[26]   The Common Procurement Vocabulary (CPV) represents the reference nomenclature applicable to public contracts while ensuring equivalence with the other

are equivalent to CPC reference Nos 7524, 7525 and 7526 and/or the services listed in Annex II B;
(c)   Euro 6 242 000 for public works contracts.

Subsidised contracts
Contracts subsidised by more than 50% by contracting authorities are covered by the Directive.[27] In particular, the Directive applies to the award of:

(a)   contracts which are subsidised directly by contracting authorities by more than 50% and the estimated value of which, net of VAT, is equal to or greater than Euro 6 242 000,
   • where those contracts involve civil engineering activities within the meaning of Annex I,
   • where those contracts involve building work for hospitals, facilities intended for sports, recreation and leisure, school and university buildings and buildings used for administrative purposes;
(b)   service contracts which are subsidized directly by contracting authorities by more than 50% and the estimated value of which, net of VAT, is equal to or greater than Euro 249 000 and which are connected to a works contract as described in the above category (a).

Member states must take the necessary measures to ensure that the contracting authorities awarding such subsidised contracts ensure compliance with the provisions of the Directive where that contract is awarded by one or more entities other than themselves. In addition, member states must comply with the Directive in cases where they themselves award that contract for and on behalf of other contracting entities.

Calculation of contract value
The Directive provides methods for calculating the estimated value of public contracts, framework agreements and dynamic purchasing systems.[28] The calculation of the estimated value of a public contract must be based on the total amount payable, net of VAT, as estimated by the contracting authority. This calculation must take account of the estimated total amount, including

---

existing nomenclatures. See Regulation 2195/2002 on the Common Procurement Vocabulary (CPV), OJ L 340, 16.12.2002. In the event of varying interpretations of the scope of the Utilities Directive, owing to possible differences between the CPV and NACE nomenclatures listed in Annex XII or between the CPV and CPC (provisional version) nomenclatures listed in Annex XVII, the NACE or the CPC nomenclature respectively takes precedence.

[27]   See Article 8 of the Public Sector Directive.
[28]   See Article 9 of the Public Sector Directive.

any form of option and any renewals of the contract.[29] Where the contracting authority provides for prizes or payments to candidates or tenderers it must take them into account when calculating the estimated value of the contract. This estimate must be valid at the moment at which the contract notice is sent out, as provided for in Article 35(2), or, in cases where such a notice is not required, at the moment at which the contracting authority commences the contract awarding procedure.[30]

Contracting authorities are under an obligation to avoid subdividing works projects or proposing the purchase of a certain quantity of supplies or services in order to escape the monetary applicability of the Directive.[31]

With regard to public works contracts, calculation of the estimated value must take account of both the cost of the works and the total estimated value of the supplies necessary for executing the works and placed at the contractor's disposal by the contracting authorities.[32]

Where a proposed work or purchase of services may result in contracts being awarded at the same time in the form of separate lots, contracting authorities must take into account the total estimated value of all such lots. Where the aggregate value of the lots is equal to or exceeds the threshold stipulated in the Directive, in that case each lot must be awarded separately in accordance with the Public Sector Directive. However, the contracting authorities may waive such application in respect of lots the estimated value of which net of VAT is less than Euro 80 000 for services or Euro 1 million for works, provided that the aggregate value of the lots does not exceed 20% of the aggregate value of the lots as a whole.

Where a proposal for the acquisition of similar supplies may result in contracts being awarded at the same time in the form of separate lots, account must be taken of the total estimated value of all such lots.

With regard to public supply contracts relating to the leasing, hire, rental or hire purchase of products,[33] the value to be taken as the basis for calculating the estimated contract value must be as follows:

(a)   in the case of fixed-term public contracts, if that term is less than or equal to 12 months, the total estimated value for the term of the contract or, if the term of the contract is greater than 12 months, the total value including the estimated residual value;

---

29   See Article 9(1) of the Public Sector Directive.
30   See Article 9(2) of the Public Sector Directive.
31   See Article 9(3) of the Public Sector Directive.
32   See Article 9(4) of the Public Sector Directive.
33   See Article 9(6) of the Public Sector Directive.

(b) in the case of public contracts without a fixed term or the term of which cannot be defined, the monthly value multiplied by 48.

For public supply or service contracts which are regular in nature or which are intended to be renewed within a given period,[34] the calculation of the esti-mated contract value must be based on the following:

(a) either the total actual value of the successive contracts of the same type awarded during the preceding 12 months or financial year adjusted, if possible, to take account of the changes in quantity or value which would occur in the course of the 12 months following the initial contract;
(b) or the total estimated value of the successive contracts awarded during the 12 months following the first delivery, or during the financial year if that is longer than 12 months.

The choice of method used to calculate the estimated value of a public contract may not be made with the intention of excluding it from the scope of the Public Sector Directive.

With regard to public service contracts,[35] the value to be taken as the basis for calculating the estimated contract value for insurance services must reflect the premium payable and other forms of remuneration; for banking and other financial services it must comprise the fees, commission, interest and other forms of remuneration; for design contracts it must include fees, commission payable and other forms of remuneration. For service contracts which do not indicate a total price, in the case of fixed-term contracts, if that term is less than or equal to 48 months, the estimated contract value must reflect the total value for their full term; in the case of contracts without a fixed term or with a term greater than 48 months, the estimated value must include the monthly value multiplied by 48.

With regard to framework agreements and dynamic purchasing systems, the value to be taken into consideration must be the maximum estimated value net of VAT of all the contracts envisaged for the total term of the framework agreement or the dynamic purchasing system.[36]

Revision of the thresholds
Revision of the thresholds will be undertaken by the Commission every two years from the entry into force of the Public Sector Directive.[37] The calculation

---

[34] See Article 9(7) of the Public Sector Directive.
[35] See Article 9(8)(a)(b) of the Public Sector Directive.
[36] See Article 9(9) of the Public Sector Directive.
[37] See Article 78 of the Public Sector Directive.

of the value of these thresholds must be based on the average daily value of
the euro, expressed in Single Drawing Rights (SDRs), over the 24 months
terminating on the last day of August preceding the revision with effect from
1 January. The value of the thresholds thus revised must, where necessary, be
rounded down to the nearest thousand euro so as to ensure that the thresholds
in force provided by the Agreement, and expressed in SDRs, are observed. The
value of the thresholds set in the national currencies of the member states
which are not participating in monetary union is normally to be adjusted every
two years from 1 January 2004 onwards. The calculation of such value must
be based on the average daily values of those currencies expressed in euro over
the 24 months terminating on the last day of August preceding the revision
with effect from 1 January. The revised thresholds and their corresponding
values in the national currencies must be published by the Commission in the
Official Journal of the European Union at the beginning of the month of
November following their revision.

The thresholds applicable to subsidised works contracts (Article 8(a)) and
subsidised service contracts (Article 8(b)), to public works concessions
(Article 56) to concession works contracts awarded by concessionaires which
are not contracting authorities (Article 63(1)) and to design contests (Article
67(1)(a)) should be aligned at the same time as the revisions covering the other
thresholds.[38]

Monitoring Requirements

Reports of contract awards

For every contract, framework agreement and every establishment of a
dynamic purchasing system, the contracting authorities must draw up a written report which must include at least the following:[39]

(a) the name and address of the contracting authority, the subject-matter and
     value of the contract, framework agreement or dynamic purchasing
     system;
(b) the names of the successful candidates or tenderers and the reasons for
     their selection;
(c) the names of the candidates or tenderers rejected and the reasons for their
     rejection;
(d) the reasons for the rejection of tenders found to be abnormally low;
(e) the name of the successful tenderer and the reasons why his tender was

---

[38] See Article 78(2) of the Public Sector Directive.
[39] Article 43 of the Public Sector Directive.

selected and, if known, the share of the contract or framework agreement which the successful tenderer intends to subcontract to third parties;

(f) for negotiated procedures, the circumstances referred to in Articles 30 and 31 which justify the use of these procedures;

(g) as far as the competitive dialogue is concerned, the circumstances as laid down in Article 29 justifying the use of this procedure;

(h) if necessary, the reasons why the contracting authority has decided not to award a contract or framework agreement or to establish a dynamic purchasing system.

The contracting authorities must take appropriate steps to document the progress of award procedures conducted by electronic means. The report, or the main features of it, must be communicated to the Commission if it so requests.

Statistical obligations

In order to permit assessment of the results of applying the public sector Directive, member states must forward to the Commission[40] a statistical report setting out public supply, services and works contracts awarded by contracting authorities during the preceding year, by no later than 31 October of each year. The content of the statistical report must include:[41]

(a) the number and value of awarded contracts covered by this Directive; the contract award procedures used; and for each of these procedures, works as given in Annex I and products and services as given in Annex II identified by category of the CPV nomenclature; the nationality of the economic operator to which the contract was awarded.

(b) the number and total value of contracts awarded pursuant to derogations to the Agreement. As far as possible, the data referred to in point (a) of the first subparagraph.

Where the contracts have been concluded according to the negotiated procedure the information provided must include the circumstances that justified use of the negotiated procedure and specify the number and value of contracts awarded by the member states and the country of origin of the successful contractor.[42]

---

[40] Article 75 of the Public Sector Directive.
[41] Article 76(1)(a) of the Public Sector Directive.
[42] See Article 76(1)(b) of the Public Sector Directive.

THE NEW CONCEPTS IN PUBLIC SECTOR PROCURE-MENT

The codified Public Sector Directive has introduced a series of new concepts which are the product of jurisprudential inferences and policy refining of the previous legal regimes. They intend to modernise public purchasing and align the procurement of government and its agencies with that of utilities which operate in a more commercially oriented environment.

Eligibility of Bodies Governed by Public Law to Tender

The new Public Sector Directive clearly accepts that entities which are covered by its rules can participate in the award of public contracts, alongside private sector undertakings. Member states should ensure that the participation of a body governed by public law as a tenderer in a procedure for the award of a public contract does not cause any distortion of competition in relation to private tenderers. The eligibility of bodies governed by public law to partici-pate in tendering procedures has been influenced by case-law.[43] There is a protection mechanism built into Article 55(e) of the Public Sector Directive, which specifies that in case of abnormally low tenders, the contracting author-ity may reject those tenders, if it establishes that the tenderer is the recipient of state aid which may have been granted illegally. The onus to prove the legit-imacy of the state aid is on the tenderer.

It should be mentioned that the previous Directives provide for an auto-matic disqualification of an 'obviously abnormally low offer'. The term has not been interpreted in detail by the Court and serves rather as an indication of a 'bottom limit'.[44] The Court, however, pronounced on the direct effect of the relevant provision requiring contracting authorities to examine the details of the tender before deciding the award of the contract and to seek from the tenderer an explanation of the price submitted.

The debate over the terminology of 'obviously abnormally low' tenders surfaced when the Court held[45] that rejection of a contract based on mathe-

---

[43]   See case C-94/99, *ARGE Gewässerschutzt v. Bundesministerium für Land-und Forstwirtschaft*, paragraph 30, judgment of 7 December 2000, where the Court ruled that directly or indirectly subsidised tenders by the state or other contracting authorities or even by the contracting authority itself can be legitimately part of the evaluation process.

[44]   Case C-76/81, *SA Transporoute et Travaux v. Minister of Public Works*, [1982] ECR 457.

[45]   See case C-103/88, *Fratelli Costanzo SpA v. Comune di Milano*, [1989] ECR 1839; case 296/89, *Impresa Dona Alfonso di Dona Alfonso & Figli snc v. Consorzio per lo Sviluppo Industriale del Comune di Monfalcone*, judgment of 18 June 1991.

matical criteria without giving the tenderer an opportunity to furnish information is inconsistent with the spirit of public procurement Directives. Following previous case-law,[46] the Court ruled that the contracting authorities must give an opportunity to tenderers to furnish explanations regarding the genuine nature of their tenders, when those tenders appear to be abnormally low. However, the Court did not analyse the meaning of 'obviously'. It seems, in the author's view, that the term 'obviously' indicates the existence of precise and concrete evidence as to the abnormality of the low tender. On the other hand, the wording 'abnormally' implies a quantitative criterion left to the discretion of the contracting authority. Nonetheless, if the tender is just 'abnormally' low, it could be argued that it is within the discretion of the contracting authority to investigate how genuine an offer a tender is. *Impresa Lombardini*[47] followed *Transporoute* and maintained the unlawfulness of mathematical criteria used to exclude a tender which appears abnormally low. Yet, it held that such criteria may be lawful if used to determine the abnormality of a low tender, provided an *inter partes* procedure between the contracting authority and the tenderer that submitted the alleged abnormal low offer offers the opportunity to clarify the genuine nature of that offer. Contracting authorities must take into account all reasonable explanations furnished and avoid limiting the grounds on which justification of the genuine nature of a tender should be made. In *ARGE*,[48] the rejection of a tender on the grounds of the abnormally low pricing attached to it got a different twist in its interpretation. Although the Court ruled that directly or indirectly subsidised tenders by the state or other contracting authorities or even by the contracting authority itself can legitimately be part of the evaluation process, it did not elaborate on the possibility of rejecting an offer which is appreciably lower than those of unsubsidised tenderers by reference to the abnormally low disqualification ground.[49]

---

[46] See case C-76/81, *Transporoute*, [1982] ECR 457, op. cit.

[47] See case C-285/99 & 286/99, *Impresa Lombardini SpA v. ANAS*, judgment of 27 November 2001.

[48] See C-94/99, *ARGE Gewässerschutzt v. Bundesministerium für Land-und Forstwirtschaft*, paragraph 30, judgment of 7 December 2000.

[49] In *ARGE* the Court adopted a literal interpretation of the Directives and concluded that if the legislature wanted to preclude subsidised entities from participating in tendering procedures for public contracts, it should have said so explicitly in the relevant Directives. See paragraphs 26 et seq. of the Court's judgment. Although the case has relevance in the fields of selection and qualification procedures and award criteria, the Court made no references to previous case-law regarding state aids in public procurement, presumably because the *Dupont de Nemours* precedent is still highly relevant.

Joint and Centralised Procurement

The Public Sector Directive aims to introduce a regime where procurement
can benefit from scale economies and streamlining planning, operation and
delivery. In the light of the diversity of public procurement contracts in
member states, contracting authorities have been given the freedom to make
provision for contracts for the design and execution of work to be awarded
jointly. The decision to award contracts jointly must be determined by qualitative and economic criteria, which may be defined by national law. According
to Article 1(10) of the Public Sector Directive, a central purchasing body is a
contracting authority which (i) acquires supplies and/or services intended for
contracting authorities or (ii) awards public contracts or concludes framework
agreements for works, supplies or services intended for contracting authorities.

Official List of Contractors

The Public Sector Directive provides for a central system of certification of
private and public organizations for the purposes of providing evidence of
financial and economic standing as well as levels of technical capacity in
public procurement selection and qualification procedures. Such systems must
be mutually recognised by all member states and registration of entities in official lists of contractors, suppliers or service providers is influenced by the
Court's case-law,[50] where an economic operator belonging to a group claims
the economic, financial or technical capabilities of other companies in the
same group in support of its application for registration. Member states may
determine the level of requirements to be met for such registrations and the
period of their validity, in particular requirements for joint and several liability where an operator relies on the financial standing of another company in
the same group.

---

[50]   See case C-76/81, *SA Transporoute et Travaux v. Minister of Public Works*,
[1982] ECR 457; case C-27/86, *Constructions et Entreprises Industrielles SA (CEI) v.
Association Intercommunale pour les Autoroutes des Ardennes*; case C-28/86, *Ing. A.
Bellini & Co. SpA v. Regie de Betiments*; case C-29/86, *Ing.A. Bellini & Co. SpA v.
Belgian State*, [1987] ECR 3347; case C-89/92, *Ballast Nedam Groep NV v. Belgische
Staat*, [1994] 2 CMLR; case C-5/97, *Ballast Nedam Groep NV v. Belgische Staat*, judg-
ment of 18 December 1997; case C-176/98, *Holst Italia v. Comune di Cagliari*, judg-
ment of 2 December 1999.

The Competitive Dialogue

The competitive dialogue is the most publicised change brought about by the new public procurement regime. Its inception is attributed to three factors: (i) the inability of open or restricted procedures to facilitate the award of complex public contracts, including concessions and public–private partnerships, (ii) the exceptional nature of negotiated procedures without prior advertisement[51] and (iii) the restrictive interpretation[52] of the grounds for using negotiated procedures with prior advertisement.

Article 29 of the Public Sector Directive establishes the competitive dialogue as an award procedure, alongside open, restricted and negotiated procedures. The competitive dialogue must be used exceptionally in cases of particularly complex contracts, where the use of open or restricted procedures will not allow the award of the contract, and the use of negotiated procedures cannot be justified. A public contract is considered to be particularly complex where the contracting authorities are not able to define in an objective manner the technical specifications which are required to pursue the project, or where they are not able to specify the legal or financial make-up of a project.

The procedure is very complex, as it has three main phases and many

---

[51]   Negotiated procedures without prior advertisement are exceptionally allowed '. . . when for technical or artistic reasons or reasons connected with the protection of exclusive rights the services could only be procured by a particular provider . . . and . . . in cases of extreme urgency brought about by events unforeseeable by the contracting authority'. In cases C-199/85, *Commission v. Italy*, [1987] ECR 1039 and C-3/88, *Commission v. Italy*, [1989] ECR 4035, the Court rejected the existence of exclusive rights and regarded the abuse of this provision as contrary to the right of establishment and freedom to provide services which are based on the principle of equal treatment and prohibit not only overt discrimination on grounds of nationality, but also all covert forms of discrimination, which, by the application of other criteria of differentiation, lead to the same result. Interestingly, in case 199/85, *Commission v. Italy*, op. cit., the Court elucidated that exclusive rights might include contractual arrangements such as know-how and intellectual property rights. For urgency reasons brought about by unforeseen events affecting contracting authorities, the Court established two tests: (i) the need for a justification test based on the proportionality principle, and (ii) the existence of a causal link between the alleged urgency and the unforeseen events (see C-199/85, *Commission v. Italy*, op. cit.; C-3/88, *Commission v. Italy*, op. cit., C-24/91, *Commission v. Spain*, [1994] CMLR 621; C-107/92, *Commission v. Italy*, judgment of 2 August 1993; C-57/94, *Commission v. Italy*, judgment of 18 May 1995; C-296/92, *Commission v. Italy*, judgment of 12 January 1994).

[52]   The grounds for using this procedure are confined to circumstances where: (i) the nature of the works or services or risks attached thereto do not permit overall pricing and (ii) the nature of the services is such that specifications cannot be established with sufficient precision. See Article 7(2)(c) of the Works Directive and Articles 11(2)(b) and 11(2)(c) of the Services Directive.

options within these phases. First, the advertisement phase according to Article 29(2) obliges contracting authorities to publish a contract notice or a descriptive document outlining their needs and the basic specifications of the project. After that phase and before launching a competitive dialogue for the award of a contract, contracting authorities may, using a technical dialogue, seek or accept advice which may be used in the preparation of the specifications, provided that such advice does not have the effect of precluding competition.

Secondly, a selection phase reduces the candidates to be invited to the competitive dialogue according to the relevant provisions of Articles 44 to 52 of the Public Sector Directive.[53] The minimum number of candidates should be three but it could be lower if there is sufficient evidence of competitiveness in the process or the limited number of initial respondents to the contract notice precludes the invitation of at least three candidates.

Thirdly, the competitive dialogue is opened by the commencement of the award phase in accordance with Article 29(3). Contracting authorities must open a dialogue with the candidates selected, the aim of which is to identify the means best suited to satisfying their needs. They may discuss all aspects of the contract with the chosen candidates, ensuring equality of treatment among all tenderers. In particular, they must not provide information in a discriminatory manner which might give some tenderers an advantage over others. Contracting authorities may not reveal to the other participants solutions proposed or other confidential information communicated by a candidate participating in the dialogue without the prior agreement of that candidate.

Contracting authorities may provide for the competitive dialogue to take place in successive stages in order to reduce the number of solutions to be discussed with the candidates in accordance with Article 29(4). They may continue the dialogue until they can identify the solution or solutions which are capable of meeting their needs. Having declared that the dialogue is concluded and having informed the participants, contracting authorities must ask them to submit their final tenders on the basis of the solution or solutions presented and specified during the dialogue.

After this phase is over (closure of the competitive dialogue), there are four stages until the contract award. First, contracting authorities must ask all remaining candidates to submit their final tenders (Article 44(4)). Secondly, these tenders need to be finalised prior to their evaluation (Article 29(6)). Thirdly, the selection of the winning tenderer must take place in accordance with the criteria stipulated in the contract notice (Article 29(7)) and fourthly

---

[53] Articles 44 to 46 of the Public Sector Directive 2004/18 govern the conduct of the procedure for verification of the suitability and choice of participants and award of contracts, criteria for qualitative selection, and suitability to pursue a professional activity.

the winning tenderer must provide further clarification and his commitment to undertake the project ((Article 29(7)).

The tenders must contain all the elements required and considered necessary for the performance of the project. They may be clarified, specified and fine-tuned at the request of the contracting authority. However, any additional information must not involve any changes to the basic features of the tender or the call for tender, nor allow for variations which are likely to distort competition or have a discriminatory effect. In the author's view, there is a great deal of uncertainty over the meaning of clarification, additional provision of tender specification and the extent of fine-tuning, to the degree of compromising the competitiveness and integrity of the procedure.

Contracting authorities must assess the tenders received on the basis of the award criteria laid down in the contract notice or the descriptive document and must choose the most economically advantageous tender in accordance with Article 53. At the request of the contracting authority, the tenderer identified as having submitted the most economically advantageous tender may be asked to clarify aspects of the tender or confirm commitments contained in the tender provided this does not have the effect of modifying substantial aspects of the tender or of the call to tender and does not risk distorting competition or discriminating against other candidates.

Overall, the competitive dialogue has addressed many of the features that are important during the award of complex projects and are currently being addressed by negotiated procedures with prior advertisement. In comparison with these procedures, the competitive dialogue also allows for a limited number of participants (three in number), introduces a staged approach to tendering and permits elimination of participants during its internal phases. However it allows significant scope for post-tender negotiations, but it restricts the award of a contract to complete offers.

Framework Procurement

The previous Utilities Directives have introduced framework agreements as a selection and tendering procedure which is influenced to a large extent by the benefits of chain-supply management and partnering schemes operating in the private sector. The new Utilities Directive has maintained the framework agreements regime in a virtually unaltered format as laid down in Article 17(3). Within the provisions of the new Utilities Directive, when an entity has established a framework agreement under the relevant procedures which are common to other public contracts covered therein, subsequent individual contracts concluded under the framework agreement may be awarded without having recourse to a call for competition. Individual contracts which have been awarded under a framework agreement could be subject to the reopening of tendering procedures, provided the contracting entity does not invite new tenderers to participate. The Directive specifically stipulates that misuse of framework agreements may distort competition and trigger the application of the relevant rules, particularly with reference to concerted practices which lead to collusive tendering.

The new Public Sector Directive has for the first time introduced framework procurement to the public sector contracting authorities. According to Article 1(5) of the Public Sector Directive, a framework agreement is an agreement between one or more contracting authorities and one or more economic operators, the purpose of which is to establish the terms and conditions of public contracts to be awarded during a given period, in particular with regard to price and, where appropriate, the quantity of supplies, works or services envisaged.

Contracting authorities may establish framework agreements in accordance with the provisions of the Public Sector Directive relating to advertising, time limits and conditions for the submission of tenders. The parties to the framework agreement must be chosen by applying the award criteria set in accordance with Article 53. Article 53 refers to the award criteria being the most economically advantageous offer or the lowest price. When the award is made to the most economically advantageous tender from the point of view of the contracting authority, various criteria are linked to the subject-matter of the public contract in question, for example, quality, price, technical merit, aesthetic and functional characteristics, environmental characteristics, running costs, cost-effectiveness, after-sales service and technical assistance, delivery date and delivery period or period of completion. When the award criterion refers to the lowest price only, no other factors should play a part. Contracting authorities may subsequently enter into contracts based on such framework agreements during their term of validity either by applying the terms set forth in the framework agreement or, if terms and condition for the conclusion of contracts have not been fixed in advance, by reopening competition between the parties to the framework agreement. The reopening of competition should comply with certain rules,[54] the aim of which is to guarantee the required flex-

---

[54]   According to Article 32(4) of the Public Sector Directive 2004/18, the conditions for reopening competition within a framework agreement include: (a) for every contract to be awarded, contracting authorities must consult in writing the economic operators capable of performing the contract; (b) contracting authorities must fix a time limit which is sufficiently long to allow tenders for each specific contract to be submitted, taking into account factors such as the complexity of the subject-matter of the contract and the time needed to send in tenders; (c) tenders must be submitted in writing, and their content must remain confidential until the stipulated time limit for reply has expired; (d) contracting authorities must award each contract to the tenderer who has submitted the best tender on the basis of the award criteria set out in the specifications of the framework agreement.

ibility and to guarantee respect for the general principles, in particular the principle of equal treatment.

Contracts based on a framework agreement must be awarded in accordance with the procedures of Article 32, which must be applied only between the contracting authorities and the economic operators originally party to the framework agreement. The duration of a framework agreement may not exceed four years, unless exceptional cases justify its extension. Framework agreements can be established between contracting authorities and a single economic operator according to Article 32(3) in exceptional circumstances which must be justified by the nature of the framework agreement, or with several economic operators according to Article 32(4). The latter must be at least three in number, provided that there are a sufficient number of economic operators to satisfy the selection criteria or there are a sufficient number of admissible tenders which meet the award criteria. Contracting authorities are under an obligation not to use framework agreements improperly or in such a way as to prevent, restrict or distort competition.

Electronic Procurement

The rapid expansion of electronic purchasing systems in private sector procurement and the continuous development of electronic purchasing techniques have made an impact on the Public Sector Directive. Electronic procurement can contribute to increasing competition and streamlining public purchasing, particularly in cases where repetitive purchasing allows efficiencies to be achieved both in time and in financial terms.

Dynamic purchasing systems

Article 1(6) of the Public Sector Directive provides for the establishment of dynamic purchasing systems. A dynamic purchasing system is an electronic process which allows contracting authorities to utilise techniques available to the private sector in order to procure supplies or services of a repetitive nature. Any economic operator which submits an indicative tender in accordance with the specification and meets the selection criteria should be allowed to join such a system. This purchasing technique allows the contracting authorities, through the establishment of a pre-selected list of tenderers, to have a particularly broad range of tenders as a result of the electronic facilities available, and to ensure, in principle, optimum use of public funds through broad competition.

The use of dynamic purchasing systems is described in Article 33 of the Public Sector Directive. In order to set up a dynamic purchasing system, contracting authorities must follow the open procedure in all its phases up to the award of the contracts. All the tenderers satisfying the selection criteria and

having submitted an indicative tender which complies with the technical specification must be admitted to the system; indicative tenders may be improved at
any time provided that they continue to comply with the overall specifications.

With a view to setting up the system and proceeding to the award of
contracts under that system, contracting authorities must use solely electronic
means in accordance with Article 42(2) to (5). For these purposes contracting
authorities must:

(a) publish a contract notice making it clear that a dynamic purchasing
     system is involved;
(b) indicate in the specification, amongst other matters, the nature of the
     purchases envisaged under that system, as well as all the necessary infor-
     mation concerning the purchasing system, the electronic equipment used
     and the technical connection arrangements and specifications;
(c) offer by electronic means, on publication of the notice and up to the
     expiry of the system, unrestricted, direct and full access to the specifica-
     tion and to any additional documents and must indicate in the notice the
     internet address at which such documents may be consulted.

Contracting authorities must give every economic operator participating in the
dynamic purchasing system the possibility of submitting an indicative tender
throughout the entire period of such system. Each specific contract must be the
subject of an invitation to tender. Before issuing the invitation to tender,
contracting authorities must publish a simplified contract notice inviting all
interested economic operators to submit an indicative tender within a time
limit of at least 15 days. The duration of a dynamic purchasing system may not
exceed four years, except in duly justified exceptional cases. Contracting
authorities are under an obligation not to levy any charges attributed to the
operation of dynamic purchasing systems on the interested economic operators admitted to such systems.

Electronic auctions
According to Article 1.7 of the Public Sector Directive an electronic auction is
a repetitive process involving an electronic device for the presentation of new
prices which are revised downwards, or new values concerning certain
elements of tenders. The presentation of such financial information occurs
after an initial full evaluation of the tenders, enabling them to be ranked using
automatic evaluation methods.

Article 54 of the Public Sector Directive stipulates the parameters for the
use of electronic auctions. In open, restricted or negotiated procedures,
contracting authorities may decide that the award of a public contract must be
preceded by an electronic auction when the contract specifications can be

established with precision. In the same circumstances, an electronic auction may be held on the reopening of competition among the parties to a framework agreement as provided for in the second indent of the second subparagraph of Article 32(4) and on the opening for competition of contracts to be awarded under the dynamic purchasing system referred to in Article 33. The electronic auction must be based (i) either solely on prices when the contract is awarded to the lowest price, or (ii) on prices and/or on the new values of the features of the tenders indicated in the specification when the contract is awarded to the most economically advantageous tender.

Contracting authorities who decide to hold an electronic auction must indicate their intention in the contract notice. The contract specifications must include, *inter alia*, the following details:

(a) the features, the values for which will be the subject of electronic auction, provided that such features are quantifiable and can be expressed in figures or percentages;

(b) any limits on the values which may be submitted, as they result from the specifications relating to the subject of the contract;

(c) the information which will be made available to tenderers in the course of the electronic auction and, where appropriate, when it will be made available to them;

(d) the relevant information concerning the electronic auction process;

(e) the conditions under which the tenderers will be able to bid and, in particular, the minimum differences which will, where appropriate, be required when bidding;

(f) the relevant information concerning the electronic equipment used and the arrangements and technical specifications for connection.

When the contract is to be awarded on the basis of the most economically advantageous tender, the invitation must provide a full evaluation framework in accordance with the respective weighting of the award criteria. The invitation must also state the mathematical formula to be used in the electronic auction to determine automatic re-rankings on the basis of the new prices or new values submitted. That formula must incorporate the weighting of all the criteria fixed to determine the most economically advantageous tender. Where variants are authorised, a separate formula must be provided for each variant. After closing an electronic auction, contracting authorities must award the contract in accordance with Article 53 on the basis of the results of the electronic auction. Contracting authorities may not have improper recourse to electronic auctions nor may they use them in such a way as to prevent, restrict or distort competition or to change the subject-matter of the contract, as specified in the contract notice and defined in the specifications.

The Award Criteria and the Introduction of Policies in Public Procurement

Contractual performance and public procurement

Conditions relating to the performance of public contracts are compatible with the Public Sector Directive provided that they are not directly or indirectly discriminatory and are indicated in the contract notice or in the contract documents. They may, in particular, be intended to favour on-site vocational training, the employment of people experiencing particular difficulty in achieving integration, the fight against unemployment or the protection of the environment.

The new Public Sector Directives and the new Utilities Directives remain silent over the possibility of expressly authorising social or environmental considerations as part of the award criteria of public contracts. Although the draft Directives, at the insistence of the European Parliament, contained specific provisions relevant to workforce matters as part of the award criteria, such provisions were omitted from the final text. The Commission has adopted a myopic view that considerations related to contractual performance cannot be used as criterion for the award of the contract. The Court had the opportunity to correct the Commission's interpretation and point its judgments in the right direction,[55] where a condition relating to the employment of long-term unemployed persons or the protection of the environment can legitimately constitute a criterion for the award of the contract. However, the new public procurement regime has failed to adopt previous jurisprudential inferences and clarify the position of contracting authorities over the legitimacy of pursuing socio-economic and environmental policies through public procurement.[56]

Examples of conditions relevant to contractual performance in public contracts may include requirements to recruit long-term job-seekers or to implement training measures for the unemployed or young persons, to comply in substance with the provisions of the International Labour Organisation (ILO) Conventions, assuming that such provisions have not been implemented in national law, and to recruit more handicapped persons than are required under national legislation.

---

[55]   See case 31/87, *Gebroeders Beentjes v. The Netherlands*, [1989] ECR 4365, at paragraph 14; case C-225/98, *Commission v. French Republic, (Nord-Pas-de-Calais)*, [2000] ECR 7445, at paragraph 52; case C-513/99, *Concordia Bus Filandia v. Helsingin Kaupunki et HKL-Bussiliikenne*, [2002] ECR 7213, at paragraph 31.

[56]   For a detailed analysis of the ordo-liberal versus the neo-classical approach in public procurement regulation, see Bovis, C., 'Public procurement and the internal market of the 21st century: economic exercise versus policy choice', chapter 17 in *EU Law for the 21st Century: Rethinking the New Legal Order*, Nebia and Tridimas (eds), Hart Publishing, 2005, pp. 290–310.

However, according to Article 19 of the Public Sector Directive, reserved contracts are regarded as a specific category of public sector contracts. This is the only concession the Commission afforded member states in relation to the socio-economic dimension of the award criteria of public contacts. Member states may reserve the right to participate in public contract award procedures to sheltered workshops or provide for such contracts to be performed in the context of sheltered employment programmes where most of the employees concerned are handicapped persons who, by reason of the nature or the seriousness of their disabilities, cannot carry on occupations under normal conditions. The contract notice must make reference to this provision.

In addition, the laws, regulations and collective agreements, at both national and Community level, which are in force in the areas of employment conditions and safety at work apply during performance of a public contract, providing that such rules, and their application, comply with Community law. In cross-border situations, where workers from one member state provide services in another member state for the purpose of performing a public contract, Directive 96/71/EC concerning the posting of workers in the framework of the provision of services[57] lays down the minimum conditions which must be observed by the host country in respect of such posted workers. If national law contains provisions to this effect, non-compliance with those obligations may be considered to be grave misconduct or an offence concerning the professional conduct of the economic operator concerned, liable to lead to the exclusion of that economic operator from the procedure for the award of a public contract.

The Most Economically Advantageous Offer

The most economically advantageous offer as an award criterion has provided the Court with the opportunity to balance the economic considerations of public procurement with policy choices. Although in numerous instances the Court has maintained the importance of the economic approach[58] in the regulation of public sector contracts, it has also recognised the relative discretion of contracting authorities to utilise non-economic considerations as award criteria.

---

[57] See OJ L 18, 12.1.97, p. 1.
[58] See case C-380/98, *The Queen and HM Treasury, ex parte University of Cambridge*, [2000] ECR 8035, at paragraph 17; case C-44/96, C-44/96, *Mannesmann Anlangenbau Austria AG et al. v. Strohal Rotationsdurck GesmbH*, [1998] ECR 73, at paragraph 33; C-360/96, *Gemeente Arnhem Gemeente Rheden v. BFI Holding BV*, [1998] ECR 6821, at paragraphs 42 and 43; C-237/99, case C-237/99, *Commission v. France*, judgment of 1 February 2001 (OPAC), at paragraphs 41 and 42.

The meaning of the most economically advantageous offer[59] includes a combination of factors chosen by the contracting authority, including price, delivery or completion date, running costs, cost-effectiveness, profitability, technical merit, product or work quality, aesthetic and functional characteristics, after-sales service and technical assistance, commitments with regard to spare parts and components and maintenance costs, security of supplies. The above list is not exhaustive and the factors listed therein serve as a guideline for contracting authorities in the weighted evaluation process of the contract award. The Court reiterated the flexible and wide interpretation of the relevant award criterion[60] and had no difficulty in declaring that contracting authorities may use the most economically advantageous offer as award criterion by choosing the factors which they want to apply in evaluating tenders,[61] provided these factors are mentioned in hierarchical order or descending sequence in the invitation to tender or the contract documents,[62] so tenderers and interested parties can clearly ascertain the relative weight of factors other than price in the evaluation process. However, factors which have no strict relevance in determining the most economically advantageous offer by reference to objective criteria do involve an element of arbitrary choice and therefore should be considered as incompatible with the Directives.[63]

A question was put before the Court in *Concordia*[64] intended to assess the integral function of the factors that comprise the most economically advantageous offer for contracting authorities. The question was as to whether, under the most economically advantageous offer, each individual award factor has to provide an economic advantage which directly benefits the contracting authority, or if it is sufficient for each individual factor to be measurable in economic terms, without the requirement that it directly provides an economic advantage to the contracting authority in the given contract.

Although there is wide discretion conferred upon contracting authorities in compiling the relevant factors, subject to the requirements of relevance to the

---

[59]   See Article 26 of Directive 93/36, Article 30 of Directive 93/37, Article 34 of Directive 93/38 and Article 36 of Directive 92/50.

[60]   Case 31/87, *Gebroeders Beentjes v. The Netherlands*, [1989] ECR 4365.

[61]   Case C-324/93, *R. v. The Secretary of State for the Home Department, ex parte Evans Medical Ltd and Macfarlan Smith Ltd*, judgment of 28 March 1995, where the national court asked whether factors concerning continuity and reliability as well as security of supplies fall under the framework of the most economically advantageous offer, when the latter is being evaluated.

[62]   See paragraph 22 of *Beentjes*.

[63]   See paragraph 37 of *Beentjes*.

[64]   See case C-513/99, *Concordia Bus Filandia v. Helsingin Kaupunki et HKL-Bussiliikenne*, [2002] ECR 7213. The case concerns *inter alia* the permissibility of environmental considerations as part of the award criteria.

contract in question and of the mentioning of these factors in the contract documents, their relative importance, in economic terms, remains in some-ways unknown. In other words, the discretion conferred upon contracting authorities would permit a wide range of factors to feature as part of the award criteria in public contracts, without the need to demonstrate a direct economic advantage to a contracting authority attributable to each of these factors. On the contrary, if each individual factor has to establish a measurable (in quantifiable terms) economic advantage to the contracting authority, which is directly attributed to its inclusion as part of the award criterion, the discretion of contracting authorities is curtailed, since they would be required to undertake and publicise in the tender or contract documents a clear cost–benefit analysis of the relevant factors that in their view comprise the most economically advantageous offer.

Social Considerations

In *Beentjes*,[65] the Court ruled that social policy considerations and in particular measures aiming at combating long-term unemployment could only be part of the award criteria for public contracts, especially in cases where the most economically advantageous offer is selected. The Court accepted that the latter award criterion contains features that are not exhaustively defined in the Directives, therefore there is discretion conferred on contracting authorities in specifying what would be the most economically advantageous offer for them. However, contracting authorities cannot refer to such measures as a selection criterion and disqualify candidates which could not meet the relevant requirements. The selection of tenderers is a process, which is based on an exhaustive list of technical and financial requirements expressly stipulated in the relevant Directives and the insertion of contract compliance as a selection and qualification requirement would be considered *ultra vires*. The Court held that a contractual condition relating to the employment of long-term unemployed persons is compatible with the Public Procurement Directives, if it has no direct or indirect discriminatory effect on tenders from other member states. Furthermore, such a contractual condition must be mentioned in the tender notice.[66] Rejection of a contract on the grounds of a contractor's inability to employ long-term unemployed persons has no relation to the checking of the contractors' suitability on the basis of their economic and financial standing and their technical knowledge and ability. The Court maintained that measures relating to employment could be utilised as a feature of the award criteria, only

---

[65] See case 31/87, *Gebroeders Beentjes BV v. The Netherlands*, op. cit.
[66] See *Bellini* case 28/86, [1987] ECR 3347.

when they are part of a contractual obligation of the public contract in question and on condition that they do not run contrary to the fundamental principles of the Treaty. The significance of that qualification has revealed the Court's potential stance over the issue of contract compliance in public procurement.

In the recent *Nord-Pas-de-Calais* case, the Court considered whether a condition linked to a local project to combat unemployment could be considered as an award criterion for the relevant contract. The Court held that the most economically advantageous offer does not preclude all possibility for the contracting authorities to use as a criterion a condition linked to the campaign against unemployment provided that that condition is consistent with all the fundamental principles of Community law, in particular the principle of non-discrimination deriving from the provisions of the Treaty on the right of establishment and the freedom to provide services.[67] Furthermore, even if such a criterion is not in itself incompatible with Directive 93/37, it must be applied in conformity with all the procedural rules laid down in that directive, in particular the rules on advertising.[68] The Court therefore accepted the employment considerations as an award criterion, part of the most economically advantageous offer, provided it is consistent with the fundamental principles of Community law, in particular the principle of non-discrimination and it is advertised in the contract notice.

The Court's rulings in *Beentjes* and *Nord-Pas-de-Calais* have opened an interesting chapter in public procurement jurisprudence. *Beentjes* started a debate on the integral dimensions of contract compliance and differentiated between the *positive* and *negative* approaches. A positive approach within contract compliance encompasses all measures and policies imposed by contracting authorities on tenderers as suitability criteria for their selection in public procurement contracts. Such positive action measures and policies intend to complement the actual objectives of public procurement, which are confined to economic and financial parameters and are based on a transparent and predictable legal background. Although the complementarity of contract compliance with the actual aims and objectives of the public procurement regime was acknowledged, the Court has been reluctant to accept such a flexible interpretation of the Directives, and based on the literal interpretation of the relevant provisions, disallowed positive actions of a social policy dimension as part of the selection criteria for tendering procedures in public procurement. However, it should be mentioned that contract compliance could not

---

[67]   See, *Beentjes*, paragraph 29.

[68]   See, to that effect, paragraph 31, where the Court stipulated that an award criterion linked to the campaign against unemployment must be expressly mentioned in the contract notice so that contractors may become aware of its existence.

only incorporate unemployment considerations, but also promote equality of opportunities and eliminate sex or race discrimination in the relevant market.[69] Indeed, the Directives on public procurement stipulate that the contracting authority may require tenderers to observe the national provisions of employment legislation when they submit their offers. The ability to observe and conform to national employment laws in a member state may constitute a ground for disqualification and exclusion of the defaulting firm from public procurement contracts. In fact, under such an interpretation, contract compliance may be a factor in the selection criteria specified in the Directives, as it contains a *negative approach* to legislation and measures relating to social policy.[70]

Environmental Considerations

In *Concordia*,[71] the Court was asked *inter alia* whether environmental considerations such as low emissions and noise levels of vehicles could be included amongst the factors in the most economically advantageous criterion, in order to promote certain types of vehicles that meet or exceed certain emission and noise levels. In his opinion,[72] the Advocate-General followed the *Beentjes*

---

[69] There are a number of legal instruments relevant to social policy at Community level that may apply to public procurement. These include, in particular, Directives on safety and health at work (for example, Council Directive 89/391 on the introduction of measures to encourage improvements in the safety and health of workers at work, and Directive 92/57 on the implementation of minimum safety and health requirements at temporary or mobile construction sites), working conditions and the application of employment law (for example, Directive 96/71/EC of the European Parliament and of the Council concerning the posting of workers in the framework of the provision of services, OJ L 18/1 of 21.1.1997, and Directive 2001/23 on the safeguarding of employees' rights in the event of transfers of undertakings, businesses or parts of undertakings or businesses, OJ L 82/16 of 22.3.2001, codifying Directive 77/187/EEC), Directive 2000/43/EC of 29.6.2000 implementing the principle of equal treatment between persons irrespective of racial or ethnic origin (OJ 2000 L 180/22) and Directive 2000/78/EC of 27.11.2000 establishing a general framework for equal treatment in employment and occupation (OJ 2000 L 303/16).

[70] It should be mentioned that adherence to health and safety laws has been considered by a British court as part of the technical requirements specified in the Works Directive for the process of selection of tenderers; see *General Building and Maintenance v. Greenwich Borough Council*, [1993] IRLR 535. Along these lines, see the Commission's Interpretative Communication on the Community law applicable to public procurement and the possibilities for integrating social considerations into public procurement, COM (2001) 566, 15/10/01.

[71] See case C-513/99, *Concordia Bus Filandia v. Helsingin Kaupunki et HKL-Bussiliikenne*, [2002] ECR 7213.

[72] See the opinion of Advocate-General Mischo delivered on 13 December 2001.

principle, establishing that contracting authorities are free to determine the factors under which the most economically advantageous offer is to be assessed and that environmental considerations could be part of the award criteria, provided they do not discriminate over alternative offers, and that they have been clearly publicised in the tender or contract documents. However, the inclusion of such factors in the award criteria should not prevent alternative offers that satisfy the contract specifications being taken into consideration by contracting authorities.[73] Criteria relating to the environment, in order to be permissible as additional criteria under the most economically advantageous offer, must satisfy a number of conditions, namely they must be objective, universally applicable, strictly relevant to the contract in question, and clearly contribute an economic advantage to the contracting authority.[74]

Under Article 6 of the EU Treaty, environmental protection requirements are to be integrated into the definition and implementation of the Community policies and activities referred to in Article 3 of the EU Treaty, in particular with a view to promoting sustainable development. The Public Sector Directive clarifies how contracting authorities may contribute to the protection of the environment and the promotion of sustainable development, whilst ensuring fairness and competition in the award of public contracts. Article 50 of the Public Sector Directive deals with environmental management standards. It provides that contracting authorities may require the production of certificates drawn up by independent bodies attesting to the compliance of the economic operator with certain environmental management standards. These must refer to the Community Eco-Management and Audit Scheme (EMAS) or to environmental management standards based on the relevant European or international standards certified by bodies conforming to Community law or the relevant European or international standards concerning certification. Contracting authorities must recognise equivalent certificates from bodies established in other member states. They must also accept other evidence of equivalent environmental management measures from economic operators.

In appropriate cases, in which the nature of the works and/or services justifies applying environmental management measures or schemes during the performance of a public contract, the application of such measures or schemes may be required. Environmental management schemes, whether or not they

---

[73]   Clearly the Advocate-General wanted to exclude any possibility of environmental considerations being part of the selection criteria or disguised as technical specifications, capable of discriminating against tenderers that could not meet them.
[74]   See the analysis of Advocate-General Mischo in his opinion of *Concordia*, paragraphs 77 to 123.

are registered under Community instruments such as Regulation (EC) No. 761/2001 (EMAS),[75] can demonstrate that the economic operator has the technical capability to perform the contract. Moreover, a description of the measures implemented by the economic operator to ensure the same level of environmental protection should be accepted as an alternative to environmental management registration schemes as a form of evidence.

Small and Medium Enterprises and Subcontracting

In order to encourage the involvement of small- and medium-sized undertakings in the public contracts procurement market, it is advisable to include provisions on subcontracting. According to Article 25 of the Public Sector Directive, the contracting authority, in the contract documents, may ask or may be required by a member state to ask the tenderer to indicate in his tender any share of the contract he may intend to subcontract to third parties and any proposed subcontractors. This indication must be without prejudice to the question of the principal economic operator's liability. The theme of public procurement and subcontracting originates in the original Works Directives where contracting authorities are allowed to specify to concessionaires a minimum percentage of the works to be subcontracted. Along these lines, Article 60 of the Public Sector Directive provides that the contracting authority may either: (a) require the concessionaire to award contracts representing a minimum of 30% of the total value of the work for which the concession contract is to be awarded to third parties, at the same time providing the option for candidates to increase this percentage, this minimum percentage being specified in the concession contract, or (b) request the candidates for concession contracts to specify in their tenders the percentage, if any, of the total value of the work for which the concession contract is to be awarded which they intend to assign to third parties.

Procurement and Culture

The award of public contracts for certain audiovisual services in the field of broadcasting should allow aspects of cultural or social significance to be taken into account which render application of procurement rules inappropriate. For these reasons, an exception must therefore be made for public service contracts for the purchase, development, production or co-production of off-the-shelf

---

[75] See Regulation (EC) No. 761/2001 of the European Parliament and of the Council of 19 March 2001 allowing voluntary participation by organisations in a Community eco-management and audit scheme (EMAS) (OJ L 114, 24.4.2001, p. 1).

programmes and other preparatory services, such as those relating to scripts or artistic performances necessary for the production of the programme and contracts concerning broadcasting times. However, this exclusion should not apply to the supply of technical equipment necessary for the production, co-production and broadcasting of such programmes. A broadcast should be defined as transmission and distribution using any form of electronic network.

Procurement and Probity

The award of public contracts to economic operators who have participated in a criminal organisation or who have been found guilty of corruption or of fraud to the detriment of the financial interests of the European Communities or of money laundering should be avoided. Where appropriate, the contracting authorities should ask candidates or tenderers to supply relevant documents and, where they have doubts concerning the personal situation of a candidate or tenderer, they may seek the co-operation of the competent authorities of the member state concerned. The exclusion of such economic operators should take place as soon as the contracting authority has knowledge of a judgment concerning such offences, rendered in accordance with national law, that has the force of *res judicata*. If national law contains provisions to this effect, non-compliance with environmental legislation or legislation on unlawful agreements in public contracts which has been the subject of a final judgment or a decision having equivalent effect may be considered an offence concerning the professional conduct of the economic operator concerned or grave misconduct. Non-observance of national provisions implementing the Council Directives 2000/78/EC[76] and 76/207/EC[77] concerning equal treatment of workers, which has been the subject of a final judgment or a decision having equivalent effect, may be considered an offence concerning the professional conduct of the economic operator concerned or grave misconduct.

Article 45 of the Public Sector Directive deals with the personal situation of the candidate or tenderer. It provides that any candidate or tenderer who has been the subject of a conviction by final judgment of which the contracting authority is aware for one or more of the reasons listed below must be excluded from participation in a public contract:

---

[76] See Council Directive 2000/78/EC of 27 November 2000 establishing a general framework for equal treatment in employment and occupation (OJ L 303, 2.12.2000, p. 16).

[77] See Council Directive 76/207/EEC of 9 February 1976 on the implementation of the principle of equal treatment for men and women as regards access to employment, vocational training and promotion, and working conditions (OJ L 39, 14.2.1976, p. 40). Directive amended by Directive 2002/73/EC of the European Parliament and of the Council (OJ L 269, 5.10.2002, p. 15).

(a) participation in a criminal organisation, as defined in Article 2(1) of Council Joint Action 98/733/JHA;[78]

(b) corruption, as defined in Article 3 of the Council Act of 26 May 1997[79] and Article 3(1) of Council Joint Action 98/742/JHA[80] respectively;

(c) fraud within the meaning of Article 1 of the Convention relating to the protection of the financial interests of the European Communities;[81]

(d) money laundering, as defined in Article 1 of Council Directive 91/308 on prevention of the use of the financial system for the purpose of money laundering.[82]

---

[78] See OJ L 351, 29.12.1998, p. 1.
[79] See OJ C 195, 25.6.1997, p. 1.
[80] See OJ L 358, 31.12.1998, p. 2.
[81] See OJ C 316, 27.11.1995, p. 48.
[82] See OJ L 166, 28.6.1991, p. 77. Directive as amended by Directive 2001/97/EC of the European Parliament and of the Council of 4 December 2001 (OJ L 344, 28.12.2001, p. 76).

5. Advertisement and publicity in public sector procurement

PUBLICATION OF NOTICES

Prior Information Notices (PINs)

Prior information notices are notices sent by contracting authorities to the Official Journal for publication or notices published by contracting authorities themselves on their buyer profile through the internet.[1]

Both prior information notices and notices on buyer profile must include the following information:[2]

(a) for public supplies contracts and as soon as possible after the beginning of the budgetary year, the estimated total value of the contracts or the framework agreements by product area which they intend to award over the following 12 months, where the total estimated value is equal to or greater than Euro 750 000. The product area must be established by the contracting authorities by reference to the CPV nomenclature;

(b) for public services contracts and as soon as possible after the beginning of the budgetary year, the estimated total value of the contracts or the framework agreements in each of the categories of services listed in Annex II A which they intend to award over the following 12 months, where such estimated total value is equal to or greater than Euro 750 000;

(c) for public works contracts and as soon as possible after the decision approving the planning of the works contracts or the framework agreements that the contracting authorities intend to award, the essential characteristics of the contracts or the framework agreements which they intend to award, the estimated value of which is equal to or greater than the threshold specified in Article 7 of the Public Sector Directive.

---

[1]   See Article 35 of the Public Sector Directive.
[2]   See Article 35(1) of the Public Sector Directive.

The notice of publication for a prior indicative notice on a buyer profile must contain the country and name of the contracting authority, the internet address of the buyer profile and any CPV nomenclature reference numbers.[3] The buyer profile may include[4] prior information notices, information on ongoing invitations to tender, scheduled purchases, contracts concluded, procedures cancelled and any useful general information, such as a contact point, a telephone and a fax number, a postal address and an e-mail address. Contracting authorities who publish a prior information notice on their buyer profiles must send the Commission notice of such publication electronically.[5] Prior information notices may not be published on a buyer profile before the dispatch to the Commission of the notice of their publication in that form; they must mention the date of that dispatch.[6]

Contracting authorities should not publish notices and their contents at national level before the date on which they are sent to the Commission for publication in the Official Journal. Notices published at national level must not contain information other than information contained in the notices dispatched to the Commission or published on a buyer profile. However, they must mention the date of dispatch of the notice to the Commission or its publication on the buyer profile.[7]

The publication of prior indicative notices is compulsory only where the contracting authorities take the option of shortening the time limits for the receipt of tenders as laid down in Article 38(4) of the Directive. Also, in the exceptional cases of contracting authorities having recourse to negotiated procedures without the prior publication of a contract notice, the publication of prior information notices or notices on buyer profile is not required.

Contract Notices

Contracting authorities which wish to award a public contract or a framework agreement by open or restricted procedures, negotiated procedures with prior advertisement, or through the procedures of a competitive dialogue must make known their intention by publishing a contract notice. Also, when contracting authorities wish to set up a dynamic purchasing system, they must publish a contract notice. Furthermore, when contracts are to be awarded based on a

---

[3]   See Annex VII A of the Public Sector Directive.
[4]   See point 2(b) of Annex VIII of the Public Sector Directive.
[5]   See the format and detailed procedures for sending notices indicated in point 3 of Annex VIII of the Public Sector Directive.
[6]   See Article 36(5), second indent of the Public Sector Directive.
[7]   See Article 36(5) of the Public Sector Directive.

dynamic purchasing system, contracting authorities must publish a simplified contract notice.[8]

Notices must include the information required in Annex VII A of the Directive and, where appropriate, any other information deemed useful by contracting authorities for publicising the award of public contracts in the standard format adopted by the Commission in accordance with the procedure referred to in Article 77(2) of the Directive. In particular, contracting authorities should provide the following information in contract notices for open and restricted procedures, competitive dialogues, and negotiated procedures with prior advertisement:

1. their name, address, telephone and fax number, and email address;
2. indication of whether the public contract is restricted to sheltered workshops, or whether its execution is restricted to the framework of protected job programmes;
3. the award procedure chosen and, where appropriate, the reasons for use of the accelerated procedure (in restricted and negotiated procedures); also, where appropriate, an indication of whether a framework agreement, or a dynamic purchasing system, is involved; finally, where appropriate, an indication of whether an electronic auction will be held, in the event of open, restricted or negotiated procedures covered by Article 30(1)(a);
4. the form of the contract;
5. the place of execution or performance of the works, of delivery of products or of the provision of services;
6. for public works contracts:

    • a description of the nature and extent of the works and general nature of the work; an indication in particular of options concerning supplementary works, and, if known, the provisional timetable for recourse to these options as well as the number of possible renewals; an indication of the size of the different lots, if the work or the contract is subdivided into several lots; a reference to nomenclature number(s);

---

[8]   A simplified contract notice for use in a dynamic purchasing system must include the following information: the country, name and e-mail address of the contracting authority, publication reference of the contract notice for the dynamic purchasing system, the e-mail address at which the technical specification and additional documents relating to the dynamic purchasing system are available, the subject of the contract and a description by reference number(s) of 'CPV' nomenclature and the quantity or extent of the contract to be awarded, the time frame for submitting indicative tenders. See Annex VII A of the Public Sector Directive.

- information concerning the purpose of the work or the contract where the latter also involves the drawing-up of projects;
- an indication, in the event of a framework agreement, of the planned duration of the framework agreement, the estimated total value of the works for the entire duration of the framework agreement and, as far as possible, the value and the frequency of the contracts to be awarded;

(b)   for public supply contracts:

- a description of the nature of the products to be supplied, indicating in particular whether tenders are requested with a view to purchase, lease rental, hire or hire purchase or a combination of these, nomenclature reference number; an indication of the quantity of products to be supplied, specifying in particular options concerning supplementary purchases and the provisional timetable for recourse to these options as well as the number of renewals; a reference to nomenclature number(s);
- in the case of regular or renewable contracts during the course of a given period, an indication of the timetable for subsequent contracts for purchase of intended supplies;
- in the event of a framework agreement, an indication of the planned duration of the framework agreement, the estimated total value of the supplies for the entire duration of the framework agreement and, as far as possible, the value and the frequency of the contracts to be awarded;

(c)   for public service contracts:

- a reference to the category and description of service by nomenclature number(s); an indication of the quantity of services to be provided, and in particular any options concerning supplementary purchases and the provisional timetable for recourse to these options as well as the number of renewals; in the case of renewable contracts over a given period, an estimate of the time frame for subsequent public contracts for purchase of intended services; in the event of a framework agreement, an indication of the planned duration of the framework agreement, the estimated total value of the services for the entire duration of the framework agreement and, as far as possible, the value and the frequency of the contracts to be awarded;
- an indication of whether the execution of the service is reserved by

law, regulation or administrative provision to a particular profession and a reference to the law, regulation or administrative provision;

- an indication of whether legal persons should indicate the names and professional qualifications of the staff to be responsible for the execution of the service;

7. in case the contracts are subdivided into lots, an indication of the possibility of tendering for one, for several or for all the lots;

8. any time limit for completion of works/supplies/services or duration of the works/supply/services contract; where possible any time limit by which works will begin or any time limit by which delivery of supplies or services will begin;

9. an indication of the admission or prohibition of variants;

10. an indication of any particular conditions to which the performance of the contract is subject;

11. in open procedures: provision of (a) name, address, telephone and telefax number and electronic address of the service from which contract documents and additional documents can be requested; (b) where appropriate, the time limit for submission of such requests; (c) where appropriate, the cost of and payment conditions for obtaining these documents; (d) the time limit for receipt of tenders or indicative tenders where a dynamic purchasing system is being used (open procedures); (e) the time limit for receipt of request to participate (restricted and negotiated procedures); (f) the address where these have to be transmitted; (g) the language or languages in which they must be drawn up; (h) persons authorised to be present at the opening of tenders; (b) date, time and place for such opening;

12. an indication of any deposit and guarantees required;

13. a reference to the main terms concerning financing and payment;

14. where applicable, the legal form to be taken by the grouping of economic operators to whom the contract is to be awarded;

15. an indication of the selection criteria regarding the personal situation of economic operators that may lead to their exclusion, and required information proving that they do not fall within the cases justifying exclusion; an indication of the selection criteria and information concerning the economic operators' personal situation, information and any necessary formalities for assessment of the minimum economic and technical standards required of the economic operator; an indication of any minimum level(s) of standards required;

16. in cases of framework agreements: a reference to the number and, where appropriate, the proposed maximum number of economic operators who will be members of the framework agreement; an indication of the dura-

tion of the framework agreement provided for, stating, if appropriate, the reasons for any duration exceeding four years;

17. in cases of a competitive dialogue or a negotiated procedure with the publication of a contract notice, an indication of a possible recourse to a staged procedure in order gradually to reduce the number of solutions to be discussed or tenders to be negotiated;

18. in cases of restricted procedures, a competitive dialogue or negotiated procedures with the publication of a contract notice, when contracting authorities exercise the option of reducing the number of candidates to be invited to submit tenders, to engage in dialogue or to negotiate, an indication of the minimum and, if appropriate, the proposed maximum number of candidates and a reference to the objective criteria to be used to choose that number of candidates;

19. in cases of open procedures, an indication of the time frame during which the tenderer must maintain its tender;

20. in cases of negotiated procedures, a reference to names and addresses of economic operators already selected by the contracting authority;

21. a reference to the award criteria to be used for award of the contract: 'lowest price' or 'most economically advantageous tender'; in cases where criteria representing the most economically advantageous tender are selected, a description of their weighting in the event that such weighting does not appear in the specifications or in the descriptive document for competitive dialogue;

22. a reference to the name and address of the body responsible for appeal and, where appropriate, mediation procedures; an indication of precise information concerning deadlines for lodging appeals, or if need be, the name, address, telephone number, fax number and e-mail address of the service from which this information may be obtained;

23. the date(s) of publication of the prior information notice; the date of dispatch of the notice;

24. an indication of whether the contract is covered by the WTO GPA Agreement.

All notices sent by contracting authorities to the Commission for publication in the Official Journal must be sent either by electronic means in accordance with the format and procedures for transmission indicated in Annex VIII, paragraph 3, or by other means. In such cases, the content of notices must be limited to approximately 650 words. In the event of recourse to the accelerated procedure set out in Article 38(8), notices must be sent either by telefax or by electronic means.

The notices must be published no later than five days after they are sent. Notices which are not transmitted by electronic means must be published not

later than 12 days after they are sent, or in the case of the accelerated procedure referred to in Article 38(8), not later than five days after they are sent.
Contracting authorities must be able to supply proof of the dates on which
notices are dispatched. The Commission must give the contracting authority
confirmation of the publication of the information sent, mentioning the date of
publication. Such confirmation must constitute proof of publication.

Contract notices must be published in full in an official language of the
Community as chosen by the contracting authority, this original language
version constituting the sole authentic text. A summary of the important
elements of each notice must be published in the other official languages. The
costs of publication of such notices by the Commission must be borne by the
Community.

Contract Award Notices

Contracting authorities which have awarded a public contract or concluded a
framework agreement must send a notice of the results of the award procedure no later than 48 days after the award of the contract or the conclusion
of the framework agreement.[9] In the case of framework agreements,
contracting authorities are not bound to send a notice of the results of the
award procedure for each contract based on that agreement. Contracting
authorities must send a notice of the result of the award of contracts based
on a dynamic purchasing system within 48 days of the award of each
contract. They may, however, group such notices on a quarterly basis. In that
case, they must send the grouped notices within 48 days of the end of each
quarter. In the case of public contracts for services listed in Annex II B, the
contracting authorities must indicate in the notice whether they agree to its
publication. For such services contracts the Commission must draw up the
rules for establishing statistical reports on the basis of such notices and for
the publication of such reports in accordance with the procedure laid down
in Article 77(2) of the Directive.

Certain information on the contract award or the conclusion of the framework agreement may be withheld from publication where release of such
information would impede law enforcement or otherwise be contrary to the
public interest, would harm the legitimate commercial interests of economic
operators, public or private, or might prejudice fair competition between
them.

---

[9]   See Article 35(4) of the Public Sector Directive.

DEADLINES FOR RECEIPT OF REQUESTS TO PARTICIPATE AND FOR RECEIPT OF TENDERS

Contracting authorities should take into account the complexity of the contract and the time required for drawing up tenders, when determining the time limits for the receipt of tenders and requests to participate.[10]

In open procedures, the minimum time limit for the receipt of tenders must be 52 days from the date on which the contract notice was sent.[11] When contracting authorities have published a prior information notice, the minimum time limit for the receipt of tenders under open procedures may, as a general rule, be shortened to 36 days.[12] The time limit must run from the date on which the contract notice was sent for publication. The shortened time limits should be permitted, provided that the prior information notice has included all the information required for the contract notice, in so far as that information is available at the time the notice is published and that the prior information notice was sent for publication between 52 days and 12 months before the date on which the contract notice was sent. Where notices are drawn up and transmitted by electronic means, the time limits for the receipt of tenders in open procedures may be shortened by seven days.[13]

The time limits for receipt of tenders referred to in open procedures may be reduced by five days where the contracting authority offers unrestricted and full direct access by electronic means to the contract documents and any supplementary documents from the date of publication of the notice, specifying in the text of the notice the internet address at which this documentation is accessible.[14] This reduction may run concurrently with the shortened period provided for receipt of tenders where notices are drawn up and transmitted by electronic means.

In restricted procedures, negotiated procedures with publication of a contract notice and the competitive dialogue:[15]

(a) the minimum time limit for receipt of requests to participate must be 37 days from the date on which the contract notice is sent;

(b) in the case of restricted procedures, the minimum time limit for the receipt of tenders must be 40 days from the date on which the invitation is sent.

---

[10] See Article 38(1) of the Public Sector Directive.
[11] See Article 38(2) of the Public Sector Directive.
[12] See Article 38(4) of the Public Sector Directive.
[13] See Article 38(5) of the Public Sector Directive.
[14] See Article 38(6) of the Public Sector Directive.
[15] See Article 38(3) of the Public Sector Directive.

When contracting authorities have published a prior information notice, the minimum time limit for the receipt of tenders under restricted procedures may be shortened to 22 days.[16] The time limit must run from the date on which the invitation to tender was sent in restricted procedures. The shortened time limits should be permitted, provided that the prior information notice has included all the information required for the contract notice, in so far as that information is available at the time the notice is published and that the prior information notice was sent for publication between 52 days and 12 months before the date on which the contract notice was sent.

Where notices are drawn up and transmitted by electronic means, the time limit for the receipt of the requests to participate in restricted and negotiated procedures and the competitive dialogue, may be shortened by seven days.[17]

The time limits for receipt of tenders referred to in restricted procedures may be reduced by five days where the contracting authority offers unrestricted and full direct access by electronic means to the contract documents and any supplementary documents from the date of publication of the notice, specifying in the text of the notice the internet address at which this documentation is accessible.[18] This reduction may run concurrently with the shortened period provided for receipt of tenders where notices are drawn up and transmitted by electronic means.

If, for whatever reason, the specifications and the supporting documents or additional information, although requested in good time, are not supplied within the time limits set in Articles 39 and 40 of the Directive, or where tenders can be made only after a visit to the site or after on-the-spot inspection of the documents supporting the contract documents, the time limits for the receipt of tenders must be extended so that all economic operators concerned may be aware of all the information needed to produce tenders.[19]

In the case of restricted procedures and negotiated procedures with publication of a contract notice, where urgency renders impracticable the time limits laid down in the Directive, contracting authorities may accelerate the award procedure[20] by specifying: (a) a time limit for the receipt of requests to participate which may not be less than 15 days from the date on which the contract notice was sent, or less than 10 days if the notice was sent by electronic means, in accordance with the format and procedure for sending notices; and (b) in the case of restricted procedures, a time limit for the receipt of tenders which must be not less than 10 days from the date of the invitation to tender.

---

[16]   See Article 38(4) of the Public Sector Directive.
[17]   See Article 38(5) of the Public Sector Directive.
[18]   See Article 38(6) of the Public Sector Directive.
[19]   See Article 38(7) of the Public Sector Directive.
[20]   See Article 38(8) of the Public Sector Directive.

TECHNICAL STANDARDS AND SPECIFICATIONS

The technical specifications must be set out in the contract documentation, such as contract notices, contract documents or additional documents.[21] Whenever possible these technical specifications should be defined so as to take into account accessibility criteria for people with disabilities or be designed for all users. Technical specifications must afford equal access for tenderers and not have the effect of creating unjustified obstacles to the opening up of public procurement to competition.

Without prejudice to mandatory national technical rules, to the extent that they are compatible with Community law, the technical specifications must be formulated:[22]

(a) either by reference to technical specifications defined in Annex VI of the Public Sector Directive and, in order of preference, to national standards transposing European standards, European technical approvals, common technical specifications, international standards, other technical reference systems established by the European standardisation bodies or – when these do not exist – to national standards, national technical approvals or national technical specifications relating to the design, calculation and execution of the works and use of the products. Each reference must be accompanied by the words 'or equivalent';

(b) or in terms of performance or functional requirements; the latter may include environmental characteristics. However, such parameters must be sufficiently precise to allow tenderers to determine the subject-matter of the contract and to allow contracting authorities to award the contract;

(c) or in terms of performance or functional requirements as mentioned in subparagraph (b), with reference to the specifications mentioned in subparagraph (a) as a means of presuming conformity with such performance or functional requirements;

(d) or by referring to the specifications mentioned in subparagraph (a) for certain characteristics, and by referring to the performance or functional requirements mentioned in subparagraph (b) for other characteristics.

Where a contracting authority makes use of the option of referring to the specifications defined in Annex VI of the Public Sector Directive and, in

---

[21] See Article 23 of the Public Sector Directive.
[22] See Article 23(3) of the Public Sector Directive.

order of preference, to national standards transposing European standards, European technical approvals, common technical specifications, international standards, other technical reference systems established by the European standardisation bodies, it cannot reject a tender on the grounds that the products and services tendered for do not comply with the specifications to which it has referred, once the tenderer proves in his tender to the satisfaction of the contracting authority, by whatever appropriate means, that the solutions which he proposes satisfy in an equivalent manner the requirements defined by the technical specifications.[23] An appropriate means might be constituted by a technical dossier from the manufacturer or a test report from a recognised body.

Where a contracting authority prescribes in terms of performance or functional requirements, it may not reject a tender for works, products or services which comply with a national standard transposing a European standard, with a European technical approval, a common technical specification, an international standard or a technical reference system established by a European standardisation body, if these specifications address the performance or functional requirements which it has laid down.[24] Within the tender documents, the tenderer must prove to the satisfaction of the contracting authority and by any appropriate means that the work, product or service in compliance with the standard meets the performance or functional requirements of the contracting authority. An appropriate means might be constituted by a technical dossier of the manufacturer or a test report from a recognised body.

Where contracting authorities lay down environmental characteristics in terms of performance or functional requirements they may use the detailed specifications, or, if necessary, parts thereof, as defined by European or (multi-) national eco-labels, or by any other eco-label, provided that those specifications are appropriate to defining the characteristics of the supplies or services that are the object of the contract, that the requirements for the label are drawn up on the basis of scientific information, that the eco-labels are adopted using a procedure in which all stakeholders, such as government bodies, consumers, manufacturers, distributors and environmental organisations, can participate, and finally they are accessible to all interested parties.[25]

Contracting authorities may indicate that the products and services bearing the eco-label are presumed to comply with the technical specifications laid down in the contract documents; they must accept any other appropriate

---

[23]   See Article 23(4) of the Public Sector Directive.
[24]   See Article 23(5) of the Public Sector Directive.
[25]   See Article 23(6) of the Public Sector Directive.

means of proof, such as a technical dossier from the manufacturer or a test report from a recognised body. Recognised bodies, within the meaning of the Directive, are test and calibration laboratories and certification and inspection bodies which comply with applicable European standards. Contracting authorities must accept certificates from recognised bodies established in other member states.[26]

Unless justified by the subject-matter of the contract, technical specifications must not refer to a specific make or source, or a particular process, or to trade marks, patents, types or a specific origin or production with the effect of favouring or eliminating certain undertakings or certain products. Such reference must be permitted on an exceptional basis, where a sufficiently precise and intelligible description of the subject-matter of the contract and such reference must be accompanied by the words 'or equivalent'.[27]

VARIANTS

Contracting authorities may allow tenderers to submit variants, only where the criterion for award is that of the most economically advantageous tender.[28] Contracting authorities must indicate in the contract notice whether or not they authorise variants, as variants should not be forwarded without prior authorisation from the contracting authority. Contracting authorities authorising variants must state in the contract documents the minimum requirements to be met by the variants and any specific requirements for their presentation. Only variants meeting the minimum requirements laid down by these contracting authorities must be taken into consideration. In procedures for awarding public supply or service contracts, contracting authorities which have authorised variants may not reject a variant on the sole ground that it would, if successful, lead to a service contract rather than a public supply contract or a supply contract rather than a public service contract.

Case Law on Technical Standards

The Court has approached very proactively the discriminatory use of specification requirements and standards.[29] It established the 'equivalent standard'

---

26   See Article 23(7) of the Public Sector Directive.
27   See Article 23(8) of the Public Sector Directive.
28   See Article 24 of the Public Sector Directive.
29   See case C-45/87, *Commission v. Ireland*, [1988] ECR 4929; also case C-359/93, *Commission v. The Netherlands*, judgment of 24 January 1995.

doctrine, where contracting authorities are prohibited from introducing technical specifications or trade marks which mention products of a certain make or source, or a particular process which favours or eliminates certain undertakings, unless these specifications are justified by the subject and nature of the contract and on condition that they are only permitted if they are accompanied by the words 'or equivalent'.

National technical standards, industrial product and service specifications and their harmonisation were considered priority areas for the internal market programme. The European Commission's White Paper for the Completion of the Internal Market stipulated that a number of Directives should be adopted and implemented with a view to eliminating discrimination based on the description of national standards. The rules on technical standards and specifications have been brought into line with the new policy, which is based on the mutual recognition of national requirements, where the objectives of national legislation are essentially equivalent, and on the process of legislative harmonisation of technical standards through non-governmental standardisation organisations (CEPT, CEN, CENELEC).[30] However, contracting authorities's persistence in specifying their procurement requirements by reference to national standards poses obstacles in public sector integration.[31] The European Commission has been for some time aware of the most notable examples of circumvention of the policy on standards and specifications.[32] These include the exclusive familiarity of national suppliers with technical data existing in a particular member state, over-specification by contracting authorities in order to exclude potential bidders and finally favouritism and discrimination by contracting authorities as a result of the availability of technical standards and specifications to certain suppliers only.

Standardisation and specification can act as a non-tariff barrier in public procurement contracts in two ways: first, contracting authorities may use apparently different systems of standards and specifications as an excuse for the disqualification of tenderers. It should be maintained here that the description of the intended supplies, works or services to be procured is made by reference to the Common Product Classification, the NACE

---

[30]   See Article 7 of Directive 88/295. See the White Paper on Completing the Internal Market, paragraphs 61–79; also Council Resolution of 7 May 1985, OJ 1985 C 136, on a new approach in the field of technical harmonisation and standards.

[31]   See the Documents of the Advisory Committee for the Opening up of Public Procurement, *Policy Guidelines on the Obligation to refer to European Standards*, CCO/91/67 final.

[32]   See the report of the Advisory Committee for the Opening up of Public Procurement, *Standards for Procurement*, CCO/92/02.

(General Industrial Classification of Economic Activities within the European Communities) and the Common Procurement Vocabulary (CPV). However, this type of description is of a generic nature and does not cover industrial specifications and standardisation requirements. Secondly, standardisation and specification requirements can be restrictively defined in order to exclude products or services of a particular origin, or to narrow the field of competition amongst tenderers. National standards are not only the subject of domestic legislation, which, of course, needs to be harmonised and mutually recognised across the common market. One of the most significant aspects of standardisation and specification appears to be the operation of voluntary standards which are mainly specified at industry level. The above category is rather difficult to harmonise, as any approximation and mutual recognition relies on the willingness of the industry in question. Voluntary standards and specifications are used quite often in the utilities sector, where the relevant procurement requirements are complex and cannot be specified solely by reference to 'statutory' standards, thus leaving a considerable margin of discretion in the hands of the contracting authorities, which may abuse it during the selection and qualification stages of the procurement process.

The European Court of Justice has condemned discriminatory use of specification requirements and standards. In the Irish *Dundalk* pipeline case,[33] the Commission had received complaints that Ireland had not complied with the Public Works Directive 71/305 and in particular with Article 10 of Directive 71/305. This provision prohibits member states from introducing into the contractual clauses relating to a given contract technical specifications, unless they are justified by the subject of the contract, which mention products of a specific make or source or a particular process which favours or eliminates certain undertakings. Such indications are only permitted if they are accompanied by the words 'or equivalent' where the authorities awarding contracts are unable to give sufficiently precise and ineligible specifications of the subject of the contract. In the *Dundalk* case, the invitation to tender referred to technical specifications which could only be adhered to by national contractors. Furthermore, they were not justified by the subject of the contract.

In another case, the Commission brought the Netherlands before the European Court of Justice[34] for failing to observe the Supplies Directive and in particular to specify, without discriminatory descriptions, the required goods for procurement. The *Neerlands Inkoopcentrum NV* had published a

---

[33] Case 45/87, *Commission v. Ireland*, [1988] ECR 4929.
[34] Case C-359/93, *Commission v. The Netherlands*, judgment of 24 January 1995.

notice in the Official Journal for the procurement of a meteorological data processing system, which it specified with a particular trade mark, without using the term 'equivalent'. The Court, following its previous case-law,[35] reiterated that Article 7(6) of the Supplies Directive 77/62 (as amended by Article 8 of Directive 89/295) intends to eliminate discriminatory descriptions of supplies by utilisation of particular trade marks, unless accompanied by the words 'or equivalent', and only in cases where reference to a particular trade mark is necessary for the description of the product in question. The Court of Justice also pronounced the compulsory and unconditional character of point 7 of Annex III to the Supplies Directive 77/62, which requires indication of authorised persons, date, time and place for the opening of tenders, in order to allow tenderers to identify their competitors and enable them to ensure that their offers are being evaluated in a transparent and equal manner.

CONTRACTUAL PERFORMANCE UNDER THE PUBLIC SECTOR DIRECTIVE

Subcontracting

In the contract documents, the contracting authority may ask or may be required by a member state to ask the tenderer to indicate in his tender any share of the contract he may intend to subcontract to third parties and any proposed subcontractors. This indication must be without prejudice to the question of the principal economic operator's liability.[36]

Socio-economic Conditions

Contracting authorities may lay down special conditions relating to the performance of a contract, provided that these are compatible with Community law and are indicated in the contract notice or in the specifications. The conditions governing the performance of a contract may, in particular, concern social and environmental considerations.[37]

---

[35] Case 45/87, *Commission v. Ireland*, [1988] ECR 4929.
[36] See Article 25 of the Public Sector Directive.
[37] See Article 26 of the Public Sector Directive.

Obligations relating to Taxes, Environmental Protection, Employment Protection Provisions and Working Conditions

A contracting authority may state in the contract documents, or be obliged by a member state to state, the body or bodies from which a candidate or tenderer may obtain the appropriate information on the obligations relating to taxes, to environmental protection, to employment protection provisions and to the working conditions which are in force in the member state, region or locality in which the works are to be carried out or services are to be provided and which must be applicable to the works carried out on site or to the services provided during the performance of the contract.[38]

A contracting authority must request the tenderers or candidates in the contract award procedure to indicate that they have taken account, when drawing up their tender, of the obligations relating to employment protection provisions and the working conditions which are in force in the place where the works are to be carried out or the service is to be provided.[39]

FEEDBACK TO CANDIDATES AND TENDERERS

Upon receiving a request in writing from any candidate or tenderer concerned, contracting authorities must inform, as soon as possible, all candidates and tenderers concerned of their decisions reached in relation to the award of a public contract, the conclusion of a framework agreement, or the admittance of participants into a dynamic purchasing system.[40]

Contracting authorities must also inform the candidates and tenderers concerned of the grounds for any decision not to conclude a framework agreement or not to award a contract for which there has been a call for competition or not to implement a dynamic purchasing system.

On request from the party concerned and within 15 days from receipt of a written request, contracting authorities must inform[41] any unsuccessful candidate of the reasons for the rejection of his application, as well as of the reasons for the rejection of his tender, including reasons for not accepting specifications referred to in Article 23(4) and (5), the reasons for its decision that specifications offered by the tenderer do not meet the 'equivalence requirement' specified in Article 23(8), or its decision that the works, supplies or services do not meet the performance or functional requirements.

---

[38] See Article 27(1) of the Public Sector Directive.
[39] See Article 27(2) of the Public Sector Directive.
[40] See Article 41(1) of the Public Sector Directive.
[41] Article 41(2) of the Public Sector Directive.

Contracting authorities must also inform any tenderer who has made an admissible tender of the characteristics and relative advantages of the tender selected as well as the name of the successful tenderer or the parties to the framework agreement.

However, contracting authorities may decide to withhold certain information regarding the contract award, the conclusion of framework agreements or admittance to a dynamic purchasing system where the release of such information would impede law enforcement, would otherwise be contrary to the public interest, would prejudice the legitimate commercial interests of economic operators, whether public or private, or might prejudice fair competition between them.[42]

---

[42]   Article 41(3) of the Public Sector Directive.

6. Qualitative selection in public sector procurement

DISQUALIFICATION AND REASONS FOR AUTOMATIC EXCLUSION

Personal Situation of Candidates or Tenderers

Contracting authorities may exclude[1] from participation in a public contract any candidate or tenderer who has been the subject of a conviction by final judgment of which the contracting authority is aware for one or more of the following reasons:[2]

(a) participation in a criminal organisation, as defined in Article 2(1) of Council Joint Action 98/733/JHA;[3]

(b) corruption, as defined in Article 3 of the Council Act of 26 May 1997[4] and Article 3(1) of Council Joint Action 98/742/JHA[5] respectively;

(c) fraud within the meaning of Article 1 of the Convention relating to the protection of the financial interests of the European Communities;[6]

(d) money laundering, as defined in Article 1 of Council Directive 91/308/EEC of 10 June 1991 on prevention of the use of the financial system for the purpose of money laundering.[7]

In addition to the above reasons, contracting authorities may exclude an economic operator from participation in a contract where that economic operator:[8]

---

[1]   See Article 45 of the Public Sector Directive.
[2]   See Article 45(1) of the Public Sector Directive.
[3]   OJ L 351, 29.12.1998, p. 1.
[4]   OJ C 195, 25.6.1997, p. 1
[5]   OJ L 358, 31.12.1998, p. 2.
[6]   OJ C 316, 27.11.1995, p. 48.
[7]   OJ L 166, 28.6.1991, p. 77, as amended by Directive 2001/97/EC of the European Parliament and of the Council of 4 December 2001 (OJ L 344, 28.12.2001, p. 76).
[8]   See Article 45(2) of the Public Sector Directive.

(a)   is bankrupt or is being wound up, where his affairs are being adminis-
      tered by the court, where he has entered into an arrangement with credi-
      tors, where he has suspended business activities or is in any analogous
      situation arising from a similar procedure under national laws and regu-
      lations;
(b)   is the subject of proceedings for a declaration of bankruptcy, for an order
      for compulsory winding up or administration by the court or of an
      arrangement with creditors or of any other similar proceedings under
      national laws and regulations;
(c)   has been convicted by a judgment which has the force of *res judicata* in
      accordance with the legal provisions of the country of any offence
      concerning his professional conduct;
(d)   has been guilty of grave professional misconduct proven by any means
      which the contracting authorities can demonstrate;
(e)   has not fulfilled obligations relating to the payment of social security
      contributions in accordance with the legal provisions of the country in
      which he is established or with those of the country of the contracting
      authority;
(f)   has not fulfilled obligations relating to the payment of taxes in accor-
      dance with the legal provisions of the country in which he is established
      or with those of the country of the contracting authority;
(g)   is guilty of serious misrepresentation in supplying the information
      required under this Section or has not supplied such information.
      Member states must specify, in accordance with their national law.

Derogation

Member states may provide for derogation from the automatic exclusion
grounds relating to participation in a criminal organisation, corruption,
fraud or money laundering for overriding requirements in the general interest.[9]

Proof of the Personal Situation of Candidates and Tenderers

Sufficient evidence of the personal situation of candidates and tenderers in
accordance with Article 45 can be provided by means of the production of an
extract from the judicial record or of an equivalent document issued by a
competent judicial or administrative authority in the country of origin of the
candidate or the tenderer proving that none of the automatic exclusion grounds

---

[9]   See the second indent of Article 45(1) of the Public Sector Directive.

relating to participation in a criminal organisation, corruption, fraud or money laundering is present.[10]

With regard to the requirements of evidence of payment of social security contributions and taxes in accordance with 2(e) and (f), a certificate issued by the competent authority in the member state concerned is adequate proof.[11]

Where the country in question does not issue extracts from the judicial record or of an equivalent document or certificates, proof of the personal situation of candidates and tenderers may be provided by a declaration on oath or, in member states where there is no provision for declarations on oath, by a solemn declaration made by the person concerned before a competent judicial or administrative authority, a notary or a competent professional or trade body, in the country of origin or in the country whence that person comes. For these purposes, member states must designate the authorities and bodies competent to issue the documents, certificates or declarations and inform the Commission, subject to data protection laws.

Ex Officio Application

Contracting authorities, where they have doubts concerning the personal situation of such candidates or tenderers, may themselves apply to the competent authorities to obtain any information they consider necessary on the personal situation of the candidates or tenderers.[12] Where the information concerns a candidate or tenderer established in a state other than that of the contracting authority, the contracting authority may seek the co-operation of the competent authorities. Such requests must relate to legal and/or natural persons, including, if appropriate, company directors and any person having powers of representation, decision or control in respect of the candidate or tenderer.

ECONOMIC AND FINANCIAL STANDING OF ECONOMIC OPERATORS

Contracting authorities may request economic operators to prove their financial and economic standing for the performance of a contract.[13] Proof of the economic operator's economic and financial standing may, as a general rule, be furnished by appropriate statements from banks or, where appropriate,

---

10 See Article 45(3)(a) of the Public Sector Directive.
11 See Article 45(3)(b) of the Public Sector Directive.
12 See Article 45(1) of the Public Sector Directive and in particular its second indent.
13 See Article 47 of the Public Sector Directive.

evidence of relevant professional risk indemnity insurance.[14] Contracting authorities may also request the presentation of balance sheets or extracts from the balance sheets, where publication of the balance sheet is required under the law of the country in which the economic operator is established.[15]

In cases where bank statements or balance sheets or extracts from balance sheets cannot be produced, a statement of the operator's overall turnover and, where appropriate, of turnover in the area covered by the contract will be sufficient. The period which such a statement should cover must be for a maximum of the last three financial years. However, depending on the date on which an undertaking was set up or the economic operator started trading, the information provided on turnovers should be acceptable.[16]

However, for the purposes of assessing the financial and economic standing of contractors, an exception to the exhaustive (and directly applicable) nature of technical capacity and qualification rules has been made. Evidence of financial and economic standing may be provided by means of references including: (i) appropriate statements from bankers; (ii) the presentation of the firm's balance sheets or extracts from balance sheets where these are published under company law provisions; and (iii) a statement of the firm's annual turnover and the turnover on construction works for the three previous financial years. The non-exhaustive character of the list of references in relation to contractors' economic and financial standing was recognised by the Court in the *CEI-Bellini* case,[17] where the value of the works which may be carried out at any one time may constitute a proof of the contractors' economic and financial standing. The contracting authorities are allowed to fix such a limit, as the provisions of the public procurement Directives do not aim to delimit the powers of member states, but to determine the references or evidence which may be furnished in order to establish the contractors' financial and economic standing. Of interest is the recent case *ARGE*,[18] where even the receipt of aid or subsidies incompatible with the Treaty by an entity may be a reason for disqualification from the selection process, as an obligation to repay illegal aid would threaten the financial stability of the tenderer in question.

The Court also maintained [19] that examination of a contractor's suitability

---

14   See Article 47(1)(a) of the Public Sector Directive.
15   See Article 47(1)(b) of the Public Sector Directive.
16   See Article 47(1)(c) of the Public Sector Directive.
17   See *Bellini* case, op. cit.
18   See case C-94/99, *ARGE Gewässerschutzt v. Bundesministerium für Land-und Forstwirtschaft*, paragraph 30, judgment of 7 December 2000.
19   Case 31/87, *Gebroeders Beentjes BV v. State of Netherlands* [1988] ECR 4635.

based on its technical capacity and qualifications and its financial and economic standing may take place simultaneously with the award procedures of a contract.[20] However, the two procedures (the suitability evaluation and bid evaluation) are totally distinct processes, which shall not be confused.[21]

Reliance on the Financial and Economic Standing of Group and/or Consortia Members

Where an economic operator is part of a group of companies or belongs to a consortium especially formed to tender for the envisaged works, supplies or services, contracting authorities may rely on the financial standing of other entities, regardless of the legal nature of the links which the economic operator has with them.[22] However, the operator which relies on the financial standing of group or consortia members must prove to the contracting authority that it will have at its disposal the resources necessary, for example, by producing an undertaking by those entities to that effect. Under the same conditions, a group of economic operators may rely on the economic and financial standing of participants in the group or of other entities.[23]

Contracting authorities must specify, in the contract notice or in the invitation to tender, the type of reference they require for proof or evidence of the economic and financial standing of economic operators and which other additional references must be provided.[24] If, for any valid reason, the economic operator is unable to provide the references requested by the contracting authority, he may prove his economic and financial standing by any other document which the contracting authority considers appropriate.[25]

TECHNICAL AND PROFESSIONAL ABILITY OF ECONOMIC OPERATORS

Evidence of the technical and professional ability of economic operators may be requested by contracting authorities.[26] Such evidence may be furnished by

---

[20]   See *Bellini* case 28/86, op. cit.

[21]   See case C-71/92, *Commission v. Spain*, judgment of 30 June 1993. Also, *Beentjes*, op. cit. at paragraphs 15 and 16, where the simultaneous application of selection of tenders and award procedures is not precluded, on condition that the two are governed by different rules.

[22]   See Article 47(2) of the Public Sector Directive.

[23]   See Article 47(3) of the Public Sector Directive.

[24]   See Article 47(4) of the Public Sector Directive.

[25]   See Article 47(5) of the Public Sector Directive.

[26]   See Articles 46 and 48 of the Public Sector Directive.

a range of documentation provided by economic operators according to the nature, quantity or importance, and use of the works, supplies or services they intend to tender for. The contracting authority must specify, in the contract notice or in the invitation to tender, which references relevant to the technical and professional ability of economic operators it wishes to consider in evaluating the suitability to perform. In particular, the ability of economic operators to provide a service or a product or to execute the envisaged works may be evaluated with reference to their skills, efficiency, experience and reliability.

The relevant provisions of the procurement Directives relating to qualitative selection and qualification criteria refer to the technical ability and knowledge of tenderers, where proof may be furnished by evidence of educational or professional qualifications, previous experience in performing public contracts and statements on the contractor's expertise.[27] The references which the tenderers may be required to produce must be specified in the notice or invitation to tender. The rules relating to technical capacity and eligibility of tenderers represent an exhaustive list and are capable of producing a direct effect.[28]

Previous Experience

For works contracts,[29] evidence of technical ability may be provided by a list of the works carried out over the past five years, accompanied by certificates of satisfactory execution for the most important works. These certificates must indicate the value, date and site of the works and must specify whether they were carried out according to the rules of the trade and properly completed. Where the recipient of the work is a contracting authority, such an authority must submit these certificates to the contracting authority directly.

For service and supplies contracts, evidence of technical ability may be provided by a list of the principal deliveries supplied or the main services provided in the past three years, with the sums, dates and recipients, whether public or private, of such supplies and services.[30] Evidence of delivery of supplies and services provided must be given by means of certificates issued or countersigned by the competent authority, where the recipient was itself a contracting authority. Where the recipient is a private purchaser, evidence must be provided by the purchaser's certification. Where the purchaser cannot

---

[27]   See Article 27 of Directive 93/37, Article 31 of Directive 93/38 and Article 22 of Directive 92/50.

[28]   See case 76/81, *SA Transporoute et Travaux v. Minister of Public Works*, [1982] ECR 457.

[29]   See Article 48(2)(a)(i) of the Public Sector Directive.

[30]   See Article 48(2)(a)(ii) of the Public Sector Directive.

provide any certification, a declaration by the economic operator should be sufficient evidence of previous experience relevant to its technical abilities.

References as a Selection Criterion

A question arose[31] as to whether Directive 93/36 precludes contracting authorities, in a procedure to award a public supply contract, from taking account of the number of references relating to the products offered by the tenderers to other customers not as a criterion for establishing their suitability for carrying out the contract but as a criterion for awarding the contract. The Court held that the Public Procurement Directives preclude any reference obtained by a contracting authority in relation to products or services offered by tenderers to other customers from being a criterion for awarding the contract. Such references may only serve as a criterion for establishing their suitability for carrying out the contract.

The Court maintained that the examination of the suitability of contractors to deliver the products which are the subject of the contract to be awarded and the awarding of the contract are two different operations in the procedure for the award of a public works contract. Article 15(1) of the Public Supplies Directive 93/36 provides that the contract is to be awarded after the supplier's suitability has been verified,[32] although the Public Procurement Directives do not rule out the possibility that examination of the tenderer's suitability and the award of the contract may take place simultaneously, provided that the two procedures are governed by different rules.[33] Article 15(1) of the Directive provides that the suitability of tenderers is to be verified by the contracting authority in accordance with the criteria of economic and financial standing and of technical knowledge or ability referred to in Articles 22, 23 and 24 of the Directive. The purpose of these articles is not to delimit the power of the member states to fix the level of financial and economic standing and technical knowledge required in order to take part in procedures for the award of public works contracts, but to determine the references or evidence which may be furnished in order to establish the supplier's financial or economic standing and technical knowledge or ability.[34]

The Court reiterated that as far as the criteria which may be used for the award of a public contract are concerned, Article 26(1) of Directive 93/36 provides that the authorities awarding contracts must base their decision either

[31] See case C-315/01, *Gesellschaft für Abfallentsorgungs-Technik GmbH (GAT) and Österreichische Autobahnen und Schnellstraßen AG (ÖSAG)*, ECR [2003] I-6351.
[32] See case C-31/87, *Beentjes* [1988], ECR 4635, paragraph 15.
[33] See case C-31/87, *Beentjes* [1988], ECR 4635, paragraph 16.
[34] See case C-31/87, *Beentjes* [1988], ECR 4635, paragraph 17.

on the lowest price only or, when the award is made to the most economically advantageous tender, on various criteria according to the contract involved, such as price, delivery date, running costs, cost-effectiveness, quality, aesthetic and functional characteristics, technical merit, after-sales service and technical assistance. The Court maintained that, as is apparent from the wording of that provision, in particular the use of the expression 'e.g.', the criteria which may be accepted as criteria for the award of a public contract to what is the most economically advantageous tender are not listed exhaustively.[35] However, although Article 26(1) of Directive 93/36 leaves it to the contracting authority to choose the criteria on which it intends to base its award of the contract, that choice may relate only to criteria aimed at identifying the offer which is the most economically advantageous.[36] However, the fact remains that the submission of a list of the principal deliveries effected in the past three years, stating the sums, dates and recipients, public or private, involved is expressly included among the references or evidence which, under Article 23(1)(a) of Directive 93/36, may be required to establish the supplier's technical capacity. Furthermore, a simple list of references, such as that called for in the invitation to tender at issue in the main proceedings, which contains only the names and number of the supplier's previous customers without other details relating to the deliveries effected to those customers, cannot provide any information to identify the offer which is the most economically advantageous within the meaning of Article 26(1)(b) of Directive 93/36, and therefore cannot in any event constitute an award criterion within the meaning of that provision. The Court therefore concluded that contracting authorities are precluded from taking account of the number of references relating to the products offered by the tenderers to other customers as a criterion for awarding the contract, but not as a criterion for establishing their suitability for carrying out the contract.

Technical Expertise

The technical and professional expertise of economic operators could be furnished by documentation providing an indication of the technicians or technical bodies involved directly or indirectly with the economic operator.[37] Emphasis should be placed on those resources responsible for quality control. In cases of public works contracts, the technical and professional expertise of

---

[35]   See case C-19/00, *SIAC Construction* [2001] ECR I-7725, paragraph 35; case C-513/99, *Concordia Bus Finland* [2002] ECR I-7213, paragraph 54.

[36]   See *Beentjes*, paragraph 19, *SIAC Construction*, paragraph 36, and *Concordia Bus Finland*, paragraph 59.

[37]   See Article 48(2)(a)(b) of the Public Sector Directive.

the economic operator can be proved by identifying those upon whom the contractor can call in order to carry out the works.

The technical capacity of economic operators can also be evidenced by means of a description of the technical facilities, measures and systems used by the supplier or service provider for ensuring quality control. Relevant to this ground of technical capacity is a description of the operator's research and development facilities.

In services, works and construction projects, the technical capacity of economic operators can be proved by a statement covering the average annual manpower of the service provider or the contractor and the number of managerial staff for the last three years. In addition, a statement of the tools, plant or technical equipment available to the service provider or contractor for carrying out the contract could also be requested by the contracting authorities.

Professional Expertise and Suitability to Pursue Professional Activities

Contracting authorities may request evidence of the educational and professional qualifications of the service provider or contractor and in particular the educational and professional qualifications of the operator's managerial staff, as well as of those persons responsible for providing the services or managing the work.

Evidence of the suitability of economic operators to pursue professional activities may be requested by contracting authorities.[38] In such cases, proof can be furnished by certified copies of the operator's enrolment on professional or trade registers prescribed in member states. In the absence of such documentation, evidence of suitability to pursue professional activities can be provided by a declaration on oath or a certificate as described in Annex IX A for public works contracts, in Annex IX B for public supply contracts and in Annex IX C for public service contracts.

For the performance of public service contracts, in so far as candidates or tenderers have to possess a particular authorisation or to be members of a particular organisation in order to be able to perform the service concerned in their country of origin, contracting authorities may require them to prove that they hold such authorisation or membership.

Reality Checks

Contracting authorities may request reality checks where the products or services to be supplied are complex or where, in exceptional circumstances,

---

[38] See Article 46 of the Public Sector Directive.

they are procured for a specific purpose.[39] Reality checks can be carried out by the contracting authorities themselves or on their behalf by a competent official body of the country in which the supplier or service provider is established. The content and purpose of a reality check is to verify the production capacities of the supplier or the technical capacity of the service provider. The checks may also cover research and development facilities available to the economic operator or measures, systems and procedures on quality control operating under that undertaking.

In cases of supplies contracts, contracting authorities may request samples, descriptions or photographs of the physical products.[40] The economic operator must be in a position to certify the authenticity of the products should the contracting authority so request. Such official recognition can be provided by certificates drawn up by official quality control institutes or agencies of recognised competence attesting to the conformity of products and clearly identifying them by reference to specifications or standards.

Location of Contractors as Selection Criterion

In *Gesellschaft für Abfallentsorgungs-Technik GmbH (GAT)*[41] a further question arose as to whether the location of the contractor can play any role in the selection and qualification stage or the award stage of public contracts. The national law asked the Court whether the principle of equal treatment under the Public Procurement Directives precludes a criterion for the award of a public supply contract according to which a tenderer's offer may be favourably assessed only if the product which is the subject of the offer is available for inspection by the contracting authority within a radius of 300 kilometres of the premises of the contracting authority. The Court maintained that such a criterion cannot constitute a criterion for the award of the contract. It put forward two reasons. First, it is apparent from Article 23(1)(d) of Directive 93/36 that for public supply contracts the contracting authorities may require the submission of samples, descriptions or photographs of the products to be supplied as references or evidence of the suppliers' technical capacity to carry out the contract concerned. Secondly, a criterion such as that which is the subject of Question 4 cannot serve to identify the most economically advantageous offer within the meaning of Article 26(1)(b) of Directive 93/36 and therefore cannot, in any event, constitute an award criterion within the meaning of that provision.

---

[39]   See Article 48(2)(d) of the Public Sector Directive.
[40]   See Article 48(2)(j) and (i) of the Public Sector Directive.
[41]   See case C-315/01, *Gesellschaft für Abfallentsorgungs-Technik GmbH (GAT) and Österreichische Autobahnen und Schnellstraßen AG (ÖSAG)*, ECR [2003] I-6351.

Evidence of Environmental Management as Selection Criterion

For public works contracts and public services contracts, and only in appropriate cases, an indication of the environmental management measures that the economic operator will be able to apply when performing the contract may be requested by the contracting authorities.[42] Should contracting authorities require the production of certificates drawn up by independent bodies attesting to the compliance of the economic operator with certain environmental management standards, they must refer to the Eco-Management and Audit Scheme (EMAS). Alternatively, they could refer to environmental management standards based on the relevant European or international standards certified by bodies conforming to Community law.[43]

In the absence of EMAS or other European or international environmental standardisation certificates, contracting authorities must recognise equivalent certificates from bodies established in member states or equivalent environmental management measures from economic operators.

Reliance on Group or Consortia

Where an economic operator is part of a group of companies or belongs to a consortium especially formed to tender for the envisaged works, supplies or services, contracting authorities may rely on the technical capacities of other entities, regardless of the legal nature of the links which the economic operator has with them.[44]

However, the economic operator must prove to the contracting authority that it will have at its disposal the resources necessary for the execution of the contract, for example, by producing an undertaking by those entities to place the necessary resources at the disposal of the economic operator. Under the same conditions a group of economic operators may rely on the abilities of participants in the group or in other entities.

Evidence of Intended Subcontracting

Contracting authorities may request economic operators to provide evidence of their intention to subcontract a proportion of the contract.[45]

---

42   See Article 48(2)(f) of the Public Sector Directive.
43   See Article 50 of the Public Sector Directive.
44   See Article 48(3) and (4) of the Public Sector Directive.
45   Article 48(2)(i) of the Public Sector Directive.

Quality Assurance Standards

In cases where contracting authorities require proof of quality assurance standards of economic operators, such proof may be furnished by the production of certificates drawn up by independent bodies attesting to the compliance of the economic operator with certain European series quality assurance standards.[46] In the event that the economic operator cannot produce such documentation, contracting authorities must recognise equivalent certificates from bodies established in member states and also accept other evidence of equivalent quality assurance measures from economic operators.

OFFICIAL LISTS OF APPROVED ECONOMIC OPERATORS

Member states may introduce official lists of approved contractors,[47] suppliers or service providers in order to assist contracting authorities with the qualitative evaluation of tenderers and candidates in public procurement contracts.[48] Economic operators may ask at any time to be registered in an official list. They must be informed within a reasonably short period of time of the decision of the authority drawing up the list or of the competent certification body.

The conditions for registration in such lists must reflect the personal situation of the candidate or tenderer to the extent of its participation in a criminal organisation, corruption, fraud, money laundering, bankruptcy, winding up, compulsory administration, professional misconduct, serious misrepresentation, ability to pursue a professional activity, economic and financial standing, technical and professional capacity, quality assurance standards, and where appropriate environmental management standards.[49] Registration in approved lists must not constitute a presumption of suitability of the registered undertakings, except for the conditions upon which their registration is based.

Economic operators belonging to a group and claiming resources made available to them by the other companies in the group may apply for registration in an official list of approved undertakings.[50] In such cases, these opera-

---

[46]   See Article 49 of the Public Sector Directive.
[47]   See Article 52(1) of the Public Sector Directive.
[48]   Member states which have official lists or certification bodies as referred to in paragraph 1 must be obliged to inform the Commission and the other member states of the address of the body to which applications should be sent.
[49]   See the provisions of Article 45(1), Article 45(2)(a) to (d) and (g), Articles 46, Article 47(1), (4) and (5), Article 48(1), (2), (5) and (6), Article 49 and Article 50.
[50]   Article 52(2) of the Public Sector Directive.

tors must prove to the authority establishing the official list that they will have these resources at their disposal throughout the period of validity of the certificate attesting to their being registered on the official list and that throughout the same period these companies continue to fulfil the qualitative selection requirements on which operators rely for their registration.

Registration in official lists of approved economic operators can be demonstrated by the issue of a certificate which must state the references which enabled the registration in the list and the classification given in that list.[51] Economic operators registered on the official lists may be requested, for each contract they tender, to submit to the contracting authority such a certificate of registration issued by the competent authority. The information which can be deduced from registration on official lists or certification may not be questioned without justification by the contracting authorities. For proof of payment of social security contributions and taxes, an additional certificate may be required of any registered economic operator whenever a contract is offered.

The *Transporoute*[52] case paved the way for the Court to elaborate on forms of selection and qualification, such as registration on lists of recognised contractors. Such lists exist in member states and tenderers may use their registration on them as an alternative means of proving their technical suitability, also before the contracting authorities of other member states. *CEI–Bellini* followed the same line,[53] although it conferred discretion on the contracting authorities to request further evidence of technical capacity, other than the mere certificate of registration on official lists of approved contractors, on the grounds that such lists might not be referring to uniform classifications.

The Court ruled in *Ballast Nedam I*[54] that a holding company which does not itself carry out works may not be precluded from registration on an official list of approved contractors, and consequently, from participating in tendering procedures, if it shows that it actually has available to it the resources of its subsidiaries necessary to carry out the contracts, unless the references of those subsidiaries do not themselves satisfy the qualitative selection criteria specified

---

[51] See Article 52(3) and (4) of the Public Sector Directive.

[52] See case 76/81, *SA Transporoute et Travaux v. Minister of Public Works*, [1982] ECR 457.

[53] See case C-27/86, *Constructions et Entreprises Industrielles SA (CEI) v. Association Intercommunale pour les Autoroutes des Ardennes*; case C-28/86, *Ing. A. Bellini & Co. SpA v. Regie de Batiments* and case C-29/86, *Ing. A. Bellini & Co. SpA v. Belgian State*, [1987] ECR 3347.

[54] See case C-89/92, *Ballast Nedam Groep NV v. Belgische Staat*, [1994] 2 CMLR.

in the Directives. *Ballast Nedam II*[55] conferred an obligation on the authorities of member states which are responsible for the compilation of lists of approved contractors to take into account evidence of the technical capacity of companies belonging to the same group, when assessing the parent company's technical capacity for inclusion on the list, provided the holding company establishes that it has available to it the resources of the companies belonging to the group that are necessary to carry out public contracts. *Holst Italia*,[56] by analogy, applied the *Ballast* principle to undertakings that belong to the same group structure but do not have the status of a holding company and the requisite availability of the technical expertise of its subsidiaries. The Court held that with regard to the qualitative criteria relevant to economic, financial and technical standing, a tenderer may rely on the standing of other entities, regardless of the legal nature of the links which it has with them, provided that it is able to show that it actually has at its disposal the resources of those entities which are necessary for performance of a public contract.

Certification

Member states may introduce certification by certification bodies established in public or private law. Such certification bodies must comply with European certification standards.[57] For any registration of economic operators of other member states on an official list or for their certification by the competent bodies, no further proof or statements can be required other than those requested from national economic operators. However, economic operators from other member states may not be obliged to undergo such registration or certification in order to participate in a public contract.[58] The contracting authorities must recognise equivalent certificates from bodies established in other member states and accept other equivalent means of proof relevant to the conditions required for registration or certification.

EXCLUSION AND REJECTION OF ECONOMIC OPERATORS

Candidates or tenderers who, under the law of the member state in which they

---

[55]   See case C-5/97, *Ballast Nedam Groep NV v. Belgische Staat*, judgment of 18 December 1997.

[56]   See case C-176/98, *Holst Italia v. Comune di Cagliari*, judgment of 2 December 1999.

[57]   See Article 52(1) of the Public Sector Directive.

[58]   Article 52(4) of the Public Sector Directive.

are established, are entitled to provide the relevant service, must not be rejected solely on the ground that, under the law of the member state in which the contract is awarded, they would be required to be either natural or legal persons.[59] However, in the case of public service and public works contracts as well as public supply contracts covering in addition services and installation operations, legal persons may be required to indicate in the tender or the request to participate, the names and relevant professional qualifications of the staff to be responsible for the performance of the contract in question.

Verification of the Suitability of Participants

Contracting authorities may require candidates and tenderers to meet minimum capacity levels.[60] The extent of the information referred to in these provisions laid down in Articles 47 and 48 and relating to the economic operators' financial and economic standing and their technical and professional capacity, as well as the minimum levels of ability required for a specific contract, must be related and proportionate to the subject-matter of the contract. These minimum levels must be indicated in the contract notice.

Market Testing and Selection of Undertakings that Assist in the Preparation of Public Contracts

The Belgian *Conseil d'État* asked the Court whether the Public Procurement Directives prevent an undertaking which has participated in the preparatory stages of a public contract from being precluded from submitting a tender for that public contract, where that undertaking has not been given an opportunity to prove that its previous involvement with the preparation of the contract has not distorted competition amongst the tenderers.[61]

Fabricom, the plaintiff in the main proceedings before the national courts, argued that the relevant Belgian law[62] contravened Community law and, in particular that they were contrary to the principle of non-discrimination.[63] That principle is applicable to all tenderers, including those who have participated in the preparatory stage of the contract. The latter should be excluded from participating in a public contract only if it appears clearly and specifically that by such participation alone they have gained an advantage which

---

[59] See Article 4(1) of the Public Sector Directive.
[60] See Article 44 of the Public Sector Directive.
[61] See joint cases C-21/03 and C-34/03, *Fabricom SA v. État Belge*, judgment of 3 March 2005.
[62] See Articles 26 and 32 of the Royal Decree of 25 March 1999.
[63] See case C324/98, *Telaustria and Telefonadress*, [2000] ECR I10745.

distorts normal competition. Thus, in Fabricom's submission, the irrefutable presumption set out in the national legislation has an effect which is disproportionate to the objective pursued, namely to ensure fair competition between tenderers. According to case-law,[64] Community law on public procurement precludes a particular tender being eliminated as a matter of course and on the basis of a criterion which is applied automatically. The exclusion of an undertaking in the particular case of participation in preparatory works must be preceded by a full and differentiated examination of the kind of preparatory works concerned, in particular as regards access to the contract specifications. Exclusion is possible only if the undertaking has obtained, through its preparatory activity, specific information relating to the contract which gives it a competitive advantage.[65]

On the other hand, the Commission contended that the provisions of Belgian law seek to avoid possible discrimination and a competitive advantage to the person who has participated in the preparatory works when he submits his tender for the same contract. If the person who carries out the preparatory work could also be the successful tenderer, he might steer the preparation of the public contract in a direction favourable to him.

The Court held that the duty to observe the principle of equal treatment lies at the very heart of the Public Procurement Directives, which are intended in particular to promote the development of effective competition in the fields to which they apply and which lay down criteria for the award of contracts which are intended to ensure such competition.[66] Furthermore, the principle of equal treatment requires that comparable situations must not be treated differently and that different situations must not be treated in the same way unless such treatment is objectively justified.[67] The Court held that a person who has been instructed to carry out research, experiments, studies or development in connection with works, supplies or services relating to a public contract (hereinafter 'a person who has carried out certain preparatory work') is not necessarily in the same situation as regards participation in the procedure for the award of that contract as a person who has not carried out such works. A person who has participated in certain preparatory works may be at an advantage when formulating his tender on account of the information concerning the

---

[64]   See joined cases C285/99 and C286/99, *Lombardini and Mantovani*, [2001] ECR I9233.

[65]   Those were the arguments of the Austrian and Finnish governments, which intervened in the joint cases C-21/03 and C-34/03, *Fabricom SA v. État Belge*, judgment of 3 March 2005.

[66]   See case C-513/99, *Concordia Bus Finland*, [2002] ECR I-7213, paragraph 81.

[67]   See case C-434/02, *Arnold André*, [2004] ECR I-2902, paragraph 68, and case C-210/03, *Swedish Match*, [2004] ECR I-1620, paragraph 70.

public contract in question which he has received when carrying out that work. However, all tenderers must have equality of opportunity when formulating their tenders.[68]

The Court, furthermore, maintained that a person may be in a situation which may give rise to a conflict of interests in the sense that he may, without even intending to do so, where he himself is a tenderer for the public contract in question, influence the conditions of the contract in a manner favourable to himself. Such a situation would be capable of distorting competition between tenderers. Taking account of the situation in which a person who has carried out certain preparatory work may find himself, therefore, it cannot be maintained that the principle of equal treatment requires that that person be treated in the same way as any other tenderer. The difference in treatment established by a national rule which consists of prohibiting, in all circumstances, a person who has carried out certain preparatory works from participating in a procedure for the award of the public contract in question is not objectively justified. Such a prohibition could be disproportionate. Equal treatment for all tenderers is ensured where there is a procedure whereby an assessment is made, in each specific case, of whether the fact of carrying out certain preparatory works has conferred on the person who carried out that work a competitive advantage over other tenderers. Such a measure is less restrictive for a person who has carried out certain preparatory work.

In that regard, the Court held that such a national rule does not afford a person who has carried out certain preparatory work any possibility of demonstrating that the principles of equal treatment and non-discrimination, as well as the competition envisaged amongst the participants in a public contract, have not been jeopardised. The Court held that such a rule goes beyond what is necessary to attain the objective of equal treatment for all tenderers, as it may have the consequence that persons who have carried out certain preparatory works are precluded from the award procedure even though their participation in the procedure entails no risk whatsoever for competition between tenderers.

The Court concluded that, on the grounds of the proportionality and objectivity principles, national laws cannot preclude an undertaking which has been instructed to carry out research, experiments, studies or development in connection with public works, supplies or services from applying to participate in or to submit a tender for those works, supplies or services and in particular where that undertaking is not given the opportunity to prove that, in the circumstances of the case, the experience which he has acquired was not capable of distorting competition. The Court expanded its conclusions to cover even

---

68   See case C-87/94, *Commission v. Belgium*, [1996] ECR I2043, paragraph 54.

public undertakings which have previously assisted other contracting authorities in the preparation of specifications related to public contracts. The Court relied on previous jurisprudence[69] and established that the Public Procurement Directives apply equally to contracts between contracting authorities and private undertakings and contracting authorities and undertakings in which public authorities have an interest.

Exclusion of a Tenderer who Participates in the Preparatory Stages of a Public Contract

The question as to whether an economic operator should be excluded from the procurement process on the grounds of its previous participation in the preparatory stages of the relevant public contract surfaced in *Fabricom*, where the Advocate-General took a different view.[70] He established in hierarchical form the principles which underlie public procurement legislation and he referred to the principles of European law which influence the interpretation of such legislation. He established that the fundamental principles of the public procurement acquis include the principle of objectivity and the principle of transparency. However, in an interesting interpretation, he positioned the principle of competition as the ultimate objective of the European Public Procurement Directives.[71] Thus, he hierarchically transposed the underlying principles of specific European rules (the public procurement legislation) within an etymological interpretation and content analysis of the wording, scheme and objectives of the Directives.[72] His teleological interpretation revealed that although the Directives provide no specific rules governing the inability of undertakings to participate in tendering procedures, and in particular, to exclude an undertaking which has previously participated in the preparation and planning of a public contract, there is a need to ensure that contracting authorities do not discriminate amongst tenderers when they evaluate their submissions and respective offers. The Advocate-General maintained that the Public Procurement Directives allow contracting authorities to request or to receive advice for the purpose of drawing up the specifications for public contracts from private undertakings, provided that competition is

---

[69]   See case C-107/98, *Teckal*, [1999] ECR I-4973.
[70]   See the Opinion of Advocate-General Léger in joint cases C-21/03 and C-34/03, *Fabricom SA v. Belgian State*, delivered on 11 November 2004.
[71]   See case 103/88, *Fratelli Costanzo*, [1989] ECR 1839, paragraph 18; joint cases C285/99, and C286/99 *Lombardini and Mantovani*, [2001] ECR I9233; case 31/87, *Beentjes*, [1988] ECR 4635.
[72]   See case C208/98 *Berliner Kindl Brauerei*, [2000] ECR I1741; case C372/98, *Cooke*, [2000] ECR I8683; and case C341/01, *Plato Plastik Robert Frank*, [2004] ECR I-4673.

not distorted.[73] Consequently the Directives view the preparatory work of private undertakings prior to the tendering procedure for a public contract, not as ineligibility grounds for participating in the tendering procedures but as a condition to allow them to do so provided that competition amongst all potential tenderers is not distorted.

Since the Public Procurement Directives provide for discretion on the part of member states to implement in detail provisions at national level in relation to the award of public contracts, such discretion should be delimited by the objectives of the Directives themselves and also the general principles of Community law.[74] The freedom of member states to transpose the Public Procurement Directives in their domestic legal systems must always observe the principle of equal treatment, which implies an obligation of transparency as a means of verification of compliance with such principles.[75] Therefore, if national provisions seek to exclude an undertaking which has previously participated in the preparation of a public contract, such provisions attempt to safeguard the fundamental objective of effective competition in public procurement. The Advocate-General posed the same question at to whether such a national provision may at the same time serve the principle of equal treatment.

The Court has held that the equal treatment principle lies at the heart of the Public Procurement Directives.[76] Accordingly, the system whereby tenderers participate on an equal basis must provide that any undertaking that wishes to be awarded a public contract must be aware beforehand that participation in preparatory work for the contract in question may have the effect of excluding the undertaking from the tendering procedures. Consequently, account must be taken of the aim of guaranteeing effective competition and balancing compliance with the principle of equality. This is

---

[73]   See the 10th recital in the preamble to Directive 97/52 and the 13th recital in the preamble to Directive 98/4, which state that contracting authorities may request advice for the purpose of drawing up public contracts, provided that that does not distort competition. Directive 97/52 has amended the public supplies, works and services Directives respectively to take into account the obligations of the Government Procurement Agreement arising out of the WTO. Directive 98/4 amended the Utilities Directive to accommodate public contacts concluded within the framework of the WTO.

[74]   See joint cases 27/86 to 29/86, *CEI and Others*, [1987] ECR 3347, paragraph 15.

[75]   See case C275/98, *Unitron Scandinavia and 3-S*, [1999] ECR I8291, paragraph 31; *Telaustria and Telefonadress*, op. cit., paragraph 61; and case C59/00, *Vestergaard*, [2001] ECR I9505.

[76]   See case C-243/89, *Commission v. Denmark*, [1993] ECR I3353, paragraph 33.

where the Advocate-General positioned the principle of effective competition on an uncompromised pedestal within the public procurement acquis. He therefore considered that, first the principle of competition must be preserved, secondly, the equality principle must be complied with, and thirdly, the application of the above principles should be subject to the principle of proportionality.

He considered that any national provision ruling on the ineligibility of an undertaking which has previously participated in the preparation of a contract seeks to prevent a situation in which competition is distorted on the grounds of the information held by the undertaking as a result of its participation in the preparation of the contract in question. He held that it is virtually impossible to envisage any means of ensuring that the information and experience required during the preparatory stage will not provide an advantage on the part of an undertaking when that undertaking submits a tender for the same contract. The knowledge acquired by the undertaking is for the most part subjective, not demonstrable, and difficult to identify. Thus, in the interest of legal certainty, in the interest of transparency, and foremost in the interest of competition, it is necessary to prevent any possibility of a privileged position of an undertaking when participating in public procurement procedures. The Advocate-General took a different view from that of the Court and concluded that ineligibility of undertakings based on the need to preserve competition serves not only principles of Community law but also corresponds to an objective of general interest.[77] He concluded that the Public Procurement Directives do not preclude national rules which exclude undertakings which have previously assisted contracting authorities in the drafting of the specifications of a public contract.

Connection of Tenderers with Undertakings that Assisted in the Preparation of Tenders

Fabricom revealed another question as to whether a contracting authority is allowed to exclude a tenderer which appears to have connections with undertakings that have carried out certain preparatory works in the procurement procedures for the award of the relevant contract, even though, when questioned on that point by the contracting authority, the undertaking can prove that it has not obtained an unfair advantage capable of distorting the normal conditions of competition.[78]

---

[77]   See paragraph 44 of the Opinion of Advocate-General Léger in joint cases C-21/03 and C-34/03, *Fabricom SA v. Belgian State*, delivered on 11 November 2004; also case C-280/93, *Germany v. Council*, [1994] ECR I4973.

[78]   See joint cases C-21/03 and C-34/03, *Fabricom SA v. État Belge*, judgment of 3 March 2005, paragraph 41.

The provisions of the Belgian legislation provided that any undertaking connected with a person who has been instructed to carry out preparatory work in connection with the public contract in question may reverse the presumption that it has a competitive advantage by providing information on which it may be established that dominant influence has not affected the contract. However, the awarding authority is not subject to any time limits and may at any time, and thus up to the end of the award procedure, eliminate the undertaking on account of the unfair advantage which it is presumed to have gained, if the evidence provided by the undertaking is deemed insufficient. That meant that the undertaking concerned would be aware of its ineligibility at the same time as the contracting authority adopted a decision to award the contract. In such a situation, a connected undertaking is unable to obtain a declaration by a court, if necessary, that in the particular case the presumption of exclusion equivalent to a reduction in competition is inapplicable, before the contract is awarded. However, it follows from the Review Directive and the Court's case-law that the member states must ensure remedies whereby the procedure or decision to award the contract by the contracting authority can be suspended.[79] Therefore, the decision to exclude a connected undertaking must be notified before the decision awarding the public contract and such advance notice must be sufficient to enable that undertaking, if it considers it appropriate, to bring an action and have the exclusion decision annulled if the relevant conditions are met. By allowing the decision to be taken to eliminate a connected undertaking which wished to tender up to the end of the procedure for examination of the tenders, in such a manner that a review can be sought only at a stage when the infringements can no longer be rectified, as the public contract has been awarded in the meantime, and at a stage where the applicant is only able to obtain damages, the effectiveness of the Review Directive is severely compromised.

The Court held that the possibility that the contracting authority might delay, until the procedure has reached a very advanced stage, taking a decision as to whether an undertaking connected with a person who has carried out certain preparatory works may participate in the procedure or submit a tender, when that authority has before it all the information which it needs in order to take that decision, deprives that undertaking of the opportunity to rely on the Community rules on the award of public contracts as against the awarding authority for a period which is solely within that authority's discretion and which, where necessary, may be extended until a time when the infringements can no longer be usefully rectified. Such a situation is obviously contrary to public procurement acquis and capable of depriving the Public Procurement

---

[79]   See case C81/98, *Alcatel Austria and Others*, [1999] ECR I7671.

Directives and in particular the remedies Directives 89/665 and 92/13 of all practical effect, as they are susceptible to giving rise to an unjustified postponement of the possibility for those concerned to exercise the rights conferred on them by the Public Procurement Directives.

CONSORTIA AND GROUP PROCUREMENT

Groups of Economic Operators

Groups of economic operators may submit tenders or put themselves forward as candidates.[80] In order to submit a tender or a request to participate, these groups may not be required by the contracting authorities to assume a specific legal form; however, the group selected may be required to do so when it has been awarded the contract, to the extent that this change is necessary for the satisfactory performance of the contract.

Reliance of Tenderers on other Sources

The Court reiterated[81] that a service provider which, with a view to being admitted to participate in a tendering procedure, intends to rely on the resources of entities or undertakings with which it is directly or indirectly linked must establish that it actually has available to it the resources of those entities or undertakings which are necessary for the performance of the contract but which it does not itself own.[82]

Substitution of Consortia Members

National law[83] which precluded the substitution of a member of a consortium which has been awarded a public contract was at the heart of the question[84] referred to the Court as to the possibility of excluding a tenderer, in the form of a consortium, from award procedures for public works contracts. Such

---

[80]   Article 4(2) of the Public Sector Directive.
[81]   See case C-126/03, *Commission v. Germany*, judgment of 18 November 2004.
[82]   See case C-176/98, *Holst Italia*, [1999] ECR I-8607, paragraph 29; case C-399/98, *Ordine degli Architetti and Others*, [2001] ECR I-5409, paragraph 92; and case C-314/01, *Siemens and ARGE Telekom & Partner*, judgment of 18 March 2004, paragraph 44.
[83]   See Law No. 1418/1984 (23 A) on public works and related matters and Presidential Decree 609/1985 (223 A).
[84]   See case C-57/01, *Makedoniko Metro and Mikhaniki*, [2003] ECR I1091.

substitution, which is always subject to approval by the contracting authority, is provided for only at the stage when the works are being carried out, that is to say the phase which follows the signing of the contract between the contractor and the contracting authority and not at a stage prior to award of the contract.

The Greek Ministry for the Environment, Planning and Public Works issued a notice of an invitation to tender, announcing the first stage (pre-selection stage) of an international tendering procedure for the appointment of a contractor for the planning and construction, self-financing and operation of an underground railway for Thessaloniki. At that stage, the awarding body selected eight groups of companies which had declared an interest, including the appellant consortium. Subsequently, the bid documentation for the second stage of the tendering procedure was approved, including the supplementary notice and the contract specifications. At that stage technical proposals, financial studies and economic and financial proposals were submitted by, among others, the consortium Makedoniko Metro in its original form, and the consortium Thessaloniki Metro (Bouygues). At the pre-selection stage, the members of the initial Makedoniko consortium were the undertakings Mikhaniki AE, Fidel SpA, Edi-Sta-Edilizia Stradale SpA and Teknocenter-Centro Servizi Administrativi-SRL. In the second stage of the tendering procedure in question, that is, after the pre-selection stage and invitation to tender, the consortium was enlarged by the addition of the undertaking AEG Westinghouse Transport Systems GmbH. In that form, the consortium submitted a bid and under that composition it was nominated as provisional contractor.

After negotiations had commenced between the Greek authorities and the consortium in its enlarged format, Makedoniko Metro enlarged its composition by adding ABB Daimler-Benz Transportation (Deutschland) GmbH to its members. After two years of negotiations with the Greek authorities and responding to rumours that members of the Fidel Group of the consortium had become insolvent and gone into liquidation, Makedoniko Metro informed the Greek authorities of the situation and the change in its composition to include different members than those with which it qualified as provisional contractor and started negotiations (Mikhaniki AE, Adtranz and Transurb Consult).

The Minister for the Environment, Planning and Public Works, acting for the awarding authority, found that Makedoniko Metro had substantially departed from the provisions of the tender documentation, terminated the negotiations and having considered that the negotiations had failed, called for negotiations with the second consortium (Thessaloniki Metro Bouygues), which was the next candidate as provisional contractor. As a result, the Makedonico Metro appealed to the Greek Council of State and applied for the awarding authority's decision to break off negotiations to be set aside. The Council of State considered that a change in the composition of a consortium was only permissible prior to submission of bids. Thus, the consortium was not entitled, in its altered composition, to apply for the decision to be set aside. Also, in its action before the Administrative Court of First Instance, Athens, Makedoniko, together with the other undertakings in the consortium, sought a declaration that the state was liable to pay the sums specified in the statement of claim by way of damages and financial compensation for the non-material losses suffered by them as a result of the above unlawful act and omission. That claim was dismissed by the Administrative Court of First Instance, Athens, on the ground that, in the new composition in which the consortium had brought the action, it was not entitled to claim compensation. Makedoniko Metro appealed against the judgment to the Administrative Court of Appeal, Athens, claiming misinterpretation and misapplication of the relevant provisions in the judgment under appeal, asked that a reference for a preliminary ruling be made to the Court of Justice of the European Communities on the interpretation of the relevant Community provisions.

Makedoniko Metro argued that the enlargement of the consortium and subsequent substitution of one its members are typical events for a complex public works contract that takes a number of years to conclude and the latest change in the composition of the consortium was irrelevant to the ability of the consortium to perform the terms and condition of the contract. The change in the composition of the consortium should neither result in such a consortium losing its status as tenderer as a result, nor in the consortium or its members being deprived of their interest in the award or in the possibility of bringing an action to enforce the rights to which they are entitled under Community law. The Greek authorities, by excluding the consortium from further negotiations, had jeopardised its chances to win the contract and violated the Public Procurement Directives, as well as the principle of the freedom to provide services.

The Greek government maintained that the Public Procurement Directives are silent as to a change in the composition of a consortium. The national law did not permit a change in composition during negotiations with the tenderer which had provisionally been selected as contractor. The only subject for negotiations with the prospective successful contractor is the final terms of the contract to be awarded and not the identity of the contractor, which is not negotiable. Therefore, Greek law legitimately provided that the identity of a provisionally selected contractor may not change.

The Commission argued that the Works Directive contains no express provisions concerning a change in the composition of a consortium after the submission of tenders. Article 21 merely provides that groups of contractors which submit tenders may not be required to assume a specific legal form prior to the award. It is therefore left to the national legislature or the individual contracting authority, to regulate the details. This applies also to public works concessions. The Commission presumed that the principle of equal treatment of tenderers would be undermined if a contracting authority could, for the benefit of one tenderer, unilaterally change the terms which are fixed in the tender documentation as not being open to variation, without reopening the whole award procedure. This would otherwise prevent the other tenderers from benefiting from the change. Therefore, the Public Procurement Directives do not allow a public contracting authority to continue to negotiate with a bidder whose composition has changed, contrary to national law or to the terms of the contract documentation. However, the Commission considered that a change in the composition of a consortium that is in breach of national law or contract documentation does not affect the exercise of rights which the consortium could claim on the basis of the Legal Remedies Directive, in particular, the right to claim damages. Under Article 1(1) of the Remedies Directive, only infringements of Community law and national rules implementing that law may be reviewed. This provision does not, therefore, require member states to provide procedures to allow review of decisions which have been taken in the context of an award procedure and which infringe rules that do not implement the Public Procurement Directives.

The Court held that, in the context of Article 234 EC, it has no jurisdiction to rule either on the interpretation of provisions of national laws or regulations or on their conformity with Community law. It may, however, supply the national court with an interpretation of Community law that will enable that court to resolve the legal problem before it.[85] It is for the Court alone, where questions are formulated imprecisely, to extract from all the information provided by the national court and from the documents in the main proceedings the points of Community law which require interpretation, having regard to the subject-matter of those proceedings.[86]

The Greek government argued that under specific circumstances a contracting authority may refrain from awarding a contract.[87] The Court found such an argument weak as, in that case, the award procedure had ended without the contract being awarded, because the contracting authority had opted for a material other than that stipulated in the tender notice, which meant a change in the subject-matter of the contract. The Court maintained the discretion which underlies the implementation of the Public Procurement Directives and the relative freedom given to the member states. The remit of the Directives is

---

[85]   See case C-17/92, *Distribuidores Cinematográficos*, [1993] ECR I-2239, paragraph 8; case C-107/98, *Teckal*, [1999] ECR I-8121, paragraph 33.

[86]   See case C-168/95, *Arcaro*, [1996] ECR I-4705, paragraph 21, and case C-107/98, *Teckal*, [1999] ECR I-8121, paragraph 34.

[87]   See case C-27/98, *Fracasso and Leitschutz*, [1999] ECR I-5697.

to co-ordinate national procedures for the award of public works contracts and not the creation of a complete system of Community rules.[88]

The Court recognised that express rules on consortia are provided only in Article 21 of the Public Works Directive, which does not expressly regulate changes in the composition of a consortium. However, that provision deals only with specific legal problems in connection with consortia. It thus affords them the right to submit tenders. Further, whilst it prohibits any requirement that consortia assume a particular legal form for the purpose of tendering, it does permit such a requirement in the event of the award of a contract. Therefore, incomplete harmonisation and the existence of only selective rules on consortia leave member states free to regulate other related matters as they see fit in accordance with their internal legal systems. This includes rules as to the composition of a consortium, such as the legal consequences of changes in its composition.

However, the Court positioned two obstacles in the way of member states' freedom to implement aspects of public procurement law which have not been expressly provided for in the relevant Directives. The principles of transparency and competition as recognised by the Court underpin the entire public procurement acquis.[89] The Court has declared that the aim of the Directives is to abolish restrictions on the freedom of establishment and the freedom to provide services in respect of public works contracts in order to open up such contracts to genuine competition between undertakings in the member states.[90] The Court has also pronounced on the requirement that contracting authorities observe the principle of non-discrimination of tenderers, which equates to the principle of equal treatment.[91]

The Court has also stated that the prohibition of discrimination implies an obligation of transparency, as a means of verification of compliance in order to allow the contracting authority to ensure that the prohibition has been observed.[92] The Court suggested that even where the principle of equal treatment cannot be observed within the Public Procurement Directives, its surro-

---

[88]   See joint cases C-285/99 and C-286/99, *Impresa Lombardini*, [2001] ECR I-9233, paragraph 33.
[89]   See the preamble to the Public Works Directive 93/37, second and tenth recitals.
[90]   See joint cases C-285/99 and C-286/99, *Impresa Lombardini*, [2001] ECR I-9233, paragraph 34; see also case C-399/98, *Ordine degli Architetti*, [2001] ECR I-5409, paragraph 52.
[91]   See joint cases C-285/99 and C-286/99, *Impresa Lombardini*, [2001] ECR I-9233, paragraph 37.
[92]   See *Impresa Lombardini*, paragraph 38; see also case C-275/98, *Unitron Scandinavia and 3-S*, [1999] ECR I-8291, paragraph 31.

gate principle of equality, which is recognised as a general principle of European law, prevails.[93]

The Court found that the equal treatment obligation prescribed in the public procurement Directives, as well as the principle of equality, would be breached, however, if the contracting authority unilaterally departed from its own rules concerning changes in the composition of consortia, particularly if it were to negotiate with a tenderer whose tender did not match the terms advertised. To that extent, an infringement of Community law can flow from the infringement of a national prohibition.

The freedom and discretion of member states to implement public procurement law in their own legal systems is also curtailed by primary Community law, in particular the fundamental freedoms and the competition provisions addressed to the state, including legislation on state aid.[94] In this context, it must be generally noted that the fundamental freedoms do not prohibit only direct or indirect discrimination, but also rules applicable without distinction which disproportionately inhibit any of the fundamental freedoms. From the application of primary Community law to the public procurement acquis two further legal principles have emerged and developed in case-law.[95] First, the principles of equivalence according to which the rules of national law must not be less favourable than those of corresponding domestic provisions. Secondly, the principle of effectiveness which obliges member states not to make the exercise of rights conferred by the system of Community law virtually impossible or excessively difficult.

The Court examined the question referred to it by considering the relevant contract for the Thessaloniki metro as a public works contract and also as a concession contract. If the contract at issue were a public works contract within the meaning of Directive 93/37, the Court found that the Directive would apply as provided in Articles 4 to 6. The only provision of Directive 93/37 dealing with groups of contractors is Article 21. That is confined, first, to stating that tenders may be submitted by groups of contractors and, second, to preventing them from being required to assume a specific legal form before the contract has been awarded to the group selected. Article 21 makes no provision about the composition of such groups. Rules about their composition are thus a matter for the member states. The same is true *a fortiori* if the

---

[93]   See the Opinion of Advocate-General in case C57/01, *Makedoniko Metro and Mikhaniki*, [2003] ECR I1091, paragraph 65.

[94]   See case C-243/89, *Commission v. Denmark*, [1993] ECR I-3353, case C-328/96, *Commission v. Austria*, [1999] ECR I-7479, and case C-225/98, *Commission v. France*, [2000] ECR I-7445.

[95]   See cases C-261/95, *Palmisani*, [1997] ECR I-4025, paragraph 27, and C-453/99, *Courage*, [2001] ECR I-6297.

contract at issue in the main proceedings is a public works concession within the meaning of Directive 93/37. The Court concluded that from Article 3(1) of the Directive, Article 21 does not even apply to public works concessions. The Court held that Directive 93/37 does not preclude national rules which prohibit a change in the composition of a group of contractors taking part in a proce-dure for the award of a public works contract or a public works concession which occurs after submission of tenders.

The Court also reiterated that Article 1(1) of Directive 89/665 requires member states to take the measures necessary to ensure that, as regards contract award procedures falling within the scope of the relevant Community directives, decisions taken by the contracting authorities may be reviewed effectively and as rapidly as possible on the grounds that such decisions have infringed Community law in the field of public procurement or national rules implementing that law. The Court ruled that member states are also required, under Article 1(3), to ensure that the review procedures are available at least to any person having or having had an interest in obtaining a particular public supply or public works contract and who has been or risks being harmed by an alleged infringement.

The Court found that the Greek authorities legitimately considered that Makedoniko Metro had departed substantially from the requirements laid down for the contract and terminated negotiations with the consortium. For the purpose of ascertaining whether the exclusion decision is covered by the expression decisions taken by the contracting authorities in Article 1(1) of Directive 89/665, the Court reiterated that the term 'decisions taken by contracting authorities' encompasses decisions taken by contracting authori-ties which are made subject to the Community law rules on public contracts.[96] The Court extended the application of the general principles of Community law, and the principle of equal treatment in particular, to the public procure-ment procedures governing the award of public contracts[97] and thus, embraced by analogy a decision taken in the context of a procedure for the award of a public contract to fall within the public procurements Directives, even in the absence of express provisions stipulating its coverage. The Court also held that the national court should be empowered to decide issues of *locus standi* in accordance with prior examination of the factual circumstances of the case in question.

---

[96]   See case C-92/00, *Hospital Ingénieure*, [2002] ECR I-5553, paragraph 37.
[97]   See case C-324/98, *Telaustria and Telefonadress*, [2000] ECR I-10745, para-graph 60, and case C-92/00, *Hospital Ingénieure*, [2002] ECR I-5553, paragraph 47.

7. Public contracts in public sector procurement

TYPES AND CATEGORIES UNDER THE PUBLIC SECTOR DIRECTIVE

One of the most important ingredients for the applicability of the Public Sector Directive is the existence of a public contract. What determines the nature of a public contract is not the legal regime that governs its terms and conditions and the relations between the parties. The crucial characteristic of a public contract for the purpose of the Public Sector Directive is the make-up of the parties to that contract. More specifically, according to and for the purposes of the Public Sector Directive, public contracts[1] are contracts for pecuniary interest concluded in writing between one or more economic operators and one or more contracting authorities and having as their object the execution of works, the supply of products or the provision of services.

Public works contracts[2] are public contracts which have as their object either the execution or both the design and execution, of works, or the completion, by whatever means, of a work corresponding to the requirements specified by the contracting authority. A work means the outcome of building or civil engineering works taken as a whole, which is sufficient of itself to fulfil an economic or technical function.

Public supply contracts[3] are public contracts having as their object the purchase, lease, rental or hire purchase, with or without option to buy, of products. A public contract having as its object the supply of products and which also covers, as an incidental matter, placement and installation operations must be considered as a public supply contract.

Public service contracts[4] are public contracts other than public works or supply contracts having as their object the provision of services referred to in Annex II of the Directive. A public contract having as its object both products

---

[1]   Article 1(2)(a) of the Public Sector Directive.
[2]   Article 1(2)(b) of the Public Sector Directive.
[3]   See Article 1(2)(c) of the Public Sector Directive.
[4]   See Article 1(2)(d) of the Public Sector Directive.

and services within the meaning of Annex II must be considered as a 'public service contract' if the value of the services in question exceeds that of the products covered by the contract. The Directive stipulates specific arrangements[5] for public service contracts listed in Annex II A. These contracts must be awarded as any other public contract covered by the Directive and in particular in accordance with Articles 23 to 55. However, for contracts which have as their object services listed in Annex II B, the Directive is applicable only[6] with respect to the setting of technical specifications (Article 23) and the requirement to file a report to the Commission after the award of the contract (Article 35(4)). Mixed contracts,[7] including services listed in Annex II A and services listed in Annex II B, must be awarded as any other public contract covered by the Directive where the value of the services listed in Annex II A is greater than the value of the services listed in Annex II B. In the reverse scenario, contracts are awarded in accordance with Article 23 and Article 35(4) of the Directive. A public contract having as its object services within the meaning of Annex II and including activities within the meaning of Annex I that are only incidental to the principal object of the contract must be considered as a public service contract.

Public works concession[8] is a contract of the same type as a public works contract except for the fact that consideration of the works to be carried out consists either solely in the right to exploit the work or in this right together with payment.

Service concession[9] is a contract of the same type as a public service contract except for the fact that consideration of the provision of services consists either solely in the right to exploit the service or in this right together with payment.

A framework agreement[10] is an agreement between one or more contracting authorities and one or more economic operators, the purpose of which is to establish the terms governing contracts to be awarded during a given period, in particular with regard to price and, where appropriate, the quantity envisaged.

A dynamic purchasing system[11] is a completely electronic process for making commonly used purchases, the characteristics of which, as generally available on the market, meet the requirements of the contracting authority,

---

5   See Article 20 of the Directive.
6   See Article 21 of the Directive.
7   See Article 22 of the Directive.
8   See Article 1(3) of the Public Sector Directive.
9   See Article 1(4) of the Public Sector Directive.
10 See Article 1(5) of the Public Sector Directive.
11 See Article 1(6) of the Public Sector Directive.

which is limited in duration and open throughout its validity to any economic operator which satisfies the selection criteria and has submitted an indicative tender that complies with the specification.

An electronic auction[12] is a repetitive process involving an electronic device for the presentation of new prices, revised downwards, or new values concerning certain elements of tenders, which occurs after an initial full evaluation of the tenders, enabling them to be ranked using automatic evaluation methods. Consequently, certain service contracts and certain works contracts having as their subject-matter intellectual performances, such as the design of works, may not be the object of electronic auctions.

THE CONCEPT OF PUBLIC CONTRACTS FROM THE STANCE OF THE EUROPEAN COURT OF JUSTICE

The Notion of Public Service Concessions

The notion of a concession is based on the fact that no remuneration is paid by the granting entity to the concessionaire. The latter must therefore simply be given the right to economically exploit the concession, although this right may be accompanied by a requirement to pay some consideration to the grantor. The main distinctive feature of a concession includes three essential characteristics. First, the beneficiary of the service provided must be third parties rather than the awarding entity itself. Secondly, the subject of the service ceded must concern a matter which is in the public interest. Finally, the concessionaire must assume the economic risk related to the performance of the service at issue.[13]

The Community legislature has viewed the absence of, at least full, consideration passing from the granting entity to the concessionaire as constituting the essence of a concession. The Public Works Directive 93/37 defines a public works concession as a contract of the same type as public works contracts, except for the fact that consideration of the works to be carried out consists either solely in the right to exploit the construction or in this right together with payment.[14] The above characteristic represents a fundamental feature of a concession whose importance is not limited to those which are concerned with public works. This feature finds expression in the fact that the

---

[12]   See Article 1(7) of the Public Sector Directive.

[13]   See case C-324/98, *Telaustria Verlags GmbH and Telefonadress GmbH v. Post & Telekom Austria AG*, judgment of 18 May 2000.

[14]   See Article 1(d) of the Public Works Directive 93/37 and the fifth recital in the preamble to that Directive.

concessionaire itself must bear the principal, or at least the substantive, economic risk attaching to the performance of the service involved. If the national court is satisfied that the economic burden or risk has effectively been passed to the concessionaire by the grantor of the concession, then there must be a very strong presumption that the arrangement concluded between them amounts to a concession rather than a contract.

The single most important indication of whether economic risk is to be borne by the concessionaire will emerge from examining the nature of the exploitation in which the supposed concession requires it to engage. *Arnhem and Rheden* provides a strong indication that the Court views the requirement to exploit the right ceded in order to obtain remuneration as the core of what constitutes a genuine concession.[15] Thus, where, for example, the public authorities effectively guarantee to indemnify the concessionaire against future losses, or where there is no effective exploitation by the concessionaire of the service whose performance is ceded, the arrangement at issue could not amount to a concession.[16]

However, there is no overriding definition of a public services concession. *Lottomatica* and *Arnhem and Rheden* reveal that, where the remuneration is fixed or determinable, the arrangement should be viewed as contractual and falling, *prima facie*, within the scope of the relevant procurement directive. In *Lottomatica*, the Italian State had published a contract notice for the purported concession of the computerisation of the Italian Lotto and maintained that, as a concession to carry out a public service, it was not covered by the Public Supplies Directive 77/62. The Court rejected this argument and held that the introduction of the computerised system in question did not involve any transfer of responsibilities to the concessionaire in respect of the various operations inherent in the lottery and that it was common ground that the contract at issue related to the supply of an integrated computerised system, including in particular the supply of certain foods to the administration. The fact that the system was to become the property of the administration at the end of the contractual relationship with the tenderer was irrelevant, because the price for the supply took the form of an annual payment in proportion to revenue.

It is, therefore, necessary in each case to look at a number of factors which

---

[15]   See case C-360/96, *Arnhem and Rheden*, [1998] ECR I-6821, paragraph 25. The Court implicitly agreed with the view of the Advocate-General that an important feature of service concessions in the Community context is that the concessionaire automatically assumes the economic risk associated with the provision and management of the services that are the subject of the concession. See paragraph 26 of the Opinion provided by Advocate-General La Pergola.

[16]   See European Commission interpretative communication of Community law on public procurement concessions, OJ 2000 C 21, p. 2, footnote 10.

will indicate whether in reality the arrangement amounts to a written contract for a pecuniary interest in respect of the provision of services. In the case of a concession, the beneficiary of the service must be a third party unconnected with the contractual relationship[17] and the concessionaire must effectively obtain at least a significant proportion of its remuneration not from the granting entity but from the exploitation of the service. Therefore, a case-by-case approach should be adopted to the question of whether a contract amounts to a concession or a service contract which takes account of all indicative factors, the most important of which is whether the supposed concession amounts to a conferral of a right to exploit a particular service as well as the simultaneous transfer of a significant proportion of the risk associated with that transfer to the concessionaire. The likelihood that the concessionaire will be able beneficially to exploit the concession would not suffice to permit a national court or tribunal to conclude that there is no economic risk. A national court or tribunal would need to be satisfied to a high degree of probability that the possibility of loss was minimal or even non-existent.

However, the requirement that the service ceded must be of public interest is more complicated. Under Community law, the service that is the subject of a service concession must also be in the general interest, so that a public authority is institutionally responsible for providing it. The fact that a third party provides the service means that the concessionaire replaces the authority granting the concession in respect of its obligations to ensure that the service is provided for the community.[18] Nevertheless, *Data-processing* held that the development of the data-processing systems for the performance of certain public activities, as well as the supply of such systems, were not in themselves public service activities, although they enabled the authorities to carry out their duties.[19]

It appears that the supposed relevance of the general interest nature of the service that is the subject of the concession derives from the definition proposed by the Commission in both its initial and amended proposals for a procurement directive concerning public service contracts, where it referred, at Article 1(h) in both cases, to the transfer by an awarding authority of the execution of a service to the public lying within its responsibility.[20] Although it is likely that there will be a public interest in most of the services that are awarded under a public service concession arrangement between a contracting

---

17   See case C-360/96, *Arnhem and Rheden*, [1998] ECR I-6821, paragraph 26.
18   See case C-360/96, *Arnhem and Rheden*, [1998] ECR I-6821, paragraphs 26 to 28.
19   See case *Commission v. Italy (Data-processing)*, [1989] ECR 4035, paragraph 26.
20   See OJ 1991 C 23, p. 1 and OJ 1991 C 250, p. 4.

authority and a private or a public undertaking, the Court held that the notion of a service to the public under a public service concession arrangement should not be construed as the same as the notion of general interest[21] or as a service of general economic interest in the sense in which that notion has been interpreted for the purposes of applying Article 90 of the EC Treaty (now Article 86 EC).[22] It should rather refer to the fact that the typical intended beneficiaries of a genuine public service concession will be third-party members of the general public or a particular category of that general public.

The Exclusion of Public Service Concessions

The legislative history of the Public Services Directive 92/50, as well as consideration of the overall scope of all the Public Procurement Directives, reveals that the Council did not wish to include concessions within the material scope of the Community instruments on public procurement. The Council rejected the Commission's proposal to include concessions within the scope of Public Services Directive 92/50.[23] The initial rationale given by the Commission for their inclusion focused on a coherent regime between the public works and public services regimes so public service concessions should be covered equally by the Public Services Directive in the same way as public works concessions are regulated by the Public Works Directives. However, during the legislative process, the Council decided to eliminate all references to public service concessions from the proposal.[24] The Commission also failed

---

[21]   See case C-324/98, *Telaustria Verlags GmbH and Telefonadress GmbH v. Post & Telekom Austria AG*, judgment of 18 May 2000.

[22]   See case C-67/96, *Albany International v. Stichting Bedrijfspensioenfonds Textielindustrie* [1999] ECR I-4532, paragraphs 102 to 107.

[23]   See Proposal for Council Directive relating to the co-ordination of procedures on the award of public service contracts, COM (90) 372 final, OJ 1991 C 23, p. 1. Special rules dealing with the situation where a concessionaire is a contracting authority were set out in Article 3 of the proposal. See also the amended proposal for Council Directive relating to the co-ordination of procedures on the award of public service contracts, COM (91) 322 final, OJ 1991 C 250, p. 4.

[24]   See Document No. 4444-92-ADD-1 of 25 February 1992. The Council felt that the differences between the various national laws on such concessions were so great that the impact of adopting the proposal would not be the same in all member states. That opposition appears to have been motivated by the fact that in some member states concessions were only granted by public or administrative acts which would therefore have fallen outside the Commission's proposed definition, which was based on concessions being granted pursuant to consensual contracts governed by private law. This was recognised by the Commission itself in its communication to the European Parliament concerning the common position; see SEC (2) 406 final of 5 March 1992.

to include public service concessions in its proposal for the initial Utilities Directive 90/531, as well as the consolidated Utilities Directive 93/38.[25] The Council rejected such inclusion on the grounds that public service concessions in the water, gas and electricity sectors were not uniformly regulated in the member states.[26]

The Court has also explicitly recognised that public service concessions were not regulated by the Utilities Directives.[27] It also maintained that a literal interpretation of the notion of public service concessions would not permit written agreements, where the consideration is obtainable wholly by exploitation or partly by both exploitation and payment from the awarding entity, to fall within the scope of Public Procurement Directives. Even if the legislative history of public service concessions were to be overlooked, a contextual construction of the notion of *contracts for pecuniary interest concluded in writing*, which would be necessary to trigger the applicability of the Public Procurement Directives, would exclude concessions.[28]

However, public service concessions should not be viewed as falling outside the scope of European Union Law, although they are excluded from the public procurement rules. Even if public service concessions fall outside the scope of the Public Procurement Directives, the awarding authorities are bound to respect the Treaty and in particular Articles 52 and 59 of the EC Treaty (now, after amendment, Articles 43 EC and 49 EC) which preclude all direct and indirect discrimination based on nationality. In other words, contracting authorities must respect the principle of equal treatment between tenderers. They must also ensure that no conditions are imposed on the tenderer that would amount to an infringement of Article 30 of the EC Treaty (now, after amendment, Article 28 EC) on the principle of free movement of goods. Entities awarding public service concessions are also under a more general obligation, which appears to derive from the objectives underlying Articles 30, 52 and 59 of the EC Treaty, to ensure the transparency of the award procedures.[29] *Unitrans Scandinavia* concerned the obligations affecting a body other than a contracting authority, but upon which special or exclusive rights to engage in a public service activity have been granted by such an

---

[25]   See proposal for a Council Directive amending Directive 90/531/EEC on the procurement procedures of entities operating in the water, energy, transport and telecommunications sectors, COM (91) 347 final, OJ 1991 C 337, p. 1.
[26]   See point 10 of Council Document No. 5250/90 of 22 March 1990, MAP 7, PRO-COOP 28.
[27]   See case C-360/96, *Arnhem and Rheden*, [1998] ECR I-6821, paragraph 26.
[28]   See case C-324/98, *Telaustria Verlags GmbH and Telefonadress GmbH v. Post & Telekom Austria AG*, judgment of 18 May 2000.
[29]   See case C-275/98, *Unitrans Scandinavia and Others v. Ministeriet for Fødevarer, Landbrug og Fiskeri*, [1999] ECR I-564, paragraph 42.

authority, when that body awards public supply contracts to third parties. The Court held that the principle of non-discrimination on grounds of nationality cannot be interpreted restrictively and that principle implies, in particular, an obligation of transparency in order to enable the contracting authority to satisfy itself that it has been complied with.

The Court also considered that substantive compliance with the principle of non-discrimination on grounds of nationality requires that the award of concessions respect a minimum degree of publicity and transparency. However, the publicity and transparency requirements for the award of public service concessions should not necessarily be equated with publication.[30] Thus, if the awarding entity addresses itself directly to a number of potential tenderers, and assuming the latter are not all or nearly all undertakings having the same nationality as that entity, the requirement of transparency would be respected. Transparency, in this context, is therefore concerned with ensuring the fundamental fairness and openness of the award procedures, particularly as regards potential tenderers who are not established in the member state of the awarding authority. It does not however require the awarding entity to apply by analogy the provisions of the most relevant of the Public Procurement Directives.

Vertical Procurement

A functional approach to the concept of contracting authority under the Public Procurement Directives[31] might imply that the public procurement rules do not apply to a contracting authority which is a prospective supplier to another contracting authority. If a contracting authority, while trading as a supplier, subcontracts certain services to a third party, the selection of that subcontractor may well be based on non-economic considerations, and it is also quite possible that, at some stage in the process, public funds will be used.[32] The fact that the matter of the subcontracting does not fall within the remits of the activities of the contracting authority[33] and might also be subject to competition[34] is immaterial.

---

30   See case C-324/98, *Telaustria Verlags GmbH and Telefonadress GmbH v. Post & Telekom Austria AG*, judgment of 18 May 2000.

31   See case C-31/87, *Beentjes*, [1988] ECR 4635, paragraph 11; and case C-360/96, *BFI Holding*, [1998] ECR I-6821, paragraph 62.

32   See case C-126/03, *Commission of the European Communities v. Federal Republic of Germany*, judgment of 18 November 2004 and the Opinion of Advocate-General, paragraph 28.

33   See cases C-107/98, *Teckal*, [1999] ECR I-8121, and C-399/98, *Ordine degli Architetti and Others*, [2001] ECR I-5409.

34   See case C-360/96, *BFI Holding*, and joined cases C-223/99 and C-260/99, *Agorà and Excelsior*, [2001] ECR I-3605.

Mannesmann Anlagenbau Austria[35] made no distinction between public contracts awarded by a contracting authority for the purposes of fulfilling its task of meeting needs in the general interest, and those which are unrelated to that task. It is immaterial that the activity in question may be unrelated to the body's task in the general interest, or may not involve any public funds. Where, under the terms of the Public Procurement Directives, a body ranks as a contracting authority, the Directives require the conduct of award procedures. Accordingly that rule applies even where the contracting authority itself is trading as a supplier on the market, and subcontracting certain parts of a contract to a third party. It is, after all, entirely possible that non-economic considerations might be involved in the selection of a subcontractor, just as it is possible that public funds might be used in the course of the operation.

Contracting authorities are free to set up legally independent entities if they wish to offer services to third parties under normal market conditions. If such entities aim to make a profit, bear the losses related to the exercise of their activities, and perform no public tasks, they are not to be classified as public bodies and hence not as contracting authorities for the purposes of the Public Procurement Directives. Their activities will therefore not be subject to the provisions of the Public Procurement Directives. A body which aims to make a profit and bears the losses associated with the exercise of its activity will not normally become involved in an award procedure on conditions which are not economically justified.[36]

It could be argued that the Public Procurement Directives do not require 'tenders within tenders'. Article 7 of the Utilities Directive 93/38 excludes contracts awarded for the purposes of resale or hire to third parties from the scope of that Directive by virtue of the fact that the purchase of the goods occurs in principle in a context of free competition, and the ensuing commercial discipline prevents a contracting authority from favouring particular tenderers on non-economic grounds. However, this provision cannot be applied by analogy to supplies, works or services public procurement contracts, as the relevant provisions stipulated in the Public Supplies, Works and Services Directives respectively establish a dividing line between their regimes and the regime of the Utilities Directive[37] and do not extend the possibility of vertical procurement to contracting authorities in the public sector.[38]

---

[35] See case C-44/96 [1998] ECR I-73.

[36] See case C-18/01, *Korhonen and Others*, [2003] ECR I-5321, paragraph 51.

[37] See Article 1(a)(ii) of the Public Services Directive 92/50 and the equivalent Articles in Council Directive 93/36 co-ordinating procedures for the award of public supply contracts (OJ 1993 L 199, p. 1) and Directive 93/37 co-ordinating procedures for the award of public works contracts (OJ 1993 L 199, p. 54).

[38] See case C-126/03, *Commission of the European Communities v. Federal Republic of Germany*, judgment of 18 November 2004.

Subcontracting

A provision in an invitation to tender which prohibits recourse to subcontracting for material parts of the contract is contrary to the Public Procurement Directives.[39] On the contrary, all Directives envisage the possibility for a tenderer to subcontract a part of the contract to third parties, as that provision states that the contracting authority may ask that tenderer to indicate in its tender any share of the contract which it may intend to subcontract.[40] Furthermore, with regard to the qualitative selection criteria, all Public Procurement Directives make express provision for the possibility of providing evidence of the technical capacity of the service provider by means of an indication of the technicians or technical bodies involved, whether or not belonging directly to the undertaking of that service provider, and which the latter will have available to it, or by indicating the proportion of the contract which the service provider may intend to subcontract.

The Court ruled[41] that a tenderer cannot be eliminated from a procedure for the award of a public service contract solely on the ground that that party proposes, in order to carry out the contract, to use resources which are not its own but belong to one or more other entities. This means that it is permissible for a service provider which does not itself fulfil the minimum conditions required for participation in the procedure for the award of a public service contract to rely, *vis-à-vis* the contracting authority, on the standing of third parties upon whose resources it proposes to draw if it is awarded the contract. However, according to the Court, the onus rests on a service provider which relies on the resources of entities or undertakings with which it is directly or indirectly linked, with a view to being admitted to participate in a tendering procedure, to establish that it actually has available to it the resources of those entities or undertakings which it does not itself own and which are necessary for the performance of the contract.[42]

Nevertheless, the Public Procurement Directives do not preclude a prohibition or a restriction on the use of subcontracting for the performance of essential parts of the contract precisely in the case where the contracting authority has not been in a position to verify the technical and economic capacities of the subcontractors when examining the tenders.[43]

---

[39]   See case C-176/98, *Holst Italia*, [1999] ECR-I-8607.

[40]   See case C-314/01, *Siemens AG Österreich, ARGE Telekom & Partner and Hauptverband der österreichischen Sozialversicherungsträger*, judgment of 18 March 2004.

[41]   See case C-176/98, *Holst Italia*, [1999] ECR-I-8607, paragraphs 26 and 27.

[42]   See case C-176/98, *Holst Italia*, [1999] ECR-I-8607, paragraph 29.

[43]   See case C-314/01, *Siemens AG Österreich, ARGE Telekom & Partner and Hauptverband der österreichischen Sozialversicherungsträger*, judgment of 18 March 2004.

Public Contracts and State Aid

Preference schemes have been indissolubly linked with regional development policies, but their interpretation by the Court has always been restrictive.[44] It appears that the Court has experimented with the question of the compatibility between state aids and free movement of goods in a number of cases where, initially, it was held that the two regimes are mutually exclusive, to the extent that the principle of free movement of goods could not apply to measures relating to state aids.[45] The acid test for such mutual exclusivity was the prior notification of such measures to the European Commission. However, the Court departed from such a position, when it applied free movement of goods provisions to a number of cases concerning state aids, which had not been notified to the Commission.[46] Surprisingly, the Court also brought notified state aids measures under the remit of the provision of free movement of goods and reconsidered the whole framework of the mutual exclusivity of states aids and free movement of goods.[47]

Public Contracts Services of General Interest

State aids jurisprudence has revealed the catalytic position of public procurement in the process of determining whether subsidies or state financing of public services represent state aids. Public procurement rules have served as a yardstick to determine the nature of an undertaking in its contractual interface when delivering public services.

The application of the state aid approach creates a *lex and policy lacuna* in the treatment of funding of services of general economic interest and normal services. In fact, it presupposes that the services of general economic interest emerge in a different market, where the state and its emanations act in a public

---

[44]   See case 84/86, *Commission v. Hellenic Republic*, not reported; case C-21/88, *Dupont de Nemours Italiana SpA v. Unita Sanitaria Locale No. 2 di Carrara*, judgment of 20 March 1990, [1990] ECR 889; case C-351/88, *Lavatori Bruneau Slr v. Unita Sanitaria Locale RM/24 di Monterotondo*, judgment of 11 July 1991; case C-360/89, *Commission v. Italy*, [1992] ECR I 3401; case C-362/90, *Commission v. Italy*, judgment of 31 March 1992.

[45]   See case C-74/76, *Ianelli & Volpi Spa v. Ditta Paola Meroni*, [1977] 2 CMLR 688.

[46]   See case C-18/84, *Commission v. France*, 1985, ECR 1339; case 103/84, *Commission v. Italy*, 1986, ECR 1759; also, case C-244/81, *Commission v. Ireland*, 1982, ECR 4005.

[47]   See Bovis, 'Public procurement as an instrument of industrial policy in the European Union', chapter 7, in Lawton (ed), *Industrial Policy and Competitiveness in Europe*, Macmillan, 1998; Fernandez Martin and Stehmann, 'Product market integration versus regional cohesion in the Community', 16 (1991), *European Law Review.*

function. Such markets are not susceptible to the private operator principle[48] which has been relied upon by the Commission and the European Courts[49] to determine the borderline between market behaviour and state intervention. European jurisprudence distinguishes the economic nature of state intervention and the exercise of public powers. The application of the private operator principle is confined to the economic nature of state intervention[50] and is justified by the principle of equal treatment between the public and private sectors.[51] Such treatment requires that intervention by the state should not be subject to stricter rules than those applicable to private undertakings. The non-economic character of state intervention[52] renders immaterial the test of private operator, for the reason that profitability, and thus the *raison d'être* of the private investment, is not present. It follows that services of general

---

[48]   See the Communication of the Commission to the Member States concerning public authorities' holdings in company capital (*Bulletin EC* 9-1984, point 3.5.1). The Commission considers that such an investment is not aid where the public authorities effect it under the same conditions as a private investor operating under normal market economy conditions. See also Commission Communication to the Member States on the application of Articles 92 and 93 of the EEC Treaty and of Article 5 of Commission Directive 80/723/EEC to public undertakings in the manufacturing sector (OJ 1993 C 307, p. 3, point 11).

[49]   See in particular case 234/84, *Belgium v. Commission*, [1986] ECR 2263, paragraph 14; case C-142/87, *Belgium v. Commission ('Tubemeuse')*, [1990] ECR I-959, paragraph 26; and case C-305/89, *Italy v. Commission ('Alfa Romeo')*, [1991] ECR I-1603, paragraph 19.

[50]   For example where the public authorities contribute capital to an undertaking (case 234/84, *Belgium v. Commission*, [1986] ECR 2263; case C-142/87, *Belgium v. Commission*, [1990] ECR I-959; case C-305/89, *Italy v. Commission*, [1991] ECR I-1603), grant a loan to certain undertakings (case C-301/87, *France v. Commission*, [1990] ECR I-307; case T-16/96, *Cityflyer Express v. Commission*, [1998] ECR II-757), provide a state guarantee (joined cases T-204/97 and T-270/97, *EPAC v. Commission*, [2000] ECR II-2267), sell goods or services on the market (joined cases 67/85, 68/85 and 70/85, *Van der Kooy and Others v. Commission*, [1988] ECR 219; case C-56/93, *Belgium v. Commission*, [1996] ECR I-723; case C-39/94, *SFEI and Others*, [1996] ECR I-3547), or grant facilities for the payment of social security contributions (case C-256/97, *DM Transport*, [1999] ECR I-3913), or the repayment of wages (case C-342/96, *Spain v. Commission*, [1999] ECR I-2459).

[51]   See case C-303/88, *Italy v. Commission*, [1991] ECR I-1433, paragraph 20; case C-261/89, *Italy v. Commission*, [1991] ECR I-4437, paragraph 15; and case T-358/94, *Air France v. Commission* [1996] ECR II-2109, paragraph 70.

[52]   For example where the public authorities pay a subsidy directly to an undertaking (case 310/85, *Deufil v. Commission*, [1987] ECR 901), grant an exemption from tax (case C-387/92, *Banco Exterior*, [1994] ECR I-877; case C-6/97, *Italy v. Commission*, [1999] ECR I-2981; case C-156/98, *Germany v. Commission*, [2000] ECR I-6857) or agree to a reduction in social security contributions (case C-75/97, *Belgium v. Commission*, [1999] ECR I-3671; case T-67/94, *Ladbroke Racing v. Commission*, [1998] ECR II-1).

economic interest cannot be part of the same demand/supply equation, as with other normal services the state and its organs procure.[53] Along the above lines, a convergence emerges between public procurement jurisprudence and the state aid approach in the light of the reasoning behind the *BFI*[54] and *Agora*[55] cases. Services of general economic interest are *sui generis*, having as main characteristics the lack of industrial and commercial character, where the absence of profitability and competitiveness are indicative of the relevant market place. As a rule, the procurement of such services should be subject to the rigour and discipline of public procurement rules and analogously, classified as state aid, in the absence of the competitive award procedures. In consequence, the application of the public procurement regime reinforces the character of services of general interest as non-commercial or industrial and the existence of public markets.[56]

The compensation approach relies heavily upon the real advantage theory to determine the existence of any advantages conferred upon undertakings through state financing. Thus, the advantages given by public authorities that threaten to distort competition are examined together with the obligations on the recipient of the aid. Public advantages thus constitute aid only if their amount exceeds the value of the commitments the recipient enters into. The compensation approach treats the costs offsetting the provision of services of general interest as the baseline over which state aids should be considered. That baseline is determined by the market price, which corresponds to the given public/private contractual interface and is demonstrable through the application of public procurement award procedures. The real advantage theory runs contrary to the apparent advantage theory which underlines Treaty provisions[57] and the approach that relies on the economic effects and the

---

[53] See the analysis in joined cases C-278/92 to C-280/92, *Spain v. Commission*, [1994] ECR I-4103.

[54] See case C-360/96, *Gemeente Arnhem Gemeente Rheden v. BFI Holding BV*, op. cit.

[55] Cases C-223/99, *Agora Srl v. Ente Autonomo Fiera Internazionale di Milano* and C-260/99, *Excelsior Snc di Pedrotti Runa & C v. Ente Autonomo Fiera Internazionale di Milano*, op. cit.

[56] See Bazex, *Le droit public de la concurrence*, RFDA, 1998; Arcelin, *L'entreprise en droit interne et communautaire de la concurrence*, Paris, Litec, 2003; Guézou, *Droit de la concurrence et droit des marchés publics: vers une notion transverale de mise en libre concurrence*, Contrats Publics, March 2003.

[57] According to Advocate-General Léger in his Opinion on the *Altmark* case, the apparent advantage theory occurs in several provisions of the Treaty, in particular in Article 92(2) and (3), and in Article 77 of the EC Treaty (now Article 73 EC). Article 92(3) of the Treaty provides that aid may be regarded as compatible with the common market if it pursues certain objectives such as the strengthening of economic and social cohesion, the promotion of research and the protection of the environment.

nature of the measures in determining the existence of state aids. The borderline of the market price, which will form the conceptual base above which
state aids would appear, is not always easy to determine, even given the existence of public procurement procedures. The state and its organs as contracting authorities (state emanations and bodies governed by public law) have
wide discretion to award public contracts under the public procurement
rules.[58] Often, price plays a secondary role in the award criteria. In cases
where the public contract is awarded to the lowest price, the element of *market
price* under the compensation approach could be determined. However, when
the public contract is to be awarded by reference to the most economically
advantageous offer,[59] the market price may be totally different from the price
the contracting authority wishes to pay for the procurement of the relevant
services. The mere existence of public procurement procedures cannot, therefore, reveal the necessary element of the compensation approach: the market
price which will determine 'excessive' state intervention and introduce state
aids regulation.

---

[58]   According to Article 26 of Directive 93/36, Article 30 of Directive 93/37,
Article 34 of Directive 93/38 and Article 36 of Directive 92/50, two criteria provide the
conditions under which contracting authorities award public contracts: *the lowest price*
or the *most economically advantageous offer*. The first criterion indicates that, subject
to the qualitative criteria and financial and economic standing, contracting authorities
do not rely on any factor other than the price quoted to complete the contract. The
Directives provide for an automatic disqualification of an 'obviously abnormally low
offer'. The term has not been interpreted in detail by the Court and serves rather as an
indication of a 'lower bottom limit' for contracting authorities accepting offers from
private sector tenderers See case 76/81, *SA Transporoute et Travaux v. Minister of
Public Works*, [1982] ECR 457; case 103/88, *Fratelli Costanzo SpA v. Comune di
Milano*, [1989] ECR 1839; case 296/89, *Impresa Dona Alfonso di Dona Alfonso &
Figli snc v. Consorzio per lo Sviluppo Industriale del Comune di Monfalcone*, judgment of 18 June 1991. In case C-94/99, *ARGE Gewässerschutzt*, the Court ruled that
directly or indirectly subsidised tenders by the state or other contracting authorities or
even by the contracting authority itself can legitimately be part of the evaluation
process. It did not elaborate on the possibility of rejection of an offer, which is appreciably lower than those of unsubsidised tenderers by reference to the abnormally low
disqualification ground. See paragraphs 26 et seq. of the Court's judgment. Although
the case has relevance in the fields of selection and qualification procedures and award
criteria, the Court made no references to previous case-law regarding state aids in
public procurement, presumably because the *Dupont de Nemours* precedent is still
highly relevant.
[59]   The meaning of the most economically advantageous offer includes a series
of factors chosen by the contracting authority, including price, delivery or completion
date, running costs, cost-effectiveness, profitability, technical merit, product or work
quality, aesthetic and functional characteristics, after-sales service and technical assistance, commitments with regard to spare parts and components and maintenance costs,
security of supplies. The above list is not exhaustive.

An indication of the application of the compensation approach is reflected in the *Stohal*[60] case, where an undertaking could provide commercial services and services of general interest, without any relevance to the applicability of public procurement rules. The rationale of the case runs parallel with the real advantage theory, to the point of recognising the different nature and characteristics of the markets under which normal (commercial) services and services of general interest are provided. The distinction begins where, for the sake of legal certainty and legitimate expectation, the activities undertakings of dual capacity are equally covered by the public procurement regime and the undertaking in question is considered as *contracting authority* irrespective of any proportion or percentage between the delivery of commercial services and services of general interest. This finding might have a significant implication for the compensation approach in state aids jurisprudence: irrespective of any costs offsetting the costs related to the provision of general interest, the entire state financing could be viewed under the state aid approach.

Finally, the *quid pro quo* approach relies on the existence of a direct and manifest link between state financing and services of general interest, an existence indicated by the presence of a public contract concluded in accordance with the provisions of the Public Procurement Directives. Apart from the obvious criticism the *quid pro quo* approach has received, its interface with public procurement appears to be the most problematic facet in its application. The procurement of public services does not always reveal a public contract between a contracting authority and an undertaking.

Public Contracts and Needs in General Interest

Although the Public Procurement Directives do not define the term 'needs in the general interest' in a contract covered by their provisions, the term is an autonomous concept in Community law[61] and represents a notion which must be assessed independently without reference to the national legal systems of the member states. The Court declared that the term 'needs in the general interest' must be appraised objectively, without regard to the legal forms of the provisions in which those needs are mentioned.[62] Having regard to the principle of legal

---

60   C-44/96, *Mannesmann Anlangenbau Austria AG et al. v. Strohal Rotationsdurck GesmbH*, op. cit. See also the analysis of the case by Bovis, C., (1999) 'Redefining Contracting Authorities under the EC Public Procurement Directives: An Analysis of the Case C-44/96, *Mannesmann Anlangenban Austria AG et al., v. Strohal Rotationsdurck Gsmbh*', 39, *Common Market Law Review*, 205–25.

61   See case C-373/00, *Adolf Truley GmbH and Bestattung Wien GmbH*, [2003] ECR I-1931.

62   See case C-360/96, *Gemeente Arnhem Gemeente Rheden v. BFI Holding BV*, [1998] ECR 6821.

certainty, it would be unacceptable that the same activity may or may not be regarded as being in the general interest depending on the member state in which it is exercised. Terms of Community law must be interpreted by reference to national concepts only in those exceptional cases in which reference is expressly or implicitly made to definitions laid down by the legal systems of the member states.[63] The need for uniform application of Community law and the principle of equality require that the terms of a provision of Community law which makes no express reference to the law of the member states for the purpose of determining its meaning and scope must normally be given an autonomous and uniform interpretation throughout the Community. That interpretation must take into account the context of the provision and the purpose of the legislation in question.[64]

The Commission has taken the view that the term 'needs in the general interest' must be defined solely on the basis of national law. It is thus for each member state, when determining the aims of its public policy, to determine what constitutes general interest and, in each individual case, the legal and factual situation of the body concerned must be examined in order to assess whether or not there is a need in the general interest. For these purposes, the Commission relies on *Mannesmann Anlagenbau Austria*,[65] in which the Court based its finding that the Austrian State printing office was established for the purpose of meeting needs in the general interest, not having an industrial or commercial character, on the relevant national provisions and on *BFI Holding*, in which the Court ruled, on the basis of, in particular, the list set out in Annex I to Directive 93/37, that the removal and treatment of household refuse is one of the services which a member state may require to be carried out by public authorities or over which it wishes to retain a decisive influence.

The Court held that the absence of competition is not a condition which must necessarily be taken into account in defining a body governed by public law.[66] The requirement that there should be no private undertakings capable of meeting the needs for which the body financed by the state, regional or local authorities or other bodies governed by public law was set up would be liable to render meaningless the term 'body governed by public law'. However, the Court stated that the existence of competition is not entirely irrelevant to the question whether a need in the general interest is other than industrial or

---

[63]   See case C-327/82, *Ekro*, [1984] ECR 107 and case C-273/90, *Meico-Fell*, [1991] ECR I-5569.

[64]   See case C-287/98, *Linster and Others*, [2000] ECR I-6917, paragraph 43, and case C-357/98, *Yiadom*, [2000] ECR I-9265, paragraph 26.

[65]   See case C-44/96, *Mannesmann Anlangenbau Austria AG et al. v. Strohal Rotationsdurck GesmbH*, [1998] ECR 73.

[66]   See *BFI Holding*, case paragraph 47.

commercial. The existence of significant competition, and in particular the fact that the entity concerned is faced with competition in the market place, may be indicative of the absence of a need in the general interest not having an industrial or commercial character. The existence of significant competition is in itself not sufficient to justify the conclusion that there is no need in the general interest, not having an industrial or commercial character. The national court must assess whether or not there is such a need, taking account of all the relevant legal and factual circumstances, such as those prevailing at the time of establishment of the body concerned and the conditions under which it exercises its activity.

Public Contracts and the Financing of Public Services

There are three approaches under which the European judiciary and the Commission have examined the financing of public services: *the state aids approach, the compensation approach and the quid pro quo approach.* The above approaches reflect not only conceptual and procedural differences in the application of state aid control measures within the common market, but also raise imperative and multifaceted questions relevant to the state funding of services of general interest.

The state aids approach[67] examines state funding granted to an undertaking for the performance of obligations of general interest. It thus regards the relevant funding as state aid within the meaning of Article 87(1) EC[68] which may however be justified under Article 86(2) EC,[69] provided that the conditions of that derogation are fulfilled and, in particular, that the funding complies with the principle of proportionality. The state aids approach provides for the most clear and legally certain procedural and conceptual framework to regulate state aids, since it positions the European Commission in the centre of that framework.

---

[67] See case C-387/92 [1994] ECR I-877; case T-106/95, *FFSA and Others v. Commission,* [1997] ECR II-229; case C-174/97 P [1998] ECR I-1303; case T-46/97 [2000] ECR II-2125.

[68] Article 87(1) EC defines state aid as 'any aid granted by a Member State or through State resources in any form whatsoever which distorts or threatens to distort competition by favouring certain undertakings or the production of certain goods . . . , in so far as it affects trade between Member States'.

[69] Article 86(2) EC stipulates that '. . . Undertakings entrusted with the operation of services of general economic interest . . . shall be subject to the rules contained in this Treaty, in particular to the rules on competition, insofar as the application of such rules does not obstruct the performance, in law or in fact, of the particular tasks assigned to them. The development of trade must not be affected to such an extent as would be contrary to the interests of the Community'.

The compensation approach[70] reflects the fact that 'compensation' is intended to cover appropriate remuneration for the services provided or the costs of providing those services. Under that approach, state funding of services of general interest amounts to state aid within the meaning of Article 87(1) EC only if and to the extent that the economic advantage which it provides exceeds such appropriate remuneration or such additional costs. European jurisprudence considers that state aids exist only if, and to the extent that, the remuneration paid, when the state and its organs procure goods or services, exceeds the market price.

The *quid pro quo* approach distinguishes between two categories of state funding; in cases where there is a direct and manifest link between state financing and clearly defined public service obligations, any sums paid by the state would not constitute state aid within the meaning of the Treaty. On the other hand, where there is no such link or the public service obligations were not clearly defined, the sums paid by the public authorities would constitute state aids.

The State Aid Approach and Public Contracts

The application of the state aid approach creates a *lex and policy lacuna* in the treatment of funding of services of general economic interest and other services which is filled by the application of the public procurement regime. In fact, it presupposes that the delivery of services of general economic interest emerge and take place in a different market, where the state and its emanations act in a public function. Such markets are not susceptible to the private operator principle[71] which has been relied upon by the Commission and the European Courts[72] to determine the borderline between market behaviour and

---

[70]   See case 240/83 [1985] ECR 531; case C-53/00, judgment of 22 November 2001; case C-280/00, judgment of 24 July 2003.

[71]   See the Communication of the Commission to the Member States concerning public authorities' holdings in company capital (*Bulletin EC* 9-1984, point 3.5.1). The Commission considers that such an investment is not aid where the public authorities effect it under the same conditions as a private investor operating under normal market economy conditions. See also Commission Communication to the Member States on the application of Articles 92 and 93 of the EEC Treaty and of Article 5 of Commission Directive 80/723/EEC to public undertakings in the manufacturing sector (OJ 1993 C 307, p. 3, point 11).

[72]   See in particular case 234/84 *Belgium v. Commission*, [1986] ECR 2263, paragraph 14; case C-142/87, *Belgium v. Commission* (*'Tubemeuse'*), [1990] ECR I-959, paragraph 26; and case C-305/89, *Italy v. Commission* (*'Alfa Romeo'*), [1991] ECR I-1603, paragraph 19.

state intervention. The state aids approach runs parallel with the assumption that services of general interest emerge and their delivery takes place within distinctive markets, which bear little resemblance to private markets in terms of competitiveness, demand and supply substitutability, structure and even regulation.

European jurisprudence distinguishes between the economic nature of state intervention and the exercise of public powers.[73] The application of the private operator principle is confined to the economic nature of state intervention[74] and is justified by the principle of equal treatment between the public and private sectors.[75] That principle requires that intervention by the state should not be subject to stricter rules than those applicable to private undertakings. The non-economic character of state intervention[76] renders immaterial the test of private operator, for the reason that profitability, and thus the *raison d'être* of private investment, is not present.

It follows that services of general economic interest cannot be part of the same demand/supply equation, as other normal services the state and its organs procure.[77] Along the above lines, a convergence emerges between public procurement jurisprudence and the state aid approach in the light of the

---

[73]   See joined cases C-278/92 to C-280/92, *Spain v. Commission*, [1994] ECR I-4103.

[74]   For example where the public authorities contribute capital to an undertaking (case 234/84, *Belgium v. Commission*, [1986] ECR 2263; case C-142/87, *Belgium v. Commission*, [1990] ECR I-959; case C-305/89, *Italy v. Commission*, [1991] ECR I-1603), grant a loan to certain undertakings (case C-301/87, *France v. Commission*, [1990] ECR I-307; case T-16/96, *Cityflyer Express v. Commission*, [1998] ECR II-757), provide a state guarantee (joined cases T-204/97 and T-270/97, *EPAC v. Commission*, [2000] ECR II-2267), sell goods or services on the market (joined cases 67/85, 68/85 and 70/85, *Van der Kooy and Others v. Commission*, [1988] ECR 219; case C-56/93, *Belgium v. Commission*, [1996] ECR I-723; case C-39/94, *SFEI and Others*, [1996] ECR I-3547), or grant facilities for the payment of social security contributions (case C-256/97, *DM Transport*, [1999] ECR I-3913), or the repayment of wages (case C-342/96, *Spain v. Commission*, [1999] ECR I-2459).

[75]   See case C-303/88, *Italy v. Commission*, [1991] ECR I-1433, paragraph 20; case C-261/89, *Italy v. Commission*, [1991] ECR I-4437, paragraph 15; and case T-358/94, *Air France v. Commission*, [1996] ECR II-2109, paragraph 70.

[76]   For example where the public authorities pay a subsidy directly to an undertaking (case 310/85, *Deufil v. Commission*, [1987] ECR 901), grant an exemption from tax (case C-387/92, *Banco Exterior*, [1994] ECR I-877; case C-6/97, *Italy v. Commission*, [1999] ECR I-2981; case C-156/98, *Germany v. Commission*, [2000] ECR I-6857) or agree to a reduction in social security contributions (case C-75/97, *Belgium v. Commission*, [1999] ECR I-3671; case T-67/94, *Ladbroke Racing v. Commission*, [1998] ECR II-1)

[77]   See the analysis in joined cases C-278/92 to C-280/92, *Spain v. Commission*, [1994] ECR I-4103.

reasoning behind the *BFI*[78] and *Agora*[79] cases. Services of general economic interest are *sui generis*, having as main characteristics the lack of industrial and commercial character, where the absence of profitability and competitiveness are indicative of the relevant market place. As a rule, the procurement of such services should be subject to the rigour and discipline of public procurement rules and analogously, classified as state aid, in the absence of the competitive award procedures. In consequence, the application of the public procurement regime reinforces the character of services of general interest as non-commercial or industrial and the existence of *marchés publics*.[80]

Of interest is the latest case, *Chronopost*,[81] where the establishment and maintenance of a public postal network such as the one offered by the French La Poste to its subsidiary Chronopost was not considered as a 'market network'. The Court arrived at this reasoning by using a market analysis, which revealed that under normal conditions it would not have been rational to build up such a network with the considerable fixed costs necessary in order to provide third parties with the kind of assistance at issue in that case. Therefore the determination of a platform under which the normal remuneration of a private operator is incurred would have constituted an entirely hypothetical exercise. As the universal network offered by La Poste was not a 'market network', there were no specific and objective references available in order to establish what normal market conditions should be. On the one hand, there was only one single undertaking, that is, La Poste, that was capable of offering the services linked to its network and none of the competitors of *Chronopost* had ever sought access to the French Post Office's network. Consequently, objective and verifiable data on the price paid within the framework of a comparable commercial transaction did not exist. The Commission's solution of accepting a price that covered all the additional costs, fixed and variable, specifically incurred by La Poste in order to provide the logistical and commercial assistance, and an adequate part of the fixed costs associated with maintaining the public postal network, represented a sound way of

---

[78]   See case C-360/96, *Gemeente Arnhem Gemeente Rheden v. BFI Holding BV*, op. cit.

[79]   Cases C-223/99, *Agora Srl v. Ente Autonomo Fiera Internazionale di Milano* and C-260/99, *Excelsior Snc di Pedrotti Runa & C v. Ente Autonomo Fiera Internazionale di Milano*, op. cit.

[80]   See Bazex, *Le droit public de la concurrence*, RFDA, 1998; Arcelin, *L'entreprise en droit interne et communautaire de la concurrence*, Paris, Litec, 2003; Guézou, *Droit de la concurrence et droit des marchés publics: vers une notion transverale de mise en libre concurrence*, Contrats Publics, March 2003.

[81]   See joined cases C-83/01 P, C-93/01 P and C-94/01, *Chronopost and Others*, [2003], not yet reported; see also the earlier judgment of the CFI case T-613/97, *Ufex and Others v. Commission*, [2000] ECR II-4055.

excluding the existence of state aid within the meaning of Article 87(1) EC. The *Chronopost* ruling did not apply the private investor principle from state aids regulation, by indirectly accepting the state aids approach and therefore the existence of *sui generis* markets within which services of general interest emerge and are delivered and which cannot feasibly be compared with private ones.

The Compensation Approach and Public Contracts

The compensation approach relies heavily upon the real advantage theory to determine the existence of any advantages conferred upon undertakings through state financing.[82] Thus, under the real advantage theory, the advantages given by the public authorities that threaten to distort competition are examined together with the obligations on the recipient of the aid. Public advantages thus constitute aid only if their amount exceeds the value of the commitments the recipient enters into. The compensation approach treats the costs offsetting the provision of services of general interest as the baseline over which state aids should be considered. That baseline is determined by the market price, which corresponds to the given public/private contractual interface and is demonstrable through the application of public procurement award procedures. The application of the compensation approach reveals a significant insight into the financing of services of general interest. A quantitative distinction emerges, over and above which state aids exist. The compensation approach introduces an applicability threshold of state aids regulation, and that threshold is the perceived market price, terms and conditions for the delivery of the relevant services.

An indication of the application of the compensation approach is reflected in the *Stohal*[83] case, where an undertaking could provide commercial services and services of general interest, without any relevance to the applicability of public procurement rules. The rationale of the case runs parallel with the real advantage theory, up to the point of recognising the different nature and characteristics of the markets under which normal (commercial) services and services of general interest are provided. The distinction begins where, for the sake of legal certainty and legitimate expectation, the activities undertakings of dual capacity are equally covered by the public procurement regime and the undertaking in question is considered as *contracting authority* irrespective of

---

[82] See Evans, *European Community Law of State Aid*, Clarendon Press, Oxford, 1997.

[83] C-44/96, *Mannesmann Anlangenbau Austria AG et al. v. Strohal Rotationsdurck GesmbH*, op. cit. See also the analysis of the case by Bovis, in 36 CMLR (1999), 205–25.

any proportion or percentage between the delivery of commercial services and services of general interest. This finding might have a significant implication for the compensation approach in state aids jurisprudence: irrespective of any costs offsetting the costs related to the provision of general interest, the entire state financing could be viewed under the state aid approach.

Nevertheless, the real advantage theory upon which the compensation approach seems to rely runs contrary to the apparent advantage theory which underlines Treaty provisions[84] and the so-called 'effects approach'[85] adopted by the Court in determining the existence of state aids. The real advantage theory seems to underpin the *quid pro quo* approach and it also creates some conceptual difficulties in reconciling jurisprudential precedent in state aids regulation.

The *Quid Pro Quo* Approach and Public Contracts

The *quid pro quo* approach appears to define state aids no longer by reference solely to the effects of the measure, but by reference to criteria of a purely formal or procedural nature. This means that the existence of a procedural or a substantive link between the state and the service in question lifts the threat of state aids regulation, irrespective of any effect the state measure has on competition. However, the Court considers that to determine whether a state measure constitutes aid, only the effects of the measure are to be taken into consideration, whereas other elements[86] typifying a measure are not relevant during the stage of determining the existence of aid, because they are not liable to affect competition. However, the relevance of these elements may appear when an assessment of the compatibility of the aid[87] with the derogating provisions of the Treaty takes place.

---

[84] According to Advocate-General Léger in his Opinion on the *Altmark* case, the apparent advantage theory occurs in several provisions of the Treaty, in particular in Article 92(2) and (3), and in Article 77 of the EC Treaty (now Article 73 EC). Article 92(3) of the Treaty provides that aid may be regarded as compatible with the common market if it pursues certain objectives such as the strengthening of economic and social cohesion, the promotion of research and the protection of the environment.

[85] See case C-173/73, *Italy v. Commission*, [1974] ECR 709; *Deufil v. Commission*, [1987] ECR 901; case C-56/93, *Belgium v. Commission*, [1996] ECR I-723; case C-241/94, *France v. Commission*, [1996] ECR I-4551; case C-5/01, *Belgium v. Commission*, [2002] ECR I-3452.

[86] For example, the form in which the aid is granted, the legal status of the measure in national law, the fact that the measure is part of an aid scheme, the reasons for the measure, the objectives of the measure and the intentions of the public authorities and the recipient undertaking.

[87] For example, certain categories of aid are compatible with the common market on condition that they are employed through a specific format. See Commission notice 97/C 238/02 on Community guidelines on state aid for rescuing and restructuring firms in difficulty (OJ 1997 C 283).

The application of the *quid pro quo* approach amounts to introducing such elements into the actual definition of aid. The presence of a direct and manifest link between state funding and public service obligations amounts to the existence of a public service contract awarded after a public procurement procedure. In addition, the clear definition of public service obligations amounts to the existence of laws, regulations or contractual provisions which specify the nature and content of the undertaking's obligations. The borderline of the market price, which will form the conceptual base above which state aids would appear, is not always easy to determine, even with the presence of public procurement procedures. The state and its organs as contracting authorities (state emanations and bodies governed by public law) have wide discretion to award public contracts under the public procurement rules.[88] Often, price plays a secondary role in the award criteria. In cases when the public contract is awarded to the lowest price,[89] the element of *market price* under the compensation approach could be determined. However, when the public contract is to be awarded by reference to the most economically advantageous offer,[90] the market price might be totally different from the price the contracting authority wishes to pay for the procurement of the relevant services. The

---

[88] According to Article 26 of Directive 93/36, Article 30 of Directive 93/37, Article 34 of Directive 93/38 and Article 36 of Directive 92/50, two criteria provide the conditions under which contracting authorities award public contracts: *the lowest price* and the *most economically advantageous offer*. The first criterion indicates that, subject to the qualitative criteria and financial and economic standing, contracting authorities do not rely on any factor other than the price quoted to complete the contract. The Directives provide for the automatic disqualification of an 'obviously abnormally low offer'. The term has not been interpreted in detail by the Court and serves rather as an indication of a 'lower bottom limit' for contracting authorities accepting offers from private sector tenderers See case 76/81, *SA Transporoute et Travaux v. Minister of Public Works*, [1982] ECR 457; case 103/88, *Fratelli Costanzo SpA v. Comune di Milano*, [1989] ECR 1839; case 296/89, *Impresa Dona Alfonso di Dona Alfonso & Figli snc v. Consorzio per lo Sviluppo Industriale del Comune di Monfalcone*, judgment of 18 June 1991.

[89] An interesting view of the lowest price representing market value benchmarking is provided by case C-94/99, *ARGE Gewässerschutzt*, op. cit., where the Court ruled that directly or indirectly subsidised tenders by the state or other contracting authorities or even by the contracting authority itself can legitimately be part of the evaluation process, although it did not elaborate on the possibility of rejection of an offer which is appreciably lower than those of unsubsidised tenderers by reference to the abnormally low disqualification ground.

[90] The meaning of the most economically advantageous offer includes a series of factors chosen by the contracting authority, including price, delivery or completion date, running costs, cost-effectiveness, profitability, technical merit, product or work quality, aesthetic and functional characteristics, after-sales service and technical assistance, commitments with regard to spare parts and components and maintenance costs, security of supplies. The above list is not exhaustive.

mere existence of public procurement procedures cannot, therefore, reveal the necessary element of the compensation approach: the market price which will determine 'excessive' state intervention and introduce state aids regulation.

Finally, the *quid pro quo* approach relies on the existence of a direct and manifest link between state financing and services of general interest, an existence indicated by the presence of a public contract concluded in accordance with the provisions of the Public Procurement Directives. Apart from the criticism it has received concerning the introduction of elements into the assessment process of state aids, the interface of the *quid pro quo* approach with public procurement appears to be the most problematic facet in its application. The procurement of public services does not always reveal a public contract between a contracting authority and an undertaking.

The *quid pro quo* approach appears to define state aids no longer by reference solely to the effects of the measure, but by reference to criteria of a purely formal or procedural nature. This means that the existence of a procedural or substantive link between the state and the service in question lifts the threat of state aids regulation, irrespective of any effect the state measure has on competition. However, the Court considers that to determine whether a state measure constitutes aid, only the effects of the measure are to be taken into consideration, whereas other elements[91] typifying a measure are not relevant during the stage of determining the existence of aid, because they are not liable to affect competition. However, the relevance of these elements may appear when an assessment of the compatibility of the aid[92] with the derogating provisions of the Treaty takes place. The application of the *quid pro quo* approach amounts to introducing such elements into the actual definition of aid. Its first criterion suggests examining whether there is a direct and manifest link between state funding and the public service obligations. In practice, this amounts to requiring the existence of a public service contract awarded after a public procurement procedure. Similarly, the second criterion suggests examining whether the public service obligations are clearly defined. In practice, this amounts to verifying that there are laws, regulations or contractual provisions which specify the nature and content of the undertaking's obligations.

---

[91]   For example, the form in which the aid is granted, the legal status of the measure in national law, the fact that the measure is part of an aid scheme, the reasons for the measure, the objectives of the measure and the intentions of the public authorities and the recipient undertaking.

[92]   For example, certain categories of aid are compatible with the common market on condition that they are employed through a specific format. See Commission notice 97/C 238/02, OJ 1997 C 283 on Community guidelines on state aid for rescuing and restructuring firms in difficulty.

Although the public procurement regime embraces activities of the *state*, which covers central, regional, municipal and local government departments, as well as *bodies governed by public law*, and public utilities, in-house contracts are not subject to its coverage. The existence of dependency, in terms of overall control of an entity by the state or another contracting authority, renders the public procurement regime inapplicable. Dependency presupposes a control similar to that which the state of another contracting authority exercises over its own departments. The 'similarity' of control denotes lack of independence with regard to decision-making. The Court in *Teckal*,[93] concluded that a contract between a contracting authority and an entity, in which the former exercises a control similar to that which it exercises over its own departments and at the same time that entity carries out the essential part of its activities with the contracting authority, is not a public contract, irrespective of that entity being a contracting authority or not. The similarity of control as a reflection of dependency reveals another facet of the thrust of contracting authorities: the non-applicability of the public procurement rules for in-house relationships.

Similar arguments lead to contracts to affiliated undertakings escaping the applicability of the Directives. Article 6 of the Services Directive provides for the inapplicability of the Directive to service contracts which are awarded to an entity which is itself a contracting authority within the meaning of the Directive on the basis of an exclusive right which is granted to the contracting authority by a law, regulation or administrative provision of the member state in question. Article 13 of the Utilities Directive provides for the exclusion of certain contracts between contracting authorities and affiliated undertakings. For the purposes of Article 1(3) of the Utilities Directive, an affiliated undertaking is one the annual accounts of which are consolidated with those of the contracting entity in accordance with the requirements of the seventh Company Law Directive.[94] These are service contracts, which are awarded to a service-provider, which is affiliated to the contracting entity, and service contracts, which are awarded to a service-provider, which is affiliated to a contracting entity participating in a joint venture formed for the purpose of carrying out an activity covered by the Directive.[95]

---

[93] See case C-107/98, *Teckal Slr v. Comune di Viano*, judgment of 18 November 1999.

[94] See Council Directive 83/349, OJ 1983 L 193/1.

[95] The explanatory memorandum accompanying the text amending the Utilities Directive (COM (91) 347-SYN 36 1) states that this provision relates, in particular, to three types of service provision within groups. These categories, which may not or may not be distinct, are: the provision of common services such as accounting, recruitment and management; the provision of specialised services embodying the know-how of the

In addition, the connection between the state and entities which operate in the utilities sector and have been privatised is also too weak to sustain the presence of a public procurement contract for the delivery of services of general interest. Privatised utilities could, in principle, be excluded from the procurement rules when a genuinely competitive regime[96] within the relevant market structure ruled out purchasing patterns based on non-economic considerations.

The Altmark Case and its Impact on Public Contracts

The European Court of Justice and the Court of First Instance have approached the subject of financing services of general interest from different perspectives. These perspectives show a degree of inconsistency but they shed light on the demarcation of competitiveness and protection with respect to the financing of public services. Also, the inconsistent precedent has opened a most interesting debate focusing on the role and remit of the state within the common market and its relation with the provision and financing of services of general interest. The conceptual link between public procurement and the financing of services of general interest reveals the policy implications and the interplay of jurisprudence between public procurement and state aids. The three approaches used by the Courts to construct the premises upon which the funding of public service obligations, services of general interest, and services for the public at large could be regarded as state aids, utilise public procurement in different ways. On the one hand, under the state aids and compensation approaches, public procurement sanitises public subsidies as legitimate contributions towards public service obligations and services of general interest. From procedural and substantive viewpoints, the existence of public procurement award procedures, as well as the existence of a public contract between the state and an undertaking, reveal the necessary links between the markets where the state intervenes in order to provide services of general inter-

---

group; the provision of a specialised service to a joint venture. The exclusion from the provisions of the Directive is subject, however, to two conditions: the service-provider must be an undertaking affiliated to the contracting authority and, at least 80% of its average turnover within the European Community for the preceding three years should derive from the provision of the same or similar services to undertakings with which it is affiliated. The Commission is empowered to monitor the application of this Article and require the notification of the names of the undertakings concerned and the nature and value of the service contracts involved.

[96]   The determination of a genuinely competitive regime is left to the utilities operators themselves. See case, C 392/93, *The Queen and HM Treasury, ex parte British Telecommunications PLC*, OJ 1993 C 287/6. This is perhaps a first step towards self-regulation which could lead to the disengagement of the relevant contracting authorities from the public procurement regime.

est. In fact, both approaches accept the *sui generis* characteristics of public markets and the role the state and its organs play within such markets. On the other hand, the *quid pro quo* approach relies on public procurement to justify the clearly defined and manifest link between the funding and the delivery of a public service obligation. It assumes that without these procedural and substantive links between public services and their financing, the financing of public services is state aids.

In most cases, public procurement connects the activities of the state with the pursuit of public interest. The subject of public contracts and their respective financing relates primarily to services of general interest. Thus, public procurement indicates the necessary link between state financing and services of general interest, a link which takes state aids regulation out of the equation. The existence of public procurement and the subsequent contractual relations ensuing from the procedural interface between the public and private sectors neutralise state aids regulation. In principle, the financing of services of general interest, when channelled through public procurement, reflects market value. However, it should be maintained that the safeguards of public procurement reflecting genuine market positions are not robust and the foundations upon which a quantitative application of state aids regulation is based are not stable. The markets within which the services of general interest emerge and are delivered reveal little evidence of similarities and do not render meaningful any comparison with private markets, where competitiveness and substitutability of demand and supply feature. The approach adopted by the European judiciary indicates the presence of *marchés publics*, *sui generis* markets where the state intervenes in pursuit of public interest. State aids regulation could be applied, as a surrogate system of public procurement, to ensure that distortions of competition do not emerge as a result of the inappropriate financing of services.

However, the debate over the delineation between market forces and protection in the financing of public services took a twist. The Court in *Altmark*,[97] followed a hybrid approach between the compensation and the *quid pro quo* approaches. It ruled that where subsidies are regarded as compensation for the services provided by the recipient undertakings in order to discharge public service obligations, they do not constitute state aids. Nevertheless for the purpose of applying that criterion, national courts should ascertain that four conditions are satisfied: first, the recipient undertaking is actually required to discharge public service obligations and those obligations have been clearly defined; secondly, the parameters on the basis of which the compensation is calculated have been established beforehand in an objective

---

[97] See case C-280/00, *Altmark Trans GmbH, Regierungspräsidium Magdeburg et Nahverkehrsgesellschaft Altmark GmbH, Oberbundesanwalt beim Bundesverwaltungsgericht* (third party), judgment of 24 July 2003.

and transparent manner; thirdly, the compensation does not exceed what is necessary to cover all or part of the costs incurred in discharging the public service obligations, taking into account the relevant receipts and a reasonable profit for discharging those obligations; fourthly, where the undertaking which is to discharge public service obligations is not chosen in a public procurement procedure, the level of compensation needed has been determined on the basis of an analysis of the costs which a typical undertaking, well run and adequately provided with appropriate means so as to be able to meet the necessary public service requirements, would have incurred in discharging those obligations, taking into account the relevant receipts and a reasonable profit for discharging the obligations.

The first criterion, which requires the existence of a clear definition of the framework within which public service obligations and services of general interest have been entrusted to the beneficiary of compensatory payments, runs consistently with Article 86(2) EC jurisprudence, where an express act of the public authority to assign services of general economic interest[98] is required. However, the second criterion, which requires the establishment of the parameters on the basis of which compensation is calculated in an objective and transparent manner, departs from existing precedent,[99] as it establishes an *ex post* control mechanism by the member states and the European Commission. The third criterion that the compensation must not exceed what is necessary to cover the costs incurred in discharging services of general interest or public service obligations is compatible with the proportionality test applied in Article 86(2) EC. However, there is an inconsistency problem, as the European judiciary is rather unclear on the question of whether any compensation for public service obligations may comprise a profit element.[100]

---

[98]   See case 127/73 *BRT v. SABAM* [1974] ECR 313, para. 20; case 66/86 *Ahmed Saeed Flugreisen v. Commission* [1989] ECR 803, para. 55.

[99]   The standard assessment criterion applied under Article 86(2) EC only requires for the application of Article 87(1) EC to frustrate the performance of the particular public service task, allowing for the examination being conducted on an *ex post facto* basis. See also the ratione behind the so-called 'electricity judgments' of the ECJ of 23 October 1997; case C-157/94 *Commission v. Netherlands*, [1997] ECR I-5699; case C-158/94 *Commission v. Italy*, [1997] ECR I-5789; case C-159/94 *Commission v. France*, [1997] ECR I-5815 and C-160/94 *Commission v. Spain*, [1997] ECR I-5851; a great deal of controversy exists as to whether the material standard of the frustration of a public service task under Article 86(2) EC had lost its strictness. See Magiera, *Gefährdung der öffentlichen Daseinsvorsorge durch das EG-Beihilfenrecht?*, FS für Dietrich Rauschning 2000.

[100]   See Opinion of Advocate-General Lenz, delivered on 22 November 1984 in case 240/83, *Procureur de la République v. ADBHU*, [1985] ECR 531 (536). In his opinion, Advocate-General Lenz held that the indemnities granted must not exceed annual uncovered costs actually recorded by the undertaking, taking into account a

Finally, the fourth criterion, which establishes a comparison between the cost structures of the recipient on the one hand and of a private undertaking, well run and adequately equipped to fulfil public service tasks, in the absence of a public procurement procedure, inserts elements of subjectivity and uncertainty that will inevitably fuel more controversy.

The four conditions laid down in *Altmark* are ambiguous. In fact they represent the hybrid link between the compensation approach and the *quid pro quo* approach. The Court appears to accept unequivocally the parameters of the compensation approach (*sui generis* markets, remuneration over and above normal market prices for services of general interest), although the link between the services of general interest and their legitimate financing requires the presence of public procurement, as procedural verification of competitiveness and cost authentication of market prices. However, the application of the public procurement regime cannot always depict the true status of the market. Furthermore, the condition relating to the clear definition of an undertaking's character in receipt of subsidies to discharge public services in an objective and transparent manner, in conjunction with the costs attached to the provision of the relevant services, could give rise to major arguments across the legal and political systems in the common market. The interface between public and private sectors in relation to the delivery of public services is in an evolutionary state across the common market. Finally, the concept of 'reasonable profit' over and above the costs associated with the provision of services of general interest could complicate matters more, since they appear as elements of subjectivity and uncertainty.

The Demarcation of Public Service Contracts

A question often arises whether the purpose of a contract is relevant in determining the applicable regime and in particular, whether, for the award of a contract with a single object but which is composed of several services, those services must be classified individually in the categories provided for in Annex I A and I B to Directive 92/50 in order to determine the regime applicable to the contract in accordance with Articles 8 to 10 of the Directive, or whether on the contrary the main purpose of the contract must be identified, in which case the ancillary services are governed by the same regime as the

---

reasonable profit. However, the Court in the *ADBHU* case did not allow for the permissibility of taking into account such a profit element. Interestingly, the approach of the Court of First Instance on Article 86(2) EC has never allowed any profit element to be taken into account, but instead focused on whether without the compensation at issue being provided the fulfillment of the specific public service tasks would have been jeopardised.

service relating to the main purpose. The Court held that the determination of the regime applicable to public service contracts composed partly of services falling within Annex I A to Directive 92/50 and partly of services falling within Annex I B to the Directive does not depend on the main purpose of those contracts and is to be made in accordance with the unequivocal test laid down by Article 10 of that Directive.[101]

The 21st recital in the preamble to Directive 92/50 states that the application of its provisions in full must be limited, for a transitional period, to contracts for services where its provisions will enable the full potential for increased cross-border trade to be realised, the contracts for other services during that period being subject only to monitoring. To that end Directive 92/50 makes a distinction between contracts for services referred to in Annex I A, which under Article 8 are awarded in accordance with the provisions of Titles III to VI, and those for services referred to in Annex I B, which under Article 9 are subject to the provisions of Articles 14 and 16. In Article 10, Directive 92/50 also provides that contracts which have as their object services listed in both Annex I A and Annex I B are to be awarded in accordance with the provisions of Titles III to VI where the value of the services listed in Annex I A exceeds the value of the services listed in Annex I B, and where this is not the case only in accordance with Articles 14 and 16.

The argument that the main purpose of a contract determines the regime applicable to it cannot be accepted, according to the Court. The Public Services Directive does not contain any definition of what constitutes the main purpose of a contract, whilst Article 10 explicitly acknowledges, on the contrary, that a contract may have as its purpose the provision of different services falling under different annexes to the directive. In that respect, the Court in *Tögel* held that the references in the annexes to Directive 92/50 to the CPC nomenclature were binding. It is thus contrary to the purpose of the directive to classify a contract composed of several services, referred to in different sections of the CPC nomenclature, according to only one of those services. The judgment in *Gestion Hotelera Internacional*,[102] in which the Court laid down the principle that the main purpose of the contract determined which directive was applicable to a given contract, provides little support. *Gestion Hotelera Internacional* is rather irrelevant in determining the applicable regime within the Public Services Directive in so far as, first, its purpose was to determine whether a contract constituted a contract for works or a contract of another type, and secondly, the criterion adopted by the Court in that judg-

---

[101]   See case C-411/00, *Felix Swoboda GmbH v. Österreichische Nationalbank*, judgment of 14 November 2002.
[102]   See case C-331/92, *Gestion Hotelera Internacional SA v. Communidad Autonoma de Canarias*, [1994] ECR 1-1329.

ment was the merely incidental nature of repair work in relation to the main purpose of the contract based on the express definition of public works contracts in accordance with the Public Works Directives. If in the context of that judgment the Court had taken the view that the determining factor for distinguishing between contracts for works and contracts for services was the predominant nature of a service in terms of value, it would have clearly so ruled, referring to Article 10 of Directive 92/50 and not to the 16th recital in the preamble thereto, which provides that when those works are incidental rather than forming the object of a contract, they do not justify treating the contract as a public works contract.

It follows from those provisions that in the context of Directive 92/50 the argument that the main purpose of a contract determines the regime applicable to it cannot be accepted. First, Directive 92/50 itself states, in the seventh recital in the preamble, that for the application of procedural rules and for monitoring purposes the field of services is best described by subdividing it into categories corresponding to particular positions of a common classification, in this case the CPC nomenclature. In paragraph 37 of the judgment in *Tögel*, the Court held that the reference made in Annexes I A and I B to Directive 92/50 to the CPC nomenclature was binding. Secondly, Article 10 of Directive 92/50 provides an unequivocal test for the determination of the regime applicable to a contract composed of several services, which is based on comparison of the value of the services referred to in Annex I A to the directive with the value of the services referred to in Annex I B.

A further question arises whether in the award of a contract having one purpose but composed of several services, the classification of those services in Annexes I A and I B to Directive 92/50 deprives the directive of its effectiveness.[103] This question also leads to uncertainty over whether there is an obligation on the part of the contracting authority, if as a result of that classification, the value of the services falling within Annex I B exceeds that of the services falling within Annex I A, to separate the services referred to in Annex I B from the contract in question and to award separate contracts in respect of them. The Court maintained that for the award of a contract with a single object but which is composed of several services, the classification of those services in Annexes I A and I B of Directive 92/50, far from depriving the award process of its effectiveness, is in accordance with the system laid down by the Directive. When, following the classification made by reference to the CPC nomenclature, the value of the services falling within Annex I B exceeds the value of the services falling within Annex I A, there is no obligation on the

---

[103] See case C-411/00, *Felix Swoboda GmbH v. Österreichische Nationalbank*, judgment of 14 November 2002.

part of the contracting authority to separate from the contract in question the services referred to in Annex I B and to award separate contracts with respect to those services.

The classification of services in Annexes I A and I B to Directive 92/50, even in the context of a contract with a single object, is in accordance with the system provided for by the directive as it appears, *inter alia*, in the seventh and 21st recitals in the preamble and in Articles 8 and 10, which envisage the application of the directive on two levels. Directive 92/50 must be interpreted as in no way requiring the separate award of a contract for the services referred to in Annex I B thereto when, in accordance with the classification made by reference to CPC nomenclature, the value of those services exceeds, for the contract in question, the value of the services referred to in Annex I A. To require such a separation in that case would effectively deprive Article 10 of Directive 92/50 of any purpose.[104] Under the second sentence of Article 10 of the Directive, the contract is subject only to Articles 14 and 16.

It would be the same if the contracting authority artificially grouped in one contract services of different types without there being any link arising from a joint purpose or operation, with the sole purpose of increasing the proportion of services referred to in Annex I B to Directive 92/50 in the contract and thus of avoiding, by way of the second sentence of Article 10, the application of its provisions in full. Moreover, that conclusion is supported by the wording of Article 7(3) of Directive 92/50, from which it is clear that the choice of the valuation method is not to be made with the intention of avoiding the application of the directive. Although that article relates to a different situation (the artificial splitting up of the contract), the purpose which inspires it (the concern to avoid any risk of manipulation) also precludes a contracting authority from artificially grouping different services in the same contract solely in order to avoid the application in full of the directive to that contract.

The classification of services in Annexes I A and I B to Directive 92/50 is primarily a question of fact for the contracting authority to determine, subject to review by the national courts which eventually must decide the regime applicable to the contract forming the object of the procedure at issue in the main proceedings on the basis of Article 10 of Directive 92/50, in particular by verifying that the services which make up that contract and the reference numbers of the CPC nomenclature correspond. In any case, Category 20 of Annex I B to Directive 92/50 cannot be interpreted as also including land transport services themselves, as they are explicitly covered by Category 2 of Annex I A to the Directive.

---

[104]   See the Opinion of the Advocate-General, paragraph 55 in case C-411/00, *Felix Swoboda GmbH v. Österreichische Nationalbank*, judgment of 14 November 2002.

Inter-administrative Agreements as Public Contracts

Exclusion of agreements between legally distinct contracting authorities from the public procurement rules is contrary to the principles of the Directives.[105] In *Commission v. Spain*, national law excluded from its scope co-operation agreements concluded either between the general state administration and Social Security, autonomous communities, local bodies, their autonomous bodies and any other public body, or between public bodies themselves. The Spanish government maintained that inter-administrative agreements are the normal way for bodies governed by public law to establish relations between each other and asserted that those relations are marginal to the concept of a contract. Furthermore, it suggested that the principle enshrined in Article 6 of the Public Services Directive 92/50 is implicitly included in the other directives on public contracts. Article 6 of the Public Services Directive provides for the inapplicability of the Directive to service contracts which are awarded to an entity which is itself a contracting authority within the meaning of the Directive on the basis of an exclusive right which is granted to the contracting authority by a law, regulation or administrative provision of the member state in question.

The Commission argued that exclusion of inter-administrative agreements from the framework of the Public Procurement Directives constitutes an incorrect transposition of the Directives, as inter-administrative agreements are of the same kind as the public contracts covered by them and that this exclusion is not found in Directives 93/36 and 93/37. The Commission relied on the definition of a contract set out in Article 1(a) of Directives 93/36 and 93/37 and the case-law of the Court, according to which, in order to show the existence of a contract, it must be determined whether there has been an agreement between two separate persons.[106]

The Court held that, according to the definitions given in Article 1(a) of Directives 93/36 and 93/37, public supply or public works contracts are contracts for pecuniary interest concluded in writing between a supplier or a contractor and a contracting authority within the meaning of Article 1(b) of the directives, for the purchase of products or the performance of a certain type of works. In accordance with Article 1(a) of Directive 93/36, it is sufficient, in principle, if the contract was concluded between a local authority and a person legally distinct from it. The position can be otherwise only in the case where the local authority exercises over the person concerned a control which is similar to that which it exercises over its own departments and, at the same

---

[105]   See case C-84/03, *Commission of the European Communities v. Kingdom of Spain*, not yet reported.

[106]   See case C-107/98, *Teckal*, [1999] ECR I-8121, paragraph 49.

time, that person carries out the essential part of its activities with the controlling local authority or authorities.[107]

Having regard to the fact that the elements constituting the definition of a
contract in Directives 93/36 and 93/37 are identical, except for the purpose of
the contract in question, the approach adopted in *Teckal* must be applied to
inter-administrative agreements covered by Directive 93/37. Consequently, if
national law excludes, *a priori*, from the scope of the Public Procurement
Directives relations between public authorities, their public bodies and non-
commercial bodies governed by public law, whatever the nature of those relations, such law constitutes an incorrect transposition of Public Procurement
Directives 93/36 and 93/37.

---

[107]   See case C-107/98, *Teckal*, [1999] ECR I-8121, paragraph 50.

8. Contracting authorities in public sector procurement

THE PUBLIC NATURE OF CONTRACTING AUTHORITIES

The term contracting authorities means the state, regional or local authorities, bodies governed by public law, associations formed by one or several of such authorities or one or several of such bodies governed by public law.[1]

A body governed by public law means any organisation which satisfies the following conditions in a cumulative manner. First, the organisation must be established for the specific purpose of meeting needs in the general interest which do not have an industrial or commercial character; secondly, it must have legal personality; and thirdly, it must be financed, for the most part, by the state, regional or local authorities, or other bodies governed by public law. Alternatively and as part of the third criterion, a body governed by public law must be subject to management supervision by the state, regional or local authorities, or other bodies governed by public law or it must have an administrative, managerial or supervisory board, more than half of whose members are appointed by the state, regional or local authorities, or by other bodies governed by public law.

Non-exhaustive lists of bodies and categories of bodies governed by public law which fulfil the three cumulative criteria for a body governed by public law are set out in Annex III of the Directive. Member states must periodically notify the Commission of any changes to their lists of bodies and categories of bodies.

A central purchasing body is a contracting authority which acquires supplies or services which are intended for contracting authorities. It may also award public contracts or conclude framework agreements for works, supplies or services intended for contracting authorities.[2]

The remit and thrust of public procurement legislation relies heavily on the connection between contracting authorities and the state. Compliance procedures brought by the European Commission against member states are a good

---

[1]   See Article 1(9) of the Public Sector Directive.
[2]   See Article 1(10) of the Public Sector Directive.

way of determining contracting authorities under public procurement law. If the state can be held responsible under Article 169 EC (now Article 226 EC) for breaches of EC law committed by the central or local government, but also for breaches by other public entities and bodies over which it exercises a certain degree of control, that responsibility denotes a degree of connection between the state and the entities in question sufficient to characterise these entities as contracting authorities for the purposes of the Public Procurement Directives.[3] A comprehensive and clear definition of the term *contracting authorities*, a factor that determines the applicability of the relevant rules, is probably the most important element of the public procurement legal framework. The structure of the Directives is such as to embrace the purchasing behaviour of all entities which have a close connection with the state. These entities, although not formally part of the state, disperse public funds in pursuit or on behalf of the public interest. The Directives describe as contracting authorities the *state*, which covers central, regional, municipal and local government departments, as well as *bodies governed by public law*. Provision has also been made to cover entities which receive more than 50% subsidies by the state or other contracting authorities.

However, that connection might be too weak to cover entities which operate in the utilities sector and have been privatised. The *Foster* principle[4] established that state accountability could not embrace privatised enterprises.[5] The enactment of the Utilities Directives[6] brought under the procurement framework entities operating in the water, energy, transport and telecommunications sectors. A wide range of these entities are covered by the term *bodies governed by public law*, which is used by the Utilities Directives for the contracting entities operating in the relevant sectors.[7] Interestingly, another category of contracting authorities under the Utilities Directives includes *public undertakings*.[8] The term indicates any undertaking over which the state may exercise direct or indirect dominant influence by means of ownership, or by means of financial participation, or by means of laws and regulations, which govern the public undertaking's operation. Dominant influence can be exercised in the

---

[3]   See case 24/91, *Commission v. Kingdom of Spain*, [1994] CMLR 621; case 247/89, *Commission v. Portugal*, [1991] ECR I 3659.

[4]   See case 188/89, *Foster v. British Gas*, [1990] ECR-1313, in which the European Court of Justice ruled that a Directive capable of having direct effect could be invoked against a body which is subject to the *control* of the state and has been delegated special powers.

[5]   This was the view of Advocate-General Lenz in case 247/89, *Commission v. Portugal*, [1991] ECR I 3659.

[6]   EC Directive 90/531, as amended by EC Directive 93/38, OJ L 199.

[7]   See Article 1(1) of Directive 93/38.

[8]   See Article 1(2) of Directive 93/38.

form of a majority holding of the undertaking's subscribed capital, in the form of majority controlling of the undertaking's issued shares, or, finally, in the form of the right to appoint the majority of the undertaking's management board. Public undertakings cover utilities operators which have been granted exclusive rights of exploitation of a service. Irrespective of their ownership, they are subject to the Utilities Directive inasmuch as the *exclusivity* of their operation precludes other entities from entering the relevant market under substantially the same competitive conditions. Privatised utilities could, in principle, be excluded from the procurement rules when a genuinely competitive regime within the relevant market structure ruled out purchasing patterns based on non-economic considerations. The determination of a genuinely competitive regime is left to the utilities operators themselves. This is perhaps a first step towards self-regulation, which could lead to the disengagement of the relevant contracting authorities from the public procurement regime.[9]

THE CONCEPT OF CONTRACTING AUTHORITIES FROM THE STANCE OF THE EUROPEAN COURT OF JUSTICE

The Functional Dimension of Contracting Authorities

Although the term contracting authorities appears rigorous and well defined, public interest functions are dispersed through a range of organisations which *stricto sensu* could not fall under the ambit of the term 'contracting authorities', since they are not formally part of the state, nor are all criteria for the definition of bodies governed by public law present. This is particularly the case with non-governmental organisations (NGOs) which operate under the auspices of the central or local government and are responsible for public interest functions.[10] The Court addressed the *lex lacuna* through its landmark case *Beentjes*.[11] The Court diluted the rigorous definition of contracting authorities for the purposes of public procurement law, by introducing a *functional dimension* to the state and its organs. In particular, it considered that a *local land consolidation committee* with no legal personality, but with its functions and compositions specifically governed by legislation, to be part of the

---

9 See case C-392/93, *The Queen and HM Treasury, ex parte British Telecommunications PLC*, OJ 1993, C 287/6.

10 See Bovis, 'Public entities awarding procurement contracts under the framework of EC Public Procurement Directives', *Journal of Business Law*, 1 (1993), 56–78.

11 Case 31/87, *Gebroeders Beentjes BV v. State of Netherlands*, [1988] ECR 4635.

state. The Court interpreted the term 'contracting authorities' in *functional terms* and considered the local land consolidation committee, which depended on the relevant public authorities for the appointment of its members, its operations being subject to their supervision and having as its main task the financing and award of public works contracts, as falling within the notion of state, even though it was not part of the state administration in *formal terms*.[12] The Court held that the aim of the public procurement rules, as well as the attainment of freedom of establishment and freedom to provide services would be jeopardised, if the public procurement provisions were to be held inapplicable, solely because entities which were set up by the state to carry out tasks entrusted to it by legislation were not formally part of its administrative organisation.

The Court in two recent cases applied the functionality test, when requested to determine the nature of entities which could not meet the criteria of bodies governed by public law, but with a distinctive public interest remit. In *Teoranta*,[13] a private company established according to national legislation to carry out the business of forestry and related activities was deemed as falling within the notion of the state. The company was set up by the state and was entrusted with specific tasks of public interest, such as managing national forests and woodland industries, as well as providing recreation, sporting, educational, scientific and cultural facilities. It was also under decisive administrative, financial and management control by the state, although the day-to-day operations were left entirely to its board. The Court accepted that since the state had at least indirect control over *Teoranta's* policies, in functional terms the latter was part of the state. In the *Vlaamese Raad*,[14] the Flemish parliament of the Belgian federal system was considered part of the 'federal' state. The Court held that the definition of the state encompasses all bodies which exercise legislative, executive and judicial powers, at both regional and federal levels. The Raad, as a legislative body of the Belgian state, although not under its direct control, was held as falling within the definition of the state and thus was regarded as a contracting authority. The fact that the Belgian government did not, at the time, exercise any direct or indirect control relating to procurement policies over the Vlaamese Raad was considered immaterial on the

---

[12]   The formality test and the relation between the state and entities under its control was established in cases C-249/81, *Commission v. Ireland*, [1982] ECR 4005; C-36/74, *Walrave and Koch v. Association Union Cycliste International et al.*, (1974) ECR 1423.

[13]   See cases C-353/96, *Commission v. Ireland* and C-306/97, *Connemara Machine Turf Co Ltd v. Coillte Teoranta*, judgment of 17 December 1998.

[14]   See case C-323/96, *Commission v. Kingdom of Belgium*, judgment of 17 September 1998.

grounds that a state cannot rely on its own legal system to justify non-compliance with EC law and particular Directives.[15]

The functional dimension of contracting authorities has exposed the Court's departure from the formality test, which has rigidly positioned an entity under state control on *stricto sensu* traditional public law grounds. Functionality, as an ingredient in assessing the relationship between an entity and the state, demonstrates, in addition to the elements of management or financial control, the importance of constituent factors such as the intention and purpose of establishment of the entity in question. Functionality depicts a flexible approach to the applicability of the procurement Directives, in that the Court through its precedence has established a pragmatic approach to the nature of the demand side of the public procurement equation.

Bodies Governed by Public Law

The above category is subject to a set of cumulative criteria[16] in order to be classified as contracting authorities for the purposes of the Directives. In particular, *bodies governed by public law* (i) must be established for the specific purpose of meeting needs in the general public interest not having an industrial or commercial character; (ii) they must have legal personality; and (iii) they must be financed, for the most part, by either the state, or regional or local authorities, or other bodies governed by public law; or subject to management supervision by these bodies, or having an administrative or supervisory board, more than half of whose members are appointed by the state, regional or local authorities or by other bodies governed by public law. There is a list of such bodies in Annex I of Directive 93/37 which is not exhaustive, in the sense that member states are under an obligation to notify the Commission of any changes to that list. The term 'bodies governed by public law' provided the Court with the opportunity to elaborate on each of the cumulative criteria and shed light on their constituent elements. The Court's jurisprudence has revealed the following thematic areas.

The Dependency Test for Bodies Governed by Public Law

To assess the existence of the third criterion of bodies governed by public law, the Court assumed that these bodies are closely dependent on the state, in terms of corporate governance, management supervision and financing.[17]

---

[15] For a similar approach, see also case C-144/97, *Commission v. France*, [1998] ECR 1-613.
[16] See Article 1(b) of Directive 93/37.
[17] This type of dependency resembles the Court's definition in its ruling on state-

These dependency features are alternative, thus the existence of one satisfies the third criterion. The Court held in *OPAC*[18] that management supervision by the state or other contracting authorities entails not only administrative verification of legality or appropriate use of funds or exceptional control measures, but the conferring of significant influence over management policy, such as the narrowly circumscribed remit of activities, the supervision of compliance, as well as overall administrative supervision. Of interest and highly relevant is the Court's analysis and argumentation relating to the requirements of management supervision by the state and other public bodies, where it maintained that entities entrusted to provide social housing in France are deemed to be bodies governed by public law, thus covered by the Public Procurement Directives.

The Court (and the Advocate-General) drew an analogy amongst the dependency features of bodies governed by public law on the state. Although the corporate governance and financing feature are quantitative (the state must appoint more than half of the members of the managerial or supervisory board or it must mostly finance the entity in question), the exercise of management supervision is qualitative. The Court held that management supervision by the state denotes dependency ties similar to the financing or governance control of the entity concerned.

Receiving public funds from the state or a contracting authority is an indication that an entity could be a body governed by public law. However, this indication is not an absolute. The Court, in the *University of Cambridge* case,[19] was asked whether (i) awards or grants paid by one or more contracting authorities for the support of research work; (ii) consideration paid by one or more contracting authorities for the supply of services comprising research work; (iii) consideration paid by one or more contracting authorities for the supply of other services, such as consultancy or the organisation of conferences; and (iv) student grants paid by local education authorities to universities in respect of tuition for named students constitute public financing for the University.

The Court held that only specific payments made to an entity by the state or other public authorities have the effect of creating or reinforcing a specific relationship or subordination and dependency. The funding of an entity within a framework of general considerations indicates that the entity has close dependency links with the state or other contracting authorities. Thus, funding

---

controlled enterprises in case 152/84, *Marshall v. Southampton and South West Hampshire Area Health Authority*, [1986] ECR 723.

[18]   See case C-237/99, *Commission v. France*, judgment of 1 February 2001.

[19]   See case C-380/98, *The Queen and HM Treasury, ex parte University of Cambridge*, judgment of 3 October 2000.

received in the form of grants or awards paid by the state or other contracting authorities, as well as funding received in the form of student grants for tuition fees for named students, constitutes public financing. The rationale for such an approach lies in the lack of any contractual consideration between the entity receiving the funding and the state or other contracting authorities which provide it, in the context of the entity's public interest activities. The Court drew an analogy with public financing received by an entity in receipt of subsidies.[20] However, if there is a specific consideration for the state to finance an entity, such as a contractual nexus, the Court suggested that the dependency ties are not sufficiently close to merit the entity financed by the state meeting the third criterion of the term 'bodies governed by public law'. Such a relationship is analogous to the dependency that exists in normal commercial relations formed by reciprocal contracts which have been negotiated freely between the parties. Therefore, funding received by Cambridge University for the supply of services for research work, or consultancies, or conference organisation cannot be deemed as public financing. The existence of a contract between the parties, apart from the specific considerations for funding, strongly indicates supply substitutability, in the sense that the entity receiving the funding faces competition in the relevant markets.

The Court stipulated that the proportion of public finances received by an entity, as one of the alternative features of the third criterion of the term 'bodies governed by public law', must exceed 50% to enable it to meet that criterion. For the purposes of assessment, there must be an annual evaluation of the (financial) status of an entity for the purposes of being regarded as a contracting authority.

Dependency, in terms of overall control of an entity by the state or another contracting authority, presupposes control similar to that which the state or another contracting authority exercises over its own departments. The 'similarity' of control denotes lack of independence with regard to decision-making. The Court in *Teckal*,[21] concluded that a contract between a contracting authority and an entity, in which the former exercises a control similar to that which it exercises over its own departments and at the same time where the entity carries out the essential part of its activities with the contracting authority, is not a public contract, irrespective of that entity being a contracting authority or not. The similarity of control as a reflection of dependency reveals another facet of the thrust of contracting authorities: the non-applicability of the public procurement rules for in-house relationships.

---

[20] See paragraph 25 of the Court's judgment as well as the Opinion of the Advocate-General, in paragraph 46.

[21] See case C-107/98, *Teckal Slr v. Comune di Viano*, judgment of 18 November 1999.

Management Supervision of Bodies Governed by Public Law

The close dependency of a body governed by public law on the state, regional or local authorities or other bodies governed by public law is recognised in the case-law of the Court.[22] More specifically, as regards the criterion of management supervision, the Court has held that that supervision must give rise to dependence on the public authorities equivalent to that which exists where one of the other alternative criteria is fulfilled, namely where the body in question is financed, for the most part, by the public authorities or where the latter appoint more than half of the members of its administrative, managerial or supervisory organs, enabling the public authorities to influence their decisions in relation to public contracts.[23]

The criterion of managerial supervision cannot be regarded as being satisfied in the case of mere review since, by definition, such supervision does not enable the public authorities to influence the decisions of the body in question in relation to public contracts. That criterion is, however, satisfied where the public authorities supervise not only the annual accounts of the body concerned but also its conduct from the point of view of proper accounting, regularity, economy, efficiency and expediency and where those public authorities are authorised to inspect the business premises and facilities of that body and to report the results of those inspections to a regional authority which holds, through another company, all the shares in the body in question.[24]

Commerciality and Needs in the General Interest and Bodies Governed by Public Law

Commerciality and its relationship with needs in the general interest is perhaps the most important theme that has emerged from the Court's jurisprudence in relation to the remit of bodies governed by public law as contracting authorities. In fact the theme sets out to explore the interface between profit-making and public interest, as features which underpin the activities of bodies governed by public law.

The criterion of the specific establishment of an entity to meet needs in the general interest which have non-commercial or industrial character has

---

[22]   See case C-380/98, *The Queen and HM Treasury, ex parte University of Cambridge*, [2000] ECR 8035, paragraph 20, and case C-237/99, *Commission v. France*, [2001] ECR 934, paragraph 44.

[23]   See case C-237/99, *Commission v. France*, paragraphs 48 and 49.

[24]   See case C-373/00, *Adolf Truley GmbH and Bestattung Wien GmbH*, [2003] ECR I-1931.

attracted the attention of the Court in some landmark cases.[25] The above criterion appears as the first of the three cumulative criteria for bodies governed by public law. The Court drew its experience from jurisprudence in the public undertakings field as well as case-law relating to public order to define the term *needs in the general interest.*[26] The Court approached the above concept by a direct analogy with the concept 'general economic interest', as defined in Article 90(2) EC.[27] The concept 'general interest' denotes the requirements of a community (local or national) in its entirety, which should not overlap with the specific or exclusive interest of a clearly determined person or group of persons.[28] However, the problematic concept of the *specificity* of the establishment of the body in question was approached by reference to the reasons and the objectives behind its establishment. Specificity of the purpose of an establishment does not mean exclusivity, in the sense that other types of activities can be carried out without escaping classification as a body governed by public law.[29]

On the other hand, the requirement of the non-commercial or industrial character of needs in the general interest has raised some difficulties. The Court had recourse to case-law and legal precedence relating to public undertakings, where the nature of industrial and commercial activities of private or public undertakings was defined.[30] The industrial or commercial character of an organisation greatly depends upon a number of criteria that reveal the thrust behind the organisation's participation in the relevant market. The state and its organs may act either by exercising public powers or by carrying out economic activities of an industrial or commercial nature by offering goods and services on the market. The key issue is the organisation's intention to achieve profitability and pursue its objectives through a spectrum of commercially motivated decisions. The distinction between the range of activities which relate to

---

[25]   See cases C-223/99, *Agora Srl v. Ente Autonomo Fiera Internazionale di Milano,* and C-260/99, *Excelsior Snc di Pedrotti runa & C v. Ente Autonomo Fiera Internazionale di Milano,* judgment of 10 May 2001; C-360/96, *Gemeente Arnhem Gemeente Rheden v. BFI Holding BV,* judgment of 10 November 1998. C-44/96, *Mannesmann Anlangenbau Austria AG et al. v. Strohal Rotationsdurck GesmbH,* judgment of 15 January 1998.

[26]   See the Opinion of Advocate-General Léger, point 65 of the *Strohal* case.

[27]   See case C-179/90, *Merci Convenzionali Porto di Genova,* [1991] ECR 1-5889; General economic interest as a concept represents 'activities of direct benefit to the public'; point 27 of the Opinion of Advocate-General van Gerven.

[28]   See Valadou, 'La notion de pouvoir adjudicateur en matière de marchés de travaux', *Semaine Juridique,* 1991, Ed. E, No. 3, p. 33.

[29]   See case C-44/96, *Mannesmann Anlangenbau Austria,* op. cit.

[30]   For example, see case 118/85, *Commission v. Italy,* [1987] ECR 2599, paragraph 7, where the Court had the opportunity to elaborate on the distinction of activities pursued by public authorities.

public authority and those which, although carried out by public persons, fall within the private domain is drawn most clearly from case-law and judicial precedence of the Court concerning the applicability of competition rules of the Treaty to the given activities.[31]

The Court in *BFI*[32] had the opportunity to clarify the element of a non-commercial or industrial character. It considered that the relationship of the first criterion of bodies governed by public law is an integral one. The non-commercial or industrial character is a criterion intended to clarify the term 'needs in the general interest'. In fact, it is regarded as a category of needs of general interest. The Court recognised that there might be needs of general interest which have an industrial and commercial character and it is possible that private undertakings can meet needs of a general interest which do not have an industrial and commercial character. The acid test for needs in the general interest not having an industrial or commercial character is that the state or other contracting authorities choose themselves to meet these needs or to have a decisive influence over their provision.

In the *Agora* case[33] the Court indicated that if an activity which meets general needs is pursued in a competitive environment, there is a strong indication that the entity which pursues it is not a body governed by public law. The reason can be found in the relationship between competitiveness and commerciality. Market forces reveal the commercial or industrial character of an activity, irrespective of whether or not the latter meets the needs of general interest. However, market competitiveness as well as profitability cannot be absolute determining factors for the commerciality or the industrial nature of an activity, as they are not sufficient to exclude the possibility that a body governed by public law may choose to be guided by considerations other than economic ones. The absence of competition is not a condition necessarily to be taken into account in order to define a body governed by public law, although the existence of significant competition in the market place may be indicative of the absence of a need in the general interest which does not carry commercial or industrial elements. The Court reached this conclusion by analysing the nature of the bodies governed by public law contained in Annex 1 of the Works Directive 93/37 and verifying that the intention of the state to establish such bodies has been to retain a decisive influence over the provision of the needs in question.

---

[31]   See case C-364/92, *SAT Fluggesellschafeten*, [1994] ECR 1-43; also case C-343/95, *Diego Cali e Figli*, [1997] ECR 1-1547.

[32]   See case C-360/96, *Gemeente Arnhem Gemeente Rheden v. BFI Holding BV*, op. cit.

[33]   See case C-223/99, *Agora Srl v. Ente Autonomo Fiera Internazionale di Milano*, op. cit.

Entities Meeting Needs of General Interest Retrospectively

A question arose before the Court as to whether an entity which was not established for the specific purpose of meeting needs in the general interest, not having an industrial or commercial character, but which has subsequently taken responsibility for such needs, which it has subsequently actually been meeting, fulfils the condition required by the first indent of the second subparagraph of Article 1(b) of Directive 93/37 so as to be capable of being regarded as a body governed by public law within the meaning of that provision. In the dispute in the main proceedings, it emerged that *Entsorgungsbetriebe Simmering GesmbH* (EBS) had taken over the operation of the main sewage treatment plant, under a contract made in 1985 with the city of Vienna. It was not disputed that the company satisfies a need in the general interest not having an industrial or commercial character. However, its treatment as a body governed by public law within the meaning of the second subparagraph of Article 1(b) of Directive 93/37 depends on the answer to be given to the question whether the condition set out in the first indent of that provision precludes an entity from being regarded as a contracting authority where it was not established for the purposes of satisfying needs in the general interest having a character other than industrial or commercial, but has undertaken such tasks as a result of a subsequent change in its sphere of activities.[34]

EBS submitted that it cannot be regarded as a body governed by public law within the meaning of the second subparagraph of Article 1(b) of Directive 93/37, on the grounds that it is clear from the actual wording of the first indent of that provision that the sole deciding factor is the task which it was given at the date of its establishment. It adds that the fact that it has, subsequently, taken responsibility for tasks in the general interest having a character other than industrial or commercial does not affect its status since it continues to carry out industrial and commercial assignments. The Commission maintained that EBS cannot be regarded as a contracting authority within the meaning of Article 1(b) of Directive 93/37, because the change in its activities stems neither from an amendment to that effect of its objects as defined in its statutes, nor from a legal obligation.

In contrast, the applicants in the main proceedings *(Universale-Bau AG)*, as well as the Austrian and Netherlands governments as intervening parties, argued that it is EBS's current activity which is to be taken into consideration and not its purpose at the date of its establishment. They asserted that a different interpretation would mean that, notwithstanding the fact that an entity

---

[34]   See case C-470/99, *Universale-Bau AG, Bietergemeinschaft Hinteregger & Söhne Bauges.mbH Salzburg, ÖSTU-STETTIN Hoch- und Tiefbau GmbH, and Entsorgungsbetriebe Simmering GesmbH*, [2002] ECR I-11617.

corresponded as a matter of fact to the definition of contracting authority in Directive 93/37, it would not be required, in awarding public works contracts, to observe the requirements of that Directive. In addition, they maintained that a functional interpretation of the term 'contracting authority' is the only one capable of preventing possible evasion, since, otherwise, Directive 93/37 could easily be circumvented by transferring tasks in the general interest having a character other than industrial or commercial not to an entity newly established for that purpose, but to an existing one which previously had another object.

The Court has held that the purpose of co-ordinating at Community level the procedures for the award of public contracts is to eliminate barriers to the freedom to provide services and goods and therefore to protect the interests of traders established in a member state who wish to offer goods or services to contracting authorities established in another member state.[35] The aim of Directive 93/37 is to avoid both the risk of preference being given to national tenderers or applicants whenever a contract is awarded by the contracting authorities and the possibility that a body financed or controlled by the state, regional or local authorities or other bodies governed by public law may choose to be guided by considerations other than economic ones.[36]

The Court has therefore held that it is in the light of those objectives that the concept of a body governed by public law in the second subparagraph of Article 1(b) of Directive 93/37 must be interpreted in functional terms.[37] Thus, in *Mannesmann Anlagenbau Austria*, in relation to the treatment of an entity which had been established for the specific purpose of meeting needs in the general interest not having an industrial or commercial character, but which also carried out commercial activities, the Court held that the condition laid down in the first indent of the second subparagraph of Article 1(b) of Directive 93/37 does not entail that the body concerned may be entrusted only with meeting needs in the general interest, not having an industrial or commercial character. In particular, the Court has held that it is immaterial that, in addition to the specific task of meeting needs in the general interest, the entity concerned is free to carry out other activities, but, on the other hand, decided that it is a critical factor that it should continue to attend to the needs which it is specifically required to meet. For the purposes of deciding whether a body satisfies the condition set out in the first indent of the second subparagraph of Article 1(b) of Directive 93/37, it is necessary to consider the activities which

---

[35]   See case C-380/98, *University of Cambridge* [2000] ECR I-8035, paragraph 16, and case C-237/99 *Commission v. France* [2001] ECR I-939, paragraph 41.

[36]   See, in particular, *University of Cambridge*, paragraph 17, and C-237/99, *Commission v. France*, paragraph 42.

[37]   See case C-237/99, *Commission v. France*, paragraph 43.

it actually carries out. In that regard, it should be pointed out that the effectiveness of Directive 93/37 would not be fully upheld if the application of the scheme of the Directive to a body which satisfies the conditions set out in the second subparagraph of Article 1(b) thereof, could be excluded owing solely to the fact that the tasks in the general interest having a character other than industrial or commercial which it carries out in practice were not entrusted to it at the time of its establishment.

The same concern to ensure the effectiveness of the second subparagraph of Article 1(b) of Directive 93/37 also militates against drawing a distinction according to whether the statutes of such an entity were or were not amended to reflect actual changes in its sphere of activity. In addition, the wording of the second subparagraph of Article 1(b) of Directive 93/37 contains no reference to the legal basis of the activities of the entity concerned.

The Court considered it appropriate to point out that, in relation to the definition of the expression 'body governed by public law' in the second subparagraph of Article 1(b) of Directive 92/50, the terms of which are identical to those contained in the second subparagraph of Article 1(b) of Directive 93/37, the Court has already held that the existence or absence of needs in the general interest not having an industrial or commercial character must be appraised objectively, the legal form of the provisions in which those needs are mentioned being immaterial in that regard.[38]

The Court regarded as irrelevant the fact that the extension of the sphere of activities of EBS did not give rise to an amendment of the provisions of its statutes concerning its objects. Although EBS's assumption of responsibility for needs in the general interest not having an industrial or commercial character has not been formally incorporated in its statutes, it is none the less set out in the contracts which EBS made with the city of Vienna and is therefore capable of being objectively established.

The Court concluded that a body which was not established to satisfy specific needs in the general interest not having an industrial or commercial character, but which has subsequently taken responsibility for such needs, and which it has since actually satisfied, fulfils the condition required by the first indent of the second subparagraph of Article 1(b) of Directive 93/37 so as to be capable of being regarded as a body governed by public law within the meaning of that provision, on condition that the assumption of responsibility for the satisfaction of those needs can be established objectively.

---

[38]   See case C-360/96, *BFI Holding*, [1998] ECR I-6821, paragraph 63.

The Dual Capacity of Contracting Authorities

The dual capacity of an entity as a public service provider and a commercial undertaking respectively, and the weighting of the relevant activity in relation to the proportion of its output, should be the decisive factor in determining whether an entity is a body governed by public law. This argument appeared for the first time before the Court in the *Strohal*[39] case. The Austrian government suggested that only if the activities in pursuit of the 'public services obligations' of an entity supersede its commercial thrust could the latter be considered as a body covered by public law and a contracting authority. In support of its argument that the relevant entity (*Österreichische Staatsdruckerei*) was not a body governed by public law, the Austrian government maintained that the proportion of public interest activities represented no more than 15–20% of its overall activities.[40]

In practice, the argument put forward implied a selective application of the Public Procurement Directives in the event of dual capacity entities. This sort of application is not entirely unjustified as, on a number of occasions,[41] the Public Procurement Directives themselves utilise thresholds or proportions considerations in order to include or exclude certain contracts from their ambit. For example, reference should be made to the relevant provisions stipulating the thresholds for the applicability of the public procurement rules as well as the provisions relating to the so-called 'mixed contracts', where the proportion of the value of the works or the supplies element in a public contract determines the applicability of the relevant Directive and finally the relevant provisions which embrace the award of works contracts subsidised *directly* by more than 50% by the state within the scope of the Directive.

However, the Court ruled out a selective application of the Directives in the case of dual capacity contracting authorities based on the principle of legal certainty. It substantiated its position on the basis that only the purpose for which an entity is established is relevant in order to classify it as a body governed by public law and not the division between its public and private activities. Thus, the pursuit of commercial activities by contracting authorities is incorporated with their public interest orientation aims and objectives, without taking into account their proportion and weighting in relation to the total

---

[39]   See case C-44/96, *Mannesmann Anlangenbau Austria v. Strohal Rotationsdurck GesmbH*, op. cit.

[40]   For a comprehensive analysis of the case, see the annotation by Bovis, in 36 CMLR (1999), 205–25.

[41]   See Article 3(1) of Directive 93/37; Article 5(1) of Directive 93/36; Article 14 of Directive 93/38; Article 7(1) of Directive 92/50; Article 6(5) of Directive 93/37; Article 2(1)(2) of Directive 93/37.

activities dispersed, and contracts awarded in pursuit of commercial purposes fall under the remit of the Public Procurement Directives. The Court recognised the fact that by extending the application of public procurement rules to activities of a purely industrial or commercial character, an onerous constraint would probably be imposed upon the relevant contracting authorities, which may also seem unjustified on the grounds that public procurement law, in principle, does not apply to private bodies which carry out identical activities.[42] The above situation represents a considerable disadvantage in delineating the distinction between private and public sector activities and their regulation, to the extent that the only determining factor appears to be the nature of the organisation in question. The Court suggested that that disadvantage could be avoided by selecting the appropriate legal instrument for the objectives pursued by public authorities. As the reasons for the creation of a body governed by public law would determine the legal framework which would apply to its contractual relations, those responsible for establishing it must restrict its thrust in order to avoid the undesirable effects of that legal framework on activities outside their scope.

The Court in *Strohal* established dualism, to the extent that it specifically implied that contracting authorities may pursue a range of activities; to procure goods, works and services destined for the public, as well as participating in commercial activities. They can pursue other activities in addition to those which meet needs of a general interest not having an industrial and commercial character. The relative importance for an entity of activities which aim to meet needs of a general interest not having an industrial or commercial character, and commercial activities is irrelevant for the characterisation of that entity as a body governed by public law. What is relevant is the intention of establishing the entity in question, which reflects on the 'specificity' requirement. Also, specificity does not mean exclusivity of purpose. Specificity indicates the intention of establishment to meet general needs. Along these lines, ownership or financing of an entity by a contracting authority does not guarantee the condition of establishment of that entity to meet needs of a general interest not having an industrial and commercial character.

Commercial Public Companies as Contracting Authorities

Sociedad Estatal de Infraestruturas y Equipamientos Penitenciarios SA (SIEPSA), a private company under the control of the Spanish government, did not follow the provisions of the Public Procurement Directives in connection

---

[42]   See Bovis, *The Liberalisation of Public Procurement in the European Union and its Effects on the Common Market*, Ashgate, 1998, chapter 1, pp. 16 et seq.

with the call for tenders for the execution of works for the Centro Educativo Penitenciario Experimental de Segovia (Experimental Educational Prison, Segovia). The question which arose in case C-283/00, *Commission v. Spain* was whether such private companies under state control should be considered as contracting authorities for the purposes of the Public Procurement Directives.[43]

The Spanish government argued that SIEPSA should not be considered as a contracting authority on the grounds that commercial companies under public control, such as SIEPSA, are not included within the notion of bodies governed by public law. That argument was based on the fact that the Utilities Directive 93/38 draws a distinction between the concept of a body governed by public law, identical in all Public Procurement Directives, and the concept of a public undertaking, the definition of which corresponds to that of a public commercial company. The Spanish government noted that the Community legislature was aware that many undertakings in the private sector, although possessing the form of a public undertaking, specifically pursue a wholly commercial object, despite their dependency on the state, and operate in the market in accordance with the rules of free competition and in conditions of equality with other private undertakings strictly for the purpose of making profits. That is why the legislature confined the Directive's ambit to bodies cumulatively satisfying the three conditions set out in Article 1(b) thereof.

While acknowledging that SIEPSA fulfils the two last conditions under Article 1(b) of the Directive, the Spanish government argued that SIEPSA possesses the attributes of a commercial company, given that its objects and tasks are typically commercial, and that it therefore meets general-interest needs of a commercial character, which does not meet the first criterion of that provision. In addition, referring to the list in Part V of Annex I to the Directive, which contains the categories of Spanish bodies governed by public law that meet the criteria laid down in the second paragraph of Article 1(b) of that Directive, the Spanish government asserted that SIEPSA does not belong to any of those categories, since it is not an independent body and since it is not subject to the Spanish laws on public procurement.

The exclusion of companies such as SIEPSA from the scope *ratione personae* of the Public Procurement Directives, according to the Spanish government, is accounted for by the circumstance that, in the Spanish legal order, it is generally the task of public bodies governed by private law, a category consisting of commercial companies under public control, such as SIEPSA, to meet general-interest needs, which explains why they are under

---

[43]   See case C-283/00, *Commission of the European Communities v. Kingdom of Spain*, [2003] ECR I-11697.

public control, but those needs are commercial or industrial in nature for, if that were not so, they could not be the object of a commercial company. The Spanish government stated that the principal task entrusted to SIEPSA, namely, the building of new prisons suited to the needs of society, consists of a general-interest requirement of a commercial character, which serves the ultimate purpose of contributing to prison policy, which is also in the general interest. SIEPSA was created in order to carry out all actions which prove necessary to the proper management of the programmes and transactions provided for in the plan for financing and constructing prisons, either by its own resources or through the resources of other undertakings. Its attributes are those of a typical commercial company, even being governed by commercial law, without prejudice to the exceptions provided for in the areas of budget, accounts and financial audit. In order to attain those objectives, SIEPSA performs transactions which must, in the Spanish government's submission, be objectively classified as commercial, such as locating and acquiring buildings to be fitted out as new prisons and the development and execution of preparatory and construction works.

The Spanish government observed that, in carrying out those activities, SIEPSA makes a profit and that the performance of those operations with a view to generating profits is a typically commercial activity which can be successfully carried out only by a company subject to the commercial rules of the private sector with which it must necessarily engage. It goes on to say that that company's activity cannot be treated as administrative, since its objective is to acquire financial means or resources like any contractor, and that is so even though in the final analysis those resources are applied for other general-interest purposes.

The Spanish government argued that, whether or not SIEPSA is subject to market competition, it carries on activities which are commercial in nature. According to case-law of the Court,[44] the absence of competition is not a condition necessarily to be taken into account in defining a body governed by public law, and therefore, an entity such as SIEPSA cannot fall within the notion of a contracting authority used by the Public Procurement Directives. The fact that state commercial companies such as SIEPSA are regulated by private law is not so much the cause as the consequence of their actual nature. It states in this regard that that company is not commercial in character because it is governed by private law, but that it is precisely the commercial character of its activity that confers on it the attributes it possesses and results in its being governed by private law. The Spanish government submitted that it is the only view that respects the autonomous definition of the criterion of

---

[44]   See case C-360/96, *BFI Holding*, [1998] ECR I-6821, paragraph 47.

the non-industrial or commercial character of needs in the general interest.[45] It contended that, since the state serves the general interest and since it has a majority shareholding in state commercial companies, it is logical to suppose that those companies will always serve the general interest to a greater or lesser extent. If, in order for the body to be classified as a contracting authority, it were sufficient that it should perform tasks in the general interest, such as contributing to the imposition of criminal penalties, then the condition that those tasks should not be industrial or commercial in character would be meaningless.

The Spanish government concluded that SIEPSA ought to receive the same treatment as undertakings supplying gas, electricity or water, sectors which satisfy essential social requirements and which are, in most cases, in the hands of private undertakings which also pursue broader objectives in the general interest.

The Commission considered that SIEPSA fulfils all the conditions laid down in Article 1(b) of the Directive and that it is therefore a contracting authority for the purposes of that Directive. The Commission noted that, when implementing Community directives in domestic law, the member states are required to respect the meaning of the words and concepts used in those measures, in order to guarantee uniform interpretation and application of Community legislation in the various member states. As a result, the Spanish authorities are bound to give the expression 'body governed by public law', used in the Directive, the meaning it has under Community law. Thus, according to the Commission, if SIEPSA is excluded from the ambit of the Community rules on the award of public procurement contracts by virtue of national law, the Public Procurement Directives have not been properly implemented into Spanish law.

The Commission claimed that the functional interpretation of the notion of contracting authority and, therefore, of body governed by public law adopted in the established case-law of the Court implies that the latter notion includes commercial companies under public control, provided that they fulfil the conditions laid down in the second paragraph of Article 1(b) of the Directive. As regards the distinction drawn by the utilities Directive 93/38 between the definitions of a body governed by public law and a public undertaking, the Commission stated that that Directive does not clarify the concept of a body governed by public law, which is identical in all public procurement Directives, but extends the scope *ratione personae* of the provisions of Community law relating to public procurement to the utilities sectors which are excluded from Directives 93/36, 93/37 and 92/50, in order to cover certain bodies carrying on significant activity in those sectors, namely, public under-

---

45   See case C-360/96, *BFI Holding*, [1998] ECR I-6821, paragraphs 32 and 36.

takings and those which enjoy special or exclusive rights granted by the authorities. In addition, the concept of a public undertaking has always been different from that of a body governed by public law, in that bodies governed by public law are created specifically to meet needs in the general interest having no industrial or commercial character, whereas public undertakings act to satisfy needs of an industrial or commercial character.

The Commission also disproved the Spanish government's interpretation, which makes the concept of body governed by public law dependent on the lists contained in Annex I to the Directive in respect of every member state, with the result that a Community concept comes to have different meanings, depending on the way in which the various lists in Annex I were drawn up. According to the Commission, the interpretation favoured by the Spanish government runs counter to the primary object of the Directive, as set out in the second recital in the preamble thereto, and is also contrary to the third paragraph of Article 1(b) thereof, according to which the lists are to be as exhaustive as possible. The Commission stressed the point that that expression cannot be understood to mean anything other than that the lists are not exhaustive and that that interpretation has been confirmed by the Court in the *BFI Holding* case.[46] From that it can be deduced that if state companies do not appear, directly or indirectly, in the list of bodies governed by public law in Part V of Annex I to the Directive, it does not mean that they fall outside the concept defined in the second paragraph of Article 1(b) for the purposes of being considered as contracting authorities. So far as the conditions laid down in the second paragraph of Article 1(b) of the Directive are concerned, the Commission observed that that provision makes no mention of the set of rules, whether public or private, under which bodies governed by public law have been formed, or of the legal form chosen, but rather refers to other standards, including the purpose for which the bodies in question were created.

The Commission submitted that SIEPSA was established for the specific purpose of meeting needs in the general interest, not having an industrial or commercial character, namely to contribute to the implementation of state prison policy through the management of programmes and actions contained in the plan for paying off the costs of establishing prisons approved by the Council of Ministers. The concept of general interest is closely linked to public order and the institutional operation of the state and even to the very essence of the state, in as much as the state holds the monopoly of power in the penal sphere, consisting of the imposition of penalties depriving persons of their liberty, and does not possess an industrial or commercial character.[47]

---

[46] See case C-360/96, *BFI Holding*, [1998] ECR I-6821, paragraph 50.
[47] See case C-44/96, *Mannesmann Anlagenbau Austria*, [1998] ECR I-73, paragraph 24.

The Commission disagreed with the Spanish government's argument that companies which, like SIEPSA, operate in the market subject to the principles of free competition in the same way as private undertakings and for the same purpose of making profits have a purely commercial object and by that token fall outside the ambit of the Community directives on public procurement. In particular, it referred by way of example to the award of works contracts for the construction of public prisons or the sale of the state's prison properties, which are two of SIEPSA's company objects and which cannot be regarded as activities subject to market competition. Furthermore, the Commission submitted that even if it should be conceded that SIEPSA carries on activity subject to free competition, that fact does not mean that it cannot be regarded as a contracting authority.[48]

The Commission claimed that the Spanish government's argument that all SIEPSA's activities are commercial is without substance. First, it stated that, contrary to the claims made by the Spanish government, SIEPSA's activity cannot be compared with private-sector activity. It explained that that company does not offer prisons in the penal establishments market (there is no such market) but rather acts as the representative of the state administration in order to assist the latter in a task of a typically state nature: the construction, management and selling of prison properties. On this subject the Commission noted that, as is clear from the company's statutes, in carrying out its tasks SIEPSA follows directives issued by the general management of the prison administration, and real property is sold and the sums so realised are used in accordance with the directives issued by the general management of state assets. Secondly, the Commission observed that the Spanish government separates the need to build prisons (from which it infers that it is of general interest and possessed of a commercial character) from the ultimate purpose, which is to contribute to penal policy (which it classifies as being in the general interest). It stated that that separation, as well as being artificial in that the two needs are closely linked, is inconsistent with the reasoning followed by the Court in other cases, in which it has declared that the collection and treatment of waste (*BFI Holding*) or the printing of official administrative documents (*Mannesmann Anlagenbau Austria*) are needs in the general interest, not having an industrial or commercial character, without separating those activities from their ultimate purpose: public health and environmental protection, on the one hand, and public order and the institutional operation of the state, on the other. Finally, the Commission claimed that even if SIEPSA's objective were profit, that aim would not prevent the company from meeting needs in the general interest not having an industrial or commercial character. While

---

[48]   See case C-360/96, *BFI Holding*, [1998] ECR I-6821, paragraph 47.

the pursuit of profit may be a distinguishing feature of the company's activities, it is not stated in the text of the Directive that that goal makes it impossible to consider that the general-interest needs to meet which SIEPSA was created have no industrial or commercial character. The Commission added that it is debatable whether the pursuit of profit is an object for a state company such as SIEPSA, which is wholly funded out of public resources, and which was created for the purpose of drawing up and implementing a plan for paying off the costs of and establishing prisons. It is obvious to the Commission that in such a sphere making a profit is not a factor which a member state would consider of prime importance.

The Court held that in order to be defined as a body governed by public law within the meaning of the second paragraph of Article 1(b) of the Directive an entity must satisfy the three cumulative conditions set out therein, requiring it to be a body established for the specific purpose of meeting needs in the general interest not having an industrial or commercial character, to possess legal personality and to be closely dependent on the state, regional or local authorities or other bodies governed by public law.[49]

The crucial point to determine whether SIEPSA is a contracting authority is whether or not the needs in the general interest to meet which SIEPSA was specifically created are commercial in character. In *Commission v. Spain* the Court rejected the Spanish government's arguments based on the fact that, under the applicable Spanish legislation, commercial companies under public control such as SIEPSA are excluded from the ambit *ratione personae* of both the Spanish rules and the Community rules on public procurement. More specifically, in order to determine whether that exclusion constitutes correct transposition of the concept of contracting authority, the Court referred to the scope of the concept of body governed by public law employed by the Public Procurement Directives.[50] In that context the Court noted that, in accordance with established case-law, in light of the dual purpose of opening up competition and of transparency pursued by the Public Procurement Directives, that concept must be given a functional and broad interpretation.[51]

The Court has held that for the purposes of settling the issue of the classification of an entity governed by public law within the meaning of the second paragraph of Article 1(b) of the Directive, it is necessary to establish only whether or not the body concerned fulfils the three conditions set out in that provision, for that body's status as a body governed by private law does not constitute a criterion capable of excluding it from being classified as a

---

[49]   See case 44/96, *Mannesmann Anlagenbau Austria*, paragraphs 20 and 21, and case C-214/00, *Commission v. Spain*, [2003] ECR I-0000, paragraph 52.

[50]   See *Commission v. Spain* case, paragraphs 48, 50 and 51.

[51]   See *Commission v. Spain* case, paragraphs 48, 50 and 51.

contracting authority for the purposes of the Directive.[52] In addition, the Court has stated that that interpretation, the only one capable of maintaining the full effectiveness of the Directive, does not disregard the industrial or commercial character of the general-interest needs which the body concerned is intended to meet, for that aspect is necessarily taken into consideration for the purpose of determining whether or not that body satisfies the condition laid down in the first indent of the second paragraph of Article 1(b) of the Directive.[53] Nor is that conclusion invalidated by the want of an express reference in the Directive to the specific category of public undertakings which is, however, used in the Utilities Directive 93/38. The Utilities Directive was adopted for the purpose of extending the application of the Community rules regulating public procurement to the water, energy, transport and telecommunications sectors which were not covered by other directives. From that point of view, by employing the concepts of public authorities, on the one hand, and public undertakings, on the other, the Community legislature adopted a functional approach similar to that adopted in Directives 92/50, 93/36 and 93/37. It was thus able to ensure that all the contracting entities operating in the sectors regulated by Directive 93/38 were included in its ambit *ratione personae*, on condition that they satisfied certain criteria, their legal form and the rules under which they were formed being in this respect immaterial.

With regard to the relevance of the Spanish government's argument that SIEPSA does not fall within any of the categories of Spanish bodies governed by public law listed in Annex I to the Directive, the Court has held that that list is in no way exhaustive, as its accuracy varies considerably from one member state to another.[54] The Court concluded that, if a specific body does not appear in that list, its legal and factual situation must be determined in each individual case in order to assess whether or not it meets a need in the general interest.

With regard to the concept of needs in the general interest, not having an industrial or commercial character, the Court has held that concept is one of Community law and must accordingly be given an autonomous and uniform interpretation throughout the Community, the search for which must take account of the background to the provision in which it appears and of the purpose of the rules in question.[55] Needs in the general interest, not having an industrial or commercial character, within the meaning of Article 1(b) of the Community directives co-ordinating the award of public contracts are gener-

---

[52] See *Commission v. Spain* case, paragraphs 54 and 55.
[53] See *Commission v. Spain* case, paragraphs 56 and 58.
[54] See case C-373/00, *Adolf Truley*, [2003] ECR I-0000, paragraph 39.
[55] See case C-373/00, *Adolf Truley*, [2003] ECR I-0000, paragraphs 36, 40 and 45.

ally needs which are satisfied otherwise than by the supply of goods and services in the market-place and which, for reasons associated with the general interest, the state chooses to provide itself or over which it wishes to retain a decisive influence.[56] The case-law makes it clear that in determining whether or not there exists a need in the general interest not having an industrial or commercial character, account must be taken of relevant legal and factual circumstances, such as those prevailing when the body concerned was formed and the conditions in which it carries on its activity, including, *inter alia*, lack of competition in the market, the fact that its primary aim is not the making of profits, the fact that it does not bear the risks associated with the activity, and any public financing of the activity in question.[57] The Court found in *Korhonen* that if the body operates in normal market conditions, aims at making a profit and bears the losses associated with the exercise of its activity, it is unlikely that the needs it aims to meet are not of an industrial or commercial nature.

To determine whether or not the needs in the general interest that SIEPSA is designed to meet are other than industrial or commercial in character the Court maintained that an intrinsic link between such needs and the public order of the state in question must be established. That intrinsic link is to be seen in particular in the decisive influence wielded by the state over the carrying through of the tasks entrusted to SIEPSA. The Court held that there is no market for the goods and services offered by SIEPSA in the planning and establishment of prisons. Activities such as paying off the costs of and establishment of prisons, which are among SIEPSA's primary objectives, are not subject to market competition. That company cannot, therefore, be regarded as a body which offers goods or services in a free market in competition with other economic agents. Even the argument which the Spanish government forwarded that SIEPSA carries on its activities for profit, cannot support the fact that it would appear inconceivable that the pursuit of such profit should in itself be the company's chief aim.

The Court went further to declare that it is unlikely that state-controlled companies such as SIEPSA should themselves have to bear the financial risks related to their activities. In fact, the state would take all necessary measures, such as measures to prevent compulsory liquidation, to protect the financial viability of such entities. In those circumstances, it is possible that in a procedure for the award of public contracts a entity such as SIEPSA should allow itself to be guided by other than purely economic considerations. Therefore, in order to safeguard against such a possibility, it is essential to apply the Public

---

[56] See *Adolf Truley*, paragraph 50, and case C-18/01, *Korhonen*, [2003] ECR I-0000, paragraph 47.

[57] See *Adolf Truley* case, paragraph 66, and *Korhonen*, paragraphs 48 and 59.

Procurement Directives.[58] The Court concluded that the needs in the general interest which the company was specifically established to meet possess a character which is other than industrial or commercial. It follows that a body such as SIEPSA must be treated as a body governed by public law for the purposes of the second paragraph of Article 1(b) of the Directive and, therefore, as a contracting authority for the purposes of the first paragraph thereof.

The Connection of Contracting Authorities with Private Undertakings

There is considerable risk of circumventing the Public Procurement Directives, if contracting authorities award their public contracts via private undertakings under their control which cannot be covered by the framework of the Directives. Under the domestic laws of the member states, there is little to prevent contracting authorities from acquiring private undertakings in an attempt to participate in market activities. In fact, in many jurisdictions the socio-economic climate is very much in favour of public–private sector partnerships, in the form of joint ventures or in the form of private financing of public projects. A classic example of such an approach is the views of the UK government in relation to the involvement of the private sector in delivering public services. A number of government documents have eulogised the so-called *Private Finance Initiative (PFI)*, which attempts to create a framework between the public and private sectors working together to deliver public services.[59] Unfortunately, the Public Procurement Directives have not envisaged such a scenario, where avoidance of the rules could be based on the fact that the entities which award the relevant contracts cannot be classified as contracting authorities within the meaning of the Directives.

The Court, prior to the *Stohal* case, did not have the opportunity to examine such corporate relationships and the effect that public procurement law has upon them. Even in *Strohal*, the Court did not rule directly on the subject, but instead it provided the necessary inferences for national courts, in order to ascertain whether such relations between public and private undertakings aim at avoiding the application of the Public Procurement Directives. Indeed, national courts, in litigation before them, must establish *in concreto* whether a contracting authority has established an undertaking in order to enter into contracts for the sole purpose of avoiding the requirements specified in public procurement law. Such conclusions must undoubtedly be based on the examination of the actual purpose for which the undertaking in question has been

---

[58]   See *Adolf Truley* case, paragraph 42, and *Korhonen*, paragraphs 51 and 52.
[59]   See in particular, *Working Together – Private Finance and Public Money*, Department of Environment, 1993. *Private Opportunity, Public Benefit – Progressing the Private Finance Initiative*, Private Finance Panel and HM Treasury, 1995.

established. The rule of thumb is the connection between the nature of a project and the aims and objectives of the undertaking which awards it. If the realisation of a project does not contribute to the aims and objectives of an undertaking, then it is assumed that the project in question is warded 'on behalf' of another undertaking, and if the latter beneficiary is a contracting authority under the framework of public procurement law, then the relevant Directives should apply. The Court followed the *Strohal* line in *Teckal*,[60] where the exercise of similar control over the management of an entity by a contracting authority prevents the applicability of the Directives.

The dual capacity of contracting authorities is irrelevant to the applicability of public procurement rules. If an entity is a contracting authority, it must apply public procurement rules irrespective of the pursuit of general interest needs or the pursuit of commercial activities. Also, if a contracting authority assigns the rights and obligations of a public contract to an entity which is not a contracting authority, that entity must follow public procurement rules. The contrary would be acceptable if the contract fell within the remit of the entity which is not a contracting authority, and the contract was entered into on its behalf by a contracting authority.

Dualism's irrelevance for the applicability of public procurement represents a safeguard for the *acquis communautaire*. Dualism could be viewed as recognition of contractualised governance, where the demarcation between public and private activities of the public sector has become difficult to define, as well as a counterbalance to commerciality. If commercialism shielded the activities of a contracting authority from the application of public procurement rules, dualism provides the necessary inferences to subject dual capacity entities to the *acquis communautaire*.

Private Law Entities as Contracting Authorities

An entity which is governed by private law but nevertheless meets all the requirements of bodies governed by public law laid down in the first, second and third indents of the second subparagraph of Article 1(b) of Directives 93/36 and 93/37 is considered a contracting authority for the purposes of the Public Procurement Directives. In *Commission v. Spain*,[61] the Commission argued that national law which excludes from the scope of the Public Procurement Directives private entities which may fulfil the requirements of contracting authorities is in default with public procurement acquis. The Commission argued that the scope *ratione personae* of the codified law does

---

[60] See case C-107/98, *Teckal Slr v. Comune di Viano*, op. cit.

[61] See case C-84/03, *Commission of the European Communities v. Kingdom of Spain*, not yet reported.

not coincide with that of Directives 93/36 and 93/37, in so far as the national law applies exclusively to bodies subject to a public law regime for the purposes of Spanish law, while the legal form of the body at issue falls outside the definition of 'body governed by public law' set out in the Public Procurement Directives. The Commission asserted that the concept 'body governed by public law' is a Community-wide concept of an autonomous nature. The Commission maintained that, according to the Court's jurisprudence,[62] a body governed by public law must be understood as a body which fulfils the three cumulative conditions set out in the second subparagraph of Article 1(b) of Directive 93/37 and that the definition of a contracting authority in Article 1 of Directives 93/36 and 93/37 must be interpreted in functional terms.[63]

The Spanish government suggested that a literal interpretation of the definition of body governed by public law does not allow the inclusion of private entities within the scope of the Public Procurement Directives. It argued that Directives 93/36 and 93/37 do not include commercial companies under public control in that definition. In support of its arguments, it relied on the Utilities Directive 93/38, which distinguishes between the notion of 'body governed by public law', which is the same in the public contracts directives, and 'public undertaking', whose definition corresponds to the definition of public commercial company. Furthermore, the Spanish government submitted that a genuine delimitation of the definition of the term 'body governed by public law' may be made only after defining needs in the general interest and, in particular, needs not having an industrial or commercial character, by means of a detailed examination of the entity in question on a case-by-case basis.

The Court held that the definition of 'body governed by public law' represents a concept of Community law which must be given an autonomous and uniform interpretation throughout the Community, and is defined in functional terms exclusively under the three cumulative conditions in the second subparagraph of Article 1(b) of Directives 93/36 and 93/37.[64] In order to determine whether a private law body is to be classified as a body governed by public law it is only necessary to establish whether the body in question satisfies the three cumulative conditions laid down in the second subparagraph of

---

[62]   See case C-44/96, *Mannesmann Anlagenbau Austria*, [1998] ECR I-73, paragraphs 17 to 35.
[63]   See case 31/87, *Beentjes*, [1988] ECR 4635 and case C-360/96, *BFI Holding*, [1998] ECR I-6821.
[64]   See case 44/96, *Mannesmann Anlagenbau Austria and Others*, paragraphs 20 and 21; case C-470/99, *Universale-Bau and Others*, [2002] ECR I-11617, paragraphs 51 to 53; case C-214/00, *Commission v. Spain*, [2003] ECR I-4667, paragraphs 52 and 53; and case C-283/00, *Commission v. Spain*, [2003] ECR I-11697, paragraph 69.

Article 1(b) of Directives 93/36 and 93/37, since an entity's private law status does not constitute a criterion for precluding it from being classified as a contracting authority for the purposes of the Public Procurement Directives.[65]

The Court has also stated that that interpretation does not amount to a disregard for the industrial or commercial character of the general interest needs which the body concerned satisfies, since that factor is necessarily taken into consideration in order to determine whether or not it satisfies the condition laid down in the first indent of the second subparagraph of Article 1(b) of Directives 93/36 and 93/37.[66] Furthermore, that conclusion is not invalidated by the want of an express reference in Directives 93/36 and 93/37 to the specific category of 'public undertakings' which is used in Directive 93/38.[67]

Semi-public Undertakings as Contracting Authorities

In *Staad Halle*,[68] a question arose as to whether, where a contracting authority intends to conclude with a company governed by private law, legally distinct from the authority and in which it has a majority capital holding and exercises a certain control, a contract for pecuniary interest relating to services within the material scope of Directive 92/50, it is always obliged to apply the public award procedures laid down by that Directive. In other words, the question prompted the criteria and their references under which the mere participation of a contracting authority, even in a minority form, in the shareholding of a private company with which it concludes a contract to be a ground for the applicability of the Public Procurement Directives. The Court held that where a contracting authority intends to conclude a contract for pecuniary interest relating to services within the material scope of Directive 92/50 with a company legally distinct from it, in whose capital it has a holding together with one or more private undertakings, the public award procedures laid down by that directive must always be applied.

The Court maintained that the obligation to apply the Public Procurement Directives in the case of semi-public undertakings is confirmed by the fact that in Article 1(c) of Directive 92/50 the term service-provider, that is, a tenderer for the purposes of the application of that directive, also includes a public body which offers services.[69]

---

[65]   See case C-214/00, *Commission v. Spain*, paragraphs 54, 55 and 60.

[66]   See case C-283/00, *Commission v. Spain*, paragraph 75.

[67]   See case C-283, *Commission v. Spain*, paragraph 76.

[68]   See case C-26/03, *Stadt Halle, RPL Recyclingpark Lochau GmbH v. Arbeitsgemeinschaft Thermische Restabfall- und Energieverwertungsanlage TREA Leuna*, judgment of 11 January 2005, not yet reported.

[69]   See case C-94/99, *ARGE*, [2000] ECR I11037, paragraph 28.

Any exception to the application of that obligation must consequently be interpreted strictly. Thus the Court has held, concerning recourse to a negotiated procedure without the prior publication of a contract notice, that Article 11(3) of Directive 92/50, which provides for such a procedure, must, as a derogation from the rules intended to ensure the effectiveness of the rights conferred by the EC Treaty in relation to public service contracts, be interpreted strictly and that the burden of proving the existence of exceptional circumstances justifying the derogation lies on the person seeking to rely on those circumstances.[70]

The Court has held, in the spirit of opening up public contracts to the widest possible competition, that the Public Procurement Directives are applicable in the case where a contracting authority plans to conclude a contract for pecuniary interest with an entity which is legally distinct from it, whether or not that entity is itself a contracting authority.[71] It is relevant to note that the other contracting party in that case was a consortium consisting of several contracting authorities, of which the contracting authority in question was also a member. A public authority which is a contracting authority has the possibility of performing the tasks conferred on it in the public interest by using its own administrative, technical and other resources, without being obliged to call on outside entities not forming part of its own departments. In such a case, there can be no question of a contract for pecuniary interest concluded with an entity legally distinct from the contracting authority. There is therefore no need to apply the Community rules in the field of public procurement.

In accordance with the Court's case-law, it is not excluded that there may be other circumstances in which a call for tenders is not mandatory, even though the other contracting party is an entity legally distinct from the contracting authority. That is the case where the public authority which is a contracting authority exercises over the separate entity concerned a control which is similar to that which it exercises over its own departments and that entity carries out the essential part of its activities with the controlling public authority or authorities.[72] It should be noted that, in the case cited, the distinct entity was wholly owned by public authorities. By contrast, the participation, even as a minority, of a private undertaking in the capital of a company in which the contracting authority in question is also a participant excludes in any event the possibility of that contracting authority exercising over that company a control similar to that which it exercises over its own departments.

In this respect, it must be observed, first, that the relationship between a

---

[70]   See joined cases C-20/01 and C-28/01, *Commission v. Germany*, [2003] ECR I3609, paragraph 58.

[71]   See case C-107/98, *Teckal*, [1999] ECR I8121, paragraphs 50 and 51.

[72]   See case C-107/98, *Teckal*, [1999] ECR I8121, paragraph 50.

public authority which is a contracting authority and its own departments is governed by considerations and requirements proper to the pursuit of objectives in the public interest. Any private capital investment in an undertaking, on the other hand, follows considerations proper to private interests and pursues objectives of a different kind. Secondly, the award of a public contract to a semi-public company without calling for tenders would interfere with the objective of free and undistorted competition and the principle of equal treatment of the persons concerned, referred to in Directive 92/50, in particular in that such a procedure would offer a private undertaking with a capital presence in that undertaking an advantage over its competitors.

Private Companies as Contracting Authorities

Companies governed by private law established for the specific purpose of meeting needs in the general interest which do not have an industrial or commercial character, have legal personality, and are financed for the most part by public authorities or other entities governed by public law or are subject to supervision by the latter, or have an administrative, managerial or supervisory board more than half of whose members are appointed by public authorities or other entities governed by public law, are considered as contracting authorities for the purposes of the Public Procurement Directives.

The Court stated, in connection with the second subparagraph of Article 1(b) of Directive 93/37, that, in order to be defined as a body governed by public law within the meaning of that provision, an entity must satisfy the three cumulative conditions set out therein, according to which it must be a body established for the specific purpose of meeting needs in the general interest, not having an industrial or commercial character, which has legal personality and is closely dependent on the state, regional or local authorities or other bodies governed by public law.[73] Moreover, the Court has repeatedly held that, in the light of the dual objective of opening up competition and transparency pursued by the directives on the co-ordination of the procedures for the award of public contracts, the term 'contracting authority', must be interpreted in functional terms.[74] The Court has also stated that, in the light of that dual purpose, the term 'body governed by public law' must be interpreted broadly.[75] The Court, for the purposes of settling the question whether various

---

[73]   See case C-44/96, *Mannesmann Anlagenbau Austria*, [1998] ECR I-73, paragraphs 20 and 21.
[74]   See case C-237/99, *Commission v. France*, [2001] ECR I-939, paragraphs 41 to 43, and case C-470/99, *Universale-Bau and Others*, [2002] ECR I-11617, paragraphs 51 to 53.
[75]   See case C-373/00, *Adolf Truley*, [2003] ECR-1931, paragraph 43.

private law entities could be classified as bodies governed by public law, has proceeded in accordance with settled case-law and merely ascertained whether those entities fulfilled the three cumulative conditions set out in the second subparagraph of Article 1(b) of Directives 92/50, 93/36 and 93/37, considering that the method in which the entity concerned has been set up was irrelevant in that regard.[76]

It is apparent from the jurisprudence of the Court that an entity's private law status does not constitute a criterion for precluding it from being classified as a contracting authority. Furthermore, it should be pointed out that the effectiveness of the Public Procurement Directives would not be fully preserved if the application of those directives to an entity which fulfils the three aforementioned conditions could be excluded solely on the basis of the fact that, under the national law to which it is subject, its legal form and rules which govern it fall within the scope of private law.

In the light of those considerations, it is not possible to interpret the term 'body governed by public law' used in the second subparagraph of Article 1(b) of Directives 92/50, 93/36 and 93/37 as meaning that member states may automatically exclude commercial companies under public control from the scope *ratione personae* of those Directives. Furthermore, it cannot be maintained that to reach that conclusion is to disregard the industrial or commercial character of the needs in the general interest which those companies meet, because that aspect is necessarily taken into consideration for the purpose of determining whether or not the entity concerned meets the condition set out in the first indent of the second subparagraph of Article 1(b) of Directives 92/50, 93/36 and 93/37. Nor is that conclusion invalidated by the lack of an express reference, in the Public Services, Supplies and Works Directives 92/50, 93/36 and 93/37 respectively, to the specific category of public undertakings which is nevertheless used in the Utilities Directive 93/38.

Private Entities for Industrial and Commercial Development as Contracting Authorities

A question was referred to the Court as to whether a limited company established, owned and managed by a regional or local authority may be regarded as meeting a specific need in the general interest, not having an industrial or commercial character, where that company's activity consists in acquiring services with a view to the construction of premises intended for the exclusive use of private undertakings, and whether the assessment of whether that condi-

---

[76] See in particular, *Mannesmann Anglagenbau Austria and Others*, paragraphs 6 and 29; case C-360/96, *BFI Holding*, [1998] ECR I-6821, paragraphs 61 and 62; and case C-237/99, *Commission v. France*, paragraphs 50 and 60.

tion is satisfied would be different if the building project in question were intended to create favourable conditions on that local authority's territory for the exercise of business activities.[77] Taitotalo is a limited company whose capital is wholly owned by the town of Varkaus (Finland), and whose objects are to buy, sell and lease real property and shares in property companies, and to organise and supply property maintenance services and other related services needed for the management of those properties and shares. The company's board has three members, who are officials of the town of Varkaus, appointed by the general meeting of the company's shareholders, at which the town has 100% of the voting rights.

The Court found that a limited company established, owned and managed by a regional or local authority meets a need in the general interest, within the meaning of the second subparagraph of Article 1(b) of Council Directive 92/50/EEC of 18 June 1992 relating to the co-ordination of procedures for the award of public service contracts, where it acquires services with a view to promoting the development of industrial or commercial activities on the territory of that regional or local authority. To determine whether that need has no industrial or commercial character, the national court must assess the circumstances which prevailed when that company was set up and the conditions in which it carries on its activity, taking account in particular of the fact that it does not aim primarily at making a profit, the fact that it does not bear the risks associated with the activity, and any public financing of the activity in question. The fact that the premises to be constructed are leased only to a single undertaking is not capable of calling into question the lessor's status as a body governed by public law, where it is shown that the lessor meets a need in the general interest not having an industrial or commercial character.

Taitotalo considered that its activity is not intended to meet needs in the general interest and in any event has an industrial or commercial character. It submitted that its sole object is to promote the conditions for the exercise of the activities of specific undertakings, not for the exercise generally of economic activity in the town of Varkaus, while the fact that it is owned and financed by a contracting authority is of no relevance, since, in the case in the main proceedings, it meets industrial or commercial needs. Taitotalo stated, in particular, that it acquired at market price the land needed for the building works at issue in the main proceedings and that the financing of the project will be taken in hand essentially by the private sector, by means of bank loans secured by mortgages. The leasing of premises for industrial or commercial

---

[77] See case C-18/01, *Arkkitehtuuritoimisto Riitta Korhonen Oy, Arkkitehtitoimisto Pentti Toivanen Oy, Rakennuttajatoimisto Vilho Tervomaa and Varkauden Taitotalo Oy*, [2003] ECR I-5321.

use cannot in any case be regarded as within the prerogatives which by their very nature are part of the exercise of public powers.[78]

According to the arguments submitted by the Finnish government, Taitotalo's activity typically appears among those which respond to a need in the general interest with no industrial or commercial character. First, Taitotalo's primary aim is not to generate profits by its activity but to create favourable conditions for the development of economic activities on the territory of the town of Varkaus, which fits in perfectly with the functions which regional and local authorities may assume by virtue of the autonomy guaranteed to them by the Finnish constitution. Secondly, the objective of Directive 92/50 would be compromised if such a company were not regarded as a contracting authority within the meaning of the Directive, as municipalities might in that case be tempted to establish, in their traditional sphere of activity, other undertakings whose contracts would be outside the scope of the Directive.

Finally, while not excluding the possibility that Taitotalo's activity may meet a need in the general interest because of the stimulus it gives to trade and the development of business activities in the territory of the town of Varkaus, the Austrian government and the Commission, as intervening parties, stated that, in view of the incomplete information available, they were unable to assess the extent to which that need had an industrial or commercial character. They therefore invited the national court to perform that assessment itself, examining in particular the competition position of Taitotalo and whether it bears the risks associated with its activity.

The Court held that the second subparagraph of Article 1(b) of Directive 92/50 draws a distinction between needs in the general interest not having an industrial or commercial character and needs in the general interest having an industrial or commercial character.[79] To give a useful answer to the questions put, it must first be ascertained whether activities such as those at issue in the main proceedings in fact meet needs in the general interest and then, if necessary, it must be determined whether such needs have an industrial or commercial character. As regards the question whether the activity at issue in the main proceedings meets a need in the general interest, it appears from the order for reference that Taitotalo's principal activity consists in buying, selling and leasing properties and organising and supplying property maintenance services and other related services needed for the management of those properties. The operation carried out by Taitotalo in the main proceedings consists, more precisely, in acquiring design and construction services in connection with a

---

[78]   See case C-44/96, *Mannesmann Anlagenbau Austria and Others*, [1998] ECR I-73; case C-237/99, *Commission v. France*, [2001] ECR I-939.

[79]   See, *inter alia*, *BFI Holding*, paragraph 36, and *Agorà and Excelsior*, paragraph 32.

building project relating to the construction of several office blocks and a multi-storey car park. That operation, which followed from the town of Varkaus's decision to create a technological development centre on its territory, and Taitotalo's stated intention to buy the land from the town once the site had been parcelled out, and to make the newly constructed buildings available to firms in the technology sector, was an activity capable of meeting a need in the general interest.

The Court held in a similar case[80] as to whether a body whose objects were to carry on and facilitate any activity concerned with the organisation of trade fairs, exhibitions and conferences could be regarded as a body governed by public law within the meaning of Article 1(b) of Directive 92/50, that activities relating to the organisation of such events meet needs in the general interest, in that an organiser of those events, in bringing together manufacturers and traders in one geographical location, is not acting solely in the individual interest of those manufacturers and traders, who are thereby afforded an opportunity to promote their goods and merchandise, but is also providing consumers who attend the events with information that enables them to make choices in optimum conditions. The resulting stimulus to trade may be considered to fall within the general interest. Similar considerations may be put forward *mutatis mutandis* with respect to the activity at issue in the main proceedings, in that it is undeniable that, in acquiring design and construction services in connection with a building project relating to the construction of office blocks, Taitotalo is not acting solely in the individual interest of the undertakings directly concerned by that project but also in that of the town of Varkaus. Activities such as those carried on by Taitotalo in the case of the main proceedings may be regarded as meeting needs in the general interest, in that they are likely to give a stimulus to trade and the economic and social development of the local authority concerned, since the location of undertakings in the territory of a municipality often has favourable repercussions for that municipality in terms of creation of jobs, increase of tax revenue and improvement in the supply and demand of goods and services.

A more difficult question, on the other hand, is whether such needs in the general interest have a character which is not industrial or commercial. While the Finnish government submitted that those needs have no industrial or commercial character, in that Taitotalo aims not so much to make a profit as to create favourable conditions for the location of undertakings in the territory of the town of Varkaus, Taitotalo put forward the contrary argument, on the grounds that it provides services precisely for commercial undertakings and that the financing of the building project in question is borne essentially by the private sector.

---

[80] See *Agorà and Excelsior*, paragraphs 33 and 34.

The Court has maintained that needs in the general interest, not having an industrial or commercial character, within the meaning of Article 1(b) of the Community directives relating to the co-ordination of procedures for the award of public contracts are generally needs which are satisfied otherwise than by the availability of goods and services in the market place and which, for reasons associated with the general interest, the state chooses to provide itself or over which it wishes to retain a decisive influence.[81] It cannot be excluded that the acquisition of services intended to promote the location of private undertakings in the territory of a particular local authority may be regarded as meeting a need in the general interest whose character is not industrial or commercial. In assessing whether or not such a need in the general interest is present, account must be taken of all the relevant legal and factual elements, such as the circumstances prevailing at the time that the body concerned was established and the conditions under which it exercises its activity. In particular, it must be ascertained whether the body in question carries on its activities in a situation of competition, since the existence of such competition may, as the Court has previously held, be an indication that a need in the general interest has an industrial or commercial character.[82]

However, it also follows from the wording of that judgment that the existence of significant competition does not of itself permit the conclusion that there is no need in the general interest not having an industrial or commercial character.[83] The same applies to the fact that the body in question aims specifically to meet the needs of commercial undertakings. Other factors must be taken into account before reaching such a conclusion, in particular the question of the conditions in which the body in question carries on its activities. If the body operates in normal market conditions, aims to make a profit, and bears the losses associated with the exercise of its activity, it is unlikely that the needs it aims to meet are not of an industrial or commercial nature. In such a case, the application of the Public Procurement Directives would not be necessary, moreover, because a body acting for profit and itself bearing the risks associated with its activity will not normally become involved in an award procedure on conditions which are not economically justified. The purpose of those directives is to avert both the risk of preference being given to national tenderers or applicants whenever a contract is awarded by the contracting authorities and the possibility that a body financed or controlled by the state, regional or local authorities or other

---

[81] See *BFI Holding*, paragraphs 50 and 51, *Agorà and Excelsior*, paragraph 37, and *Adolf Truley*, paragraph 50.
[82] See *BFI Holding*, paragraphs 48 and 49.
[83] See *Adolf Truley*, paragraph 61.

bodies governed by public law may choose to be guided by other than economic considerations.[84]

The Court considered that there are few differences between companies such as Taitotalo and limited companies owned by private operators, in that they bear the same economic risks as the latter and may similarly be declared bankrupt, the regional and local authorities to which they belong rarely allow such a thing to happen and will, if appropriate, recapitalise those companies so that they can continue to look after the tasks for which they were established, essentially the improvement of the general conditions for the pursuit of economic activity in the local authority area in question. The Court also held that while it is not impossible that the activities of companies such as Taitotalo may generate profits, the making of such profits can never constitute the principal aim of such companies, since under Finnish law they must always aim primarily to promote the general interest of the inhabitants of the local authority area concerned. In such conditions, and having regard to the fact mentioned by the national court that Taitotalo received public funding to carry out the building project at issue in the main proceedings, it appears probable that an activity such as that pursued by Taitotalo in this case meets a need in the general interest not having an industrial or commercial character. The Court asserted that it is for the national court to assess the circumstances which prevailed when that body was set up and the conditions in which it carries on its activity, including in particular whether it aims to make a profit and bears the risks associated with its activity.

The fact that the activity at issue represents only a minor part of Taitotalo's activities would be of no relevance to the description of the entity as a contracting authority, in so far as that company continues to look after needs in the general interest. The status of a body governed by public law is not dependent on the relative importance, within that body's activity, of the meeting of needs in the general interest not having an industrial or commercial character.[85] The Court reached the conclusion that a limited company established, owned and managed by a regional or local authority meets a need in the general interest, within the meaning of the second subparagraph of Article 1(b) of Directive 92/50, where it acquires services with a view to promoting the development of industrial or commercial activities in the territory of that regional or local authority. To determine whether that need has no industrial or commercial character, the national court must assess the circumstances which

---

[84] See case C-380/98, *University of Cambridge*, [2000] ECR I-8035, paragraph 17; case C-470/99, *Universale-Bau and Others*, [2002] ECR I-11617, paragraph 52; and *Adolf Truley*, paragraph 42.

[85] See *Mannesmann Anlagenbau Austria and Others*, paragraphs 25, 26 and 31; *BFI Holding*, paragraphs 55 and 56; and *Adolf Truley*, paragraph 56.

prevailed when that company was set up and the conditions in which it carries on its activity, taking account in particular of the fact that it does not aim primarily at making a profit, the fact that it does not bear the risks associated with the activity, and any public financing of the activity in question.

The question as to whether the fact that the offices to be constructed are leased only to a single undertaking would not affect the lessor's status as a body governed by public law, where it is shown that the lessor meets a need in the general interest not having an industrial or commercial character.

Transfer of Undertakings and Contracting Authorities

The relevance of the Acquired Rights Directive[86] to the public procurement regime became clear when contracting authorities started *testing the market* in an attempt to define whether the provision of works or services from a commercial operator could be cheaper than that from the in-house team. This is the notion of *contracting out*, an exercise which aims at achieving potential savings and efficiency gains for contracting authorities. The application of the transfer of undertakings rules in contracting out cases has the important consequence that the external bidder (if successful) must engage the authority's former employees on the same conditions as they enjoyed under the authority itself.

The initial Directive proclaimed its inapplicability in cases where the undertaking was not in the nature of a commercial venture; this proviso was interpreted as exclusive of contracting out by government. The impact of the Transfer of Undertakings Directive in the context of public procurement was felt in a landmark decision of the Court,[87] which maintained that the Directive does not permit such a limitation. Thus it became apparent that contracting out by government and other public authorities was covered, and a transfer of an undertaking may take place where the government contracts out to the private sector a function previously carried out in-house[88] and vice versa, namely where the contracting authority takes back in-house a service formerly contracted out. The circumstances under which a transfer of an undertaking through contracting out occurs depend upon the transfer retaining its identity.[89] However, the 'retention of identity' test can only be satisfied when the

---

[86]   Directive 77/62, OJ C 61/26 [1977], as amended by Directive 98/50, OJ L 132 [1998] and consolidated by Directive 2001/23 OJ L 82/16 [2001].

[87]   Case C-29/91, *Dr Sophie Redmond Stichting v. Bartol*, [1992] IRLR 369.

[88]   Case C-382/92, *Commission v. United Kingdom*, [1994] ECR 1.

[89]   Case 24/85, *Spijkers v. Gebroders Benedik Abbatoir CV*, [1986] ECR 1, 1123. Case C-209/91, *Rask v. ISS Kantinservice*, [1993] ECR 1. Case C-392/92, *Schmidt v. Spar und Leihkasse der fruherer Amter Bordersholm, Kiel und Cronshagen*, [1994] ECR 1, 1320.

undertaking transferred represents *substantially the same* or *similar activities*,[90] as well as relating to a *stable economic entity*.[91] The existence of a contractual link or relation between the parties to a transfer of an undertaking is not a decisive criterion to establish the applicability of the Directive.[92]

Serious concerns have been raised over the compatibility of the public procurement and the transfer of undertakings regimes.[93] It appeared that there was a clear antithesis between the drivers of two regimes in achieving savings on the one hand, whilst protecting employees on the other. However, the *Liikenne*[94] case confirmed the compatibility of the two regimes.[95] The Court's jurisprudence relating to the applicability of transfer of undertakings to public procurement has positioned transfers amongst contractual terms and conditions of a contract, thus obliging contracting authorities to inform tenderers appropriately, so the latter can factor all relevant financial consequences into their bid.

---

[90]   Case C-392/92, *Schmidt v. Spar und Leihkasse der fruherer Amter Bordersholm, Kiel und Cronshagen*, [1994] ECR 1, 1320.

[91]   Case C-48/94, *Rygaard v. Stro Molle Akustik*, judgment of 19 September 1995.

[92]   See case C-324/86, *Tellerup*, judgment of 10 February 1998.

[93]   See the analysis of Bovis, 'The compatibility of socio-economic policies with competitive tendering: the case of contract compliance and transfer of undertakings', chapter 21, in Collins, Davies and Rideout (eds), *Legal Regulation of the Employment Relations*, Kluwer, 2000.

[94]   See case C-172/99, judgment of 25 January 2001, points 21 to 22.

[95]   See also the conclusions of Advocate-General Léger in case C-172/99, in particular paragraphs 28 to 37; and also paragraph 22 of the judgment in this case.

9. Award procedures in public sector procurement

PROCEDURES AND THE CHOICE OF PARTICIPANTS

Contracting authorities must award public contracts by applying principally open or restricted procedures. In the specific circumstances expressly provided for in Article 29 of the Directive, contracting authorities may award their public contracts by means of a competitive dialogue. In the specific cases and circumstances referred to expressly in Articles 30 and 31 of the Directive, they may apply a negotiated procedure, with or without publication of a contract notice.[1]

In restricted procedures, negotiated procedures with publication of a contract notice and in the competitive dialogue procedure, contracting authorities may limit the number of suitable candidates they will invite to tender, to negotiate or to conduct a dialogue with, provided a sufficient number of suitable candidates are available.[2] The contracting authorities must indicate in the contract notice the objective and non-discriminatory criteria or rules they intend to apply, the minimum number of candidates they intend to invite and, where appropriate, the maximum number.

In the restricted procedure the minimum number of tenderers must be five. In the negotiated procedure with publication of a contract notice and the competitive dialogue procedure the minimum number of candidates must be three. In any event the number of candidates invited must be sufficient to ensure genuine competition. The contracting authorities must invite a number of candidates at least equal to the minimum number set in advance.[3] Where the number of candidates meeting the selection criteria and the minimum levels of ability is below the minimum number, the contracting authority may continue the procedure by inviting the candidate(s) with the required capabilities. However, when the number of candidates is below the minimum number, contracting authorities may not include other economic oper-

---

[1] Article 28, paragraph 2 of the Public Sector Directive.
[2] See Article 44(3) of the Public Sector Directive.
[3] Article 44(3), second indent of the Public Sector Directive.

ators who did not request to participate, or candidates who do not have the required capabilities.

Where contracting authorities exercise the option of reducing the number of solutions to be discussed or of tenders to be negotiated, provided for in Articles 29(4) and 30(4) of the Directive, they must apply the award criteria stated in the contract notice, in the specifications or in the descriptive document.[4] In the final stage, the number of candidates invited to participate or tender must ensure genuine competition to the extent that there are enough solutions or suitable candidates.

OPEN PROCEDURES

Open procedures, alongside restricted procedures, are from the normal award procedures stipulated in the Directive and contracting authorities must first have recourse to them in awarding public contracts.[5] The normal character of the open procedure does not mean that it is a mandatory award procedure. Rather, it indicates its priority over other procedures such as negotiated procedures or the competitive dialogue.

Open procedures are those award procedures where any interested economic operator may submit a tender.[6] After publishing a notice, contracting authorities must await a minimum of 52 days from the date on which the contract notice was published for the receipt of tenders.[7] When contracting authorities have published a prior information notice (PIN), the minimum time limit for the receipt of tenders may, as a general rule, be shortened to 36 days. The time limit must run from the date on which the contract notice was sent in open procedures.[8]

The shortened time limit should be permitted on two conditions.[9] First, contracting authorities must have dispatched the prior information notice for publication between 52 days and 12 months before the date on which the relevant contract notice was sent for publication. Secondly, the prior information notice has to include all the information required for the contract notice, in so far as that information is available at the time the prior information notice is published.

Where notices are drawn up and transmitted by electronic means, the time

---

[4] See Article 44(4) of the Public Sector Directive.
[5] Article 28(2) of the Public Sector Directive.
[6] Article 1(11)(a) of the Public Sector Directive.
[7] See Article 38(2) of the Public Sector Directive.
[8] Article 38(4) of the Public Sector Directive.
[9] See Article 38(4) of the Public Sector Directive.

limits for the receipt of tenders in open procedures may be shortened by seven days. The time limits for receipt of tenders may be reduced by a further five days where the contracting authority offers unrestricted and full direct access by electronic means to the contract documents and any supplementary documents from the date of publication of the notice, specifying in the text of the notice the internet address at which this documentation is accessible.[10]

Specifications, Additional Documents and Information

Where contracting authorities do not offer unrestricted and full direct access by electronic means to the specifications and any supporting documents, the specifications and supplementary documents must be sent to economic operators within six days of receipt of the request to participate, provided that the request was made in good time before the deadline for the submission of tenders.[11]

Provided that it has been requested in good time, additional information relating to the specifications and any supporting documents must be supplied by the contracting authorities or competent departments not later than six days before the deadline fixed for the receipt of tenders.[12]

Extension of Time Limits

Contracting authorities may extend the time limits and deadlines applicable to open procedures for the receipt of tenders if, for whatever reason, the specifications and the supporting documents or additional information, although requested in good time, are not supplied within six days of receipt of the request to participate.[13] In cases where additional information relating to the specifications and any supporting documents were requested but not provided within six days of receipt of the request to participate, the contracting authority may also extend the time limits for the receipt of tenders.

Extension of time limits can be provided also where the submission of tenders is possible only after a visit to the site or after on-the-spot inspection of the documents supporting the contract documents.

---

[10]   Article 38(5) of the Public Sector Directive.
[11]   Article 39(1) of the Public Sector Directive.
[12]   See Article 39(2) of the Public Sector Directive.
[13]   See Article 38(7) of the Public Sector Directive.

RESTRICTED PROCEDURES

Alongside open procedures, restricted procedures represent the norm in award procedures for public procurement contracts.[14] Restricted procedures are those procedures in which any economic operator may request to participate and whereby only those economic operators invited by the contracting authority may submit a tender.[15]

Contracting authorities using restricted procedures must set the minimum time limit for receipt of requests to participate at 37 days from the date on which the contract notice is sent for publication.[16] The minimum time limit for the receipt of tenders must be 40 days from the date on which the invitation is sent to the participant tenderers.[17]

When contracting authorities have published a prior information notice, the minimum time limit for the receipt of tenders may, as a general rule, be shortened to 22 days. The time limit must run from the date on which the invitation to tender was sent to the participants.[18] The shortened time limit should be allowed if contracting authorities have fulfilled two conditions. First, the prior information notice has to include all the information required for the contract notice, in so far as that information is available at the time the notice is published. Secondly, the prior information notice must have been sent for publication between 52 days and 12 months before the date on which the contract notice was sent.

In cases where contracting authorities utilise electronic means to draw up and transmit notices in accordance with the format and procedures for transmission indicated in Annex VIII of the Directive, the time limit for the receipt of requests to participate may be shortened by seven days.[19]

In cases where the contracting authority offers unrestricted and full direct access by electronic means to the contract documents and any supplementary documents from the date of publication of the notice, by specifying in the text of the notice the internet address at which this documentation is accessible, the time limit for receipt of tenders may be reduced by five days.[20]

The reduction in the time limit for the receipt of requests to participate in cases where contracting authorities utilise electronic means to draw up and transmit notices and the reduction in the time limit for receipt of tenders in

---

[14]   Article 28(2) of the Public Sector Directive.
[15]   See Article 1(11)(b) of the Public Sector Directive.
[16]   Article 38(3)(a) of the Public Sector Directive.
[17]   See Article 38(3)(b) of the Public Sector Directive.
[18]   Article 38(4) of the Public Sector Directive.
[19]   Article 38(5) of the Public Sector Directive.
[20]   Article 38(6) of the Public Sector Directive.

cases where contracting authorities offer unrestricted and full direct access by electronic means to the contract documents and any supplementary documents may run concurrently.

Extension of Time Limits

Contracting authorities may extend the time limits and deadlines specified for the receipt of tenders in restricted procedures if, for whatever reason, the specifications and the supporting documents or additional information, although requested in good time, are not supplied within the time limits set in Article 38(4)(5) of the Directive.[21] Extension of time limits can be provided also where the submission of tenders is possible only after a visit to the site or after on-the-spot inspection of the documents supporting the contract documents.

Accelerated Restricted Procedure on Grounds of Urgency

Where for reasons of urgency contracting authorities cannot adhere to the time limits specified in the Directive for the receipt of requests to participate and for the receipt of tenders respectively, an accelerated form of the restricted procedure may be used.[22]

Contracting authorities may stipulate a time limit for the receipt of requests to participate which may not be less than 15 days from the date on which the contract notice was sent, or less than 10 days if the notice was sent by electronic means, in accordance with the format and procedure for sending notices laid down in Annex VIII. Contracting authorities may also stipulate a time limit for the receipt of tenders which must be not less than 10 days from the date of the invitation to tender.

Invitation to Submit a Tender under Restricted Procedures

Contracting authorities must simultaneously and in writing invite the selected candidates to submit their tenders.[23] The invitation to the candidates should include a copy of the specifications and any supporting documents, or a reference to allow the invited parties to access by electronic means the specifications and the supporting documents.[24]

Where an entity other than the contracting authority responsible for the award procedure has the specifications and any supporting documents, the

---

21 Article 38(7) of the Public Sector Directive.
22 See Article 38(8) of the Public Sector Directive.
23 Article 40(1) of the Public Sector Directive.
24 Article 40(2) of the Public Sector Directive.

invitation must provide the address from which the specifications and the supporting documents may be requested and, where appropriate, the deadline for requesting such documents, and the sum payable for obtaining them and any payment procedures.[25] The entity that is responsible for dispatching the relevant documentation, upon receipt of a request from economic operators that have been invited to tender, must send any documentation relevant to the specifications and any supporting documents to the economic operators without delay.

Any additional information relevant to the specifications or any supporting documents must be sent by the contracting authority or the competent department not less than four days before the deadline fixed for the receipt of tenders, provided that it is requested in good time.[26]

The Content of the Invitation to Tender in Restricted Procedures

Apart from the copy of the specifications and any supporting documents, or a reference to allow the invited parties to access by electronic means the specifications and the supporting documents, contracting authorities must provide,[27] as a minimum requirement, the following information in the invitation to submit tenders:

(a) a reference to the contract notice published;
(b) the deadline for the receipt of the tenders, the address to which the tenders must be sent and the language or languages in which the tenders must be drawn up;
(c) a reference to any documents or certificates to be submitted in support of the economic operator's personal situation, economic and financial standing and technical and professional capacity according to Articles 44, 47 and 48 of the Directive, or documents in support of verifiable declarations by the tenderer where the official documentation and certification cannot be provided in accordance with Article 44;
(d) the relative weighting of criteria for the award of the contract or, where appropriate, the descending order of importance for such criteria, if they are not given in the contract notice, the specifications or the descriptive document.

---

[25] See Article 40(3) of the Public Sector Directive.
[26] Article 40(4) of the Public Sector Directive.
[27] See Article 40(5) of the Public Sector Directive.

CASE-LAW ON RESTRICTED PROCEDURES

Restricted Procedures and Weighting of Criteria

A question arose[28] as to whether, in the context of a restricted procedure, a contracting authority which has laid down in advance the rules on the weighting of criteria for selecting the candidates who will be invited to tender, is obliged to state them in the contract notice or the tender documents. The relevant contracting authority had instead deposited the documents specifying those methods with a notary.

The applicants in the main proceedings before the national court claimed that the procedure followed by the contracting authority not to reveal to the candidates either the detailed rules of the scoring procedure or the importance of the different criteria for ranking the applications to take part is incompatible with the principles of transparency and objectivity. They claimed that the respective importance of the different ranking criteria must, in any event, appear in the contract notice, so as to exclude any arbitrariness in the contracting authority's decision and to enable the candidates to scrutinise the lawfulness thereof and to make use of their right of review.

The contracting authority submitted that a procedure such as depositing with a notary documents specifying the detailed rules for evaluating the applications to take part is sufficient guarantee of compliance with the principles of non-discrimination and objectivity. They submitted that, whilst it is clear from the principles of non-discrimination and objectivity that the contracting authority must prescribe in advance the procedure which it will use to choose the candidates and that such method of selection may not be subsequently changed, these principles do not require the contracting authorities to divulge the precise details of the rules for evaluating the candidatures. The contracting authority maintained that it had set out the principal criteria for ranking the applications to take part in order of importance, and that it was precisely to encourage lawful and fair competition that it did not make known in advance to the candidates the precise detailed rules for evaluating the applications.

The Court held that in the context of a restricted procedure, contracting authorities which have laid down in advance the rules for weighting the criteria for selecting the candidates who will be invited to tender are obliged to state them in the contract notice or tender documents. The Court maintained that the Public Procurement Directives contain no specific provision relating to the requirements for prior advertisement concerning the criteria for selecting the candidates who will be invited to tender in the context of a restrictive

---

[28]   See case C-470/99, *Universale-Bau and Others*, [2002] ECR I-11617.

procedure.[29] The Public Procurement Directives have as their prime aim simply to co-ordinate national procedures for the award of public works contracts, although it does not lay down a complete system of Community rules on the matter.[30] The Directives nevertheless aim to abolish restrictions on the freedom of establishment and on the freedom to provide services in respect of public works contracts in order to open up such contracts to genuine competition between undertakings in the member states.[31] The Court reiterated that the criteria and conditions which govern public contracts must be given sufficient publicity by the contracting authorities.[32]

The Court reiterated that the principle of equal treatment which underlies the Public Procurement Directives on procedures for the award of public contracts implies an obligation of transparency in order to enable verification that it has been complied with.[33] That obligation of transparency which is imposed on the contracting authority consists in ensuring, for the benefit of any potential tenderer, a degree of advertising sufficient to enable the services market to be opened up to competition and the impartiality of procurement procedures to be reviewed.[34] The Court held that the procedure for awarding a public contract must comply, at every stage, particularly that of selecting the candidates in a restricted procedure, both with the principle of equal treatment of the potential tenderers and with the principle of transparency so as to afford all tenderers equality of opportunity in formulating the terms of their applications to take part in the award procedures.[35]

The Court maintained that the Public Procurement Directives require advertising requirements in respect of the criteria both for selecting candidates and for awarding the contract.[36] Thus, in relation, first, to the selection criteria, Article 7(2) of Directive 93/37, which concerns negotiated procedures, requires that the candidates are to be selected according to known qualitative criteria. Secondly, in relation to the award criteria for both negotiated and

---

[29]   See case C-470/99, *Universale-Bau and Others*, [2002] ECR I-11617, paragraph 87.
[30]   See joined cases C-285/99 and C-286/99, *Lombardini and Mantovani*, [2001] ECR I-9233, paragraph 33.
[31]   See joined cases, C-285/99 and C-286/99, *Lombardini and Mantovani*, [2001] ECR I-9233, paragraph 34.
[32]   See case 31/87, *Beentjes*, [1988] ECR 4635, paragraph 21.
[33]   See case C-324/98, *Telaustria and Telefonadress*, [2000] ECR I-10745, paragraph 61, and case C-92/00, *HI*, [2002] ECR I-5553, paragraph 45.
[34]   See case C-324/98, *Telaustria and Telefonadress*, [2000] ECR I-10745, paragraph 62.
[35]   See case C-87/94, *Commission v. Belgium*, [1996] ECR I-2043, paragraph 54.
[36]   See the 10th and 11th recitals in the preamble to the Public Works Directive 93/37.

restricted procedures,[37] the public procurement rules provide that they form part of the minimum information which must be mentioned in the letter of invitation to tender, if they do not already appear in the contract notice. Similarly, for all types of procedure, where the award of the contract is made to the most economically advantageous tender, Article 30(2) of Directive 93/37, which applies to both the open procedure and the restricted and negotiated procedures, imposes on the contracting authority the obligation to state in the contract documents or in the contract notice all the criteria it intends to apply to the award, where possible in descending order of importance. The Court stated that where the contracting authority has set out a ranking in order of importance of the criteria which it intends to use for the award, it may not confine itself to a mere reference thereto in the contract documents or in the contract notice, but must, in addition, inform the tenderers of the ranking which it has used.

With respect to the Utilities Directive 90/531 and in particular Article 27(2), the terms of which are substantially the same as those of Article 30(2) of Directive 93/37, the requirement thus imposed on the contracting authorities is intended precisely to inform all potential tenderers, before the preparation of their tenders, of the award criteria to be satisfied by these tenders and the relative importance of those criteria, thus ensuring the observance of the principles of equal treatment of tenderers and of transparency.[38]

The Court finally concluded that in the context of a restricted procedure, the contracting authority which has laid down prior to the publication of the contract notice the rules for the weighting of the selection criteria it intends to use is obliged to bring them to the prior knowledge of the candidates.

THE COMPETITIVE DIALOGUE

In the case of particularly complex contracts, contracting authorities may provide that where contracting authorities consider that the use of the open or restricted procedure will not allow the award of the contract, the use of the competitive dialogue procedure is required.[39]

Competitive dialogue is a procedure in which any economic operator may request to participate and whereby the contracting authority conducts a dialogue with the candidates admitted to that procedure, with the aim of developing one

---

[37] See Article 13(2)(e) of the Public Works Directive 93/97.

[38] See case C-87/94, *Commission v. Belgium*, [1996] ECR I-2043, paragraphs 88 and 89.

[39] See Article 29(1) of the Public Sector Directive.

or more suitable alternatives capable of meeting its requirements, and on the basis of which the candidates chosen are invited to tender.[40]

A public contract is considered to be particularly complex where the contracting authorities are not able to define objectively the technical means of the contract.[41] In particular, to formulate the technical specifications required for the performance of the contract, contracting authorities must take into account any mandatory national technical rules, to the extent that they are compatible with Community law.[42] In addition, the technical specifications must be formulated by sufficiently precise parameters having reference to the performance or functional requirements, including environmental characteristics, of the works, supplies or services. The requirement of sufficient precision in the formulation of the technical specifications must be present in order to allow tenderers to determine the subject-matter of the contract and also to allow contracting authorities to award the contract. In such cases, where the technical specifications cannot be formulated with sufficient precision that they are capable of satisfying their needs or the objectives of the contracting authority, the contract is deemed to be particularly complex.[43]

A public contract is also considered particularly complex in cases where contracting authorities cannot determine the performance or functional requirements of a project in conformity with the technical standards defined in Annex VI of the Directive and, in order of preference, national standards transposing European standards, European technical approvals, common technical specifications, international standards, or any equivalent standard.[44] In such cases, the inability to comply with the required technical standards precludes the contracting authority from determining the technical specifications necessary for the performance of the contract and as a consequence, the needs and objectives of the contracting authority cannot be met.[45] Therefore, the public contract is deemed to be particularly complex.

Finally, when contracting authorities cannot objectively specify the legal or the financial make-up of a project, the contract is deemed to be particularly complex.

Conduct of the Competitive Dialogue

When contracting authorities wish to use the competitive dialogue as an award procedure, they must publish a notice for the contract setting out their needs

---

[40] Article 1(11)(c) of the Public Sector Directive.
[41] See Article 1(11)(c), second indent of the Public Sector Directive.
[42] Article 23(3) of the Public Sector Directive.
[43] Article 23(3)(b) of the Public Sector Directive.
[44] See Article 23(3)(c) of the Public Sector Directive.
[45] Article 23(3)(d) of the Public Sector Directive.

and requirements.[46] The notice must define in a clear and objective manner the needs and requirements to be achieved through the contract. Alternatively, a descriptive document may be used to stipulate the contracting authority's need and requirements. Contracting authorities may specify prices or payments to the participants in the dialogue.[47]

The preliminary phase of the competitive dialogue is to select a number of candidates with which contracting authorities may commence a dialogue with the aim of identifying the means best suited to meeting their needs and requirements. The selection process should take place in accordance with the usual selection provisions found in Articles 44 to 52 of the Directive, covering *inter alia* the personal situation of the candidates, their suitability to pursue a professional activity, their economic and financial standing and their technical and professional ability. The Directive does not specify the minimum number of candidates to be invited to participate in the competitive dialogue. However, the number of candidates should be adequate in order to provide sufficient competition and to identify enough solutions from which the solution which meets the needs and requirements of the contracting authority will emerge.

Opening of the Competitive Dialogue

The most important requirement in this phase is the equal treatment of candidates by the contracting authority.[48] They may discuss all aspects of the contract with the chosen candidates. However, they must not provide information in a discriminatory manner which may give some candidates an advantage over others.

The opening of the competitive dialogue commences when contracting authorities simultaneously and in writing invite the selected candidates to take part in the dialogue.[49] The invitation to the candidates must include a copy either of the specifications or of the descriptive document and any supporting documents or a reference in order to access by electronic means the specifications and any supporting documents.[50] Where an entity other than the contracting authority responsible for the award procedure has the specifications, the descriptive document or any supporting documents, the invitation must state the address from which those documents may be requested and, if appropriate,

---

46   See Article 29(2) of the Public Sector Directive.
47   Article 29(8) of the Public Sector Directive.
48   Article 29(3) of the Public Sector Directive.
49   See the requirements laid down in Article 40 of the Public Sector Directive.
50   Article 40(2) of the Public Sector Directive.

the deadline for requesting such documents, and the sum payable for obtaining them and any payment procedures.

The invitation to participate in the dialogue must contain also[51] a reference to the contract notice published; the address and the date set for the start of consultation and the language or languages used; a reference to any additional documents to be submitted, either in support of or supplementing verifiable declarations by the participants that they meet minimum capacity levels required for the contract, levels which must be related and proportionate to the subject-matter of the contract and previously indicated in the contract notice; the relative weighting of criteria for the award of the contract or, where appropriate, the descending order of importance of such criteria, if they are not given in the contract notice, the specifications or the descriptive document.

The deadline for the receipt of the tenders, the address to which the tenders must be sent and the language or languages in which the tenders must be drawn up must not appear in the invitation to participate in the dialogue but instead in the invitation to submit a tender.

In principle, contracting authorities may not reveal to the other participants solutions proposed or other confidential information communicated by a candidate participating in the dialogue without that candidate's prior agreement.[52] The dialogue should be continued until the contracting authority can identify the solution or solutions, if necessary after comparing them, which are capable of meeting its needs.[53]

The dialogue with the selected candidates can take place in a single stage or in successive stages.[54] The reason for the successive stages in the competitive dialogue is to reduce the number of solutions to be discussed by the contracting authority and the candidates. When contracting authorities wish to have recourse to successive stages during the competitive dialogue, their intention must be mentioned in the contract notice or the descriptive document. In order to reduce the solutions on offer during the competitive dialogue, contracting authorities must apply the award criteria in the contract notice or the descriptive document. Contracting authorities must ensure that the elimination of solutions proposed by candidates does not jeopardise a genuine competition, which is necessary for the final tendering stage of the competitive dialogue.[55]

---

51 Article 40(5) of the Public Sector Directive.
52 See Article 29(3), second indent of the Public Sector Directive.
53 See Article 29(5) of the Public Sector Directive.
54 Article 29(4) of the Public Sector Directive.
55 Article 44(4) of the Public Sector Directive.

Closure of the Competitive Dialogue

When a particular solution or a number of solutions have been identified, the contracting authority must declare that the dialogue is concluded.[56] It must communicate its decision to all candidates that have participated and at the same time ask them to submit their final tenders on the basis of the solution or solutions presented and specified during the dialogue. The minimum number of candidates which could be invited to submit tenders is three.

Submission of Final Tenders

The tenders submitted by the invited candidates must contain all the elements required and necessary for the performance of the project, as identified in the solution or the solutions during the dialogue between the contracting authorities and the candidates.[57]

These tenders may be clarified, specified and fine-tuned at the request of the contracting authority. However, such clarification, specification, fine-tuning or additional information may not involve changes to the basic features of the tender or the call for tender, variations in which are likely to distort competition or have a discriminatory effect.

For the assessment of the tenders, contracting authorities must apply the criteria specified in the contract notice or the descriptive document.[58] After the assessment exercise of the tenders, the contracting authority must identify the candidate that submitted the most economically advantageous tender in accordance with Article 53 of the Directive.

Award of the Contract

Contracting authorities may award the contract straightaway or seek clarifications of any aspects of the tender or commitments contained which were contained in the tender.[59] A public contract awarded under the procedures of the competitive dialogue must be based solely on the most economically advantageous tender as the award criterion. The candidate which submitted the most economically advantageous tender, at the request of the contracting authority, may be asked to clarify aspects of the tender or confirm commitments contained in the tender provided this does not have the effect of modifying substantial aspects of the tender or of the call for tender and does not risk distorting competition or causing discrimination.

---

[56] See Article 29(6) of the Public Sector Directive.
[57] See Article 29(6), second indent of the Public Sector Directive.
[58] Article 29(7) of the Public Sector Directive.
[59] Article 29(7), second indent of the Public Sector Directive.

NEGOTIATED PROCEDURES

Negotiated procedures are the award procedures under which contracting authorities consult the economic operators of their choice and negotiate the terms of contract with one or more of these.[60] There are two types of negotiated procedures. Negotiated procedures with prior publication of a contract notice and negotiated procedures without prior publication of a contract notice.[61]

Grounds for Use of the Negotiated Procedure with Prior Publication of a Contract Notice

Contracting authorities may award their public contracts by negotiated procedure, after publication of a contract notice, in the following cases:[62]

(a) in the event of irregular tenders in response to an open or restricted procedure or a competitive dialogue in so far as the original terms of the contract are not substantially altered;

(b) in the event of the submission of the tenders which are unacceptable and have been rejected under national provisions compatible with the provisions of the Directive and in particular the nature of economic operators (Article 4), variants included in the tender (Article 24), subcontracting (Article 25), the obligations of economic operators relating to taxes, environmental protection, employment protection and working conditions (Article 27) and provisions of Chapter VII of the Directive on the economic operator's personal situation, economic and financial standing and technical and professional capacity of economic operators.

(c) in exceptional cases, when the nature of the works, supplies or services or the risks attached to the performance of the contract do not permit prior overall pricing;

(d) in the case of services, *inter alia* services within category 6 of Annex II A (insurance services and banking and investment services, except financial services in connection with the issue, sale, purchase or transfer of securities or other financial instruments, and central bank services), and intellectual services such as services involving the design of works, in so far as the nature of the services to be provided is such that contract specifications cannot be established with sufficient precision to permit

---

[60] See Article 1(11)(d) of the Public Sector Directive.
[61] Article 38(8) of the Public Sector Directive.
[62] See Article 31 of the Public Sector Directive.

the award of the contract by selection of the best tender according to the rules governing open or restricted procedures;

(e)   in respect of public works contracts, for works which are performed solely for purposes of research, testing or development and not with the aim of ensuring profitability or recovering research and development costs.

Accelerated Negotiated Procedures on Grounds of Urgency

Where for urgency reasons contracting authorities cannot adhere to the time limits specified in the Directive for the receipt of requests to participate and for the receipt of tenders respectively, an accelerated form of the negotiated procedure may be used.[63]

Contracting authorities may stipulate a time limit for the receipt of requests to participate which may not be less than 15 days from the date on which the contract notice was sent, or less than 10 days if the notice was sent by electronic means, in accordance with the format and procedure for sending notices indicated in Annex VIII of the Directive.

Invitation to Negotiate

In negotiated procedures with publication of a contract notice, contracting authorities must simultaneously and in writing invite the selected candidates to negotiate. The invitation to the candidates must include either a copy of the specifications and any supporting documents or a reference to accessing the specifications and any related documents, when they are made directly available by electronic means.[64] The invitation to negotiate must contain, as a minimum requirement, the following information:

(a)   a reference to the contract notice published;

(b)   the deadline for the receipt of tenders; the address to which the tenders must be sent and the language or languages in which the tenders must be drawn up;

(c)   a reference to any documents or certificates to be submitted in support of the economic operator's personal situation, economic and financial standing and technical and professional capacity according to Articles 44, 47 and 48 of the Directive, or documents in support of verifiable declarations by the tenderer in the case that official documentation and certification cannot be provided in accordance with Article 44;

---

63   See the provisions laid down in Article 38(8) of the Public Sector Directive.
64   Article 44 of the Public Sector Directive.

(d) the relative weighting of criteria for the award of the contract or, where appropriate, the descending order of importance of such criteria, if they are not given in the contract notice, the specifications or the descriptive document.

Where an entity other than the contracting authority responsible for the award procedure has the specifications or any supporting documents, the invitation to negotiate must specify the address from which those specifications and those documents may be requested and, if appropriate, the deadline for requesting such documents and any payment necessary for obtaining them.[65] Upon receipt of such a request, the entity that has the specifications or any supporting documents must dispatch them to the economic operators participating in the negotiations without delay.

Any additional information on the specifications or the supporting documents must be sent by the contracting authority or the competent department at least six days before the deadline for the receipt of tenders, provided that such information is requested in good time. In the event of an accelerated negotiated procedure, that period must be four days.

Conduct of Negotiated Procedures with Prior Publication

In negotiated procedures with publication of a contract notice the minimum time limit for receipt of requests to participate must be 37 days from the date on which the contract notice is sent to the Official Journal.[66] Where notices are drawn up and transmitted by electronic means in accordance with the format and procedures for transmission indicated in Annex VIII, the time limits for the receipt of tenders may be shortened by seven days.[67] In the case of negotiated procedures with publication of a contract notice where urgency renders impracticable the time limits specified above, contracting authorities may stipulate a time limit for the receipt of requests to participate which may not be less than 15 days from the date on which the contract notice was sent, or less than 10 days if the notice was sent by electronic means, in accordance with the format and procedure for sending notices described in Annex VIII of the Directive.[68]

During the negotiations with participants, contracting authorities must ensure that all tenderers receive equal treatment. In particular, contracting authorities must not provide any information in a discriminatory manner which may give some tenderers an advantage over others.[69]

---

[65] Article 44(2) of the Public Sector Directive.
[66] Article 38(3) of the Public Sector Directive.
[67] Article 38(5) of the Public Sector Directive.
[68] Article 38(8) of the Public Sector Directive.
[69] See Article 30(3) of the Public Sector Directive.

Contracting authorities may provide for the negotiated procedure to take place in successive stages in order to reduce the number of tenders to be negotiated by applying the award criteria in the contract notice or the specifications. The contract notice or the specifications must indicate whether contracting authorities wish to use successive stages in the procedure.[70]

The outcome of the negotiated procedures with prior publication must lead to the adaptation of the tenders and offers submitted by the participants to the needs and requirements of the contracting authority, which must have been set out in the contract notice, the specifications and any additional documents.[71] Following this process, the contracting authority must seek the best tender in accordance with Article 53(1) of the Directive and award the contact based on either the most economically advantageous offer or the lowest price.

Case-Law on Negotiated Procedures with Prior Publicity

The process of liberalising public procurement relies to a great extent on the principle of objectivity in the award of public contracts. The Court had the opportunity to reflect on award procedures under the relevant Directives and subject the negotiated procedures, particularly those without prior advertisement, to a restrictive interpretation. According to the previous procurement Directives, negotiated procedures without prior notification shall be used restrictively inter alia '... when for technical or artistic reasons or reasons connected with the protection of exclusive rights the services could only be procured by a particular provider ... and ... in cases of extreme urgency brought about by events unforeseeable by the contracting authority'.

The Court reinforced its restrictive interpretation of the above two reasons to which contracting authorities might be allowed to have recourse and maintained their exceptional character rather than their prohibitive use, and the onerous obligation of contracting authorities to justify them.

The presence of technical or artistic reasons, or reasons which are connected with the protection of exclusive rights, and as a result allow for a contracting authority to negotiate without prior advertisement with a particular contractor or service provider, has attracted the attention of the Court in two instances.[72] The Court rejected the existence of exclusive rights in both cases and regarded the abuse of this provision as contrary to the right of establishment and freedom to provide services which are based on the principle of equal treatment and prohibit not only overt discrimination on grounds of

---

70   Article 30(4) of the Public Sector Directive.
71   See Article 30(2) of the Public Sector Directive.
72   See cases C-199/85, *Commission v. Italy*, [1987] ECR 1039; also C-3/88, *Commission v. Italy*, [1989] ECR 4035.

nationality, but also all covert forms of discrimination, which, by the application of other criteria of differentiation, lead to the same result. Interestingly, the Court elucidated that exclusive rights might include contractual arrangements such as know-how and intellectual property rights (case 199/85, *Commission v. Italy*).

Urgency reasons brought about by unforeseen events affecting contracting authorities received similarly restrictive interpretation.[73] The Court maintained the need for a justification test based on the proportionality principle (case 199/85, *Commission v. Italy*), as well as the existence of a causal link between the alleged urgency and the unforeseen events.[74]

Grounds for Use of Negotiated Procedures

In *Commission v. Spain*,[75] the use of negotiated procedures based on grounds not provided by the Directives was examined. The Commission took the view that the Spanish law has authorised the use of the negotiated procedure in two cases, namely for the award of contracts following procedures declared unsuccessful and the award of supply contracts for uniform goods.

First, the grounds concerning the award of contracts following unsuccessful procedures were examined and were deemed to contravene the exhaustive list of grounds for the use of negotiated procedures stipulated in the Public Procurement Directives. The national law provided that contracting authorities might also have recourse to negotiated procedures, in so far as it had not been possible to award the contract during an open or restricted procedure or where the candidates were not allowed to tender, provided that there were no modifications of the original conditions of the contract apart from the price, which could not be increased by more than 10%. In the Commission's view, by permitting an increase in the original tender price of up to 10% in relation to the earlier open or restricted procedures, the national law contravened Directives 93/36 and 93/37, since they allowed a substantial alteration of one of the original conditions of the contract, namely the price. The Commission maintained that the list of cases in respect of which the negotiated procedure might be used was limited. The interpretation of the concept of 'non-substantial alteration' must therefore be restrictive. The Spanish government

---

[73] See C-199/85, *Commission v. Italy*, op. cit.; C-3/88, *Commission v. Italy*, op. cit. C-24/91; *Commission v. Spain*, [1994] CMLR 621; C-107/92, *Commission v. Italy*, judgment of 2 August 1993; C-57/94, *Commission v. Italy*, judgment of 18 May 1995; C-296/92, *Commission v. Italy*, judgment of 12 January 1994.

[74] See case C-107/92, *Commission v. Italy*, judgment of 2 August 1993.

[75] See case C-84/03, *Commission of the European Communities v. Kingdom of Spain*, not yet reported.

asserted that for the purposes of legal certainty, the Spanish legislature transformed the vague notion of 'substantial modifications to the original conditions of the contract' into a well-defined notion, since in the wording of the Public Procurement Directives, there is no indication as to which price modifications must be regarded as substantial and which do not merit such a classification.

The Court ruled that the negotiated procedure is exceptional in nature and, therefore, must be applied only in cases which are set out in an exhaustive list.[76] It held that Articles 6(3)(a) of Directive 93/36 and Article 7(3)(a) of Directive 93/37 exhaustively list the cases in which the negotiated procedure may be used without prior publication of a tender notice. The derogations from the rules intended to ensure the effectiveness of the rights conferred by the Treaty in connection with public works contracts must be interpreted strictly.[77] To prevent the directives at issue being deprived of their effectiveness, the member states cannot, therefore, use the negotiated procedure in cases not provided for in Directives 93/36 and 93/37, or add new conditions to the cases expressly provided for by those Directives, which make that procedure easier to use. The Court held that the national law has added a new condition to the provisions of Directives 93/36 and 93/37 capable of undermining both their scope and their exceptional character. Such a condition cannot be regarded as a non-substantial alteration of the original terms of the contracts as provided for in Article 6(3)(a) of Directive 93/36 and Article 7(3)(a) of Directive 93/37.

Secondly, the grounds concerning the award of supply contracts for uniform goods as a justification for the use of negotiated procedures were also deemed to be in contravention of the Public Procurement Directives. Spanish law provided that the negotiated procedure might be used without prior publication of a tender notice in respect of goods whose uniformity had been held to be necessary for their common use by the administration. The use of that procedure was possible in so far as the type of goods had been chosen in advance and independently, pursuant to a call for tenders.

The Commission submitted that the award of supply contracts for uniform goods disregarded the provisions of Article 6(2) and (3) of Directive 93/36, which sets out in an exhaustive manner the cases in which the negotiated procedure may be applied. The Spanish government contended that the calls for tenders seeking to determine the type of uniform goods are similar to framework contracts and do not differ in any way from the tendering procedures following a contract under a framework agreement, although framework agreements are not covered by the Public Supplies Directive 93/36.

---

[76] The Court referred to the 12th recital in the preamble to Directive 93/36 and the eighth recital in the preamble to Directive 93/37.

[77] See case C-57/94, *Commission v. Italy*, [1995] ECR I-1249, paragraph 23, and case C-318/94, *Commission v. Germany*, [1996] ECR I-1949, paragraph 13.

The Court reiterated that the negotiated procedure may be used only in the cases exhaustively listed in Article 6(2) and (3) of Directive 93/36, whereas Article 6(4) of that Directive states that 'in all other cases, the contracting authorities shall award their supply contracts by the open procedure or by the restricted procedure'. The Court found that the provision at issue concerning the award of supply contracts for uniform goods did not correspond either to the case mentioned in Article 6(2) of Directive 93/36 or to one of the five situations listed in Article 6(3) in which the use of a negotiated procedure without prior publication of a tender notice is expressly permitted. It also stated that the concept of framework agreement does not come within the scope of those exceptions. The Court repeated its consistent jurisprudence that the provisions which authorise derogations from the rules intended to ensure the effectiveness of the rights conferred by the Treaty in the field of public supply contracts must be strictly interpreted.[78] The Court concluded that the law at issue, to the extent that it authorises use of the negotiated procedure without prior publication of a tender notice for the procedures involving goods whose uniformity has been held to be necessary for their common use by the public authorities, provided that the choice of the type of goods has been made in advance, pursuant to a call for tenders, constitutes an incorrect transposition of Article 6(2) and (3) of Directive 93/36.

Justifications for Use of Negotiated Procedures

The municipality of Bockhorn in Lower Saxony concluded a contract for the collection of its waste water for a term of at least 30 years from 1997 with the energy distribution undertaking *Weser-Ems AG* without recourse to the Public Procurement Directives. Also the city of Braunschweig, also in Lower Saxony, concluded a contract with *Braunschweigsche Kohlebergwerke* for residual waste disposal by thermal processing for a period of 30 years from 1999. The Commission brought two actions[79] under Article 226 EC for declarations that by failing to invite tenders for the award of the contract, Germany had failed to observe the relevant provisions of the Public Services Directive 92/50 in relation to the publication and advertisement of contracts[80] and those provisions in relation to the award of public contracts by negotiated procedures without prior advertisement.[81]

---

[78]   See case C-71/92, *Commission v. Spain*, [1993] ECR I-5923, paragraph 36.

[79]   See joined cases C-20/01 and C-28/01, *Commission of the European Communities v. Federal Republic of Germany*, [2003] ECR I-3609.

[80]   See Article 8 in conjunction with Articles 15(2) and 16(1) of Directive 92/50, OJ 1992 L 209, p. 1.

[81]   See Articles 8 and 11(3)(b) of Directive 92/50.

The German government and the municipality of Bockhorn did not contest the applicability of the relevant public procurement provisions in relation to the advertisement of the contract with *Weser-Ems AG.* The Court therefore pronounced on Germany's failure to observe the Public Services Directive. However, the competent authorities of the city of Braunschweig took the view that Directive 92/50 applied, but relied on Article 11(3) thereof to release them from their obligation to publish a contract notice, and award the contract by a negotiated procedure. They argued that the conditions to which Article 11(3)(b) of Directive 92/50 applied were met, since for technical reasons thermal treatment of waste could be entrusted only to *Braunschweigsche Kohlebergwerke*. It had been an essential criterion of the award of the contract that the incineration facilities were close to the city of Braunschweig in order to avoid transport over longer distances. Furthermore, the city authorities justified the choice of the award procedure at issue with an argument based on the guarantee that waste would be disposed of.

The German government argued that only *Braunschweigsche Kohlebergwerke* was in a position to satisfy the quite lawfully selected criterion that the waste disposal facility should be close to the relevant region. The criterion was not automatically discriminatory, since it was not impossible for undertakings established in other member states to meet the requirement. The German government submitted that a contracting authority is entitled to take account of environmental criteria in its considerations relating to the award of a public contract when it determines which type of service it is proposing to acquire.

The Commission submitted that the criteria allowing a negotiated procedure to be used without publication of a prior contract notice, as provided for in Article 11(3)(b) of Directive 92/50, were not met. Neither the location of the undertaking selected, on account of its proximity to the place where the services were to be provided, nor the fact that award of the contract was urgent, provided a basis for the application of that provision in this instance. The Commission argued that the principle provided for in Article 130r(2) of the EC Treaty (now, after amendment, Article 174 EC), that environmental damage should as a priority be rectified at source, should be read in the light of that provision as a whole, according to which environmental protection requirements must be integrated into the definition and implementation of other Community policies. Article 130r(2) does not provide that Community environmental policy is to take precedence over other Community policies in the event of a conflict between them. Nor, in the context of a procedure for the award of public contracts, can ecological criteria be used for discriminatory ends. As to the argument that the contracting authority justified its choice of the award procedure at issue with an argument based on the guarantee that waste would be disposed of, the Commission maintained that the city's argument refuted the argument that the procedure had been chosen on account of environmental considerations and the proximity of the waste disposal facility.

The Court declared that the argument forwarded by the German government that *Braunschweigsche Kohlebergwerke* was actually the only undertaking to which the contract could be awarded and that a further award procedure would not affect that outcome could not be accepted. It stated that the provisions of Article 11(3) of Directive 92/50, which authorise derogations from the rules intended to ensure the effectiveness of the rights conferred by the Treaty in relation to public service contracts, must be interpreted strictly and that the burden of proving the existence of exceptional circumstances justifying a derogation lies upon the person seeking to rely on those circumstances.[82] Article 11(3)(b) of Directive 92/50 cannot apply unless it is established that for technical or artistic reasons, or for reasons connected with the protection of exclusive rights, only one undertaking is actually in a position to perform the contract concerned. Since no artistic reason, nor any reason connected with the protection of exclusive rights, had been put forward in this instance, it was appropriate solely to ascertain whether the reasons relied on by the German government were capable of constituting technical reasons for the purposes of Article 11(3)(b).

The Court maintained that a contracting authority may take account of criteria relating to environmental protection at the various stages of a procedure for the award of public contracts.[83] Therefore, it is not impossible that a technical reason relating to the protection of the environment may be taken into account in an assessment of whether the contract at issue may be awarded to a given supplier. However, the procedure used where there is a technical reason of that kind must comply with the fundamental principles of Community law, in particular the principle of non-discrimination as it follows from the provisions of the Treaty on the right of establishment and the freedom to provide services.[84] The risk of a breach of the principle of non-discrimination is particularly high where a contracting authority decides not to put a particular contract out to tender.

The Court noted also that, in the absence of any evidence to that effect, the choice of thermal waste treatment cannot be regarded as a technical reason substantiating the claim that the contract could be awarded to only one particular supplier. Secondly, the argument regarding the proximity of the waste

---

[82] See case C-318/94, *Commission v. Germany*, [1996] ECR I-1949, paragraph 13.

[83] See case C-513/99, *Concordia Bus Finland*, [2002] ECR I-7213, paragraph 57.

[84] See case C-513/99, *Concordia Bus Finland*, [2002] ECR I-7213, paragraph 63.

disposal facility as a necessary consequence of the city of Braunschweig's decision that residual waste should be treated thermally is not borne out by any evidence and cannot therefore be regarded as a technical reason justifying the use of negotiated procedures without prior publicity. The Court held that the German government had not proved that the transport of waste over a greater distance would necessarily constitute a danger to the environment or to public health. The Court finally concluded that the fact that a particular supplier is close to the contracting authority's area can likewise not amount, on its own, to a technical reason for justifying the use of negotiated procedures without prior publicity in accordance with Article 11(3)(b) of Directive 92/50.

Causality of Condition Justifying the Use of Negotiated Procedures

The Court pointed out that Article 11(3)(d) of Directive 92/50, as a derogation from the rules intended to ensure the effectiveness of the rights conferred by the EC Treaty in relation to public service contracts, must be interpreted strictly and that the burden of proving the existence of exceptional circumstances justifying a derogation lies on the person seeking to rely on those circumstances.[85] The application of Article 11(3) of the Directive is subject to three cumulative conditions. It requires the existence of an unforeseeable event, extreme urgency rendering the observance of time limits laid down by other procedures impossible, and a causal link between the unforeseeable event and the extreme urgency.[86] The Court maintained that where the causality link is not present, accelerated restricted procedures should be used.[87]

Use of Negotiated Procedure for Technical Reasons

Under Article 7(3)(b) of Directive 93/37, negotiated procedures without prior publication may be allowed when, for technical or artistic reasons or for reasons connected with the protection of exclusive rights, the works may only be carried out by a particular contractor. The definition of the condition that the works may 'only be carried out by a particular contractor' should be interpreted restrictively. According to the Court's case-law, that constitutes derogation and should therefore apply only where there exist exceptional

---

85　See joint cases C-20/01 and C-28/01, *Commission v. Germany*, [2003] ECR I-3609, paragraph 58.

86　See case C-107/92, *Commission v. Italy*, [1993] ECR I-4655, paragraph 12, and case C-318/94, *Commission v. Germany*, [1996] ECR I-1949, paragraph 14.

87　See case C-24/91, *Commission v. Spain*, [1992] ECR I-1989, paragraph 14; case C-107/92, *Commission v. Italy*, [1993] ECR I-4655, paragraph 13.

circumstances.[88] Contracting authorities cannot justify the use of negotiated procedures without prior publicity by simply invoking technical constraints in non-specific terms.[89] Instead they must explain in detail why, in the circumstances of the case, technical reasons made it absolutely necessary for the contract to be awarded to a particular contractor. The burden of proof of the existence of exceptional circumstances lies on the person seeking to rely on them.[90] In the absence of such a justification, contracting authorities might abuse the negotiated procedures without prior publicity in order to avoid calls for tender, and thus subvert the general purpose of the Public Procurement Directives.

Extreme Urgency as a Reason for Negotiated Procedure

Under Article 7(3)(c) of Directive 93/37 negotiated procedures without prior publicity may be allowed in so far as is strictly necessary when, for reasons of extreme urgency brought about by events unforeseen by the contracting authorities in question, the time limit laid down for the open, restricted or negotiated procedures cannot be kept. The circumstances invoked to justify extreme urgency must not in any event be attributable to the contracting authorities. The Court maintained that the wording of the relevant provision ('strictly necessary', 'extreme urgency', 'events unforeseen') attaches strict conditions to any reliance on it and must be construed narrowly.[91] The extreme urgency to conclude a contract by negotiated procedures without prior publicity must not be attributed to the contracting authority. Thus, organisational issues and internal considerations on the part of the contacting authority cannot justify any urgency requirements. The burden of proof of the existence of extreme urgency not attributable to the contracting authority lies on the contracting authority itself.[92]

---

[88]   See case C-57/94, *Commission v. Italy*, [1995] ECR I-1249, paragraph 23. See also case C-318/94, *Commission v. Germany*, [1996] ECR I-1949, paragraph 13. Similarly Advocate-General Jacobs at paragraph 64 of his Opinion of 23 March 2000 in case C-337/98, *Commission v. France*, [2000] ECR I-8377, 8379.

[89]   In case C-385/03, *Commission v. Italy*, the Italian government stated that the competent authority wished to forestall any damage to or deterioration of the works already completed, and to avoid difficult questions as to the respective liability of a number of contractors. Those arguments were rejected by the Court.

[90]   See case C-57/94, *Commission v. Italy*, [1995] ECR I-1249, paragraph 23.

[91]   See case 199/85, *Commission v. Italy*, [1987] ECR 1039, paragraph 14. See also case C-318/94, *Commission v. Germany*, [1996] ECR I-1949, paragraph 13.

[92]   See case C-57/94, *Commission v. Italy*, [1995] ECR I-1249, paragraph 23.

Repetition of Similar Works within Three Years

Under Article 7(3)(e) of Directive 93/37 negotiated procedures without prior publicity may be allowed for new works consisting of the repetition of similar works entrusted to the undertaking to which the same contracting authorities awarded an earlier contract, provided that such works conform to a basic project for which a first contract was awarded. This procedure may only be adopted during the three years following the conclusion of the original contract and subject to notice which should be given in the original invitation to tender. The Court held that in the light of a comparison of the language versions of that provision, the expression 'conclusion of the original contract' must be understood as meaning the time when the original contract was entered into and not as referring to the completion of the works to which the contract relates. As the Court has consistently held,[93] all language versions of a Community provision must be, in principle, recognised as having the same weight. It follows that the correct starting-point for the three-year period should be determined not by considering a single language version in isolation, but on the basis of an overview of all language versions. That interpretation is confirmed by the objective of the provision in question and its place in the scheme of the Directive. First, as it is a derogating provision which falls to be strictly interpreted, the interpretation which restricts the period during which the derogation applies must be preferred rather than that which extends it. That objective is met by the interpretation which takes the starting point as being the date on which the original contract is entered into rather than the, necessarily later, date on which the works which are its subject-matter are completed. Secondly, legal certainty, which is desirable where procedures for the award of public procurement contracts are involved, requires that the date on which the period in question begins can be defined in a certain and objective manner. While the date on which a contract is entered into is certain, numerous dates may be treated as representing the completion of the works and thus give rise to a corresponding level of uncertainty. Moreover, while the date on which the contract is entered into is clearly established at the outset, the date of completion of the works, whatever definition is adopted, may be altered by accidental or voluntary factors for so long as the contract is being carried out.

---

[93] See cases C-296/95, *EMU Tabac and Others*, [1998] ECR I-1605, paragraph 36, and C-257/00, *Givane and Others*, [2003] ECR I-345, paragraph 36.

Grounds for Use of the Negotiated Procedure without Prior Publication of a Contract Notice

Contracting authorities may award public contracts by a negotiated procedure without prior publication of a contract notice in the following cases:[94]

(1) for public works contracts, public supply contracts and public service contracts:

(a) when no tenders or no suitable tenders or no applications have been submitted in response to an open procedure or a restricted procedure, provided that the initial conditions of the contract are not substantially altered and on condition that a report is sent to the Commission if it so requests;

(b) when, for technical or artistic reasons, or for reasons connected with the protection of exclusive rights, the contract may be awarded only to a particular economic operator;

(c) in so far as is strictly necessary when, for reasons of extreme urgency brought about by events unforeseeable by the contracting authorities in question, the time limit for the open, restricted or negotiated procedures with prior publication of a contract notice cannot be complied with. The circumstances invoked to justify extreme urgency must not in any event be attributable to the contracting authority;

(d) where they include in the negotiated procedure all of, and only, the tenderers which satisfy the selection and qualification criteria of Articles 45 to 52 of the Directive and have submitted acceptable tenders as a result of prior open or restricted procedures or competitive dialogue;

(2) for public supply contracts:

(a) when the products involved are manufactured purely for the purpose of research, experimentation, study or development; this provision does not extend to quantity production to establish commercial viability or to recover research and development costs;

(b) for additional deliveries by the original supplier which are intended either as a partial replacement of normal supplies or installations or as an extension of existing supplies or installations where a change of supplier would oblige the contracting authority to acquire material having different technical characteristics, which would result in incompatibility or disproportionate technical difficulties in operation and maintenance; the length of such contracts as well as that of recurrent contracts may not, as a general rule, exceed three years;

---

[94] See the requirements laid down in Article 31 of the Public Sector Directive.

(c)   for supplies quoted and purchased on a commodity market;
(d)   for the purchase of supplies on particularly advantageous terms, from
      either a supplier which is definitively winding up its business activities,
      or the receivers or liquidators of a bankruptcy, an arrangement with cred-
      itors, or a similar procedure under national laws or regulations;

(3) for public service contracts:
when the contract concerned follows a design contest and must, under the
applicable rules, be awarded to the successful candidate or to one of the
successful candidates; in the latter case, all successful candidates must be
invited to participate in the negotiations;

(4) for public works contracts and public service contracts:
(a)   for additional works or services not included in the project initially
      considered or in the original contract but which have, through unforeseen
      circumstances, become necessary for the performance of the works or
      services described therein, on condition that the award is made to the
      economic operator performing such works or services:

      •   when such additional works or services cannot be technically or
          economically separated from the original contract without major
          inconvenience to the contracting authorities, or
      •   when such works or services, although separable from the perfor-
          mance of the original contract, are strictly necessary for its comple-
          tion.

      However, the aggregate value of contracts awarded for additional works
      or services may not exceed 50% of the amount of the original contract;
(b)   for new works or services consisting in the repetition of similar works or
      services entrusted to the economic operator to whom the same contract-
      ing authorities awarded an original contract, provided that such works or
      services are in conformity with a basic project for which the original
      contract was awarded according to the open or restricted procedure.
      Contracting authorities wishing to apply negotiated procedures without
      prior publication of a notice for the possibility of awarding additional
      works to the successful candidate must make their intention known in the
      contract notice that led to the award of the original contract under open
      or restricted procedures.

The total estimated cost of subsequent works or services must be taken into
consideration by the contracting authorities when they calculate the contract
value in accordance with the thresholds applicable under the provisions of

Article 7 of the Directive. Negotiated procedures without prior publication of a notice can be used for the award of new works or services consisting of the repetition of similar works or services entrusted to the economic operator to whom the same contracting authorities awarded an original contract only during the three years following the conclusion of the original contract.

Case-Law on Negotiated Procedures without Prior Publicity

The central issue in *Commission v. Italy*[95] was the utilisation of negotiated procedures without prior advertisement and an assessment of the conditions stipulated in the relevant Directives, in particular whether, in the case of new works consisting of the repetition of similar earlier works, it is permissible and if so, subject to what conditions, for a negotiated procedure to be conducted without prior publication of a contract notice.

The rules governing negotiated procedures without prior publication are defined restrictively in Article 7(3) and (4) of Directive 93/37. Negotiated procedures without prior publication are allowed when, for technical or artistic reasons or for reasons connected with the protection of exclusive rights, the works may only be carried out by a particular contractor; in so far as is strictly necessary when, for reasons of extreme urgency brought about by events unforeseen by the contracting authorities in question, the time limit laid down for the open, restricted or negotiated procedures cannot be kept. The circumstances invoked to justify extreme urgency must not in any event be attributable to the contracting authorities; the circumstances cover cases for new works consisting of the repetition of similar works entrusted to the undertaking to which the same contracting authorities awarded an earlier contract, provided that such works conform to a basic project for which a first contract was awarded. This procedure may only be adopted during the three years following the conclusion of the original contract and subject to notice which should be given in the original invitation to tender.

The Court reiterated the exceptional character of negotiated procedures by reference to Article 7(4) of Directive 93/37 which provides that, in principle, public works contracts are to be awarded by the open procedure or the restricted procedure – and *not*, therefore, by the negotiated procedure. Only in exceptional cases is it permissible to use the negotiated procedure without prior publication of a contract notice. These cases are listed exhaustively in Article 7(3) of the Directive.[96]

---

[95] See case C-385/03, *Commission v. Italy*, 14 September 2004.
[96] See case C-323/96, *Commission v. Belgium*, [1998] ECR I-5063, paragraph 34.

DESIGN CONTESTS

Design contests are those procedures which enable the contracting authority to acquire a plan or design selected by a jury after being put out to competition with or without the award of prizes. The plan or design should be mainly in the disciplines of town and country planning, architecture and engineering or data processing.[97]

Scope and Thresholds

The following contracting authorities can organise design contests:[98]

(a)   contracting authorities which are listed as central government authorities in Annex IV of the Directive, starting from a threshold equal to or greater than Euro 162 000;

(b)   contracting authorities not listed in Annex IV of the Directive, starting from a threshold equal to or greater than Euro 249 000;

(c)   all the contracting authorities, starting from a threshold equal to or greater than Euro 249 000, where contests concern services in the field of research and development,[99] telecommunications services,[100] or services listed in Annex II B.[101]

Conduct of Design Contests

Contracting authorities which wish to carry out a design contest must make

---

[97]   See Article 1(11)(e) of the Public Sector Directive.

[98]   See the provisions of Article 67 of the Public Sector Directive.

[99]   See category 8 of Annex II A of the Directive for research and development services, except research and development services other than those where the benefits accrue exclusively to the contracting authority for its use in the conduct of its own affairs on condition that the service provided is wholly remunerated by the contracting authority.

[100]   Telecommunication services capable of being awarded through design contests have positions which in the CPV are equivalent to reference No. CPC 7524, 7525 and 7526.

[101]   Services described in Annex II B include the following: hotel and restaurant services, rail transport services, water transport services, supporting and transport services, legal services, personnel and placement supply services (except employment contracts), investigation and security services (except armoured services), education and vocational education services, health and social services, recreational, cultural and sporting services, or other services (except contracts for the acquisition, development, production or co-production of programmes by broadcasting organisations and contracts for broadcasting time).

known their intention by means of a contest notice. The usual advertisement and publicity requirements stipulated in Article 36 of the Directive apply to design contests.[102] The notices relating to organisation of design contests must contain the following information:[103]

1. name, address, fax number and e-mail address of the contracting authority and those of the service from which the additional documents may be obtained;
2. description of the project;
3. type of contest: open or restricted;
4. in the event of an open contest: time limit for the submission of projects;
5. in the event of a restricted contest:

   (a) number of participants contemplated;
   (b) names of the participants already selected, if any;
   (c) criteria for the selection of participants;
   (d) time limit for requests to participate;

6. if appropriate, indicate that the participation is restricted to a specified profession;
7. criteria which will be applied in the evaluation of the projects;
8. names of any members of the jury who have already been selected;
9. indicate whether the jury's decision is binding on the contracting authority;
10. number and value of any prizes;
11. payments to be made to all participants, if any;
12. indicate whether any contracts following the contest will or will not be awarded to the winner or winners of the contest.

Design contests could be arranged as part of a procedure leading to the award of a public service contract or as a competition with prizes or payments to participants.[104] The value of the public service contract subject to a design contest should be net of VAT, including any possible prizes and/or payments to participants. The total amount of the prizes and payments to the participants of a design contest, including the estimated value of the public services contract which might be subsequently concluded should not exceed the stipulated thresholds.

---

[102] Article 69 of the Public Sector Directive.
[103] See the format and template of information required in Annex VII D of the Public Sector Directive.
[104] See Article 67(2) of the Public Sector Directive.

After the conclusion of the design contest, contracting authorities must publish a notice of the results including the following information:[105] reference of the contest notice, description of the project, total number of participants, number of foreign participants, the winner(s) of the contest, any prizes awarded to the winner(s).

The admission of participants to design contests must not be limited either by reference to the territory or part of the territory of a member state or on the grounds that, under the law of the member state in which the contest is organised, they would be required to be either natural or legal persons.[106] For the selection of competitors, where design contests are restricted to a limited number of participants, contracting authorities are obliged to lay down clear and non-discriminatory selection criteria. In any event, the number of candidates invited to participate must be sufficient to ensure genuine competition.

Contracting authorities cannot utilise design contests to award (i) public contracts in the water, energy, transport and postal services sectors (Article 12), (ii) contracts with the principal purpose of permitting the contracting authorities to provide or exploit public telecommunications networks or to provide to the public one or more telecommunications services (Article 13), (iii) secret contracts and contracts requiring special security measures (Article 14) and (iv) contracts awarded pursuant to international rules (Article 15).[107]

Composition of the Jury

The jury in a design contest should be composed exclusively of natural persons who are independent of participants in the contest.[108] Where participants in a contest are required to have a particular professional qualification, at least a third of the members of the jury must have that qualification or an equivalent qualification.

Decisions of the Jury

The jury must be autonomous in its decisions or opinions. In its decision-making process, it should examine the plans and projects submitted by the candidates anonymously and solely on the basis of the criteria indicated in the contest notice.[109] It should record its ranking of projects in a report, signed by its members, made according to the merits of each project, together with its

---

[105]   See Article 69(2) of the Public Sector Directive.
[106]   Article 66(2) of the Public Sector Directive.
[107]   Article 68 of the Public Sector Directive.
[108]   Article 73 of the Public Sector Directive.
[109]   See Article 74 of the Public Sector Directive.

remarks and any points which may need clarification. Anonymity must be observed until the jury has reached its opinion or decision. Candidates may be invited, if need be, to answer questions which the jury has recorded in the minutes to clarify any aspects of the projects. The organiser of a design contest must keep complete minutes of the dialogue between jury members and candidates.

Communication between Participants and the Jury

Communications, exchanges and the storage of information relevant to a design contest must ensure that the integrity and the confidentiality of all information communicated by the participants in a contest are preserved and that the jury ascertains the contents of plans and projects only after the expiry of the time limit for their submission.[110] For the electronic receipt of plans and projects, the Directive stipulates that information relating to the specifications which are necessary for the presentation of plans and projects by electronic means, including encryption, must be available to the parties concerned. Member states may introduce or maintain voluntary arrangements for accreditation intended to improve the level of the certification service provided for such devices.[111]

FRAMEWORK AGREEMENTS

A framework agreement is an agreement between one or more contracting authorities and one or more economic operators, the purpose of which is to establish the terms and conditions governing contracts to be awarded during a given period, in particular with regard to price and, where appropriate, the quantity envisaged.[112]

Conduct of Framework Agreements

Contracting authorities may not use framework agreements improperly or in such a way as to prevent, restrict or distort competition.[113] The duration of a framework agreement may not exceed four years.[114] That period may be extended in exceptional circumstances which should be duly justified particularly by reference to the subject of the framework agreement.

---

110 Article 71(2) of the Public Sector Directive.
111 Article 71(3) of the Public Sector Directive.
112 See the definition provided in Article 1(5) of the Public Sector Directive.
113 Article 32(2), fifth indent of the Public Sector Directive.
114 Article 32(2), fourth indent of the Public Sector Directive.

The conclusion of a framework agreement should follow all the phases specified in the Directive in relation to advertisement and publication, selection and qualification of economic operators and award procedures.[115] Contracting authorities must select the parties to the framework agreement by applying the award criteria laid down in Article 53 of the Directive.

After the award of a framework agreement, individual contracts between the contracting authority and the participant(s) to such a framework agreement must be awarded in accordance with specific procedures covering singe-operator framework agreements and multi-operator framework agreements respectively.[116] Those procedures may only be applied between the contracting authorities and the economic operators originally party to the framework agreement.

When awarding contracts based on a framework agreement, especially a single-operator framework agreement, the parties must ensure that no substantial amendments to the terms and conditions laid down in that framework agreement should be allowed.[117]

Award of Contracts-Based Framework Agreements

Where a framework agreement is concluded with a single economic operator, contracts based on that agreement must be awarded within the limits of the terms laid down in the framework agreement.[118] For the award of those contracts, contracting authorities may consult the operator party to the framework agreement in writing, requesting it to supplement its tender as necessary.

Where a framework agreement is concluded with several economic operators, contracting authorities must ensure that the minimum number of operators to be included in the framework agreement is three, provided that a sufficient number of economic operators can satisfy the selection criteria and submit admissible tenders which meet the award criteria.[119]

Contracts based on framework agreements concluded with several economic operators may be awarded without re-opening any tendering/competition stage by application of the terms laid down in the framework agreement.[120]

Alternatively, in cases where the framework agreement does lay down all

---

[115] See Article 32(2) of the Public Sector Directive.
[116] Article 32(4) of the Public Sector Directive.
[117] Article 32(3) of the Public Sector Directive.
[118] See the provisions laid down in Article 32(3) of the Public Sector Directive.
[119] Article 32(4) of the Public Sector Directive.
[120] Article 32(4), second indent of the Public Sector Directive.

the terms and conditions of individual contracts, contracting authorities may stipulate that the parties to the framework agreement should compete on the basis of the same and, if necessary, more precisely formulated terms, and, where appropriate, other terms referred to in the specifications of the framework agreement. The reopening of competition should follow a specific procedure:

(a) for every contract to be awarded, contracting authorities must consult in writing the economic operators capable of performing the contract;

(b) contracting authorities must determine a time limit which is sufficiently long to allow tenders for each specific contract to be submitted, taking into account factors such as the complexity of the subject-matter of the contract and the time needed to send in tenders;

(c) tenders must be submitted in writing, and their content must remain confidential until the stipulated time limit for reply has expired;

(d) contracting authorities must award each contract to the tenderer who has submitted the best tender on the basis of the award criteria set out in the specifications of the framework agreement.

DYNAMIC PURCHASING SYSTEMS

A dynamic purchasing system is a completely electronic process for making commonly used purchases of products. The characteristics of such products should be such as to meet the requirements of contracting authorities by reference to their products' general availability in the market and their standardised specifications.[121] A dynamic purchasing system must be of limited duration and open throughout its validity to any economic operator which satisfies the selection criteria and has submitted an indicative tender that complies with the specification.[122] The costs of setting and running a dynamic purchasing system are borne by the contracting authority. No charges for set-up costs or participating costs for the duration of the dynamic purchasing system may be billed to the interested economic operators or to parties to the system.[123]

Setting up a Dynamic Purchasing System

In order to set up a dynamic purchasing system, contracting authorities must

---

[121] See Article 1(6) of the Public Sector Directive.
[122] Article 3(4) of the Public Sector Directive.
[123] Article 33(7), second indent of the Public Sector Directive.

follow the rules of the open procedure in all its phases up to the award of the contracts.[124] Contracting authorities must:

(a) publish a contract notice with the clear intention of setting up a dynamic purchasing system;
(b) indicate in the specifications, amongst other matters, the nature of the purchases envisaged under that system, as well as all the necessary information concerning the purchasing system, the electronic equipment used and the technical connection arrangements and specifications;
(c) offer by electronic means, on publication of the notice and up to the expiry of the system, unrestricted, direct and full access to the specifications and to any additional documents and must indicate in the notice the internet address at which such documents may be consulted.

With a view to setting up the system and to awarding contracts under that system, contracting authorities must use solely electronic means.[125] The means of communication chosen must be generally available and may under no circumstances restrict the economic operators' access to the tendering procedure. The tools to be used for communicating by electronic means, as well as their technical characteristics, must be non-discriminatory, generally available and interoperable with the information and communication technology products in general use.[126]

Devices used for the electronic receipt of requests to participate and devices used for the electronic transmission and receipt of tenders must ensure the availability of information regarding the specifications necessary for the electronic submission of tenders and requests to participate, including any encryption requirements.[127] Member states may introduce or maintain voluntary accreditation schemes aimed at enhanced levels of certification service provision for these devices.

Such electronic devices must also conform to the requirements of Annex X of the Directive[128] and in particular they must guarantee, through technical means and appropriate procedures, that:

(a) electronic signatures relating to tenders, requests to participate and the

---

[124] Article 33(3) of the Public Sector Directive.
[125] See Article 42(2) to (5) of the Directive.
[126] See the provisions of Article 42(4) of the Public Sector Directive.
[127] Article 42(5) of the Public Sector Directive.
[128] See Annex X of the Directive on Requirements relating to devices for the electronic receipt of tenders, request for participation and plans and projects in contests.

forwarding of plans and projects comply with national provisions adopted pursuant to Directive 1999/93; contracting authorities may require that electronic tenders be accompanied by an advanced electronic signature;

(b)   the exact time and date of the receipt of tenders, requests to participate and the submission of plans and projects can be determined precisely;

(c)   no person can have access to data transmitted before the time limits laid down;

(d)   if data access prohibition is infringed, the infringement must be clearly detectable;

(e)   only authorised persons may set or change the dates for opening data received;

(f)   during the different stages of the contract award procedure or of the contest access to all data submitted must be possible only through simultaneous action by authorised persons;

(g)   simultaneous action by authorised persons must give access to data transmitted only after the prescribed date;

(h)   data received and opened in accordance with these requirements must remain accessible only to authorised persons.

Under a dynamic purchasing system, communication and the exchange and storage of information must be carried out in such a way as to ensure that the integrity of data and the confidentiality of tenders and requests to participate are preserved, and that the contracting authorities examine the content of tenders and requests to participate only after the time limit set for submitting them has expired.[129] Tenderers or candidates for a dynamic purchasing system must submit in hard copy the documents, certificates and declarations referred to in Articles 45 to 50 and Article 52, if they do not exist in electronic format, before expiry of the time limit laid down for submission of tenders or requests to participate.

The Conduct of Dynamic Purchasing Systems

A dynamic purchasing system may not last for more than four years, except in duly justified exceptional cases. Contracting authorities may not resort to this system to prevent, restrict or distort competition.[130]

Admission into a dynamic purchasing system is subject to two requirements: (a) meeting and satisfying the selection and qualification criteria and

---

[129]   Article 42(3) of the Public Sector Directive.
[130]   Article 33(7) of the Public Sector Directive.

(b) submitting an indicative tender which complies with the specification or any possible additional documents.[131] Admittance to a dynamic purchasing system or the rejection of an economic operator's indicative tender must be communicated to the relevant economic operator at the earliest possible opportunity. Throughout the entire period of a dynamic purchasing system, contracting authorities must give any economic operator that has met and satisfied the selection and qualification requirements, the possibility of submitting an indicative tender and of being admitted to the system.

The Indicative Tenders

In order to issue an invitation to tender to those economic operators admitted into a dynamic purchasing system, contracting authorities must publish a simplified contract notice inviting all interested economic operators to submit an indicative tender within 15 days from the date on which the simplified notice was sent. Contracting authorities may not proceed with tendering until they have completed evaluation of all the indicative tenders received by that deadline.[132]

Indicative tenders may be improved at any time provided that they continue to comply with the specification. Contracting authorities must complete the evaluation of indicative tenders within a maximum of 15 days from the date of their submission.[133] However, they may extend the evaluation period provided that no invitation to tender is issued in the meantime.

The Award of Contracts under Dynamic Purchasing Systems

Each specific contract awarded under a dynamic purchasing system must be the subject of an invitation to tender. Contracting authorities, after evaluating the indicative tenders and admitting economic operators into the dynamic purchasing system, must invite tenders from those admitted to the system for each specific contract to be awarded under the system.[134]

A time limit for the submission of tenders must be set by the contracting authorities. The evaluation of tenders should be based on the award criteria set out in the contract notice for the establishment of the dynamic purchasing system.[135] The award of contracts under a dynamic purchasing system must reflect the best tender on the basis of those criteria which may, if appropriate,

131   Article 33(2) of the Public Sector Directive.
132   Article 33(5) of the Public Sector Directive.
133   See Article 33(4), first indent of the Public Sector Directive.
134   See Article 33(5) of the Public Sector Directive.
135   Article 33(6) of the Public Sector Directive.

be formulated more precisely in the invitation to tender extended to the economic operators admitted into the dynamic purchasing system.

ELECTRONIC AUCTIONS

An electronic auction is a repetitive process involving an electronic device for the presentation of new prices, revised downwards, and/or new values concerning certain elements of tenders, which occurs after an initial full evaluation of the tenders, enabling them to be ranked using automatic evaluation methods. Consequently, certain service contracts and certain works contracts having as their subject-matter intellectual performances, such as the design of works, may not be the object of electronic auctions.[136]

Contracting authorities may hold electronic auctions on the reopening of competition among the parties to a framework agreement, as well as on the opening for competition of contracts to be awarded under the dynamic purchasing system.[137] Contracting authorities which decide to hold an electronic auction must indicate their intention in the contract notice.

In open, restricted or negotiated procedures contracting authorities may decide that the award of a public contract must be preceded by an electronic auction when the contract specifications can be established with precision.[138] The specifications must include, *inter alia*, the following details:[139]

(a) the features, the values for which will be the subject of electronic auction, provided that such features are quantifiable and can be expressed in figures or percentages;

(b) any limits on the values which may be submitted, as they result from the specifications relating to the subject of the contract;

(c) the information which will be made available to tenderers in the course of the electronic auction and, where appropriate, when it will be made available to them;

(d) the relevant information concerning the electronic auction process;

(e) the conditions under which the tenderers will be able to bid and, in particular, the minimum differences which will, where appropriate, be required when bidding;

(f) the relevant information concerning the electronic equipment used and the arrangements and technical specifications for connection.

---

[136] Article 1(7) of the Public Sector Directive.
[137] Article 54(2) of the Public Sector Directive.
[138] Article 54(2), first indent of the Public Sector Directive.
[139] Article 54(3) of the Public Sector Directive.

Organization of Electronic Auctions

Before proceeding with an electronic auction, contracting authorities must make a full initial evaluation of the tenders in accordance with the award criteria set and with the weighting attached to them for evaluation purposes.[140] All tenderers who have submitted admissible tenders must be invited simultaneously by electronic means to submit new prices and/or new values; the invitation must contain all relevant information concerning individual connection to the electronic equipment being used and must state the date and time of the start of the electronic auction. The electronic auction may take place in a number of successive phases. The electronic auction may not start sooner than two working days after the date on which invitations are sent out.

The invitation must also state the mathematical formula to be used in the electronic auction to determine automatic re-rankings on the basis of the new prices or new values submitted by the participants.[141] That formula must incorporate the weighting of all the criteria fixed to determine the most economically advantageous tender, as indicated in the contract notice or in the specifications; for that purpose, any ranges must, however, be reduced beforehand to a specified value. Where variants are authorised, a separate formula must be provided for each variant.

Throughout each phase of an electronic auction the contracting authorities must instantaneously communicate to all tenderers at least sufficient information to enable them to ascertain their relative rankings at any moment. They may also communicate other information concerning other prices or values submitted, provided that that is stated in the specifications.

They may also at any time announce the number of participants in that phase of the auction. However, they must not disclose the identities of the tenderers during any phase of an electronic auction.

Closure of Electronic Auctions

The closure of electronic auctions is the next phase that contracting authorities have to follow prior to the award of the contract. The closure of the auction is a necessary procedural requirement integral to the award of contracts in such award procedures and should be observed rigorously.[142]

There are three possible ways in which electronic auctions should be drawn to a close. First, the indication of such closure could be stipulated in the invitation to take part in the auction, where contracting authorities clearly define

---

[140]   Article 54(4) of the Public Sector Directive.
[141]   See Article 54(6) of the Public Sector Directive.
[142]   See Article 54(7) of the Public Sector Directive.

the date and time of the closure in advance. Secondly, the auction can be closed when participants to the auction do not furnish any more new prices or new values which meet the requirements concerning minimum differences stipulated by the contracting authority in the invitation to participate in the auction. In such an event, the contracting authorities must affirm in the invitation to take part in the auction the time which they will allow to elapse after receiving the last submission before they close the electronic auction. Thirdly, an electronic auction may be drawn to a close when the number of phases in the auction, which must be prescribed by the contracting authorities in the invitation to take part in the auction, has been completed. The closure of an auction as a result of the lapse of its predetermined phases must be based on a clear indication in the timetable of each phase of the auction, which must also be stated in the invitation to take part in the auction.

After closing an electronic auction contracting authorities must award the contract on the basis of the results of the electronic auction. Contracting authorities may not have improper recourse to electronic auctions nor may they use them in such a way as to prevent, restrict or distort competition or to change the subject-matter of the contract, as put up for tender in the published contract notice and defined in the specification.[143]

Award Criteria in Electronic Auctions

After the closure of an electronic auction, contracting authorities must award the contract based on the following criteria:[144]

- either solely on prices when the contract is awarded to the lowest price,
- or on prices or on the new values of the features of the tenders indicated in the specification when the contract is awarded to the most economically advantageous tender.

Contracting authorities must stipulate in the invitation to participate in the electronic auction the criteria they will apply to the award of the contract. When the contract is to be awarded on the basis of the most economically advantageous tender, the invitation to participate in an electronic auction must include the relative weighting of the criteria or factors that the contracting authority considers relevant for the evaluation process.[145]

---

[143] Article 54(8) of the Public Sector Directive.
[144] See the details specified in Article 54(8) of the Public Sector Directive.
[145] Article 54(5) of the Public Sector Directive.

PUBLIC HOUSING SCHEMES

Contracting authorities may utilise a special award procedure for the award of public contracts relating to the design and construction of subsidised housing schemes. A public housing scheme is a project which, due to its size and complexity and the estimated duration of the work involved, requires that planning be based from the outset on close collaboration within a team comprising representatives of the contracting authority, experts and the contractor responsible for carrying out the works. The purpose of such a special award procedure is to select the contractor most suitable for integration into the team.[146]

Conduct of Public Housing Schemes Award

Contracting authorities must publish a contract notice in accordance with the standard advertisement and publicity requirements stipulated in the Directive. In the contract notice, they must include a description of the works to be carried out as accurately as possible, in order to enable interested contractors to form a valid and realistic idea of the project.

They also need to include the requirements envisaged in relation to the personal situation of the candidates, their technical and professional capacity and their economic and financial standing in order to perform the public housing scheme contract.

Award of Public Housing Schemes

Where such a procedure is adopted for the award of public housing schemes, contracting authorities must comply with the principles of transparency, equality and non-discrimination stipulated in Article 2 of the Directive. In addition, they must observe the rules on advertising and transparency, in particular the publication of notices (Article 35), the form and manner of publication of notices (Article 36), the time limits for receipt of requests to participate (Article 38), specifications, additional documents and information in relation to open procedures (Article 39), rules applicable to information and communication with candidates and tenderers (Articles 41 and 42) and rules on the content of reports (Article 43).

Finally, before the selection of the successful operator to be intergrated into the team responsible for delivering the public housing scheme, contracting authorities must observe the provisions of the Directive relevant to the

---

[146]   See the provisions of Article 34 of the Public Sector Directive.

personal situation of the candidates or tenderers (Article 45), their suitability to pursue a professional activity (Article 46), their economic and financial standing (Article 47), their technical and professional ability (Article 48), their quality assurance standards (Article 49), their environmental management standards (Article 50). Contracting authorities must also consider candidates which belong to official lists of approved economic operators established by member states or provide certification by bodies established under public or private law in accordance with Article 52 of the Directive.

PUBLIC WORKS CONCESSIONS

Scope and Remit

Public works concession is a contract of the same type as a public works contract except for the fact that the consideration for the works to be carried out consists either solely in the right to exploit the work or in this right together with payment.[147] The Directive applies to all public works concession contracts concluded by contracting authorities where the value of the contracts is equal to or greater than Euro 6 242 000. For the purposes of calculating the contract value, the rules applicable to public works contracts defined in Article 9 of the Directive apply.[148] The Directive does not apply to works concession contracts in the water, energy, transport and postal services sectors (Article 12), to contracts with the principal purpose of permitting the contracting authorities to provide or exploit public telecommunications networks or to provide to the public one or more telecommunications services (Article 13), secret contracts and contracts requiring special security measures (Article 14) and contracts awarded pursuant to international rules (Article 15).[149]

The Nature of the Concessionaire

A concessionaire could be an undertaking which is a contracting authority in accordance with the provision of the Directive.[150] Where the concessionaire is a contracting authority, it must comply with the provisions laid down by this Directive for public works contracts in the case of works to be carried out by third parties. However, it is possible that the concessionaire could be an entity

---

[147] Article 1(3) of the Public Sector Directive.
[148] See Article 56 of the Public Sector Directive.
[149] For the exclusions, see Article 57(a)(b) of the Public Sector Directive.
[150] Article 62 of the Public Sector Directive.

which is not a contracting authority. In such cases, the applicability of the Directive is extended to cover the procurement of the necessary works.[151]

Groups of undertakings which have been formed to obtain the concession or undertakings related to them must not be considered third parties.[152] The term 'related undertaking' means any undertaking over which the concessionaire can exert a dominant influence, whether directly or indirectly, or any undertaking which can exert a dominant influence on the concessionaire or which, as the concessionaire, is subject to the dominant influence of another undertaking as a result of ownership, financial participation or the rules which govern it. A dominant influence on the part of an undertaking is presumed when, directly or indirectly in relation to another undertaking, it: (a) holds a majority of the undertaking's subscribed capital; (b) controls a majority of the votes attached to the shares issued by the undertaking; or (c) can appoint more than half of the undertaking's administrative, management or supervisory body.

The exhaustive list of such undertakings must be included in the application for the concession. That list must be brought up to date following any subsequent changes in the relationship between the undertakings.[153]

Advertisement and Publicity of Public Works Concessions

When contracting authorities wish to award a public works concession contract, they must utilise the advertisement and publicity provisions stipulated in the Directive and must make known their intention by means of a notice.[154] Notices of public works concessions must contain the information referred to in Annex VII C and, where appropriate, any other information deemed useful by the contracting authority, in accordance with the standard forms adopted by the Commission pursuant to the procedure in Article 77(2) of the Directive.

Contract notices for the award of public works concessions must follow the standards procedure stipulated within Article 36(2) to (8). In cases where the envisaged works concession contract is not covered by the Directive, contracting authorities may still publish the notice in accordance with Article 37 on the non-mandatory publication of notices.[155]

---

[151]   Article 63(1) of the Public Sector Directive.
[152]   See the provisions of Article 63(2) of the Public Sector Directive.
[153]   Article 63(2), second indent of the Public Sector Directive.
[154]   Article 64 of the Public Sector Directive.
[155]   Article 64(3) of the Public Sector Directive.

Award Procedures for Public Works Concessions

The Public Sector Directive does not provide for a specific award procedure envisaged for public works concession. Contracting authorities are free to select the standard procedures specified for the award of public contracts. However, contracting authorities must allow a time limit of not less than 52 days from the date of dispatch of the notice for the presentation of applications for the concession.[156] In cases where dispatch of the notice was transmitted by electronic means, the time limit may be shortened by seven days according to Article 38(5).

Member states must ensure that public works concessionaires which are not contracting authorities apply the advertising rules defined in Article 64 when awarding works contracts to third parties where the value of such contracts is equal to or greater than Euro 6 242 000. Works concessionaires which are not contracting authorities and which wish to award works contracts to third parties must use notices in accordance with the standard publication procedures stipulated in the Directive. Notices must contain the information referred to in Annex VII C and, where appropriate, any other information deemed useful by the works concessionaire, in accordance with the standard form adopted by the Commission in accordance with the procedure in Article 77(2). When recourse to negotiated procedures without notification is justified according to Article 31, the advertising of contract notices is not required. The values of contracts awarded by concessionaires which are not contracting authorities must be calculated in accordance with the rules applicable to public works contracts laid down in Article 9 of the Directive.

In works contracts awarded by a works concessionaire which is not a contracting authority, the time limit for the receipt of requests to participate, fixed by the concessionaire, must be not less than 37 days from the date on which the contract notice was dispatched and the time limit for the receipt of tenders not less than 40 days from the date on which the contract notice or the invitation to tender was dispatched.

Subcontracting in Concession Contracts

The contracting authority may require the concessionaire to award contracts representing a minimum of 30% of the total value of the work for which the concession contract is to be awarded, to third parties, at the same time providing the option for candidates to increase this percentage, this minimum percentage being specified in the concession contract. Also, the contracting

---

[156]   See Article 59 of the Public Sector Directive.

authority may request the candidates for concession contracts to specify in their tenders the percentage, if any, of the total value of the work for which the concession contract is to be awarded which they intend to assign to third parties.[157]

Additional Works Awarded to the Concessionaire

Additional works which have not been included in the concession contract when initially considered but subsequently have, through unforeseen circumstances, become necessary for the performance of the work concession are allowed to be awarded by the contracting authority to the concessionaire[158] subject to the following conditions: (a) the additional works cannot be technically or economically separated from the initial contract without major inconvenience to the contracting authorities, or (b) when such works, although separable from the performance of the initial contract, are strictly necessary for its completion. The aggregate value of contracts awarded for additional works may not exceed 50% of the amount of the original works concession contract.

---

[157] Article 60 of the Public Sector Directive.
[158] See Article 61 of the Public Sector Directive.

10. Award criteria in public sector procurement

OVERVIEW

Throughout the evolution of public procurement acquis, the procedural phase of the procurement process culminated in the application of objectively determined criteria which demonstrate the logic behind the behaviour of the contracting authorities. There are two criteria on which the contracting authorities must base the award of public contracts;[1] (a) the most economically advantageous tender and (b) the lowest price.

THE MOST ECONOMICALLY ADVANTAGEOUS TENDER

When the award is made to the tender that is most economically advantageous from the point of view of the contracting authority, various criteria linked to the subject-matter of the public contract in question, for example, quality, price, technical merit, aesthetic and functional characteristics, environmental characteristics, running costs, cost-effectiveness, after-sales service and technical assistance, delivery date and delivery period or period of completion, can be taken into consideration. The above-listed criteria which constitute the parameters of the most economically advantageous offer are not exhaustive.[2]

For the purposes of defining what constitutes the most economically advantageous offer, the contracting authority must specify in the contract notice or in the contract documents or, in the case of a competitive dialogue, in the descriptive document, the relative weighting which it gives to each of the criteria chosen to determine the most economically advantageous tender. Those weightings can be expressed by providing a range with an appropriate maximum spread. Where, in the opinion of the contracting authority, weighting is not possible for demonstrable reasons, the contracting authority must indicate in the contract notice or contract documents or, in the case of a

---

[1] Article 53 of the Public Sector Directive.
[2] Article 53(1)(a) of the Public Sector Directive.

competitive dialogue, in the descriptive document, the criteria in descending order of importance.[3]

The meaning of the most economically advantageous offer includes a series of factors chosen by the contracting authority, including price, delivery or completion date, running costs, cost-effectiveness, profitability, technical merit, product or work quality, aesthetic and functional characteristics, after-sales service and technical assistance, commitments with regard to spare parts and components and maintenance costs, security of supplies. The above list is not exhaustive and the factors listed therein serve as a guide to contracting authorities in the weighted evaluation process of the contract award.

The Court's Stance on the Meaning of the Most Economically Advantageous Tender

The Court reiterated the flexible and wide interpretation of the relevant award criterion[4] and had no difficulty in declaring that contracting authorities may use the most economically advantageous offer as award criterion by choosing the factors which they want to apply in evaluating tenders,[5] provided these factors are mentioned, in hierarchical order or descending sequence, in the invitation to tender or the contract documents,[6] so tenderers and interested parties can clearly ascertain the relative weight of factors other than price in the evaluation process. However, factors which have no strict relevance in determining the most economically advantageous offer by reference to objective criteria do involve an element of arbitrary choice and therefore should be considered as incompatible with the Directives.[7]

Social Considerations as Award Criteria

The most economically advantageous offer as an award criterion has provided the Court with the opportunity to balance the economic considerations of public procurement with policy choices. Although in numerous instances the

---

[3]   Article 53(2) of the Public Sector Directive.
[4]   Case 31/87, *Gebroeders Beentjes v. The Netherlands*, op. cit., paragraph 19.
[5]   Case C-324/93, *R. v. The Secretary of State for the Home Department, ex parte Evans Medical Ltd and Macfarlan Smith Ltd*, judgment of 28 March 1995, where the national court asked whether factors concerning continuity and reliability as well as security of supplies fall under the framework of the most economically advantageous offer, when the latter is being evaluated.
[6]   See paragraph 22 of *Beentjes*.
[7]   See paragraph 37 of *Beentjes*.

Court has maintained the importance of the economic approach[8] in the regulation of public sector contracts, it has also recognised the relative discretion of contracting authorities in utilising non-economic considerations as award criteria. In *Beentjes*,[9] the Court ruled that social policy considerations and in particular measures aimed at combating long-term unemployment could only be part of the award criteria for public contracts, especially in cases where the most economically advantageous offer is selected. The Court accepted that the latter award criterion contains features that are not exhaustively defined in the Directives, therefore there is discretion conferred on contracting authorities to specify what would be the most economically advantageous offer for them. However, contracting authorities cannot refer to such measures as a selection criterion and disqualify candidates which could not meet the relevant requirements. The selection of tenderers is a process, based on an exhaustive list of technical and financial requirements expressly stipulated in the relevant Directives, and the insertion of contract compliance as a selection and qualification requirement would be considered *ultra vires*. The Court held that a contractual condition relating to the employment of long-term unemployed persons is compatible with the Public Procurement Directives, if it has no direct or indirect discriminatory effect on tenders from other member states. Furthermore, such a contractual condition must be mentioned in the tender notice.[10] Rejection of a contract on the grounds of a contractor's inability to employ long-term unemployed persons has no relation to the checking of contractors' suitability on the basis of their economic and financial standing and their technical knowledge and ability. The Court maintained that measures relating to employment could be utilised as a feature of the award criteria only when they are part of a contractual obligation of the public contract in question and on condition that they do not run contrary to the fundamental principles of the Treaty. The significance of that qualification has revealed the Court's potential stance over the issue of contract compliance in public procurement.

In the recent *Nord-Pas-de-Calais* case, the Court considered whether a condition linked to a local project to combat unemployment could be considered as an award criterion for the relevant contract. The Commission alleged that the French Republic had infringed Article 30(1) of Directive 93/37 purely and simply by referring to the criterion linked to the campaign against unemployment as an award criterion in some of the disputed contract notices.

---

[8]   See cases C-380/98, (*Cambridge University*) at paragraph 17, C-44/96, (*Strohal*), paragraph 33; C-360/96, (*BFI*), paragraphs 42 and 43; C-237/99, (*OPAC*), paragraphs 41 and 42.

[9]   See case 31/87, *Gebroeders Beentjes BV v. The Netherlands*, [1989] ECR 4365.

[10]   See *Bellini* case 28/86, [1987] ECR 3347.

Under Article 30(1) of Directive 93/37, the criteria on which contracting authorities are to base the award of contracts are the lowest price only or, when the award is made to the most economically advantageous tender, various criteria according to the contract, such as price, period for completion, running costs, profitability and technical merit.

The Court held that the most economically advantageous offer does not preclude all possibility for the contracting authorities to use as a criterion a condition linked to the campaign against unemployment provided that that condition is consistent with all the fundamental principles of Community law, in particular the principle of non-discrimination deriving from the provisions of the Treaty on the right of establishment and the freedom to provide services.[11] Furthermore, even if such a criterion is not in itself incompatible with Directive 93/37, it must be applied in conformity with all the procedural rules laid down in that Directive, in particular the rules on advertising.[12] The Court therefore accepted employment considerations as an award criterion, part of the most economically advantageous offer, provided they are consistent with the fundamental principles of Community law, in particular the principle of non-discrimination and that they are advertised in the contract notice.

Environmental Considerations as Award Criteria

In *Concordia*,[13] the Court was asked *inter alia* whether environmental considerations such as low emissions and noise levels of vehicles could be included amongst the factors in the most economically advantageous criterion, in order to promote certain types of vehicles that meet or exceed certain emission and noise levels. The Court followed the *Beentjes* principle, and established that contracting authorities are free to determine the factors under which the most economically advantageous offer is to be assessed and that environmental considerations could be part of the award criteria, provided they do not discriminate between alternative offers, and that they have been clearly publicised in the tender or contract documents. However, the inclusion of such factors in the award criteria should not prevent alternative offers that satisfy the contract specifications being taken into consideration by contracting authorities. Clearly the Court wanted to exclude any possibility of environ-

---

[11]   See, *Beentjes*, paragraph 29.
[12]   See, to that effect, paragraph 31 of the judgment, where the Court stipulated that an award criterion linked to the campaign against unemployment must be expressly mentioned in the contract notice so that contractors may become aware of its existence.
[13]   See case C-513/99, Concordia *Bus Filandia v. Helsingin Kaupunki et HKL-Bussiliikenne*, op. cit.

mental considerations being part of the selection criteria or disguised as technical specifications, capable of discriminating against tenderers that could not meet them. Criteria relating to the environment, in order to be permissible as additional criteria under the most economically advantageous offer, must satisfy a number of conditions, namely they must be objective, universally applicable, strictly relevant to the contract in question, and clearly contribute an economic advantage to the contracting authority.[14]

Ecological Criteria

A question arose as to whether Article 36(1) of Directive 92/50 or Article 34(1)(a) of Directive 93/3 which define the most economically advantageous offer as an award criterion would allow the inclusion of a reduction in nitrogen oxide emissions or the noise level of vehicles in such a way that if those emissions or that noise level is below a certain ceiling additional points may be awarded for the comparison of tenders.[15]

The Court considered that in public procurement the criteria for the decision must always be of an economic nature. If the objective of the contracting authority is to satisfy ecological or other considerations, it should have recourse to procedures other than public procurement procedures. The Commission contended that the criteria for the award of public contracts which may be taken into consideration when assessing the economically most advantageous tender must satisfy four conditions. They must be objective, apply to all the tenders, be strictly linked to the subject-matter of the contract in question, and be of direct economic advantage to the contracting authority. On the other hand, it was submitted before the Court that it is permissible to include ecological factors in the criteria for the award of a public contract. The Public Procurement Directives and in particular Article 36(1)(a) of Directive 92/50 and Article 34(1)(a) of Directive 93/38 list merely as examples factors which the contracting authorities may take into account when awarding public contracts.[16] Thus the protection of the environment could well be included amongst the factors which determine the most economically advantageous offer. In addition, reference was made to Article 6 EC, which requires envi-

---

[14] See the analysis in the opinion of the Advocate-General, paragraphs 77 to 123.

[15] See case C-513/99, *Concordia Bus Finland*, [2002] ECR I-7213.

[16] Article 36(1)(a) of Directive 92/50 and Article 34(1)(a) of Directive 93/38 provide that the criteria on which the contracting authority may base the award of contracts may, where the award is made to the economically most advantageous tender, be various criteria relating to the contract, such as, for example, quality, technical merit, aesthetic and functional characteristics, technical assistance and after-sales service, delivery date, delivery period or period of completion, or price.

ronmental protection to be integrated into the other policies of the Community. Finally, the protection of the environment could have direct economic links with policies associated with health and social affairs in the member states.

It also emerged that the award criteria based on the most economically advantageous offer may introduce two essential restrictions. First, the criteria chosen by the contracting entity must relate to the contract to be awarded and make it possible to determine the most economically advantageous tender. Secondly, the criteria must be directly linked to the subject-matter of the contract, have effects which can be measured objectively, must be quantifiable at the economic level and must be capable of guiding the discretion of the contracting entity on an objective basis without including elements of arbitrary choice.

The Court held that in order to determine whether and under what conditions the contracting authority may, in accordance with Article 36(1)(a), take into consideration criteria of an ecological nature, the criteria which may be used as criteria for the award of a public contract to the economically most advantageous tender are not listed exhaustively.[17] Secondly the Court maintained that Article 36(1)(a) cannot be interpreted as meaning that each of the award criteria used by the contracting authority to identify the economically most advantageous tender must necessarily be of a purely economic nature. It cannot be excluded that factors which are not purely economic may influence the value of a tender from the point of view of the contracting authority. That conclusion is also supported by the wording of the provision, which expressly refers to the criterion of the aesthetic characteristics of a tender. In the light of Article 130r(2) EC and Article 6 EC, which lay down that environmental protection requirements must be integrated into the definition and implementation of Community policies and activities, the Court concluded that Article 36(1)(a) of Directive 92/50 does not exclude the possibility of the contracting authority using criteria relating to the preservation of the environment when assessing the economically most advantageous tender.

However, that does not mean that any criterion of that nature may be taken into consideration by contracting authorities. While Article 36(1)(a) of Directive 92/50 leaves it to the contracting authority to choose the criteria on which it proposes to base the award of the contract; that choice may, however, relate only to criteria aimed at identifying the economically most advantageous tender.[18] Since a tender necessarily relates to the subject-matter of the contract, it follows that the award criteria which may be applied in accordance with that provision must themselves also be linked to the subject-matter of the

---

[17]   See case C-19/00, *SIAC Construction*, [2001] ECR I-7725, paragraph 35.

[18]   See *Beentjes*, paragraph 19, *Evans Medical and Macfarlan Smith*, paragraph 42, and *SIAC Construction*, paragraph 36.

contract. The Court has held that, in order to determine the economically most advantageous tender, the contracting authority must be able to assess the tenders submitted and take a decision on the basis of qualitative and quantitative criteria relating to the contract in question.[19] It is also clear that an award criterion having the effect of conferring on the contracting authority an unrestricted freedom of choice as regards the award of the contract to a tenderer would be incompatible with Article 36(1)(a) of Directive 92/50.[20]

The criteria adopted to determine the economically most advantageous tender must be applied in conformity with all the procedural rules laid down in Directive 92/50, in particular the rules on advertising. It follows that, in accordance with Article 36(2) of that Directive, all such criteria must be expressly mentioned in the contract documents or the tender notice, where possible in descending order of importance, so that operators are in a position to be aware of their existence and scope.[21] Such criteria must comply with all the fundamental principles of Community law, in particular the principle of non-discrimination as it follows from the provisions of the Treaty on the right of establishment and the freedom to provide services.[22]

The Court concluded that where the contracting authority decides to award a contract to the tenderer who submits the economically most advantageous tender, it may take criteria relating to the preservation of the environment into consideration, provided that they are linked to the subject-matter of the contract, do not confer an unrestricted freedom of choice on the authority, are expressly mentioned in the contract documents or the tender notice, and comply with all the fundamental principles of Community law, in particular the principle of non-discrimination.

The Court also found that the principle of equal treatment does not preclude taking into consideration criteria concerned with the protection of the environment because the contracting entity's own transport undertaking is one of the few undertakings that actually perform the terms and conditions of the contract. The principle of equal treatment is not breached even if, following a procedure for the award of a public contract, only one tender remains,[23] or even in a case where only a comparatively small number of tenderers are able to satisfy the award criteria. It appears, however, that there is a limit to the permissibility of certain minimum ecological standards where the criteria

---

[19] See case 274/83, *Commission v. Italy,* [1985] ECR 1077, paragraph 25.

[20] See *Beentjes*, paragraph 26, and *SIAC Construction*, paragraph 37.

[21] See *Beentjes*, paragraphs 31 and 36, and case C-225/98, *Commission v. France*, [2000] ECR I-7445, paragraph 51.

[22] See *Beentjes*, paragraph 29, and *Commission v. France*, paragraph 50.

[23] See case C-27/98, *Fracasso and Leitschutz*, [1999] ECR I-5697, paragraphs 32 and 33.

applied restrict the market for the services or goods to be supplied to the point where there is only one tenderer remaining.[24]

Variants

The obligation to set out the minimum specifications required by a contracting authority in order to take variants into consideration is not satisfied where the contract documents merely refer to a provision of national legislation requiring an alternative tender to ensure the performance of work which is qualitatively equivalent to that for which tenders are invited, without further specifying the comparative parameters on the basis of which such equivalence is to be assessed.[25]

According to the Public Procurement Directives,[26] where the criterion for the award of the contract is that of the most economically advantageous tender, contracting authorities may take account of variants which are submitted by a tenderer and meet the minimum specifications required by the contracting authorities. Contracting authorities must state in the contract documents the minimum specifications to be respected by the variants and any specific requirements for their presentation and they must indicate in the tender notice if variants are not permitted. Contracting authorities may not reject the submission of a variant on the sole grounds that it has been drawn up with technical specifications defined by reference to national standards transposing European standards, to European technical approvals or to common technical specifications referred to in the Public Procurement Directives.[27]

Where the contracting authority has not excluded the submission of variants, it is under an obligation to set out in the contract documents the minimum specifications with which those variants must comply. Consequently, a reference made in the contract documents to a provision of national legislation cannot satisfy the requirements of transparency and equal treatment of tenderers wishing to forward a variant bid.[28] Tenderers may be deemed to be informed in the same way of the minimum specifications with which their variants must comply in order to be considered by the contracting authority

---

[24]   See case 45/87, *Commission v. Ireland*, [1988] ECR 4929.

[25]   See case C-421/01, *Traunfellner GmbH and Österreichische Autobahnen und Schnellstraßen Finanzierungs-AG (Asfinag)*, [2003] ECR I-11941.

[26]   See Article 19 of the Public Works Directive 93/37 and the equivalent provisions in all Public Procurement Directives.

[27]   See Article 10(2) or the reference to national technical specifications in Article 10(5)(a) and (b) of the Public Works Directive 93/37 and the equivalent provisions in all Public Procurement Directives.

[28]   See case 31/87, *Beentjes*, [1988] ECR 4635, paragraph 35, and case C-225/98, *Commission v. France*, [2000] ECR I-7445, paragraph 73.

only where those specifications are set out in the contract documents. This involves an obligation of transparency designed to ensure compliance with the principle of equal treatment of tenderers, which must be complied with in any procurement procedure governed by the Directive.[29]

A question arose as to whether a contracting authority can reject an alternative tender which differs from a tender conforming to the contract specifications in that it proposes different technical specifications, without specifying the comparative parameters to be used to assess the equivalence of all tenders.[30] The Court asserted that consideration of variants is subject to fulfilment of the requirement that the minimum specifications with which those variants must comply be set out in the contract documents and that a mere reference in those documents to a provision of national legislation is insufficient to satisfy that requirement. Variants may not be taken into consideration where the contracting authority has failed to comply with the requirements with respect to the statement of minimum specifications, even if they have not been declared inadmissible in the tender notice. The Court held that award criteria based on the most economically advantageous offer can apply only to variants which have been properly taken into consideration by a contracting authority.

Criteria Related to the Subject-matter of the Contract

A question arose as to whether a contracting authority can apply, and under what conditions, in its assessment of the most economically advantageous tender for a contract for the supply of electricity, a criterion requiring that the electricity supplied be produced from renewable energy sources.[31] In principle, that question referred to the possibility of a contracting authority laying down criteria that pursue advantages which cannot be objectively assigned a direct economic value, such as advantages related to the protection of the environment. The Court held that each of the award criteria used by the contracting authority to identify the most economically advantageous tender must not necessarily be of a purely economic nature.[32] The Court therefore accepted that where the contracting authority decides to award a contract to the tenderer

---

[29]   See case C-19/00, *SIAC Construction*, [2001] ECR I-7725, paragraphs 41 and 42.

[30]   See case C-421/01, *Traunfellner GmbH and Österreichische Autobahnen und Schnellstraßen Finanzierungs-AG (Asfinag)*, [2003] ECR I-11941.

[31]   See case C-448/01, *EVN AG, Wienstrom GmbH and Republik Österreich*, judgment of 4 December 2003.

[32]   See case C-513/99, *Concordia Bus Finland*, [2002] ECR I-7123, paragraph 55.

who submits the most economically advantageous tender it may take into consideration ecological criteria, provided that they are linked to the subject-matter of the contract, do not confer an unrestricted freedom of choice on the authority, are expressly mentioned in the contract documents or the tender notice, and comply with all the fundamental principles of Community law, in particular the principle of non-discrimination.[33] The Court concluded that the Public Procurement Directives do not preclude a contracting authority from applying, in the context of the assessment of the most economically advantageous tender for a contract for the supply of electricity, a criterion requiring that the electricity supplied be produced from renewable energy sources, provided that that criterion is linked to the subject-matter of the contract, does not confer an unrestricted freedom of choice on the authority, is expressly mentioned in the contract documents or the contract notice, and complies with all the fundamental principles of Community law, in particular the principle of non-discrimination.

The criterion requiring that the electricity supplied be produced from renewable energy sources had a number of characteristics which posed further questions as to their compatibility with public procurement acquis. In particular, the criterion that the electricity supplied should be produced from renewable energy sources had a weighting of 45%; was not accompanied by requirements which permit the accuracy of the information contained in the tenders to be effectively verified, and could not necessarily achieve the objective pursued; did not impose a defined supply period; and required tenderers to state how much electricity they can supply from renewable energy sources to a non-defined group of consumers, and allocated the maximum number of points to whichever tenderer stated the highest amount, where the supply volume is taken into account only to the extent that it exceeded the volume of consumption to be expected in the context of the contract to which the invitation to tender relates.

With regard to the fact that the criterion that the electricity supplied should be produced from renewable energy sources had a weighting of 45%, the question posed was whether a consideration such as the protection of the environment which is not capable of being assigned a direct economic value, could have such a significant influence on the award decision. The Court held that it is open to the contracting authority when choosing the most economically advantageous tender to choose the criteria on which it proposes to base the award of contract, provided that the purpose of those criteria is to identify the most economically advantageous tender and that they do not confer on the

---

[33]   See case C-513/99, *Concordia Bus Finland*, [2002] ECR I-7123, paragraph 69.

contracting authority an unrestricted freedom of choice as regards the award of the contract to a tenderer.[34] Such criteria must be applied in conformity with both the procedural rules and the fundamental principles laid down in Community law.[35] The Court maintained that contracting authorities are free not only to choose the criteria for awarding the contract but also to determine the weighting of such criteria, provided that the weighting enables an overall evaluation to be made of the criteria applied in order to identify the most economically advantageous tender.

With reference to the award criterion requiring that the electricity supplied be produced from renewable energy sources and its relative weighting of 45% in the evaluation process of determining the most economically advantageous offer, the Court held that the use of renewable energy sources for producing electricity is useful for protecting the environment in so far as it contributes to the reduction in emissions of greenhouse gases which are amongst the main causes of climate change which the European Community and its member states have pledged to combat.[36] Therefore, the importance of the objective pursued by that criterion justified its weighting of 45% and did not present an obstacle to an overall evaluation of the criteria applied in order to identify the most economically advantageous tender.

The award criterion requiring that the electricity supplied be produced from renewable energy sources was not accompanied by requirements which permit the accuracy of the information contained in the tenders to be effectively verified, and as a result it was deemed that it could not necessarily serve the objective pursued. That posed a serious question as to the compatibility of such a criterion with public procurement rules. The Court held that an award criterion which is not accompanied by requirements which permit the information provided by the tenderers to be effectively verified is contrary to the principles of Community law in the field of public procurement and particularly the principle of equal treatment, which underlies[37] the Public Procurement Directives and implies that tenderers must be in a position of equality both when they formulate their tenders and when those tenders are being assessed by the contracting authority.[38] More specifically, that means that when tenders are being assessed, the award criteria must be applied objectively and uniformly

---

[34]   See case 31/87, *Beentjes*, [1988] ECR 4635, paragraphs 19 and 26; case C-19/00, *SIAC Construction*, [2001] ECR I-7725, paragraphs 36 and 37; and *Concordia Bus Finland*, paragraphs 59 and 61.

[35]   See *Beentjes*, paragraphs 29 and 31, and *Concordia Bus Finland*, paragraphs 62 and 63.

[36]   See case C-379/98, *PreussenElektra*, [2001] ECR I-2099, paragraph 73.

[37]   See case C-470/99, *Universale-Bau and Others*, [2002] ECR I-11617, paragraph 91, and case C-315/01, *GAT*, [2003] ECR I-0000, paragraph 73.

[38]   See *SIAC Construction*, paragraph 34.

to all tenderers.[39] The principle of equal treatment also implies an obligation of transparency in order to enable verification that it has been complied with, which consists in ensuring, *inter alia*, review of the impartiality of procurement procedures.[40] Objective and transparent evaluation of the various tenders depends on the contracting authority relying on the information and proof provided by the tenderers, being able to verify effectively whether the tenders submitted by those tenderers meet the award criteria. The Court concluded that where a contracting authority lays down an award criterion indicating that it neither intends, nor is able, to verify the accuracy of the information supplied by the tenderers, it infringes the principle of equal treatment, because such a criterion does not ensure the transparency and objectivity of the tender procedure. However, the fact that an award criterion such as the requirement to supply electricity from renewable energy sources is not objectively verifiable cannot be regarded as incompatible with public procurement law simply because it does not necessarily achieve the objective pursued, in so far as it is not necessarily capable of helping to increase the amount of electricity produced from renewable energy sources.

The fact that in the invitation to tender the contracting authority omitted to determine the period in respect of which tenderers had to state the amount of electricity from renewable energy sources which they could supply, would result in an infringement of the principles of equal treatment and transparency if that omission made it difficult or even impossible for tenderers to interpret the exact scope of the criterion in question in a uniform manner. The Court held that it is for the national courts to determine the clarity of formulation of award criteria constituting the most economically advantageous offer to satisfy the requirements of equal treatment and transparency of procedures for awarding public contracts.

With regard to the requirement of the award criterion consisting in the allocation of points for the total amount of electricity from renewable energy sources in excess of the volume expected though the particular contract in question, the Court held that such a requirement is incompatible with Community legislation on public procurement. The fact that the amount of electricity in excess of the expected annual consumption is decisive to the determination of the most economically advantageous offer is liable to confer an advantage on tenderers who, owing to their larger production or supply capacities, are able to supply greater volumes of electricity than other tenderers. That criterion is thus liable to result in unjustified discrimination against tenderers whose tender is fully able to meet the requirements linked

---

[39]   See *SIAC Construction*, paragraph 44.
[40]   See *Universale-Bau and Others*, paragraphs 91 and 92.

to the subject-matter of the contract. Such a limitation on the circle of economic operators in a position to submit a tender would have the effect of thwarting the objective of opening up the market to competition pursued by the directives co-ordinating procedures for the award of public supply contracts.

The Court maintained that a criterion relating to the reliability of supplies is a legitimate factor in determining the most economically advantageous offer for a contracting authority.[41] However, the capacity of tenderers to provide the largest amount of electricity possible from renewable sources in excess of the amount laid down in the invitation to tender cannot legitimately be given the status of an award criterion. The award criterion applied did not relate to the service which is the subject-matter of the contract, namely the supply of an amount of electricity to the contracting authority corresponding to its expected annual consumption as laid down in the invitation to tender, but to the amount of electricity that the tenderers have supplied, or will supply, to other customers. An award criterion that relates solely to the amount of electricity produced from renewable energy sources in excess of the expected annual consumption, as laid down in the invitation to tender, cannot be regarded as linked to the subject-matter of the contract. The applicants in the main proceedings submitted that the award criterion in question is in fact a disguised selection criterion inasmuch as it concerns the tenderers' capacity to supply as much electricity as possible from renewable energy sources and, in that way, ultimately relates to the tenderers themselves.

The Court concluded that Community legislation on public procurement does not preclude a contracting authority from applying, in the context of the assessment of the most economically advantageous tender for a contract for the supply of electricity, an award criterion with a weighting of 45% which requires that the electricity supplied be produced from renewable energy sources. The fact that that criterion does not necessarily serve to achieve the objective pursued is irrelevant in that regard. On the other hand, public procurement law does preclude such a criterion where it is not accompanied by requirements which permit the accuracy of the information contained in the invitation to tender document to be effectively verified and it contains factors for its assessment which are not directly linked to the subject-matter of the procurement in question.

---

[41] See case C-448/01, *EVN AG, Wienstrom GmbH and Republik Österreich*, judgment of 4 December 2003, paragraph 70.

THE LOWEST PRICE

When the lowest price has been selected as the award criterion, contracting authorities must not refer to any other qualitative consideration when deliberating the award of a contract. The lowest price is the sole quantitative benchmark that intends to differentiate the offers made by tenderers.[42] However, contracting authorities can reject a tender, if they regard the price attached to it as abnormally low.

ABNORMALLY LOW TENDERS

In cases where tenders appear to be abnormally low in relation to the goods, works or services, the contracting authority must request in writing details of the constituent elements of the tender which it considers relevant before it rejects those tenders.[43]

The clarification details[44] may relate in particular to:

(a)   the economics of the construction method, the manufacturing process or the services provided;
(b)   the technical solutions chosen and/or any exceptionally favourable conditions available to the tenderer for the execution of the work, for the supply of the goods or services;
(c)   the originality of the work, supplies or services proposed by the tenderer;
(d)   compliance with the provisions relating to employment protection and working conditions in force at the place where the work, service or supply is to be performed;
(e)   the possibility of the tenderer obtaining state aid.

Where a contracting authority establishes that a tender is abnormally low because the tenderer has obtained state aid, the tender can be rejected on that ground alone only after consultation with the tenderer where the latter is unable to prove, within a sufficient time limit fixed by the contracting authority, that the aid in question was granted legally.[45] Where the contracting authority rejects a tender in these circumstances, it must inform the Commission of their decision.

---

[42]   See Article 53(1)(b) of the Public Sector Directive.
[43]   Article 55 of the Public Sector Directive.
[44]   Article 55(1) of the Public Sector Directive.
[45]   Article 55(3) of the Public Sector Directive.

The Court's Stance on the Rejection of an Abnormally Low Offer

Although the previous Public Procurement Directives provided for an automatic disqualification of an 'obviously abnormally low offer', the term did not receive detailed clarification by the European Commission. Neither has the term been interpreted in detail by the Court and its remit has served as an indication of a 'lower limit'.[46] The Court, however, pronounced on the direct effect of the relevant provision requiring contracting authorities to examine the details of the tender before deciding the award of the contract. The contracting authorities are under duty to seek from the tenderer an explanation for the price submitted or to inform him that his tender appears to be abnormally low and to allow a reasonable time within which to submit further details, before making any decision as to the award of the contract.

The debate over the terminology of 'obviously abnormally low' tenders surfaced when the Court held[47] that rejection of a contract based on mathematical criteria without giving the tenderer an opportunity to furnish information is inconsistent with the spirit of the Public Procurement Directives. Following previous case-law,[48] the Court ruled that the contracting authorities must give an opportunity to tenderers to furnish explanations regarding the genuine nature of their tenders, when those tenders appear to be abnormally low. Unfortunately, the Court did not proceed to an analysis of the wording 'obviously'. It rather seems that the term 'obviously' indicates the existence of precise and concrete evidence as to the abnormality of the low tender. On the other hand, the wording 'abnormally' implies a quantitative criterion left to the discretion of the contracting authority. However, if the tender is just 'abnormally' low, it could be argued that it is within the discretion of the contracting authority to investigate the genuine offer of a tender. *Impresa Lombardini*[49] followed the precedence established by *Transporoute* and maintained the unlawfulness of mathematical criteria used to exclude a tender which appears abnormally low. Nevertheless, it held that such criteria may be lawful if used to determine the abnormality of a low tender, provided an *inter partes* procedure between the contracting authority and the tenderer that submitted the alleged abnormally low offer offers the opportunity to clarify the genuine

---

[46] See case C-76/81, *SA Transporoute et Travaux v. Minister of Public Works*, [1982] ECR 457.

[47] See case C-103/88, *Fratelli Costanzo SpA v. Comune di Milano*, [1989] ECR 1839; case 296/89, *Impresa Dona Alfonso di Dona Alfonso & Figli snc v. Consorzio per lo Sviluppo Industriale del Comune di Monfalcone*, judgment of 18 June 1991.

[48] See case C-76/81, *Transporoute*, [1982] ECR 417, op. cit.

[49] See case C-285/99 & 286/99, *Impresa Lombardini SpA v. ANAS*, judgment of 27 November 2001.

nature of that offer. Contracting authorities must take into account all reasonable explanations furnished and avoid limiting the grounds on which justification of the genuine nature of a tender should be made. Both the wording and the aim of the Public Procurement Directives direct contracting authorities to seek explanation and reject unrealistic offers, informing the Advisory Committee[50]. In *ARGE*,[51] the rejection of a tender based on the abnormally low pricing attached to it had a different twist in its interpretation. Although the Court ruled that tenders directly or indirectly subsidised by the state or other contracting authorities or even by the contracting authority itself can be legitimately part of the evaluation process, it did not elaborate on the possibility of the rejection of an offer which is appreciably lower than those of unsubsidised tenderers by reference to the abnormally low disqualification ground.[52]

---

[50] The Advisory Committee for Public Procurement was set up by Decision 77/63 (OJ 1977 L 13/15) and is composed of representatives of the member states belonging to the authorities of those states and has as its task the supervision of the proper application of Public Procurement Directives by member states.

[51] See case C-94/99, *ARGE Gewässerschutzt*, op. cit.

[52] In *ARGE* the Court adopted a literal interpretation of the Directives and concluded that if the legislature wanted to preclude subsidised entities from participating in tendering procedures for public contracts, it should have said so explicitly in the relevant Directives. See paragraphs 26 et seq. of the Court's judgment. Although the case has relevance in the fields of selection and qualification procedures and award criteria, the Court made no reference to previous case-law regarding state aids in public procurement, presumably because the *Dupont de Nemours* precedent is still highly relevant.

11. Utilities procurement

THE CONCEPTS OF THE NEW UTILITIES DIRECTIVE

As a result of the liberalisation process in public utilities across the European Union and the introduction of sector-specific regulation covering the operational interface of such entities, regulation of their purchasing practices no longer requires the rigidity and disciplined structure of that of public sector authorities. Under the remit of flexibility envisaged by the new regime, utilities procurement has undergone a dramatic restructuring with effects varying from the relaxation of the competitive tendering regime to the total disengagement of the public procurement rules in industries that operate under competitive conditions, especially in the telecommunications and water sectors. The new Utilities Procurement Directive does not regard telecommunication utilities as contracting entities, since the sector has been subjected to competitive forces adequate enough to ensure its commercial operation.

The previous Utilities Directive 98/38/EC covered certain contracts awarded by contracting entities operating in the telecommunications sector. One of the consequences of telecommunications regulation has been the introduction of effective competition, both *de jure* and *de facto*, in this sector. The Commission, being aware of this development, has published a list of telecommunications services[1] which may already be excluded from the scope of the existing Utilities Directive by virtue of Article 8 of the existing Utilities Directive.

There are three milestones in EU telecommunications regulation. The first of these comprises the actions which followed the 1987 Green Paper[2] and opened the door for partial sector liberalization and set in motion the process of an integrated telecommunications market. Although the corporate structure of operators was left untouched and voice telephony and television broadcasting were excluded, some fundamental principles were established and the

---

[1]   See OJ L 336, 23.12.1994, p. 1.
[2]   See European Commission, Towards a Dynamic Economy – Green Paper on the Development of the Common Market for Telecommunications Services and Equipment, COM (87) 290.

necessary conditions for subsequent regulatory reforms were created. In particular, these comprised the liberalisation of terminal equipment,[3] community-wide interoperability,[4] the separation of regulatory and operation functions of public telecommunications operators,[5] the application of competition law to public telecommunications operators and private sector providers[6] and the installation of an Open Network Provision (OPN) to determine the level of competitiveness between public monopolies and private telecommunications providers.[7] The period that followed the 1992 Review[8] and the 1994 Green Paper[9] resulted, gradually, in a full liberalisation of alternative infrastructures,[10] cable television networks and mobile networks. Voice telephony regulation and the liberalisation of the relevant market were envisaged as the next phase.

Secondly, came the fully liberalised period, a period which includes the introduction of a competition regime in the telecommunications sectors with the so-called full competition Directive (Directive 96/19/EC).[11] This period witnessed significant regulatory adjustments in the field of Open Network Provision, such as interconnectivity and licensing provisions and voice tele-

---

[3] Directive 88/301/EEC on liberalising terminal equipment in telecommunications is the first instrument that followed the 1987 Green Paper. The Directive required the abolition of exclusive rights for import, marketing, connection, bringing into service or maintenance of telecommunications terminal equipment.

[4] See Directive 91/263/EEC replacing Directive 86/361/EEC on the initial stage of the mutual recognition of type approval for telecommunications terminal equipment. The Directive has been consolidated by Directive 98/13/EC on telecommunications terminal equipment and satellite earth station equipment, including mutual recognition of its conformity. The system has been replaced by a mutual recognition framework by virtue of Directive 99/5/EC on radio equipment and telecommunications terminal and mutual recognition of their conformity.

[5] See Directive 90/388/EC (the Services Directive) as subsequently amended. The original Directive did not apply to television or radio broadcasting, telex mobile telephony paging, satellite services and voice telephony.

[6] See the Commission's Guidelines on the application of EC Competition Rules in the telecommunications sector, OJ 1991 C 233/2.

[7] See Directive 90/387/EEC on the OPN Framework and Directive 92/44/EEC on the OPN Leased Lines.

[8] See European Commission, Review of the Situation in the Telecommunications Services Sector, 1992, SEC (92) 1048 final.

[9] See European Commission, Part I – Principles and Timetable, 1994, COM (94) 440 final and Part II – A Common Approach to the Provision of Infrastructures for Telecommunications in the European Union, 1995, COM (94) 682 final.

[10] Telecommunications infrastructure owned by parties different from local telecommunications operators.

[11] See Directive 96/19/EC, OJ L74, 1996 amending Directive 90/388/EEC with regard to the implementation of full competition in telecommunications markets.

phony and universal service liberalisation.[12] In addition, common frameworks for interconnection of networks and licensing and authorisation were provided by Directive 97/33/EC[13] (the so-called Interconnection Directive) and by Directive 97/13/EC[14] (the so-called Licensing Directive) respectively. The advent of competitiveness in the relevant markets introduced the notion of significant market power (SMP) in telecommunications markets,[15] a development which will provide a regulatory yardstick for future generations of legal, and policy instruments.

Thirdly, the current phase of telecommunications regulation embraces the notion of convergence and the creation of a common regulatory framework for telecommunications, media and information technologies.[16] The most significant legislative measure has been the adoption of the Competition Directive 2002/76/EC,[17] on competition in the markets for electronic communications networks and services. The Directive consolidates all previous instruments and its main purpose is to reaffirm the obligation of member states to abolish exclusive and special rights in the field of telecommunications. Furthermore, four additional Directives consolidate the telecommunications regime and, in particular, the Framework Directive 2002/21/EC[18] on a common regulatory framework for electronic communications networks and services, the Authorisation Directive 2002/20/EC,[19] the Universal Service Directive

---

[12]   The envisaged regulatory adjustments were enacted by virtue of Directive 97/51/EC, OJ 1997 L 295/23 and Directive 98/10/EC on the application of OPN to voice telephony and universal service for telecommunications in a competitive environment.

[13]   See Directive 97/33/EC, OJ 1997 L 199/32.

[14]   See Directive 97/13/EC, OJ 1997 L 117/15.

[15]   See Article 4(3) of the Interconnection Directive 97/33/EC regarding universal service and operability through the applications of OPN.

[16]   See European Commission, Green Paper on the Convergence of Telecommunications, Media and Information Technologies COM (97) 623.

[17]   See Directive 2002/76/EC, OJ 2002 L 249/21, which consolidates the Services Directive 90/388/EEC as amended by the Satellite Directive 94/46/EC, the Cable Directive 95/51/EC, the Mobile Directive 96/2/EC, the full Competition Directive 96/19/EC and the Cable Ownership Directive 1999/64 amending the Services Directive in relation to the requirement that telecommunications networks and cable TV networks owned by a single operator are separate legal entities.

[18]   See Directive 2002/21/EC, OJ 2002 L 108/33, which effectively replaces the OPN Framework Directive 90/387/EEC, as amended by 9751/EC, and repeals Directives 90/387/EEC, 92/44, the Interconnection Directive 97/33/EC, the Licensing Directive 97/13/EC, the Voice Telephony Directive 98/10/EC and the Telecommunications Data Protection Directive 97/66/EC.

[19]   See Directive 2002/20/EC, which effectively repeals all existing licensing and authorisation instruments.

2002/22/EC[20] on universal service and users' rights relating to electronic communications networks and services and the Access Directive 2002/19/EC[21] on access to interconnection of electronic communications networks and associated facilities.

The regulatory process of telecommunications in the European Union is centred on the national regulatory authorities (NRAs), which will provide the necessary interface for implementing Community principles in line with national legal frameworks and market conditions. As a consequence of the above progress in the telecommunications sector and its relevant markets, the Commission considers that it is no longer necessary to regulate purchases by entities operating in this sector.

On the other hand, Directive 93/38/EC excludes from its scope purchases of voice telephony, telex, mobile telephone, paging and satellite services. Those exclusions were introduced to take account of the fact that the services in question could frequently be provided by only one service provider in a given geographical area because of the absence of effective competition and the existence of special or exclusive rights. The introduction of effective competition in the telecommunications sector removes the justification for these exclusions. The Commission has therefore included the procurement of such telecommunications services within the remit of the new Utilities Directive.

Conversely, the postal sector which was previously excluded from procurement regulation is now covered, but not until 1 January 2009 in order to allow sufficient time for transitional measures in the postal services sector of member states. Taking into account the further opening up of Community postal services to competition and the fact that such services are provided through a network by contracting authorities, public undertakings and other undertakings, contracts awarded by contracting entities providing postal services should be subject to the rules of this Directive, create a framework for sound commercial practice and allow greater flexibility than is offered by the new Utilities Directive 2004/18/EC. For a definition of the activities in question, it is necessary to take into account the definitions of Directive 97/67/EC on common rules for the development of the internal market of Community postal services and the improvement of quality of service.[22]

---

[20]   See Directive 2002/22/EC, OJ 2002 L 108/51 which replaces the relevant provisions of the Interconnection Directive 97/33/EC and the Voice Telephony Directive 98/61/EC

[21]   See Directive 2002/19, OJ 2002 L108/7, which replaces the relevant provisions of the Interconnection Directive 97/33/EC and OPN Leased Lined Directive 92/44/EC.

[22]   See OJ L 15, 21.1.1998, p. 14. Directive as last amended by Regulation (EC) No. 1882/2003 (OJ L 284, 31.10.2003, p. 1).

The new concepts of Directive 2004/17 embrace the links of the state with utilities through special or exclusive rights and the notion of affiliated undertakings as a potential subject of utilities procurement coverage. Finally, the new regime introduces grounds for exemption for entities operating in competitive markets.

Special or Exclusive Rights in the Utilities

The remit and thrust of public procurement legislation has traditionally relied on the connection between contracting authorities and the state. However, that connection might be too weak to cover entities which operate in the utilities sector and have been privatised. The *Foster* principle[23] established that state accountability could not embrace privatised enterprises.[24] The enactment of the Utilities Directives[25] brought under the procurement framework entities operating in the water, energy, transport and telecommunications sectors. A wide range of these entities are covered by the term *bodies governed by public law*, which is used by the existing Utilities Directives for the contracting entities operating in the relevant sectors.[26] Interestingly, another category of contracting authorities under the existing Utilities Directives includes *public undertakings*.[27] The term indicates any undertaking over which the state may exercise direct or indirect dominant influence by means of ownership, or by means of financial participation, or by means of laws and regulations, which govern the public undertaking's operation. Dominant influence can be exercised in the form of a majority holding of the undertaking's subscribed capital, in the form of majority control of the undertaking's issued shares, or, finally in the form of the right to appoint the majority of the undertaking's management board. Public undertakings may cover utilities operators which have been granted exclusive rights of exploitation of a service. Irrespective of their ownership, they are subject to the Utilities Directive inasmuch as the *exclusivity* of their operation precludes other entities from entering the relevant market under substantially the same competitive conditions.

Entities in the utilities sector enjoying special or exclusive rights conferred upon them by member states have been covered by the utilities procurement

---

[23] See case 188/89, *Foster v. British Gas*, [1990] ECR-1313, in which the European Court of Justice ruled that a Directive capable of having direct effect could be invoked against a body which is subject to the *control* of the state and has been delegated special powers.

[24] This was the view of Advocate-General Lenz in case 247/89, *Commission v. Portugal*, [1991] ECR I 3659.

[25] EC Directive 90/531, as amended by EC Directive 93/38, OJ L 199.

[26] See Article 1(1) of Directive 93/38.

[27] See Article 1(2) of Directive 93/38.

regime. The intention of the legislature was to eliminate government interference in the purchasing behaviour of the recipients of such rights arising from the pressure exercised by the respective governments as a condition of granting the special or exclusive rights and the inability of the recipient entity to resist such pressure as a result of the non-competitive environment of its operation. Traditionally, special or exclusive rights were demonstrable when the right to expropriate property or the right to place utility networks on, under or over highways were conferred upon the recipient. Also, a connection with an entity enjoying special or exclusive rights brought any supplier of a utility network within the remit of utilities procurement.

For the purposes of the new Utilities Directive and in accordance with Article 2(3), 'special or exclusive rights' mean rights granted by a competent authority of a member state by way of any legislative, regulatory or administrative provision, the effect of which is to limit the exercise of activities defined in Articles 3 to 7[28] to one or more entities, and which substantially affects the ability of other entities to carry out such activity.

The new Utilities Directive provides a more restrictive definition of the notion of special or exclusive rights than its predecessor. The consequences of the definition are threefold: first, the availability of a procedure for the expropriation or use of property and the ability of an entity to place network equipment on, under or over a public highway for the purpose of constructing networks or port or airport facilities, do not automatically constitute exclusive or special rights within the meaning of the Directive; secondly, a special or exclusive right does not exist merely due to the fact that an entity supplies drinking water, electricity, gas or heat to a network which is itself operated by an entity enjoying special or exclusive rights granted by a competent authority of a member state; and thirdly, rights granted by a member state, through acts of concession, to a limited number of undertakings on the basis of objective, proportionate and non-discriminatory criteria that allow any interested party fulfilling those criteria to enjoy those rights are not considered special or exclusive rights.

The practical implication of the definition of special or exclusive rights under the new Utilities Directive is the non-applicability of the regime to the entities that do not meet the conditions but are still covered by the existing regime.

The influence of the Court's jurisprudence in the restrictive application of special or exclusive rights is evident. The Court's approach in the *British*

---

[28]   The activities covering special or exclusive rights embrace the following utilities sectors: gas, heat and electricity, water, postal services, transport services, exploration for, or extraction of, oil, gas, coal or other solid fuels, as well as ports and airports.

Telecommunications[29] case does not allow the application of the sector-specific definition of leased (licensed) lines in the telecommunications sector to the respective utilities procurement definition of special or exclusive right. In that case the Court ruled that special or exclusive rights under the Leased Lines Directive[30] did not exist as a result of the licences conferred by member states upon entities.

The situation could be more complicated as entities compete for special or exclusive rights such as concessions or public–private partnerships on the basis of objective, proportionate and non-discriminatory criteria which can restrict market access to other undertakings and by definition limit the number of interested parties. The analogous application of the *British Telecommunications* judgment is dubious, as the Court remained silent over such a scenario. The Commission has however indicated[31] that where member states do not enjoy discretion in the conferral of special or exclusive rights, by definition they cannot detrimentally influence the procurement behaviour of the recipient of such rights and as a consequence the utilities procurement regime need not apply.

Affiliated Undertakings

Article 13 of the existing Utilities Directive provides for the exclusion of certain contracts between contracting authorities and affiliated undertakings. An affiliated undertaking, for the purposes of Article 1(3) of the Utilities Directive, is an undertaking whose accounts are consolidated with those of the contracting entity in accordance with the requirements of the Seventh Company Law Directive.[32] These are service contracts which are awarded to a service-provider which is affiliated to the contracting entity and service contracts which are awarded to a service-provider which is affiliated to a contracting entity participating in a joint venture formed for the purpose of carrying out an activity covered by the Directive.

The explanatory memorandum of the Utilities Directive[33] stated that this provision relates to three types of service provision within groups. These categories, which may or may not be distinct, are: the provision of common

---

[29] See case C-302/94, *R v. Secretary of State for Trade and Industry ex parte British Telecommunications plc*, [1996] ECR 6417.

[30] See EC Directive 92/44, OJ 1992 L 165/27.

[31] See European Commission, Explanatory Memorandum of the Proposal for the Directive Co-coordinating the Procurement Procedures of Entities Operating in the Water, Energy and Transport Sectors, COM (2000) 276 final.

[32] See Council Directive 83/349 (OJ 1983 L193/1).

[33] See COM (91) 347-SYN 36 1.

services such as accounting, recruitment and management; the provision of specialised services embodying the know-how of the group; the provision of a specialised service to a joint venture. The exclusion from the provisions of the Directive is subject, however, to two conditions: the service-provider must be an undertaking affiliated to the contracting authority and at least 80% of its average turnover arising within the European Community for the preceding three years should derive from the provision of the same or similar services to undertakings with which it is affiliated. The Commission is empowered to monitor the application of this Article and require the notification of the names of the undertakings concerned and the nature and value of the service contracts involved.

Interestingly, the new utilities regime also excludes from its remit contracts awarded to affiliated undertakings. Article 23 of the new Utilities Directive excludes contracts awarded by a contracting entity to an affiliated undertaking, or by a joint venture, formed exclusively of a number of contracting entities for the purpose of carrying out activities which are covered by the Utilities Directive for an undertaking which is affiliated to one of these contracting entities.

Under the new utilities procurement regime, the term 'affiliated undertaking' means any undertaking the annual accounts of which are consolidated with those of the contracting entity in accordance with the requirements of the Seventh Council Directive 83/349 on consolidated accounts.[34] In cases of entities which are not subject to that Directive, affiliated undertaking means any undertaking over which the contracting entity may exercise, directly or indirectly, a dominant influence within the meaning of Article 2(1)(b), or any undertaking over which the contracting entity may exercise a dominant influence by virtue of ownership, financial participation, or the rules which govern it.

Competitive Markets in Utilities

Privatised utilities could, in principle, be excluded from the procurement rules where a genuinely competitive regime[35] within the relevant market structure ruled out purchasing patterns based on non-economic considerations. The new

---

[34]   See OJ L 193, 18.7.1983, p. 1, as last amended by Directive 2001/65/EC (OJ L 283, 27.10.2001, p. 28).

[35]   The determination of a genuinely competitive regime is left to the utilities operators themselves. See case, C 392/93, *The Queen and HM Treasury, ex parte British Telecommunications PLC*, OJ 1993 C 287/6. This is perhaps a first step towards self-regulation, which could lead to the disengagement of the relevant contracting authorities from the public procurement regime.

Utilities Directive should not apply to markets where the participants pursue an activity which is directly exposed to competition in markets to which access is not limited within the relevant member state. The new Utilities Directive has therefore introduced a procedure, applicable to all sectors covered by its provisions, that will enable the effects of current or future opening up to competition to be taken into account. Such a procedure should provide legal certainty for the entities concerned, as well as an appropriate decision-making process, ensuring, within short time limits, uniform application of standards that result in the disengagement of the relevant procurement rules.

Direct exposure to competition should be assessed on the basis of objective criteria, taking account of the specific characteristics of the sector concerned. The implementation and application of appropriate Community legislation liberalising a utility sector will be considered to provide sufficient grounds for determining if there is free access to the market in question. Such appropriate legislation should be identified in an annex which will be provided by the Commission. The Commission will in particular take into account the possible adoption of measures entailing a genuine opening up to competition of sectors other than those for which legislation is already mentioned in Annex XI, such as that of railway transport services. Where free access to a given market does not result from the implementation of appropriate Community legislation, it should be demonstrated that such access is uninhibited *de jure and de facto*.

Article 30 of the new Utilities Directive provides for the procedure for establishing whether a given activity of a utility entity is directly exposed to competition. The question of whether an activity is directly exposed to competition shall be decided on the basis of criteria that are in conformity with the Treaty provisions on competition, such as the characteristics of the goods or services concerned, the existence of alternative goods or services, the prices and the actual or potential presence of more than one supplier of the goods or services in question. When a member state considers that access to the relevant market activity is free, it must notify the Commission and provide all relevant facts, and in particular details of any law, regulation, administrative provision or agreements, where appropriate, together with the position adopted by an independent national authority that is competent in relation to the regulation of the activity concerned. The Commission can issue a Decision which verifies that the relevant activity is provided in a competitive environment. Such verification is also presumed if the Commission has not adopted a Decision concerning the inapplicability of the Utilities Directive within a certain period.[36]

---

[36] According to Article 68(2), for the adoption of a Decision the Commission shall be allowed a period of three months commencing on the first working day following the date on which it receives the notification or the request. However, this period

The disengagement of the utilities procurement regime as a result of the operation of the relevant entities in competitive markets by virtue of Article 30 of the new Utilities Directive does not apply to the WTO Government Procurement Agreement. This represents a legal *lacuna* as the procedural flexibility envisaged in the European procurement regulatory regime does not cover entities covered under the GPA. Rectification of the problem would require amendment of the GPA with the conferral of concessions and reciprocal access rights to the GPA signatories.

THE REMIT OF THE UTILITIES DIRECTIVE

The Utilities Directive[37] applies to the award of contracts between contractors, suppliers or service providers and contracting entities. The terms contractor, supplier or service provider mean either a natural or a legal person, or a contracting entity, or a group of such persons or entities which offers on the market, respectively, the execution of works, products or services. The term 'economic operator' covers equally the concepts of contractor, supplier and service provider and it is used for simplification purposes.[38]

Types and Categories of Utilities Contracts

Supply, works and service contracts in the utilities sectors are contracts for pecuniary interest concluded in writing between, on the one hand, one or more of the contracting entities referred to in the Utilities Directive, and on the other hand, one or more contractors, suppliers, or service providers.[39]

Works contracts are contracts having as their object either the execution, or both the design and execution, of works related to one of the activities within the meaning of Annex XII of the Directive or a work, or the realisation by whatever means of a work, corresponding to the requirements specified by the contracting entity.[40] A work means the outcome of building or civil engineering works taken as a whole which is sufficient of itself to fulfil an economic or technical function.

Supply contracts are contracts having as their object the purchase, lease, rental or hire-purchase, with or without the option to buy, of products. A

---

may be extended once by a maximum of three months in duly justified cases, in particular if the information contained in the notification or request or in the documents annexed thereto is incomplete.

[37]   See Directive 2004/17, OJ 2004 L 134/1.
[38]   See Article 1(7) of the Utilities Directive.
[39]   See Article 1(2)(a) of the Utilities Directive.
[40]   See Article 1(2)(b) of the Utilities Directive.

contract having as its object the supply of products, which also covers, as an incidental matter, placement and installation operations must be considered to be a supply contract.[41]

Service contracts are contracts having as their object the provision of services referred to in Annex XVII of the Directive. A contract having as its object both products and services within the meaning of Annex XVII of the Directive is considered to be a service contract if the value of the services in question exceeds that of the products covered by the contract.[42] A contract having as its object services within the meaning of Annex XVII of the Directive and including activities within the meaning of Annex XII of the Directive that are only incidental to the principal object of the contract must be considered to be a service contract.

The Utilities Directive stipulates specific arrangements[43] for service contracts listed in Annex XVII A. These contracts must be awarded as any other contract covered by the Directive and in particular in accordance with Articles 34 to 59. However, for contracts which have as their object services listed in Annex XVII B, the Directive is applicable only[44] with respect to the setting of technical specifications (Article 34) and the requirement to file a report to the Commission after the award of the contract (Article 43). Mixed contracts[45] including services listed in Annex XVII A and services listed in Annex XVII B must be awarded as any other public contract covered by the Directive where the value of the services listed in Annex XVII A is greater than the value of the services listed in Annex XVII B. In the reverse scenario, contracts are awarded in accordance with Article 34 and Article 43 of the Utilities Directive.[46]

A works concession is a contract of the same type as a works contract except for the fact that the consideration for the works to be carried out consists either solely in the right to exploit the work or in that right together with payment.[47] A service concession is a contract of the same type as a service contract except for the fact that the consideration for the provision of services consists either solely in the right to exploit the service or in that right together with payment.[48]

A framework agreement is an agreement between one or more contracting

---

[41]   See Article 1(2)(c) of the Utilities Directive.
[42]   See Article 1(2)(d) of the Utilities Directive.
[43]   See Article 31 of the Utilities Directive.
[44]   See Article 32 of the Utilities Directive.
[45]   See Article 33 of the Utilities Directive.
[46]   See Article 1(2)(d), second indent of the Utilities Directive.
[47]   See Article 1(3)(a) of the Utilities Directive.
[48]   See Article 1(3)(b) of the Utilities Directive.

entities and one or more economic operators, the purpose of which is to establish the terms governing contracts to be awarded during a given period, in particular with regard to price and, where appropriate, the quantities envisaged.[49]

A dynamic purchasing system is a completely electronic process for making commonly used purchases, the characteristics of which, as generally available on the market, meet the requirements of the contracting entity, which is limited in duration and open throughout its validity to any economic operator which satisfies the selection criteria and has submitted an indicative tender that complies with the specification.[50]

An electronic auction is a repetitive process involving an electronic device for the presentation of new prices, revised downwards, and/or new values concerning certain elements of tenders, which occurs after an initial full evaluation of the tenders, enabling them to be ranked using automatic evaluation methods.[51] Consequently, certain service contracts and certain works contracts having as their subject-matter intellectual performances, such as the design of works, may not be the object of electronic auctions.

Design contests are those procedures which enable the contracting entity to acquire, mainly in the fields of town and country planning, architecture, engineering or data processing, a plan or design selected by a jury after having been put out to competition with or without the award of prizes.[52]

The Common Procurement Vocabulary (CPV) represents the reference nomenclature applicable to public and utilities contracts while ensuring equivalence with the other existing nomenclatures.[53]

Types of Economic Operators

The terms 'contractor', 'supplier' and 'service-provider' mean any natural or legal person or public entity or group of such persons and/or bodies which offers in the market, respectively, the execution of works and/or a work, products or services.[54] The term 'economic operator' covers equally the concepts

---

[49] See Article 1(4) of the Utilities Directive.
[50] See Article 1(5) of the Utilities Directive.
[51] See Article 1(6) of the Utilities Directive.
[52] See Article 1(10) of the Utilities Directive.
[53] See Regulation 2195/2002 on the Common Procurement Vocabulary (CPV), OJ L 340,16.12.2002. In the event of varying interpretations of the scope of the Utilities Directive, owing to possible differences between the CPV and NACE nomenclatures listed in Annex XII or between the CPV and CPC (provisional version) nomenclatures listed in Annex XVII, the NACE or the CPC nomenclature respectively must take precedence.
[54] See Article 1(7) of the Utilities Directive.

of contractor, supplier and service-provider. It is used merely in the interest of simplification.[55] An economic operator who has submitted a tender must be designated a 'tenderer'. One which has sought an invitation to take part in a restricted or negotiated procedure or a competitive dialogue must be designated a 'candidate'.[56]

Candidates or tenderers who, under the law of the member state in which they are established, are entitled to provide the relevant service, must not be rejected solely on the grounds that, under the law of the member state in which the contract is awarded, they would be required to be either natural or legal persons.[57] However, in the case of service and works contracts as well as supply contracts covering in addition services or installation operations, legal persons may be required to indicate, in the tender or the request to participate, the names and relevant professional qualifications of the staff to be responsible for the performance of the contract in question.[58]

Groups of economic operators may submit tenders or put themselves forward as candidates. In order to submit a tender or a request to participate, these groups may not be required by the contracting entities to assume a specific legal form; however, the group selected may be required to do so when it has been awarded the contract, to the extent to which this change is necessary for the satisfactory performance of the contract.[59]

Economic operators based in third countries which have concluded agreements within the World Trade Organisation must enjoy conditions as favourable as those member states offer to operators based in countries which are signatories to the Government Procurement Agreement.[60]

Economic operators and third countries
A special regime[61] under the Utilities Directive applies for supplies contracts that include products originating in third countries with which the European Union has not concluded either multilateral or bilateral agreements to enable comparable and effective access for Community undertakings to the markets of those third countries.

Where two or more tenders, after their evaluation in accordance with the award criteria, appear as equivalent, contracting entities must give preference

---

55   See Article 1(7), second indent of the Utilities Directive.
56   See Article 1(7), third indent of the Utilities Directive.
57   See Article 11(1) of the Utilities Directive.
58   See Article 11(1), second indent of the Utilities Directive.
59   See Article 11(2) of the Utilities Directive.
60   See Article 12 of the Utilities Directive.
61   See Article 58 of the Utilities Directive.

to the tender that consist of products originating[62] in third countries, provided that the proportion of the products does not exceed 50%. In order to assess the equivalence of tenders, if the price difference does not exceed 3%, those tenders are considered equivalent by contracting entities.[63]

However, contracting entities may reject tenders for supplies where the proportion of the products originating in third countries exceeds 50% of the total value of the products constituting the tender. Products include software used in telecommunications network equipment. In addition, preference must not be given to a tender when its acceptance would oblige the contracting entity to acquire equipment which has technical characteristics different from those of existing equipment, resulting in incompatibility, technical difficulties in operation and maintenance, or disproportionate costs.[64]

By virtue of a Decision adopted by the Council to extend the benefit of the provisions of the Utilities Directive to third countries, products originating in those countries should not count towards determining the 50% proportion of products originating in third countries required for the preferential treatment of tenders for supplies contracts.[65]

The progress made in multilateral or bilateral negotiations regarding access for Community undertakings to the markets of third countries in the activities covered by the Utilities Directive, the results which such negotiations may have achieved and the implementation in practice of all the agreements which have been concluded between third countries and the European Union are subjects of an annual report submitted by the Commission to the Council.[66] The Council, acting by a qualified majority on a proposal from the Commission, may amend the special regime under the Utilities Directive for supplies contracts that include products originating in third countries in the light of such developments.[67]

Relations with third countries

In cases where third countries do not grant community undertakings effective access comparable to that granted by the European Community to undertakings from that country, nor the same competitive opportunities as are available

---

[62] For the source of products and their origin from third countries, see Regulation 2913/92 establishing the Community Customs Code, OJ L 302, 19.10.1992, p. 1, as last amended by Regulation 2700/2000, OJ L 311, 12.12.2000, p. 17.

[63] See Article 58(3) of the Utilities Directive.

[64] See Article 58(2) of the Utilities Directive.

[65] See Article 58(4) of the Utilities Directive.

[66] Such a report should first be submitted in the second half of the first year following the entry into force of this Directive (summer 2007). See Article 58(5) of the Utilities Directive.

[67] See Article 58(5) of the Utilities Directive.

to national undertakings and instead grant undertakings from other third countries more favourable treatment than Community undertakings, the Commission must approach the third country concerned in an attempt to remedy the situation.[68]

Member states must inform the Commission of any general difficulties, in law or in fact, encountered and reported by their undertakings in securing the award of service contracts in third countries,[69] as well as of any difficulties, in law or in fact, encountered and reported by their undertakings and which are due to the non-observance of the international labour law conventions[70] related to Convention 87 on Freedom of Association and the Protection of the Right to Organise, Convention 98 on the Right to Organise and Collective Bargaining, Convention 29 on Forced Labour, Convention 105 on the Abolition of Forced Labour, Convention 138 on Minimum Age, Convention 111 on Discrimination (Employment and Occupation), Convention 100 on Equal Remuneration, Convention 182 on Worst Forms of Child Labour.[71]

The Commission may at any time propose, on its own initiative or at the request of a member state,[72] that the Council decide to suspend or restrict the award of service contracts to undertakings governed by the law of the third country in question; undertakings affiliated to the undertakings governed by the law of the third country and having their registered office in the Community but having no direct and effective link with the economy of a member state or undertakings submitting tenders which have as their subject services originating in the third country in question.[73]

The Council may adopt a Decision by qualified majority, to suspend or restrict the award of service contracts to undertakings governed by the law of the third country in question over a period to be laid down in the Decision.[74]

The Commission must report to the Council before 31 December 2005, and periodically thereafter, on the opening up of service contracts in third countries and on progress in negotiations with these countries on this subject, particularly within the framework of the WTO.[75]

---

[68] See Article 59(3) of the Utilities Directive.
[69] See Article 59(1) of the Utilities Directive.
[70] See Article 59(4) of the Utilities Directive.
[71] See Annex XXIII of the Utilities Directive.
[72] See Article 59(5), second indent of the Utilities Directive.
[73] See Article 59(5)(a) and (b) of the Utilities Directive.
[74] See Article 59(1) of the Utilities Directive.
[75] See Article 59(2) of the Utilities Directive.

Utilities as Contracting Entities

For the purposes of the Utilities Directive, contracting entities include the state, regional or local authorities, bodies governed by public law, associations formed by one or several such authorities or one or several of such bodies governed by public law.[76]

A body governed by public law means any body which is established for the specific purpose of meeting needs in the general interest which do not have an industrial or commercial character; a body governed by public law must also have legal personality and must be financed, for the most part, by the state, regional or local authorities, or other bodies governed by public law.[77] With respect to the latter requirement, a body governed by public law may also be subject to management supervision by the state, regional or local authorities, or by other bodies governed by public law or may have an administrative, managerial or supervisory board, more than half of whose members are appointed by those bodies.

Contracting entities also include public undertakings. A public undertaking is any undertaking over which the contracting authorities may exercise directly or indirectly a dominant influence by virtue of their ownership of it, their financial participation therein, or the rules which govern it.[78]

Contracting authorities exercise dominant influence upon public undertakings when directly or indirectly, in relation to an undertaking, they hold the majority of the undertaking's subscribed capital, or control the majority of the votes attached to shares issued by the undertaking, or can appoint more than half of the undertaking's administrative, management or supervisory body.

A central purchasing body[79] is a contracting authority within the meaning of the Utilities Directive[80] or a contracting authority within the meaning of the Public Sector Directive[81] which acquires supplies or services intended for contracting entities, or awards public contracts, or concludes framework agreements for works, supplies or services intended for contracting entities.

The Utilities Directive also includes as contracting entities undertakings which, although they are not contracting authorities or public undertakings themselves, operate on the basis of special or exclusive rights granted by a

---

[76] See Article 2(1)(a) of the Utilities Directive.
[77] See Article 2(1)(a), second indent of the Utilities Directive.
[78] See Article 2(1)(b) of the Utilities Directive.
[79] See Article 1(8) of the Utilities Directive.
[80] See Article 2(1)(a) of the Utilities Directive
[81] See Article 1(9) of the Public Sector Directive 2004/18/EC.

competent authority of a member state.[82] These special or exclusive rights are conveyed upon the relevant undertaking by a competent authority of a member state by means of legislative, regulatory or administrative provisions which aim to limit the exercise of activities covered by the Utilities Directive to one or more entities. The conferral of special or exclusive rights substantially affects the ability of other entities to carry out such activities in the market place.

Lists of contracting entities

The non-exhaustive lists of contracting entities within the meaning of this Directive are contained in Annexes I to X of the Utilities Directive. Member states must notify the Commission periodically of any changes to their lists.[83]

Principles of Awarding Contracts in Utilities

The Utilities Directive establishes three principles which cover the award of contracts. In particular, contracting authorities must treat economic operators equally and in a non-discriminatory manner and act in a transparent way.[84]

The principle of confidentiality is also enshrined in the Utilities Directive, where specific provisions[85] allow for discretion on the part of contracting entities to impose requirements with a view to protecting the confidential nature of information which they make available, in the context of the provision of technical specifications to interested economic operators.

The Utilities Directive also provides for the obligation[86] to observe confidentiality in accordance with the national law to which the contracting authority is subject. Contracting authorities must not disclose information forwarded to it by economic operators which they have designated as confidential; such information includes, in particular, technical or trade secrets and the confidential aspects of tenders. This obligation is without prejudice to the provisions of the Directive relevant to the advertising of awarded contracts and to the information to candidates and tenderers set out in Articles 43 and 49 of the Utilities Directive.

---

[82] See Article 2(3) of the Utilities Directive.
[83] See Article 8 of the Utilities Directive.
[84] See Article 10 of the Utilities Directive.
[85] See Article 13 of the Utilities Directive.
[86] See Article 13(2) of the Utilities Directive.

THE SUBSTANTIVE APPLICABILITY OF THE UTILITIES DIRECTIVE

Activities Covered

The gas and heat sector

The provision of fixed networks or the operation of fixed networks in order to provide a service to the public in connection with the production, transport or distribution of gas or heat, as well as the supply of gas[87] or heat to such networks[88] are activities covered by the Utilities Directive. However, the supply of gas or heat to networks which provide a service to the public by a contracting entity fall outside[89] the remit of the Utilities Directive when the production of gas or heat by the entity concerned is the unavoidable consequence of carrying out an activity unrelated to the activities covered by the Utilities Directive,[90] and when supply to the public network is aimed only at the economic exploitation of such production and amounts to less than 20% of the entity's average turnover for the preceding three years.[91]

The electricity sector

The Utilities Directive applies to activities dealing with the provision of fixed networks[92] or the operation of fixed networks intended to provide a service to the public in connection with the production, transport or distribution of electricity or the supply of electricity to such networks.[93] The supply of electricity to networks which provide a service to the public by a contracting entity is not covered[94] by the Directive when the production of electricity by the entity concerned takes place because its consumption is necessary for carrying out an activity unrelated to the activities covered by the Utilities Directive[95] and also when supply to the public network depends only on the entity's own consumption and has not exceeded 30% of the entity's total production of energy during the past three years.[96]

---

[87]   See Article 3(1)(a) of the Utilities Directive.
[88]   See Article 3(1)(b) of the Utilities Directive.
[89]   See Article 3(2) of the Utilities Directive.
[90]   See Article 3(2)(a) of the Utilities Directive.
[91]   See Article 3(2)(b) of the Utilities Directive.
[92]   See Article 3(3)(a) of the Utilities Directive.
[93]   See Article 3(3)(b) of the Utilities Directive.
[94]   See Article 3(4) of the Utilities Directive.
[95]   See Article 3(4)(a) of the Utilities Directive.
[96]   See Article 3(4)(b) of the Utilities Directive.

The water sector

The provision of fixed networks or the operation of fixed networks intended to provide a service to the public in connection with the production, transport or distribution of drinking water[97] or the supply of drinking water to such networks are activities covered by the Utilities Directive.[98] In addition, the Utilities Directive applies to contracts or design contests awarded or organised by entities which pursue an activity related to the provision of fixed networks or the operation of fixed networks in order to provide a service to the public in connection with the production, transport or distribution of gas or heat, and which are connected with hydraulic engineering projects, irrigation or land drainage,[99] provided that the volume of water to be used for the supply of drinking water represents more than 20% of the total volume of water made available by such projects or irrigation or drainage installations, or are connected with the disposal or treatment of sewage.[100]

However, the supply of drinking water to networks which provide a service to the public by a contracting entity is not covered by the Utilities Directive in cases where the production of drinking water by the entity concerned takes place because its consumption is necessary for carrying out an activity unrelated to the activities covered by the Utilities Directive[101] and where supply to the public network depends only on the entity's own consumption and has not exceeded 30% of the entity's total production of drinking water during the past three years.[102]

Transport services

The Utilities Directive applies to activities relating to the provision or operation of networks providing a service to the public in the field of transport by railway, automated systems, tramway, trolley bus, bus or cable.[103] A transport services network is a network where the service is provided under operating conditions laid down by a competent authority of a member state, such as conditions on the routes to be served, the capacity to be made available or the frequency of the service.[104]

The Directive does not apply to entities providing bus transport services to the public which were excluded from the scope of the previous Utilities

---

[97]   See Article 4(1)(a) of the Utilities Directive.
[98]   See Article 4(1)(b) of the Utilities Directive.
[99]   See Article 4(2)(a) of the Utilities Directive.
[100]   See Article 4(2)(b) of the Utilities Directive.
[101]   See Article 4(3)(a) of the Utilities Directive.
[102]   See Article 4(3)(b) of the Utilities Directive.
[103]   See Article 5(1) of the Utilities Directive.
[104]   See Article 5(2) of the Utilities Directive.

Directive 93/38 according to Article 2(4). In particular, where other entities are free to provide bus transport services to the public either in general or in a particular geographical area, under the same conditions as those applying to the contracting entities, the Directive assumes that the relevant activities are performed in a sufficiently competitive market and specifically excludes them from its coverage. The exclusion of such activities in the bus transport sector from the remit of the new Utilities Directive is justified by reference to the effects of the competition which already exists in the relevant markets and the need to prevent the existence of a multitude of specific arrangements applying to that sector.

Postal services

The Utilities Directive applies to activities relating to the provision of postal services,[105] consisting of the clearance, sorting, routing and delivery of postal items. A postal item[106] is an item addressed in the final form in which it is to be carried, irrespective of weight. In addition to items of correspondence, such items also include for instance books, catalogues, newspapers, periodicals and postal packages containing merchandise with or without commercial value, irrespective of weight. Postal services may comprise any postal services[107] which are or may be reserved on the basis of Article 7 of Directive 97/67/EC, as well as other postal services which may not be reserved on the basis of Article 7 of Directive 97/67/EC.

In addition to the postal services relating to the clearance, sorting, routing and delivery of postal items, the Utilities Directive covers services ancillary[108] to postal services and in particular, mail service management services (services both preceding and subsequent to dispatch, such as mailroom management services), added-value services linked to and provided entirely by electronic means (including the secure transmission of coded documents by electronic means, address management services and transmission of registered electronic mail), services concerning postal items such as direct mail bearing no address, financial services including in particular postal money orders and postal giro transfers,[109] philatelic services, and finally logistics services (services combining physical delivery or warehousing with other non-postal functions), on condition that such services are provided by an entity which

---

[105]   See Article 6(2)(b) of the Utilities Directive.
[106]   See Article 6(2)(a) of the Utilities Directive.
[107]   See Article 6(2)(b), second indent of the Utilities Directive.
[108]   See Article 6(2)(c) of the Utilities Directive.
[109]   See the services defined in category 6 of Annex XVII A and in Article 24(c) of the Utilities Directive.

also provides postal services and that such logistics services are not directly exposed to competition in markets to which access is not restricted.[110]

Exploration for, or extraction of, oil, gas, coal or other solid fuels
Activities relating to the exploitation of a geographical area for the purpose of exploring for oil, gas, coal or other solid fuels or extracting oil, gas, coal or other solid fuels are covered by the Utilities Directive.[111]

Ports and airports
The construction of airports and maritime or inland ports or other terminal facilities for carriers by air, sea or inland waterways are activities covered by the Utilities Directive.[112]

Contracts covering several activities
A contract which is intended to cover several activities included within the remit of the Utilities Directive must be subject to the rules applicable to the activity for which it is principally intended.[113] However, in cases where one of the activities covered by a contract falls within the scope of the Public Sector Directive 2004/18, and if it is objectively impossible to determine for which activity the contract is principally intended, the contract must be awarded in accordance with the provisions laid down in the Public Sector Directive.[114]

On the other hand, if one of the activities for which the contract is intended is subject to the Utilities Directive and other activities are not covered by either the Utilities Directive or the Public Sector Directive, and if it is objectively impossible to determine for which activity the contract is principally intended, the contract must be awarded in accordance with the provisions laid down in the Utilities Directive.[115]

---

[110] To decide whether an activity is directly exposed to competition, the criteria that must be used refer to the characteristics of the goods or services concerned, the existence of alternative goods or services, the prices and the actual or potential presence of more than one supplier of the goods or services in question and must be in conformity with the Treaty provisions on competition. See the conditions set out in Article 30(1) of the Utilities Directive.

[111] See Article 7(a) of the Utilities Directive.
[112] See Article 7(b) of the Utilities Directive.
[113] See Article 9 of the Utilities Directive.
[114] See Article 9(2) of the Utilities Directive.
[115] See Article 9(3) of the Utilities Directive.

Activities excluded from the Utilities Directive

Contracts awarded for purposes of resale or lease to third parties
The Utilities Directive does not apply to contracts awarded for purposes of resale or lease to third parties, provided that the contracting entity enjoys no special or exclusive right to sell or lease the subject of such contracts, and other entities are free to sell or lease it under the same conditions as the contracting entity.[116]

The contracting entities must notify the Commission at its request of all the categories of products or activities which they regard as excluded for purposes of resale or lease to third parties. The Commission, for information purposes and subject to any commercial confidentiality aspects pointed out by contracting entities, may periodically publish in the Official Journal of the European Union lists of the categories of products and activities which it considers to be covered by this exclusion.[117]

Contracts awarded for purposes other than the pursuit of an activity covered or for the pursuit of such an activity in a third country
The Utilities Directive does not apply to contracts which contracting entities award for purposes other than the pursuit of their activities covered by the Utilities Directive or for the pursuit of such activities in a third country,[118] in conditions not involving the physical use of a network or geographical area within the Community. The contracting entities must notify the Commission at its request of all the categories of such activities which they regard as excluded for the above purposes. The Commission, for information purposes and subject to any commercial confidentiality aspects pointed out by contracting entities, may periodically publish in the Official Journal of the European Union lists of the categories of products and activities which it considers to be covered by this exclusion.[119]

Contracts which are secret or require special security measures
Contracts which are declared to be secret by a member state are not covered by the Utilities Directive. These secret contracts must be performed on the basis of special security measures which should be in place in accordance with the laws, regulations or administrative provisions in force in the member state concerned.[120] Alternatively, secret contracts could be awarded on the basis of the protection of the security interests of a member state.

---

[116]   See Article 19(1) of the Utilities Directive.
[117]   See Article 19(2) of the Utilities Directive.
[118]   See Article 20(1) of the Utilities Directive.
[119]   See Article 20(2) of the Utilities Directive.
[120]   See Article 21 of the Utilities Directive.

Contracts awarded pursuant to international rules

The Utilities Directive does not apply to contracts governed by different procedural rules and awarded pursuant to an international agreement[121] concluded in accordance with the Treaty between a member state and one or more third countries and covering supplies, works, services or design contests intended for the joint implementation or exploitation of a project by the signatory states;[122] the Utilities Directive is also inapplicable to contracts concluded pursuant to a signed international agreement relating to the stationing of troops and concerning the undertakings of a member state[123] or a third country or contracts concluded pursuant to the particular procedure of an international organisation.[124]

Contracts awarded to an affiliated undertaking, to a joint venture or to a contracting entity forming part of a joint venture

The Utilities Directive does not apply to contracts awarded by a contracting entity to an affiliated undertaking.[125] An affiliated undertaking is an undertaking the annual accounts of which are consolidated with those of the contracting entity in accordance with the requirements of the Seventh Council Directive[126] on consolidated accounts, or, in the case of entities not subject to that Directive,[127] any undertaking over which the contracting entity may exercise, directly or indirectly, a dominant influence[128] or which may exercise a dominant influence over the contracting entity or which, in common with the contracting entity, is subject to the dominant influence of another undertaking by virtue of ownership, financial participation, or the rules which govern it.

The Utilities Directive does not apply to contracts awarded by a joint venture, formed exclusively by a number of contracting entities for the

---

[121]   See Article 22(a) of the Utilities Directive.

[122]   All agreements covering supplies, works, services or design contests must be communicated to the Commission, which may consult the Advisory Committee for Public Contracts referred to in Article 68 of the Utilities Directive.

[123]   See Article 22(b) of the Utilities Directive.

[124]   See Article 22(c) of the Utilities Directive.

[125]   See Article 23(2)(a) of the Utilities Directive.

[126]   See Directive 83/349 OJ L 193, 18.7.1983, p. 1. Directive as last amended by Directive 2001/65/EC of the European Parliament and of the Council, OJ L 283, 27.10.2001, p. 28.

[127]   See Article 23(1) of the Utilities Directive.

[128]   According to Article 2(1)(b) of the Utilities Directive, contracting authorities exercise a dominant influence upon public undertakings when directly or indirectly, in relation to an undertaking, they hold the majority of the undertaking's subscribed capital, or control the majority of the votes attaching to shares issued by the undertaking, or can appoint more than half of the undertaking's administrative, management or supervisory body.

purpose of carrying out activities covered by the Utilities Directive to an undertaking which is affiliated with one of these contracting entities.[129]

Types of contracts cover service contracts provided that at least 80% of the average turnover of the affiliated undertaking with respect to services for the preceding three years derives from the provision of such services to undertakings with which it is affiliated;[130] supplies contracts provided that at least 80% of the average turnover of the affiliated undertaking with respect to supplies for the preceding three years derives from the provision of such supplies to undertakings with which it is affiliated;[131] works contracts provided that at least 80% of the average turnover of the affiliated undertaking with respect to works for the preceding three years derives from the provision of such works to undertakings with which it is affiliated.[132]

When the turnover of an affiliated undertaking is not available for the past three years, as a result of the date on which an affiliated undertaking was created or commenced activities, it will be sufficient for that undertaking to demonstrate the required turnover by means of financial projections.[133] Where more than one undertaking affiliated with the contracting entity provides the same or similar services, supplies or works, the required turnover percentages must be calculated taking into account the total turnover deriving respectively from the provision of services, supplies or works by those affiliated undertakings.[134]

The Utilities Directive is inapplicable to contracts awarded by a joint venture,[135] formed exclusively by a number of contracting entities for the purpose of carrying out activities covered by the Utilities Directive, to one of these contracting entities, or by a contracting entity to such a joint venture of which it forms part, provided that the joint venture has been set up in order to carry out the activity concerned over a period of at least three years and that the instrument setting up the joint venture stipulates that the contracting entities which form it will be part thereof for at least the same period.

The Commission may request[136] from member states notification of the names of affiliated undertakings or joint ventures concerned, the nature and value of the contracts involved and such proof as may be deemed necessary by the Commission that the relationship between the undertaking or joint

---

[129]   See Article 23(2)(b) of the Utilities Directive.
[130]   See Article 23(3)(a) of the Utilities Directive.
[131]   See Article 23(3)(b) of the Utilities Directive.
[132]   See Article 23(3)(c) of the Utilities Directive.
[133]   See Article 23(3), second indent of the Utilities Directive.
[134]   See Article 23(3), third indent of the Utilities Directive.
[135]   See Article 23(4) of the Utilities Directive.
[136]   See Article 23(5) of the Utilities Directive.

ventures to which contracts are awarded and the contracting entity complies with the requirements of the Utilities Directive and in particular Article 23.

Contracts relating to certain services excluded from the scope of this Directive

The Utilities Directive does not cover service contracts for (a) the acquisition or rental, by whatever financial means, of land, existing buildings or other immovable property or related real estate rights. Nevertheless, financial service contracts concluded at the same time as, before or after the contract of acquisition or rental, in whatever form, are covered by the Utilities Directive; (b) arbitration and conciliation services; (c) financial services in connection with the issue, sale, purchase or transfer of securities or other financial instruments, in particular transactions by the contracting entities to raise money or capital; (d) employment contracts; (e) research and development services other than those where the benefits accrue exclusively to the contracting entity for its use in the conduct of its own affairs, on condition that the service provided is wholly remunerated by the contracting entity.[137]

Service contracts awarded on the basis of an exclusive right

The Utilities Directive does not apply to service contracts awarded to an entity which is itself a contracting authority within the meaning of Article 2(1)(a)[138] or to an association of contracting authorities on the basis of an exclusive right which they enjoy pursuant to a published law, regulation or administrative provision which is compatible with the Treaty.[139]

Contracts awarded by certain contracting entities for the purchase of water and for the supply of energy or of fuels for the production of energy

The Utilities Directive does not apply to contracts for the purchase of water[140] if awarded by contracting entities engaged in the provision of fixed networks or the operation of fixed networks intended to provide a service to the public in connection with the production, transport or distribution of drinking water or the supply of drinking water to such networks.[141]

---

[137] See Article 24 of the Utilities Directive.

[138] For the purposes of the Utilities Directive, contracting entities include the state, regional or local authorities, bodies governed by public law, associations formed by one or several such authorities or one or several of such bodies governed by public law.

[139] See Article 25 of the Utilities Directive.

[140] See Article 26(a) of the Utilities Directive.

[141] See Article 4(1) of the Utilities Directive.

The Utilities Directive does not apply to contracts for the supply of energy or of fuels for the production of energy,[142] if awarded by contracting entities engaged in the provision of fixed networks or the operation of fixed networks in order to provide a service to the public in connection with the production, transport or distribution of gas or heat, as well as the supply of gas or heat to such networks;[143] the provision of fixed networks or the operation of fixed networks intended to provide a service to the public in connection with the production, transport or distribution of electricity or the supply of electricity to such networks;[144] or the exploitation of a geographical area for the purpose of exploring for oil, gas, coal or other solid fuels or extracting oil, gas, coal or other solid fuels.[145]

Contracts subject to special arrangements
The Kingdom of the Netherlands, the United Kingdom, the Republic of Austria and the Federal Republic of Germany have established special arrangements for entities exploiting geographical areas for the purpose of exploring for or extracting oil, gas, coal or other solid fuels by virtue of Decisions 93/676, 97/367, 2002/205 and 2004/73. The Utilities Directive does not apply to entities operating in the sectors covered by the special arrangements.[146] However, the member states concerned must ensure, by way of the conditions of authorisation or other appropriate measures, that the excluded entities observe the principles of non-discrimination and competitive procurement in respect of the award of supplies, works and service contracts, in particular as regards the information which they make available to economic operators concerning their procurement intentions.[147] These entities must communicate[148] to the Commission all relevant information relating to the contracts they award under the parameters of the special arrangement regime.[149]

---

[142] See Article 26(b) of the Utilities Directive.
[143] See Article 3(1) of the Utilities Directive.
[144] See Article 3(3) of the Utilities Directive.
[145] See Article 7(a) of the Utilities Directive.
[146] See Article 27 of the Utilities Directive.
[147] See Article 27(a) of the Utilities Directive.
[148] See Article 27(b) of the Utilities Directive.
[149] See the conditions defined in Commission Decision 93/327, OJ L 129, 27.5.1993, p. 25, defining the conditions under which contracting entities exploiting geographical areas for the purpose of exploring for or extracting oil, gas, coal or other solid fuels must communicate to the Commission information relating to the contracts they award.

Reserved contracts

Member states may reserve the right to participate in contract award procedures to sheltered workshops or provide for such contracts to be performed in the context of sheltered employment programmes where most of the employees concerned are handicapped persons who, by reason of the nature or the seriousness of their disabilities, cannot carry on occupations under normal conditions.[150] The notice used to make the call for competition must make reference to the intention of contracting entities to reserve contracts for the specific requirements stipulated in Article 28 of the Utilities Directive.

Contracts and framework agreements awarded by central purchasing bodies

Contracting entities which purchase works, supplies or services from or through a central purchasing body do not have to follow the provisions of the Utilities Directive,[151] provided that the central purchasing body has complied with the relevant procurement regime laid down in the Utilities Directive or in the Public Sector Directive, where appropriate.[152]

Contracts for an activity directly exposed to competition

Contracts intended to enable a contracting entity to pursue an activity covered by the Utilities Directive do not fall within its remit if, in the member state in which the activity is performed, it is directly exposed to competition in markets to which access is not restricted.[153]

Access to a market is deemed not to be restricted[154] if the member state has implemented and applied specific provisions of Community legislation mentioned in Annex XI of the Utilities Directive regarding the opening up of the relevant markets and in particular, in the sector of transport or distribution of gas or heat, Directive 98/30[155] concerning common rules for the internal market in natural gas; in the sector of production, transmission or distribution of electricity, Directive 96/92[156] concerning common rules for the internal market in electricity; in the postal sector, Directive 97/67[157] on common rules for the development of the internal market of Community postal services and the improvement of quality of service; and finally in the exploration of gas or

---

[150] See Article 28 of the Utilities Directive.
[151] See Article 29(1) of the Utilities Directive.
[152] See Article 29(2) of the Utilities Directive.
[153] See Article 30(1) of the Utilities Directive.
[154] See Article 30(3) of the Utilities Directive.
[155] See OJ L 204, 21.7.1998, p. 1
[156] See OJ L 27, 30.1.1997, p. 20
[157] See OJ L 15, 21.1.1998, p. 14, last amended by Directive 2002/39/EC, OJ L 176, 5.7.2002, p. 21.

oil and in the extraction for gas or oil sectors, Directive 94/22[158] on the conditions for granting and using authorisations for the prospecting, exploration and
production of hydrocarbons. If free access to a given market cannot be
presumed on the basis of compliance with the above legislation, then it must
be demonstrated that access to the market in question is free *de facto* and *de
jure*.[159]

Procedure for establishing whether an activity is directly exposed to competition

The question of whether an activity is directly exposed to competition must be
decided on the basis of criteria that are in conformity with the Treaty provisions on competition, such as the characteristics of the goods or services
concerned, the existence of alternative goods or services, the prices and the
actual or potential presence of more than one supplier of the goods or services
in question.[160]

Notification by member states

When a Member State considers that an activity is directly exposed to competition, it must notify the Commission and inform of all relevant facts, and in
particular of any law, regulation, administrative provision or agreement
concerning compliance with the legislation regarding the opening up of the
relevant markets as set out in Annex XI of the Utilities Directive. In addition
to the above notification requirement, member states, where appropriate, must
furnish a position adopted by an independent national authority that is competent in relation to the activity concerned in their territory.[161]

When an activity in a member state is already the subject of a notification
procedure, further requests concerning the same activity in the same member
state before the expiry of the period begun when the first notification was
made to the Commission, are not considered as new procedures and they will
not be treated in the context of the first request.[162]

Decision by the Commission

After the notification, the Commission can adopt a Decision[163] establishing
the fact that an activity is directly exposed to competition and therefore the
Utilities Directive does not apply within a period of three months. For the

---

[158]   See OJ L 164, 30.6.1994, p. 3
[159]   See Article 30(3), second indent of the Utilities Directive.
[160]   See Article 30(2) of the Utilities Directive.
[161]   See Article 30(4) of the Utilities Directive.
[162]   See Article 30(6), second indent of the Utilities Directive.
[163]   See Article 30(6), first indent of the Utilities Directive.

adoption of a Decision the Commission must allow a period of three months commencing on the first working day following the date on which it receives the notification or the request. However, this period may be extended once by a maximum of three months in duly justified cases, in particular if the information contained in the notification or the request or in the documents justifying the alleged competitive environment of an activity is incomplete or if the facts as reported are subject to any substantive changes. This extension must be limited to one month where an independent national authority that is competent in the activity concerned has established the applicability of Article 30(1) of the Utilities Directive and in particular that the activity concerned is directly exposed to competition in markets to which access is not restricted.

However, the inapplicability of the Directive is also presumed when that period has expired without the Commission adopting a decision.[164] Where free access to a given market is presumed on the basis of compliance with the legislation regarding the opening up of the relevant markets as set out in Annex XI of the Utilities Directive[165] and where an independent national authority that is competent in the activity concerned has established that the relevant activity is directly exposed to competition in markets to which access is not restricted, the Utilities Directive is inapplicable if the Commission does not adopt a Decision declaring the inapplicability of Article 30(1) of the Utilities Directive.

The Commission may also begin the procedure for adoption of a Decision establishing that a given activity is directly exposed to competition on its own initiative.[166] In such a case, the Commission must inform the member state concerned.

Publicity requirements
The Commission must adopt detailed rules for applying the provisions referred to in Article 30 of the Utilities Directive concerning activities which are directly exposed to competition, prior to adopting a Decision. Such requirements include the publication of notices in the Official Journal which, for information purposes, state the date on which the three-month period required for the adoption of a Decision begins, and in case this period is extended, any extension granted.[167] In addition the notice must contain any arrangements for forwarding positions adopted by an independent national authority that is competent in the activity concerned and any relevant information which should be forwarded to the Commission to determine either compliance with the required legislation

---

164 See Article 30(4) of the Utilities Directive.
165 See Article 30(3), first subparagraph of paragraph of the Utilities Directive.
166 See Article 30(5) of the Utilities Directive.
167 See Article 30(6) of the Utilities Directive.

of opening up the relevant market in which an activity is performed or any *de facto* or *de jure* conditions which should be taken into account by the Commission in establishing whether an activity is directly exposed to competition.

Works and service concessions

The Utilities Directive does not apply to works and service concessions[168] which are awarded by contracting entities carrying out one or more of the activities covered by the Utilities Directive and in particular activities including gas, heat and electricity, water, transport services, postal services, exploration for oil, gas or other solid fuels, extraction of oil, gas or other solid fuels and provision of ports and airports referred to in Articles 3 to 7, where those concessions are awarded for carrying out those activities.

The Monetary Applicability of the Utilities Directive

Contract thresholds

The Utilities Directive applies to contracts which have a value[169] excluding value-added tax (VAT) estimated at:

(a)   Euro 499 000 in the case of supply and service contracts;
(b)   Euro 6 242 000 in the case of works contracts.

Contract value calculation

The Directive provides methods for calculating the estimated value of contracts, framework agreements and dynamic purchasing systems.[170] The calculation of the estimated value of a contract must be based on the total amount payable, net of VAT, as estimated by the contracting entity. This calculation must take account of the estimated total amount, including any form of option and any renewals of the contract.[171] Where the contracting entity provides prizes or payments to candidates or tenderers it must take them into account when calculating the estimated value of the contract.

Contracting entities are under an obligation to avoid subdividing works projects or proposing the purchase of a certain quantity of supplies or services in order to circumvent the monetary applicability of the Directive.[172]

With regard to framework agreements and dynamic purchasing systems,

---

[168]   See Article 30(6), third indent of the Utilities Directive.
[169]   See Article 16 of the Utilities Directive.
[170]   Article 17 of the Utilities Directive.
[171]   Article 17(1) of the Utilities Directive.
[172]   Article 17(3) of the Utilities Directive.

the value to be taken into consideration must be the maximum estimated value net of VAT of all the contracts envisaged for the total term of the framework agreement or the dynamic purchasing system.[173]

With regard to works contracts, calculation of the estimated value must take account of both the cost of the works and the total estimated value of the supplies or services necessary for executing the works.[174] The value of supplies or services which are not necessary for the performance of a particular works contract may not be added to the value of the works contract when to do so would result in removing the procurement of those supplies or services from the scope of the Utilities Directive.

Where a proposed work or purchase of services may result in contracts being awarded at the same time in the form of separate lots, contracting entities must take into account the total estimated value of all such lots.[175] Where the aggregate value of the lots is equal to or exceeds the threshold stipulated in the Directive, in that case each lot must be awarded separately in accordance with the Utilities Directive. However, the contracting entities may waive such application in respect of lots the estimated value of which net of VAT is less than Euro 80 000 for services or Euro 1 million for works, provided that the aggregate value of those lots does not exceed 20% of the aggregate value of the lots as a whole.

Where a proposal for the acquisition of similar supplies may result in contracts being awarded at the same time in the form of separate lots, account must be taken of the total estimated value of all such lots.

In the case of supply or service contracts which are regular in nature or which are intended to be renewed within a given period, the calculation of the estimated contract value must be based on the following: either (a) the total actual value of successive contracts of the same type awarded during the preceding 12 months or financial year, adjusted, if possible, to take account of the changes in quantity or value which would occur in the course of the 12 months following the initial contract; or (b) the total estimated value of the successive contracts awarded during the 12 months following the first delivery, or during the financial year if that is longer than 12 months. The basis for calculating the estimated value of a contract including both supplies and services must be the total value of the supplies and services, regardless of their respective shares. The calculation must include the value of the installation operations.

With regard to supply contracts relating to the leasing, hire, rental or hire

---

[173]   Article 17(9) of the Utilities Directive.
[174]   Article 17(4) of the Utilities Directive.
[175]   Article 17(6) of the Utilities Directive.

purchase of products,[176] the value to be taken as a basis for calculating the estimated contract value must be as follows:

(a)   in the case of fixed-term contracts, if that term is less than or equal to 12 months, the total estimated value for the term of the contract or, if the term of the contract is greater than 12 months, the total value including the estimated residual value;

(b)   in the case of contracts without a fixed term or the term of which cannot be defined, the monthly value multiplied by 48.

With regard to service contracts,[177] the value to be taken as a basis for calculating the estimated contract value for insurance services must reflect the premium payable and other forms of remuneration; for banking and other financial services it must comprise the fees, commissions, interest and other forms of remuneration; for design contracts it must include fees, commission payable and other forms of remuneration. For service contracts which do not indicate a total price, in the case of fixed-term contracts, if that term is less than or equal to 48 months, the estimated contract value must reflect the total value for their full term; in the case of contracts without a fixed term or with a term greater than 48 months, the estimated value must include the monthly value multiplied by 48.

Revision of the thresholds

Revision of the thresholds will be undertaken by the Commission every two years from the entry into force of the Utilities Directive.[178] The calculation of the value of these thresholds must be based on the average daily value of the Euro, expressed in SDRs, over the 24 months terminating on the last day of August preceding the revision with effect from 1 January. The value of the thresholds thus revised must, where necessary, be rounded down to the nearest thousand Euros so as to ensure that the thresholds in force provided for by the Agreement, expressed in SDRs, are observed. The value of the thresholds set in the national currencies of the member states which are not participating in monetary union is normally to be adjusted every two years from 1 January 2004 onwards. The calculation of such value must be based on the average daily values of those currencies expressed in Euro over the 24 months terminating on the last day of August preceding the revision with effect from 1 January. The revised thresholds and their corresponding values in the national

---

[176]   Article 17(6) of the Utilities Directive.
[177]   Article 17(8)(a)(b) of the Utilities Directive.
[178]   See Article 69 of the Utilities Directive.

currencies must be published by the Commission in the Official Journal of the European Union at the beginning of the month of November following their revision.

MONITORING REQUIREMENTS

Information Concerning Awards

Contracting entities must keep appropriate information on each contract which must be sufficient to permit them at a later date to justify decisions taken in connection with:

(a) the qualification and selection of economic operators and the award of contracts;

(b) the use of procedures without a prior call for competition by virtue of Article 40(3);

(c) the non-application of Chapters III to VI of this Title by virtue of the derogations provided for in Chapter II of Title I and in Chapter II of this Title.

Contracting entities must record and document the progress of award procedures conducted by electronic means. The information must be kept for at least four years from the date of award of the contract so that the contracting entity will be able, during that period, to provide the necessary information to the Commission.

Statistical obligations

Member states must ensure, in accordance with the arrangements to be laid down under the procedure provided for in Article 68(2), that the Commission receives every year a statistical report concerning the total value, broken down by member state and by category of activity to which Annexes I to X refer, of the contracts awarded below the thresholds set out in Article 16 but which would be covered by this Directive were it not for those thresholds.

As regards the categories of activity to which Annexes II, III, V, IX and X refer, member states must ensure that the Commission receives a statistical report on contracts awarded no later than 31 October 2004 for the previous year, and before 31 October of each year thereafter, in accordance with arrangements to be laid down under the procedure provided for in Article 68(2). The statistical report must contain the information required to verify the proper application of the Agreement.

The information required under the first subparagraph must not include information concerning contracts for the research and development services listed in category 8 of Annex XVII A, for telecommunications services listed in category 5 of Annex XVII A whose CPV positions are equivalent to the CPC reference numbers 7524, 7525 and 7526, or for the services listed in Annex XVII B.

The arrangements under paragraphs 1 and 2 must be laid down in such a way as to ensure that: (a) in the interests of administrative simplification, contracts of lesser value may be excluded, provided that the usefulness of the statistics is not jeopardised; (b) the confidential nature of the information provided is respected.

Monitoring mechanisms
In conformity with Council Directive 92/13 co-ordinating the laws, regulations and administrative provisions relating to the application of Community rules on the procurement procedures of entities operating in the water, energy, transport and telecommunications sectors, member states must ensure implementation of this Directive by effective, available and transparent mechanisms. For this purpose they may, among other things, appoint or establish an independent body.

12. Publicity and advertisement in utilities procurement

NOTICES

Periodic Indicative Notices

Periodic indicative notices are notices sent for publication by contracting entities to the Official Journal or notices published by contracting entities themselves on their buyer profile through the internet.[1]

Both periodic indicative notices and notices on buyer profiles must include the following information:[2]

(a) for public supplies contracts and as soon as possible after the beginning of the budgetary year, the estimated total value of the contracts or the framework agreements by product area which contracting entities intend to award over the following 12 months, where the total estimated value is equal to or greater than euro 750 000. The product area must be established by the contracting entities by reference to the CPV nomenclature;

(b) for public services contracts and as soon as possible after the beginning of the budgetary year, the estimated total value of the contracts or the framework agreements in each of the categories of services listed in Annex XVII A which contracting entities intend to award over the following 12 months, where such estimated total value is equal to or greater than euro 750 000;

(c) for public works contracts and as soon as possible after the decision approving the planning of the works contracts or the framework agreements that the contracting entities intend to award, the essential characteristics of the contracts or the framework agreements which they intend to award, the estimated value of which is equal to or greater than the threshold specified in Article 16 of the Utilities Directive.

---

[1] Article 41 of the Utilities Directive.
[2] See Article 41(1) of the Utilities Directive.

The notice of publication for a prior indicative notice on a buyer profile must contain the country and name of the contracting authority, the internet address of the buyer profile and any CPV nomenclature reference numbers.[3] The buyer profile may include[4] periodic indicative notices, information on ongoing invitations to tender, scheduled purchases, contracts concluded, procedures cancelled and any useful general information, such as a contact point, a telephone and a fax number, a postal address and an e-mail address. Contracting entities which publish a periodic indicative notice on their buyer profile must send the Commission, electronically, a notice of such publication.[5] Periodic indicative notices may not be published on a buyer profile before the dispatch to the Commission of the notice of their publication in that form; they must mention the date of that dispatch.[6]

Contracting entities should not publish notices and their contents at national level before the date on which they are sent to the Commission for publication in the Official Journal.[7] Notices published at national level must not contain information other than information contained in the notices dispatched to the Commission or published on a buyer profile. However, they must mention the date of dispatch of the notice to the Commission or its publication on the buyer profile.[8]

The publication of prior indicative notices is compulsory only where the contracting entities take the option of shortening the time limits for the receipt of tenders as laid down in Article 45 of the Utilities Directive. Also, in exceptional cases where contracting entities have recourse to procedures without the prior publication of a contract notice, the publication of periodic indicative notices or notices on buyer profile are not required.[9]

Contracting entities may publish or arrange for the Commission to publish periodic indicative notices relating to major projects without repeating information previously included in a periodic indicative notice, provided that it is clearly pointed out that these notices are additional ones.[10]

Notices sent by contracting entities to the Commission must be sent either by electronic means in accordance with the format and procedures for transmission indicated in Annex XX of the Utilities Directive, or by other means.[11]

---

[3] See Annex XV A of the Utilities Directive.
[4] See point 2(b) of Annex XX of the Utilities Directive.
[5] See the format and detailed procedures for sending notices indicated in point 3 of Annex XX of the Utilities Directive.
[6] See Article 36(5), second indent of the Utilities Directive.
[7] See Article 42(5) of the Utilities Directive.
[8] Article 44, second indent of the Utilities Directive.
[9] See Article 45(5) of the Utilities Directive.
[10] See Article 41(2) of the Utilities Directive.
[11] See Article 44(3) of the Utilities Directive.

Notices drawn up and transmitted by electronic means in accordance with the format and procedures for transmission indicated in point 3 of Annex XX of the Utilities Directive will be published within five days of dispatch. Notices which are not transmitted by electronic means will be published not later than 12 days after they are transmitted.[12] However, in exceptional cases, the contract notices utilised as a call for competition according to Article 42(1)(c) of the Utilities Directive must be published within five days in response to a request by the contracting entity, provided that the notice has been sent by fax.

Notices on the Existence of Qualification System

Where contracting entities choose to set up a qualification system in accordance with Article 53 of the Utilities Directive, the system must be the subject of a notice as referred to in Annex XIV, indicating the purpose of the qualification system and how to access the rules concerning its operation.[13] According to Annex XIV of the Utilities Directive, information to be included in the notice on the existence of a qualification system must comprise:

1. the name, address, telegraphic address, electronic address, telephone number, telex and fax number of the contracting entity;
2. an indication, where appropriate, as to whether the contract is reserved for sheltered workshops or whether its performance is reserved in the context of sheltered employment programmes;
3. a statement on the purpose of the qualification system, including the description of the goods, services or works or categories to be procured through the system by reference to nomenclature numbers;
4. a statement on the conditions to be fulfilled by the economic operators in view of their qualification pursuant to the system and the methods according to which each of those conditions will be verified. Where the description of such conditions and verification methods is voluminous and based on documents available to interested economic operators, a summary of the main conditions and methods and a reference to those documents will be sufficient;
5. an indication of the period of validity of the qualification system and the formalities for its renewal;
6. a reference to the fact that the notice acts as a call for competition;
7. an address where further information and documentation concerning the qualification system can be obtained;

---

12 See Article 44(3), second indent of the Utilities Directive.
13 See Article 41(3) of the Utilities Directive.

8.   a reference concerning the name and address of the body responsible for appeal and, where appropriate, mediation procedures. In addition, precise information should be provided concerning time limits for lodging appeals, or the name, address, telephone number, fax number and e-mail address of the service from which this information may be obtained;

9.   an indication of award criteria, where known, for award of the contract. Criteria representing the most economically advantageous tender as well as their weighting or, where appropriate, the order of importance of these criteria, must be mentioned where they do not appear in the specifications or will not be indicated in the invitation to tender or to negotiate;

10. any other relevant information.

Where the system is of more than three years duration, the notice must be published annually. Where the system is of a shorter duration, an initial notice will be adequate.

Notices used as a Call for Competition

In the case of supply, works or service contracts, the call for competition may be made by means of a periodic indicative notice or by means of a notice on the existence of a qualification system, or by means of a contract notice in accordance with Annex XXX of the Utilities Directive.[14]

When a call for competition is made by means of a periodic indicative notice, the notice must refer specifically to the supplies, works or services which are the subject of the contract to be awarded. It must indicate that the contract will be awarded by restricted or negotiated procedure without further publication of a notice of a call for competition and invite interested economic operators to express their interest in writing.[15] The period indicative notice must be published not more than 12 months prior to the date on which the invitation to negotiate or submit a tender is sent for publication according to Article 47(5) of the Utilities Directive. Moreover, the contracting entity must meet the time limits laid down in Article 45 with respect to the receipt of requests to participate in award procedures and the receipt of tenders.

When a call for competition is made by means of a notice on the existence of a qualification system, tenderers in a restricted procedure or participants in a negotiated procedure must be selected from the qualified candidates in accordance with such a system.[16]

---

[14]   See Article 42 of the Utilities Directive.
[15]   See Article 42(3) of the Utilities Directive.
[16]   See Article 42(1)(b) of the Utilities Directive.

In particular, when a call for competition is made by means of a contract notice, contracting entities should provide the following information in contract notices for open and restricted procedure and negotiated procedures with prior advertisement:[17]

1. name, address, telephone and fax number, and e-mail address;
2. an indication of whether the public contract is restricted to sheltered workshops, or whether its execution is restricted to the framework of protected job programmes;
3. the award procedure chosen and where appropriate, the reasons for use of the accelerated procedure (in restricted and negotiated procedures); also, where appropriate, an indication of whether a framework agreement or a dynamic purchasing system is involved; finally, where appropriate, an indication of whether an electronic auction will be held, in the event of open, restricted or negotiated procedures covered by Article 30(1)(a);
4. the form of the contract;
5. the place of completion or performance of the works, of delivery of products or of the provision of services;
6. (a) for public works contracts:
   - a description of the extent of the works and general nature of the work; an indication in particular of options concerning supplementary works, and, if known, the provisional timetable for recourse to these options as well as the number of possible renewals; an indication of the size of the different lots, if the work or the contract is subdivided into several lots; a reference to nomenclature number(s);
   - information concerning the purpose of the work or the contract where the latter also involves the drawing-up of projects;
   - an indication, in the event of a framework agreement, of the planned duration of the framework agreement, the estimated total value of the works for the entire duration of the framework agreement and, as far as possible, the value and the frequency of the contracts to be awarded.
   (b) for public supply contracts:
   - a description of the nature of the products to be supplied, indicating in particular whether tenders are requested with a view to purchase, lease rental, hire or hire-purchase or a

---

[17] See Article 42(1)(c) of the Utilities Directive.

combination of these, nomenclature reference number; an indication of the quantity of products to be supplied, specifying in particular options concerning supplementary purchases and the provisional timetable for recourse to these options as well as the number of renewals; a reference to nomenclature number(s);

- in the case of regular or renewable contracts during the course of a given period, an indication of the timetable for subsequent contracts for purchase of intended supplies;
- in the event of a framework agreement, an indication of the planned duration of the framework agreement, the estimated total value of the supplies for the entire duration of the framework agreement and, as far as possible, the value and the frequency of the contracts to be awarded;

(c) for public service contracts:

- a reference to the category and description of service by nomenclature number(s); an indication of the quantity of services to be provided, and in particular any options concerning supplementary purchases and the provisional timetable for recourse to these options as well as the number of renewals; in the case of renewable contracts over a given period, an estimate of the time frame for subsequent public contracts for purchase of intended services; in the event of a framework agreement, an indication of the planned duration of the framework agreement, the estimated total value of the services for the entire duration of the framework agreement and, as far as possible, the value and the frequency of the contracts to be awarded;
- an indication of whether the execution of the service is reserved by law, regulation or administrative provision to a particular profession and a reference to the law, regulation or administrative provision;
- an indication of whether legal persons should indicate the names and professional qualifications of the staff to be responsible for the execution of the service;

7. where the contracts are subdivided into lots, an indication of the possibility of tendering for one, for several or for all the lots;

8. any time limit for completion of works/supplies/services or duration of the works/supply/services contract; where possible any time limit by which works will begin or any time limit by which delivery of supplies or services will begin;

9. an indication of admission or prohibition of variants;

10. an indication of any particular conditions to which the performance of the contract is subject;

11. in open procedures: provision of (a) name, address, telephone and telefax number and electronic address of the service from which contract documents and additional documents can be requested; (b) where appropriate, the time limit for submission of such requests; (c) where appropriate, the cost of and payment conditions for obtaining these documents; (d) the time limit for receipt of tenders or indicative tenders where a dynamic purchasing system is being used (open procedures); (e) the time limit for receipt of a request to participate (restricted and negotiated procedures); (f) the address where these have to be sent; (g) the language or languages in which they must be drawn up; (h) persons authorised to be present at the opening of tenders; (b) date, time and place of such opening;

12. an indication of any deposit and guarantees required;

13. a reference to the main terms concerning financing and payment;

14. where applicable, the legal form to be taken by the grouping of economic operators to whom the contract is to be awarded;

15. an indication of the selection criteria regarding the personal situation of economic operators that may lead to their exclusion, and required information proving that they do not fall within the cases justifying exclusion; an indication of the selection criteria and information concerning the economic operators' personal situation, information and any necessary formalities for assessment of the minimum economic and technical standards required of the economic operator; an indication of any minimum level(s) of standards required;

16. in cases of framework agreements: a reference to the number and, where appropriate, proposed maximum number of economic operators who will be members of the framework agreement; an indication of the duration of the framework agreement provided for, stating, if appropriate, the reasons for any duration exceeding four years;

17. in cases of negotiated procedures with the publication of a contract notice, an indication of possible recourse to a staged procedure in order gradually to reduce the number of solutions to be discussed or tenders to be negotiated;

18. in cases of restricted procedures or negotiated procedures with the publication of a contract notice, when contracting entities exercise the option of reducing the number of candidates to be invited to submit tenders, to engage in dialogue or to negotiate, an indication of the minimum and, if appropriate, the proposed maximum number of candidates and a reference to the objective criteria to be used in choosing that number of candidates;

19.   in cases of open procedures, an indication of the time frame during which the tenderers must submit their tender;
20.   in cases of negotiated procedures, a reference to the names and addresses of economic operators already selected by the contracting authority;
21.   a reference to the award criteria to be used in the award of the contract: 'lowest price' or 'most economically advantageous tender'; in cases where criteria representing the most economically advantageous tender are selected, a description of their weighting in the event that such weighting does not appear in the specifications;
22.   a reference to the name and address of the body responsible for appeal and, where appropriate, mediation procedures; an indication of the precise information concerning deadlines for lodging appeals, or if need be the name, address, telephone number, fax number and e-mail address of the service from which this information may be obtained;
23.   the date(s) of publication of the prior information notice; the date of dispatch of the notice;
24.   an indication of whether the contract is covered by the WTO GPA Agreement.

Contract notices must be published in full in an official language of the Community as chosen by the contracting entity, this original language version constituting the sole authentic text. A summary of the important elements of each notice will be published in the other official languages.

When contracting entities wish to set up a dynamic purchasing system, they must publish a contract notice. Furthermore, when contracts are to be awarded based on a dynamic purchasing system, contracting entities must publish a simplified contract notice.[18]

Notices and their contents may not be published at national level before the date on which they are sent to the Commission. Notices published at national level must not contain information other than that contained in the notices dispatched to the Commission or published on a buyer profile, but must mention the date of dispatch of the notice to the Commission or its publication on the buyer profile. Periodic indicative notices may not be published on a

---

[18]   A simplified contract notice for use in a dynamic purchasing system must include the following information: the country, name and e-mail address of the contracting authority, publication reference of the contract notice for the dynamic purchasing system, the e-mail address at which the technical specification and additional documents relating to the dynamic purchasing system are available, the subject of contract and a description by reference number(s) of 'CPV' nomenclature and the quantity or extent of the contract to be awarded the time frame for submitting indicative tenders. See Annex XIII D of the Utilities Directive.

buyer profile before the dispatch to the Commission of the notice of publication in that form; they must mention the date of that dispatch.

Contract Award Notices

Contracting entities which have awarded a contract or a framework agreement must, within two months of the award of the contract or framework agreement, send a contract award notice to the Commission.[19] In the case of contracts awarded under a framework agreement, contracting entities are not obliged to send a notice of the results of the award procedure for each contract based on that agreement. Contracting entities must send a contract award notice based on a dynamic purchasing system within two months after the award of each contract.[20] They may, however, group such notices on a quarterly basis. In that case, they must send the grouped notices within two months of the end of each quarter.[21]

The Commission must respect any sensitive commercial aspects which the contracting entities may point out when forwarding this information, concerning the number of tenders received, the identity of economic operators, or prices. Where contracting entities award a research and development service contract through procedures without a call for competition, they may limit information to be provided with reference to the research and development services.[22] In particular, they may, on grounds of commercial confidentiality, limit the information to be provided in the contract award notice concerning the nature and quantity of the services supplied. In cases where a research and development contract is awarded through negotiated procedures with prior notice, contracting entities must ensure that any information published under a contract award notice is similar in detail and description to the information contained in the notice of the call for competition.[23]

Contract award notices of contracts based on a qualification system must also contain information similar in detail and description to the information contained in the list of qualified service providers drawn up in accordance with Article 53(7) of the Utilities Directive.[24]

For contracts awarded for services listed in Annex XVII B of the Utilities Directive, contracting entities must indicate in the contract notice whether they agree to publication of a contract award notice.[25]

---

[19]   See the content and conditions of such notices in Annex XVI of the Utilities Directive.
[20]   See Article 43 of the Utilities Directive.
[21]   See Article 43(1) of the Utilities Directive.
[22]   See Article 43(2) of the Utilities Directive.
[23]   See Article 43(3) of the Utilities Directive.
[24]   See Article 43(3), fourth indent of the Utilities Directive.
[25]   See Article 43(4) of the Utilities Directive.

TIME LIMITS FOR THE RECEIPT OF REQUESTS TO PARTICIPATE AND FOR THE RECEIPT OF TENDERS

In determining the time limits for requests to participate and the receipt of tenders, contracting entities must take particular account of the complexity of the contract and the time required for drawing up tenders.[26]

Time Limits for Open Procedures

When contracting entities wish to award a contract through open procedures, the minimum time limit for the receipt of tenders must be 52 days from the date on which the contract notice was sent for publication to the Commission.[27] Where notices are drawn up and transmitted by electronic means in accordance with the format and procedures for transmission indicated in Annex XX of the Utilities Directive, the time limits for the receipt of tenders in open procedures may be reduced by seven days.[28]

The time limits for the receipt of tenders in open procedures may be further reduced by five days where the contracting entity offers unrestricted and full direct access to the contract documents and any supplementary documents by electronic means from the date on which the notice used as a means of calling for competition is published, in accordance with Annex XX of the Utilities Directive. The notice should specify the internet address at which this documentation is accessible.[29]

If contracting entities have published a periodic indicative notice, the minimum time limit for the receipt of tenders in open procedures must be, as a general rule, not less than 36 days. In cases where the periodic indicative notice has included, in addition to the information required by Annex XV A, part I, all the information required by Annex XV A, part II, in-so-far as the latter information is available at the time the notice is published, and that the notice has been sent for publication between 52 days and 12 months before the date on which the contract notice referred to in Article 42(1)(c) is sent for publication, a reduced time limit for the receipt of tenders is permitted, provided that it will not be less than 22 days from the date on which the notice was sent.[30]

In open procedures, the cumulative effect of the reductions provided for the receipt of tenders may in no case result in a period for the receipt of tenders of

---

26   See Article 45 of the Utilities Directive.
27   See Article 45(1) of the Utilities Directive.
28   See Article 45(5) of the Utilities Directive.
29   See Article 45(6) of the Utilities Directive.
30   See Article 45(4) of the Utilities Directive.

less than 15 days from the date on which the contract notice is sent. However, if the contract notice is not transmitted by fax or electronic means, the cumulative effect of the reductions may in no case result in a time limit for receipt of tenders in an open procedure of less than 22 days from the date on which the contract notice is transmitted.

In open procedures, where contracting entities do not offer unrestricted and full direct access by electronic means in accordance with Article 45(6) of the Utilities Directive to the specifications and any supporting documents, the specifications and supporting documents must be sent to economic operators within six days of receipt of the request, provided that the request was made in good time before the time limit for the submission of tenders. Provided that it has been requested in good time, contracting entities must supply additional information relating to the specifications not later than six days before the time limit for the receipt of tenders.[31]

Request to Participate or Negotiate

In restricted procedures with a prior call for competition, the time limit for the receipt of requests to participate, in response to a contract notice used as a call for competition and published under Article 42(1)(c) of the Utilities Directive, must be no less than 37 days from the date on which the notice was sent for publication.[32]

In negotiated procedures with a prior call for competition, the time limit for the receipt of requests to negotiate in response to an invitation by contracting entities under Article 47(5), must be no less than 37 days from the date on which the invitation was sent for publication. If notices were sent for publication by means other than electronic means or fax, the time limit may be no less than 22 days; on the other hand, if notices are transmitted by electronic means or fax the time limit must be no less than 15 days from the dispatch of the notice.[33]

Where notices are drawn up and transmitted by electronic means in accordance with the format and procedures for transmission indicated in Annex XX of the Utilities Directive, the time limits for the receipt of requests to participate in restricted and negotiated procedures may be reduced by seven days.[34]

The cumulative effect of the reductions may in no case result in a time limit on receipt of requests to participate, in response to a notice published under Article 42(1)(c), or in response to an invitation by the contracting entities

---

[31] See Article 45(8) of the Utilities Directive.
[32] See Article 45(3)(a) of the Utilities Directive.
[33] See Article 45(3)(a), second indent of the Utilities Directive.
[34] See Article 45(5) of the Utilities Directive.

under Article 47(5) of the Utilities Directive, of less than 15 days from the date on which the contract notice or invitation is sent.[35]

Receipt of Tenders in Restricted and Negotiated Procedures

The time limit for the receipt of tenders may be set by mutual agreement between the contracting entity and the selected candidates, provided that all candidates have the same time to prepare and submit their tenders.[36] Where it is not possible to reach agreement on the time limit for the receipt of tenders, the contracting entity should determine a time limit which, as a general rule, must be at least 24 days and in no case must be less than 10 days from the date of the invitation to tender.[37]

The time limits for the receipt of tenders in restricted and negotiated procedures may be further reduced by five days where the contracting entity offers unrestricted and full direct access to the contract documents and any supplementary documents by electronic means from the date on which the notice used as a means of calling for competition is published, in accordance with Annex XX of the Utilities Directive. The notice should specify the internet address at which this documentation is accessible.[38]

In restricted and negotiated procedures, the cumulative effect of the reductions to the time limits to submit tenders may in no case, except that of a time limit set by mutual agreement, result in a time limit for the receipt of tenders of less than 10 days from the date of the invitation to tender.[39]

Extensions to Time Limits for the Receipt of Tenders

If, for whatever reason, the contract documents and the supporting documents or additional information, although requested in good time, have not been supplied within the time limits set in Articles 46 and 47 of the Utilities Directive, or where tenders can be made only after a visit to the site or after on-the-spot inspection of the documents supporting the contract documents, the time limits for the receipt of tenders must be extended accordingly, except in the case of a time limit set by mutual agreement in accordance with paragraph 3(b), so that all economic operators concerned may be aware of all the information needed for the preparation of a tender.[40]

---

[35]   See Article 45(8) of the Utilities Directive.
[36]   See Article 45(3)(b) of the Utilities Directive.
[37]   See Article 45(3)(c) of the Utilities Directive.
[38]   See Article 45(6) of the Utilities Directive.
[39]   See Article 45(8), second indent of the Utilities Directive.
[40]   See Article 45(9) of the Utilities Directive.

INVITATIONS TO SUBMIT A TENDER OR TO NEGOTIATE

In restricted procedures and negotiated procedures, contracting entities must simultaneously and in writing invite the selected candidates to submit their tenders or to negotiate.[41] The invitation to the candidates must include either a copy of the specifications and any supporting documents,[42] or a reference to accessing the specifications and any supporting documents, when they are made directly available by electronic means in accordance with Article 45(6) of the Utilities Directive.[43]

Where the specifications or any supporting documents are held by an entity other than the contracting entity responsible for the award procedure, the invitation must indicate the address from which those specifications and documents may be requested and, if appropriate, the closing date for requesting such documents, the sum payable for obtaining them and any payment procedures.[44]

The additional information on the specifications or the supporting documents must be sent by the contracting entity or the competent department not less than six days before the final date for the receipt of tenders, provided that it is requested in good time.[45] In addition, the invitation must include at least the following:[46]

(a) where appropriate, the time limit for requesting additional documents, as well as the amount and terms of payment of any sum to be paid for such documents;

(b) the final date for receipt of tenders, the address to which they are to be sent, and the language or languages in which they are to be drawn up;

(c) a reference to any published contract notice;

(d) an indication of any documents to be attached;

(e) the criteria for the award of the contract, where they are not indicated in the notice on the existence of a qualification system used as a means of calling for competition;

(f) the relative weighting of the contract award criteria or, where appropriate, the order of importance of such criteria, if this information is not given in the contract notice, the notice on the existence of a qualification system or the specifications.

---

[41] See Article 47 of the Utilities Directive.
[42] See Article 47(1) of the Utilities Directive.
[43] See Article 47(2) of the Utilities Directive.
[44] See Article 47(2), second indent of the Utilities Directive.
[45] See Article 47(3) of the Utilities Directive.
[46] See Article 47(4) of the Utilities Directive.

When a call for competition is made by means of a periodic indicative notice,[47] contracting entities must subsequently invite all candidates to confirm their interest on the basis of detailed information on the contract concerned before beginning the selection of tenderers or participants in negotiations. This invitation must include at least the following information:

(a) nature and quantity, including all options concerning complementary contracts and, if possible, the estimated time available for exercising these options for renewable contracts, the nature and quantity and, if possible, the estimated publication dates of future notices of competition for works, supplies or services to be put out to tender;

(b) type of procedure: restricted or negotiated;

(c) where appropriate, the date on which the delivery of supplies or the execution of works or services is to commence or terminate;

(d) the address and closing date for the submission of requests for tender documents and the language or languages in which they are to be drawn up;

(e) the address of the entity which is to award the contract and the information necessary for obtaining the specifications and other documents;

(f) economic and technical conditions, financial guarantees and information required from economic operators;

(g) the amount and payment procedures for any sum payable for obtaining tender documents;

(h) the form of the contract which is the subject of the invitation to tender: purchase, lease, hire or hire-purchase, or any combination of these; and

(i) the contract award criteria and their weighting or, where appropriate, the order of importance of such criteria, if this information is not given in the indicative notice or the specifications or in the invitation to tender or to negotiate.

TECHNICAL SPECIFICATIONS

The technical specifications must be set out in the contract documentation, such as contract notices, contract documents or additional documents.[48] Whenever possible these technical specifications should be defined so as to take into account accessibility criteria for people with disabilities or design for all users. Technical specifications must afford equal access for tenderers and

---

[47] See Article 47(5) of the Utilities Directive.
[48] Article 34 of the Utilities Directive.

not have the effect of creating unjustified obstacles to the opening up of public procurement to competition.

Without prejudice to mandatory national technical rules, to the extent that they are compatible with Community law, the technical specifications must be formulated:[49]

(a) either by reference to technical specifications defined in Annex XXI of the Utilities Directive and, in order of preference, to national standards transposing European standards, European technical approvals, common technical specifications, international standards, other technical reference systems established by the European standardisation bodies or – when these do not exist – to national standards, national technical approvals or national technical specifications relating to the design, calculation and execution of the works and use of the products. Each reference must be accompanied by the words 'or equivalent';

(b) either in terms of performance or functional requirements; the latter may include environmental characteristics. However, such parameters must be sufficiently precise to allow tenderers to determine the subject-matter of the contract and to allow contracting entities to award the contract;

(c) either in terms of performance or functional requirements as mentioned in subparagraph (b), with reference to the specifications mentioned in subparagraph (a) as a means of presuming conformity with such performance or functional requirements;

(d) or by referring to the specifications mentioned in subparagraph (a) for certain characteristics, and by referring to the performance or functional requirements mentioned in subparagraph (b) for other characteristics.

Where a contracting entity makes use of the option of referring to the specifications defined in Annex XXI of the Utilities Directive and, in order of preference, to national standards transposing European standards, European technical approvals, common technical specifications, international standards, other technical reference systems established by the European standardisation bodies, it cannot reject a tender on the grounds that the products and services tendered for do not comply with the specifications to which it has referred, once the tenderer proves in his tender to the satisfaction of the contracting entity, by whatever appropriate means, that the solutions which he proposes satisfy in an equivalent manner the requirements defined by the technical specifications.[50] An appropriate means might be constituted by a

---

[49] See Article 34(3) of the Utilities Directive.
[50] Article 34(4) of the Utilities Directive.

technical dossier of the manufacturer or a test report from a recognised body.

Where a contracting entity prescribes in terms of performance or functional requirements, it may not reject a tender for works, products or services which comply with a national standard transposing a European standard, with a European technical approval, a common technical specification, an international standard or a technical reference system established by a European standardisation body, if these specifications address the performance or functional requirements which it has laid down.[51] Within the tender documents, the tenderer must prove to the satisfaction of the contracting entity and by any appropriate means that the work, product or service in compliance with the standard meets the performance or functional requirements of the contracting entity. An appropriate means might be constituted by a technical dossier of the manufacturer or a test report from a recognised body.

Where contracting entities lay down environmental characteristics in terms of performance or functional requirements they may use the detailed specifications, or, if necessary, parts thereof, as defined by European or (multi-) national eco-labels, or by any other eco-label, provided that those specifications are appropriate to define the characteristics of the supplies or services that are the object of the contract, that the requirements for the label are drawn up on the basis of scientific information, that the eco-labels are adopted using a procedure in which all stakeholders, such as government bodies, consumers, manufacturers, distributors and environmental organisations can participate, and finally they are accessible to all interested parties.[52]

Contracting entities may indicate that the products and services bearing the eco-label are presumed to comply with the technical specifications laid down in the contract documents; they must accept any other appropriate means of proof, such as a technical dossier of the manufacturer or a test report from a recognised body. Recognised bodies, within the meaning of the Directive, are test and calibration laboratories and certification and inspection bodies which comply with applicable European standards. Contracting entities must accept certificates from recognised bodies established in other member states.[53]

Unless justified by the subject-matter of the contract, technical specifications must not refer to a specific make or source, or a particular process, or to trade marks, patents, types or a specific origin or production with the effect of favouring or eliminating certain undertakings or certain products. Such reference must be permitted on an exceptional basis, where a sufficiently precise

---

[51] Article 34(5) of the Utilities Directive.
[52] See Article 34(6) of the Utilities Directive.
[53] Article 34(7) of the Utilities Directive.

and intelligible description of the subject-matter of the contract and such reference must be accompanied by the words 'or equivalent'.[54]

Any technical specifications regularly referred to in the supply, works or service contracts of contracting entities, or the technical specifications which they intend to apply to specific contracts covered by periodic indicative notices within the meaning of Article 41(1) of the Utilities Directive, must be made available on request to interested economic operators. Where the technical specifications are based on documents available to interested economic operators, the inclusion of a reference to those documents is sufficient proof of the requirements stipulated in Article 35 of the Utilities Directive in relation to communication of technical specifications.

VARIANTS

Contracting entities may allow tenderers to submit variants, only where the criterion for award is that of the most economically advantageous tender.[55] Contracting entities must indicate in the specifications whether or not they authorise variants. Contracting entities authorising variants must state in the contract documents the minimum requirements to be met by the variants and any specific requirements for their presentation. In procedures for awarding public supply or service contracts, contracting entities which have authorised variants may not reject a variant on the sole ground that it would, if successful, lead to a service contract rather than a public supply contract or a supply contract rather than a public service contract.

CONTRACTUAL PERFORMANCE

Subcontracting

In the contract documents, contracting entities may ask or may be required by a member state to invite tenderers to indicate in their tender any share of the contract they may intend to subcontract to third parties and any proposed subcontractors. This indication must be without prejudice to the question of the principal economic operator's liability.[56]

---

[54] See Article 34(8) of the Utilities Directive.
[55] Article 36 of the Utilities Directive.
[56] See Article 37 of the Utilities Directive.

Socio-economic Conditions

Contracting entities may lay down special conditions relating to the performance of a contract, provided that these are compatible with Community law
and are indicated in the contract notice or in the specifications. The conditions
governing the performance of a contract may, in particular, concern social and
environmental considerations.[57]

**Obligations relating to Taxes, Environmental Protection, Employment
Protection Provisions and Working Conditions**

Contracting entities may state in the contract documents, or be obliged by a
member state to state, the body or bodies from which a candidate or tenderer
may obtain the appropriate information on the obligations relating to taxes, to
environmental protection, to the employment protection provisions and to the
working conditions which are in force in the member state, region or locality
in which the works are to be carried out or services are to be provided and
which must be applicable to the works carried out on site or to the services
provided during the performance of the contract.[58]

A contracting entity must request the tenderers or candidates in the contract
award procedure to indicate that they have taken account, when drawing up
their tender, of the obligations relating to employment protection provisions
and the working conditions which are in force in the place where the works are
to be carried out or the service is to be provided.[59]

---

[57]   Article 38 of the Utilities Directive.
[58]   Article 39(1) of the Utilities Directive.
[59]   Article 39(2) of the Utilities Directive.

13. Qualification and qualitative selection in utilities procurement

QUALIFICATION SYSTEMS

Contracting entities may resort to qualifications systems in order to select the economic operators to invite them to submit a tender or to negotiate the award of a contract. The Utilities Directive provides for discretion on the part of contracting entities to establish and operate a system of qualification of economic operators. The operation of such systems must be based on objective criteria and rules for qualification which are to be established by the contracting entity.[1]

Contracting entities which establish or operate such a system must ensure that economic operators are at all times able to request participation in the qualification system.[2] The criteria and rules for qualification must be made available to economic operators on request. The updating of these criteria and rules must be communicated to interested economic operators. Where a contracting entity considers that the qualification system of certain other entities or bodies meets its requirements, it must communicate to interested economic operators the names of such other entities or bodies.[3]

Establishment of Qualification Systems

Qualification systems may involve different stages.[4]

Qualification with reference to technical specifications

In qualifications systems, contracting entities may determine criteria and rules for the selection of candidates to be invited to tender or negotiate which include technical specifications.[5] In such cases the provisions of Article 34 of the Utilities Directive must apply.

---

[1]   See Article 53 of the Utilities Directive.
[2]   See Article 53(1) of the Utilities Directive.
[3]   See Article 53(2) of the Utilities Directive.
[4]   See Article 53(2) of the Utilities Directive.
[5]   See Article 53(2), second indent of the Utilities Directive.

The technical specifications must be set out in the contract documentation, such as contract notices, contract documents or additional documents.[6] Whenever possible these technical specifications should be defined so as to take into account accessibility criteria for people with disabilities or be designed for all users. Technical specifications must afford equal access for tenderers and not have the effect of creating unjustified obstacles to the opening up of public procurement to competition.

Without prejudice to mandatory national technical rules, to the extent that they are compatible with Community law, the technical specifications must be formulated:[7]

(a)   either by reference to technical specifications defined in Annex XXI of the Utilities Directive and, in order of preference, to national standards transposing European standards, European technical approvals, common technical specifications, international standards, other technical reference systems established by the European standardisation bodies or when these do not exist, to national standards, national technical approvals or national technical specifications relating to the design, calculation and execution of the works and use of the products. Each reference must be accompanied by the words 'or equivalent';

(b)   either in terms of performance or functional requirements; the latter may include environmental characteristics. However, such parameters must be sufficiently precise to allow tenderers to determine the subject-matter of the contract and to allow contracting entities to award the contract;

(c)   or in terms of performance or functional requirements as mentioned in subparagraph (b), with reference to the specifications mentioned in subparagraph (a) as a means of presuming conformity with such performance or functional requirements;

(d)   or by referring to the specifications mentioned in subparagraph (a) for certain characteristics, and by referring to the performance or functional requirements mentioned in subparagraph (b) for other characteristics.

Where a contracting entity makes use of the option of referring to the specifications defined in Annex XXI of the Utilities Directive and, in order of preference, to national standards transposing European standards, European technical approvals, common technical specifications, international standards, other technical reference systems established by the European standardisation bodies, it cannot reject a tender on the grounds that the products and services

---

6   Article 34 of the Utilities Directive.
7   See Article 34(3) of the Utilities Directive.

tendered for do not comply with the specifications to which it has referred, once the tenderer proves in his tender to the satisfaction of the contracting entity, by whatever appropriate means, that the solutions which he proposes satisfy in an equivalent manner the requirements defined by the technical specifications.[8] An appropriate means might be constituted by a technical dossier of the manufacturer or a test report from a recognised body.

Where a contracting entity prescribes in terms of performance or functional requirements, it may not reject a tender for works, products or services which comply with a national standard transposing a European standard, with a European technical approval, a common technical specification, an international standard or a technical reference system established by a European standardisation body, if these specifications address the performance or functional requirements which it has laid down.[9] Within the tender documents, the tenderer must prove to the satisfaction of the contracting entity and by any appropriate means that the work, product or service in compliance with the standard meets the performance or functional requirements of the contracting entity. An appropriate means might be constituted by a technical dossier of the manufacturer or a test report from a recognised body.

Where contracting entities lay down environmental characteristics in terms of performance or functional requirements they may use the detailed specifications, or, if necessary, parts thereof, as defined by European or (multi-) national eco-labels, or by any other eco-label, provided that those specifications are appropriate to define the characteristics of the supplies or services that are the object of the contract, that the requirements for the label are drawn up on the basis of scientific information, that the eco-labels are adopted using a procedure in which all stakeholders, such as government bodies, consumers, manufacturers, distributors and environmental organisations can participate, and finally they are accessible to all interested parties.[10]

Contracting entities may indicate that the products and services bearing the eco-label are presumed to comply with the technical specifications laid down in the contract documents; they must accept any other appropriate means of proof, such as a technical dossier of the manufacturer or a test report from a recognised body. Recognised bodies, within the meaning of the Directive, are test and calibration laboratories and certification and inspection bodies which comply with applicable European standards. Contracting entities must accept certificates from recognised bodies established in other member states.[11]

---

[8] Article 34(4) of the Utilities Directive.
[9] Article 34(5) of the Utilities Directive.
[10] See Article 34(6) of the Utilities Directive.
[11] Article 34(7) of the Utilities Directive.

Unless justified by the subject-matter of the contract, technical specifications must not refer to a specific make or source, or a particular process, or to trade marks, patents, types or a specific origin or production with the effect of favouring or eliminating certain undertakings or certain products. Such reference must be permitted on an exceptional basis, where a sufficiently precise and intelligible description of the subject-matter of the contract and such reference must be accompanied by the words 'or equivalent'.[12]

Any technical specifications regularly referred to in the supply, works or service contracts of contracting entities, or the technical specifications which they intend to apply to specific contracts covered by periodic indicative notices within the meaning of Article 41(1) of the Utilities Directive must be made available on request to interested economic operators.[13] Where the technical specifications are based on documents available to interested economic operators, the inclusion of a reference to those documents is sufficient proof of the requirements stipulated in Article 35 of the Utilities Directive in relation to communication of technical specifications.

The criteria and rules in relation to qualifications systems based on technical specifications may be updated as required.[14]

Qualification with reference to exclusion criteria

When establishing a qualification system, contracting entities may utilise as criteria the exclusion criteria listed in Article 45 of the Public Sector Directive 2004/18 and the terms and conditions set out within that provision.[15] Where contracting entities are also contracting entities within the meaning of Article 2(1)(a) of the Utilities Directive, namely, entities such as the state, regional or local entities, bodies governed by public law, associations formed by one or several such entities or one or several of such bodies governed by public law, it is mandatory to utilise as criteria for a qualification system those criteria and rules relevant to automatic exclusion grounds relating to participation in a criminal organisation, corruption, fraud or money laundering listed in Article 45(1) of Directive 2004/18.

In particular, the criteria and rules for qualification in relation to exclusion criteria may include reasons for automatic exclusion of economic operators in relation to their personal situation.

---

12 See Article 34(8) of the Utilities Directive.
13 See Article 35 of the Utilities Directive.
14 See Article 53(2), second indent of the Utilities Directive.
15 See Article 53(3) of the Utilities Directive.

Personal Situation of Economic Operators

Contracting entities may exclude[16] from participation in a public contract any candidate or tenderer who has been the subject of a conviction by final judgment of which the contracting authority is aware for one or more of the following reasons:[17]

(a) participation in a criminal organisation, as defined in Article 2(1) of Council Joint Action 98/733/JHA;[18]

(b) corruption, as defined in Article 3 of the Council Act of 26 May 1997[19] and Article 3(1) of Council Joint Action 98/742/JHA[20] respectively;

(c) fraud within the meaning of Article 1 of the Convention relating to the protection of the financial interests of the European Communities;[21]

(d) money laundering, as defined in Article 1 of Council Directive 91/308/EEC of 10 June 1991 on prevention of the use of the financial system for the purpose of money laundering.[22]

In addition to the above reasons, contracting entities may exclude an economic operator from participation in a contract where that economic operator:[23]

(a) is bankrupt or is being wound up, where his affairs are being administered by the court, where he has entered into an arrangement with creditors, where he has suspended business activities or is in any analogous situation arising from a similar procedure under national laws and regulations;

(b) is the subject of proceedings for a declaration of bankruptcy, for an order for compulsory winding up or administration by the court or of an arrangement with creditors or of any other similar proceedings under national laws and regulations;

(c) has been convicted by a judgment which has the force of *res judicata* in accordance with the legal provisions of the country of any offence concerning his professional conduct;

---

16   See Article 45 of the Public Sector Directive.
17   Article 45(1) of the Public Sector Directive.
18   OJ L 351, 29.12.1998, p. 1.
19   OJ C 195, 25.6.1997, p. 1
20   OJ L 358, 31.12.1998, p. 2.
21   OJ C 316, 27.11.1995, p. 48.
22   OJ L 166, 28.6.1991, p. 77, as amended by Directive 2001/97/EC of the European Parliament and of the Council of 4 December 2001 (OJ L 344, 28.12.2001, p. 76).
23   Article 45(2) of the Public Sector Directive.

(d)   has been guilty of grave professional misconduct proven by any means which the contracting entities can demonstrate;

(e)   has not fulfilled obligations relating to the payment of social security contributions in accordance with the legal provisions of the country in which he is established or with those of the country of the contracting authority;

(f)   has not fulfilled obligations relating to the payment of taxes in accordance with the legal provisions of the country in which he is established or with those of the country of the contracting entity;

(g)   is guilty of serious misrepresentation in supplying the information required under this Section or has not supplied such information. Member states must specify, in accordance with their national law, the ramifications of misrepresentation in supplying false information.

Derogation

Member States may provide for derogation from the automatic exclusion grounds relating to participation in a criminal organisation, corruption, fraud or money laundering for overriding requirements in the general interest.[24]

Proof of the Personal Situation of Economic Operators

Sufficient evidence of the personal situation of candidates and tenderers in accordance with Article 45 can be provided by means of the production of an extract from the judicial record or of an equivalent document issued by a competent judicial or administrative authority in the country of origin of the candidate or the tenderer proving that none of the automatic exclusion grounds relating to participation in a criminal organisation, corruption, fraud or money laundering is present.[25]

With regard to the requirements for evidence of payment of social security contributions and taxes, a certificate issued by the competent authority in the member state concerned is adequate proof.[26]

Where the country in question does not issue extracts from the judicial record or of an equivalent document or certificates, proof of the personal situation of candidates and tenderers may be provided by a declaration on oath or, in member states where there is no provision for declarations on oath, by a solemn declaration made by the person concerned before a competent judicial or administrative authority, a notary or a competent professional or trade body,

---

[24]   See the second indent of Article 45(1) of the Public Sector Directive.
[25]   Article 45(3)(a) of the Public Sector Directive.
[26]   Article 45(3)(b) of the Public Sector Directive.

in the country of origin or in the country whence that person comes. For these purposes, member states must designate the entities and bodies competent to issue the documents, certificates or declarations and inform the Commission, subject to data protection laws.

Ex Officio Application

Contracting entities, where they have doubts concerning the personal situation of such candidates or tenderers, may themselves apply to the competent entities to obtain any information they consider necessary on the personal situation of the candidates or tenderers.[27] Where the information concerns a candidate or tenderer established in a state other than that of the contracting entity, the contracting entity may seek the co-operation of the competent entities. Such requests must relate to legal and/or natural persons, including, if appropriate, company directors and any person having powers of representation, decision or control in respect of the candidate or tenderer.

Qualification with Reference to Economic and Financial Capacity

In cases where contracting entities set as criteria and rules for qualification those which include requirements relating to economic and financial capacity, economic operators may where necessary rely on the capacity of other entities, irrespective of the legal nature or the link between them and those entities.[28]

However, in this case the economic operator which wishes to rely on the economic and financial capacity of others must prove to the contracting entity that these resources will be available to it throughout the period of the validity of the qualification system.[29] Such proof can be furnished, for example, by producing an undertaking by those entities to that effect. Under the same conditions, a group of economic operators[30] may rely on the capacity of participants in the group or of other entities.

---

[27]   See Article 45(1) of the Public Sector Directive and in particular its second indent.

[28]   See Article 53(4) of the Utilities Directive.

[29]   See Article 53(4), second indent and Article 54(5) of the Utilities Directive.

[30]   See Article 11 of the Utilities Directive; groups of economic operators may submit tenders or put themselves forward as candidates. In order to submit a tender or a request to participate, these groups may not be required by the contracting entities to assume a specific legal form; however, the group selected may be required to do so when it has been awarded the contract, to the extent to which this change is necessary for the satisfactory performance of the contract.

Qualification with Reference to Technical and Professional Ability

Where the criteria and rules for qualification include requirements relating to technical or professional ability, economic operators may rely, where necessary, on the capacity of other entities, whatever the legal nature or the link between them and those entities.[31] In this case the economic operator must provide evidence to the contracting entity, by producing an undertaking of certificates from the entities it wishes to rely on for technical and professional ability qualification purposes, that the required resources will be available to it throughout the period of validity of the qualification system. As with qualification with reference to economic and financial capacity, a group of economic operators may rely on the technical and professional abilities of participants in the group or of other entities.[32]

Contracting entities must keep written records of qualified economic operators. Such records may be divided into categories according to the type of contract for which the qualification is valid.[33]

Operation of Qualification Systems

When establishing or operating a qualification system,[34] contracting entities must in particular observe the provisions of Article 41(3) concerning notices on the existence of a system of qualification. The qualification system must be the subject of a notice as referred to in Annex XIV, indicating the purpose of the qualification system and how to have access to the rules concerning its operation. According to Annex XIV of the Utilities Directive, information to be included in the notice on the existence of a qualification system must comprise:

1. the name, address, telegraphic address, electronic address, telephone number, telex and fax number of the contracting entity;
2. an indication, where appropriate, as to whether the contract is reserved for sheltered workshops or whether its performance is reserved in the context of sheltered employment programmes;
3. a statement on the purpose of the qualification system, including the description of the goods, services or works or categories to be procured through the system by reference to nomenclature numbers;
4. a statement on the conditions to be fulfilled by the economic operators

---

31   See Article 53(5) of the Utilities Directive.
32   See Article 54(6) of the Utilities Directive.
33   See Article 53(7) of the Utilities Directive.
34   See Article 53(8) of the Utilities Directive.

in view of their qualification pursuant to the system and the methods according to which each of those conditions will be verified. Where the description of such conditions and verification methods is voluminous and based on documents available to interested economic operators, a summary of the main conditions and methods and a reference to those documents will be sufficient;

5. an indication of the period of validity of the qualification system and the formalities for its renewal;

6. a reference to the fact that the notice acts as the call for competition;

7. an address where further information and documentation concerning the qualification system can be obtained;

8. a reference concerning the name and address of the body responsible for appeal and, where appropriate, mediation procedures. In addition, precise information should be provided concerning time limits for lodging appeals, or the name, address, telephone number, fax number and e-mail address of the service from which this information may be obtained;

9. an indication of the award criteria, where known, for award of the contract. Criteria representing the most economically advantageous tender as well as their weighting or, where appropriate, the order of importance of these criteria, must be mentioned where they do not appear in the specifications or will not be indicated in the invitation to tender or to negotiate;

10. any other relevant information.

Where the system is of more than three years duration, the notice must be published annually. Where the system is of a shorter duration, an initial notice will be sufficient.[35]

Contracting entities must also adhere to the requirements concerning the information to be delivered to economic operators that have applied for qualification, as laid down in Article 49(3), (4) and (5) of the Utilities Directive, when they operate a qualifications system.[36] More specifically, contracting entities which establish and operate a system of qualification must inform applicants of their decision as to qualification within a period of six months. If the decision will take longer than four months from the presentation of an application, contracting entities must inform the applicant, within two months of the application, of the reasons justifying the longer period and of the date by which the operator's application will be accepted or refused.

Disqualified applicants whose qualification is refused must be informed of

---

[35] See Article 41(3) of the Utilities Directive.
[36] See Article 53(8) of the Utilities Directive.

the contracting entity's decision and the reasons for refusal as soon as possible and under no circumstances more than 15 days later than the date of the decision. The reasons must be based on the objective criteria for qualification referred to in Article 53(2) of the Utilities Directive, established by the contracting entity and referring to reasons and grounds for automatic exclusions relating to participation in a criminal organisation, corruption, fraud or money laundering, or criteria relevant to economic and financial standing, or criteria concerning technical and professional ability.[37]

Contracting entities which establish and operate a system of qualification may bring the qualification of an economic operator to an end only for reasons based on the criteria for qualification referred to in Article 53(2) of the Utilities Directive. Any intention to bring qualification to an end must be notified in writing to the economic operator beforehand, at least 15 days before the date on which qualification is due to end, together with the reason or reasons justifying the proposed action.[38]

When operating a qualification system, contracting entities must also observe the requirements concerning the selection of participants when a call for competition is made by means of a notice on the existence of a qualification system in accordance with Article 51(2) of the Utilities Directive.[39] When a call for competition is made by means of a notice on the existence of a qualification system and for the purpose of selecting participants in award procedures for the specific contracts which are the subject of the call for competition, contracting entities must select economic operators in accordance with the provisions of Article 53. In restricted or negotiated procedures,[40] they also need to apply to such qualified economic operators such criteria as those which may be based on the objective need of the contracting entity to reduce the number of candidates to a level which is justified by the need to balance the particular characteristics of the procurement procedure with the resources required to conduct it.[41] The number of candidates selected must, however, take account of the need to ensure adequate competition.

Finally, contracting entities operating qualification systems must respect the principle of mutual recognition[42] concerning administrative, technical or financial conditions, certificates, tests and evidence, as laid down in Article 52 of the Utilities Directive.

---

37   See Article 49(4) of the Utilities Directive.
38   See Article 49(5) of the Utilities Directive.
39   See Article 53(8) of the Utilities Directive.
40   See Article 51(2)(b) of the Utilities Directive.
41   See Article 54(3) of the Utilities Directive.
42   See Article 52 of the Utilities Directive.

MUTUAL RECOGNITION

Contracting entities must recognise equivalent certificates from bodies established in other member states. They must also accept other evidence of equivalent quality assurance measures from economic operators. For works and service contracts, and only in appropriate cases, the contracting entities may require, in order to verify the economic operator's technical abilities, an indication of the environmental management measures which the economic operator will be able to apply when carrying out the contract.[43] In such cases, should the contracting entities require the production of certificates drawn up by independent bodies attesting to the compliance of the economic operator with certain environmental management standards, they must refer to the EMAS or to environmental management standards based on the relevant European or international standards certified by bodies conforming to Community law or the relevant European or international standards concerning certification.[44]

When selecting participants for a restricted or negotiated procedure, in reaching their decision as to qualification or when the criteria and rules are being updated, contracting entities must not impose administrative, technical or financial conditions on certain economic operators which would not be imposed on others or require tests or evidence which would duplicate objective evidence already available.[45]

Where they request the production of certificates drawn up by independent bodies attesting to the compliance of the economic operator with certain quality assurance standards, contracting entities must refer to quality assurance systems based on the relevant European standards series certified by bodies conforming to the European standards series concerning certification.[46]

CRITERIA FOR QUALITATIVE SELECTION

The criteria for qualitative selection of economic operators by contracting entities in open, restricted or negotiated procedures must be established in accordance with the objective rules and criteria which are available to interested economic operators.[47]

In restricted or negotiated procedures, the criteria may be based on the

---

[43]   See Article 52(2) of the Utilities Directive.
[44]   See Article 52(3) of the Utilities Directive.
[45]   See Article 52(1) of the Utilities Directive.
[46]   See Article 52(3) second indent of the Utilities Directive.
[47]   See Article 54 of the Utilities Directive.

objective need[48] of the contracting entity to reduce the number of candidates to a level which is justified by the need to balance the particular characteristics of the procurement procedure with the resources required to conduct it. However, the number of candidates selected must take into account the need to ensure adequate competition.

The criteria may include the exclusion criteria relating to participation in a criminal organisation, corruption, fraud or money laundering, criteria referring to the economic and financial capacity of the economic operators, or criteria relating to the technical or professional abilities of economic operators.[49]

---

[48]   See Article 54(3) of the Utilities Directive.
[49]   See Article 54(4), (5) and (6) of the Utilities Directive.

14. Award procedures and award criteria in utilities procurement

AWARD PROCEDURES

Use of Open, Restricted and Negotiated Procedures

Contracting entities may choose any of the procurement procedures described in Article 1(9)(a), (b) and (c) of the Utilities Directive, namely open, restricted and negotiated procedures, provided[1] that a call for competition has been made in accordance with Article 42 of the Utilities Directive. In the case of open procedures, any interested economic operator may submit a tender; in the case of restricted procedures, any economic operator may request to participate and only candidates invited by the contracting entity may submit a tender; finally, in the case of negotiated procedures, the contracting entity consults the economic operators of its choice and negotiates the terms of the contract with one or more of these contractors.[2]

Contracting entities may use a procedure without a prior call for competition in the following cases:[3]

(a) when no tenders or no suitable tenders or no applications have been submitted in response to a procedure with a prior call for competition, provided that the initial conditions of contract are not substantially altered;
(b) where a contract is purely for the purpose of research, experiment, study or development, and not for the purpose of securing a profit or of recovering research and development costs, and in so far as the award of such a contract does not prejudice the competitive award of subsequent contracts which, in particular, seek those ends;
(c) when, for technical or artistic reasons, or for reasons connected with the protection of exclusive rights, the contract may be executed only by a particular economic operator;

---

[1] See Article 40(3) of the Utilities Directive.
[2] See Article 1(9) of the Utilities Directive.
[3] See Article 40(3) of the Utilities Directive.

(d)   in so far as is strictly necessary when, for reasons of extreme urgency brought about by events unforeseeable by the contracting entities, the time limits laid down for open procedures, restricted procedures and negotiated procedures with a prior call for competition cannot be adhered to;

(e)   in the case of supply contracts for additional deliveries by the original supplier which are intended either as a partial replacement of normal supplies or installations or as an extension of existing supplies or installations, where a change of supplier would oblige the contracting entity to acquire material having different technical characteristics which would result in incompatibility or disproportionate technical difficulties in operation and maintenance;

(f)   for additional works or services not included in the project initially awarded or in the contract as first concluded but which have, through unforeseen circumstances, become necessary to the performance of the contract, on condition that the award is made to the contractor or service-provider executing the original contract when such additional works or services cannot be technically or economically separated from the main contract without great inconvenience to the contracting entities, or when such additional works or services, although separable from the performance of the original contract, are strictly necessary to its later stages;

(g)   in the case of works contracts for new works consisting in the repetition of similar works assigned to the contractor to which the same contracting entities awarded an earlier contract, provided that such works conform to a basic project for which a first contract was awarded after a call for competition; as soon as the first project is put up for tender, notice must be given that this procedure might be adopted and the total estimated cost of subsequent works must be taken into consideration by the contracting entities when they calculate the applicable contract value thresholds in accordance with the provisions of Articles 16 and 17 of the Utilities Directive;

(h)   for supplies quoted and purchased in a commodity market;

(i)   for contracts to be awarded on the basis of a framework agreement, provided that the framework agreement itself has been awarded in accordance with the Utilities Directive as provided in Article 14(2);

(j)   for bargain purchases, where it is possible to procure supplies by taking advantage of a particularly advantageous opportunity available for a very short time at a price considerably lower than normal market prices;

(k)   for purchases of supplies under particularly advantageous conditions from either a supplier definitively winding up his business activities or the receivers or liquidators of a bankruptcy, an arrangement with creditors or a similar procedure under national laws or regulations;

(l)   when the service contract concerned is part of the follow-up to a design contest organised in accordance with the provisions of the Utilities Directive and must, in accordance with the relevant rules, be awarded to the winner or to one of the winners of that contest; in the latter case, all the winners must be invited to participate in the negotiations.

FRAMEWORK AGREEMENTS

A framework agreement is an agreement between one or more contracting entities and one or more economic operators, the purpose of which is to establish the terms governing contracts to be awarded during a given period, in particular with regard to price and, where appropriate, the quantities envisaged.[4] Contracting entities may regard a framework agreement as a contract within the remit of the Utilities Directive.[5] Framework agreements should not be misused in order to hinder, limit or distort competition.[6]

In cases where contracting entities have awarded a framework agreement in accordance with the Utilities Directive, the award of contracts based on that framework agreement may be pursued though an award procedure without prior call for competition.[7] Where a framework agreement has not been awarded in accordance with the provisions of the Utilities Directive, contracting entities must not utilise such award procedures.

DYNAMIC PURCHASING SYSTEMS

A dynamic purchasing system is a completely electronic process for making commonly used purchases of products. The characteristics of such products should be such as to meet the requirements of contracting entities by reference to their products' general availability in the market and their standardised specifications.[8] A dynamic purchasing system must have limited duration and be open throughout its validity to any economic operator which satisfies the selection criteria and has submitted an indicative tender that complies with the specification. The costs of setting and running a dynamic purchasing system are borne by the contracting entity. No charges for the set-up costs or participating

---

4   See Article 1(4) of the Utilities Directive.
5   See Article 14 of the Utilities Directive.
6   See Article 14(4) of the Utilities Directive.
7   See Article 14(2) and Article 40(3)(i) of the Utilities Directive.
8   See Article 1(7) of the Utilities Directive.

costs for the duration of the dynamic purchasing system may be billed to the interested economic operators or to parties to the system.[9]

Setting up a Dynamic Purchasing System

In order to set up a dynamic purchasing system, contracting entities must follow the rules of the open procedure in all its phases up to the award of the contracts.[10] Contracting entities must:

(a) publish a contract notice with their clear intention of setting up a dynamic purchasing system;
(b) indicate in the specifications, amongst other matters, the nature of the purchases envisaged under that system, as well as all the necessary information concerning the purchasing system, the electronic equipment used and the technical connection arrangements and specifications;
(c) offer by electronic means, on publication of the notice and up to the expiry of the system, unrestricted, direct and full access to the specifications and to any additional documents and indicate in the notice the internet address at which such documents may be consulted.

With a view to setting up the system and to awarding contracts under that system, contracting entities must use solely electronic means.[11] The means of communication chosen must be generally available and may under no circumstances restrict the economic operators' access to the tendering procedure. The tools to be used for communicating by electronic means, as well as their technical characteristics, must be non-discriminatory, generally available and interoperable with the information and communication technology products in general use.[12]

Devices used for the electronic receipt of requests to participate and devices used for the electronic transmission and receipt of tenders must ensure the availability of information regarding the specifications necessary for the electronic submission of tenders and requests to participate, including any encryption requirements.[13] Member states may introduce or maintain voluntary accreditation schemes aiming at enhanced levels of certification service provision for these devices.

Such electronic devices must also conform to the requirements of Annex

---

9   Article 15(7), second indent of the Utilities Directive.
10 Article 15(3) of the Utilities Directive.
11 See Article 48(2) to (5) of the Directive.
12 See the provisions of Article 48(4) of the Utilities Directive.
13 Article 48(5) of the Utilities Directive.

XXIV of the Utilities Directive[14] and in particular they must guarantee, through technical means and appropriate procedures, that:

(a) electronic signatures relating to tenders, requests to participate and the forwarding of plans and projects comply with national provisions adopted pursuant to Directive 1999/93; contracting entities may require that electronic tenders be accompanied by an advanced electronic signature.

(b) the exact time and date of the receipt of tenders, requests to participate and the submission of plans and projects can be determined precisely;

(c) no person can have access to data transmitted before the time limits laid down;

(d) if data access prohibition is infringed, the infringement must be clearly detectable;

(e) only authorised persons may set or change the dates for opening data received;

(f) during the different stages of the contract award procedure or of the contest, access to all data submitted must be possible only through simultaneous action by authorised persons;

(g) simultaneous action by authorised persons must give access to data transmitted only after the prescribed date;

(h) data received and opened in accordance with these requirements must remain accessible only to authorised persons.

Under a dynamic purchasing system, communication and the exchange and storage of information must be carried out in such a way as to ensure that the integrity of data and the confidentiality of tenders and requests to participate are preserved, and that the contracting entities examine the content of tenders and requests to participate only after the time limit set for submitting them has expired.[15]

The Conduct of Dynamic Purchasing Systems

A dynamic purchasing system may not last for more than four years, except in duly justified exceptional cases. Contracting entities may not resort to this system to prevent, restrict or distort competition.[16]

---

[14]   See Annex XXIV of the Directive on Requirements relating to devices for the electronic receipt of tenders, request for participation and plans and projects in contests.

[15]   Article 48(3) of the Utilities Directive.

[16]   Article 15(7) of the Utilities Directive.

Admission into a dynamic purchasing system is subject to two requirements: (a) meeting and satisfying the selection and qualification criteria and (b) submitting an indicative tender which complies with the specification or any possible additional documents.[17] Admittance to a dynamic purchasing system or the rejection of an economic operator's indicative tender must be communicated to the relevant economic operator at the earliest possible opportunity. Throughout the entire period of a dynamic purchasing system, contracting entities must give any economic operator that has met and satisfied the selection and qualification requirements, the possibility of submitting an indicative tender and of being admitted to the system.

The Indicative Tenders

In order to issue an invitation to tender to those economic operators admitted into a dynamic purchasing system, contracting entities must publish a simplified contract notice inviting all interested economic operators to submit an indicative tender within 15 days from the date on which the simplified notice was sent. Contracting entities may not proceed with tendering until they have completed evaluation of all the indicative tenders received by that deadline.[18]

Indicative tenders may be improved at any time provided that they continue to comply with the specification. Contracting entities must complete the evaluation of indicative tenders within a maximum of 15 days from the date of their submission.[19] However, they may extend the evaluation period provided that no invitation to tender is issued in the meantime.

The Award of Contracts under Dynamic Purchasing Systems

Each specific contract awarder under a dynamic purchasing system must be the subject of an invitation to tender. Contracting entities, after evaluating the indicative tenders and admitting economic operators into the dynamic purchasing system, must invite tenders from those admitted to the system for each specific contract to be awarded under the system.[20]

A time limit for the submission of tenders must be set by the contracting entities. The evaluation of tenders should be based on the award criteria set out in the contract notice for the establishment of the dynamic purchasing system.[21] The award of contracts under a dynamic purchasing system must

---

[17] Article 15(2) of the Utilities Directive.
[18] Article 15(5) of the Utilities Directive.
[19] See Article 15(4), first indent of the Utilities Directive.
[20] See Article 15(5) of the Utilities Directive.
[21] Article 15(6) of the Utilities Directive.

reflect the best tender on the basis of those criteria which may, if appropriate, be formulated more precisely in the invitation to tender extended to the economic operators admitted into the dynamic purchasing system.

ELECTRONIC AUCTIONS

An electronic auction is a repetitive process involving an electronic device for the presentation of new prices, revised downwards, and/or new values concerning certain elements of tenders, which occurs after an initial full evaluation of the tenders, enabling them to be ranked using automatic evaluation methods. Consequently, certain service contracts and certain works contracts having as their subject-matter intellectual performances, such as the design of works, may not be the object of electronic auctions.[22]

Contracting entities may hold electronic auctions on the opening for competition of contracts to be awarded under the dynamic purchasing system.[23] Contracting entities which decide to hold an electronic auction must indicate their intention in the contract notice.

In open, restricted or negotiated procedures contracting entities may decide that the award of a public contract must be preceded by an electronic auction when the contract specifications can be established with precision.[24] The specifications must include, *inter alia*, the following details:[25]

(a) the features, the values for which will be the subject of electronic auction, provided that such features are quantifiable and can be expressed in figures or percentages;

(b) any limits on the values which may be submitted, as they result from the specifications relating to the subject of the contract;

(c) the information which will be made available to tenderers in the course of the electronic auction and, where appropriate, when it will be made available to them;

(d) the relevant information concerning the electronic auction process;

(e) the conditions under which the tenderers will be able to bid and, in particular, the minimum differences which will, where appropriate, be required when bidding;

(f) the relevant information concerning the electronic equipment used and the arrangements and technical specifications for connection.

---

22   Article 1(6) of the Utilities Directive.
23   Article 56(2) of the Utilities Directive.
24   Article 56(2), first indent of the Utilities Directive.
25   Article 56(3) of the Utilities Directive.

Organization of Electronic Auctions

Before proceeding with an electronic auction, contracting entities must make a full initial evaluation of the tenders in accordance with the award criteria set and with the weighting attached to them for evaluation purposes.[26] All tenderers who have submitted admissible tenders must be invited simultaneously by electronic means to submit new prices and/or new values; the invitation must contain all relevant information concerning individual connection to the electronic equipment being used and must state the date and time of the start of the electronic auction. The electronic auction may take place in a number of successive phases. The electronic auction may not start sooner than two working days after the date on which invitations are sent out.

The invitation must also state the mathematical formula to be used in the electronic auction to determine automatic re-rankings on the basis of the new prices or new values submitted by the participants.[27] That formula must incorporate the weighting of all the criteria fixed to determine the most economically advantageous tender, as indicated in the contract notice or in the specifications; for that purpose, any ranges must, however, be reduced beforehand to a specified value. Where variants are authorised, a separate formula must be provided for each variant.

Throughout each phase of an electronic auction the contracting entities must instantaneously communicate to all tenderers at least sufficient information to enable them to ascertain their relative rankings at any moment. They may also communicate other information concerning other prices or values submitted, provided that that is stated in the specifications.

They may also at any time announce the number of participants in that phase of the auction. However, they must not disclose the identities of the tenderers during any phase of an electronic auction.

Closure of Electronic Auctions

The closure of electronic auctions is the next phase that contracting entities have to follow prior to the award of the contract. The closure of the auction is a necessary procedural requirement integral to the award of contracts in such award procedures and should be observed rigorously.[28]

There are three possible ways in which electronic auctions should be drawn to a close. First, the indication of such closure could be stipulated in the invitation to take part in the auction, where contracting entities clearly define the

---

[26] Article 56(4) of the Utilities Directive.
[27] See Article 56(6) of the Utilities Directive.
[28] See Article 56(7) of the Utilities Directive.

date and time of the closure in advance. Secondly, the action can be closed when participants to the auction do not furnish any more new prices or new values which meet the requirements concerning minimum differences stipulated by the contracting authority in the invitation to participate in the auction. In such an event, the contracting entities must affirm in the invitation to take part in the auction the time which they will allow to elapse after receiving the last submission before they close the electronic auction. Thirdly, an electronic auction may be drawn to a close when the number of phases in the auction, which must be prescribed by contracting entities in the invitation to take part in the auction, has been completed. The closure of an auction as a result of the lapse of its predetermined phases must be based on a clear indication of the timetable for each phase of the auction which must also be stated in the invitation to take part in the auction.

After closing an electronic auction contracting entities must award the contract on the basis of the results of the electronic auction. Contracting entities may not have improper recourse to electronic auctions nor may they use them in such a way as to prevent, restrict or distort competition or to change the subject-matter of the contract, as put up for tender in the published contract notice and defined in the specification.[29]

Award Criteria in Electronic Auctions

After the closure of an electronic auction, contracting entities must award the contract based on the following criteria:[30]

- either solely on prices when the contract is awarded to the lowest price,
- or on prices or on the new values of the features of the tenders indicated in the specification when the contract is awarded to the most economically advantageous tender.

Contracting entities must stipulate in the invitation to participate in the electronic auctions the criteria they will apply to the award of the contract. When the contract is to be awarded on the basis of the most economically advantageous tender, the invitation to participate in an electronic auction must include the relative weighting of the criteria or factors that the contracting authority considers relevant for the evaluation process.[31]

---

[29]   Article 56(8) of the Utilities Directive.
[30]   See the details specified in Article 54(8) of the Utilities Directive.
[31]   Article 54(5) of the Utilities Directive.

DESIGN CONTESTS

Design contests are those procedures which enable the contracting authority to acquire a plan or design selected by a jury after being put out to competition with or without the award of prizes. The plan or design should be mainly in the disciplines of town and country planning, architecture and engineering or data processing.[32]

Scope and Thresholds

Design contests could be arranged as part of a procurement procedure leading to the award of a service contract or as a competition with prizes or payments to participants.[33] The value of the service contract subject to a design contest should be Euro 499 000 net of VAT, including any possible prizes or payments to participants. The total amount of the prizes and payments to the participants in a design contest, including the estimated value of the services contract, which might subsequently be concluded,[34] should not exceed the stipulated threshold of Euro 499 000.

Design contests excluded[35] from the Utilities Directive include contests for service contracts which are awarded for purposes other than the pursuit of an activity covered by the Utilities Directive, or service contracts awarded for the pursuit of an activity covered by the Utilities Directive in a third country;[36] contests for service contracts which are secret or require special security measures;[37] and finally contests for service contracts awarded pursuant to international rules.[38] Design contests organised as part of a procurement process for an activity which is directly exposed to competition[39] are also excluded from the Utilities Directive

Conduct of Design Contests

Contracting entities which wish to carry out a design contest must make

---

[32] See Article 1(10) of the Utilities Directive.
[33] See Article 61(1) and (2) of the Utilities Directive.
[34] See Article 40(3) of the Utilities Directive.
[35] See Article 62 of the Utilities Directive.
[36] See Article 20 of the Utilities Directive.
[37] See Article 21 of the Utilities Directive.
[38] See Article 22 of the Utilities Directive.
[39] See Articles 30(1) and 30(4), second and third indent and 30(5), fourth indent of the Utilities Directive.

known their intention by means of a contest notice.[40] The notices relating to organisation of design contests must contain the following information:[41]

1. name, address, fax number and e-mail address of the contracting entity and those of the service from which the additional documents may be obtained;
2. description of the project;
3. type of contest: open or restricted;
4. in the event of an open contest: time limit for the submission of projects;
5. in the event of a restricted contest:
    (a) number of participants contemplated;
    (b) names of the participants already selected, if any;
    (c) criteria for the selection of participants;
    (d) time limit for requests to participate;
6. if appropriate, an indication that participation is restricted to a specified profession;
7. criteria which will be applied in the evaluation of the projects;
8. names of any members of the jury who have already been selected;
9. indication of whether the jury's decision is binding on the contracting entity;
10. number and value of any prizes;
11. payments to be made to all participants, if any;
12. indication of whether any contracts following the contest will or will not be awarded to the winner or winners of the contest.

After the conclusion of the design contest, contracting entities must publish a notice of the results including the following information:[42] reference to the contest notice, description of the project, total number of participants, number of foreign participants, the winner(s) of the contest, any prizes awarded to the winner. The notice of the results of a design contest must be forwarded to the Commission by contracting entities within two months of the closure of the design contest, pointing out any sensitive commercial aspects which might concern the number of projects or plans received, the identity of the economic operators and the prices tendered.

The admission of participants to design contests must not be limited either by reference to the territory or part of the territory of a member state or on the grounds that, under the law of the member state in which the

---

[40]   See Article 63 of the Utilities Directive.
[41]   See the format and template of information required in Annex XVIII of the Utilities Directive.
[42]   See Article 63(2) of the Utilities Directive and Annex XIX.

contest is organized, they would be required to be either natural or legal persons.[43] For the selection of competitors, where design contests are restricted to a limited number of participants, contracting entities are obliged to lay down clear and non-discriminatory selection criteria. In any event, the number of candidates invited to participate must be sufficient to ensure genuine competition.[44]

Composition of the Jury

The jury in a design contest should be composed exclusively of natural persons who are independent of participants in the contest.[45] Where a particular professional qualification is required from participants in a contest, at least a third of the members of the jury must have that qualification or an equivalent qualification.

Decisions of the Jury

The jury must be autonomous in its decisions or opinions. In its decision-making process, it examines the plans and projects submitted by the candidates anonymously and solely on the basis of the criteria indicated in the contest notice.[46] It records its ranking of projects in a report, signed by its members, made according to the merits of each project, together with its remarks and any points which may need clarification. Anonymity must be observed until the jury has reached its opinion or decision. Candidates may be invited, if need be, to answer questions which the jury has recorded in the minutes to clarify any aspects of the projects. The organiser of a design contest must keep complete minutes of the dialogue between jury members and candidates.

Communication between Participants and the Jury

Communications, exchanges and the storage of information relevant to a design contest must ensure that the integrity and the confidentiality of all information communicated by the participants in a contest are preserved and that the jury ascertains the contents of plans and projects only after the expiry of the time limit for their submission.[47] For the electronic receipt of plans and

---

43 Article 60(2) of the Utilities Directive.
44 Article 65(2) of the Utilities Directive.
45 Article 65(3) of the Utilities Directive.
46 See Article 66 of the Utilities Directive.
47 Article 64(2) of the Utilities Directive.

projects, the Directive stipulates that the information relating to specifications which is necessary for the presentation of plans and projects by electronic means, including encryption, must be available to the parties concerned. Member states may introduce or maintain voluntary arrangements for accreditation intended to improve the level of the certification service provided for such devices.[48]

AWARD CRITERIA

There are two criteria on which the contracting entities must base the award of contracts;[49] (a) the most economically advantageous tender and (b) the lowest price.

The Most Economically Advantageous Tender

When the award is made to the most economically advantageous tender from the point of view of the contracting authority, various criteria linked to the subject-matter of the public contract in question, for example, quality, price, technical merit, aesthetic and functional characteristics, environmental characteristics, running costs, cost-effectiveness, after-sales service and technical assistance, delivery date and delivery period or period of completion, can be taken into consideration. The above-listed criteria, which constitute the parameters of the most economically advantageous offer, are not exhaustive.[50]

For the purposes of defining what constitutes a most economically advantageous offer, the contracting authority must specify in the contract notice or in the contract documents or, in the case of a competitive dialogue, in the descriptive document, the relative weighting which it gives to each of the criteria chosen to determine the most economically advantageous tender. Those weightings can be expressed by providing a range with an appropriate maximum spread. Where, in the opinion of the contracting authority, weighting is not possible for demonstrable reasons, the contracting authority must indicate in the contract notice or contract documents or, in the case of a competitive dialogue, in the descriptive document, the criteria in descending order of importance.[51] The relative weighting or order of importance must be specified, as appropriate, in the notice used as a means of calling for competition, in the invitation to confirm the interest referred to in Article 47(5) of the

---

48 Article 64(3) of the Utilities Directive.
49 Article 55 of the Utilities Directive.
50 Article 55(1)(a) of the Utilities Directive.
51 Article 55(2) of the Utilities Directive.

Utilities Directive, in the invitation to tender or to negotiate, or in the specifications.

The Lowest Price

When the lowest price has been selected as the award criterion, contracting entities must not refer to any other qualitative consideration when deliberating the award of a contract. The lowest price is the sole quantitative benchmark that intends to differentiate between the offers made by tenderers.[52] However, contracting entities can reject a tender, if they regard the price attached to it as abnormally low.

Abnormally Low Tenders

Where tenders appear to be abnormally low in relation to the goods, works or services, the contracting entity must request in writing details of the constituent elements of the tender which it considers relevant before it rejects those tenders.[53]

The clarification details[54] may relate in particular to:

(a) the economics of the construction method, the manufacturing process or the services provided;
(b) the technical solutions chosen and/or any exceptionally favourable conditions available to the tenderer for the execution of the work, for the supply of the goods or services;
(c) the originality of the work, supplies or services proposed by the tenderer;
(d) compliance with the provisions relating to employment protection and working conditions in force at the place where the work, service or supply is to be performed;
(e) the possibility of the tenderer obtaining state aid.

Where a contracting entity establishes that a tender is abnormally low because the tenderer has obtained state aid, the tender can be rejected on that ground alone only after consultation with the tenderer where the latter is unable to prove, within a sufficient time limit fixed by the contracting entity, that the aid in question was granted legally.[55] Where the contracting entity rejects a tender in these circumstances, it must inform the Commission of its decision.

---

[52] See Article 55(1)(b) of the Utilities Directive.
[53] Article 57 of the Utilities Directive.
[54] Article 57(1) of the Utilities Directive.
[55] Article 57(3) of the Utilities Directive.

15. Compliance with public procurement rules

THE REMEDIES DIRECTIVES

The public procurement sector is by nature decentralised and requires decentralised control. In most member states there are already specific remedies for breach of public procurement laws, and it is the responsibility of all the member states to provide legal remedies to the parties concerned, capable of enforcing the provisions of the Public Procurement Directives.

National courts can claim jurisdiction for a member state's failure to fulfil Treaty obligations, when primary and secondary Community legislation is directly applicable and directly effective. Direct applicability of Community law means that there is no need for implementing measures to be taken by member states,[1] whereas direct effectiveness implies the reliance of individuals upon Community law before national courts.[2] Individuals may avail themselves of legal remedies before national courts relying on provisions of Community law armed with direct effectiveness. With respect to Public Procurement Directives, actions may be launched by individuals against the state, central government, local government and other contracting authorities, provided that the particular provisions of the Directives upon which individuals rely produce *vertical direct effect*. The verticality of direct effectiveness implies the responsibility of the state *vis-à-vis* individuals, arising from obligations stipulated in the particular Directive in question and assimilates the direct effect of the Directives with the direct applicability of Regulations. Direct effectiveness in its vertical dimension provides for access to justice for individuals against the state in situations where judicial review is otherwise unattainable, due to the fact that Directives are addressed to member states

---

[1] See Winter, 'Direct applicability and direct effectiveness of EC law', 9 (1972) *CMLRev*, 425.

[2] See the Court's judgment in case C-26/62, *NV Algemene Transport-en Expeditie Onderneming Van Gend en Loos v. Nederlandse Administratie der Belastigen*, [1963] ECR 1. Also cases 57/65, *Alfons Luttucke GmbH v. Haupzollampt Saarlouis*, [1966] ECR 205, and C-28/67, *Firma Molkerei Zentrale Westfalen/Lippe GmbH v. Haupzollampt Paderborn*, [1968] ECR 143.

only, thus requiring legislative incorporation into domestic legal systems in order to confer rights and duties upon individuals. On the other hand, *horizontal direct effectiveness* may allow individuals to rely on Community law in actions against other individuals.[3] Interestingly the Court rejected the argument that Directives may produce horizontal direct effect[4] on the grounds that their binding nature exists only in relation to the member states to which they are addressed.

The legal nature of Directives precludes them from being directly applicable, as member states are required to introduce implementing measures, and the direct effectiveness of their provisions depends on three cumulative conditions, as defined by the European Court of Justice:[5] (i) the sufficient clearness and precision of their provisions, (ii) their unconditionality and finally, (iii) the lack of discretion on the part of member states when implementing them. The concept of direct effectiveness is closely linked with the normative character of Community law. However, access to justice before national fora based upon reliance on directly effective Community law requires judicial precedent set by the European Court of Justice. Judicial control at domestic level relies heavily on the utilisation of the Court's rulings as a guide for the direct effectiveness or the interpretation of provisions of the relevant Directives through Article 177 EC proceedings. In cases where there is no clear precedent, clarification and interpretation of provisions of the relevant Directives are needed, thus the national court embarks upon a reference procedure asking for the assistance of the European Court of Justice.

Public procurement litigation, which has been the subject of domestic judicial control, is based on the doctrine of vertical direct effectiveness of the provisions of Public Procurement Directives and focuses particularly on the *post*-implementation era,[6] when the Directives have been transplanted into the domestic legal orders. Individuals claim the existence of direct effectiveness,

---

[3]   The concept of horizontal direct effect has been defined by the Court of Justice in case C-13/61, *Kledingverkoopbedrijf de Geus en Uitdenbogerd v. Robert Bosch GmbH*, [1962] ECR 45.

[4]   See case C-152/84, *Marshal v. Southampton and South West Hampshire Area Health Authority*, [1986] ECR 723.

[5]   See cases C-6/64, *Costa v. ENEL*, [1964] ECR 585; 27/67, *Firma Fink-Frucht GmbH v. Haupzollamt Munchen Landsbergerstrasse*, [1968] ECR 223; C-13/68, *SpA Salgoil v. Italian Ministry for Foreign Trade*, [1968] ECR 453; C-41/74, *Van Duyn v. Home Office*, [1974] ECR 1337.

[6]   Most Directives provide for a period between their enactment and their coming into force in order to give member states the time necessary to adjust their national systems to Community standards and also gear their legislative machinery with a view to introducing laws implementing the Directives. See Lauwaars, *Lawfulness and legal force of Community Decisions*, A.W.Sijthoff, 1973, pp. 28–37.

requesting the court to apply the provision of the Directive in question directly, irrespective of any implementing measure adopted by the state. In most cases national courts feel safer to ask the European Court of Justice for a reference regarding the direct effect of the relevant provision, even if the case is obviously clear or a materially identical reference has previously been made to the Court.[7] The majority of cases initiated before national courts and later referred to the European Court of Justice relate to the meaning and definition of the term 'contracting authorities' and the application of selection and award criteria defined in the Public Procurement Directives. Until the completion of the internal market in 1992, there had been nine cases before national courts relying on Public Procurement Directives' provisions, which were referred to the Court of Justice for a preliminary ruling under Article 177 EC. In five other cases before national courts,[8] the latter dealt with them without having recourse to 177 proceedings. The post-internal market era has witnessed litigation which was mainly concerned with the interpretation and clarification of provisions of the Public Procurement Directives.

Decentralised judicial control of the public procurement regime has revealed the perpetuation by some member states of preferential and discriminatory procurement as a major and persisting obstacle to the integration of public markets in the European Union. Failure to comply with the provisions of the relevant Directives, as well as incorrect application of them by contracting authorities, constitute the most important non-tariff barrier in the European integration process. While technical standards and specifications have been harmonised to a considerable degree to eliminate any potential ground for discrimination based on nationality, the movement of goods and services related to public markets appears more distorted than the movement of goods and services destined for private markets.

The aim of the European institutions should be to provide for the possibility of having uniform remedies in all member states, of harmonising procedures or at least of co-ordinating national laws and administrative provisions relating to the application of procedures for reviewing public procurement contracts.[9] Uniformity of application, as far as legal remedies are concerned, is a desirable situation but it is an ideal which is difficult to achieve, since there

---

7   See case C-283/81, *Srl CILFIT v. Minisrty of Health*, [1982] ECR 3415. The theories of *acte eclaire* and *acte claire*.

8   See case No. 10475 *SA.SHV Belgium v. La Maison Ideale et Société Nationale du Longement*; judgment of 24 June 1986 of the Belgian *Conseil d'Etat*; case 194/84, *P. Steinhauser v. Ville de Biarritz*, before the Tribunal Administratif du Pau; judgment of 24 December 1987 before the District Court of Maastricht; and finally, an arbitration award of the Raad van Arbitrage of 31/3/87.

9   This is the aim of Article 100 EC and to a certain point of Article 100A EC.

are different ways, already established, for solving public procurement disputes. It is almost impossible to have one law applicable in all member states due to separate legal traditions and procedures. Any attempt to abolish existing national systems would be extremely difficult, useless and a waste of time. Similarly, harmonisation of national procedures concerning the availability of legal remedies for breach of public procurement contracts is neither possible nor necessary. In order to achieve harmonisation, that is, approximation of national legal orders, one should start from a common point; in other words, the national legal orders to be harmonised should be homogeneous.

In the case of public procurement, the existing national remedies are addressed to civil or administrative courts or administrative bodies or arbitrators. Furthermore, the national law applicable in each member state varies from civil to public administrative law. Finally, the cost of initiating proceedings differs from member state to member state, depending on the cost of living or the judicial cost in each country. Under those conditions, it is hardly possible to achieve harmonisation. What remains is to co-ordinate these national legal remedies with a view to ensuring a procedure and a sanction for the application of the underlying Public Procurement Directives.

In an attempt to give an answer to these questions, the Council enacted a Directive on the harmonisation of laws, regulations and administrative provisions relating to the application of review procedures on the award of public works and public supply contracts (Directive 89/665 EC).[10] In addition, Directive 92/13[11] extends the remedies and review procedures covered by Directive 89/665 to the water, energy, transport and telecommunication sectors. According to the Remedies Directives, member states should be left to implement procedures consistent with their own judicial practices to achieve effective and rapid review rules. This approach is consistent with the provisions in Article 189 EC that a directive shall be binding as to the result to be achieved, leaving the form and methods at the discretion of member states. In some member states, highly developed systems of monitoring public procurement procedures already exist. Both Directives aim at co-ordinating existing procedures and procedures to be introduced with a view to a uniform application of the underlying Directives concerning public supplies, public works, and utilities. It seems that neither Directive has a direct effect.

The Principles of the Remedies Directives

The enactment of the Remedies Directives has brought a different dimension

---

[10]   See OJ 1989 L 395.
[11]   See OJ 1992 L 76/7.

to the application of public procurement rules. Such a dimension relies on the decentralised compliance and enforcement of the substantive regime. Directive 89/665[12] on the co-ordination of the laws, regulations and administrative provisions relating to the application of review procedures to the award of public supply and public works contracts and Directive 92/13[13] co-ordinating the laws, regulations and administrative provisions relating to the application of community rules on the procurement procedures of entities operating in the water, energy, transport and telecommunications sectors require member states to introduce effective remedies and means of enforcement for suppliers, contractors and service providers who believe that they have been harmed by an infringement of the substantive procurement rules.

Existing arrangements at both national and Community levels for ensuring the application of the substantive public procurement rules have been inadequate in ensuring compliance with the relevant Community provisions. Their inadequacy is highlighted in their inability to correct infringements and ensure an efficient application of the award procedures by contracting authorities. The absence or inadequacy of effective remedies at national level has a detrimental effect on the opening up of public procurement by deterring undertakings from participating in award procedures for public contract and submitting tenders. The opening up of public procurement to community-wide competition demands also a substantial increase in the levels of transparency at national level regarding the availability of redress to the supply side of the public procurement equation (tenderers and participants). Such increased levels of transparency must be accompanied by non-discriminatory measures introduced within national legal systems which provide interested parties, at least, with the same treatment in public procurement litigation, as in other forms of litigation.

The Remedies Directives are based on three fundamental principles: the principle of effectiveness, the principle of non-discrimination and the principle of procedural autonomy.

The Principle of Effectiveness

In both Remedies Directives, effective review of decisions or acts of contracting authorities is the essential requirement of compliance with the substantive public procurement rules. The principle of effectiveness includes two individual features; first, the swift resolution of disputes and secondly, the enforceability of decisions. In particular, Article 1 of Directive 89/665 (public sector

---

[12]   See OJ 1989 L 395/33.
[13]   See OJ 1992 L 76/14.

Remedies Directive) and Article 1 of Directive 92/13 (utilities Remedies Directive) stipulate that member states must take any measures necessary to ensure that decisions taken by the contracting authorities may be reviewed effectively and as rapidly as possible and can be effectively enforced[14] on the grounds that such decisions have infringed Community law in the field of public procurement or national implementing laws.

The Principle of Non-discrimination

There is an explicit obligation conferred upon member states to avoid introducing review procedures for decisions of contracting authorities and utilities, as well as procedures for the recovery of damages which differ, in a discriminatory context, from review procedures for other administrative acts and procedures for the recovery of damages under national law.[15]

The Principle of Procedural Autonomy

The Remedies Directive leaves member states with wide discretion as to the creation of the appropriate forum to receive complaints and legal actions against decisions of contracting authorities and utilities, as well as action for damages in public procurement cases.[16]

The Remit of the Remedies Directives

According to Article 1 of Directive 89/665 and Article 1 of Directive 93/13, member states must ensure effective and rapid review of decisions taken by contracting authorities which infringe public procurement provisions. Undertakings seeking relief from damages in the context of a procedure for the award of a contract should not be treated differently under national rules implementing European public procurement laws and under other national rules. This means that the measures to be taken concerning the review procedures should be similar to national review proceedings, without any discriminatory character.

Any person having or having had an interest in obtaining a particular public supply or public works contract and who has been or risks being harmed by an alleged infringement of public procurement provision must be entitled to seek review before national courts. This is laid down in the third paragraph of

---

14   See Article 2(7) of Directive 89/665 and Article 2(8) of Directive 92/13.
15   See Article 1(2) of Directive 89/665 and Article 1(2) of Directive 92/13.
16   See Article 2(2) of Directive 89/665 and Article 2(2) of Directive 92/13.

Article 1 of Directive 89/665 and Article 3 of Directive 92/13 and in both cases is followed by a stand-still provision concerning the prior notification by the person seeking review to the contracting authority of the alleged infringement and of his intention to seek review. However, with respect to admissibility aspects, there is no qualitative or quantitative definition of the interest of a person in obtaining a public contract. As to the element of potential harm by an infringement of public procurement provisions, it should be cumulative with the first element, that of interest. The prior notification should intend to exhaust any possibility of amicable settlement before the parties have recourse to national courts.

However, by virtue of Article 2 of Directive 89/665 and Article 2 of Directive 92/13, the measures concerning the review procedures shall include interim measures, by way of interlocutory procedures, with the aim of correcting the alleged infringement or preventing further damage. Provision shall be made for measures to suspend or to ensure the suspension of the procedure for the award of a public contract or the implementation of any decision taken by the contracting authority. In most member states, suspension of a contract would be achieved through an injunction. National courts have the power to grant an injunction to restrain unlawful acts. It should be borne in mind that suspension of the whole procedure or of the implementation of any decision will create some problems.

First, review procedures should not have an automatic suspensive character. Indeed, Article 2(3) in both Directives so reads. Secondly, in practical terms, a disappointed tender would ask the court to order the contracting authority to reconsider its bid and not to enter into a contract in the meantime. Often, this will cause disproportionate hardship. Therefore, the national courts or administrative bodies should take into account the probable consequences for all interests likely to be harmed as well as the public interest. In fact, Article 2(4) in both instruments introduces the principle of proportionality. The provision stipulates that where any grant of a review measure causes negative consequences, such consequences must not exceed the benefits. For the sake of history, it is worth mentioning that Article 3 of the draft Directive 89/665[17] gave the Commission the right to suspend a contract award procedure for a period of up to three months. Since this would have led to legal uncertainty, while at the same time national courts have suspensive powers, it has been deleted from the final text.

In addition to interim measures correcting the alleged infringement or suspending the award procedure, Article 2(1)(b) provides measures to set aside unlawfully taken decisions by the contracting authority, including the removal

---

[17]   See COM (88) 733 final.

of discriminatory technical, economic or financial specifications in the invitation to tender, the contract document or any other document relating to the award procedure. The present texts of the Directives are not sufficiently clear in respect of the execution of the contract itself. It could be argued that contracts may be set aside, even after having been awarded. The effect of annulling contracts would be to render uncertain for several years the basis for proceeding with important public works and could cause damage extending well beyond the authority under challenge. The Commission has made clear its intention that contracts once awarded should not be at risk of being overturned. However, the fact of setting aside a decision leaving the contract unaffected causes serious doubts as to the validity of the contract. In some continental legal orders, the theory of detachable acts has been developed and permits the validity of administrative acts leading to the making of a contract to be considered distinct from the contract itself and for them to be open to challenge on grounds of their illegality, without affecting the validity of the contract. In these legal orders, the challenge to the unlawful decision is a prerequisite to an action for damages. In other jurisdictions, the setting aside of the decision without touching the contract will create problems, as the legal basis of the contract has been removed.

It is at the discretion of the national court to decide whether it should set aside the decision to enter into a contract or simply declare illegalities in the award procedure and therefore grant damages. Directive 92/13 recognises explicitly the theory of detachable acts and provides in Article 2(d) that prior to an award of damages, the contested decision must first be set aside or declared illegal. The power to order the removal of discriminatory specifications in the contract documents is a different matter. Such an order should not be made in a way which would hinder the procurement process and it should ensure that the procedure is in accordance with the Community principle of non-discrimination.

Set Aside and Annulment of Decisions

The possibility to set aside the act awarding the contract is provided in most member states. In some jurisdictions, administrative courts have power to set aside unlawful administrative acts and deal with claims concerning the act awarding the contract. With respect to the contract itself, they follow the theory of detachable acts, whereby the validity of administrative acts leading to the conclusion of a public contract may be viewed in isolation from the contract itself and challenged on grounds of unlawfulness, without the validity of the contract necessarily being affected. However, in other jurisdictions the validity of the contract may be automatically affected if the award decision is set aside.

The theory of detachable act, which operates in French-influenced continental jurisdictions, presents considerable weaknesses when applied to public procurement cases. Under that theory, the public procurement process is subject to both public and private law jurisdiction. The above jurisdictional separation lies in the fact that the decision of a contracting authority under which a particular public contract is awarded is considered an administrative act which is subject to the jurisdiction of public law and as such is separated from the contract itself, which falls under civil law jurisdiction. However, it is undisputed that the administrative act awarding the contract constitutes an integral part of the whole procurement process and forms the legal justification for the conclusion of the contract between the contracting authority and the successful tenderer. By the separation, both jurisdictional and actual, of the act of awarding the contract and the contract itself, there is the possibility that the whole procurement process could be thrown into legal uncertainty in the event that the legality of the awarding act is contested. If the contract itself has not yet been concluded, its suspension represents the most logical solution and, in principle, falls under the same jurisdiction as the action to annul the awarding decision. If the act is annulled, then the contract remains without legal basis. Where the contract itself has not yet been concluded, this does not represent a major problem. The administrative act will be reissued by the contracting authority without defaults this time. However, a question remains as to whether the contracting authority is liable to compensate the contractor previously successful at the award stage of the procurement process, when the reissued act awards the contract to a different tenderer. If, for example, the act awarding the contract is declared illegal and the contracting authority is ordered to re-open the tendering process for its award, the contracting authority should compensate the existing contractor for losses of profits, should the contract finally be awarded to another tenderer. The issue remains unclear, although, in proceedings concerning interim measures before it, the European Court of Justice did not consider the successful contractor's knowledge of the illegality of the awarding act and it was not considered to be a relevant factor in determining whether the contract should be set aside.[18]

Problems arise when the parties have concluded the agreement (by signing the relevant contract) or even when the contract is at its performance stage. An action to annul the administrative act which awarded the contract would probably shake the entire legal foundation of the latter. Two elements deserve attention here: first, if the administrative act is annulled, the legal basis of the concluded contract or the contract under performance disappears. This means

---

[18] See case C-199/85, *Commission v. Italy* [1987] ECR 1039. Also, case 272/91R, *Commission v. Italy*, order of 12 June 1992.

that the contract, as a private law covenant, cannot be executed; therefore it should be suspended. Even in the event of the reissued act awarding the contract to the same contractor, this new administrative act cannot *stricto sensu* be the legal foundation of the contract already awarded by the first one. The second element refers to the prejudice to the harm of the public interest as a result of the amount of legal uncertainty which covers the period during which the case concerning the legality of the awarding act is pending, as well as the period during which the performance of the contract is suspended.

On the other hand, the *doctrine of severance* utilised in common law juris-dictions may have more balanced results. In contrast with the theory of detach-able acts, the doctrine of severance allows the courts, in principle, to separate the defaulting parts of a contract, thus saving the legitimate ones. If the contract is viable only with the latter then it could be legally executed, other-wise it should be declared null and void. The viability, in legal terms, of a public procurement contract after severance of any unlawful or illegal parts of the procurement process may insert an element of *qualitative evaluation* of the stages under which public contracts are awarded. Such evaluation, perhaps, would classify in hierarchical order the relative importance of violation of procurement law. For example, a breach of the time limits for the receipt of tenders under open procedures could not in itself be a sufficient reason to nullify the award of a public contract. However, violations of rules relating to the qualification of tenderers or the selection and award criteria cannot be severed by other legitimate parts of a public contract, as they affect its substan-tive validity considerably. The doctrine of severance cannot be applied in legal systems where public law and private law jurisdiction coexist. In such a case the doctrine could hardly provide any assistance.

The Award of Damages under the Remedies Directives

Article 2(1)(c) in both Directives provides for the award of damages to persons harmed by an infringement of public procurement law. The purpose behind this provision is to mobilise interested contractors in order to supervise the application of Public Procurement Directives.

As already mentioned above, European law does not require the provision of a remedy for the award of damages when there is a breach of a directly effective rule. The reasons for that absence vary: in some cases the national court has held that the authority in breach of Community law did not owe any obligation directly to the plaintiff or that the plaintiff's losses were the results of foreseeable economic risk; in others, the award of damages has been seen as an unacceptable fetter on the freedom of authorities to enact legislative measures or administrative rules in good faith, pursuant to their general duty to safeguard the public interest, such as human health. Damages may be available as a consequence of provisions of national law which make a national authority liable to compensate for breach of its obligations. Procuring authorities are subject to a duty to observe European rules and are liable for damages in breach of those rules. In the context of the Remedies Directives, a question arises as to whether an aspiring contractor seeking damages should prove that he would have been accepted as a tender or that he would have won the contract, if not for the infringement.

Under the restrictive procedures, a limited number of contractors or suppliers are invited to tender pursuant to Article 22 of the Public Works Directive or Article 19 of the Public Supplies Directive. Where a contractor or a supplier has applied as a candidate, but has not been invited to tender and the contracting authority has infringed the Directive, the assessment of loss would be difficult since tender costs have not been incurred and the contractor or supplier might not, in any case, have been awarded the contract.

In the case where he has submitted a tender, it may be easier to show that he has suffered a quantifiable loss in respect of which he should be indemnified, at least so far as the expenses of tendering are concerned. Any additional loss would be more difficult to prove. Under the utilities Remedies Directive, the undertaking claiming damages must prove the infringement of public procurement law and the effect of this infringement on his chance of being awarded the contract. He does not have to prove that, in the absence of the infringement he would have been awarded it.[19]

Where the complaint is that the procuring authority has failed to accept the most economically advantageous tender, as required by the Public Procurement Directives, there is probably no alternative; the procuring authority will be required to advise unsuccessful tenderers of the reason for their failure. Then, it is for the unsuccessful tenderers to assess whether these reasons are so defective as to justify legal proceedings for compensation. It should be recalled that the criteria laid down in the public procurement Directives are wide-ranging, leaving a great deal of discretion to the contracting authority. The burden of proof will be on the unsuccessful tenderer to persuade the court that his tender was more economically advantageous than that of the winning tender. On the other hand, where the potential tenderer complains of unlawful exclusion from the tendering process, he should be entitled, on proof, to recovery of costs actually incurred, which will usually not be substantial. Under the draft Remedies Directive on the utilities sectors, the amount of damages refunded should be deemed to be 1% of the value of the contract, in a case where a contractor is preparing a bid or participating in an award procedure, unless he proves that his costs were greater. This provision has been

---

[19]   See Recital 11 of Directive 92/13.

deleted from the final text of Directive 92/13. It should be noted that the draft Directive 89/665 mentioned three grounds of action for damages: the cost of unnecessary studies, forgone profits and lost opportunities. The final text of the Directive, interestingly, remains silent and refers only to award of damages generally (Article 2(1)(c)). There have been fears that the inclusion of forgone profits and lost opportunities could have led to speculative and wasteful litigation.

There are two observations relating to damages litigation in public procurement. First, as is generally admitted, undertakings will be hesitant to bring a contracting authority before a court, since they want to maintain good relations in the future. Litigation between a supplier and a contracting authority often results in an irrevocable break in their relationship. Secondly, if damages are too greatly and too readily awarded, contracting authorities would find themselves proceeding so extremely carefully as to seriously impede any public work or supplies contract. It remains to be seen how, in practice, national courts will deal with the matter. Since there are a number of different jurisdictions throughout the Community, it also follows that there would be great differences in the amounts awarded as compensation by national courts. This could prevent some undertakings from taking any proceedings in member states that provide for low sanctions. In this case, the member state is obliged to introduce more effective procedures, similar though not necessarily identical to those of the rest of the member states of the Community. The Commission could launch an action under Article 169 EC and request the Court to declare that a member state has not conformed to the Remedies Directive.

The Remedies Directives provide that member states should establish judicial or administrative bodies responsible for their enforcement. Member states, therefore, have a choice as to the forum and procedures provided for hearing disputes or otherwise achieving the required result. In addition, they require that all decisions taken by bodies responsible for review procedures shall be effectively enforced.

As explained above, since contracting authorities are involved in a public contract, in many continental jurisdictions public law will be applied and the dispute is to be addressed before administrative courts. In other cases, civil law applies in public procurement litigation, whereas in the Netherlands, for example, there is a remarkably swift arbitration system for construction contracts. Consequently, the question of enforcement of the decisions is relevant to the choice of forum. Normally, national courts have the power, the prerogative and the means to enforce their decisions. An administrative body, without judicial powers to order discovery or injunctions, could not ensure effective enforcement of its decisions. In the case of arbitration, the winning party, in order to have the arbitration award enforced, has to go before national courts and exhaust the relevant proceedings. Moreover, there are some doubts as to the consistency of tribunals' decisions. National courts are skilled at construing contracts and statutory provisions, knowledgeable about the principles of damages and staffed by judges. On the other hand, an administrative body or a tribunal, normally staffed by lawyers and laymen experienced in public procurement, is a swift, flexible and rapid institution with simple proceedings to resolve disputes, since it will deal exclusively with this matter.

Where the Remedies Directive in the utilities sectors[20] is really novel is in Chapter 2. Member states are required to give the contracting entities the possibility of having their purchasing procedures and practices *attested* to by persons authorised by law to exercise this function. Indeed, this attestation mechanism may investigate in advance possible irregularities identified in the award of a public contract and allow the contracting authorities to correct them. The latter may include the attestation statement in the notice inviting tenders published in the Official Journal. The system appears flexible and cost-efficient and may prevent wasteful litigation. Quite promisingly, the attestation procedure under Directive 92/13 will be the essential requirement for the development of European standards of attestation.[21]

The Role of the European Commission under the Remedies Directives

As mentioned above, under the draft Directive 89/665, the Commission had extensive powers, namely to intervene in an administrative or judicial procedure and to suspend unilaterally the procedure for the award of a public procurement contract. Those powers were indeed far beyond the provision of Article 100A EC Treaty and could only be justified under Article 235 EC. The Commission's intervention was a novel provision since it has no power to be a party or to intervene in a trial before national courts. The *vires* of this provision was questioned, since the draft Directive was unclear at that particular point; it did not specify whether the Commission would have had a certain right to intervene or whether its intervention was subject to invitation or the permission of the court. In the latter case, it would have been considered as *amicus curiae*, advising the court upon the right interpretation of European Community law. On the other hand, it could be argued that the Commission's intervention would have been desirable, since it can only be heard in a case of interim measures before the Court of Justice or under the proceedings of Article 169 EC. Interim measures may be taken by the Court only if the case in question is pending before it, and an Article 169 EC action is a heavy,

---

[20] See Directive 92/13, OJ 1992 L 76/7.
[21] See Article 7 of EC Directive 92/13.

cumbersome and time-consuming procedure, as far as public procurement cases are concerned.

The Commission's suspension power could lead to legal uncertainty and undermine the independence of the courts. Control by both court and the Commission simultaneously is not desirable. In the final text of Directive 89/665, all these powers have been deleted and the Commission has been left with the right to invoke the procedure of Article 3 by way of notification of an infringement of Community law provisions to a member state requiring its correction. The same regime is provided for in Directive 92/13 (Article 8).

Interestingly, the Commission's action is limited. It can only notify a clear and manifest infringement of Community law provisions in the field of public procurement, before a contract has been concluded. The former requirement introduces a kind of qualitative test. Clear and manifest infringement probably means an outspoken breach of a relevant provision. Unclear and ambiguous situations will fall outside the scope of the notification procedure. The latter requirement serves the principle of legal certainty, since after the contract has been concluded it is extremely costly and undesirable to start investigating it, probably with a view to suspending it.

After 21 days in the case of Directive 89/665 and 30 days in the case of Directive 92/13 from the Commission's notification to a member state, the latter is obliged to communicate to the former: (i) its confirmation that an infringement has been corrected or (ii) a justification as to why no correction has been made or (iii) a notice that a suspension of the award procedure has been ordered. When the suspension is lifted, the member state is obliged to inform the Commission. It is apparent that the Commission's role has been limited on the insistence of member states and, from a power to intervene or to suspend award procedures, the Commission's powers consist of the mere possibility of notification.

There have been two cases[22] where the Commission has utilised the procedure provided in Article 3 of Directive 89/665. The Court had the opportunity to declare that the special procedure of Article 3 is a preliminary measure which can neither derogate from nor replace the powers of the Commission to initiate proceedings under Article 169 EC. In both cases, the communication of the Commission's position under Article 3 of Directive 89/665 served as the reasoned opinion for the subsequent compliance proceedings under Article 169 EC.

The Commission's role is really innovative under Directive 92/13, where provision has been made for a conciliation procedure, apart from the attempt

---

[22]   See case C-359/93, *Commission v. The Netherlands*, judgment of 24 January 1995; case C-79/94, *Commission v. Greece*, judgment of 4 May 1995.

to achieve an amicable settlement laid down in Article 1(3), as an endeavour to avoid any litigation between the parties. The conciliation procedure shall be distinguished from the judicial/administrative procedures at national level. Interestingly, there is no provision concerning the relationship between the two proceedings, and if the same person were to initiate conciliation and judicial review proceedings under the Directive simultaneously, the relation between them is unclear. Article 11(2)(a) of the Directive stipulates that conciliation proceedings shall be without prejudice to proceedings under Articles 169 or 170 EC and the rights of the parties or any other person under national laws (Article 11(2)(b). Any person having an interest and feeling that a breach of relevant public procurement law rules occurs may notify the Commission or the competent authorities of a member state. The possibility of the interested person choosing either the Commission or a member state's authorities creates some uncertainty, since it is admitted that the whole public procurement problem is decentralised. The Commission or the national authorities may refer the case to the Advisory Committee for Public Contracts[23] or the Advisory Committee on Telecommunications.[24] These Committees will set up working groups with a view to reaching an agreement between the parties.

The degree of compliance with Public Procurement Directives is closely related to the degree of enforcement of their provisions at national level. Enforcement concerns legal remedies available to individuals before national courts, in particular actions for damages. Judicial review concerning the administrative part of a public procurement contract is subject to public law in almost all member states.[25] The award of damages to an aggrieved contractor reflects the approach of each national legal system *vis-à-vis* state liability.

NATIONAL LEGAL STRUCTURES AND PUBLIC PROCUREMENT LITIGATION

The Profile of National Legal Structures

Access to justice for individuals before domestic fora in public procurement cases is of paramount importance as it constitutes the mechanism for judicial control at national level. Existing national legal systems channel public

---

[23] This Committee has been set up by EC Council Decision 71/306 (OJ 1971 L 185) as amended by EC Council Decision 77/63 (OJ 1977 L 152).

[24] See Article 31 of EC Directive 90/531.

[25] The notable exception is Denmark, where there is no distinction between administrative and civil disputes in a public contract.

procurement disputes through either public law review proceedings or through civil law review proceedings as a result of the conceptual predisposition of public market transactions. In principle, and to a certain degree in practice, arbitration through the operation of non-judicial fora and alternative dispute resolution systems appears in many jurisdictions. Although a detailed investigation of the domestic procedural and substantive legal regimes of member states is provided in Chapter 16 of this work, the following analysis intends to expose the main difference between national legal systems when dealing with public procurement disputes. The level and degree of access to justice for interested parties is exposed by reference to the remedies and actions available to them for review procedures, interim measures and finally, actions for the award of damages.

French law regards public procurement contracts as subject to the exclusive jurisdiction of administrative courts.[26] Administrative courts are competent to deal with actions concerning the award of public procurement in most cases, even where the awarded contract itself is governed by private law. Indeed, the action is not directed against the contract, but against the decision adopted by the awarding authority (which is normally a public administration), and which is 'severable' from the contract itself.

There are two types of action available: an action for annulment and an action for damages. Both can be lodged at the same time, provided the time limits required have been met. Interim measures may be ordered in cases of urgency. An action for annulment may be brought before the competent administrative court within two months of the issue of the administrative act in question. French courts apply the *théorie de l'act détachable* and separate the act awarding the contract or the act calling for tender or the act that approves the award, or preparatory acts before the award of the contract in question, from the contract itself. Thus, they focus on the administrative part of the public procurement contract. The most common ground on which to base an action for annulment is *excès de pouvoir*, a concept which hardly coincides with misuse of powers found in English law. *Excès de pouvoir* means the grave disregard of the limits by the authority in question, which would have acted in a manner beyond the competence and the powers attributed to it. In addition to the above-mentioned grounds, the plaintiff may plead the direct effect of a provision of a Directive. Although the *Conseil d'Etat* has recognised the supremacy of Community law over national law, sometimes it is reluctant to pronounce on the direct effectiveness of Directives, thus follow-

---

26　　For a detailed analysis of the French legal order with respect to Public Procurement regulation see the report of Brechon-Moulènes in the 14th FIDE Congress on Application in the Member States of the Directives on Public Procurement, Madrid, 1990.

ing a restrictive interpretation of Article 189 EC. On the merits, the plaintiff may attack the external legality of the administrative act, as well as its internal legality. The former provides the following grounds: (i) incompetence of the awarding authority, (ii) irregularities as to its composition and function, (iii) any violation of a rule relating to the award of the contract in question (this should be a substantial one capable of nullifying the act). As to the internal legality, four grounds may be invoked against the authority: (i) the material inaccuracy of the act, (ii) a lack of respect for the principle of equality among the candidates, (iii) *détournement de pouvoir* (misuse of powers attributed to the authority) and (iv) manifestly wrong exercise of its discretion. On these grounds the plaintiff may achieve the annulment of the detachable act (awarding act, or the act calling for tender etc.), but not the annulment of the contract itself. An action for damages should also be addressed to the administrative courts. To award compensation, they look for a *faute de service* (a wrongful act of the administration). With respect to public procurement, such a *faute* includes: (i) the illegal selection of a candidate and (ii) the illegal award of a contract. The plaintiff must prove the existence of actual damages, in particular damages resulting from the preparation for the bid, expecting profits had the contract been awarded to him and finally, damages for the bad reputation attaching to his undertakings in a case where the authority illegally rejected its offer and revealed the reasons for that rejection. It must be said that the causal link between the damage and the *faute* must be proved by the plaintiff.

Before the contract is concluded, an action may be lodged before the president of the administrative court ('pre-contractual action'). The president must decide within 20 days and may suspend the award procedure, make injunctions to the administration and annul all measures taken by the awarding authority,[27] in particular decisions covering technical specifications. Where the awarding authority is operating in the utilities sectors and is an entity governed by private law or in certain cases governed only partially by public law, the president of the competent court (which is the administrative court, the commercial or civil court, depending on the nature of the awarding authority) may only make an injunction to the awarding entity and impose a periodic penalty payment in order to comply with its obligations.[28]

After the contract is concluded, an action for annulment of the decision of the administrative authority to conclude such a contract may be lodged before

---

[27]   See Article L 22 of the Code of administrative courts and administrative courts of appeal.

[28]   See Article L 23 of the Code of administrative courts and administrative courts of appeal, or Article 11-1 of Act 91-3 of 3 January 1991, as subsequently amended, and Articles 1441-1 to 1441-3 of the new civil procedure code.

the administrative court. However, the contract does not disappear when the decision to conclude it is set aside. Only the parties to the contract may lodge an action before the administrative court (or the civil or commercial court in cases where the contract is governed by private law) in order to have the contract declared void. An injunction or a periodic penalty payment may be imposed by the court having set aside the decision to award the contract, in order to force the administrative authority to lodge such an action. Finally, an interested party which has suffered an economic loss because of the violation of the public procurement rules may lodge an action in order to ask for damages.

Litigation on the award of public contracts is relatively frequent in France. The nature of disputes includes cases concerning alleged incomplete or unlawful amendment of tender material, communication with undertakings before or during the tender procedure, confusion between selection and award criteria and whether reservations in tender proposals actually constitute alternative proposals. The existing remedies do not provide aggrieved contractors with the possibility of being awarded a contract which should have been awarded to them, had the contracting authorities complied with public procurement rules.

The pre-contractual action was conceived in order to give a more effective remedy. It has been negatively affected by the case-law of the *Conseil d'Etat*. The *Conseil d'Etat* held that where the contract had been concluded after the action was lodged, but before the judge rendered its decision, the action was inadmissible. This is considered to constitute an incentive for the awarding authority to try to sign the contract as quickly as possible, especially when it is informed that there is a risk that its choice may be challenged before the administrative court. Moreover, French law provides that before lodging a pre-contractual action, the applicant must request the awarding authority to comply with its obligations, and if the authority does not reply, then the action may be lodged only ten days after this demand. This delays the action and increases the risk that it may be considered inadmissible. Consequently, in many cases, possible actions are not lodged because their chances of success are considered to be too low.

In Belgium, the incorporation of the provisions of Public Procurement Directives through *Arrêtes Royaux* has created a nexus of rights and duties which are enforceable before the *Conseil d'Etat*, in case of an action for annulment, and before tribunals and ordinary courts in case of an action for damages.[29] The Belgian remedial system in the field of public procurement reveals a split of competencies between the administrative courts and the civil

---

[29] See the report of Hannequart and Delvaux in 14th FIDE Congress, op. cit.

courts. Actions for annulment of decisions by the administrative authorities may be lodged before the *Conseil d'Etat*.[30] Decisions taken by the awarding authority before the conclusion of the contract, and in particular the decision of awarding the contract, are considered to be decisions of an administrative authority. However, the question whether an entity normally governed by private law is to be considered as an administrative authority because of its obligation to comply with the public procurement rules has not been settled.[31] As in French law, the annulment of the decision does not affect the contract that may be cancelled by the competent court (in Belgium the civil court) only at the request of the parties to the contract.

An action for annulment does not suspend the application of the challenged act. An action may be lodged before the *Conseil d'Etat* in order for application of the act to be suspended.[32] Such an action may be lodged at the latest with the action for annulment. In spite of this power of the *Conseil d'Etat*, civil courts may also grant interim measures, at least in certain circumstances.

Actions for damages must be lodged before civil courts that are the only ones competent to deal with matters concerning 'subjective rights'. In cases where the award criterion is the lowest price, a bidder that should have been awarded the contract if the law had not been infringed is automatically entitled to compensation equal to 10% of the amount of its bid.[33] In other cases, the candidate or bidder may claim compensation for the loss of the chance to win the contract.

Actions for annulment before the Belgian *Conseil d'Etat* are time-consuming exercises (often in excess of two years), and the judgment is usually not rendered before the contract has been signed and at least partially implemented. The authority of the judge is limited because of the discretionary power that the awarding authority is recognised to have in most of the cases. However, the rate of success of actions is far from negligible. The most common ground for annulment seems to be the lack of a statement of reasons in the challenged decision. Actions for a suspension of the decisions of the awarding authorities have been a matter of controversy between the Flemish-speaking and the French-speaking chambers of the *Conseil d'Etat* since the entry into force of the Act of 1991. This dispute turns on the question of whether or not the loss of a contract, and any resulting financial impact on the company concerned, constitutes an irreparable damage, which justifies a suspension of the award procedure.

---

[30] See Article 14 of the Co-ordinated laws on the *Conseil d'Etat*.
[31] See Act of 24 December 1993, which is notably applicable to certain entities governed by private law, which operate in the so-called 'excluded sectors'.
[32] See Act of 19 July 1991, codified in Article 17 of the co-coordinated laws on the Conseil d'Etat.
[33] See Article 15 of the Act of 24 December 1993.

The Belgian administrative law accepts the theory of detachable acts. Under this doctrine, the courts are allowed to separate the defaulting part of an act, seeking to save the remaining legitimate part(s). (To some extent, this doctrine is also recognised in common law jurisdictions, where it is known as the doctrine of severance.) Under *la théorie de l'acte détachable*, the decision of the administration awarding a public procurement contract constitutes an act separable from the contract itself. In fact, only those administrative acts that award contracts fall under the jurisdiction of the *Conseil d'Etat*, which may annul them on the grounds of excess or misuse of powers (*excès ou détournement de pouvoir*), or order their suspension in the form of interim measure, as the case may be. On the other hand, the contract itself falls under the jurisdiction of private law in a case where disputes and grievances concerning damages may arise between the parties. It should be mentioned that in both cases (before the *Conseil d'Etat* and tribunals or ordinary courts) third parties may also avail themselves of the appropriate remedies provided they can show and prove the existence of a legal-legitimate interest. This means that third parties (mainly unsuccessful tenderers) must prove not only a personal link with the dispute in question, but also the legal consequences arising from this personal link. In respect of public law jurisdiction, the *Conseil d'Etat* may annul the decision awarding a public procurement contract either because of substantial irregularities that derogate from the framework of powers attributed to the contracting authority, or because of non-substantial irregularities due to arbitrary exercise of its margin of appreciation. A successful request for annulment of the act awarding the contract will normally open the door for an action for damages under private law, as the *Conseil d'Etat* will pronounce on the illegality of that act. Before the tribunals and ordinary courts the plaintiff should prove, apart from the existence of a legal interest, the wrongful act of the contracting authority (*faut de service*), the actual damage caused by that act and the existence of a causal link between the wrongful act and the damage suffered.

Both public and private law regulate the settlement of public procurement disputes in Luxembourg. The control of the award of public contracts (the act awarding them) relies on the jurisdiction of the *Conseil d'Etat*, which may annul on grounds of want of authority, infringement of essential procedural requirement, *ultra vires* and misuse of powers, the act or decision awarding a contract or any unilateral administrative act carried out under the award procedure. In principle, the *Conseil d'Etat* may suspend the execution of the contract or order any other appropriate interim measure. Damages resulting from a breach of the rules governing public procurement are under the jurisdiction of ordinary courts. Private law regulates state liability in public procurement as a quasi-tort[34] and action for damages before ordinary courts

---

[34] See Article 1382 of the Civil Code.

normally requires the prior annulment of the act awarding the contract by the *Conseil d'Etat*.

Under Greek law, all administrative disputes (disputes where one party is the state, legal or regional authorities and bodies governed by public law) fall under the jurisdiction of administrative tribunals and of the *Conseil d'Etat*. The latter also has unlimited jurisdiction to examine the legality of the act awarding the contracts. Thus, applying *la théorie de l'act détachable*, the *Conseil d'Etat* may annul the awarding (administrative) act of a contract, as it considers it an act separable from the contract itself. In such a case, an aggrieved participant in the tender may sue for damages before the administrative courts. He may also sue directly before ordinary (civil) courts,[35] seeking compensation and contesting the legality of the award at the same time, but in that case he will not be able to ask for the suspension of the latter. It should be noted that the power to annul the act awarding the contract is exclusively vested in the hands of the *Conseil d'Etat*.[36]

In Spain, review procedures for public procurement contracts are channelled through administrative and judicial routes. Under the former, the *Bureau of Supervision of Projects* is vested with the power to examine technical aspects in the award of the contract in question and to adjudicate possible disputes arising therein; in addition, the Intervention of the State, another administrative organ, deals with aspects concerning the financial control of the award, the formal legality of the contract and the decision awarding it. Furthermore, in the adjudication stage within the administrative review procedures, the *Mesa de Contratacio* (also an administrative organ) is empowered, upon request from one of the parties concerned, to pronounce on the validity of the offers, on the conditions for participation in the tender competition, and on the qualitative criteria for the selection of the tenderer to whom the contract has been awarded. It also has the power to make a provisional award of contracts based on the criterion of the best (lowest) price, and it may modify the conditions of the award in case of infringement of the law or in case of an abnormally low or disproportionate price with regard to the project. The lengthy administrative review proceedings constitute a requirement of admissibility in order to pursue judicial review at a later stage.[37] Judicial review denotes the involvement of Administrative Tribunals, where the dispute has not been settled through the administrative stage or in the case of a claim for

---

[35] In both cases the action will be based on Article 105 of the Introductory Law to the Civil Code, which lays down state liability (non-fault liability) for illegal actions performed by its organs in pursuit of the exercise of official authority.

[36] For a general introduction to the Hellenic Administrative Law, see the report of Stathopoulos in the FIDE Congress, op. cit.

[37] The latter must be lodged within two months of dismissal of the former.

damages. Under the former, the Tribunals have competence to declare the act awarding a public contract void, mainly on grounds of want of authority, failure to comply with procedural or substantive requirements, *ultra vires* and misuse of powers. What is interesting is that such a declaration results in the contract itself being rendered void. An action for damages must fulfil very strict requirements, as Spanish courts are very stringent in awarding compensation for damages which can be attributed to the state. Interim measures are available on request of the applicant in accordance with a separate procedure before the same forum.

In the Spanish legal system, actions before the courts may be lodged only after an administrative complaint to a superior authority, if there is one. The competent courts are the administrative courts. They may set aside the decisions taken by the awarding authority, and in particular decisions awarding contracts. Contrary to French and Belgian laws, the contract normally becomes void as a result of the fact that the decision to conclude it has been set aside. However, the administrative authority may decide, on the grounds of public interest, to continue with implementation of the contract.

Administrative complaints and actions for annulment do not have the effect of suspending the execution of the administrative decision at stake. However, interim measures may be granted both at the stage of the administrative review procedure and by the administrative court. In particular, the decisions of the awarding authority may be suspended. In cases where no other remedy is available that can correct the effects of the violation of public procurement rules, the court may also grant compensation for damages. Specific remedies rules have been provided for by the act on utilities procurement.[38] An administrative complaint must first be lodged before the administrative authority that is in charge of controlling the awarding entity (which may be an entity established under private law). Certain trends appear from the case-law published in the Supreme Court report and in law journals. Litigation is not rare in this field, but cases concerning award procedures are much less frequent than cases concerning disputes over the performance of public contracts.

Traditionally, the courts have been quite reluctant to grant interim measures. This is a serious problem, since the Spanish administrative court procedures can result in long delays. Actions often take between two and five years to reach a conclusion. Nevertheless, the application of the new Act on administrative courts, which is intended to make the adoption of interim measures easier, could lead Spanish courts to grant such measures more frequently in the future. The annulment of the decisions of the awarding authority is not in itself satisfactory for the complainant, especially when it

---

[38]   See Act 48/1998 on Utilities Procurement of December 1998.

takes place several years later. Actions for damages have so far been infrequently successful. In cases where damages are granted, they are usually equal to 6% of the amount of the bid. Such awards are not regarded as a sufficient incentive for bidders who are victims of a violation of the public procurement rules to go to court.

In Portugal, administrative courts have jurisdiction over matters concerning the validity, interpretation and annulment of the act which awards a public procurement contract. Portuguese law follows to a large extent the notion of *administrative act* which emanates from the French *droit administratif.* The relative importance of the awarding act is reflected also in the fact that it constitutes the most crucial stage in the public procurement process. The plaintiff may submit before administrative courts an application for annulment of the act awarding the contract, which is subject to an appeal before the same courts. It is also possible to lodge an action for damages before administrative courts, after the administrative law review process has been exhausted and the act awarding the relevant public contract has been found to be unlawful. Damages are in most cases nominal, to the extent that the courts award compensation only with respect to the exact amount the plaintiff has suffered as a result of the unlawful behaviour of the contracting authority. Substantive disputes arising out of a public contract between the successful tenderer and the contracting authority are the subject of the civil law jurisdiction. Interim relief in relation to the award of public contracts is in theory available to affected parties, although the administrative courts are often reluctant to award measures which have the effect of suspending an awarding act. Such reluctance is probably due to the relatively slow process of judicial review of the administrative act which awards a public contract and the need to avoid prejudicing the public interest.

In the Italian legal system, apart from the administrative redress available to aggrieved contractors, where the hierarchical superior authority is entitled to review the legality and substance of the act awarding a public contract, there are legal remedies available to aggrieved contractors before administrative and ordinary courts. The Italian system is interesting, as in cases where an injury caused by an administrative act relates to a right of the contractor or a third party, ordinary courts have jurisdiction; where, on the other hand, the dispute concerns the legality of the administrative act awarding the contract, then ordinary courts take over. Administrative courts have not only the power to suspend the award of the contract, by means of interim measure, but also to set aside it or any other administrative act performed in the course of the awarding procedure. Action for damages brought by the contractor or a third party against the contracting authority before ordinary courts is admissible only when a 'subjective' right is in breach. State responsibility embraces contractual and pre-contractual liability, but it is only for the successful tenderer who has been awarded the contract to seek remuneration. Unsuccessful tenderers are not entitled to pursue an action for damages as they have only a 'lawful interest' and not a 'subjective right'. Actions for damages before ordinary courts are allowed to proceed on condition of a previous delivery of judgment concerning the annulment of the act awarding the contract by an administrative court.

In the public procurement field, a distinction must be made between two phases, that is, the procedure for selecting the contractor and the execution of the contract once it has been awarded. Under Italian law, private citizens do not have unrestricted rights to bring cases against the government, but can only claim an interest in the government acting appropriately and in compliance with the law (what are known as 'legitimate interests'). From a judicial standpoint, this has always been a key distinction, and there are two different courts with jurisdiction in such cases, depending on whether citizens' individual rights or legitimate interests are concerned. In particular, Administrative Tribunals which handle appeals against illegal acts of government and thereby safeguard the legitimate interests of citizens, are organised on a regional basis. These administrative courts may not award compensation for damages (which is traditionally granted by ordinary courts and only for the infringement of plaintiffs' individual rights), but may only annul illegal acts.

Consequently, any matters that arise during the tendering phase are the jurisdiction of administrative courts since enterprises may only challenge government action on the basis of the defence of their legitimate interest. However, during the execution of the contract phase, the government is deemed to act as a normal private party, and is therefore liable, like any contracting party, if it fails to meet its contractual obligations.

As a result, in such cases claims are brought before the ordinary courts. With regard to public works contracts, an accelerated procedure has been introduced in Italy that has reduced the appeals process from 60 days to 30 days, from the time at which the appeal against the illegal act is lodged. The administrative court can then make an immediate ruling to suspend the act being appealed. Furthermore, under the influence of the Compliance Directives 89/665 and 92/13, an important innovation has recently been introduced by Legislative Decree 80/1998, which has given the administrative courts exclusive jurisdiction over all procedures for awarding contracts for public works, supplies and services related to the management of public services. Administrative courts can also award compensation for damages in these fields. In practice, appeals most often contest procedures for awarding contracts or calls for tenders and specifications that the parties concerned consider to be directly harmful to their legal positions. However, this field is continually changing, as is shown by a recent ruling of the Supreme Court of Appeal that allows damages to be awarded when parties' legitimate interests are harmed by an illegal act of government, thus overturning one of the most long-standing tenets of Italian law. There is also growing use of extra-judicial methods in the public procurement sector. These methods of resolving conflicts that arise during the execution of the contract generally consist of arbitration and in special cases of 'amicable agreements'. They undoubtedly make it possible to resolve conflicts more rapidly than through the ordinary courts, even though their cost is often considerable.

Under Danish law, there is no distinction between administrative and civil disputes in public procurement contracts. There are no administrative courts. The decision awarding a public procurement contract may be reviewed by a higher administrative authority. This sort of review is not a judicial one, but rather seeks the adjudication and conciliation of the dispute. The offended party or third parties (unsuccessful tenderers) may resort to ordinary courts seeking compensation for damage caused by a wrongful act of the authority awarding contracts. There are no statutory rules governing state liability but well-established judicial precedent regulates the issue. The plaintiff has the burden of proof as regards the wrongful act of the administration, the actual damage suffered and the causal link between the wrongful act and the damage. Compensation covers any economic loss caused by the fault of the contracting authorities, but the plaintiff's contribution (negligence) to that loss may reduce or exempt the state from an obligation to compensate.

A specific system for public procurement review has existed in Denmark[39] since 1995. The Public Procurement Review Board was established to implement the public procurement regime. The system allows complaints in the first instance to be brought before the normal courts or the Public Procurement Review Board which has been established as an independent entity by the Ministry of Industry and Trade. The decisions of the Board can be appealed to the normal courts. The Public Procurement Review Board is assisted by the Competition Board, which is part of the Ministry of Industry and Trade and is responsible for administering the law and acting as the secretariat to the Public Procurement Review Board.

The Public Procurement Review Board can decide on any alleged infringement of the Public Procurement Directives, including those concerning the utilities sector,[40] as well as the relevant Treaty provisions concerning, for

---

[39] See *Lovbekendtgoerelse nr.1166 af 20 December 1995 om Klagenaevnet for Udbud*. Detailed rules on the activities of the Board are contained in a Decree issued by the Minister of Trade and Industry – *Bekendtgoerelse nr. 26 af 23 Januar 1996 om Klagenaevnet for Udbud*.

[40] An important modification in this respect is that complaints regarding contracts involving the utility entities dealing with exploration of oil and gas fall outside the competence of PPB but can be lodged at a specific Commercial Court (*Soe- og Handelsretten*).

example, the free movement of goods. This means that the Board can review tenders below the thresholds defined in the Directives. The Public Procurement Review Board is composed of judges and independent experts and is headed by a judge. The status and procedures of the Board are similar to those of national courts with the possibility for both parties to submit written observations in support of their claims. Any person with an interest in a particular contract can lodge a complaint with the Public Procurement Review Board. This includes situations where the complaint is that a contract has been made without any tender procedure at all. The Competition Board and certain business organisations can also register complaints.

The Public Procurement Review Board can take all the types of decision foreseen in the Directives, including suspension of tender procedures and annulment of unlawful decisions of the contracting entity. Normal courts determine the effects of such decisions on the relation between parties in cases when a contract exists according to general Danish rules on contractual relationships. The Public Procurement Review Board cannot take decisions about damages, which is the responsibility of the courts. Since 1996 the Competition Board has dealt with approximately 100 cases annually. It can act on the basis of any complaint from any person and on its own initiative lodge complaints with the Public Procurement Review Board. The Board has no power of decision, but usually the contracting entity will comply with the Board's recommendations.

To ensure the application of Public Procurement Directives both at '*Bund*' and at '*Länder*' levels, Germany has enacted administrative instructions[41] that are legally binding by means of and through pertinent budgetary laws. Under the principle of legality of administration,[42] the state and local authorities are entitled to act on their own initiative where a violation of provisions of Public Procurement Directives occurs. Nationals and non-nationals (from other EC member states or non-EC member states) enjoy the same treatment, as a consequence of the principle of equal treatment laid down in the German Basic Law. Disputes concerning the award of public contracts fall under the jurisdiction of administrative control. The power of supervision over acts and decisions of the contracting authorities is based on similar principles at the *Bund* and *Länder* levels.[43] The organs finally responsible for the administration, the state and the *Länder*, exert their supervision over inferior authorities controlling the legality of acts awarding public contracts. In particular, they

---

[41]   '*Verdingungsordnung fur Leistungen- ausgenommen Bauleistungen* for public works and '*Verdingungsordnung fur Bauleistungen*' for public supplies contracts.
[42]   Article 20, paragraph 3 of the German Basic Law.
[43]   The constitutionally established right of organisation, Article 65, sentence 2 of the German Basic Law.

have powers to suspend the act awarding a public contract, to order new tendering procedures, to rescind the act that invites tenders for a public contract, even to invite tenders on their own initiative in cases where the contracting authority does not comply with the instructions given within a certain time. What is interesting is the fact that once the contract has been awarded, administrative control is no longer applicable. The award is considered to be the acceptance of the contractor's or the supplier's offer and according to principles of German Law, the contractor must not be burdened with the uncertainty of a potential cancellation of the contract due to the violation of rules by the contracting authority. Thus, aggrieved contractors may only apply for damages against public authorities before ordinary courts. Their claim requires a fault on the part of the contracting authority in concluding the contract or in its preparation – *culpa in contrahendo.*[44] The claim is based on the relationship of confidence, which resembles that of contract, arising between the contracting authority and the contractor by virtue of the invitation to tender. The amount of damages depends on the actual damage which the contractor can prove. The damage may be limited to the cost of taking part in the tendering process. This might be the case when the supervisory administrative authority cancels an illegitimate invitation for tender. On the other hand, if the contractor can prove that the contracting authority has illegally discriminated against him in awarding the contract to another contractor, then he is entitled to damages to the amount of his lost profits, on condition that he can substantiate that he would have been awarded the contract, had the contracting authority not discriminated. If the contracting authority holds a monopoly or a dominant position, the applicant who has been denied the award of the contract may base his claims for damages against the former also on the provisions of the 'Statute against Distortions of Trade' or on the 'Statute against Unfair Competition'. He may suspend the award process by requesting the court for an injunction.

By virtue of the Fourth Chapter of the Act against Restraints of Competition[45] review procedures that guarantee effective remedies for complaints against violations of the procurement rules have been established. The Act grants bidders the right to complain against infringements of the procurement rules during an award procedure, thus enforcing compliance with the procurement rules. Since 1 January 1999, 'Procurement Chambers' (*Vergabekammer*) have been in charge of deciding about complaints lodged in connection with an award procedure. This (independent) administrative review body is an integral part of the German Federal Cartel Office

---

[44] See Paragraph 242 of the Civil Codebook.
[45] See *Gesetz gegen Wettbewerbsbeschränkungen* of 26 August 1998, Federal Gazette (*Bundesgesetzblatt*) 1998, I, p. 2512.

(*Bundeskartellamt*). It is also possible that other parties, in particular other bidders, may formally participate in the proceedings. The parties involved have standing to appeal against the Procurement Chamber's decision. A procedure for judicial review of the Chamber's decisions was introduced by the Act. New bodies, the 'Procurement Senates' (*Vergabesenate*), were established at the level of the Higher Court of Appeals (*Oberlandesgericht*). These senates form part of the ordinary courts in Germany.

As Germany is a federal state, review bodies have to be established at both the federal level (that is, at the Federal Cartel Office) and the state level. The 16 German states have chosen very different solutions for the establishment of Procurement Chambers. The respective Higher Court of Appeals in the state is in charge of appeals. The remedies against an infringement of the procurement rules have proved to be very efficient since the award procedure is suspended during the proceedings in the Procurement Chamber and, if the complainant is successful, also during the proceeding in the Higher Court of Appeals. Both the Procurement Chambers and the Higher Court of Appeals are bound by very strict time limits in order to guarantee a speedy resolution of procurement disputes. The Procurement Chambers have to decide within five weeks after a complaint has been lodged. On the basis of the information available, it appears that such time limits have been observed in only a very few cases. The Higher Court of Appeals has also to make a decision within a reasonable period but this period is not precisely defined in law.

In the Netherlands, the judicial review of the award of public contracts is subject to the control of civil courts and also to arbitration. Supplies and services contracts are under the jurisdiction of ordinary courts, whereas public works contracts are channelled through a special institution (*Raad van Arbitrage*).[46] The appropriate forum for judicial control of public procurement is determined by virtue of the laws implementing the relevant Directives. In practice, the legal *forum* which handles the majority of public procurement disputes is the *Raad van Arbitrage*, as the laws implementing the Directives contain arbitral clauses under which the jurisdiction of civil courts is secondary. Both the civil courts and the *Raad van Arbitrage* are competent in awarding damages to aggrieved tenderers, on condition that the applicant can prove that he would have won the contract.

By virtue of a Resolution on public procurement,[47] the Dutch legal system entrusted public procurement compliance at domestic level to the Dutch Court

---

[46] See the report of Glazener, Pijnacker Hordijk and van der Riet in the FIDE Congress, op. cit.

[47] See *Besluit overheidsaanschaffingen* of 4 June 1993 on public procurement of goods, works and services and *Besluit aanbestedingen Nutssector* on public procurement in the utilities sectors of 6 April 1993.

of Justice and the Council of Arbitration (the latter for remedies concerning works). Interim measures such as suspension of the tendering procedure are handled by the Dutch Court of Justice through urgent procedures or injunctive relief (*spoedprocedure, kortgeding*). When arbitration is required, especially in construction projects, the Dutch system offers a form of accelerated arbitration (*spoed arbitrage*). Damage awards vary between 6% and 17% of the total contract value. The party claiming has to prove that it suffered genuine damage and to provide evidence that it had a good chance of winning the contract had the contracting authority followed the provisions of the Public Procurement Directives.

In the United Kingdom, an aggrieved contractor could initiate judicial review proceedings against a contracting authority under public law or seek redress through private actions, in a case where there has been a breach of a statutory duty. In addition to the remedies which have been created under the statutory instruments implementing the Directives specifically for enforcing the procurement rules, an aggrieved contractor may also make use of the more general remedies which may be used in order to ensure that public bodies act lawfully.

Remedies which are required to be available under the Compliance Directive in the United Kingdom include: (i) provision for the court to 'set aside' a decision or action which is in breach of the Regulations. The effect of an order of set aside will be that the decision or action has no legal effect and cannot be acted upon. For example, if the government makes an award decision in breach of the Regulations, and that award decision is set aside, the government may not go ahead and conclude a contract with the selected firm, but must take the award decision again in a lawful manner; (ii) provision that the court may order the contracting authority to amend any document. Thus if a contract document contains unlawful specifications, for example, the court may order the authority to amend them. This is a useful power: it allows a firm effectively to ensure documents are amended without the need to strike down the whole call for tenders; (iii) finally, provision that a remedy in damages must be available to disappointed contractors who suffer loss.

Among the main remedies available in an action for judicial review are *certiorari, prohibition* and *mandamus*. The first will annul with retrospective effect, an order or decision of a person or a body of persons having legal authority to determine questions affecting the rights of subjects; the second has a prospective effect, prohibiting an administrative authority from acting either at all or in the way it proposes; the latter is an order requiring a public body to do something on condition that the applicant has first called on it unsuccessfully to do its duty.

The right of damages under judicial review is not an independent remedy. What is peculiar in comparison with continental legal systems is that the High

Court or the Court of Appeal must be satisfied that the claim for damages before it fulfils all the conditions in order to be successful under private law; that means the breach of a statutory duty. The award of damages is at the discretion of the court and when the applicant (aggrieved contractor) claims damages alternatively (in a case where the application for annulment of the act awarding the contract is dismissed), the court may order the continuation of proceedings as if they had begun by writ. Action for damages in tort represents the private way of judicial redress of public procurement cases in the United Kingdom. Such actions can be based on breach of statutory duty or negligence. The plaintiff is entitled to compensation for the loss he suffered, on condition that he can prove that the tort has caused his loss.

In Ireland, the appropriate *forum* for the review of public procurement cases is the High Court, which has general jurisdiction over administrative, civil or criminal cases. The Irish legal system does not provide for an administrative law forum. However, a number of *ad hoc* administrative tribunals have been established and are under the supervision of the High Court. Judicial remedies available to aggrieved contractors in public procurement cases before the High Court include the general public law remedies in the form of *certiorari, prohibition* and *mandamus*. Through these remedies the Court has the power to quash unlawful administrative decisions (practically the same results with setting aside a decision under the Compliance Directive), to prevent an unlawful decision being made, and to order a decision to be taken in a lawful manner. The general remedies of *declaration*, where the Court simply declares the legal position in the case before it, and *injunction* are also available. The challenge of an unlawful administrative act through the above public law remedies requires prior application for judicial review. However, declarations and injunctions are also available in plenary proceedings. Damages may be sought by the applicant on grounds of deliberate breach of public law rules by virtue of the tort of misfeasance in public office.[48]

The Swedish legal system has established review procedures for both dimensional (those with values above the thresholds stipulated by the Directives) and sub-dimensional (those with values below the thresholds stipulated by the Directives) public procurement contracts. Prior to the conclusion of a public procurement contract, administrative courts are responsible for dealing with public procurement cases. The County Administrative Court is a judicial body dealing with issues of public law and has jurisdiction to hear disputes on public procurement. The County Court may decide to suspend a tender proceeding until the complaint has been reviewed by the court and a final decision taken. The County Court will abstain from suspending the

---

[48]   See the report of Mary Robinson in the FIDE Congress, op. cit.

proceedings if the negative consequences of such a decision are judged to be greater than the advantages, that is, the damage to the procuring entity is greater than the advantage to the complainant. The County Court may decide to cancel the tender proceedings and order re-tendering. It may also order the correction by the contracting entity of deficiencies found in the tender proceedings. In the case of a complaint procedure brought against a public utility, the decision may also include a fine.

A decision of the County Court may be challenged in higher administrative courts and in such cases the tender proceeding will be suspended until the court takes its final decision. Before contract signing, there are no time limits for filing a complaint, nor is there any maximum period of time for the County Court or higher courts to finalise the complaint review. After the contract is signed, the only remaining remedy available to aggrieved contractors is to request damages in an ordinary (civil) court. Such a request must be filed within one year of signing the contract. To be successful in court, the supplier must prove not only that the contracting entity acted unlawfully but also that the supplier in question would have been awarded the contract if the tender proceedings had been carried out lawfully. If the supplier succeeds in proving his case, he is entitled to compensation for loss incurred.

The Award of Damages at National Level in Breach of European Law

In the absence of specific remedies available to individuals before national courts in order to rectify infringements of Community law, two questions arise with respect to the award of damages suffered by individuals as a result of the state's violation of Community law. The first question is whether an infringement of a directly effective primary or secondary Community provision may be used by individuals before national courts as grounds for an action for damages against the state. The second question approaches the problem from a different perspective; if the infringed provision does not produce a direct effect, is, then, the state liable to compensate individuals who have suffered as a result of its infringement or of its wrongful implementation of Community law?

In public procurement cases, Article 30 EC establishing the free movement of goods and Article 52 concerning the right of establishment, produce a direct effect.[49] Also, the European Court of Justice has recognised that specific (substantive) provisions of the relevant Directives produce a direct effect. There are also cases in which national courts have awarded compensation to

---

[49]   This occurred at the end of the transitional period (31/12/69); see also cases 2/74, *Reyners v. Belgian State*, [1974] ECR 631 and 33/74, *Van Bisbergen v. Bestuur van de Bedrijfsvereninging voor de Metaalinijverheid*, [1974] ECR 1299.

individuals who suffered damages due to a mere breach of Community law.[50]
More intriguing are those cases before national courts where infringement of
Community law has already been pronounced directly by the European Court
of Justice through a proceeding under Article 169 EC. In those cases, national
courts are confronted with national legislation, the incompatibility of which
with Community law has been unequivocally and authoritatively declared by
the Court. Is the existence of incompatible national legislation grounds for an
action for damages before national courts?

The whole matter goes further to question whether the European Court of
Justice may require the courts of the member states to make declarations of
invalidity in respect of national legislation found to infringe Community law
or to make declaration of awards of damages to the victims. By virtue of
Article 171 EC Treaty, the Court said in the *Waterkeyn* case[51] that national
courts are bound to draw the '*necessary inferences*' from judgments under
Article 169 EC. What is meant by this term is not clear. In the *Waterkeyn* case,
the Court did not expressly require national courts to declare invalid a national
law or an administrative rule that violates directly effective primary or
secondary Community legislation. On the other hand, there is a strong suggestion, in the same case, that such measures should be considered invalid.

The assertion of a national rule that violates Community law as valid, probably justified by the public interest, would leave individuals with the possibility of being compensated only through judicial review based on the system of
non-fault liability, where a wrongful act is not required. This appears contrary
to the principles of good faith and legitimate expectation and beyond the spirit
of the Treaty.[52] On the other hand, if national courts recognise the unlawful
nature of an infringement of Community law as such, they should, normally,
open the door to compensation on the basis of fault.

With respect to the second question, that of the possibility of relying upon
a provision of Community law that does not have a direct effect, as grounds
for an action for damages against the state before national courts, the Court in
one of its most important recent judgments[53] answered in the affirmative. The

---

50   See case C-213/89, *The Queen v. Minister of Agriculture, Fisheries and Food*,
[1990] ECR I-2433; also case C-14/68, *Wilhem v. Bundeskartellampt*, [1969] ECR 1 at
27; case 78/70, *Deutsche Grammophon GmbH v. Metro-SB Grossmarkte GmbH*,
[1971] ECR 1 at 31; case 44/84, *Hurd v. Jones*, [1986] ECR 29.
51   See cases 314–316/81 & 82, *Procureur de la République et al. v. Waterkeyn*,
[1982] ECR 4337.
52   All the above-mentioned principles, legal certainty, legitimate expectation,
Community loyalty and Community solidarity are inherent in the fundamental provision of Article 5 EC.
53   Judgment on the joint cases 6/90 and 9/90 (*Francovich and Bonifaci v. Italian
Republic*).

cases referred to it concerned the non-implementation by Italy of a Directive on the protection of employees in the event of the insolvency of their employer and reached the Court through a reference under Article 177 EC. The questions the Court faced, at the request of national courts, were (i) whether provisions of the Directive in question were capable of producing direct effect, thus being relied upon by individuals and (ii) the above being answered in the negative, whether individuals had a right to receive compensation from the member state for the negative effects of its failure to implement the Directive. The Court found that the provisions of the Directive were not sufficiently clear, precise and unconditional to produce a direct effect, thus answering the first question in the negative. In considering whether an individual has a right to be compensated by a state that has failed to implement a Directive, the Court held that, in principle, an individual is entitled to compensation in such circumstances.[54] In order to find state liability, it relied on Article 5 of the EC Treaty, the principle of Community loyalty and solidarity, which provides that member states are under an obligation to take all the necessary measures to ensure that Community law is properly applied. It has been held by the Court[55] that Article 5 EC (especially its negative obligation) is capable of producing a direct effect, but only in conjunction with other substantive Treaty provisions or in circumstances in which this obligation is further developed in implementing legislation or through case-law. Based on the above considerations, as well as on the doctrine of the useful effect (*effet utile*) of Community rules and the rights being acknowledged therein, and which would be weakened if individuals were not provided with the possibility of compensation in the case of their rights being affected by a violation of Community law by a member state, the Court proceeded further and examined the specific conditions that should be met in order for an individual suffering damages to be entitled to compensation by the defaulting state.

Three conditions should be fulfilled: first, the result required by the Directive must involve the granting of rights to individuals; secondly, these rights must be identifiable on the basis of the provisions of the Directive and thirdly, there must be a clear causal link between the breach of its obligations by the member state and the damage suffered by the individual concerned. The above conditions being met, then an individual may benefit from a right to compensation at national level based on Community law which is not directly effective. The amount of compensation payable should be determined by

---

54   See also case C-213/89, *The Queen v. Minister of Agriculture, Fisheries and Food*, [1990] ECR I-2433.

55   See case C-14/68, *Wilhem v. Bundeskartellampt*, [1969] ECR 1 at 27; case 78/70, *Deutsche Grammophon GmbH v. Metro-SB Grossmarkte GmbH* [1971] ECR 1 at 31; case C-44/84, *Hurd v. Jones*, [1986] ECR 29.

national courts in accordance with relevant domestic legislation. The *Francovich* judgment was a landmark decision with respect to state liability under Community law. Individuals may rely upon Community law which does not produce direct effect before their national courts. The European Court of Justice laid down the required conditions for the admissibility of an action for damages before national courts submitted by an individual claiming damages against a member state which has failed to implement a Directive, hereby injuring a right conferred therein. How strict the national courts will be when confronted with such actions remains to be seen. Obviously, harmonisation of domestic provisions on the award of compensation will be required.

What appears to be the most important element is the importance that is given to the interest of individuals. According to the judgment of the Court in the *Francovich* case,[56] the individual must be granted rights conferred by the Directive itself. This means that member states and their competent national authorities must not have any discretion in determining the content and extent of such rights. Here, it should be recalled that lack of discretion in the hands of a member state is perhaps the most fundamental condition for the direct effect of provisions of Directives. Thus, the relevant provisions of the Directive should be close to producing direct effect, being deprived of it due to their conditionality or to their insufficient clarity and precision.

The whole issue came to be tested in 1993, when the Divisional Court of the Queen's Bench Division of the Supreme Court of England and Wales made a reference to the European Court of Justice on the interpretation of Directive 90/531 concerning procurement procedures in the utilities. The national case[57] was concerned with the definition of the relevant provision of the Directive relating to the application of procurement rules to entities operating in the telecommunication sector. Also a request was made for clarification of the possibility of the award of damages to individuals in case of wrongful implementation of the relevant provision by member states. In the preliminary ruling, the European Court of Justice elucidated the member states' obligation to award damages to individuals who suffered from wrongful implementation of Directives. The Court held that the conditions laid down in the *Brasserie du Pêcheur* and *Factortame* cases[58] concerning state liability applied where a member state had incorrectly implemented a Directive. However, in this case

---

[56]   See joint cases, C-6/90 and 9/90, *Francovich and Bonifaci v. Italian Republic*, [1993] ECR 61.

[57]   See case C-392/93, *The Queen and HM Treasury, ex parte British Telecommunications PLC*, OJ 1993 C 287/6.

[58]   See cases C-46 & 48/93, *Brasserie du Pêcheur SA v. Germany, Regina v. Secretary of State for Transport, ex parte Factortame LTD*, 5 March 1996, [1996] 1 CMLR 889.

the breach of Community law was not sufficiently serious, as the relevant provision of the Utilities Directive (Article 8(1)) was imprecisely worded and reasonably capable of bearing the interpretation given to it by the UK government in good faith, no guidance had been available from previous case-law as to the interpretation of the relevant provision, and the Commission had not raised the matter when the national relevant legislation was adopted. The Court therefore held that no liability could be attributed to the state in question.

Since many provisions of the Public Procurement Directives are deemed to produce a direct effect, the question of whether an infringement of them can be considered as sufficient grounds for an action for damages at national level is combined with the duty of national courts to afford an effective protection mechanism in the form of remedies for the protection of rights conferred on individuals by directly effective Community law.

16. Enforcement of public procurement rules

ENFORCEMENT OF PUBLIC PROCUREMENT RULES AT EUROPEAN LEVEL

The implementation of public procurement Directives by member states through the enactment of national legislation is subject to judicial control at Community level. The European Commission, by virtue of Article 226 EC may initiate proceedings, on its own initiative[1] or in response to a complaint, against a defaulting member state for failure to fulfil its obligations under the Treaty. Existence of specific legal interest is not required[2] as a condition of the admissibility of the action, since it is in the general interest of the Commission to observe, supervise and ensure the correct application of Community law.

Even where the national litigation (*Farmaindustria v. Consejeria de salud de la Junta de Andalucia*)[3] was withdrawn, the Commission proceeded to launch an action against Spain for failure to comply with the provisions of the Public Supplies Directive 77/62, on the basis of the incompatibility with the principles and provisions of public procurement law of a framework agreement entered into by the Spanish public authorities and the national association of pharmaceutical companies (*Farmaindustria*), under which are prices and other terms and conditions governing the direct purchase of pharmaceutical products destined for social security institutions and the indirect purchase of such products for institutions non-related to social security.

The enactment of the Remedies Directives[4] has introduced a special procedure of a centralised nature, the so-called *correction procedure*. Under the Remedies Directives, there is an opportunity for the European Commission to

---

[1] Individuals cannot force the Commission to bring a state before the Court under the Article 169 EC procedure, case C-48/65, *Alfons Luttucke GmbH v. Commission*, [1966] ECR 19.

[2] See case C-167/73, *Commission v. France*, [1974] ECR 359.

[3] See case C-179/89, *Farmaindustria v. Consejeria de salud de la Junta de Andalucia*, [1989] OJ C 160/10.

[4] See the Public Works and Public Supplies Compliance Directive 89/665, OJ 1989 L 395, and the Utilities Compliance Directive 92/13, OJ 1992 L 76/7.

intervene in cases where it feels there has been a breach of the procurement rules under the provisions laid out in Article 3 of the public sector Remedies Directive and Article 8 of the utilities Remedies Directive. However, as far as the public sector Compliance Directive is concerned, the relevant provision applies only where there appears to have been a breach of the rules relating to contracts covered by the public works Directive (93/37/EC) and the public supplies Directive (93/36/EC). There seems to be nothing in the Public Services Directive to make a particular provision applicable to public services contracts, although the rest of the Remedies Directive applies to award procedures under the Services Directive, as well as to those covered by the Public Works and Supplies Directives. This was, apparently, due to an oversight in the drafting stages and was not intentional. The oversight in relation to public sector services is not, however, important, since the provision adds nothing to the powers which the Commission has already had under Article 169 EC. In effect, the corrective procedure may be invoked whenever the Commission considers that there has been a *clear and manifest* breach of the public procurement law. When the procedure is invoked, the Commission must notify both the relevant state and the contracting authority of the reasons which have led it to this conclusion, and request that the infringement be corrected (Article 3 (2)). The member state concerned must reply within 21 days of receipt of notification, and must either confirm that the infringement has been corrected or give an explanation as to why no correction has been made (unless the award procedure has already been suspended, in which case it is simply required to notify the Commission of this). Failure by a member state to give a reply which is to the satisfaction of the Commission does not attract any specific sanctions under Article 3, nor does the Commission enjoy any special powers where this 'corrective mechanism' is invoked. It was originally proposed that the Commission should be able to suspend the relevant award procedure on its own initiative, but the proposal was dropped because of opposition from the member states. Thus, if a satisfactory reply is not received, the Commission may initiate proceedings under Article 226 EC in the usual way. It is the Commission's practice to treat a notification of a breach given under the Article 3 procedure as a 'letter of infringement' for the purpose of the Article 226 EC procedure. If the member state does not give a satisfactory reply within the 21 day period stated in Article 3, a reasoned opinion will be issued on expiry of that period. It is submitted that 21 days is a 'reasonable' period for a state to prepare a response, and that the Commission's practice in this respect is consistent with the requirements of Article 226 EC. The effect of the corrective procedure under the Remedies Directives appears to demonstrate in an official manner that a member state is in breach of the law whether it provides a satisfactory reply or not. The corrective procedure does not in practice facilitate the powers of the Commission to effectively enforce public procurement law.

Proceedings before the European Court of Justice

The European Commission has an important role to play in ensuring that the
public procurement rules are complied with and enforced, and positively encour-
ages complaints from aggrieved undertakings. In practice, the Commission
follows all genuine complaints with the member state concerned, in an attempt
to negotiate an amicable and satisfactory solution. A complaint to the
Commission is, thus, always a potentially useful avenue of redress for an
aggrieved contractor. In those cases where no satisfactory solution can be
reached, the Commission may, as a last resort, consider bringing compliance
proceedings before the European Court of Justice, under the provisions of
Article 226 EC. Proceedings are brought against member states as such, and not
against the particular contracting authorities which are responsible for the
breach. Thus, states are not only held responsible for breaches of Community
law committed by the central or local government but also for breaches by other
public authorities and bodies over which they exercise a certain degree of
control. Based on the Court's case-law, it appears likely that the state will be held
responsible under Article 226 EC for the award procedures of bodies which are
defined as 'contracting authorities' for the purposes of the Public Procurement
Directives, since these are all bodies which have sufficient connection with
central authority for that authority to be held accountable for all their activities.

However, it may be that the state will not be held accountable for all those
bodies which are caught as 'contracting authorities' under the Utilities
Directive.[5] In particular, in many member states entities operating in the
telecommunications, energy, water and transport sectors, which have been
privatised, may have insufficient connection with the state. A leading case
which has defined the ambit of the state from a functional perspective is *Foster
v. British Gas*,[6] in which the European Court of Justice ruled that a Directive
capable of having direct effect could be invoked against a body which is
subject to the *control* of the state and has been delegated special powers. The
House of Lords then held that this applied to the British Gas Corporation
(publicly controlled entity), the predecessor of British Gas (privatised utility).
However, it is not clear that the privatised utilities could be covered by the
Foster principle,[7] thus state accountability under the compliance proceedings
of Article 169 EC (now Article 226 EC) could not embrace privatised enterprises.[8] Nevertheless, it may be pointed out that in those cases where the state

---

5   See Directive 93/38 EC.
6   See case *Foster v. British Gas*, [1990] ECR-1313.
7   See Trepte, *Public Procurement in the EC*, CCH Europe, 1993, pp. 197–8.
8   This was the view of Advocate-General Lenz in case C-247/89, *Commission
v. Portugal*, [1991] ECR I 3659.

is not generally held responsible for the activities of a contracting authority, the state may be held accountable where it exercises some specific control (for example, auditing, regulation) over the contractual activities of the entity concerned.

Interim Measures before the European Court of Justice

The postponement of a particular procurement procedure leading to the award of a public contract or the postponement of the performance of the contract after an award is made can be sought by obtaining an order through interim measures, until the substantial or the procedural disputes have been finally settled. Interim measures refer to the case where aggrieved tenderers challenge the legality of the selection or the award stages of public procurement and wish to delay the process in order to avoid damage. Interim measures are very important legal remedies in public procurement cases. Where contracting authorities refuse to delay the award procedure and no interim relief is available, by the time the substantive or procedural matter has been finally determined by national courts or by the Court, it is likely that the contract will have been finalised. If this is the case, then in practice it would not be possible to reopen the award procedure, and an action for damages would generally be the only remedy available to those who have been prejudiced by the breach.[9] Perhaps even more important than the outcome in a particular case, the availability of interim relief is also likely to act as an important deterrent to a breach of the rules, possibly more than any award of damages or any financial penalty. Although the availability of interim measures may be more important in the context of national review procedures than in the context of procedures before the European Court of Justice, since the prospect of an action under Article 226 EC would seem much more remote a possibility than a national review action, the overall thrust of interim measures at a centralised level appears as an effective *modus* of judicial control in public procurement.

On application by the European Commission the Court may grant interim measures under a general power which is found in Article 186 EC. The detailed rules governing the application are set out in Articles 83–8 of the Rules of Procedure of the European Court of Justice. Applications are made to the President of the Court, who may hear the matter himself or refer it to the Court. However, it is not possible for the Commission to apply for interim relief until Article 226 EC proceedings have actually been instituted before the

---

[9] This is certainly likely to happen in the context of proceedings before the Court of Justice, where the average length of proceedings for cases decided in 1991 was 24.2 months. See Proceedings of the Court of Justice and of the Court of First Instance of the European Communities No. 23191, 30 January 1992.

Court. This is arguably implicit in Article 186 EC, and is stated in Article 83(2) of the Rules of Procedure, which permits an application only if made by a party to a case before the European Court.

It should be maintained that the Commission must follow certain formal requirements before compliance proceedings under Article 169 EC can be instituted, which are concerned notably with providing an opportunity for the state concerned to dispute the allegations made and to redress any breach. There might be some delay between observation of the breach, and commencement of proceedings and the opportunity to obtain interim relief.

It has been suggested that this delay might cause considerable problems, to the extent that contracting authorities might rush to conclude a contract before interim relief could be sought to suspend the award procedure, and in this way make it difficult for the Court to affect the outcome of the procedure. It was partly in response to this fear that a proposal was originally made in the Compliance Directive to allow the Commission to suspend the procedure of its own motion when a breach appeared to be *clear* and *manifest*; but the suggestion was eventually dropped. That fear was based on the assumption that the Court might not consider itself to have the power to prevent the performance of a contract once it had actually been concluded. It now seems, however, that this fear was groundless, since the Court does indeed have the power to suspend the implementation and performance of a concluded contract. This was accepted by the Court in the *Lottmatica* case.[10] This case concerned the award by the Italian government of a concession contract for the establishment and operation of a computerised lottery system. Participation in the competition was limited to firms (or groups of firms) which had a majority of their shares in Italian public ownership, which condition the Commission contended contravened Articles 52 and 59 EC. It was also alleged that there had been a breach of Article 30 EC, and of some of the provisions of the Supplies Directive. Article 169 EC (now Article 226 EC) proceedings were instituted, and interim relief sought under Article 186 EC. At the relevant time the award decision by the contracting authorities had already been made, and it seems that the contract might actually have been entered into. The application for interim relief thus requested not simply the suspension of the award procedure, but also suspension of (i) the legal effects of the Ministerial Decree awarding the contract and also (ii) the legal effects of *any contract actually concluded*. This relief was granted by the President in the order of 31 January (a later application to have the order discharged was rejected on 12 June 1992). Thus the Court was prepared to order the parties to suspend the execution of an actual contract. It is suggested that this decision also seems to indi-

---

10   See case C-272/91R, orders of 31 January 1992 and 12 June 1992.

cate that a public contract would be required to be set aside if the action is successful at the final hearing concerning the substantive requirements of the alleged breach. If this appears to be the case, the inevitable delay between the opening of negotiations over an alleged breach (initiation of compliance procedures) and any application to suspend the award procedure (interim measures) would not be of much practical importance, if the power to set aside an illegally awarded public contract, either at the interim relief stage or at the substantive stage, is vested in the Court of Justice.

However, interim relief is not given automatically in every case. There are a number of conditions which must be met. First, the applicant must establish a *prima-facie* case, which means that the application should not be '*manifestly without foundation*'. It must then be shown that the need for measures is 'urgent'. A second condition will be satisfied when it can be shown that interim measures are needed to prevent '*serious and irreparable*' damage to the applicant. There is some doubt over whether, in the case of actions brought by the Commission, it is necessary in order to meet this requirement to show some specific and concrete damage to Community interests, or whether it is sufficient that there is a *prima-facie* breach of Community law, the effects of which are irreversible. In public procurement cases it will often be difficult to show any concrete effect on the competitive market structure brought about by a breach of the law which relates merely to an isolated award procedure. However, specific and concrete damage to Community interests can be demonstrated by serious and irreparable injury to tenderers interested in the particular contract. Although third party interests cannot, in principle, be taken into account in applications for interim measures, this is permissible where the European Commission is the applicant, as it represents all affected interests in the Community.[11] This approach, however, raises the question of whether the damage to interested parties is indeed irreparable, given the availability of remedies for the award of damages before national courts. In the three cases concerning interim measures before it, the Court did not make clear the basis for its decision in this respect – whether it relied on damage to individual contractors, or simply took the view that it is appropriate to award interim measures in order to prevent any irreversible breach of Community law.[12]

Another important consideration for the award of interim measures is the '*balance of interests*' of the relevant parties. This condition requires the Court to examine the merits of the case against any injury which would be caused by an award of interim measures and in particular the possible harm to the public interest which would be caused by the delay to the procurement of goods,

---

[11] See case 61/77R, *Commission v. Ireland*, [1977] ECR 1411.
[12] See case 45/87R, *Commission v. Ireland*, [1987] ECR 1369; and case 194/88R, *Commission v. Italy*, [1988] ECR 5647.

works or services in question. Balancing the interests of the relevant parties in a public procurement case appears to be a difficult exercise, as the hierarchical classification of the interests in question would determine the outcome of the interim relief proceedings.

On the one hand, the economic interests of a tenderer or a number of tenderers which might be prejudiced by the unlawful behaviour of a contracting authority could be protected by recourse to decentralised judicial control, in the sense that aggrieved contractors may generally obtain damages in actions before national courts or some sort of interim relief, as the case may be. On this side of the balance, the adverse effects arising from the violation of Community law should also be added. On the other hand, every public procurement project serves the public interest and the possible suspension of its award or the set aside of the particular contract could cause unnecessary delays which may inevitably have an effect upon public interest aspects such as public health, public safety, the protection of the environment.

Balancing, on the one hand, individual economic interest damaged by breaches of Community law against the general public interest potentially harmed by delays in the provision of public service has revealed the priorities of European institutions, particularly the European Court of Justice, in the process of the integration of the Community. The reluctance of some member states to recognise the relative importance of individual interests harmed through violations of European law was reflected in the early case-law of the European Court of Justice. In the *Dundalk* pipeline case,[13] which concerned the award of a contract for the construction of a water pipeline, although interim relief was initially granted in order to assess the situation, at a later stage, the Court refused the suspension of the contract on the basis of a possible threat to public health and safety caused by the shortage of water and the potential delay of the project. Along the same lines, in an earlier case,[14] the Court was also reluctant to delay the award of a construction project on the grounds of public interest. The case concerned an Ethiopian government contract for the construction of a hydro-electric dam, which was subject to the supervision of the Commission under the terms of the Lomé Convention. One of the aggrieved tenderers sought interim measures against the Commission in an attempt to secure the suspension of the procedure. Interim relief was refused by the Court on the basis that delays in the award procedures would inevitably reflect upon the conclusion of the contract and the public interest would be prejudiced as a result. In both cases where interim measures were refused, the Court emphasised the potential damage to the public interest

---

13   See case C-45/87, *Commission v. Ireland*, [1988] ECR 4929.
14   See case 118/83R, *CMC Co-operativa Muratori e Cementisti v. Commission*, [1983] ECR 2583.

which would be caused by delays in public procurement and that counter-balanced any adverse effects of Community Law violations on individual economic interests and the principles stipulated in the Treaties.

However, the balancing exercise between individual economic interests and public interest at large revealed a completely different dimension in two cases, where a refusal of interim relief on the grounds of public interest is likely to be the exception rather than the rule. The first case is *Commission v. Italy (La Spezia)*,[15] which concerned a contract for the renovation of a waste disposal plant. The Court awarded interim measures despite acceptance of the fact that damage to both public health and the environment might result from the delay. The differentiating factor which distinguishes this case from *Dundalk* was that the urgency of the renovations was due to the fault of the contracting authorities themselves in not acting earlier on the matter, although it might be that the Court would normally refuse interim measures in cases where there is no fault by contracting authorities and there is an immediate and serious threat to public health. However, in this case the Court prioritised the individual economic interests and the violation of Community procurement law over the possible prejudice to the public interest as a result of delays in the procurement process. The Court is not only the guardian of the public interest of the subjects of European Law, but also, and more importantly, it is the guarantor of the success in the European Integration process. *La Spezia* certainly showed the commitment of European Institutions to the principles and rule of public sector integration and could be seen to pave the way for interim relief where the prejudice to public interest is less serious, even when there is no fault on the part of the contracting authority. As was noted above, relief has now also been given in the case *Commission v. Italy* (Lottomatica)[16]. In this case Italy argued that the measures requested should be refused on the balance of interests because of, first, the loss of revenue which the government would suffer and, second, the fact that delay to the computerised lottery system would delay the government's fight against illegal gambling schemes. However, these arguments were quickly dismissed by the Court on the basis that the interests of the Community should prevail over those of member states. *Lottomatica* seems to have redefined the concept of public interest in applications for interim measures relating to public procurement projects to an extent that the concept should be narrowly construed.

The spirit of *Dundalk* returned in interim measures litigation in the *Wallonia* case, interestingly after the completion of the internal market. The Commission initiated interim measures against Belgium[17] under Article 185

---

[15] See case 194/88R, *Commission v. Italy*, [1988] ECR 4547.
[16] See case 272/91R, *Commission v. Italy*, order of 12 June 1992.
[17] See case C 87/94R, *Commission v. Belgium*, order of 22 April 1994.

EC in order to suspend the award of a contract relating to the purchase of buses for public transport in Wallonia. The Commission had already opened proceedings under Article 169 EC (now Article 226 EC) against Belgium for infringement of the Utilities Directive 90/531, particularly the selection of tender offers and their evaluation. The Commission argued that interim measures with suspension of the award procedures were justified by conditions of manifest urgency dictated by the possibility of serious and irreparable damage to an aggrieved tenderer. The Court, in balancing the interest of the parties in question, ruled that the performance and completion of the contract should take precedence over potential economic damage, on the grounds of public interest. The contract concerned with the purchase and operation of new buses by a transport authority and delays in its execution could seriously harm the lives of individual commuters who rely on the modernisation of the transport fleet. The President of the Court refused the interim measures requested.

The Consequences of a Judgment by the Court of Justice

Compliance procedures before the European Court of Justice lack an enforcement character to the extent that the Court only pronounces on the failure of the defaulting member state to comply with Community law, although as a result of the Maastricht Treaty, there is the possibility of periodic fines of a dissuasive character imposed on a member state which is in default of the Court's judgment. The nature of the Court's judgment is to give the state in question the opportunity to take all the necessary measures to avoid future violations, rather than penalise it for the particular breach. Unfortunately, the compliance procedure under Article 226 EC represents a rather soft approach to monitoring the correct application of and adherence to Community law, when it comes to member states' infringement of the spirit and the letter of the Treaties. A mere declaration of a member state's inability to comply with its obligations apparently does not create the right level of confidence in the centralised judicial control system nor does it reflect the degree of commitment by European institutions in the European integration process. Failure by a member state to take into account the outcome of compliance procedures may bring an action under Article 228 EC, where the member state concerned comes under an obligation to take all the necessary measures to comply with the judgment. Here again, the Court's decision has a declaratory character and no specific enforcement measures are attached to it.

In public procurement cases, the European Commission has instigated compliance procedures in order to have the Court declare the failure of a member state to align general legal measures or specific administrative practices with primary and secondary Community law relevant to public procurement. It follows that after the Court's judgment, and under Article 228 EC, there is a concrete obligation imposed upon the member state in question to repeal any legislation and to abandon any unlawful practices that might contravene the Court's judgment. If this is not done, the member state concerned may be brought before the Court in a further Article 226 EC action, based this time on a breach of Article 228 EC.

An issue which is less clear, however, and which deserves careful consideration, is whether there is an obligation imposed on a member state to set aside any contract which has actually been concluded and which has not yet been finally performed. This assumption would imply that the relevant award procedure should be reopened and conducted in a lawful manner. The main argument in favour of setting aside a public contract is confidence in the legal system in observing and enforcing public procurement law. On the other hand, the main argument against is the unfairness which this may cause to the successful tenderer or to the public interest as a result of the delay. It should be mentioned here that under the Remedies Directives, the question of whether national courts or review bodies should be allowed to set aside a contract which has already been awarded or concluded is expressly left to the discretion of member states.

It is suggested, however, that where the Court pronounces the failure of a member state to implement public procurement law in an appropriate manner under Article 226 EC, the duty of the member state under Article 228 EC to comply with the judgment reflects an obligation to set aside a contract which is affected by the judgment. This argument is substantiated by virtue of the *Lottomatica* case, where the Court exercised its powers under Articles 185, 186 EC to *suspend* a concluded contract. The same line of argumentation is found in the opinion of Advocate-General Lenz in the *Commission v. Italy* case.[18] This case concerned an alleged breach of the procurement rules relating to a contract for the construction of a waste recycling plant. The crucial question which was raised was whether the state in question had complied with the reasoned opinion issued by the Commission. Apparently it had not, thus the Advocate-General suggested that compliance with the reasoned opinion presupposed the setting aside of the contract. Although the substantial case before the Court was compliance procedures under Article 226 EC, the requirements of an action for failure to act under Article 228 EC do not preclude the conclusion that the content of the obligation to comply with a reasoned opinion is the same as that under Article 228 EC. In both cases knowledge on the part of the successful tenderer of any illegality or its complicity in a particular breach were not considered to be relevant factors in determining whether the contract should be set aside.

---

[18]   See case C-199/85, *Commission v. Italy*, [1987] ECR 1039.

ENFORCEMENT OF PUBLIC PROCUREMENT RULES AT NATIONAL LEVEL

Pre-judicial Stages in Review Procedures

The Court stated[19] that, even though Article 1(3) of Directive 89/665 expressly allows member states to determine the detailed rules according to which they must make the review procedures provided for in that Directive available to any person having or having had an interest in obtaining a particular public contract and who has been or risks being harmed by an alleged infringement, it none the less does not authorise them to give the term 'interest in obtaining a public contract' an interpretation which may limit the effectiveness of that Directive.[20] However, a person who has participated in a contract award procedure, but subsequently failed to initiate pre-judicial proceedings, such as conciliation or mediation proceedings, to settle a contested act or decision of a contracting authority must not be regarded as having lost his interest in obtaining the contract and therefore being precluded from lodging an action to contest the legality of the contract awarding decision or any decision of the contracting authority. The fact that access to the review procedures provided for by the Directive is made subject to prior referral to a pre-judicial stage such as conciliation, or mediation, would be contrary to the objectives of establishing fast and effective review mechanisms under the Remedies Directives.

In another case,[21] the national court sought clarification from the European Court of Justice to ascertain whether Article 1(3) of Directive 89/665 precludes an undertaking which has participated in a public procurement procedure from being considered as having lost its interest in obtaining that contract on the ground that, before bringing a review procedure under that directive, it failed to initiate a pre-judicial dispute resolution such as conciliation. The Court examined whether under the framework of Directive 89/665, it is necessary to make a tenderer's interest in obtaining a specific contract, and therefore its right to have access to the review procedures established by that Directive, dependent on the condition that it has beforehand exhausted pre-judicial review procedures. The Court maintained that Directive 89/665 is intended to strengthen the existing mechanisms, both at national and

---

[19]   See case C-230/02, *Grossmann Air Service, Bedarfsluftfahrtunternehmen GmbH & Co. KG and Republik Österreich*, judgment of 12 February 2004.

[20]   See case C-410/01, *Fritsch, Chiari & Partner and Others*, ECR [2003] I-11547, paragraphs 31 and 34.

[21]   See case C-410/01, *Fritsch, Chiari & Partner, Ziviltechniker GmbH and Others and Autobahnen- und Schnellstraßen-Finanzierungs-AG (Asfinag)*, ECR [2003] I-11547.

Community level, to ensure the effective application of Community rules on public procurement, in particular at a stage when infringements can still be remedied. To that effect, Article 1(1) of the Remedies Directive 89/665 requires member states to guarantee that unlawful decisions of contracting authorities can be subjected to effective and swift judicial review.[22]

The Court found that making access to the review procedures provided by Directive 89/665 conditional on prior application to a body which has no judicial character such as a conciliation commission, is contrary to the aims and objectives of the Remedies Directive and in particular the objective of speed and effectiveness in judicial review of acts or decisions of contracting authorities. First, prior application to a non-judicial body which has the aim to conciliate disputes arising between contracting authorities and aggrieved tenderers inevitably has the effect of delaying the introduction of the review procedures which Directive 89/665 requires member states to establish. Secondly, a non-judicial review body such as a conciliation commission has none of the powers which Article 2(1) of Directive 89/665 requires member states to grant the bodies responsible for carrying out those review procedures, so that referral to it does not ensure the effective application of the Community Directives on public procurement.

Interim Measures

The Remedies Directives require Member States to ensure that interim measures are available to aggrieved tenderers and candidates in procurement award procedures. The most important function of interim measures in public procurement is the ability to suspend an award procedure, particularly prior to the conclusion of the contract in question. Such possible suspension is a demonstrable factor of the ability of aggrieved tenderers to review the actions and the behavior of contracting authorities and utilities, without necessarily having recourse to an action for damages, which, in all Member States, appears as the only possible remedy available after the conclusion of the contract.

Suspension of the award procedure aims at the possible annulment of the act which has awarded a public contract, or any other act or measure of a contracting authority or a utility which forms part of the procurement process for the award of such contracts. It is widely accepted that a public contract, once concluded, is not subject to any set aside or annulment actions. For this reason, without interim orders, an aggrieved tenderer or candidate would be

---

[22] See case C-470/99, *Universale-Bau and Others*, [2002] ECR I-11617, paragraph 74.

left with very few options to challenge an alleged infringement of the procurement rules, which has a detrimental impact upon his right to participate and tender for public contracts.

Under Article 2(4) of Directive 89/665 and Article 2(4) of Directive 92/13, member states have discretion in allowing the competent judicial or administrative authorities to take into account the likely consequences of the interim measures upon the parties to the dispute and to balance their respective interests in contrast to the public interest at large. For these purposes, the courts in most member states apply a balance of interests test, where the complainant may have to show, *prima facie*, that he is likely to suffer serious and possibly irreparable harm if interim measures are not granted. Furthermore, that harm must outweigh the inconvenience or any harm or damages which the interim order would cause both to the awarding authority and to the public interest at large. The complainant might also have to show that the harm which he is likely to suffer, if the interim order is not granted, could not be adequately compensated through financial damages.

Interim Measures from the Court's Jurisprudence

Obligation to allow sufficient time between contract award and contract conclusion

The Court investigated[23] the obligations required by the Remedies Directives 89/665/EEC and 92/13/EEC to transpose legislation at domestic level relating to the award of public contracts and provide a procedure whereby all unsuccessful tenderers may have the award decision set aside. The Court took the view that the provisions of Article 2(1)(a) and (b) of Directive 89/665 require member states to provide a review procedure so that an applicant may set aside a decision of a contracting authority to award a public contract to a third party, prior to the conclusion of the contract. That right of review for tenderers must be independent of the possibility of them bringing an action for damages once the contract has been concluded.[24]

According to the Court's analysis, a legal system of a member state that makes it impossible to contest an award decision because the award decision and the conclusion of the contract occur at the same time, deprives interested parties of any possible review in order to have an unlawful award decision set aside or to prevent the contract from being concluded. Complete legal protection requires that it be possible for unsuccessful tenderers to examine in suffi-

---

23   See case C-212/02, *Commission of the European Communities v. Republic of Austria*, judgment of 24 June 2004.
24   See case C-81/98, *Alcatel Austria and Others*, [1999] ECR I-7671, paragraph 43.

cient time the validity of the award decision. A reasonable period must elapse between the time when the award decision is communicated to unsuccessful tenderers and the conclusion of the contract in order, in particular, to allow an application to be made for interim measures prior to the conclusion of the contract. Complete legal protection also presupposes an obligation to inform tenderers of the award decision. A decision of the contracting authority which is notified only to the person to whom the contract is awarded may, as a general rule, not be contested as unsuccessful tenderers have not become aware of that decision. National legislation relating to access to administrative documents which merely requires that tenderers be informed only as regards decisions which directly affect them cannot offset the failure to require that all tenderers be informed of the contract award decision prior to conclusion of the contract, so that a genuine possibility to bring an action is available to them. The effect of such national legislation is to preclude the possibility of an action to have the award decision set aside and, consequently, is incompatible with the public procurement rules. Member states are therefore required to put in place appropriate procedures to enable unlawful decisions or the act of contracting authorities to be set aside and, in accordance with Articles 1(3) of Directives 89/665 and 92/13, to ensure that review procedures are available at least to any person having an interest in obtaining a public contract. That effectiveness depends not only on the existence of a sufficiently long interval in which tenderers may react to the award decision but also on the obligation to keep tenderers informed of the award decision.

Admissibility requirements of interim measures

The Court examined[25] review procedures under the Remedies Directive 89/665/EEC and in particular interim measures and the possibility of applying for interim measures after an action to set aside or annul an act or a decision of a contracting authority has been initiated. The Commission claimed that the scope *ratione materiae* of Directive 89/665 has been improperly reduced since the Spanish review provisions[26] precluded a challenge to certain unlawful decisions taken by contracting authorities. In particular, national law limited the possibility of appealing against procedural acts, or administrative measures which do not bring administrative proceedings to an end. As the

---

[25]   See cases C-214/00, *Commission of the European Communities v. Kingdom of Spain*, ECR [2003] I-4667; C-236/95, *Commission v. Greece*, [1996] ECR I-4459.

[26]   See Article 107 of Law 30/1992 and Article 25(1) of Law 29/1998, which stipulate that procedural acts are not open to administrative appeal or administrative appeal proceedings unless they decide, directly or indirectly, the substance of the case, make it impossible to continue the procedure, make it impossible to put up a defence, or cause irreparable harm to legitimate rights or interests.

EU public procurement law

Court stated, the Remedies Directive does not provide for any derogation in that regard.[27] In support of its argument, the Commission referred to Articles 1(1), 2(1)(b) and 8 of Directive 89/665, from which it follows that it must be ensured that any allegedly illegal measure may be reviewed effectively and, in particular, as rapidly as possible.

The Commission maintained that the wording of the provisions of the Remedies Directive such as 'any allegedly illegal measure' refers to all types of act alleged to be illegal, not only to definitive acts. Furthermore, the expression 'reviewed effectively and . . . as rapidly as possible' supports the conclusion that the possibility of seeking review of procedural acts is one of the best means of ensuring the effectiveness and rapidity of review procedures, since to wait for the outcome of the contract award procedure is the best way of weakening, or even undermining, the effectiveness and speediness of the review procedures envisaged by Directive 89/665.

The Spanish government contested the Commission's interpretation of the term procedural act. It considered that a procedural act, by definition, does not cause any harm to the interested party but is at most a preparatory step to a decision which will be favourable or unfavourable to him. Thus, a procedural act does not imply the adoption of a position but is part of a procedure initiated in order to reach a decision. In that regard, the Spanish government states that, if an act which appears to be a procedural act entailed the adoption of a position *per se*, it would cease to be a procedural act in the strict sense and would be reviewable. The Spanish government claimed that the national provisions concerning the possibility of challenging procedural acts are not specific to the award of public contracts, but apply equally to all procedures. The government pointed out that that device, which seeks to avoid procedures being paralysed by successive claims and appeals at the stage of preparatory measures which do not yet definitively affect the rights of those concerned, is not only found within the Spanish legal system but is also common to all the legal systems of the member states.[28]

The Court maintained that the national law[29] did not allow judicial review of procedural acts that are not open to administrative appeal or administrative appeal proceedings unless they decide, directly or indirectly, the substance of

---

[27] See case C-81/98, *Alcatel Austria and Others*, [1999] ECR I-7671.

[28] The Spanish government points out that that conception of precluding the review of procedural acts is embedded in Community case-law. See case C-282/95, *Guérin automobiles v. Commission*, [1997] ECR I-1503. The Court has also held that the preparatory nature of the act against which the action is brought is one of the grounds for inadmissibility of an action for annulment, and that that is a ground which the Court may examine of its own motion; see case 346/87, *Bossi v. Commission*, [1989] ECR 303.

[29] See Article 107 of Law 30/1992 and Article 25(1) of Law 29/1998.

the case, make it impossible to continue the procedure, make it impossible to put up a defence, or cause irreparable harm to legitimate rights or interests. Therefore, those provisions have the effect of excluding procedural acts from the scope *ratione materiae* of Directive 89/665, unless they fulfil one of the above-mentioned conditions. Since Directive 89/665 does not expressly define the scope of the term 'decisions taken by contracting authorities', the question whether procedural acts which do not fulfil one of the above-mentioned conditions constitute decisions in respect of which the member states must provide review procedures within the meaning of Directive 89/665 must be examined in the light of the aims of the Directive. In that regard, the Court pointed out that the sixth recital in the preamble and Article 1(1) of Directive 89/665 seek to ensure that adequate procedures exist in all the member states to permit the setting aside of decisions taken by contracting authorities in infringement of Community law on the award of public contracts or of national rules transposing that law, and also the compensating of persons harmed by such an infringement. The review procedures to which the Remedies Directive refers must be conducted effectively and as rapidly as possible and must be available to any person having or having had an interest in obtaining a particular public contract and who has been or risks being harmed by an alleged infringement.

The Court found that the Spanish legislation enabled interested parties to bring actions against not only definitive acts but also procedural acts, if such acts decide, directly or indirectly, the substance of the case, make it impossible to continue the procedure or to put up a defence, or cause irreparable harm to legitimate rights or interests and as a result that legislation provided adequate judicial protection for individuals harmed by infringements of the relevant rules of Community law or of the national rules transposing that law.

The Commission also argued that the national provisions which transpose Article 2(1)(a) of Directive 89/665 into Spanish law[30] do not provide for an urgent procedure independent of the lodging of an appeal, designed to suspend the procedure for the award of a public contract or the implementation of any decision adopted by the contracting authorities and in particular do not provide any opportunity for applying for interim measures in the absence of an appeal on the merits. The Court has pointed out that it must be possible to adopt, independently of any prior action, any interim measures.[31]

The Commission claimed that, in administrative appeals, the only interim measure which may be adopted is suspension of operation. Secondly, in administrative appeal proceedings, the court hearing the application for interim relief tends not to adopt measures other than suspension of operation.

---

[30] See Articles 111 of Law 30/1992 and 129 to 136 of Law 29/1998.
[31] See case C-236/95, *Commission v. Greece*, [1996] ECR I-4459, paragraph 11.

The Commission stated that, according to Spanish case-law, interim measures cannot relate to the substance, because they must not anticipate the outcome of the main proceedings. However, the rule that interim measures must be neutral as regards the substance of the main proceedings has the consequence that, contrary to the requirements of Article 2(1)(a) of Directive 89/665, the court hearing the application for interim relief cannot take all the measures necessary to correct an infringement.

The Spanish government did not dispute that both the rules of administrative procedure and the rules governing administrative appeal proceedings have the effect that the adoption of an interim measure is linked to the prior lodging of an appeal and cannot, under any circumstances, be requested separately. However, it argued that although interim measures may be requested and granted even before an appeal is lodged, that requirement does not imply that those measures are independent of the latter, since the person concerned is required to lodge such an appeal against the act he considers unlawful within a period of 10 days of notification of the decision granting the measures requested. He must then request confirmation of those measures and, if he does not lodge the appeal within the time limit, the interim measures will automatically lapse.

With regards to the suspension effects of legal proceedings, the Spanish government claimed that administrative appeal proceedings are not initiated by application, but by a simple written document which must indicate the act challenged or allege inertia on the part of the authority, and in which the interested party may request suspension of the operation of the contested act without necessarily having to lodge a separate application. Once an appeal is lodged, the court will ask the authority to forward the administrative file and it is only after the applicant in the review proceedings is in possession of the case-file that the time limit within which he must formulate his application and set out the grounds for review will begin to run.

The Court, in order to ascertain whether the Spanish legislation was consistent with Directive 89/665, referred to the fifth recital in the preamble to the Remedies Directive, which stipulates the short duration of the procedures for the award of public contracts, meaning that infringements of the relevant rules of Community law or national rules transposing that law which mar those procedures need to be dealt with urgently. For these purposes, Article 2(1)(a) of the Remedies Directive requires member states to empower the review bodies to take, at the earliest opportunity and by way of interlocutory procedures, interim measures with the aim of correcting the alleged infringement or preventing further damage to the interests concerned, including measures to suspend or to ensure the suspension of the procedure for the award of a public contract or the implementation of any decision taken by the contracting authorities.

In *Commission v. Greece*,[32] which concerned the compliance with Directive 89/665 of national legislation which restricted interim judicial protection to proceedings for suspension of the operation of an administrative act and made the suspension conditional on bringing an action for the annulment of the contested act, the Court had the opportunity to define the scope of the obligations arising in that regard under that Directive. In particular, it found that, under Article 2 of Directive 89/665, the member states are under a duty more generally to empower their review bodies to take, independently of any prior action, any interim measures, including measures to suspend or to ensure the suspension of the procedure for the award of the public contract in question.[33] The Court found that, although the Spanish legislation provides for the possibility of adopting positive interim measures, it nevertheless cannot be regarded as a system of interim judicial protection which is adequate to remedy effectively any infringements that might have been committed by the contracting authorities, since, as a general rule, it requires proceedings on the merits to be brought beforehand as a condition for the adoption of an interim measure against a decision of a contracting authority. That finding is not affected by the fact that, where suspension is sought by way of legal proceedings, it may be done merely by a written document and the application initiating the proceedings may be formulated after the request for granting of the interim measure, since the requirement that that formality be completed beforehand cannot be regarded as consistent with the requirements of Directive 89/665. Consequently, member states, by making the possibility of interim measures being granted in relation to decisions adopted by contracting authorities subject to the need first to appeal against the decision of the contracting authority, are in breach of Articles 1 and 2 of Directive 89/665.

Set Aside and Annulment

The Remedies Directives also stipulate that national courts or administrative tribunals must be given the power to set aside or annul acts of contracting authorities. Such orders aim at nullifying the decision of the contracting authority or a utility which awards a contract, prior to its conclusion. A set aside or annulment order cannot attack the contract itself, as the latter represents a pact between the contracting authority and a third party. In most legal orders, a set aside or annulment order will be reached after application of a balance of interest test. However, many legal systems rely predominantly on the mere lawfulness of the administrative act of the contracting authority or

---

[32] See case C-236/95, *Commission v. Greece*, [1996] ECR I-4459.
[33] See case C-236/95, *Commission v. Greece*, [1996] ECR I-4459, paragraph 11.

the utility and do not involve any test which weights interests and potential harm and damages.

Set Aside and Annulment Orders from the Court's Jurisprudence

Meaning and content of decisions for review

The Court examined the level of judicial protection afforded to third parties having an interest under the Remedies Directive 89/665/EEC and verified that any remedies available to them against decisions taken by contracting authorities extend also to decisions taken outside a formal award procedure and decisions prior to a formal call for tenders,[34] in particular the decision on whether a particular contract falls within the personal and material scope of the Public Procurement Directives. The national court asked whether Article 1(1) of Directive 89/665 could be interpreted as meaning that the member states' obligation to ensure that effective and rapid remedies are available against decisions taken by contracting authorities extends also to decisions taken outside a formal award procedure and decisions prior to a formal call for tenders, in particular the decision on whether a particular contract falls within the material scope of Public Procurement Directives, and from what moment during a procurement procedure the member states are obliged to make a remedy available to a tenderer, candidate or an interested party.

The Court examined the scope of the concept 'decisions taken by the contracting authorities' stipulated in Article 1(1) of Directive 89/665 on the basis of the wording of the relevant provisions of the Directive and the objective of effective and rapid judicial protection pursued by it. Although that concept is not expressly defined in the Remedies Directive, the wording of Article 1(1) of Directive 89/665 provided ample confidence in assuming that every decision of a contracting authority falling under the Community rules in the field of public procurement and liable to infringe them is subject to the judicial review provided for in Article 2(1)(a) and (b) of that Directive.[35] It thus embraces generally the decisions of a contracting authority without distinguishing between those decisions according to their content or time of adoption. In addition, the Court ascertained that Article 2(1)(b) of Directive 89/665 provides for the possibility of annulling unlawful decisions of the contracting authorities in relation to the technical and other specifications not only in the invitation to tender but also in any other document relating to the

---

[34] See case C-26/03, *Stadt Halle, RPL Recyclingpark Lochau GmbH v. Arbeitsgemeinschaft Thermische Restabfall und Energieverwertungsanlage TREA Leuna*, judgment of 11 January 2005.

[35] See case C92/00, *Hospital Ingenieure*, [2002] ECR I5553, paragraph 37; case C57/01, *Makedoniko Metro and Mikhaniki*, [2003] ECR I1091, paragraph 68.

award procedure in question. That provision can therefore include documents containing decisions of the contracting authority taken at a stage prior to the call for tenders.

That broad meaning of the concept of a decision taken by a contracting authority is confirmed by the Court's case-law. The Court has already held that Article 1(1) of Directive 89/665 does not lay down any restriction with regard to the nature and content of the decisions it refers to.[36] Nor may such a restriction be inferred from the wording of Article 2(1)(b) of that Directive.[37] Moreover, a restrictive interpretation of the concept of a decision amenable to review would be incompatible with the provision in Article 2(1)(a) of that Directive which requires the member states to make provision for interim relief procedures in relation to any decision taken by the contracting authorities.[38] In line with this broad interpretation of the concept of a decision amenable to review, the Court has held that the contracting authority's decision prior to the conclusion of the contract as to the tenderer to whom the contract will be awarded must in all cases be open to review, regardless of the possibility of obtaining an award of damages once the contract has been concluded.[39]

The Court has also held that a contracting authority's decision to withdraw an invitation to tender for a public service contract must be open to a review procedure.[40] *A contrario*, a contracting authority's decision not to initiate an award procedure may be regarded as the counterpart of its decision to terminate such a procedure. Where a contracting authority decides not to initiate an award procedure on the grounds that the contract in question does not fall within the scope of the relevant Community rules, such a decision constitutes the very first decision amenable to judicial review.[41] Therefore, any act of a contracting authority adopted in relation to a public service contract and capable of producing legal effects constitutes a decision amenable to review within the meaning of Article 1(1) of Directive 89/665, regardless of whether that act is adopted outside a formal award procedure or as part of such a procedure.

---

[36] See case C81/98, *Alcatel Austria and Others*, [1999] ECR I7671, paragraph 35.

[37] See case C81/98, *Alcatel Austria and Others*, [1999] ECR I7671, paragraph 32.

[38] See case C92/00, *Hospital Ingénieure*, [2002] ECR I5553, paragraph 49.

[39] See case C81/98, *Alcatel Austria and Others*, [1999] ECR I7671, paragraph 43.

[40] See case C92/00, *Hospital Ingénieure*, [2002] ECR I5553, paragraph 55.

[41] See the Opinion of Advocate-General Stix-Hackl, point 23 in case C-26/03, *Stadt Halle, RPL Recyclingpark Lochau GmbH v. Arbeitsgemeinschaft Thermische Restabfall und Energieverwertungsanlage TREA Leuna*, delivered on 23 September 2004.

The approach under which an act or a decision of a contracting authority does not require judicial protection because it falls outside the framework of a formal award procedure is incorrect according to the Court, as the effect of such approach would be to make the application of the Public Procurement Remedies Directive optional, at the option of contracting authorities, even though that application is mandatory where the relevant conditions are satisfied. Such an option could lead to the most serious breach of Community law in the field of public procurement on the part of a contracting authority as it would substantially reduce the effective and rapid judicial protection aimed at by the Remedies Directives, and would interfere with the objectives of free movement of services and open and undistorted competition.

On the other hand, decisions or acts of contracting authorities which constitute a mere preliminary study of the market or which are purely preparatory and form part of the internal reflections of the contracting authority with a view to a public award procedure are not amenable to review.

The Court also elaborated on the availability of the Remedies Directive 89/665/EEC in relation to the scope of reviewing judicially a decision of a contracting authority to withdraw an invitation to tender.[42] The Court determined that the decision of the contracting authority to withdraw the invitation to tender for a public service contract should be open to a review procedure, and should be capable of being annulled, on the ground that it has infringed Community law on public contracts or national rules implementing that law. The Remedies Directives preclude national legislation from limiting review of the legality of the withdrawal of an invitation to tender to mere examination of whether it was arbitrary. The determination of the time to be taken into consideration for assessing the legality of the decision by the contracting authority to withdraw an invitation to tender is a matter for national law, provided that the relevant national rules are not less favourable than those governing similar domestic actions and that they do not make it practically impossible or excessively difficult to exercise rights conferred by Community law.

The national court (*Vergabekontrollsenat*) requested clarification from the European Court of Justice asking whether Article 1(1) of Directive 89/665 requires the decision of the awarding authority to withdraw the invitation to tender for a public service contract to be open to review proceedings, and to annulment in appropriate cases, on the ground that it infringed Community law on public contracts or the national rules transposing that law. In that respect, whereas Article 2(1)(b) of Directive 89/665 delimits the scope of the

---

[42]   See case C-92/00, *Hospital Ingénieure Krankenhaustechnik Planungs- GmbH (HI) and Stadt Wien*, ECR [2002] I-5553.

Directive, it does not define the unlawful decisions of which annulment may be sought, confining itself to listing measures which member states are required to take for the purposes of the review proceedings referred to in Article 1 of the Remedies Directive.[43]

The Austrian government and the Commission maintained that member states are required to establish procedures allowing review proceedings to be brought against the withdrawal of an invitation to tender for a public service contract if that withdrawal is governed by Directive 92/50. In that respect, they considered that such withdrawal falls exclusively under national legal rules and therefore does not fall within the scope of Directive 89/665.

In particular, the Commission states that, in its proposal for a Council Directive 87/C 230/05 co-ordinating the laws, regulations and administrative provisions relating to the application of Community rules on procedures for the award of public supply and public works contracts,[44] it expressly proposed that the obligation of member states to establish review procedures should extend not only to decisions taken by the contracting authorities in breach of Community law but also to those infringing national legal rules. However, in the course of the legislative process, the obligation to establish a review mechanism was limited to its present scope, so as to cover only decisions which infringe 'Community law on public contracts or the national rules which transpose that law'.

The Austrian government argued that the conclusion that a decision to withdraw an invitation to tender does not constitute a decision within the meaning of Directive 89/665 is confirmed by Article 2(1)(b) of that Directive, which exclusively concerns decisions which the contracting authority adopts during the procedure for the award of a public contract, whereas a decision to withdraw an invitation to tender brings such a procedure to an end. Thus, where an invitation to tender is withdrawn unlawfully, the national legislature is required, under Directive 89/665, only to ensure that the candidates and tenderers are given a right to damages.

The Court as a preliminary observation reiterated that Article 1(1) of Directive 89/665 places an obligation on member states to lay down procedures enabling review of decisions taken in a tender procedure on the ground that those decisions infringed Community law on public contracts or national rules transposing that law. It follows that, if a decision taken by a contracting authority in a procedure for awarding a public contract is made subject to the Community law rules on public contracts and is therefore capable of infringing

---

[43] See case C-81/98, *Alcatel Austria and Others v. Bundesministerium für Wissenschaft und Verkehr*, [1999] ECR I-7671, paragraphs 30 and 31
[44] See OJ 1987 C 230, p. 6.

them, Article 1(1) of Directive 89/665 requires that that decision be capable of forming the subject-matter of an action for annulment.

Therefore, in order to determine whether a decision of a contracting authority to withdraw an invitation to tender for a public service contract may be regarded as one of those decisions in respect of which member states are required, under Directive 89/665, to establish annulment action procedures, the Court examined whether such a decision falls within Community law rules on public contracts. In that respect, the Court noted that the provisions found in the Public Procurement Directives provide, *inter alia*, that where the contracting authorities have decided to abandon an award procedure,[45] they also stipulate that contracting authorities must inform candidates and tenderers of the reasons for their decision as soon as possible.

The Court has defined the scope of the obligation to notify reasons for abandoning the award of a contract in the context of the Public Works Directive 93/37,[46] where it held that public procurement rules[47] do not provide that the option of the contracting authority to decide not to award a contract put out to tender is limited to exceptional cases or must necessarily be based on serious grounds.[48] It follows that, although a contracting authority is required to notify candidates and tenderers of the grounds for its decision if it decides to withdraw the invitation to tender for a public contract, there is no implied obligation on that authority to carry the award procedure to its conclusion.

However, even though, apart from the duty to notify the reasons for the withdrawal of the invitation to tender, the public procurement rules contain no specific provision concerning the substantive or formal conditions for that decision, the fact remains that the latter decision is still subject to fundamental rules of Community law, and in particular to the principles laid down by the EC Treaty on the right of establishment and the freedom to provide services. In that regard, the Court has consistently held that the purpose of co-ordinating at Community level the procedures for the award of public contracts is to eliminate barriers to the freedom to provide services and goods and therefore to protect the interests of traders established in a member state who wish to offer goods or services to contracting authorities established in another member state.[49]

---

[45]   See Article 12(2) of the Public Services Directive 92/50 and Article 8(2) of the Public Works Directive 93/37 relating specifically to the decision to withdraw an invitation to tender.

[46]   See OJ 1993 L 199, p. 54.

[47]   In particular Article 8(2) of Directive 93/37.

[48]   See case C-27/98, *Fracasso and Leitschutz v. Salzburger Landesregierung*, [1999] ECR I-5697, paragraphs 23 and 25.

[49]   See case C-380/98, *University of Cambridge*, [2000] ECR I-8035, paragraph 16; case C-19/00, *SIAC Construction*, [2001] ECR I-7725, paragraph 32.

The Court's case-law also demonstrates that the principle of equal treatment which underlies the directives on procedures for the award of public contracts, implies in particular an obligation of transparency in order to enable verification that it has been complied with.[50] In that respect, it should be noted that the duty to notify reasons for a decision to withdraw an invitation to tender is dictated precisely by concern to ensure a minimum level of transparency in the contract-awarding procedures to which that Directive applies and hence compliance with the principle of equal treatment. Even though the Public Procurement Directives do not specifically govern the detailed procedures for withdrawing an invitation to tender for a public contract, the contracting authorities are nevertheless required, when adopting such a decision, to comply with the fundamental rules of the Treaty in general, and the principle of non-discrimination on the ground of nationality.[51]

Since the decision by a contracting authority to withdraw an invitation to tender for a public service contract is subject to the relevant substantive rules of Community law, the Court concluded that it also falls within the rules laid down by Directive 89/665 in order to ensure compliance with the rules of Community law on public contracts. That finding is corroborated, first, by the wording of the provisions of Directive 89/665. The Court pointed out that the provision in Article 1(1) of that Directive does not lay down any restriction with regard to the nature and content of the decisions referred to therein.[52] Nor can such a restriction be inferred from the wording of Article 2(1)(b) of that Directive.[53] Moreover, a restrictive interpretation of the category of decisions in relation to which member states must ensure the existence of review procedures would be incompatible with Article 2(1)(a) of the same directive, which requires member states to make provision for interim relief procedures in relation to any decision taken by the contracting authorities.

The Court held that the general frameworks of Directive 89/665 require a broad interpretation, in so far as Article 2(5) of that Directive authorises member states to provide that, where damages are claimed on the grounds that a decision by the contracting authority was taken unlawfully, the contested decision must first be set aside. To accept that member states are not required

---

[50]   See case C-275/98, *Unitron Scandinavia and 3-S v. Ministeriet for Fødevarer, Landbrug og Fiskeri,* [1999] ECR I-8291, paragraph 31; case C-324/98, *Telaustria and Telefonadress v. Telekom Austria,* [2000] ECR I-10745, paragraph 61.

[51]   See case C-324/98, *Telaustria Verlags GmbH and Telefonadress GmbH v. Post & Telekom Austria AG,* paragraph 60, concerning the conclusion of public service concessions.

[52]   See case C81/98, *Alcatel Austria and Others,* [1999] ECR I7671, paragraph 35.

[53]   See case C81/98, *Alcatel Austria and Others,* [1999] ECR I7671, paragraph 32.

to lay down review procedures for annulment in relation to decisions withdrawing invitations to tender would amount to authorising them, by availing themselves of the option provided for in the provision mentioned in the paragraph above, to deprive tenderers adversely affected by such decisions, adopted in breach of the rules of Community law, of the possibility of bringing actions for damages. Any other interpretation would undermine the effectiveness of Directive 89/665. As the first and second recitals in its preamble show, that directive is designed to reinforce existing arrangements at both national and Community level for ensuring effective application of Community Directives on the award of public contracts, in particular at the stage where infringements can still be rectified, and it is precisely in order to ensure compliance with those directives that Article 1(1) of Directive 89/665 requires the member states to establish effective review procedures that are as rapid as possible.[54] The full attainment of the objective pursued by Directive 89/665 would be compromised if it were lawful for contracting authorities to withdraw an invitation to tender for a public service contract without being subject to the judicial review procedures designed to ensure that the directives laying down substantive rules concerning public contracts and the principles underlying those directives are genuinely complied with.

The Court concluded that the decision to withdraw an invitation to tender for a public service contract is one of those decisions in relation to which member states are required under Directive 89/665 to establish review procedures for annulment, for the purposes of ensuring compliance with the rules of Community law on public contracts and national rules implementing that law.

The national court also asked the European Court of Justice whether Directive 89/665 precludes national rules from limiting review of the legality of the withdrawal of an invitation to tender to mere examination of whether that decision was arbitrary. The Court held that Directive 89/665 provides for the co-ordination of existing mechanisms in member states in order to ensure the full and effective application of the directives laying down substantive rules concerning public contracts, and does not expressly define the scope of the remedies which the member states must establish for that purpose. Therefore, the question of the extent of the judicial review exercised in the context of the national review procedures covered by Directive 89/665 must be examined in the light of the aims and objectives of the Remedies Directive. In that respect, the latter requires member states to establish review procedures that are appropriate in the event of procedures for the award of public contracts being unlawful. Therefore, the Court maintained that, with reference to the

---

[54] See case C-81/98, *Alcatel Austria and Others*, [1999] ECR I7671, paragraphs 33 and 34.

aim of strengthening remedies pursued by Directive 89/665, and in the absence of indications to the contrary, the scope of the judicial review to be exercised in the context of the review procedures referred to therein cannot be interpreted restrictively.

Even in cases where the relevant national legislation gives the contracting authorities wide discretion in relation to the withdrawal of invitations to tender, the national courts must be able, pursuant to Directive 89/665, to verify the compatibility of a decision to withdraw an invitation to tender with the relevant rules of Community law. In those circumstances, the Court held that neither the letter nor the spirit of Directive 89/665 allows for discretion on the part of member states to reduce the review of the legality of a decision of a contracting authority to withdraw an invitation to tender to a mere examination of the arbitrariness of such a decision. The Court therefore concluded that Directive 89/665 precludes national legislation from limiting the review of the legality of the withdrawal of an invitation to tender to mere examination of whether that withdrawal was arbitrary.

Impact of the theory of detachable acts

The Court covered the review procedures concerning the award of public contracts under the Remedies Directive 89/665/EEC and the effects of a decision by a contracting authority to award a public contract based on grounds which are incompatible with Community law upon the legality and validity of the contract itself.[55] The national court (Austrian *Bundesvergabeamt*) sought to ascertain whether Article 2(7) of Directive 89/665, which provided for effective enforcement of decisions annulling or setting aside acts or decisions of contracting authorities which award or lead to the award of public contracts, allows for a contract concluded at the end of an award procedure, the proper conduct of which is affected by the incompatibility with Community law of a provision in the invitation to tender, to be treated as void if the applicable national law declares contracts that are illegal to be void.

The Court maintained that if a clause in the invitation to tender, such as a prohibition on the part of the successful tenderer to have recourse to subcontracting in order to perform the contract in question, is in fact contrary to the Public Procurement Directives, it would then be a matter for the legal systems of member states to take the measures necessary to ensure that decisions taken by the contracting authorities may be reviewed effectively and as rapidly as possible in the case where those decisions may have infringed Community law on public procurement in accordance with Articles 1(1) and 2(7) of Directive 89/665.

---

[55] See case C-314/01, *Siemens AG Österreich, ARGE Telekom & Partner and Hauptverband der österreichischen Sozialversicherungsträger*, judgment of 18 March 2004.

It follows that, in the case where a clause in the invitation to tender is incompatible with Community rules on public procurement, the national legal system of the member state in question must provide for the possibility of relying on that incompatibility in the review procedures referred to in Directive 89/665. However, the Court did not pronounce on the potential effect of such incompatibility on the legality and validity of a concluded contract, indicating the fact that in most cases, the principle *pact servanta sunt* as applied in the jurisprudence of member states, will be sufficient to save the concluded contract from nullity, even in the event of it being awarded on erroneous or illegal grounds.

The Court also discussed the review proceeding under the Remedies Directive 89/665/EEC for unlawful decisions of contracting authorities. It examined the possibility of annulment of a decision or an act of a contracting authority only in the case of material influence on the outcome of the tender procedure and pronounced on the significance of the illegality of an award criterion and as a consequence the obligation of the contracting authority to cancel the invitation to tender.[56]

The national court requested clarification from the European Court of Justice whether Article 2(1)(b) of Directive 89/665 precludes a provision of national law, which makes the annulment in review proceedings of an unlawful decision by a contracting authority dependent on proof that the unlawful decision materially influenced the outcome of the procurement procedure and whether the answer to that question must differ if the proof of that influence derives from an examination by the review body of whether the ranking of the tenders actually submitted would have been different had they been re-evaluated disregarding the unlawful award criterion. The object of the review proceedings before the European Court of Justice related, *inter alia*, to the annulment of the invitation to tender in its entirety and the annulment of a series of individual conditions in the contract documents and of a number of decisions of the contracting authority relating to the requirements established by the award and selection criteria used in that tender procedure.

The Court found, in the light of the information provided by the national court (the Austrian *Bundesvergabeamt*) that all the decisions whose annulment was sought in the main proceedings had a decisive effect on the outcome of the tender procedure. On the other hand, the Court declined to provide a ruling on the question of the annulment of a series of individual conditions in the contract documents and of a number of decisions of the contracting authority relating to the requirements established by the award and selection criteria

---

[56]   See case C-448/01, *EVN AG, Wienstrom GmbH and Republik Österreich*, judgment of 4 December 2003.

used in that tender procedure, since it considered such a question hypothetical and, accordingly, inadmissible.

However, the Court elaborated on the requirement of contracting authorities to cancel the invitation to tender if it transpires in review proceedings under Article 1 of Directive 89/665 that a decision relating to one of the award criteria laid down by that authority is unlawful. According to the *Bundesvergabeamt*, if it is assumed that the review of the effects of unlawful decisions relating to award criteria is contrary to Community law, the only alternative where such a decision is unlawful seems to be cancellation of the invitation to tender, since otherwise the tender procedure would be carried out on the basis of weighting of criteria which were neither laid down by the authority nor known by the tenderers.

The Austrian government submitted that Community law does not recognise an express obligation to cancel invitations to tender, just as the directives on public procurement do not lay down a tendering obligation, and concludes that it is for the member states, acting in accordance with the principles of Community law, to lay down rules determining whether, where a decision relating to an award criterion is recognised to be unlawful, the contracting authority is obliged to cancel the invitation to tender. On the other hand, the Commission considered that if, after the tenders have been submitted or opened, the review body declares a decision relating to an award criterion unlawful, the contract cannot be awarded on the basis of the invitation to tender and the only option is to cancel the invitation to tender. Any amendment to the criteria would have an effect on the evaluation of the tenders, whereas the tenderers would no longer have the possibility of adapting their tenders, prepared at a completely different time and in different circumstances and on the basis of different criteria. The only option would therefore be to start the entire tender procedure afresh.

The Court noted that a finding that a decision relating to an award criterion is unlawful does not always lead to the annulment of that decision. As a result of the option granted to member states under Article 2(6) of Directive 89/665 providing that, after the conclusion of a contract following its award, the powers of the body responsible for the review procedures are to be limited to awarding damages to any person harmed by an infringement, where the review proceedings are instituted after the conclusion of the contract and the member state concerned has made use of the option, if the review body finds that a decision relating to an award criterion is unlawful, it may not annul that decision, but only award damages. Nevertheless, prior to the conclusion of the relevant contract, the situation appears different. The question focuses on whether Community legislation on public procurement requires the contracting authority to cancel an invitation to tender where it transpires in review proceedings under Article 1 of Directive 89/665 that a decision relating to one of the award criteria laid down by that authority is unlawful and it is therefore annulled by the review body.

The Court has held that the principles of equal treatment and transparency of tender procedures imply an obligation on the part of contracting authorities to interpret the award criteria in the same way throughout the procedure.[57] As far as the award criteria themselves are concerned, it is *a fortiori* clear that they must not be amended in any way during the tender procedure. As a consequence, where a national review body annuls a decision relating to an award criterion, the contracting authority cannot validly continue the tender procedure leaving aside that criterion, since that would be tantamount to amending the criteria applicable to the procedure in question. Therefore, the Court pronounced that there is a requirement on contracting authorities to cancel an invitation to tender if it transpires in review proceedings under Article 1 of Directive 89/665 that a decision relating to one of the award criteria laid down by a contracting authority is unlawful and it is therefore annulled by the review body.

Locus standi and interest to review acts
The Court stated[58] that the persons to whom review procedures must be available include, at a minimum, any person having or having had an interest in obtaining a public contract who has been or risks being harmed by an alleged infringement.[59] The formal capacity of tenderer or candidate is thus not required.

The Court also dealt with the scope of review procedures for the award of public contracts under Articles 1(3) and 2(1)(b) of the Remedies Directive 89/665/EEC and in particular the persons to whom review procedures must be available.[60] The case provided a definition of interest in obtaining a public contract, as a condition for *locus standi* under the Remedies Directive.

The national court asked the European Court of Justice whether Articles 1(3) and 2(1)(b) of Directive 89/665 must be interpreted as precluding a person from being regarded, once a public contract has been awarded, as having lost his right of access to the review procedures provided for by the Directive if he did not participate in the award procedure for that contract on

---

[57] See case *SIAC Construction*, ECR I-7725, paragraph 43
[58] See C-26/03, *Stadt Halle, RPL Recyclingpark Lochau GmbH v. Arbeitsgemeinschaft Thermische Restabfall und Energieverwertungsanlage TREA Leuna*, judgment of 11 January 2005.
[59] See case C212/02, *Commission v. Austria*, [2004], paragraph 24, Judgement of 24 June, not yet reported.
[60] See case C-230/02, *Grossmann Air Service, Bedarfsluftfahrtunternehmen GmbH & Co. KG and Republik Österreich*, judgment of 12 February 2004.

the ground that he was not in a position to supply all the services for which bids were invited, because there were allegedly discriminatory specifications in the documents relating to the invitation to tender, but he did not seek review of those specifications before the contract was awarded.

The Court maintained that an assessment of an aggrieved tenderer's interest in reviewing a decision or an act of a contracting authority should be examined on the basis that he did not participate in the contract award procedure, as well as that he did not appeal against the invitation to tender before the award of the contract.

The failure to participate in the contract award procedure

In accordance with Article 1(3) of Directive 89/665, the member states are required to ensure that the review procedures provided for are available at least to any person having or having had an interest in obtaining a particular public contract and who has been or risks being harmed by an alleged infringement of the Community law on public procurement or national rules transposing that law. It follows that member states are not obliged to make those review procedures available to any person wishing to obtain a public contract, but instead, require that the person concerned has been or risks being harmed by the alleged infringement.[61]

In that sense, participation in a contract award procedure may, in principle, with regard to Article 1(3) of Directive 89/665, validly constitute a condition which must be fulfilled before the person concerned can show an interest in obtaining the contract at issue or that he risks suffering harm as a result of the allegedly unlawful nature of the decision to award that contract. If he has not submitted a tender, it will be difficult for such a person to show that he has an interest in challenging that decision or that he has been harmed or risks being harmed as a result of that award decision. However, where an undertaking has not submitted a tender because there were allegedly discriminatory specifications in the documents relating to the invitation to tender, or in the contract documents, which have specifically prevented it from being in a position to provide all the services requested, it would be entitled to seek review of those specifications directly, even before the procedure for awarding the contract concerned is terminated.

The Court maintained that, on the one hand, it would be too much to require an undertaking allegedly harmed by discriminatory clauses in the documents relating to the invitation to tender to submit a tender, before being able to avail itself of the review procedures provided for by Directive 89/665 against such specifications, in the award procedure for the contract at issue, even though its

---

[61] See case C-249/01, *Hackermüller*, [2003] ECR I-6319, paragraph 18.

chances of being awarded the contract are non-existent by reason of the existence of those specifications. On the other hand, it is clear from the wording of Article 2(1)(b) of Directive 89/665 that the review procedures to be organised by the member states in accordance with the Directive must, in particular, set aside decisions taken unlawfully, including the removal of discriminatory technical, economic or financial specifications. It must, therefore, be possible for an undertaking to seek review of such discriminatory specifications directly, without waiting for the contract award procedure to be terminated.

Absence of proceedings against the invitation to tender

The national court sought to ascertain whether Article 1(3) of Directive 89/665 must be interpreted as meaning that it precludes a person who not only has not participated in the award procedure for a public contract but has not sought any review of the decision of the contracting authority determining the specifications of the invitation to tender, from being regarded as having lost his interest in obtaining the contract and, therefore, the right of access to the review procedures provided for by the Directive.

The European Court of Justice examined the absence of proceedings against the invitation to tender in the light of the purpose of Directive 89/665 and in particular its intentions to strengthen the existing mechanisms, both at national and Community level, to ensure the effective application of Community directives relating to public procurement, in particular at a stage when infringements can still be remedied. To that effect, Article 1(1) of that directive requires member states to guarantee that unlawful decisions of contracting authorities may be subjected to effective review which is as swift as possible.[62]

It must be pointed out that the fact that a person does not seek review of a decision of the contracting authority determining the specifications of an invitation to tender which in his view discriminate against him, in so far as they effectively disqualify him from participating in the award procedure for the contract at issue, but awaits notification of the decision awarding the contract and then challenges it before the body responsible, on the ground specifically that those specifications are discriminatory, indicates a conduct which is incompatible with the spirit and objective of the Remedies Directive 89/665. Such conduct, in so far as it may delay, without any objective reason, the commencement of the review procedures which member states were required to institute by Directive 89/665, impairs the effective implementation of the Community directives on the award of public contracts.

---

[62]   See case C-81/98, *Alcatel Austria and Others*, [1999] ECR I-7671, paragraphs 33 and 34, case C-470/99, *Universale-Bau and Others*, [2002] ECR I-11617, paragraph 74, and case C-410/01, *Fritsch, Chiari & Partner and Others*, [2003] ECR I-6413, paragraph 30.

In those circumstances, a refusal to acknowledge the interest in obtaining the contract in question and, therefore, the right of access to the review procedures provided for by Directive 89/665 of a person who has not participated in the contract award procedure, or sought review of the decision of the contracting authority laying down the specifications of the invitation to tender, does not impair the effectiveness of that directive.

Therefore, once a public contract has been awarded, an aggrieved tenderer may be regarded as having lost his right of access to the review procedures provided by the Directive if he did not participate in the award procedure for that contract on the ground that he was not in a position to supply all the services for which bids were invited, because there were allegedly discriminatory specifications in the documents relating to the invitation to tender, but he did not seek review of those specifications before the contract was awarded.

The Court examined the material scope of Article 1(3) of the Remedies Directive 89/665/EEC with a view to determining the persons to whom review procedures must be available and providing a definition of interest in obtaining a public contract.[63]

The Court pointed out that the fact that Article 1(3) of Directive 89/665 expressly allows member states to determine the detailed rules according to which they must make the review procedures available to any person having or having had an interest in obtaining a particular public contract and who has been or risks being harmed by an alleged infringement none the less does not authorise them to give the term 'interest in obtaining a public contract' an interpretation which may limit the effectiveness of that directive.[64] Thus, Article 1(3) of Directive 89/665 precludes an undertaking which has participated in a public procurement procedure from being considered as having lost its interest in obtaining that contract on the ground that, before bringing review procedures for setting aside or annulling an act or a decision of a contracting authority, it failed to exhaust pre-judicial proceedings.

The Court examined the scope of Article 1(3) of the Remedies Directive 89/665 in respect of review procedures concerning the award of public contracts and the *locus standi* of persons that are eligible to bring such review procedures before the competent national forum.[65]

---

[63] See case C-410/01, *Fritsch, Chiari & Partner, Ziviltechniker GmbH and Others and Autobahnen- und Schnellstraßen-Finanzierungs-AG (Asfinag)*, ECR [2003] I-11547.

[64] See case C-470/99, *Universale-Bau and Others*, [2002] ECR I-11617, paragraph 72.

[65] See C-249/01, *Werner Hackermüller and Bundesimmobiliengesellschaft mbH (BIG), Wiener Entwicklungsgesellschaft mbH für den Donauraum AG (WED)*, ECR [2003] I-6319;

The Court pointed out that, under Article 1(3) of Directive 89/665, member states are required to ensure that the review procedures laid down by the directive are available at least to any person having or having had an interest in obtaining a particular public contract and who has been or risks being harmed by an alleged infringement of the Community law on public procurement or the national rules implementing that law. Therefore, it is apparent that the provision does not oblige the member states to make those review procedures available to any person wishing to obtain a public contract but allows them to require, in addition, that the person concerned has been or risks being harmed by the infringement he alleges. The Court concluded that Article 1(3) of Directive 89/665 does not preclude the review procedures laid down by the directive being available to persons wishing to obtain a particular public contract only if they have been or risk being harmed by the infringement they allege.

The national court also sought to ascertain whether a tenderer seeking to contest the lawfulness of the decision of the contracting authority not to consider his bid as the best bid may be refused access to the review procedures laid down by Directive 89/665 on the ground that his bid should have been eliminated at the outset by the contracting authority for other reasons and that, therefore, he neither has been nor risks being harmed by the unlawfulness which he alleges.

The Court reiterated that Directive 89/665 is intended to strengthen the existing mechanisms, both at national and Community levels, to ensure the effective application of the directives relating to public procurement, in particular at a stage when infringements can still be remedied. To that effect, Article 1(1) of that directive requires member states to guarantee that unlawful decisions of contracting authorities can be subjected to effective review which is as swift as possible.[66] The full achievement of the objective of Directive 89/665 would be compromised if it were permissible for a body responsible for the review procedures provided for by the directive to refuse access to them to a tenderer alleging the unlawfulness of the decision by which the contracting authority had not considered its bid as being the best bid, on the ground that the same contracting authority was wrong not to eliminate that bid even before making the selection of the best bid. The Court pointed out that there can be no doubt that a decision by which the contracting authority eliminates the bid of a tenderer even before making that selection is a decision of which it must be possible to seek review under Article 1(1) of Directive 89/665, since that provision applies to all decisions taken by contracting

---

[66]   See case C81/98, *Alcatel Austria and Others*, [1999] ECR I7671, paragraphs 33 and 34, and case C-470/99, *Universale-Bau and Others*, [2002] ECR I-11617, paragraph 74.

authorities which are subject to the rules of Community law on public procurement,[67] and makes no provision for any limitation as regards the nature and content of those decisions.[68] Therefore, if the tenderer's bid had been eliminated by the contracting authority at a stage prior to that of the selection of the best bid, he would have had to be allowed, as a person who has been or risks being harmed by that decision to eliminate his bid, to challenge the lawfulness of that decision by means of the review procedures provided by Directive 89/665.

In those circumstances, if a review body were to refuse access to those procedures to a tenderer, the effect would be to deny him not only his right to seek review of the decision he alleges to be unlawful but also the right to challenge the validity of the ground for exclusion raised by that body to deny him the status of a person who has been or risks being harmed by the alleged unlawfulness. Admittedly, if in order to mitigate that situation the tenderer is afforded the right to challenge the validity of that ground of exclusion in the review procedure he instigates in order to challenge the lawfulness of the decision by which the contracting authority did not consider his bid as being the best bid, it is possible that at the end of that procedure the review body may reach the conclusion that the bid should actually have been eliminated at the outset and that the tenderer's application should be dismissed on the ground that, in the light of that circumstance, he neither has been nor risks being harmed by the infringement he alleges. However, if the contracting authority has not taken a decision to exclude the tenderer's bid at the appropriate stage of the award procedure, the method of proceeding described in the previous paragraph must be regarded as the only one likely to guarantee the tenderer the right to challenge the validity of the ground for exclusion on the basis of which the review body intends to conclude that he neither has been nor risks being harmed by the decision he alleges to be unlawful and, accordingly, to ensure the effective application of the Community directives on public procurement at all stages of the award procedure.

The Court concluded that Article 1(3) of Directive 89/665 does not permit a tenderer to be denied access to the review procedures laid down by the Directive in order to contest the lawfulness of the decision of the contracting authority which did not consider his bid on the ground that it should have been eliminated at the outset for different reasons. The fact that the tenderer has neither been harmed nor does he risk being harmed by the alleged unlawful-

---

[67] See case C-92/00, *Hospital Ingenieure*, [2002] ECR I-5553, paragraph 37, and case C-57/01, *Makedoniko Metro and Michaniki*, [2003] ECR I-1091, paragraph 68.

[68] See case C81/98, *Alcatel Austria and Others*, [1999] ECR I7671, paragraph 35 and case C-92/00, *Hospital Ingénieure*, [2002] ECR I-5553, paragraph 49.

ness of the decision of the contracting authority is immaterial to his right to challenge such decision. Thus, in the review procedures available under Article 1(3) of Directive 89/665, the tenderer must be allowed to challenge the grounds of his exclusion on the basis that the lack of harm or risk of being harmed by such unlawful exclusion does not bear any significance to the admissibility of his claim.

Time limits to enact review proceedings

In an interesting case,[69] the national court asked whether Directive 89/665 precludes national legislation which provides that any application for review of the decision of a contracting authority must be commenced within a specific time limit and that any irregularity in the award procedure relied upon in support of such application must be raised within the same period.

The Court noted that whilst the objective of Directive 89/665 is to guarantee the existence, in all member states, of effective remedies for infringements of Community law in the field of public procurement or of the national rules implementing that law, so as to ensure the effective application of the directives on the co-ordination of public procurement procedures, it contains no provision specifically covering time limits for the applications for review which it seeks to establish. It is therefore for the internal legal order of each member state to establish such time limits. However, since there are detailed procedural rules governing the remedies intended to protect rights conferred by Community law on candidates and tenderers harmed by decisions of contracting authorities, they must not compromise the effectiveness of Directive 89/665.

The Court reiterated that Directive 89/665 is intended to strengthen the existing mechanisms, both at national and Community levels, to ensure the effective application of the directives relating to public procurement, in particular at a stage when infringements can still be corrected. To that effect, Article 1(1) of that directive requires member states to guarantee that unlawful decisions of contracting authorities can be subjected to effective review which is as swift as possible. The full implementation of the objective sought by Directive 89/665 would be undermined if candidates and tenderers were allowed to invoke, at any stage of the award procedure, infringement of the rules of public procurement, thus obliging the contracting authority to restart the entire procedure in order to correct such infringements. Moreover, the setting of reasonable limitation periods for bringing proceedings must be regarded as satisfying, in principle, the requirement of effectiveness under

---

[69]   See case C-470/99, *Universale-Bau AG, Bietergemeinschaft*, ECR [2002] I-11617.

Directive 89/665, since it is an application of the fundamental principle of legal certainty.[70] The Court found that Directive 89/665 does not preclude national legislation which provides that any application for review of a contracting authority's decision must be commenced within a time limit laid down to that effect and that any irregularity in the award procedure relied upon in support of such application must be raised within the same period, provided that the time limit in question is reasonable.

In another case,[71] the national court finally asked the European Court of Justice what time is to be taken into consideration for assessing the legality of the decision by the contracting authority to withdraw an invitation to tender. The Court maintained that in the absence of specific Community rules governing the decisive moment for the purposes of assessing the legality of the decision to withdraw an invitation to tender, it is for the domestic legal system of each member state to determine the decisive moment for the purposes of assessing the legality of the withdrawal decision, provided that the relevant national rules are not less favourable than those governing similar domestic actions (principle of equivalence) and that they do not make it practically impossible or excessively difficult to exercise rights conferred by Community law (principle of effectiveness).[72] The Court pronounced that determination of the time to be taken into consideration for assessing the legality of the decision by the contracting authority to withdraw an invitation to tender is a matter for national law, provided that the relevant national rules are not less favourable than those governing similar domestic actions and that they do not make it practically impossible or excessively difficult to exercise rights conferred by Community law.

Actions for Damages

Article 2(1)(c) in both Directives provides for award of damages to persons harmed by an infringement of public procurement law. The purpose behind this provision is to mobilise the interested contractors in order to supervise the application of Public Procurement Directives. The Public Procurement Directives do not require the provision of a remedy for the award of damages when there is a breach of a directly effective rule. The reasons for that absence

---

[70] See case C-261/95, *Palmisani*, [1997] ECR I-4025, paragraph 28, and case C-78/98, *Preston and Others*, [2000] ECR I-3201, paragraph 33.

[71] See C-92/00, *Hospital Ingénieure Krankenhaustechnik Planungs- GmbH (HI) and Stadt Wien*, ECR [2002] I-5553.

[72] See case C-390/98, *Banks v. Coal Authority and Secretary of State for Trade and Industry*, [2001] ECR I-6117, paragraph 121; case C-453/99, *Courage and Crehan*, [2001] ECR I-6297, paragraph 29.

vary: in some cases the national court has held that the authority in breach of Community law did not owe any obligation directly to the plaintiff or that the plaintiff's losses were the results of foreseeable economic risk; in others, the award of damages has been seen as an unacceptable fetter on the freedom of authorities to enact legislative measures or administrative rules in good faith, pursuant to their general duty to safeguard the public interest, such as human health. Damages may be available as a consequence of provisions of national law which make a national authority liable to compensate for breach of its obligations. Procuring authorities are subject to a duty to observe European rules and are liable for damages in breach of those rules. In the context of the Compliance Directives, a question arises as to whether an aspiring contractor seeking damages should prove that he would have been accepted as a tenderer or he would have won the contract, if not for the infringement.

The Directives provide that member states should establish judicial or administrative bodies responsible for their enforcement. Member states, therefore, have a choice as to the forum and procedures provided for hearing disputes or otherwise achieving the required result. In addition, they require that all decisions taken by bodies responsible for review procedures must be effectively enforced.

Damages largely remain to be determined by national law and practice. However, a pattern has emerged where a complainant seeking damages must prove that the contracting authority has committed an infringement of the procurement rules and as a direct result and consequence of that infringement, has suffered harm or loss. In some legal orders, the complainant does not have to prove a breach of procurement rules on the part of the contracting authority, if a previous set aside or annulment judgment of administrative court or tribunal has declared the awarding decision unlawful.

An aggrieved tenderer should in principle be entitled to recover the costs he has incurred in preparing his tender and participating in the award procedure (bid costs), as well as any loss of profit he would have achieved, had he been awarded the contract. In most member states, the burden of proof concerning damages is set at a relatively high level. The mere presence of a breach of procurement procedures, which could be proved by the applicant or through a previous set aside or annulment order of the awarding decision of a contracting authority would be sufficient grounds to trigger the award of damages relating to bid costs and costs necessary for the preparation and submission of a tender.

However, the most important issue emerging from actions for damages in the legal systems of member states relates to the burden of proof on the part of the aggrieved tenderer seeking damages. In most legal orders, the recovery of damages relating to losses of profit is subject to the complainant proving that, in the absence of the alleged breach, he would have been awarded the contract. The public sector Remedies Directive 89/665 is silent on this issue, whereas Directive 92/13 provides some clarification as regards the recovery of bid costs as against utilities. Directive 92/13 provides that where an aggrieved tenderer establishes that an infringement deprived him of a real chance of winning the contract, he is entitled (at least) to damages covering his bid costs. General principles and relevant case-law in a number of member states suggest that this real chance test would apply more generally to any claim for damages under either Remedies Directive.

Damages from the Court's Jurisprudence

Ex proprio motu investigation and causality

The Court covered review procedures concerning the award of public contracts under the Remedies Directive 89/665/EEC and in particular the power of the body responsible for review procedures to consider infringements of its own motion.[73] The national court asked the European Court of Justice whether Directive 89/665 precludes the national court responsible for hearing review procedures, in an action brought by a tenderer with the ultimate aim of obtaining damages, for a declaration that the decision to award a public contract is unlawful, from raising of its own motion the unlawfulness of a decision of the contracting authority other than the one contested by the tenderer. On the other hand, the directive does preclude the court from dismissing an application by a tenderer on the ground that, owing to the unlawfulness raised of its own motion, the award procedure was, in any event, unlawful and that the harm the tenderer may have suffered would therefore have been caused even in the absence of the unlawfulness alleged by the tenderer.

In that regard, it is appropriate to recall that, as is apparent from the first and second recitals in the preamble, Directive 89/665 is intended to strengthen the existing mechanisms, both at national and Community levels, to ensure the effective application of Community directives relating to public procurement, in particular at a stage when infringements can still be remedied. To that effect, Article 1(1) of that directive requires member states to guarantee that unlawful decisions of contracting authorities can be subjected to effective review which is as swift as possible.[74] However, Directive 89/665 lays down only the minimum conditions to be satisfied by the review procedures established in

---

[73]   See case C-315/01, *Gesellschaft für Abfallentsorgungs-Technik GmbH (GAT) and Österreichische Autobahnen und Schnellstraßen AG, (ÖSAG)*, ECR [2003] I-6351.

[74]   See case C-81/98, *Alcatel Austria and Others*, [1999] ECR I-7671, paragraphs 33 and 34, and case C-470/99, *Universale-Bau and Others*, [2002] ECR I-11617, paragraph 74.

domestic law to ensure compliance with the requirements of Community law concerning public contracts.[75]

If there is no specific provision governing the matter, it is therefore for the domestic law of each member state to determine whether, and in what circumstances, a court responsible for review procedures may raise *ex proprio motu* unlawfulness which has not been raised by the parties to the case brought before it. Neither the aims of Directive 89/665 nor the requirement it lays down that both parties be heard in review procedures precludes the introduction of that possibility in the domestic law of a member state.

The Court declared that, first, it cannot be inconsistent with the objective of that directive, which is to ensure compliance with the requirements of Community law on public procurement by means of effective and swift review procedures, for the court responsible for the review procedures to raise *ex proprio motu* unlawfulness affecting an award procedure, without waiting for one of the parties to do so. Secondly, the requirement that both parties be heard in review procedures does not preclude the court responsible for those procedures from being able to raise *ex proprio motu* unlawfulness which it is the first to find, but simply means that before giving its ruling the court must observe the right of the parties to be heard on the unlawfulness raised *ex proprio motu*.

From the Court's stance, it follows that Directive 89/665 does not preclude the court responsible for hearing review procedures, in an action brought by a tenderer with the ultimate aim of obtaining damages, for a declaration that the decision to award a public contract is unlawful, from raising of its own motion the unlawfulness of a decision of the contracting authority other than the one contested by the tenderer. However, it does not necessarily follow that the court may dismiss an application by a tenderer on the ground that, by reason of the unlawfulness raised of its own motion, the award procedure was in any event unlawful and that the harm the tenderer may have suffered would therefore have been caused even in the absence of the unlawfulness alleged by the tenderer.

On the one hand, as is apparent from the case-law of the Court, Article 1(1) of Directive 89/665 applies to all decisions taken by contracting authorities which are subject to the rules of Community law on public procurement[76] and makes no provision for any limitation as regards the nature and content of those decisions.[77] On the other hand, among the review procedures which Directive 89/665 requires the member states to introduce for the purposes of

---

[75]   See case C-327/00, *Santex*, [2003] ECR I-1877, paragraph 47.

[76]   See case C-92/00, *HI*, [2002] ECR I-5553, paragraph 37, and case C-57/01, *Makedoniko Metro and Michaniki*, [2003] ECR I-1091, paragraph 68.

[77]   See case C-81/98, *Alcatel Austria and Others*, [1999] ECR I-767, paragraph 35, and case C-92/00, *Hospital Ingénieure*, [2002] ECR I5553, paragraph 49.

ensuring that the unlawful decisions of contracting authorities may be the subject of review procedures which are effective and as swift as possible is the procedure enabling damages to be granted to the person harmed by an infringement, which is expressly stated in Article 2(1)(c). Therefore, a tenderer harmed by a decision to award a public contract, the lawfulness of which he is contesting, cannot be denied the right to claim damages for the harm caused by that decision on the ground that the award procedure was in any event defective owing to the unlawfulness, raised *ex proprio motu*, of another (possibly previous) decision of the contracting authority.

That conclusion is all the more obvious if a member state has exercised the power conferred on member states by the second subparagraph of Article 2(6) of Directive 89/665 to limit, after the conclusion of the contract following the award, the powers of the court responsible for the review procedures to award damages. In such cases, the unlawfulness alleged by the tenderer cannot be subject to any of the penalties provided for under Directive 89/665. The Court concluded that Directive 89/665 does not preclude the court responsible for hearing review procedures, in an action brought by a tenderer, with the ultimate aim of obtaining damages, for a declaration that the decision to award a public contract is unlawful, from raising of its own motion the unlawfulness of a decision of the contracting authority other than the one contested by the tenderer. However, the directive does preclude the court from dismissing an application by a tenderer on the ground that, owing to the unlawfulness raised of its own motion, the award procedure was in any event unlawful and that the harm which the tenderer may have suffered would therefore have been caused even in the absence of the unlawfulness alleged by the tenderer.

Dissuasive Penalty Payments

Under Article 2(1) of Remedies Directive 92/13, applicable to utilities, member states were given the option of introducing an alternative remedy to the usual combination of interim measures and set aside orders which must be made available, at least prior to the conclusion of the contract. Instead of those two remedies, member states could legislate for the availability of dissuasive penalty payments where an infringement is not corrected or prevented. The option of dissuasive penalty payments has only been taken up by three member states, Denmark (as regards offshore oil and gas utilities only), France and Luxembourg.

Complaints to the European Commission

Under the Remedies Directives, the Commission may invoke a corrective procedure when, prior to a contract being concluded, it considers that a clear and manifest infringement of EU procurement rules has been committed. In such a case, the Commission will notify the awarding authority and the relevant member state government of the circumstances of the alleged infringement. The Commission will set a time limit of at least 21 days for public sector contracting authorities or 30 days for entities operating in the utility sectors, within which the national government has to respond. In practice the awarding authority is called upon to justify its conduct, rectify the infringement or suspend the award procedure.

In cases where the Commission is not satisfied with the explanations or actions of the awarding authority or the government of the respective member state, it may commence formal proceedings against the latter under Article 234 EC, seeking a declaration by the European Court of Justice for failure on the part of the member state to observe and comply with Community law. In particularly serious cases, the Commission might also ask the European Court of Justice to grant interim measures.

Conciliation Procedure for Utilities

Where a dispute arises in relation to procurement award procedures in the utilities sectors, an aggrieved tenderer may initiate the conciliation procedure specified in the Remedies Directive 92/13 for the utilities sectors. Recourse to the conciliation procedure involves the following steps: the aggrieved tenderer forwards a request for use of the conciliation procedure to the European Commission; the Commission asks the utility in question to state whether it is willing to take part in the conciliation procedure. The procedure can only continue if the utility gives its consent; the Commission proposes a conciliator drawn from a list of independent persons. Both sides must state whether they accept the conciliator and each side designates an additional conciliator; aggrieved tenderer, the utility and any other relevant candidate or tenderer have the opportunity to make representations to the conciliators; finally, the conciliator endeavours to reach an agreement between the parties which is in accordance with Community law.

The conciliation procedure must be distinguished from any pre-judicial administrative procedures at national level. Interestingly, there is no provision concerning the relationship between the two proceedings, and in a case where the same person were to initiate conciliation and judicial review proceedings under the Directive simultaneously, the relation between them is unclear. The utility or the aggrieved tenderer may withdraw from the procedure at any time.

COMPLIANCE WITH AND ENFORCEMENT OF THE RULES UNDER THE WTO GOVERNMENT PROCUREMENT AGREEMENT

The extra-territoriality of the legal regime regulating the public procurement of the member states of the Community has been achieved by virtue of the special intergovernmental agreements concluded between the European Community and members/signatories to the GATT Agreement. It was initially the GATT Agreement on Government Procurement (AGP), which was concluded during the Tokyo Round of negotiations, that provided third-country contractors with access to European public markets. The AGP was amended by virtue of the WTO Government Procurement Agreement (GPA) during the Uruguay Round. In principle, access to the public sector markets of the member states has been guaranteed, as far as the framework of provisions in relation to procedural and substantive stages of public procurement is concerned. However, even the most comprehensive set of rules would be ineffective, if its enforcement appeared not sufficient. Access to justice for third-country providers under the GATT/WTO agreements is thus equally important as the principles of access to the public markets of the member states of the Community.

Both the WTO Government Procurement Agreement and its predecessor (the GATT AGP) are considered intergovernmental instruments which are addressed to states and do not intend to confer rights and duties upon individuals as such. Irrespective of the clearness and precision, the unconditionality of their provision and the lack of discretion reserved to states for their implementation, international agreements are not deemed to produce a direct effect,[78] thus depriving individuals from taking advantage of directly effective provisions in litigation before national courts. The Decision of the European Council, which incorporates the WTO GPA into Community law, specifically stipulates that the provisions under the GPA do not have direct effect. However, there is apparently a contradiction between the difficulties arising from applying the theory of direct effectiveness to the GPA provisions and the spirit and wording of the agreement. Express provision of remedies for aggrieved providers is made under Article XX of the GPA, where the remedies provided should be as favourable as those conferred upon Community contractors. Also, Article III of the GPA stipulates that signatories to the agreement should not be treated in a less favourable manner than national providers

---

[78]   See cases C-21–24/72, *International Fruit Co NV v. Produktschap voor Groenten en Fruit*, [1972] ECR 1236. Also case C-280/93, *Germany v. Council*, judgment of 5 October 1994.

or providers from other parties. How in practice these provisions concerning access to justice at national level for third-party providers will operate remains to be seen.

As with its predecessor, the WTO Government Procurement Agreement has created an intergovernmental mechanism for settling disputes arising from its application. The mechanism is referred to as the Understanding on Rules and Procedures Governing the Settlement of Disputes (DSU) and is attached to Annex II of the Agreement. The mechanism provides for a dispute settlement procedure between parties to the Agreement, that is states and not individuals. The DSU apparently elevates the pre-contractual or the contractual dispute between a third-party provider and a contracting authority to a grievance of an intergovernmental dimension. To invoke the Dispute Settlement Understanding, a state must first exhaust all possible ways of settling the dispute in an amicable manner by means of direct consultation and negotiations with the state allegedly in breach. If settlement cannot be reached, the state may then request the WTO Dispute Settlement Body for a Panel to be established in order to hear the case. The Panel is appointed in consultation with the parties and comprises persons with experience in the area of government procurement. The Panel has as its task the provision of a report to the parties concerned, which is then adopted by the Dispute Settlement Body. The latter would then request the state in breach to repeal all the measures which contravene the principles of the WTO Government Procurement Agreement. If it fails to do so, the Dispute Settlement Body may authorise *unilateral suspension* of the application of the GPA or any other agreement under the WTO in the territory of the state affected by the violation.

17. Public procurement as a policy instrument

OVERVIEW

The regulation of public procurement in the European Union reveals various dimensions, as a discipline of European law and policy, directly relevant to the fundamental principles of the common market and as a policy instrument in the hands of member states. The purpose of the regulation of public procurement is to insert a regime of competitiveness into the relevant markets and eliminate all non-tariff barriers to intra-community trade that emanate from preferential purchasing practices which favour national undertakings. Apart from reasons relating to accountability for public expenditure, avoidance of corruption and political manipulation, the regulation of public procurement represents best practice in the delivery of public services by the state and its organs.

Public procurement is a powerful exercise. It carries the power of acquisition; it epitomises economic freedom; it depicts the nexus of trade relations amongst economic operators; it represents the process necessary to deliver public services; it demonstrates strategic policy options. Public procurement as a discipline expands from a simple topic of the common market, to a multi-faceted tool of European regulation and governance covering policy choices and revealing an interesting interface between centralised and national governance systems. This is where the legal effects of public procurement regulations will be felt most.

Procurement Regulation and Economic Policy

Viewing public procurement through the prism of an economic exercise, its regulation displays strong neo-classical influences. Such influences embrace the merit of efficiency in the relevant market and the presence of competition, mainly price competition, which would create optimal conditions for welfare gains. The connection between public procurement regulation and the neo-classical approach to economic integration in the common market is reflected in the criterion for awarding public contracts based on the lowest offer. This feature of the public procurement legal framework focuses on price competition being inserted into the relevant markets, and assisted by the transparency requirement to advertise public contracts above certain thresholds, it would result in production and distribution efficiencies and drive the market towards an optimal allocation of resources.

The lowest offer as an award criterion of public contracts is a quantitative method of achieving market equilibrium between the demand and supply sides. The supply side competes in costs terms to deliver standardised (at least in theory) works, services and goods to the public sector. Price competition is bound to result in innovation in the relevant industries, where through investment and technological improvements, firms could reduce production and/or distribution costs. The lowest offer criterion could be seen as the necessary stimulus to encourage the relevant market participants to improve their competitive advantages.

The lowest offer award criterion reflects, and presupposes, low barriers to entry in a market and provides a type of predictable accessibility to product or geographical markets. This is a desirable characteristic in a system such as public procurement regulation which is charged with integrating national markets and creating a common market for public contracts which is homogeneous and transparent. In addition, the low barriers to entering a market, together with the competitive and transparent price benchmarking for awarding public contracts through the lowest offer criterion would inevitably attract new undertakings in public procurement markets. This can be seen as an increase of the supply-side pool, a fact which would provide comfort and confidence to the demand side (the public sector) in relation to the competitive structure of an industry. Nevertheless, the increased number of participants in public tenders could have adverse effects. Assuming that the financial and technical capacity of firms is not an issue,[1] the demand side (the public sector) will have to bear the cost of tendering and in particular the costs relating to the evaluation of offers. However, the demand side in public procurement often omits risk assessment tests during the evaluation process. The Directives remain vague as to the methods for assessing financial risk, leaving a great deal of discretion in the hands of contracting authorities. Evidence of financial and economic standing may be provided by means of references including: (i) appropriate statements from bankers; (ii) the presentation of the firm's balance sheets or extracts from the balance sheets where these are

---

[1]   See case C-27/86, *Constructions et Entreprises Industrielles SA (CEI) v. Association Intercommunale pour les Autoroutes des Ardennes*; case C-28/86, *Ing.A. Bellini & Co. SpA v. Regie de Betiments*; case C-29/86, *Ing. A. Bellini & Co. SpA v. Belgian State*, [1987] ECR 3347.

published under company law provisions; and (iii) a statement of the firm's annual turnover and the turnover on construction works for the three previous financial years. The more participants enter the market for the award of public contracts, the bigger the costs attributed to the tendering process that would have to be borne by the public sector.

None the less, competitiveness in an industry is not reflected solely by reference to low production costs.[2] Efficiencies which might result through production or distribution innovations are bound to have a short-term effect on the market for two reasons: if the market is bound to clear with reference to the lowest price, there would be a point where the quality of deliverables is compromised (assuming a product or service remains standardised). Secondly, the viability of industries which tend to compete primarily on a cost basis is questionable. Corporate mortality will increase and the market could revert to oligopolistic structures.

The welfare gains emanating from a neo-classical approach to public procurement regulation encapsulate the actual and potential savings the public sector (and consumers of public services at large) would enjoy through a system that forces the supply side to compete on costs (and price). These gains, however, must be counterbalanced by the costs of tendering (administrative and evaluative costs borne by the public sector), the costs of competition (costs related to the preparation and submission of tender offers borne by the private sector) and litigation costs (costs relevant to prospective litigation borne by both aggrieved tenderers and the public sector). If the cumulative costs exceed any savings attributed to the lowest offer criterion, the welfare gains are negative.

A neo-classical perspective on public procurement regulation reveals the zest of policy makers for establishing conditions which calibrate market clearance on price grounds. Price competitiveness in public procurement raises a number of issues with anti-trust law and policy. If the maximisation of savings is the only (or the primary) achievable objective for the demand side in the public procurement process, the transparent/competitive pattern cannot provide any safeguards in relation to under-priced (and anti-competitive) offers.

The price-competitive tendering reflects on the dimension of public procurement regulation as an economic exercise. On the one hand, when the supply side responds to the perpetually competitive purchasing patterns by lowering prices, the public sector could face a dilemma: *what would be the lowest offer it can accept?* The public sector faces a considerable challenge in

---

2   See Lawton (ed), *Industrial Policy and Competitiveness in Europe*, Macmillan, 1998.

evaluating and assessing low offers other than 'abnormally low' ones.[3] It is difficult to identify dumping or predatory pricing disguised behind a low offer for a public contract. On the other hand, even if there is an indication of anti-competitive price fixing, the European public procurement rules do not provide for any kind of procedure to address the problem. The anti-trust rules take over and the suspension of the award procedures (or even the suspension of the contract itself) would be subject to a thorough and exhaustive investigation by the competent anti-trust authorities.

Evidence of the neo-classical approach in public procurement regulation can be found in Guidelines[4] issued by the European Commission. The Commission adopted a strict interpretation of the rules and focused member states on an economic approach to the application of the Public Procurement Directives. The Commission has championed the neo-classical approach for two reasons: first, to bring about an acceptable level of compliance by member states with the public procurement regime and secondly, to follow the assumptions made through the internal market process that procurement represents a significant non-tariff barrier and its regulation can result in substantial savings for the public sector.

It is interesting to follow the Commission's approach[5] in litigation before the European Court of Justice, where as an applicant in compliance procedures, or as an intervening party in reference procedures, it consistently regarded public procurement regulation as an economic exercise. The backbone of such an approach has been the price approach to the award of public contracts, predominantly through the lowest offer award criterion, but also

---

[3]   The European rules provide an automatic disqualification for an 'obviously abnormally low offer'. The term has not been interpreted in detail by the judiciary at European and domestic levels and serves rather as a 'lower bottom limit'. The contracting authorities are under a duty to seek from the tenderer an explanation for the price submitted or else to inform him that his tender appears to be abnormally low and to allow a reasonable time within which to submit further details, before making any decision as to the award of the contract. See case 76/81, *SA Transporoute et Travaux v. Minister of Public Works*, [1982] ECR 457; case 103/88, *Fratelli Costanzo SpA v. Comune di Milano*, [1989] ECR 1839; case 296/89, *Impresa Dona Alfonso di Dona Alfonso & Figli snc v. Consorzio per lo Sviluppo Industriale del Comune di Monfalcone*, [1991] ECR 2967; case C-285/99 & 286/99, *Impresa Lombardini SpA v. ANAS*, [2001] ECR 9233.

[4]   See Commission Communication, Public Procurement, 22 September 1989, C 311 89.

[5]   See the Commission's arguments in the *Bentjees* case (case 31/87, *Gebroeders Beentjes BV v. State of Netherlands*, [1988] ECR 4635), Nord-Pas-de-Calais (case C-225/98, *Commission v. French Republic*, [2000] ECR 7445), and the Concordia C-513/99, *Concordia Bus Filandia v. Helsingin Kaupunki et HKL-Bussiliikenne*, [2002] ECR 7213.

through the most economically advantageous offer criterion, where factors other than price can play a role in the award process. Even in the latter category, where some degree of flexibility is envisaged by the legal regime, the Commission has been sceptical of any attempts to apply so-called 'qualitative' factors in the award process. Along these lines, the European Court of Justice pursued a neo-classical approach to public procurement regulation through its rulings relating to (i) compliance procedures against member states for not observing the publicity and mandatory advertisement requirements, (ii) procedures concerning standardisation and technical specifications[6] and (iii) procedures relating to the notion of abnormally low offers.[7]

Public Procurement Regulation and Anti-trust

The regulatory weaponry for private markets evolves around anti-trust law and policy, where the influence of the neo-classical economic approach has been evident.[8] Public markets are fora where the structural and behavioural remedial tools of competition law also apply. However, they focus on the supply side (the industry) which *ipso facto* is subject to the relevant rules relating to cartels and abusive dominance.

There is a conceptual difference relating to the application of anti-trust in public markets. The demand side (the public sector, the state and its organs) can hardly be embraced by its remit, except in the case of state aids and illegal subsidies. In private markets, anti-trust law and policy seek to punish cartels and the abusive dominance of undertakings. The focus of the remedial instruments of anti-trust is the supply side, which is conceived as the commanding part of the supply/demand equation due to the fact that it instigates and often controls demand for a product. In private markets, the demand side of the equation (the consumers at large) is susceptible to exploitation and market equilibria are prone to distortion as a result of collusive behaviour by undertakings or an abusive monopoly position. On the other hand, the structure of public markets reveals a different picture. In the supply/demand equation, the dominant part appears to be the demand side (the state and its organs as purchasers), which initialises demand through purchasing, while the supply side (the industry) fights for access to the relevant markets.

---

6 See case C-45/87, *Commission v. Ireland*, [1988] ECR 4929; Also case C-359/93, *Commission v. The Netherlands*, [1995] ECR 151.

7 See case 76/81, *SA Transporoute et Travaux v. Minister of Public Works*, [1982] ECR 457; case 103/88, *Fratelli Costanzo SpA v. Comune di Milano*, [1989] ECR 1839; case 296/89, *Impresa Dona Alfonso di Dona Alfonso & Figli snc v. Consorzio per lo Sviluppo Industriale del Comune di Monfalcone*, [1991] ECR 2967; case C-285/99 & 286/99, *Impresa Lombardini SpA v. ANAS*, [2001] ECR 9233.

8 See Posner, *Antitrust Law*, 2nd edition, Chicago, 2000.

In public markets, market segmentation occurs as a result of concerted practices attributed to the demand side. Since such concerted practices by member states and their contracting authorities (for example, excluding foreign competition, application of buy-national policies, and application of national standards policies) focus on the origin of a product or a service or the nationality of a contractor, market segmentation in public markets tends to possess geographical characteristics and results in the division of the European public market into different national public markets.

The regulation of public markets requires more than the control of the supply side through anti-trust. The primary objective is *market access* and the abolition of barriers and obstacles to trade. Therefore, the regulation aims at the demand side, which effectively controls access and can segment the relevant market. Whereas price competition is the main characteristic of anti-trust,[9] public procurement regulation first pursues market access. This perspective reflects on the *sui generis* nature of public markets and has provided the basis for developing a regulatory system which is strongly influenced by neo-classical economics, whilst at the same time integrating the relevant market. Such a system also has strong public law characteristics, to the extent that it has been branded as public competition law (*droit public de la concurrence*).[10]

The vehicle of harmonisation has been entrusted with carrying public procurement regulation forward. Directives, as legal instruments, have been utilised to provide the framework of the *acquis communautaire*, but at the same time afford the necessary discretion to the member states as to the forms and methods of their implementation. This is where the first deviation of anti-trust from the traditional economic approach to public procurement occurs. Anti-trust law and policy are enacted through the principle of uniformity across the common market, utilising directly applicable regulations. By allowing discretion to the member states, an element of public policy is inserted into the equation, which often has decentralised features. Traditionally, discretion afforded by Directives takes into account national particularities and sensitivities as well as the readiness of domestic administrations to implement acquis before a certain deadline. In addition, individuals, who are also subject to the

---

9   See Monti, 'Article 81 EC and public policy', 39 (2002), *Common Market Law Review*, where it is argued that public policy considerations balance the legality test of *ab initio* illegal restrictive agreements by virtue of Article 81(1)(2) EC with a set of requirements contained in Art 81(3) EC and also developed by the EC Commission in its jurisdictional capacity to provide individual exemptions.

10   See Bazex, *Le droit public de la concurrence*, RFDA, 1998; Arcelin, *L'entreprise en droit interne et communautaire de la concurrence*, Litec, 2003; Guézou, 'Droit de la concurrence et droit des marchés publics: vers une notion transversale de mise en libre concurrence', *Contrats Publics*, March 2003.

rights and duties envisaged by the Directives, do not have access to justice, unless the provisions of Directives produce a direct effect.

However, the public policy dimension of public procurement regulation is not exhausted by the nature of the legal instruments of the regime. The genuine connection of an ordo-liberal perspective[11] with public procurement regulation is reflected in the award criterion relating to the most economically advantageous offer. The public sector can award contracts by reference to 'qualitative' criteria, in conjunction with price, and thus can legitimately deviate from the strict price competition environment set by the lowest offer criterion.[12] There are three themes emanating from such an approach: one reflects on public procurement's role as a complimentary tool of the European integration process; the second regards public procurement as an instrument of contract compliance; last, the ordo-liberal perspective can reveal a rule of reason in public procurement, where the integration of public markets in the European Union serves as a conveyer belt for common policies, such as environmental policy, consumer policy, social policy, industrial policy and takes into account a flexible and wider view of national and community priorities, and a type of 'European public policy'.

Policy makers at both European and national levels have not overlooked the effects of public procurement on the formulation of the industrial policy of the European Union. The objective of public procurement regulation has to a large extent acquired an industrial policy background, which mainly focuses on the achievement of savings for the public sector and the much desired restructuring and adjustment of the European industrial base. However, public spending in the form of procurement is indissolubly linked with adjacent policies and agendas in all member states. The most important policy associated with public purchasing is social policy. Such an argument finds justification for two reasons: the first relates to the optimal utilisation of human resources in industries supplying the public sector; the second reason acquires a strategic dimension, in the sense that public purchasing serves aims and objectives stipulated in the European Treaties, such as social cohesion, combating of long-term unemployment, and finally the achievement of acceptable standards of living.

---

[11]   See Jacquemin and de Jong, *European Industrial Organization*, Macmillan, 1997; Möschel, 'Competition law from an ordo point of view', in Peacock and Willgerodt, *German Neo-liberals and the Social Market Economy*, Macmillan, 1989.

[12]   See Commission Interpretative Communication on the Community law applicable to public procurement and the possibilities for integrating social considerations into public procurement, COM (2001) 566, 15 October 2001. Also, Commission Interpretative Communication on the Community law applicable to public procurement and the possibilities for integrating environmental considerations into public procurement, COM (2001) 274, 4 July 2001.

The underlying objectives of the European regime on public procurement relating to enhanced competition and unobstructed market access in the public sector at first sight appear incompatible with the social dimension of European integration, particularly in an era where recession and economic stagnation have revealed the combating of unemployment as a main theme of European governance.

As mentioned above, the award of public contracts can be based on two criteria: (i) the lowest price or (ii) the most economically advantageous offer. Contracting authorities have absolute discretion in adopting the award criterion under which they wish to award their public contracts. The lowest price award criterion is mostly used when the procurement process is relatively straightforward. On the other hand, the most economically advantageous offer award criterion is suited to more complex procurement schemes.

The most economically advantageous offer as an award criterion represents a flexible framework for contracting authorities wishing to insert a qualitative parameter into the award process for a public contract. Needless to say, price, as a quantitative parameter, plays an important role in the evaluation stage of tenders, as the meaning of 'economically advantageous' could well embrace financial considerations in the long run. So, if the qualitative criteria of a particular bid compensate for its higher price, potential savings in the long run could not be precluded. It is not clear whether the choice of the two above-mentioned award criteria has been intentional with a view to providing contracting authorities with a margin of discretion to take into account social policy objectives when awarding their public contracts, or if it merely reflects an element of flexibility which is considered necessary in modern purchasing transactions. If the most economically advantageous offer represents elements relating to quality of public purchasing other than price, an argument arises here supporting the fact that the enhancement of the socio-economic fabric is a 'qualitative' element which can fall within the framework of the above criterion. This argument would remove the assumption that the award of public contracts is a purely *economic exercise*. On the other hand, if one is to insist that public procurement should reflect only *economic choices*, the social policy considerations that may arise from the award of public contracts would certainly have an economic dimension attached to them, often in public service activities which are parallel to public procurement. To what extent contracting authorities should contemplate such elements remains unclear.

The regulation of public procurement and the integration of the public markets of the member states do not operate in a vacuum. Irrespective of the often publicised nature of public procurement as the most significant non-tariff barrier to the functioning of the common market and the clinical presentation of arguments in favour of an integrated public market across the

European Union,[13] public purchasing is indissolubly linked with national policies and priorities.[14] In the history of European economic integration, public procurement has been an important part of member states' industrial policies. It has been utilised as a policy tool[15] in order to support indigenous suppliers and contractors and protect national industries and the related workforce. The legislation on public procurement in the early days clearly allowed for 'preference schemes' in less favoured regions of the common market which were experiencing industrial decline. Such schemes required the application of award criteria based on considerations other than the lowest price or the most economically advantageous offer, subject to their compatibility with Community law inasmuch as they did not run contrary to the principle of free movement of goods and to competition law considerations with respect to state aid. Since the completion of the internal market (1992) they have been abolished, as they have been deemed capable of contravening, directly or indirectly, the basic principle of non-discrimination on grounds of nationality.

The public procurement legal framework can also accommodate *contract compliance* through its award criteria and in particular the most economically advantageous offer. The most economically advantageous offer as an award criterion has provided the Court with the opportunity to balance the economic considerations of public procurement against policy choices. Although in numerous instances the Court has maintained the importance of the economic approach[16] in the regulation of public sector contracts, it has also recognised the relative discretion of contracting authorities in utilising non-economic considerations as part of the award criteria.

The term *contract compliance*[17] could be best defined as the range of secondary policies relevant to public procurement which aim at combating

---

[13] See European Commission, Special Sectoral Report No. 1, Public Procurement, Brussels, November 1997.

[14] See European Commission, Public Procurement: Regional and Social Aspects COM (89) 400.

[15] See Articles 29(4) and 29(a) of the EC Public Works Directive 71/305; also Article 26 of EC Public Supplies Directive 77/62.

[16] See case C-380/98, *The Queen and HM Treasury, ex parte University of Cambridge*, judgment of 3 October 2000, at paragraph 17; case C-44/96, *Mannesmann Anlangenbau Austria AG et al. v. Strohal Rotationsdurck GesmbH*, judgment of 15 January 1998, paragraph 33; case C-360/96, *Gemeente Arnhem Gemeente Rheden v. BFI Holding BV*, judgment of 10 November 1998, at paragraphs 42 and 43; C-237/99, *Commission v. France*, judgment of 1 February 2001, at paragraphs 41 and 42.

[17] See Bovis, 'The compatibility of compulsory tendering with transfer of undertakings: the case of contract compliance and the acquired rights directive', chapter 21, in Collins, Davies and Rideout (eds), *Legal Regulation of the Employment Relations*, Kluwer, 2000.

discrimination on grounds of sex, race, religion or disability.[18] When utilised in public contracts, contract compliance is a system whereby, unless the supply side (the industry) complies with certain conditions relating to social policy measures, contracting authorities can lawfully exclude tenderers from selection, qualification and award procedures. The potential of public purchasing as a tool capable of promoting social policies has been regarded with considerable scepticism. Policies relevant to affirmative action or positive discrimination have caused a great deal of controversy, as they in practice accomplish very little in rectifying labour market equilibria. In addition to the practicability and effectiveness of such policies, serious reservations have been expressed with regard to their constitutionality,[19] since they could limit, actually and potentially, the principles of economic freedom and freedom of transactions.[20]

Contract compliance legislation and policy are familiar to most European member states, although the enactment of Public Procurement Directives has changed the situation dramatically.[21] The position of European institutions on contract compliance has been addressed in three instances before the European Court of Justice.[22] The Court maintained that contract compliance with reference to domestic or local employment cannot be used as a selection criterion in tendering procedures for the award of public contracts. The selection of tenderers is a process which is based on an exhaustive list of technical and financial requirements expressly stipulated in the relevant Directives and the insertion of contract compliance as a selection and qualification requirement would be considered *ultra vires*. The Court ruled that social policy considerations can only be part of award criteria in public procurement, and especially

---

[18]   See ILEA Contract Compliance Equal Opportunities Unit, *Contract Compliance: A Brief History*, London, 1990.

[19]   In particular in the US, see case 93-1841, *Adarand Constructors v. Pena*, 1995 Annual Volume of US Supreme Court. The United States Supreme Court questioned the constitutionality of the application of contract compliance as a potential violation of the equal protection component of the Fifth Amendment's Due Process Clause and ordered the Court of Appeal to reconsider the employment of socio-economic policy objectives in the award of federal public procurement contracts.

[20]   For an overview of social policy in North American systems, see Cnossen and Bovis, 'The framework of social policy in federal states: An analysis of the law and policy on industrial relations in USA and Canada', 12 (1996), *International Journal of Comparative Labour Law and Industrial Relations*.

[21]   For example, in the United Kingdom, every initiative relating to contract compliance has been outlawed by virtue of the Local Government Act 1988. Contract compliance from a public law perspective has been examined by Daintith, in 'Regulation by contract: The new prerogative', 32 (1979), CLP, 41.

[22]   See case 31/87, *Gebroeders Beentjes BV v. The Netherlands*, [1989] ECR 4365. Also see case C-360/89, *Commission v. Italy*, judgment of 3 July 1992.

in cases where the most economically advantageous offer is selected, provided that they do not run counter to the basic principles of the Treaty and that they have been mentioned in the tender notice.

The Court's approach has also opened up an interesting debate on the integral dimensions of contract compliance and the differentiation between the *positive* and *negative* approaches. The concept of positive approach within contract compliance encompasses all measures and policies imposed by contracting authorities on tenderers as suitability criteria for their selection in public procurement contracts. Such positive action measures and policies intend to complement the actual objectives of public procurement which are confined to economic and financial parameters and are based on a transparent and predictable legal background. Although the complementarity of contract compliance with the actual aims and objectives of the public procurement regime was acknowledged, the Court (and the European Commission) were reluctant to accept such an over-flexible interpretation of the Directives and based on the literal interpretation of the relevant provisions disallowed positive actions of a social policy dimension as part of the selection criteria for tendering procedures in public procurement.

However, contract compliance can not only incorporate unemployment considerations, but also promote equality of opportunities and eliminate sex or race discrimination in the relevant market.[23] There are a number of legal instruments relevant to social policy at Community level that may apply to public procurement. These include issues relevant to safety and health at work, working conditions and the application of employment law, the posting of workers within the framework of the provision of services, the safeguarding of employees' rights in the event of transfers of undertakings, businesses or parts of undertakings or businesses, the principle of equal treatment between persons irrespective of racial or ethnic origin and the establishment of a general framework for equal treatment in employment and occupation.

---

[23]   See in particular, Directives on safety and health at work (for example, Council Directive 89/391 on the introduction of measures to encourage improvements in the safety and health of workers at work, and Directive 92/57 on the implementation of minimum safety and health requirements at temporary or mobile construction sites), working conditions and the application of employment law (for example, Directive 96/71/EC of the European Parliament and of the Council concerning the posting of workers in the framework of the provision of services, OJ L 18/1 of 21.1.1997, and Directive 2001/23 on the safeguarding of employees' rights in the event of transfers of undertakings, businesses or parts of undertakings or businesses, OJ L 82/16 of 22.3.2001, codifying Directive 77/187/EEC), Directive 2000/43/EC of 29.6.2000 implementing the principle of equal treatment between persons irrespective of racial or ethnic origin (OJ 2000 L 180/22) and Directive 2000/78/EC of 27.11.2000 establishing a general framework for equal treatment in employment and occupation (OJ 2000 L 303/16).

Indeed, the Directives on Public Procurement stipulate that the contracting authority may require tenderers to observe national provisions of employment legislation when they submit their offers. The inability to observe and conform to national employment laws in a member state may constitute a ground for disqualification and exclusion of the defaulting firm from public procurement contracts.[24] In fact, under such an interpretation, contract compliance may be a factor in selection criteria specified in the Directives, as it contains a *negative approach* to legislation and measures relating to social policy.

There are arguments in favour and against incorporating social policy considerations in public procurement.[25] The most important argument in favour focuses on the ability of public procurement to promote parts of the member states' social policy, with particular reference to long-term unemployment, equal distribution of income, social exclusion and the protection of minorities. Under such a positively oriented approach, public purchasing could be regarded as an instrument of policy in the hands of national administrations with a view to achieving social equilibria. Contract compliance in public procurement could also cancel the stipulated aims and objectives of the liberalisation of the public sector. The regulation of public markets focuses on economic considerations and competition. Adherence to social policy factors could derail the whole process, as the public sector will pay more for its procurement through extra or hidden costs for the implementation of contract compliance in purchasing policies.[26]

The nomination of regional or national firms in the award process of public contracts, as well as the promotion of socio-economic considerations relevant to policies of member states under such premises could, legitimately, elevate preferential procurement as an instrument of industrial policy. This might shift the debate from the potential violation of internal market provisions, such as state aids and the free movement principles, towards the overall compatibility of the regime with national or common market-wide industrial policies, thus positioning preferential public procurement within the remit of anti-trust.

---

[24]   It should be mentioned that adherence to health and safety laws has been considered by a British court as part of the technical requirements specified in the Works Directive for the process of selection of tenderers; see *General Building and Maintenance v. Greenwich Borough Council*, [1993] IRLR 535. Along these lines, see the Commission's Interpretative Communication on the Community law applicable to public procurement and the possibilities for integrating social considerations into public procurement, COM (2001) 566, 15/10/01.

[25]   See Kruger, Nielsen, and Brunn, *European Public Contracts in a Labour Law Perspective*, DJOF Publishing, 1997.

[26]   See Bovis, 'Social policy considerations and the European public procurement regime', 3 (1998), *International Journal of Comparative Labour Law and Industrial Relations*.

Secondly, there is a fundamental change in perceptions about the role and responsibilities expected from governments in delivering public services. The public sector not only initiates and facilitates the delivery of public services but can also be actively involved in the actual delivery process. Such changes, in practical terms viewed through the evolution of public–private partnerships,[27] are translated into a new contractual interface between public and private sectors, which in turn encapsulates an era of *contractualised governance*. Of interest is the recent case *ARGE*[28] where even the receipt of aid or subsidies incompatible with the Treaty by an entity may be a reason for disqualification from the selection process, as an obligation to repay an illegal aid would threaten the financial stability of the tenderer in question. The Court maintained that if the legislature wanted to preclude subsidised entities from participating in tendering procedures for public contracts, it should have said so explicitly in the relevant Directives.

Public Procurement Regulation and State Aid

The frequently exposed nature of public procurement as the most significant non-tariff barrier to the functioning of the common market[29] and the presentation of arguments in favour of an integrated public market across the European Union[30] have contributed to the debate that public purchasing is indissolubly linked with national policies and priorities.[31] In the history of European economic integration, public procurement has been an important part of

---

[27] An example of such an approach is the views of the UK government in relation to the involvement of the private sector in delivering public services. The so-called *Private Finance Initiative (PFI)*, has been utilised as a procurement and contractual system in order to create a framework for the public and private sectors working together in delivering public services. See in particular, *Working Together – Private Finance and Public Money*, Department of Environment, 1993. *Private Opportunity, Public Benefit – Progressing the Private Finance Initiative*, Private Finance Panel and HM Treasury, 1995.

[28] See case C-94/99, *ARGE Gewässerschutzt v. Bundesministerium für Land- und Forstwirtschaft*, judgment of 7 December 2000.

[29] See European Commission, White Paper for the Completion of the Internal Market, (COM) 85 310 final, 1985. Also Commission of the European Communities, The Cost of Non-Europe, Basic Findings, Vol. 5, Part A; The Cost of Non-Europe in Public Sector Procurement, Official Publications of the European Communities, Luxembourg, 1988. Also the Cecchini Report, *1992 The European Challenge, The Benefits of a Single Market*, Wildwood House, 1988.

[30] See European Commission, Special Sectoral Report no 1, Public Procurement, Brussels, November 1997.

[31] See European Commission, Public Procurement: Regional and Social Aspects COM (89) 400.

member states' industrial policies. It has been utilised as a policy tool[32] in order to support indigenous suppliers and contractors and preserve national industries and the related workforce. The legislation on public procurement in the early days clearly allowed for 'preference schemes' in less favoured regions of the common market which were experiencing industrial decline. Such schemes required the application of award criteria based on considerations other than the lowest price or the most economically advantageous offer, subject to their compatibility with Community law inasmuch as they did not run contrary to the principle of free movement of goods and to competition law considerations with respect to state aids. Since the completion of the internal market in 1992 they have been abolished, as they have been deemed capable of contravening directly the basic principle of non-discrimination on grounds of nationality.

There has been a great deal of controversy over the issue of the compatibility of preferential procurement with EU law. The justification of preference schemes as a way of promoting regional development policies has revealed the interaction of public procurement with state aid.[33] Preferential procurement reflects protectionism, and as such is regarded as a non-tariff barrier. However, protectionist public procurement, when strategically exercised, has resulted in the evolution of vital industries for the state in question.[34] Preferential public procurement can be seen through a multi-dimensional prism. First, it appears in the form of an exercise which aims at preserving some domestic sectors or industries at the expense of the principles of the European integration process. Impact assessment studies undertaken by the European Commission showed that the operation of preference schemes had a minimal effect on the economies of the regions where they had been applied, both in terms of the volume of procurement contracts, as well as in terms of real economic growth attributed to the operation of such schemes.[35] Thus, in such a form, preferential public procurement perpetuates the sub-optimal allocation of resources and represents a welfare loss for the economy of the relevant state. On the other hand, preferential purchasing in the form of strategic investment in the sustainability of selected industries might represent a viable instrument of industrial policy, to the extent that the infant industry, when specialised and

---

[32] See Articles 29(4) and 29(a) of the EC Public Works Directive 71/305; also Article 26 of EC Public Supplies Directive 77/62.

[33] See, Fernandez-Martin and Stehmann, 'Product market integration versus regional cohesion in the community', 16 (1991), *European Law Review*.

[34] See Bovis, *The Liberalisation of Public Procurement in the European Union and its Effects on the Common Market*, Ashgate-Dartmouth, 1998.

[35] European Commission, Public Procurement: Regional and Social Aspects (COM (89) 400)

internationalised, would be in a position to counterbalance any welfare losses during its protected period. In the above form, preferential public procurement, as an integral part of industrial policy could possibly result in welfare gains.[36]

Preference schemes have been indissolubly linked to regional development policies, but their interpretation by the European Court of Justice has always been restrictive.[37] Although the utilisation of public procurement as a tool of regional development policy may breach, directly or indirectly, primary Treaty provisions on free movement of goods, the right of establishment and the freedom to provide services, it is far from clear whether the European Commission or the Court could accept the legitimate use of public procurement as a means of state aid. Prior notification to the European Commission of the measures or policies intended to be used as state aid apparently does not legitimise such measures or absolve them from adherence to the judicially well-established framework of the four freedoms. The parallel applicability of rules relating to state aid and the free movement of goods, in the sense that national measures conceived as state aid must not violate the principle of free movement of goods, renders the thrust of regional policies through state aid practically ineffective. It appears that the Court has experimented with the question of the compatibility between state aid and free movement of goods in a number of cases where, initially, it was held that the two regimes were mutually exclusive, to the extent that the principle of free movement of goods could not apply to measures relating to state aid.[38] The acid test for such mutual exclusivity was the prior notification of such measures to the European Commission. However, the Court departed from such a position when it applied free movement of goods provisions to a number of cases concerning state aid, which had not been notified to the Commission.[39] Surprisingly, the Court also brought notified state aid measures under the remit of the provision of free movement of

---

[36]   See Commission of the European Communities, *Statistical Performance for keeping watch over public procurement*, 1992.

[37]   See case 84/86, *Commission v. Hellenic Republic*, not reported; case C-21/88, *Dupont de Nemours Italiana SpA v. Unita Sanitaria Locale No. 2 di Carrara*, judgment of 20 March, 1990, [1990] ECR 889; case C-351/88, *Lavatori Bruneau Slr v. Unita Sanitaria Locale RM/24 di Monterotondo*, judgment of 11 July 1991; case C-360/89, *Commission v. Italy*, [1992] ECR I 3401; case C-362/90, *Commission v. Italy*, judgment of 31 March 1992.

[38]   See case C-74/76, *Ianelli & Volpi Spa v. Ditta Paola Meroni*, [1977] 2 CMLR 688.

[39]   See case C-18/84, *Commission v. France*, 1985, ECR 1339; case 103/84, *Commission v. Italy*, 1986, ECR 1759; also, case C-244/81, *Commission v. Ireland*, 1982, ECR 4005.

goods and reconsidered the whole framework of the mutual exclusivity of states aid and free movement of goods.[40]

State aid jurisprudence has revealed the catalytic position of public procurement in the process of determining whether subsidies or state financing of public services represent state aid. The significance of the subject is epitomised in the attempts of the European Council[41] to provide a policy framework of greater predictability and increased legal certainty in the application of the state aid rules to the funding of services of general interest. Along the above lines, public procurement rules have served as a yardstick to determine the nature of an undertaking in its contractual interface when delivering public services. The funding of services of general interest by the state may materialise in different forms, such as the payment of remuneration for services under a public contract, the payment of annual subsidies, preferential fiscal treatment or lower social contributions. The most common form is the existence of a contractual relation between the state and the undertaking charged with delivering public services. The above relation should, under normal circumstances, pass through the remit of the public procurement framework, not only as an indication of market competitiveness but mainly as a demonstration of the nature of the deliverable services as services of 'general interest having non industrial or commercial character'.

There are three ways in which the European judiciary and the Commission have examined the financing of public services: *the state aid approach, the compensation approach and the quid pro quo approach.* The above approaches not only reflect conceptual and procedural differences in the application of state aid control measures within the common market, but also raise imperative and multifaceted questions relevant to the state funding of services of general interest.

The state aid approach[42] examines state funding granted to an undertaking

---

40   See Bovis, 'Public procurement as an instrument of industrial policy in the European Union', chapter 7, in Lawton (ed), *Industrial Policy and Competitiveness in Europe*, Macmillan, 1998; Fernandez Martin and Stehmann, 'Product market integration versus regional cohesion in the Community', op. cit.

41   See the Conclusions of the European Council of 14 and 15 December 2001, paragraph 26; Conclusions of the Internal Market, Consumer Affairs and Tourism Council meeting of 26 November 2001 on services of general interest; Commission Report to the Laeken European Council on Services of General Interest of 17 October 2001, COM (2001) 598; Communication from the Commission on the application of the State aid rules to public service broadcasting, OJ 2001 C 320, p. 5; see also the two general Commission Communications on Services of General Interest of 1996 and 2000 in OJ 1996 C 281, p. 3 and OJ 2001 C 17, p. 4.

42   See case C-387/92 [1994] ECR I-877; case T-106/95 *FFSA and Others v. Commission*, [1997] ECR II-229; case C-174/97 P [1998] ECR I-1303; case T-46/97 [2000] ECR II-2125.

for the performance of obligations of general interest. It thus regards the relevant funding as state aid within the meaning of Article 87(1) EC,[43] which may however be justified under Article 86(2) EC,[44] provided that the conditions of that derogation are fulfilled and, in particular, that the funding complies with the principle of proportionality. The state aid approach provides the most clear and legally certain procedural and conceptual framework to regulate state aid, since it positions the European Commission in the centre of that framework.

The compensation approach[45] reflects a 'compensation' being intended to cover an appropriate remuneration for the services provided or the costs of providing those services. Under this approach state funding of services of general interest amounts to state aid within the meaning of Article 87(1) EC, only if and to the extent that the economic advantage which it provides exceeds such an appropriate remuneration or such additional costs. European jurisprudence considers that state aid exists only if, and to the extent that, the remuneration paid, when the state and its organs procure goods or services, exceeds the market price.

The *quid pro quo* approach distinguishes between two categories of state funding; in cases where there is a direct and manifest link between state financing and clearly defined public service obligations, any sums paid by the state would not constitute state aid within the meaning of the Treaty. On the other hand, where there is no such link or the public service obligations were not clearly defined, the sums paid by the public authorities would constitute state aid.

The choice between the state aid approach and the compensation approach does not only reflect a theoretical debate; it mainly reveals significant practical ramifications in the application of state aid control within the common market. Whilst it is generally accepted that the pertinent issue of substance is whether the state funding exceeds what is necessary to provide an appropriate remuneration or to offset the extra costs caused by the general interest obligations, the two approaches have very different procedural implications. Under

---

[43]   Article 87(1) EC defines state aid as 'any aid granted by a Member State or through State resources in any form whatsoever which distorts or threatens to distort competition by favoring certain undertakings or the production of certain goods . . ., in so far as it affects trade between Member States'.

[44]   Article 86(2) EC stipulates that '. . . Undertakings entrusted with the operation of services of general economic interest . . . shall be subject to the rules contained in this Treaty, in particular to the rules on competition, insofar as the application of such rules does not obstruct the performance, in law or in fact, of the particular tasks assigned to them. The development of trade must not be affected to such an extent as would be contrary to the interests of the Community'.

[45]   See case 240/83 [1985] ECR 531; case C-53/00, judgment of 22 November 2001; case C-280/00, judgment of 24 July 2003.

the compensation approach, state funding which does not constitute state aid escapes the clutches of EU state aid rules and need not be notified to the Commission. More importantly, national courts have jurisdiction to pronounce on the nature of the funding as state aid without the need to wait for an assessment by the Commission of its compatibility with acquis. Under the state aid approach the same measure would constitute state aid and must be notified in advance to the Commission. Moreover, the derogation in Article 86(2) EC is subject to the same procedural regime as the derogations in Article 87(2) and (3) EC, which means that new aid cannot be implemented until the Commission has declared it compatible with Article 86(2) EC. Measures which infringe that stand-still obligation constitute illegal aid. Another procedural implication of the compensation approach is that national courts must offer to individuals the certain prospect that all appropriate conclusions will be drawn from the infringement of the last sentence of Article 88(3) EC, as regards the validity of the measures giving effect to the aid, the recovery of financial support granted in disregard of that provision and possible interim measures.

The *quid pro quo* approach[46] positions at the centre of the analysis of state funding of services of general interest a distinction between two different categories: (i) the nature of the link between the financing granted and the general interest duties imposed and (ii) the degree of clarity in defining those duties. The first category would comprise cases where the financing measures are clearly intended as a *quid pro quo* for clearly defined general interest obligations, or in other words where the link between, on the one hand, the state financing granted and, on the other hand, clearly defined general interest obligations imposed is direct and manifest. The clearest example of such a direct and manifest link between state financing and clearly defined obligations are public service contracts awarded in accordance with public procurement rules. The contract in question should define the obligations of the undertakings entrusted with the services of general interest and the remuneration which they will receive in return. Cases falling into that category should be analysed according to the compensation approach. The second category consists of cases where it is not clear from the outset that the state funding is intended as a *quid pro quo* for clearly defined general interest obligations. In those cases the link between state funding and the general interest obligations imposed is either not direct or not manifest or the general interest obligations are not clearly defined.

The *quid pro quo* approach appears at first sight consistent with the general

---

[46]   See Opinion of Advocate General Jacobs in case C-126/01, *Ministre de l'économie, des finances et de l'industrie v. GEMO SA*, 30 April 2002.

case-law on the interpretation of Article 87(1) EC. Also it gives appropriate weight to the importance of services of general interest, within the remit of Article 16 EC and of Article 36 of the EU Charter of Fundamental Rights. On the other hand, the *quid pro quo* approach presents a major shortcoming: it introduces elements[47] of the nature of public financing into the process of determining the legality of state aid. According to state aid jurisprudence, only the effects of the measure are to be taken into consideration,[48] and as a result of the application of the *quid pro quo* approach legal certainty could be undermined.

The application of the state aid approach creates a *lex and policy lacuna* in the treatment of funding of services of general economic interest and normal services. In fact, it presupposes that the services of general economic interest emerge in a different market, where the state and its emanations have a public function. Such markets are not susceptible to the private operator principle[49] which has been relied upon by the Commission and the European

---

[47]   For example the form in which the aid is granted (see cases C-323/82 *Intermills v. Commission*, [1984] ECR 3809, paragraph 31; case C-142/87, *Belgium v. Commission*, cited in note 18, paragraph 13; and case 40/85 *Belgium v. Commission*, [1986] ECR I-2321, paragraph 120, the legal status of the measure in national law). See Commission Decision 93/349/EEC of 9 March 1993 concerning aid provided by the United Kingdom Government to British Aerospace for its purchase of Rover Group Holdings over and above those authorised in Commission Decision 89/58/EEC authorising maximum aid to this operation subject to certain conditions (OJ 1993 L 143, p. 7, point IX), the fact that the measure is part of an aid scheme (case T-16/96, *Cityflyer Express v. Commission*, [1998] ECR II-757), the reasons for the measure and the objectives of the measure (case C-173/73, *Italy v. Commission*, [1974] ECR 709; *Deufil v. Commission*, [1987] ECR 901; case C-56/93, *Belgium v. Commission*, [1996] ECR I-723; case C-241/94, *France v. Commission*, [1996] ECR I-4551; case C-5/01, *Belgium v. Commission* [2002] ECR I-3452) and the intentions of the public authorities and the recipient undertaking (Commission Decision 92/11/EEC of 31 July 1991 concerning aid provided by the Derbyshire County Council to Toyota Motor Corporation, an undertaking producing motor vehicles (OJ 1992 L 6, p. 36, point V)).

[48]   See case C-173/73 *Italy v. Commission* [1974] ECR 709, paragraph 27; *Deufil v. Commission*, [1987] ECR 901; case C-56/93 *Belgium v. Commission*, [1996] ECR I-723 paragraph 79; case C-241/94 *France v. Commission* [1996] ECR I-4551, paragraph 20; and case C-5/01 *Belgium v. Commission* [2002] ECR I-3452, paragraphs 45 and 46.

[49]   See the Communication of the Commission to the Member States concerning public authorities' holdings in company capital (*Bulletin EC* 9-1984, point 3.5.1). The Commission considers that such an investment is not aid where the public authorities authorized it under the same conditions as a private investor operating under normal market economy conditions. See also Commission Communication to the Member States on the application of Articles 92 and 93 of the EEC Treaty and of Article 5 of Commission Directive 80/723/EEC to public undertakings in the manufacturing sector (OJ 1993 C 307, p. 3, point 11).

courts[50] to determine the borderline between market behaviour and state intervention.

European jurisprudence distinguishes between the economic nature of state intervention and the exercise of public powers. The application of the private operator principle is confined to the economic nature of state intervention[51] and is justified by the principle of equal treatment between the public and private sectors.[52] Such treatment requires that intervention by the state should not be subject to stricter rules than those applicable to private undertakings. The non-economic character of state intervention[53] renders immaterial the test of private operator, for the reason that profitability, and thus the *raison d'être* of private investment, is not present. It follows that services of general economic interest cannot be part of the same demand/supply equation as other normal services the state and its organs procure.[54] Along the above lines, a convergence emerges between public procurement jurisprudence and the state aid approach in the light of the reasoning behind the *BFI*[55] and

---

[50]   See in particular case 234/84 *Belgium v. Commission*, [1986] ECR 2263, paragraph 14; case C-142/87 *Belgium v. Commission* ('*Tubemeuse*'), [1990] ECR I-959, paragraph 26; and case C-305/89 *Italy v. Commission* ('*Alfa Romeo*'), [1991] ECR I-1603, paragraph 19.

[51]   For example, where the public authorities contribute capital to an undertaking (case 234/84, *Belgium v. Commission*, [1986] ECR 2263; case C-142/87, *Belgium v. Commission*, [1990] ECR I-959; case C-305/89, *Italy v. Commission*, [1991] ECR I-1603), grant a loan to certain undertakings (case C-301/87, *France v. Commission*, [1990] ECR I-307; case T-16/96, *Cityflyer Express v. Commission*, [1998] ECR II-757), provide a state guarantee (joined cases T-204/97 and T-270/97, *EPAC v. Commission*, [2000] ECR II-2267), sell goods or services on the market (joined cases 67/85, 68/85 and 70/85, *Van der Kooy and Others v. Commission*, [1988] ECR 219; case C-56/93, *Belgium v. Commission*, [1996] ECR I-723; case C-39/94, *SFEI and Others*, [1996] ECR I-3547), or grant facilities for the payment of social security contributions (case C-256/97, *DM Transport*, [1999] ECR I-3913), or the repayment of wages (case C-342/96, *Spain v. Commission*, [1999] ECR I-2459).

[52]   See case C-303/88, *Italy v. Commission*, [1991] ECR I-1433, paragraph 20; case C-261/89, *Italy v. Commission*, [1991] ECR I-4437, paragraph 15; and case T-358/94, *Air France v. Commission*, [1996] ECR II-2109, paragraph 70.

[53]   For example where the public authorities pay a subsidy directly to an undertaking (case 310/85, *Deufil v. Commission*, [1987] ECR 901), grant an exemption from tax (case C-387/92, *Banco Exterior*, [1994] ECR I-877; case C-6/97 *Italy v. Commission* [1999] ECR I-2981; case C-156/98 *Germany v. Commission* [2000] ECR I-6857) or agree to a reduction in social security contributions (case C-75/97, *Belgium v. Commission*, [1999] ECR I-3671; case T-67/94, *Ladbroke Racing v. Commission*, [1998] ECR II-1).

[54]   See the analysis in the joined cases C-278/92 to C-280/92, *Spain v. Commission*, [1994] ECR I-4103.

[55]   See case C-360/96, *Gemeente Arnhem Gemeente Rheden v. BFI Holding BV*, op. cit.

Agora[56] cases. Services of general economic interest are *sui generis*, having as their main characteristics the lack of industrial and commercial character, where the absence of profitability and competitiveness are indicative of the relevant market place. As a rule, the procurement of such services should be subject to the rigour and discipline of public procurement rules and analogously, classified as state aid, in the absence of the competitive award procedures. In consequence, the application of the public procurement regime reinforces the character of services of general interest as non-commercial or industrial and the existence of public markets.[57]

The compensation approach relies heavily upon the real advantage theory to determine the existence of any advantages conferred on undertakings through state financing. Thus, the advantages given by public authorities that threaten to distort competition are examined together with the obligations on the recipient of the aid. Public advantages thus constitute aid only if their amount exceeds the value of the commitments the recipient enters into. The compensation approach treats the costs offsetting the provision of services of general interest as the baseline over which state aids should be considered. That baseline is determined by the market price, which corresponds to the given public/private contractual interface and is demonstrable through the application of public procurement award procedures.

The real advantage theory runs counter to the apparent advantage theory which underlines Treaty provisions[58] and the approach that relies on the economic effects and the nature of the measures in determining the existence of state aid. The borderline of the market price, which will form the conceptual base above which state aid would appear, is not always easy to determine, even in the presence of public procurement procedures. The state and its organs as contracting authorities (state emanations and bodies governed by public law) have wide discretion to award public contracts under the public

---

[56]   Cases C-223/99, *Agora Srl v. Ente Autonomo Fiera Internazionale di Milano* and C-260/99, *Excelsior Snc di Pedrotti Runa & C v. Ente Autonomo Fiera Internazionale di Milano*, op. cit.

[57]   See Bazex, *Le droit public de la concurrence*, RFDA, 1998; Arcelin, *L'entreprise en droit interne et communautaire de la concurrence*, Litec, 2003; Guézou, 'Droit de la concurrence et droit des marchés publics: vers une notion transverale de mise en libre concurrence', *Contrats Publics*, March 2003.

[58]   According to Advocate-General Léger in his Opinion on the *Altmark* case, the apparent advantage theory occurs in several provisions of the Treaty, in particular in Article 92(2) and (3), and in Article 77 of the EC Treaty (now Article 73 EC). Article 92(3) of the Treaty provides that aid may be regarded as compatible with the common market if it pursues certain objectives such as the strengthening of economic and social cohesion, the promotion of research and the protection of the environment.

procurement rules.[59] In *ARGE Gewässerschutzt*, the Court ruled that directly or indirectly subsidised tenders by the state or other contracting authorities or even by the contracting authority itself can legitimately be part of the evaluation process; it did not elaborate on the possibility of the rejection of an offer, which is appreciably lower than those of unsubsidised tenderers by reference to the abnormally low disqualification ground. Although the case has relevance in the fields of selection and qualification procedures and award criteria, the Court made no references to previous case-law regarding state aids in public procurement, presumably because the *Dupont de Nemours* precedent is still highly relevant.

Often, price plays a secondary role in the award criteria. In cases where the public contract is awarded to the lowest price, the element of *market price* under the compensation approach could be determined. However, when the public contract is to be awarded by reference to the most economically advantageous offer, the market price might be totally different than the price the contracting authority wishes to pay for the procurement of the relevant services. The meaning of the most economically advantageous offer includes a series of factors chosen by the contracting authority, including price, delivery or completion date, running costs, cost-effectiveness, profitability, technical merit, product or work quality, aesthetic and functional characteristics, after-sales service and technical assistance, commitments with regard to spare parts and components and maintenance costs, security of supplies. The above list is not exhaustive. The mere existence of public procurement procedures cannot, therefore, reveal the necessary element of the compensation approach: the market price which will determine the 'excessive' state intervention and introduce state aids regulation.

An indication of the application of the compensation approach is reflected in the *Stohal*[60] case, where an undertaking could provide commercial services and services of general interest, without any relevance to the applicability of

---

[59]   According to the Public Procurement Directives, two criteria provide the conditions under which contracting authorities award public contracts: *the lowest price* or the *most economically advantageous offer*. The first criterion indicates that, subject to qualitative criteria and financial and economic standing, contracting authorities do not rely on any factor other than the price quoted to complete the contract. The Directives provide an automatic disqualification of an 'obviously abnormally low offer'. See case 76/81, *SA Transporoute et Travaux v. Minister of Public Works*, [1982] ECR 457; case 103/88, *Fratelli Costanzo SpA v. Comune di Milano*, [1989] ECR 1839; case 296/89, *Impresa Dona Alfonso di Dona Alfonso & Figli snc v. Consorzio per lo Sviluppo Industriale del Comune di Monfalcone*, judgment of 18 June 1991.

[60]   C-44/96, *Mannesmann Anlangenbau Austria AG et al. v. Strohal Rotationsdurck GesmbH*, op. cit. See also the analysis of the case by Bovis, in 36 CMLR (1999), pp. 205–25.

the public procurement rules. The rationale of the case runs parallel to the real advantage theory, up to the point of recognising the different nature and characteristics of the markets under which normal (commercial) services and services of general interest are provided. The distinction begins where, for the sake of legal certainty and legitimate expectation, the activities undertakings of dual capacity are equally covered by the public procurement regime and the undertaking in question is considered as *contracting authority* irrespective of any proportion or percentage between the delivery of commercial services and services of general interest. This finding might have a significant implication for the compensation approach in state aid jurisprudence: irrespective of any costs offsetting the costs related to the provision of general interest, the entire state financing could be viewed under the state aid approach.

Finally, the *quid pro quo* approach relies on the existence of a direct and manifest link between state financing and services of general interest, indicated by the presence of a public contract concluded in accordance with the provisions of the Public Procurement Directives. Apart from the obvious criticism the *quid pro quo* approach has received, its interface with public procurement appears as the most problematic facet in its application. The procurement of public services does not always reveal a public contract between a contracting authority and an undertaking.

Public Procurement Regulation and Industrial Policy

The implementation of industrial policies through public purchasing focuses on either the sustainability of strategic national industries, or the development of infant industries. In both cases, preferential purchasing patterns can provide the economic and financial framework for the development of such industries, at the expense of competition and free trade. Although the utilisation of public procurement as a means of industrial policy in member states may breach, directly or indirectly, primary Treaty provisions on the free movement of goods and the right of establishment and the freedom to provide services, it is far from clear whether the European Commission and the European Court of Justice could accept public procurement as legitimate state aids.

The industrial policy dimension of public procurement is also reflected in the form of strategic purchasing by public utilities. Public utilities in the European Union, which for the most part are monopolies, are accountable for a substantial magnitude of procurement, in terms of volume and in terms of price. Responsible for this are the expensive infrastructure and high technology products that it is necessary to procure in order to deliver their services to the public. Given the fact that most of the suppliers to public utilities depend almost entirely on their procurement and that, even when some degree of privatisation has been achieved, the actual control of the utilities is still vested in the state, the first constraint in liberalising public procurement in the European Union is apparent. Utilities, in the form of public monopolies or semi-private enterprises, appear prone to perpetuate long-standing over-dependency purchasing patterns with certain domestic suppliers. Reflecting the above observations, it is worth bearing in mind that until 1991 utilities were not covered by European legislation on procurement. The delay in their regulation can be attributed to the resistance from member states over privatising their monopolies and the uncertainty of the legal regime that would follow their privatisation.

Nevertheless, the public procurement legal framework is positively in favour of strategic sub-contracting.[61] Sub-contracting plays a major role in the opening up of public markets as it is the most effective way for small and medium-sized enterprises to participate in public procurement. All Directives on public procurement, influenced by the Commission's Communications on sub-contracting and small and medium enterprises, encourage the use of sub-contracting in the award of public contracts. For example, in public supplies contracts, the contracting entity in the invitation to tender may ask the tenderers about their intention to sub-contract to third parties as part of the contract. In public works contracts, contracting authorities awarding the principal contract to a concessionaire may require the sub-contracting to third parties of at least 30% of the total work provided by the principal contract. A public works concession is defined by the Works Directive as a written contract between a contractor and a contracting authority concerning either the execution or both the execution and design of a work and for which remunerative considerations consist, at least partly, in the right of the *concessionaire* to exploit exclusively the finished construction works for a period of time. The regulation of concession contracts was introduced into the *acquis communautaire* by virtue of Directive 89/440 which amended Directive 71/305. In fact, it incorporated the Voluntary Code of Practice, which was adopted by the Representatives of Member States meeting within the Council in 1971.[62] The Code was a non-binding instrument and contained rules on the advertising of contracts and the principle that contracting authorities awarding the principal contract to a concessionaire were to require him to subcontract to third parties at least 30% of the total work provided by the principal contract.

---

[61]   See European Commission, *SME TASK FORCE: SMEs and Public Procurement*, Brussels, 1988; European Commission, *Pan European Forum on Sub-Contracting in the Community*, Brussels, 1993. Also, Mardas, 'Sub-contracting, small and medium sized enterprises (SMEs) and public procurement in the European community', 3 (1994), *Public Procurement Law Review*, CS 19.

[62]   See OJ 1971 C 82/13.

The industrial policy dimension of public procurement revolves around public monopolies in the member states which predominately operate in the utilities sectors (energy, transport, water and telecommunications) and have been assigned the exclusive exploitation of the relevant services in their respective member states. The legal status of these entities varies from legal monopolies, where they are constitutionally guaranteed, to delegated monopolies, where the state confers certain rights on them. During the last decade they have been the target of a sweeping process of transformation from underperforming public corporations to competitive enterprises. Public monopolies very often possess a monopsony position. As they are state-controlled enterprises, they tend to perform under different management patterns than private firms. Their decision making responds not only to market forces but mainly to political pressure. Understandably, their purchasing behaviour follows, to a large extent, parameters reflecting current trends in domestic industrial policies. Public monopolies in the utilities sector have sustained national industries in member states through exclusive or preferential procurement. The sustainability of 'national champions', or in other terms, strategically perceived enterprises, could only be achieved through discriminatory purchasing patterns. The privatisation of public monopolies, which absorb, to a large extent, the output of such industries will most probably disrupt such patterns. It will also result in industrial policy imbalances as it would be difficult for 'national champions' to secure new markets to replace the traditional long dependency on public monopolies. Finally, it will take time and effort to diversify their activities or to convert to alternative industrial sectors.

The protected and preferential purchasing frameworks between monopolies and 'national champions' and the output dependency patterns and secured markets of the latter have attracted considerable foreign direct investment, to the extent that European Union institutions face the dilemma of threatening to discontinue the investment flow when liberalising public procurement in the common market. However, it could be argued that the industrial restructuring following the opening up of the procurement practices of public monopolies would possibly attract similar levels of foreign direct investment, which would be directed towards supporting the new structure. The liberalisation of public procurement in the European Union has as one of its main aims the restructuring of industries suffering from over-capacity and sub-optimal performance. However, the industries supplying public monopolies and utilities are themselves, quite often, public corporations. In such cases, procurement dependency patterns between state outfits, when disrupted, can result in massive unemployment attributed to the supply side's inability to secure new customers. The abolition of a monopsony position might often bring about the collapse of the relevant sector.

Industrial policies through public procurement can also be implemented with reference to defence industries, particularly for procurement of military equipment. The Procurement Directives cover dual-use equipment purchased by the armed forces, but explicitly exclude from their ambit the procurement of military equipment. It should also be mentioned here that every member state in the European Union pursues its own military procurement policy by virtue of Article 223 of the Treaty of Rome. However, the Maastricht Treaty on European Union has created a framework within which a common European Defence Policy should be established, defence contracts and procurement of military equipment by member states should be harmonised, to the extent that a centralised mechanism regulating them should take over independent national military procurement practices.

Attempts have been made to liberalise, to a limited extent, the procurement of military equipment at European level under the auspices of the European Defence Equipment Market (EDEM). This initiative is a programme of gradual liberalisation of defence industries in the relevant countries and has arisen through the operation of the Independent European Programme Group, which has been a forum of industrial co-operation in defence industry matters amongst European NATO members. Apart from collaborative research and development in defence technology, the programme has envisaged the introduction of a competitive regime in defence procurement and a modest degree of transparency, subject to the draconian primary Treaty provisions of Article 223. Award of defence procurement contracts under the EDEM should follow a similar rationale as civilian procurement, particularly in the introduction of award criteria based on economic and financial considerations and a minimum degree of publicity for contracts in excess of Euro 1 million.

The establishment of a Common European Defence Policy could possibly bring about the integration of defence industries in the European Union and this will inevitably require a change in governments' policies and practices. Competitiveness, public savings considerations, value for money, transparency and non-discrimination should be the principles of the centralised mechanism regulating defence procurement in Europe. The establishment of a centralised defence agency with specific tasks of *contractorisation, facilities management* and *market testing* represent examples of new procurement policies which would give an opportunity to the defence industry to adopt its practices in the light of the challenges, risks, policy priorities and directions of the modern era. In particular, risk management and contracting arrangements measuring reliability of deliveries and cost compliance, without penalising the supply side, are themes which could revolutionise defence procurement and play a significant role in linking such strategic industries with national and European-wide industrial policies.

Public procurement as a discipline expands from a simple internal market topic to a multifaceted tool of European regulation and governance covering policy choices and revealing an interesting interface between centralised and national governance systems.

Index

abnormally low tenders
  Public Sector Directive 170, 268, 286, 287
  Utilities Directive 366
accelerated negotiated award procedures 242
accelerated restricted award procedures 232
advertisement
  competition, notices used as call for 326
  contract award notices
    generally 66
    Public Sector Directive 112, 113, 114, 120
    Utilities Directive 323, 324, 325, 328, 335
  contract notices, under Public Sector Directive 112, 113, 114, 120
  generally 66
  restricted award procedures 232, 233
  Public Sector Directive, under
    contract award notices 118
    contract notices 113, 114, 115, 116, 117, 118
    public works concessions 270
  Utilities Directive, under
    periodic indicative notices, under Utilities Directive 323
    prior information notices 112, 113
  Utilities Directive, under competition, notices used as call for 326
    contract award notices 331
    periodic indicative notices 323
    qualification system, notices on existence of 325
affiliated undertakings, contracts to
  exclusions, under Utilities Directive 295, 296, 311, 312
  utilities procurement, in 44, 45

AGP *see* GATT Agreement on Government Procurement
Airports
  Utilities Directive, applicability of 294, 309, 318
annulment of contracting authorities' acts 381–97
annulment of decisions
  see also set aside; set aside of contracting authorities' acts 419–27
anti-trust dimension 5–10
award criteria
  ecological criteria 277, 278
  environmental considerations 107, 108, 276, 277, 278
  generally 79, 80
  lowest offer, disqualification 286, 287
  Public Sector Directive, under 273
    abnormally low tenders 286
    electronic auctions 100, 101
    generally informing candidates and tenderers 66
    lowest price 286
    most economically advantageous tender 103, 104, 274
  public sector procurement, in
    social considerations as 105, 106, 274, 275, 276
    subject matter of contract and 281, 282
  Utilities Directive, under
    abnormally low tenders 366
    in dynamic purchasing systems 357, 358
    in electronic auctions 359, 360, 361
    lowest price 366
    most economically advantageous tender 365
  variants in 280, 281
award of contract
  Public Sector Directive, under
    generally 273–86